Lecture Notes in Computer Science 13572

More information about this series at https://link.springer.com/bookseries/558

Helmut Seidl · Zhiming Liu ·
Corina S. Pasareanu (Eds.)

Theoretical Aspects of Computing – ICTAC 2022

19th International Colloquium
Tbilisi, Georgia, September 27–29, 2022
Proceedings

 Springer

Editors
Helmut Seidl
TU München
Munich, Germany

Zhiming Liu (ID)
Southwest University
Chongqing, China

Corina S. Pasareanu
NASA Ames Research Center
Moffett Field, CA, USA

ISSN 0302-9743   ISSN 1611-3349 (electronic)
Lecture Notes in Computer Science
ISBN 978-3-031-17714-9   ISBN 978-3-031-17715-6 (eBook)
https://doi.org/10.1007/978-3-031-17715-6

This Springer imprint is published by the registered company Springer Nature Switzerland AG
The registered company address is: Gewerbestrasse 11, 6330 Cham, Switzerland

Preface

After more than two years of COVID-19, the pandemic seems, at the time of writing, more or less under control - suggesting a return to having in-person conferences as before the pandemic. However, the current war in Ukraine and its potential expansion towards Georgia also rendered this year's edition of ICTAC a challenge.

This volume contains the papers presented at ICTAC 2022: the 19th International Colloquium on Theoretical Aspects of Computing held during September 27–30, 2022, in Tbilisi, Georgia. The International Colloquia on Theoretical Aspects of Computing (ICTAC) is a series of annual events founded in 2003 by the United Nations University International Institute for Software Technology. Its purpose is to bring together practitioners and researchers from academia, industry, and government to present research results and exchange experience and ideas. Beyond these scholarly goals, another main purpose is to promote cooperation in research and education between participants and their institutions from developing and industrial regions.

This year ICTAC was part of the Computational Logic Autumn Summit (CLAS), which took place in Tbilisi - the capital of Georgia. As a venue we had Ivane Javakhishvili Tbilisi State University (TSU), the oldest and most prominent educational and research institution in Georgia, and the whole South Caucasus. TSU was founded in 1918 and has now more than 22,000 students. CLAS was organized by TSU together with the Kurt Gödel Society and sponsored by Amazon, AnyDesk, Runtime Verification Inc, and Springer. We were honored to have six distinguished guests as invited speakers:

- Volker Diekert and Manfred Kufleitner (University of Stuttgart, Germany)
- Miaomiao Zhang (Tongji University, China)
- Marsha Chechik (University of Toronto, Canada)
- Bernhard Beckert (Karlsruhe Institute of Technology, Germany)
- Dmitriy Traytel (University of Copenhagen, Denmark).

ICTAC 2022 received 52 submissions (including eight short papers) from authors in 27 different countries. Each submission received between two and four reviews, where the average was 2.9. Out of all submissions, 23 full-length papers were accepted. The committee also accepted two short papers. Apart from the paper presentations and invited talks, ICTAC 2022 continued the tradition of previous ICTAC conferences in holding a five-day school on eight important topics in theoretical aspects of computing, formal methods and verification, formal models of concurrency, and security in concurrency. These courses were as follows:

- Gödel logics - the dominance of order, given by Matthias Baaz (TU Wien, Austria)
- Parity Games, given by Volker Diekert and Manfred Kufleitner (University of Stuttgart, Germany)
- Nominal techniques, given by Maribel Fernandez (King's College London, UK)

- A logical basis for the verification of imperative programs, given by Tudor Jebelean (RISC, Johannes Kepler University Linz, Austria)
- The semantically reflected digital twin, given by Einar Broch Johnsen (University of Oslo, Norway)
- Learning meets verification, given by Martin Leucker (University of Lübeck, Germany)
- Logical framework with union and intersection types, given by Luigi Liquori (Inria, France)
- To prove with a proof assistant or not to prove, given by Dmitriy Traytel (University of Copenhagen, Denmark)

We thank all the authors for submitting their papers to the conference, and the Program Committee members and external reviewers for their excellent work in the review, discussion, and selection process. We are indebted to all the members of the Organizing Committee for their hard work in all phases of the conference. We also acknowledge our gratitude to the Steering Committee for their constant support.

We are also indebted to EasyChair, which greatly simplified the assignment and reviewing of the submissions as well as the production of the material for the proceedings. Finally, we thank Springer for their cooperation in publishing the proceedings.

August 2022

Helmut Seidl
Zhiming Liu
Corina S. Pasareanu

Organization

Program Committee

Luis Barbosa	University of Minho, Portugal
Lei Bu	Nanjing University, China
Zhenbang Chen	National University of Defense Technology, China
Deepak D'Souza	Indian Institute of Science, Bangalore, India
Yunwei Dong	Northwestern Polytechnical University, China
Maribel Fernandez	King's College London, UK
Simon Foster	University of York, UK
Fei He	Tsinghua University, China
Joost-Pieter Katoen	RWTH Aachen University, Germany
Johannes Kinder	Bundeswehr University Munich, Germany
Peter Lammich	TU Munich, Germany
Guoqiang Li	Shanghai Jiao Tong University, China
Zhiming Liu (Chair)	Southwest University, China
Francesco Logozzo	Meta, USA
Yannic Noller	National University of Singapore, Singapore
Corina S. Pasareanu (Chair)	Carnegie Mellon University, NASA, and KBR, USA
Colin Paterson	University of York, UK
Helmut Seidl	TU Munich, Germany
Martina Seidl (Chair)	Johannes Kepler University Linz, Austria
Vaibhav Sharma	University of Minnesota, USA
Volker Stolz	Høgskulen på Vestlandet, Norway
Youcheng Sun	Queen's University Belfast, UK
Caterina Urban	Inria, France
Heike Wehrheim	University of Oldenburg, Germany
Naijun Zhan	Institute of Software, Chinese Academy of Sciences, China
Miaomiao Zhang	Tongji University, China

On Safety, Assurance and Reliability: A Software Engineering Perspective (Abstract of Invited Talk)

Marsha Chechik

Department of Computer Science, University of Toronto, Canada
chechik@cs.toronto.edu

Abstract. From financial services platforms to social networks to vehicle control, software has come to mediate many activities of daily life. Governing bodies and standards organizations have responded to this trend by creating regulations and standards to address issues such as safety, security and privacy. In this environment, the compliance of software development to standards and regulations has emerged as a key requirement. Compliance claims and arguments are often captured in assurance cases, with linked evidence of compliance. Evidence can come from test cases, verification proofs, human judgement, or a combination of these. That is, we try to build (safety-critical) systems carefully according to well justified methods and articulate these justifications in an assurance case that is ultimately judged by a human.

Building safety arguments for traditional software systems is difficult—they are lengthy and expensive to maintain, especially as software undergoes change. Safety is also notoriously noncompositional—each subsystem might be safe but together they may create unsafe behaviors. It is also easy to miss cases, which in the simplest case would mean developing an argument for when a condition is true but missing arguing for a false condition. Furthermore, many ML-based systems are becoming safety-critical. For example, recent Tesla self-driving cars misclassified emergency vehicles and caused multiple crashes. ML-based systems typically do not have precisely specified and machine-verifiable requirements. While some safety requirements can be stated clearly: "the system should detect all pedestrians at a crossing", these requirements are for the entire system, making them too high-level for safety analysis of individual components. Thus, systems with ML components (MLCs) add a significant layer of complexity for safety assurance.

I argue that safety assurance should be an integral part of building safe and reliable software systems, but this process needs support from advanced software engineering and software analysis. In this talk, I outline a few approaches for development of principled, tool-supported methodologies for creating and managing assurance arguments. I then describe some of the recent work on specifying and verifying reliability requirements for machine-learned components in safety-critical domains.

Contents

VeriMon: A Formally Verified Monitoring Tool

David Basin[1], Thibault Dardinier[1], Nico Hauser[1], Lukas Heimes[1],
Jonathan Julián Huerta y Munive[2], Nicolas Kaletsch[1], Srđan Krstić[1],
Emanuele Marsicano[1], Martin Raszyk[3], Joshua Schneider[1],
Dawit Legesse Tirore[4], Dmitriy Traytel[2(✉)], and Sheila Zingg[1]

[1] Department of Computer Science, ETH Zürich, Zurich, Switzerland
[2] Department of Computer Science, University of Copenhagen,
Copenhagen, Denmark
traytel@di.ku.dk
[3] DFINITY Foundation, Zurich, Switzerland
[4] Computer Science Department, IT University of Copenhagen,
Copenhagen, Denmark

Abstract. A runtime monitor observes a running system and checks
whether the sequence of events the system generates satisfies a given
specification. We describe the evolution of VeriMon: an expressive and
efficient monitor that has been formally verified using the Isabelle proof
assistant.

1 Introduction

The goal of runtime verification (RV) is to gain confidence in the correctness of a
given execution of a running system. This is a lightweight alternative to full formal
verification which must consider all possible executions. In RV, monitors are tools
that take as input an execution represented as a sequence of events called trace,
analyze the trace with respect to a given specification, and output verdicts, i.e.,
satisfactions or violations of the specification. Monitors support a wide range of
specification languages [8], including automaton-based, (temporal-)logic-based,
and (recursive-)rule-based formalisms.

A monitor's specification language must be *expressive* to allow users to formulate the desired properties in a concise, natural, and intuitive way. At the
same time and often in direct conflict with the expressiveness requirement, monitors must be *time-* and *memory-efficient*. Expressive and efficient monitors use
complex, optimized algorithms, whose correctness is not obvious. Yet a monitor
must be *trustworthy* to be used as a verification tool.

VeriMon [1,18,20] is an expressive, efficient, and trustworthy monitor. Its
specification language is based on the expressive metric first-order temporal logic
(MFOTL) [2], but it additionally incorporates automata-based and rule-based
features. It uses efficient algorithms for evaluating the temporal operators Since
and Until, n-ary conjunctions (as multi-way joins), and aggregations such as

H. Seidl et al. (Eds.): ICTAC 2022, LNCS 13572, pp. 1–6, 2022.
https://doi.org/10.1007/978-3-031-17715-6_1

sums or averages. Finally, it is trustworthy as it has been formally verified using the Isabelle/HOL proof assistant [15]. Proof assistants are tools that mechanically check the correctness of human-written mathematical proofs, e.g., of an algorithm's correctness. They are built around a small, well-understood inference kernel through which all reasoning must pass, which provides the highest level of trustworthiness.

Here, we describe VeriMon's origins and evolution, outline some planned next steps, and discuss the advantages of formally verifying monitors.

2   Evolution

VeriMon originated from a certain dissatisfaction with existing monitoring tools. Specifically, we have been using the efficient MFOTL monitor MonPoly [2,3] for years. But every so often, we would discover and fix an implementation bug. While annoying, this was not the most pressing issue. More importantly, MonPoly became an impenetrable black box: extending its specification language or improving its algorithms became extremely difficult for us as the implementation included various undocumented and non-obvious performance optimizations and the original implementors had moved on. (A typical fate of academic software!)

Eventually, we decided to start from scratch aiming at establishing the correctness of a much simplified algorithm, which did not include performance optimizations and supported a restricted specification language. To this end, we formulated in Isabelle the syntax and semantics of MFOTL, defined a core monitoring algorithm as a functional program, and proved the algorithm sound (all produced verdicts are correct according to the semantics) and complete (all verdicts that hold under the semantics are eventually produced). To obtain an executable program, we used Isabelle's code generator [10] to extract 2 800 lines of OCaml code from our formalization consisting of 3 000 lines of Isabelle definitions and proofs. The extracted code included two main functions (and their dependencies): *init* that initialized the monitor's state for a given abstract syntax tree of an MFOTL specification and *step* that updates the monitor's state upon incoming events while outputting verdicts. The first version of VeriMon [18] augmented this verified core with MonPoly's unverified specification and log parsers and modules for type-checking, rewriting, and preprocessing specifications and for printing verdicts.

After this kick-start, the first target was to align VeriMon's variant of MFOTL with MonPoly's, which included inequalities and aggregation operators. Having formally established and thus understood the algorithmic invariants for other non-temporal operators made these extensions straightforward [1, §2–3]. At that point, we were in the position of extending VeriMon, one feature at a time, often carried out mostly by undergraduate students. Today, VeriMon incorporates:

– Regular expression matching operators generalizing MFOTL's temporal operators and representing a form of automaton-based specifications [1, §4];
– A non-recursive let operator, invaluable for structuring policies [20, §3];

– A recursive let operator that requires all recursive occurrences to be guarded by past temporal operators and can encode rule-based specifications [20, §4].

We are currently working on adding support for dual temporal operators (Release and Trigger) [13]. All these extensions do not only introduce new operators, but also extend the correctness proof to cover the new features.

The first version of VeriMon was extremely inefficient. We have spent considerable time and energy on verifying performance optimizations. VeriMon became the incubator for developing and proving correct algorithms for the evaluation of Since and Until [1, §6][16, §4.4] and aggregations over those that asymptotically improved over MonPoly's algorithms. We also used insights from databases and incorporated a worst-case optimal multi-way join algorithm [1, §5]. Overall, VeriMon still tends to be slower and use more memory than MonPoly, but it is easy to construct examples in which the better algorithms reverse the picture. In the meantime, some of these algorithms have also found their way into MonPoly.

We have also made progress on reducing the amount of VeriMon's unverified code by verifying a type inference algorithm and a specification rewriting module.

Since the first version, VeriMon's publicly available code base[1] grew significantly. The formalization now spans over 45 000 lines of Isabelle definitions and proofs. The extracted code amounts to over 11 000 lines of OCaml. Thanks to the transpiler `js_of_ocaml` [19], we can now run VeriMon in every web browser.[2] This is not recommended for realistic applications (due to the suboptimal performance and the increased trusted code base which then includes `js_of_ocaml` and the browser's JavaScript engine), but extremely useful for demonstrations.

3   Future Directions

We plan to improve VeriMon along the three discussed dimensions. For trustworthiness, the missing ingredients are the specification and log parsers. Once verified, they will allow us to run VeriMon without relying on MonPoly's unverified code.

To further improve efficiency, we will use database-style indices to speed up joins and other operations on tables, the main computations in VeriMon aside from the temporal operator evaluation. Furthermore, we plan to lift the recently developed algorithms for the regular expression matching operators in the propositional metric temporal logic setting [16, §3] to VeriMon's first-order setting.

In terms of expressiveness, we aim to generalize VeriMon's time domain from natural numbers to an arbitrary domain meeting minimal well-formedness conditions. This will improve the flexibility of VeriMon's metric intervals used to express quantitative temporal constraints. We also intend to verify and incorporate algorithms for a Datalog-style recursive let operator. Finally, VeriMon, like MonPoly, operates on finite tables and thus can only handle the *monitorable*

---

[1] https://bitbucket.org/jshs/monpoly/src/master/.

[2] https://traytel.bitbucket.io/verimon.

fragment of MFOTL [2, §4.2]. While other approaches, which can handle full MFOTL by replacing tables with automatic structures or binary decision diagrams, exist [2,11,12], we believe that working with finite tables is a major source of efficiency for VeriMon. Thus, we plan to verify and integrate in Veri-Mon the recent approach of rewriting arbitrary MFOTL specifications into the monitorable fragment [16, §4.3].

4 Discussion

The obvious benefit of working with a formally verified algorithm is the absence of bugs. This benefit is no longer given when the verified code is combined with unverified code. Indeed, we found and fixed several issues in the unverified glue code connecting VeriMon's data structures to MonPoly's in VeriMon's early days. Yet, the glue code is only a few hundred lines and it is much easier to localize the problem there compared to the thousands of lines of code comprising the actual monitor.

A bigger danger for verified tools are misunderstandings in the semantics. For example, VeriMon used to compute averages as $a + b/2$ because it reused the same faulty Isabelle definition in the semantics and the algorithm, which omitted a pair of parentheses by mistake. To avoid such issues, the formalized semantics of the specification language must be carefully inspected, including all auxiliary definitions. Fortunately, and again in contrast to the actual monitoring algorithm, VeriMon's semantics comprises only a few hundred lines of Isabelle definitions.

A major asset for VeriMon's usability is its tight integration with MonPoly. Both tools are compiled into a single binary, which distinguishes the used algorithm via a flag. This resulted in a standard workflow, in which users run Mon-Poly and rerun using VeriMon in case MonPoly's output looks suspicious. We have also performed such a comparative execution on a larger scale on random inputs. This differential testing revealed discrepancies [1,18,20] pointing to bugs and an unusual (but specified) semantics in the unverified tools MonPoly and DejaVu [12].

We see extensibility as the main advantage of a formally verified monitor. The verification of the first version of VeriMon has already identified several notions and their properties central to the verification. Adding new features then reduced to extending these notions while updating the proofs of their properties. Along similar lines, we replaced inefficient algorithms by efficient ones using refinement, which allowed us to reuse the proofs of the inefficient algorithms' correctness.

Several of VeriMon's features, such as the non-recursive let operator and the improved algorithms for Since and Until, have been propagated back to MonPoly and have guided the design of a new monitoring tool implemented in C++, CPPMon.[3]

We are happy to start seeing other work in the community that uses proof assistants [4–6,17], deductive verifiers [9], or SMT solvers [7,14] to improve the

---

[3] https://github.com/matthieugras/cppmon.

trustworthiness of monitors. We believe that formal verification is the only way towards a landscape of tools that are reliable and maintainable: not just one-paper wonders.

Acknowledgments. Research on VeriMon has been supported by the Swiss National Science Foundation grant "Big Data Monitoring" (167162), the US Air Force grant "Monitoring at Any Cost" (FA9550-17-1-0306), and a Novo Nordisk Foundation Start Package grant (NNF20OC0063462). The authors are listed in alphabetical order regardless of individual contributions or seniority.

References

1. Basin, D., Dardinier, T., Heimes, L., Krstić, S., Raszyk, M., Schneider, J., Traytel, D.: A formally verified, optimized monitor for metric first-order dynamic logic. In: Peltier, N., Sofronie-Stokkermans, V. (eds.) IJCAR 2020. LNCS (LNAI), vol. 12166, pp. 432–453. Springer, Cham (2020). https://doi.org/10.1007/978-3-030-51074-9_25

2. Basin, D., Klaedtke, F., Müller, S., Zălinescu, E.: Monitoring metric first-order temporal properties. J. ACM **62**(2), 15:1–15:45 (2015). https://doi.org/10.1145/2699444

3. Basin, D., Klaedtke, F., Zălinescu, E.: The MonPoly monitoring tool. In: Reger, G., Havelund, K. (eds.) RV-CuBES 2017. Kalpa Publications in Computing, vol. 3, pp. 19–28. EasyChair (2017). https://doi.org/10.29007/89hs

4. Blech, J.O., Falcone, Y., Becker, K.: Towards certified runtime verification. In: Aoki, T., Taguchi, K. (eds.) ICFEM 2012. LNCS, vol. 7635, pp. 494–509. Springer, Heidelberg (2012). https://doi.org/10.1007/978-3-642-34281-3_34

5. Bohrer, R., Tan, Y.K., Mitsch, S., Myreen, M.O., Platzer, A.: VeriPhy: verified controller executables from verified cyber-physical system models. In: Foster, J.S., Grossman, D. (eds.) PLDI 2018, pp. 617–630. ACM (2018). https://doi.org/10.1145/3192366.3192406

6. Chattopadhyay, A., Mamouras, K.: A verified online monitor for metric temporal logic with quantitative semantics. In: Deshmukh, J., Ničković, D. (eds.) RV 2020. LNCS, vol. 12399, pp. 383–403. Springer, Cham (2020). https://doi.org/10.1007/978-3-030-60508-7_21

7. Dauer, J.C., Finkbeiner, B., Schirmer, S.: Monitoring with verified guarantees. In: Feng, L., Fisman, D. (eds.) RV 2021. LNCS, vol. 12974, pp. 62–80. Springer, Cham (2021). https://doi.org/10.1007/978-3-030-88494-9_4

8. Falcone, Y., Krstić, S., Reger, G., Traytel, D.: A taxonomy for classifying runtime verification tools. Int. J. Softw. Tools Technol. Transf. **23**(2), 255–284 (2021). https://doi.org/10.1007/s10009-021-00609-z

9. Finkbeiner, B., Oswald, S., Passing, N., Schwenger, M.: Verified Rust monitors for Lola specifications. In: Deshmukh, J., Ničković, D. (eds.) RV 2020. LNCS, vol. 12399, pp. 431–450. Springer, Cham (2020). https://doi.org/10.1007/978-3-030-60508-7_24

10. Haftmann, F., Nipkow, T.: Code generation via higher-order rewrite systems. In: Blume, M., Kobayashi, N., Vidal, G. (eds.) FLOPS 2010. LNCS, vol. 6009, pp. 103–117. Springer, Heidelberg (2010). https://doi.org/10.1007/978-3-642-12251-4_9

11. Havelund, K., Peled, D., Ulus, D.: First order temporal logic monitoring with BDDs. In: Stewart, D., Weissenbacher, G. (eds.) FMCAD 2017, pp. 116–123. IEEE (2017). https://doi.org/10.23919/FMCAD.2017.8102249

12. Havelund, K., Peled, D., Ulus, D.: DejaVu: a monitoring tool for first-order temporal logic. In: MT@CPSWeek 2018, pp. 12–13. IEEE (2018). https://doi.org/10.1109/MT-CPS.2018.00013

13. Huerta y Munive, J.J.: Relaxing safety for metric first-order temporal logic via dynamic free variables. In: Thao, D., Stolz, V. (eds.) RV 2022. LNCS, Springer (2022) (to appear)

14. Laurent, J., Goodloe, A., Pike, L.: Assuring the guardians. In: Bartocci, E., Majumdar, R. (eds.) RV 2015. LNCS, vol. 9333, pp. 87–101. Springer, Cham (2015). https://doi.org/10.1007/978-3-319-23820-3_6

15. Nipkow, T., Wenzel, M., Paulson, L.C. (eds.): Isabelle/HOL - A Proof Assistant for Higher-Order Logic. LNCS, vol. 2283. Springer, Heidelberg (2002). https://doi.org/10.1007/3-540-45949-9

16. Raszyk, M.: Efficient, Expressive, and Verified Temporal Query Evaluation. Ph.D. thesis, ETH Zürich (2022). https://doi.org/10.3929/ethz-b-000553221

17. Rizaldi, A., et al.: Formalising and monitoring traffic rules for autonomous vehicles in isabelle/HOL. In: Polikarpova, N., Schneider, S. (eds.) IFM 2017. LNCS, vol. 10510, pp. 50–66. Springer, Cham (2017). https://doi.org/10.1007/978-3-319-66845-1_4

18. Schneider, J., Basin, D., Krstić, S., Traytel, D.: A formally verified monitor for metric first-order temporal logic. In: Finkbeiner, B., Mariani, L. (eds.) RV 2019. LNCS, vol. 11757, pp. 310–328. Springer, Cham (2019). https://doi.org/10.1007/978-3-030-32079-9_18

19. Vouillon, J., Balat, V.: From bytecode to JavaScript: the js_of_ocaml compiler. Softw. Pract. Exp. **44**(8), 951–972 (2014). https://doi.org/10.1002/spe.2187

20. Zingg, S., Krstić, S., Raszyk, M., Schneider, J., Traytel, D.: Verified first-order monitoring with recursive rules. In: TACAS 2022. LNCS, vol. 13244, pp. 236–253. Springer, Cham (2022). https://doi.org/10.1007/978-3-030-99527-0_13

Generalized Test Tables: A Domain-Specific Specification Language for Automated Production Systems

Bernhard Beckert[1], Mattias Ulbrich[1], Birgit Vogel-Heuser[2],
and Alexander Weigl[1(✉)]

[1] Karlsruhe Institute of Technology, Karlsruhe, Germany
{beckert,ulbrich,weigl}@kit.edu
[2] Technical University of Munich, Munich, Germany
vogel-heuser@tum.de

Abstract. We give an overview of Generalized Test Tables (GTTs), a specification language derived from existing table-based test case description methods commonly used in the domain of automated production systems. We cover syntax and semantics of GTTs as well as their use for formal verification, and introduce an extension, Relational Test Tables (RTTs), which allow the specification of relations between code variants.

Keywords: Formal specification · Relational verification

1 Introduction

Motivation. Over the past few decades, the reach and power of formal software verification have increased considerably, driven by advances in the domains of satisfiability (SAT) and satisfiability modulo theories (SMT) solving. We have seen tremendous progress in the verification of real-word systems. For example, deductive verification has successfully been used to verify relevant library code [4, 6] (and to discover subtle and relevant bugs during the process [12]). At the same time, it has become increasingly clear that full functional verification is an elusive goal for almost all application scenarios. In practice, the validation of software remains dominated by testing and simulation.

Verification methods and tools are available that fully cover industrial languages and can handle realistic systems, but their effective application requires considerable training on part of the user. The main challenge to their successful practical use is the need for formal specification: It is exceedingly difficult and time consuming to specify real systems' functionalities. Not verification, but specification is the real bottleneck in functional verification.

A formal specification must capture the desired properties (requirements) precisely. In addition, the user must provide auxiliary specifications such as interfaces of modules or components, loop invariants etc. Typically, the size of required specifications is a multiple of that of the code to be verified. To avoid

H. Seidl et al. (Eds.): ICTAC 2022, LNCS 13572, pp. 7–13, 2022.
https://doi.org/10.1007/978-3-031-17715-6_2

the need for specifications, one may (a) use pre-defined requirements (e.g., "no arithmetic overflow occurs"), (b) use bounded verification, which requires fewer auxiliary specifications, and (c) use regression verification, where the old version of a program is used as specification of the new version. But all these approaches compromise on full functional verification. Full functional verification still needs a full formal specification.

One promising way to alleviate the difficulties with writing specifications are domain-specific specification languages that are adapted to the specifics of an application domain both with regard to system properties and to the methods commonly used in that domain to describe them. For example, assertion languages such as the Java Modeling Language (JML) [13] or SPEC# [1] adopt the syntax of the specified programming language, which is an important step, but fall short of adapting to the specification methodology of a particular domain.

Overview. In the following, we give an overview of Generalized Test Tables (GTTs) [3], which are a specification language derived from existing table-based test case descriptions commonly used in the domain of automated production systems. We cover syntax and semantics of GTTs as well as their use for formal verification (Sect. 3). We also introduce Relational Test Tables [15], which extend GTTs to specify the relation of code variants and versions (Sect. 4).

2   The Domain of Automated Production Systems

Automated Production Systems (aPS) drive safety- and mission-critical industrial processes, e.g., energy systems or automated manufacturing systems. The logic of an aPS is defined in software that is executed on real-time capable controllers. These controllers periodically read sensor stimuli and cyclically execute the same program to produce actuator signals (i.e., they are sample-based reactive systems). Software for aPS are commonly written using special-purpose languages from IEC 61131-3, which defines five textual and graphical programming languages for the domain of programmable logic controllers.

In practice, the quality assurance of aPS software is dominated by testing and simulation of individual test cases. These test cases are described in form of test tables defining a sequence of concrete inputs and the expected outputs. Commonly, these test tables are written and maintained in a spreadsheet application. Each test table corresponds to a single concrete run of the system.

3   Generalized Test Tables

GTTs are an extension of the concept of (concrete) test tables for the specification of correct functional behavior, where each GTT describes a family of concrete test tables. The main idea is to replace the concrete values in the table cells by abstract expressions, thus enabling a table to capture not just a single test case but many similar test cases, i.e., a scenario. Despite the additional

#	ASSUME		ASSERT		⏲	
	Tc [°C]	Tt [°C]	P	B		
1	$(Tc - Tb) > d$	$[10, 60 + d]$	TRUE	FALSE	30s	$\rceil$ [0, 1] $\lceil$
2	$> Tb, < Tc[-1]$	$> Tb[-1], < 60 + d$	TRUE	FALSE	–	
3	$\leq Tb$	$\leq 60 - d$	FALSE	TRUE	$\geq 30s$	$\rceil$ [0, 1] $\lceil$ $-\infty$
4	$\leq Tb$	$\leq 60 + d$	FALSE	TRUE	–	
5	–	$> 60 - d, \leq 60 + d$	FALSE	FALSE	$[1\text{min}, -]_p$	

Fig. 1. A GTT for a heating system [16].

syntax, we aim to preserve the intuitiveness and comprehensibility of concrete test tables. In particular for system design engineers who are experts in test case specification but are not familiar with formal temporal and first-order logic, this eases writing specifications. As the engineers are used to maintaining test tables with spreadsheet applications, we use a mixture of expressions common in spreadsheets and the IEC standard.

Figure 1 shows a GTT for a heating system consisting of a solar thermal collector and an auxiliary gas burner, and Fig. 2 shows a concrete test table that is an instance of this GTT. The GTT describes the scenario in which the water temperature Tt (input variable) in the water tank is insufficient. The system is designed to target a temperature between $60 - d$ and $60 + d$ °C. The temperature Tt can be increased either by pumping warm water from the collector (output variable P) or activating the gas burner (output variable B). We decide to use the collector if the temperature in the collector Tc (input variable) is above Tt (by more than d °C). If so, we pump hot water from the collector to the tank (row 1) increasing the tank temperature and decreasing the collector temperature (row 2). Otherwise, if the collector temperature is insufficient (lower than $Tc < Tt$), we use the gas burner (row 3 and 4). The system has to use the gas burner if the tank temperature is below $60 - d$ °C for at least 30 s., and the system is allowed to use the gas burner if the temperature is below $60 + d$ °C. Row 5 specifies that the system should stand still if the target temperature has been reached. The process is repeated indefinitely.

#	ASSUME		ASSERT		⏲
	Tc [°C]	Tt [°C]	P	B	
1	76	65	TRUE	FALSE	30s
2	73	66	TRUE	FALSE	1
3	73	66	TRUE	FALSE	1
4	72	67	TRUE	FALSE	1
5	71	68	TRUE	FALSE	1
6	70	70	TRUE	FALSE	1
7	25	70	FALSE	FALSE	1

Fig. 2. A concrete test table for the GTT for a heating system in Fig. 1.

Typically, the columns of GTT belong to one of two categories: one for the input variables and one for the output variables—or, more abstractly, one for assumptions and one for assertions. Each cell contains (comma separated) constraints on the designated column variable. Each constraint is a complete or abbreviated Boolean expression. The expressions may contain the input and output variables and global parameters and are evaluated using the semantics of IEC 61131-3. For example, the constraint "[10, 60 + d]" restricts the boiler temperature Tt (column variable) to the depicted range and is an abbreviation for $10 \leq Tt \wedge Tt \leq 60 + d$ for an arbitrary d. The variable d is a global parameter (with an arbitrary value that is fixed for the table). A system needs to conform to every possible instantiation of a global parameter, in the sense of an universal quantification. A "don't-care" ("—") constraint signals that the value may be chosen arbitrarily. References to values of past I/O cycles can be made using square brackets, e.g., "$< Tc[-1]$" specifies that the collector temperature is strictly decreasing compared to the last cycle.

The table rows form the steps of a (test) protocol which are consecutively applied from top to bottom, considering the "duration column" on the right of the table. The duration column defines how often a row or a group of rows can be repeated, e.g., "—" denotes a (finite) repetition for zero-or-more cycles, "[1,—]" a repetition for at least one cycle, and "$-_\infty$" is the infinite repetition (ω). If multiple successor rows are "active", i.e., can be chosen next, the protocol branches non-deterministically.

Informally, a software system is *not* compliant with a GTT, if the software responds with an output which violates all currently active table rows—assuming that all inputs (up to the current point in time) have always fulfilled the input constraints of at least one row that was active when the input occurred. Formally, the compliance of software to a GTT is defined as a two-party turn-based game in which the challenger (the environment) chooses the input values and the system computes the output values. The first party who plays a faulty turn, i. e., emitting an input or output which does not satisfy any current assumptions or assertions, looses the game. The software complies to a GTT if it implements a winning strategy, i.e., never loses this game.

Our main purpose for GTTs is the static verification with a model-checker [3, 9], but they are also suitable for runtime verification [16], and for the generation of concrete test cases [17].

4   Relational Test Tables

Not every required property is functional, i.e., a property that specifies the behavior for single program runs, e. g., an invariant that needs to hold in every reachable state or an LTL formula that needs to hold for any execution trace. Properties like regression verification [7], information flow or the behavior after a restart define the relation between multiple runs [5][1]. Such relational properties

---

[1] Or sometimes called multi-property [11] or hyper-properties [10] if all program runs origin from the same program.

#	CTRL		ASSUME		ASSERT	⊕
	a	b	I	b» Reset	O	
1	▶	▶	=	a» Reset	=	≥ 1 ⌐∞
2	◀0	▶	=	TRUE	=	1 ⌐

Fig. 3. This RTT specifies that resetting with *Reset* results into the same behavior, as running the system from its initial state. The program runs a and b are from the same program.

are expressible with Relational Test Tables RTTs [15], which are an extension of GTTs.

There is an implicit universal quantification over the program runs, which arise by the execution of the same or of different programs. This allows us to express various kinds of properties like

Absence of regression. The new system behaves exactly as the old system modulo the intended changes (bug fixes etc.).

(Secure) information flow. A stored secret is never leaked into observable output variables.

Robustness. Two similar input values result in similar output.

Most important for the engineer is that relational properties allow the use of existing software for functional specification. Instead of writing multiple GTTs, the engineer can use existing similar programs, and describe how the verification subject should behave in relation to them.

RTTs are an extension of GTTs to allow the specification of relational properties [15], which extend the syntax of GTTs to cope with the multiple program runs. Figure 3 shows an RTT, which specifies that a given software is robust after a software reset. The reset is triggered by setting the input variable `Reset` to true. After a reset, the program should behave identically to the system as started in the initial state (hard reset). Hence, we verify that every variable is correctly reset.

RTTs have a new column type, called control columns: Control columns define the name and number of program runs. Their cell content controls the associated runs. One can normally execute ▶, pause the program run ‖ (stuttering), or reset its state back to that of a previous table row r ◀r. Control commands allow to break up the synchronous (lock-step) execution of program runs. In addition to GTTs, each program variable is qualified with the identifier of the corresponding program run.

The RTT in Fig. 3 uses two program runs (a, b) of the same program. The first row describes that both runs behaves equally (equality = on **O**) as long as the input variables (equality on = on **I**) and the *Reset* are equal for at least one cycle. The reset is triggered after an arbitrary amount of time by switching to row 2: Then, *Reset* is set to true in program run b, while the program state of program run a is set to the initial state (as it was at the beginning of row 1). Equality of input and output should remain the same. The table requires that, after the hard reset for a and the soft reset for b, the output remains the same if the input remains the same. Because of the row group, we repeat this process infinitely often.

The semantics of RTTs is defined by reduction to GTTs using product programs [2]. The control commands are handled by program transformation of the original software. Application on typical examples from software engineering can be found in [15].

5   Conclusion

GTTs and RTTs arise from the idea to re-use an already established language for the specification and verification of reactive systems. This includes capturing the original semantics of test tables and extending it to use in formal tools. If this process succeeds, we gain a domain specific language that preserves intuitiveness and comprehensibility of the original language but allows formal specification and verification. A complete explanation of GTTs and RTTs can be found in [14]. Their integration into the development process for aPS is discussed in [8].

References

1. Barnett, M., Leino, K.R.M., Schulte, W.: The Spec# programming system: an overview. In: Barthe, G., Burdy, L., Huisman, M., Lanet, J.-L., Muntean, T. (eds.) CASSIS 2004. LNCS, vol. 3362, pp. 49–69. Springer, Heidelberg (2005). https://doi.org/10.1007/978-3-540-30569-9_3
2. Barthe, G., Crespo, J.M., Kunz, C.: Relational verification using product programs. In: Butler, M., Schulte, W. (eds.) FM 2011. LNCS, vol. 6664, pp. 200–214. Springer, Heidelberg (2011). https://doi.org/10.1007/978-3-642-21437-0_17
3. Beckert, B., Cha, S., Ulbrich, M., Vogel-Heuser, B., Weigl, A.: Generalised test tables: a practical specification language for reactive systems. In: Polikarpova, N., Schneider, S. (eds.) IFM 2017. LNCS, vol. 10510, pp. 129–144. Springer, Cham (2017). https://doi.org/10.1007/978-3-319-66845-1_9
4. Beckert, B., Schiffl, J., Schmitt, P.H., Ulbrich, M.: Proving JDK's dual pivot quicksort correct. In: Paskevich, A., Wies, T. (eds.) VSTTE 2017. LNCS, vol. 10712, pp. 35–48. Springer, Cham (2017). https://doi.org/10.1007/978-3-319-72308-2_3
5. Beckert, B., Ulbrich, M.: Trends in relational program verification. In: Principled Software Development, pp. 41–58. Springer, Cham (2018). https://doi.org/10.1007/978-3-319-98047-8_3
6. de Boer, M., de Gouw, S., Klamroth, J., Jung, C., Ulbrich, M., Weigl, A.: Formal specification and verification of JDK's identity hash map implementation. In: ter Beek, M.H., Monahan, R. (eds.) Integrated Formal Methods - 17th International Conference, IFM 2022, Lugano, Switzerland, June 7–10, 2022, Proceedings. Lecture Notes in Computer Science, vol. 13274, pp. 45–62. Springer, Cham (2022). https://doi.org/10.1007/978-3-031-07727-2_4
7. Butler, M., Conchon, S., Zaïdi, F. (eds.): ICFEM 2015. LNCS, vol. 9407. Springer, Cham (2015). https://doi.org/10.1007/978-3-319-25423-4

8. Cha, S.: Application concept and evaluation of a formal specification approach usable by engineers for retrofitting production automation by software changes. Ph.D. thesis, Technical University of Munich, Germany (2021). https://nbn-resolving.org/urn:nbn:de:bvb:91-diss-20210519-1595575-0-5

9. Cha, S., Weigl, A., Ulbrich, M., Beckert, B., Vogel-Heuser, B.: Applicability of generalized test tables: a case study using the manufacturing system demonstrator xppu. Automatisierungstechnik **66**(10), 834–848 (2018). https://doi.org/10.1515/auto-2018-0028

10. Clarkson, M.R., Schneider, F.B.: Hyperproperties. J. Comput. Secur. **18**(6), 1157–1210 (2010). https://doi.org/10.3233/JCS-2009-0393

11. Goudsmid, O., Grumberg, O., Sheinvald, S.: Compositional model checking for multi-properties. In: Henglein, F., Shoham, S., Vizel, Y. (eds.) VMCAI 2021. LNCS, vol. 12597, pp. 55–80. Springer, Cham (2021). https://doi.org/10.1007/978-3-030-67067-2_4

12. de Gouw, S., Rot, J., de Boer, F.S., Bubel, R., Hähnle, R.: OpenJDK's Java.utils.Collection.sort() is broken: the good, the bad and the worst case. In: Kroening, D., Păsăreanu, C.S. (eds.) CAV 2015. LNCS, vol. 9206, pp. 273–289. Springer, Cham (2015). https://doi.org/10.1007/978-3-319-21690-4_16

13. Leavens, G.T.: Tutorial on JML, the java modeling language. In: Stirewalt, R.E.K., Egyed, A., Fischer, B. (eds.) 22nd IEEE/ACM International Conference on Automated Software Engineering (ASE 2007), 5–9 November 2007, Atlanta, Georgia, USA, p. 573. ACM (2007). https://doi.org/10.1145/1321631.1321747

14. Weigl, A.: Formal Specification and Verification for Automated Production Systems. Ph.D. thesis, Karlsruhe Institute of Technology, Germany (2021). https://nbn-resolving.org/urn:nbn:de:101:1-2021122204023164080066

15. Weigl, A., Ulbrich, M., Cha, S., Beckert, B., Vogel-Heuser, B.: Relational test tables: A practical specification language for evolution and security. In: Bae, K., Bianculli, D., Gnesi, S., Plat, N. (eds.) FormaliSE@ICSE 2020: 8th International Conference on Formal Methods in Software Engineering, Seoul, Republic of Korea, 13 July 2020, pp. 77–86. ACM (2020). https://doi.org/10.1145/3372020.3391566

16. Weigl, A., Ulbrich, M., Tyszberowicz, S., Klamroth, J.: Runtime verification of generalized test tables. In: Dutle, A., Moscato, M.M., Titolo, L., Muñoz, C.A., Perez, I. (eds.) NFM 2021. LNCS, vol. 12673, pp. 358–374. Springer, Cham (2021). https://doi.org/10.1007/978-3-030-76384-8_22

17. Weigl, A., Wiebe, F., Ulbrich, M., Ulewicz, S., Cha, S., Kirsten, M., Beckert, B., Vogel-Heuser, B.: Generalized test tables: A powerful and intuitive specification language for reactive systems. In: 15th IEEE International Conference on Industrial Informatics, INDIN 2017, Emden, Germany, 24–26 July 2017, pp. 875–882. IEEE (2017). https://doi.org/10.1109/INDIN.2017.8104887

Reachability Games and Parity Games

Volker Diekert[(✉)] [iD] and Manfred Kufleitner[iD]

University of Stuttgart, FMI, Stuttgart, Germany
{diekert,kufleitner}@fmi.uni-stuttgart.de

Abstract. Parity games are positionally determined. This is a fundamental and classical result. In 2010, Calude et al. showed a breakthrough
result for finite parity games: the winning regions and their positional
winning strategies can be computed in quasi-polynomial time.

   In the present paper we give a self-contained and detailed proofs for
both results. The results in this paper are not meant to be original. The
positional determinacy result is shown for possibly infinite parity games
using the ideas of Zielonka which he published in 1998. In order to show
quasi-polynomial time, we follow Lehtinen's register games, which she
introduced in 2018. Although the time complexity of Lehtinen's algorithm is not optimal, register games are conceptually simple and interesting in their own right. Various of our proofs are either new or simpli-
fications of the original proofs. The topics in this paper include the definition and the computation of optimal attractors for reachability games,
too.

1 Introduction

A game on a graph is played by two players who move from one vertex to another.
The vertices are often called *positions*. Every move needs to follow an edge in
the graph. Each position belongs to one of the players and the owner of the
position chooses the next move. The resulting sequence of moves can be finite
or infinite. Basically, there can be two reasons for a game to be finite: the game
ends in a sink (i.e., a vertex where no moves are possible) or one of the players
has won the game. The other situation is that the game continues indefinitely.
Infinite games also have a winner; the winner depends on the sequence of vertices
visited during the game or, alternatively, on the sequence of moves (i.e., edges)
taken by the players. When considering infinite duration games, then a typical
approach in the literature is to avoid finite games by disallowing both sinks and
finite winning sequences. In this paper, we take a slightly different approach.
We allow game graphs to be infinite and to have sinks, and we consider winning
conditions which allow both finite and infinite games. This way, we are able to
discuss reachability games and parity games in a uniform way.

   A *strategy* is a rule for choosing a player's next move; the chosen move can
depend on the current position (i.e., the current vertex in the graph) and all
previous moves. Players *follow* a strategy if, whenever it is their turn, they
always use the strategy's suggestion as their next move. A strategy is *winning*
if, by following the strategy, the player wins against all possible replies of the

© The Author(s), under exclusive license to Springer Nature Switzerland AG 2022
H. Seidl et al. (Eds.): ICTAC 2022, LNCS 13572, pp. 14–35, 2022.
https://doi.org/10.1007/978-3-031-17715-6_3

opponent. This depends on the starting position; there might be some starting positions where the strategy is winning and others where it is not winning. A game is *determined* if for every starting position exactly one of the players has a winning strategy. Not all games are determined; the example by Gale and Stewart of a non-determined game relies on the axiom of choice [6].

After introducing a general framework for games on graphs, we consider reachability games and parity games in more depth. The objective for one of the players in a *reachability game* is to eventually visit a position in a given target set R; the objective of the other player is to never visit a position in R. In a *parity game*, there is a finite set of non-negative integers and each vertex is colored with one of these integers; the colors are also called *priorities*. A game which ends in a sink is losing for the owner of the sink (i.e., a player loses immediately if they cannot move); all other games are infinite. In an infinite game, the largest color which is seen infinitely often determines the winner. One player wins if this color is even and the other player wins if it is odd. Among the numerous applications of parity games, we mention the following two: parity games play an important role in model-checking modal μ-calculus [7, Part V], and they can be used for proving the complementation lemma in Rabin's Tree Theorem [15]; see e.g. [16].

Martin's Determinacy Theorem shows that if the winning condition in a game on graphs is a Borel set, then the game is determined [11]. This includes both reachability games and parity games. However, the winning strategies from the Borel Determinacy Theorem need to store all the previous moves. Gurevich and Harrington proved that *finite-memory strategies* suffice for parity games over finite game graphs [8]: at every starting position, exactly one of the players has a winning strategy which only takes into account the current position and a fixed number of bits of information about the past (and this fixed number of bits can be updated move by move). Independently of one another, Emerson and Jutla [3] and Mostowski [13] further improved this result by showing *positional determinacy* (or *memoryless determinacy*) of finite parity games. In a *positional* strategy, the next move only depends on the current position. Positional strategies are also known as *memoryless*. Positional determinacy means that, for every starting position, exactly one of the players has a positional winning strategy. Zielonka showed memoryless determinacy for infinite parity games in which every vertex has only a finite number of successors [18], but he also observed that only some minor adjustments are necessary to generalize this result to arbitrary infinite graphs. Therefore we consider parity games over arbitrary graphs confirming his observation. The present proof is based on notes of the first author when he attended a lecture by Zielonka held in Paris on January 19th, 1996. As a tool for our proof, we show that reachability games are positionally determined. The result is well-known and considered to be folklore. For the sake of completeness, we include the proof.

Algorithmically solving a game usually means one of two things. Firstly, given a starting position, one wants to know the winner of the game (i.e., the player with a winning strategy). And secondly, we can solve a game by computing winning regions and winning strategies for the two players. Since a solution to the first problem typically also involves the computation of a winning strategy, the two problems are equivalent in practice. We only consider solutions of games with finite game graphs. It is folklore that reachability games can be solved in time $\mathcal{O}(n+m)$ for game graphs with n vertices and m edges; see e.g. [7, Exercise 2.6]. We give a version of this algorithm which computes *optimal* strategies. There is a large and increasing number of algorithms for solving parity games; we refer to the Oink project by van Dijk [17] for an overview. Nowadays, Zielonka's algorithm [18] is considered to be the most classical one. It is relatively easy to describe and it is often fast in practice [5]. However, Friedmann showed that there are instances where Zielonka's algorithm uses an exponential number of steps [4]. In the same paper, Friedmann gave an upper bound of $\mathcal{O}(n^d)$ on the number of recursive calls in Zielonka's algorithms for parity games with n vertices and d colors. Since every recursive call involves solving two reachability games, this yields a running time of $\mathcal{O}(n^d(n+m)) \subseteq \mathcal{O}(n^{d+2})$. We give an analysis of Zielonka's algorithm which shows that its running time is in $\mathcal{O}(n^{d-1}(n+m)) \subseteq \mathcal{O}(n^{d+1})$.

Calude et al. [1] showed that parity games with n vertices can be solved in quasi-polynomial time $2^{\log^{\mathcal{O}(1)}(n)}$. This led to a series of quasi-polynomial algorithms; see e.g. [10,14] for brief overviews. We give a version of Lehtinen's algorithm [9]. Her quasi-polynomial time algorithm is conceptually simpler than the algorithm by Calude et al. but less efficient in the worst case. Lehtinen's algorithm uses Zielonka's algorithm on a larger game graph but with $2 + 2\lceil \log_2 n \rceil$ colors, only. The resulting running time is $n^{\mathcal{O}(\log n)} d^{\mathcal{O}(\log^2 n)}$ for a game with n vertices and largest color d. This is not optimal. For instance, the recent modification of Zielonka's algorithm [10, Theorem 3.3] has a running time of $\mathcal{O}\left(n^{6.9+2\log\left(1+\frac{d}{2\log n}\right)}\right)$.

As usual, we use *random access machines* to measure the time complexity of algorithms; see e.g. [2, Chapter 2.2].

2   Games on Graphs

A *game graph* $G = (V_0, V_1, E)$ is a directed graph such that the *vertices* $V = V_0 \cup V_1$ are partitioned into two sets V_0 and V_1 with $V_0 \cap V_1 = \emptyset$. We allow V to be infinite. The set of *edges* is $E \subseteq V \times V$. Depending on the setting, the game graph might have additional information such as labeled edges or a coloring of the vertices. A *sink* is a vertex $v \in V$ without outgoing edges. The set of all finite paths in the graph (V, E) is denoted by E^*; and E^∞ is the set of all finite of infinite paths. We consider E^∞ to be a subset of $V^+ \cup V^\omega$, i.e., a path $\alpha \in E^\infty$ is either a non-empty finite sequence $\alpha = v_1 \cdots v_k$ or an infinite sequence $\alpha = v_1 v_2 \cdots$ of vertices v_j such that any two consecutive vertices v_j, v_{j+1} satisfying the edge relation $(v_j, v_{j+1}) \in E$. Similarly, we have $E^* \subseteq V^+$. There are two *players*, player 0 and player 1. The vertices in V_i *belong* to player $i \in \{0, 1\}$. A *position* is a vertex $u \in V$. At position u, player $i \in \{0, 1\}$ with $u \in V_i$ chooses $v \in V$ with $(u, v) \in E$. The next position is v and the game continues at this position. This is called a *move* of player i. We use the term *position* rather than vertex for an element $v \in V$ to emphasize that v is part of a sequence of moves; on the other hand, for graph properties such as paths we use the term *vertex*.

A set of *games* C is a subset of E^∞ such that every path in E^∞ has a unique prefix in C. This prefix does not need to be proper. Note that no path in C has a proper prefix in C; i.e., either a game is infinite or the game immediately ends as soon as a finite sequence of moves defines a path in C. A *winning condition* is a partition $C = C_0 \cup C_1$. Here, C_i is the set of games which player i wins, and we have $C_0 \cap C_1 = \emptyset$. The winning condition C_i of player i does *not depend on finite prefixes* if for every $p\beta \in C$, we have that $\beta \in C_i$ implies $p\beta \in C_i$. We note that this property of C_i also depends on C_{1-i} because we consider all games in $C = C_0 \cup C_1$. A *game* (G, u, C_0, C_1) consists of a game graph G, an initial position $u \in V$, and a winning condition C_0, C_1. The latter gives the set of games as $C = C_0 \cup C_1$. If the winning condition is clear from the context, then the game is denoted by (G, u); if $G = (V_0, V_1, E)$, then we usually do not distinguish between (G, u) and (V_0, V_1, E, u) in the sense that both describe the same game. Remember that, by abuse of notation, a *game* is also a sequence in C. A game (in the sense of a sequence in C) on (G, u) is created by moves of the players, starting at position u; the game is either infinitely long, or it finishes immediately if the current sequence of positions yields a path in $C \cap E^*$. Note that every game has a unique winner $i \in \{0, 1\}$ because if the game reaches a sink (in particular, there was no previous point at which a player has won the game), then the path leading to this sink needs to be in C.

Intuitively, a strategy for player i defines its next move; this move can depend on the current position $v_k \in V_i$ as well as the sequence of the previous positions $v_1, \ldots, v_{k-1}$. More formally, it is a partial map $\sigma : E^* \to V$ such that after the moves $v_1 \cdots v_k$ with $v_k \in V_i$, the next move of player i is $v_{k+1} = \sigma(v_1 \cdots v_k)$. In particular, the strategy is required to satisfy $(v_k, v_{k+1}) \in E$. It does not have to be defined on all paths in V^*V_i because some configurations might not be reachable if player i always moves according to the strategy. Moreover, we sometimes do not care for certain positions how player i moves. This is the case if all moves at this position lead to winning games, or if all games at this position immediately end. In this paper, we are mostly interested in strategies which do not take the previous moves into account and only depend on the current position: A *positional strategy* for player i is a partial map $\sigma : W \to W$ for $W \subseteq V$ such that if $\sigma(w)$ is defined, then $w \in W \cap V_i$ and $(w, \sigma(w)) \in E$; i.e., the strategy only suggests legal moves and only for player i. The set W is called the *support* of σ. A path $\alpha = v_1 v_2 \cdots \in E^\infty$ with $v_1 \in W$ follows a strategy $\sigma : W \to W$ for player i if for all prefixes $v_1 \cdots v_j v_{j+1}$ of α such that $\sigma(v_j)$ is defined, we have $v_{j+1} = \sigma(v_j)$. In other words, whenever possible, player i applies σ for choosing their next move. Remember that if $\sigma(v_j)$ is defined, then $v_j \in W \cap V_i$. Note that we allow α to leave and re-enter W. A positional strategy $\sigma : W \to W$ for player i is *winning* if all games α which start in W and follow σ are in C_i. In this case, we say that σ is a *i-strategy*. If $\sigma : W \to W$ is an i-strategy and $\sigma(w)$ is not defined for $w \in W \cap V_i$, then all games starting in W, following i, and visiting w at some point are winning for player i. This means that the only reason for σ to be undefined at a position $w \in W \cap V_i$ is that the choice of the next move does not matter. For instance, this is the case if player i wins as soon as the position w is reached. If $\sigma_0 : W_0 \to W_0$ is a 0-strategy and $\sigma_1 : W_1 \to W_1$ is a 1-strategy, then $W_0 \cap W_1 = \emptyset$; otherwise, a game starting in $W_0 \cap W_1$ and following both strategies would be winning for both players.

We can identify a positional strategy $\sigma : W \to W$ with the subgraph (W, F) where the set of edges is $F = \{(w, \sigma(w)) \mid \sigma(w) \text{ is defined}\}$; note that $F \subseteq E$. Similarly, a positional strategy can be built-in into the game graph by replacing the edges E by $E' = F \cup \{(u, v) \in E \mid \sigma(u) \text{ is not defined}\}$. We order i-strategies by $(W', F') \leq (W, F)$ if $W' \subseteq W$ and $F' \subseteq F$. By Zorn's Lemma, there exist maximal i-strategies. Maximal i-strategies (W, F) have the following property: Whenever, for a position $w \in W \cap V_i$, the set of neighbors $\{v \in W \mid (w, v) \in E\}$ in W is nonempty, then there exists an edge $(w, v) \in F$. Otherwise, all possible (W, F)-following continuations (even those leaving W) from w would lead to winning games for player i. By adding an edge (w, v) to F which stays inside W, the resulting strategy would generate a subset of those continuations but with more edges, thereby contradicting the maximality of (W, F). Therefore, maximal strategies always choose a move except if $w \in W \cap V_i$ is a sink or if all outgoing edges leave W.

Proposition 1. *If the winning condition C_i does not depend on finite prefixes, then the support of maximal i-strategies is unique. This means, if (W_1, F_1) is maximal and (W_2, F_2) is an arbitrary i-strategy, then we have $W_2 \subseteq W_1$.*

Proof. Let (W_1, F_1) be maximal and (W_2, F_2) be an arbitrary i-strategy. Let $W_3 = W_1 \cup W_2$ and $F_3 = F_1 \cup \{(u, v) \in F_2 \mid u \in W_2 \setminus W_1\}$, i.e., at positions in $W_1 \cap W_2$, we give preference to the strategy (W_1, F_1). Consider a game α which starts in W_3 and follows (W_3, F_3). If α never visits a position in W_1, then α follows the i-strategy (W_2, F_2). Hence, $\alpha \in C_i$ in this case. If $\alpha = p\beta$ such that β starts at a position in W_1, then β follows the i-strategy (W_1, F_1). As before, we see that $\beta \in C_i$. Since the winning condition does not depend on finite prefixes, we have $\alpha = p\beta \in C_i$. Thus, (W_3, F_3) is an i-strategy. By maximality of (W_1, F_1) and since $(W_1, F_1) \leq (W_3, F_3)$, we have $(W_1, F_1) = (W_3, F_3)$ and thus $W_2 \subseteq W_3 = W_1$. □

In the above situation, the support of a maximal i-strategy is called the *winning region* of player i. A game is *positionally determined* if, for $i \in \{0, 1\}$, there exist i-strategies (W_i, F_i) such that $V = W_0 \cup W_1$. Since W_0 and W_1 are the supports of winning strategies for different players, we have $W_0 \cap W_1 = \emptyset$. Positional determinacy is also known as *memoryless determinacy* in the literature. If a game G is positionally determined and player i has an arbitrary (not necessarily positional) winning strategy for (G, v), then i also has a positional winning strategy for (G, v): the opponent $1 - i$ cannot win (G, v) with a positional strategy against player i's arbitrary strategy. Since G is positionally determined, one of the players has a positional winning strategy for (G, v); and this has to be player i because it is not player $1 - i$. By *solving* a game (G, v), we mean deciding which player has a winning strategy (if it exists at all); if G is positionally determined, then exactly one of the players has a positional winning strategy (and the other player loses no matter which strategy they use).

Remark 1. Sometimes one needs to distinguish whether there is one winning strategy for all starting positions in the winning region or whether for every starting position in the winning region there exists an individual winning strategy. Proposition 1 shows that these two properties are equivalent for positional strategies and winning conditions which do not depend on finite prefixes.   ◇

3   Reachability Games and Attractors

Let $G = (V_0, V_1, E)$ be a game graph, and let $V = V_0 \cup V_1$. Let $M \subseteq E^\infty$ be the paths which cannot be extended to the right (the identifier M is for *maximal* paths). In other words, we have $\alpha \in M$ if either α is infinite or α ends in a sink. In a *reachability game*, the objective of one of the players is to reach a position in $R \subseteq V$. Suppose that player i wins at all positions in R in which case we call R the *target set* of player i. More formally, the winning condition for player i is $C_i = (V \setminus R)^* R \cap E^*$, and the winning condition for player $1 - i$ is $C_{1-i} = M \cap (V \setminus R)^\infty$. The winning conditions does not depend on finite prefixes.

Theorem 1. *Reachability games are positionally determined.*

Proof. Let (W_i, F_i) be a maximal i-strategy. Note that $R \subseteq W_i$. Let $W_{1-i} = V \setminus W_i$. It remains to show that player $1 - i$ has a positional winning strategy with support W_{1-i}. If $u \in W_{1-i} \cap V_i$, then there exists no edge $(u, v) \in E$ with $v \in W_i$; otherwise $(W_i \cup \{u\}, F_i \cup \{(u, v)\})$ is a bigger i-strategy than (W_i, F_i). Next, we consider $u \in W_{1-i} \cap V_{1-i}$. If u is a sink, then all games ending in u are winning for player $1 - i$ since it is impossible to reach a position in R. If u is not a sink, then there exists an edge $(u, v) \in E$ with $v \in W_{1-i}$; otherwise $(W_i \cup \{v\}, F_i)$ is a bigger i-strategy than (W_i, F_i). We set $\sigma(u) = v$. This leads to a strategy $\sigma : W_{1-i} \to W_{1-i}$ such that $\sigma(u)$ is defined for all $u \in W_{1-i} \cap V_{1-i}$ which are not a sink. Every game α starting in W_{1-i} and following σ never leaves W_{1-i}. It follows that α cannot enter a position in R and, hence, $\alpha \in C_{1-i}$.   □

Example 1. We consider the following reachability game with vertices $V_0 = \{a, c, e\}$ and $V_1 = \{b, d, f\}$, edges $E = \{ad, da, be, eb, de, ed, bc, ef, fc\}$ where xy denotes the pair (x, y), and target set $R = \{c, f\}$ of player 0. A graphical representation is

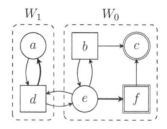

Round vertices belong to player 0 and square vertices belong to player 1. Double borders are used for states in the target set. The winning regions are $W_0 = \{b, c, e, f\}$ and $W_1 = \{a, d\}$ and the (in this case unique) positional strategies are (W_i, F_i) with $F_0 = \{da\}$ and $F_1 = \{ef\}$, indicated by thicker arrows.   ◇

The proof of Theorem 1 suggests that the winning regions of the two players can be defined more explicitly. A set of vertices $A \subseteq V$ is i-*attracting* if the following two conditions hold:

1. If $u \in V_i$ and there exists an edge $(u, v) \in E$ with $v \in A$, then $u \in A$.
2. If $u \in V_{1-i}$ is not a sink and all edges $(u, v) \in E$ satisfy $v \in A$, then $u \in A$.

The i-*attractor* of $R \subseteq V$ is the smallest set of vertices which is i-attracting and contains R. It is well-defined because V is i-attracting, and the intersection of all sets which both contain R and are i-attracting also satisfies both properties. The i-attractor of R in a game graph G is denoted by $\mathrm{attr}_i(G, R)$.

Proposition 2. *Let (W, F) be a maximal i-strategy for reaching the target set R within a game graph G. Then we have $W = \mathrm{attr}_i(G, R)$.*

Proof. Let $A = \mathrm{attr}_i(G, R)$ and $B = V \setminus A$. Since (W, F) is maximal, the set W is i-attracting and it contains R; see the proof of Theorem 1 for details. This shows $A \subseteq W$. For the converse, we show $B \subseteq V \setminus W$ by giving a $(1 - i)$-strategy $\sigma : B \to B$. Consider a position $u \in B$. We have $u \notin R$ because $R \subseteq A$. In particular, if u is a sink, then reaching u is winning for player $1 - i$. Therefore, we can assume that u is not a sink. If $u \in V_i$, then there is no edge $(u, v) \in E$ with $v \in A$ because A is i-attracting. Similarly, if $u \in V_{1-i}$, then there exists an edge $(u, v) \in E$ with $v \notin A$ and we can set $\sigma(u) = v$. Every game which starts in B and follows the strategy σ stays in B. Therefore, player $1 - i$ wins at all positions in B since he can avoid reaching a position in R. This shows $B \subseteq V \setminus W$ and, hence, $W \subseteq A$.   □

A consequence of Theorem 1 and Proposition 2 is that player $1 - i$ wins at all positions in $V \setminus \mathrm{attr}_i(G, R)$.

4   Optimal Strategies for Reachability Games

In this section, we consider reachability games where the set of positions V is finite. We still assume that player i's winning objective is to reach a position in $R \subseteq V$. Let (W_i, F_i) be a maximal i-strategy. Then for all starting positions $u \in W_i$, there is a maximal number of moves which are necessary for games which follows (W_i, F_i) to reach a position in R. We are interested in a strategy for player i which minimizes this number. We do not aim at optimizing maximal $(1 - i)$-strategies (W_{1-i}, F_{1-i}) because usually games starting in W_{1-i} and following (W_{1-i}, F_{1-i}) are infinite; the only other case is that the game ends in a sink and if we would want to optimize the number of moves when targeting a sink, we could apply the same algorithms as below for player $1 - i$ reaching this set of sinks.

The *winning distance* is a function $d : V \to \mathbb{N} \cup \{\infty\}$ defined by:

- $d(u) = 0$ for $u \in R$,
- $d(u) = \min \{1 + d(v) \mid (u,v) \in E \}$ for $u \in V_i \setminus R$,
- $d(u) = \max \{1 + d(v) \mid (u,v) \in E \}$ for $u \in V_{1-i} \setminus R$.

Here, we let $\min \emptyset = \max \emptyset = \infty$ and $1 + \infty = \infty$. A similar concept as the winning distance is the *rank* of a position which is only defined for elements of the attractor [18, p.146]. Since d occurs on both sides of the definition, we need to show that the winning distance is well-defined.

Lemma 1. *The winning distance is unique and well-defined. Moreover, we have $d(u) < \infty$ if and only if $u \in W_i$.*

Proof. A straightforward induction on $n \in \mathbb{N}$ shows that if $d(u) \leq n$, then $u \in W_i$. Next, we show that $u \in W_i$ implies $d(u) < \infty$. Since V is finite, the i-attractor of R can be computed by starting with R and successively adding positions which contradict the current set to be i-attracting; this is repeated until the set does not change anymore. By using this naive algorithm, every time we add a position u, we can define $d(u) < \infty$ (and possibly update previously defined values $d(v)$; these updates only affects positions v satisfying $d(v) > d(u)$ before and after the update). Since $W_i = \text{attr}_i(G, R)$, we have $d(u) < \infty$ for all $u \in W_i$. This concludes the second part of the lemma. Moreover, we have shown that there exists at least one winning distance.

Suppose that d and d' are two different winning distances. Then there exists $u \in V$ with $d(u) \neq d'(u)$. At least one of $d(u)$ and $d'(u)$ is in $\mathbb{N}$; therefore, we have $u \in W_i$ which shows that both $d(u)$ and $d'(u)$ are in $\mathbb{N}$. Among all $u \in V$ with $d(u) \neq d'(u)$, let n be minimal such that either $d(u) > n = d'(u)$ or $d'(u) > n = d(u)$. Without loss of generality, suppose that $d'(u) > n = d(u)$. We have $u \notin R$ because $d'(u) > 0$. If $u \in V_i \setminus R$, then there exists an edge $(u, v) \in E$ with $n - 1 = d(v) = d'(v)$; the latter equality holds by minimality of n. This edge yields $d'(u) \leq n$, a contradiction. Let now $u \in V_{1-i}$, then all edges $(u, v) \in E$ satisfy $d(v) \leq n - 1$ and hence $d(v) = d'(v)$, again by minimality of n. Note that there exists at least one such edge since $\max \emptyset = \infty$ but $d(u) < \infty$. As before, this shows $d'(u) \leq n$, a contradiction. Therefore $d(u) \neq d'(u)$ is not possible. $\square$

The following example shows that the second claim of Lemma 1 does not directly hold for infinite graphs. For finite game graphs, attractors are often defined as $\bigcup_{k \geq 0} \{v \in V \mid d(v) \leq k \}$; see e.g. [18, p.145]. The example also shows that this approach does not work directly for graphs where positions can have infinitely many successors. Depending on the purpose, ordinal numbers might be used for a generalization of the winning distance towards infinite graphs.

Example 2. Let $V = V_1 = \mathbb{N} \cup \{a, b\}$, i.e., all positions belong to player 1. Let $R = \{0\} \subseteq \mathbb{N}$ be the target set of player 0. The edges are $\{(i+1, i) \in \mathbb{N}^2 \mid i \geq 0 \} \cup \{(b, i) \mid i \in \mathbb{N} \} \cup \{(a, b)\}$.

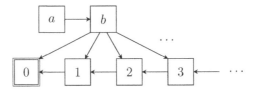

All positions in V are winning for player 0: all paths eventually end in 0 because $\mathbb{N}$ is well-ordered. The winning distance of the vertex $n \in \mathbb{N}$ is $d(n) = n$; in particular, the winning distances of the successors of b are unbounded. Therefore, the winning distance of b cannot be a natural number. Also note that the winning distance of a would need to be greater than $d(b)$.   ◇

Lemma 2. *Let (W_i, F_i) be a maximal i-strategy for a reachability game in a finite game graph and let $d : V \to \mathbb{N} \cup \{\infty\}$ be the winning distance. For every $u \in W_i$, there exists a game α starting in u and following (W_i, F_i) which uses at least $d(u)$ moves.*

Proof. This is trivial if $d(u) = 0$. Let now $d(u) > 0$; in particular $u \notin R$. First, consider the case $u \in V_i$. Let $(u, v) \in F_i$. Then $1 + d(v) \geq d(u)$ and, by induction, there exists a game β starting at v and following (W_i, F_i) such that β uses at least $d(v)$ moves. Then $\alpha = u\beta$ is a game which starts at u and which follows (W_i, F_i) and uses at least $1 + d(v) \geq d(u)$ moves.

Next, let $u \in V_{1-i}$. Then there exists at least one edge $(u, v) \in E$ because $u \in W_i \setminus R$. Among the neighbors of u, we choose v with $d(u) = 1 + d(v)$; the position v exists by definition of $d(u)$. By induction, there exists a game β starting at v and following (W_i, F_i) such that β uses at least $d(v)$ moves; as before, $\alpha = u\beta$ is the desired game.   □

When trying to optimize the worst-case number of moves necessary to reach R, then Lemma 2 shows that one cannot be better than the winning distance. A maximal i-strategy $\sigma : W_i \to W_i$ actually achieves this bound if and only if for all $u \in W_i \cap V_i$ we have that $\sigma(u) = v$ implies $d(u) = 1 + d(v)$. In this case, we say that σ is *optimal*. For player $1 - i$, every maximal winning strategy is optimal.

Proposition 3. *Consider a reachability game with n vertices and m edges. Then we can compute optimal positional winning strategies for both players in time $\mathcal{O}(n + m)$. In particular, this computation yields attractors.*

Proof. We basically use an adaption of the breadth-first search algorithm (and if all positions belong to player i, then it actually is the usual breadth-first search algorithm; see e.g. [2, Chapter 20.2]). Our algorithm uses the following data structures:

– A set $\mathcal{P}$ which is initialized as $\mathcal{P} = \big\{ \big(\{u \in V \mid (u, v) \in E\}, v \big) \mid v \in V \big\}$. For every $v \in V$, the set $\mathcal{P}$ gives access to its predecessors. We assume that for a given $v \in V$, we have access to the pair $(U, v) \in \mathcal{P}$ in constant time. We will successively remove edges in $\mathcal{P}$ such that the remaining edges define strategies for the respective players. If we say that we remove an edge (u, v) from $\mathcal{P}$, then what we actually do is replacing the pair $(U, v) \in \mathcal{P}$ by $(U \setminus u, v)$.

- A function $n : V_{1-i} \to \mathbb{N}$ which gives the number of neighbors (i.e., successors, not predecessors) of a vertex in V_{1-i} in the graph defined by $\mathcal{P}$. Initially, we let $n(u)$ be the out-degree of u.
- A function $D : V \to \mathbb{N} \cup \{\infty\}$ which is the current estimate of the winning distance d. Initially, we have $D(u) = 0$ for $u \in R$ and $D(u) = \infty$ for $u \notin R$. For each vertex u, the value $D(u)$ is assigned a new value at most once; if such an assignment occurs, then before this assignment, we have $D(u) = \infty$ and after this assignment we have $D(u) = d(u) < \infty$. If at some point we have $D(u) < \infty$ for $u \in V_{1-i} \setminus R$, then $n(u) = 0$.
- A FIFO queue $\mathcal{Q}$ of vertices in V. Initially, $\mathcal{Q}$ contains the vertices in R in some arbitrary order. The queue $\mathcal{Q}$ contains the vertices which still need to propagate their distance D to their predecessors. An invariant of $\mathcal{Q}$ will be that it only contains vertices v with $D(v) = d(v) < \infty$ and that vertices with smaller winning distance are closer to the front of the queue than vertices with larger winning distance.

After this initialization, the algorithm proceeds as follows. While $\mathcal{Q} \neq \emptyset$ do:

1. $v \leftarrow$ delete-first($\mathcal{Q}$) and let $(U, v) \in \mathcal{P}$.
2. For all $u \in U$ do
   - If $u \in V_i$, then
     (a) If $D(u) = \infty$, then $D(u) \leftarrow 1 + D(v)$ and append u to $\mathcal{Q}$;
     (b) else we remove the edge (u, v) from $\mathcal{P}$.
   - If $u \in V_{1-i}$, then
     (c) We remove the edge (u, v) from $\mathcal{P}$ and set $n(u) \leftarrow n(u) - 1$.
     (d) If $n(u) = 0$, then $D(u) \leftarrow 1 + D(v)$ and append u to $\mathcal{Q}$.

For $u \in V_i$, we set $D(u) = 1 + D(v)$ when considering the first edge (u, v); and for $u \in V_{1-i}$, we set $D(u) = 1 + D(v)$ when considering the last remaining edge (u, v). In both cases, the invariant on the order of the elements in $\mathcal{Q}$ ensures that $D(u) = d(u)$. In step 2d, if $n(u) = 0$, we could remember the move (u, v) since, even though it is losing for player $1 - i$, always choosing these moves achieves a maximal winning distance for player i (it might be a natural desire of player $1 - i$ to delay the defeat for as long as possible).

Every vertex $v \in V$ is added at most once to the queue $\mathcal{Q}$. In the sum of all iterations of the loop in step 2, we consider every edge of the graph at most once. Since the initialization is also possible in linear time, the running time of the above algorithm is $\mathcal{O}(n + m)$.

After running the algorithm, $D = d$ is the winning distance and thus the winning positions are $W_i = \{u \in V \mid D(u) < \infty\}$ and $W_{1-i} = \{u \in V \mid D(u) = \infty\}$. The winning strategy $\sigma_i : W_i \to W_i$ for player i at a position $u \in (W_i \cap V_i) \setminus R$ is given by $\sigma_i(u) = v$ with $(u, v) \in E$ and $D(u) = 1 + D(v)$; note that in this case, after the algorithm stops, there exists exactly one pair $(U, v) \in \mathcal{P}$ such that $D(v) < \infty$ and $u \in U$. The winning strategy $\sigma_{1-i} : W_{1-i} \to W_{1-i}$ for player $1-i$ at a non-sink position $u \in W_{1-i} \cap V_{1-i}$ is given by $\sigma_{1-i}(u) = v$ with $(u, v) \in E$

such that $v \in W_{1-i}$; note that if u is not a sink, then there exists at least one such edge because $n(u) > 0$. Moreover, after the algorithm terminates, every such edge is represented by a pair $(U, v) \in \mathcal{P}$ with $u \in U$. In other words, winning strategies for both player i and $1 - i$ are given by the edges in $\mathcal{P}$; however, for player i, we need to exclude the edges leading to positions outside W_i.   □

5 Parity Games

The game graph $G = (V_0, V_1, E, \chi)$ of a *parity game* is equipped with a vertex coloring $\chi : V \to \{1, \ldots, d\}$ for an integer $d \geq 1$. The coloring χ helps to formulate the winning conditions of the players. Sometimes, if we prefer the smallest color to be even, the coloring has the form $\chi : V \to \{0, \ldots, d-1\}$. The identifier d is for *dimension*. In the literature, the colors are called *priorities*, too. The subgraph of G *induced* by a set of vertices $W \subseteq V$ is $G[W] = (V_0 \cap W, V_1 \cap W, E', \chi')$ with $E' = \{(u, v) \in E \mid u, v \in W\}$ and $\chi' : W \to \{1, \ldots, d\}$ is the restriction of χ. Similarly, $G - W$ is the subgraph of G induced by $V \setminus W$. In a parity game, player 0 is called EVEN and player 1 is called ODD. The set of games C contains all infinite paths and all finite paths ending in a sink. EVEN wins all finite games which end in a sink in V_1 and infinite games where the largest color which is seen infinitely often is even. Symmetrically, ODD wins all finite games which end in a sink in V_0 and all infinite games where the largest color which is seen infinitely often is odd. The winning condition regarding sinks means that if players cannot move, they lose immediately.

Whenever there are two colors q and $q+2$ such that there is no position with color $q+1$, then we can identify q and $q+2$ (for instance, by using the color q for all vertices with color $q+2$). In particular, we can assume that the dimension d is the number of different colors in the game graph.

Remark 2. In Sect. 7, we consider edge colorings for parity games. In this setting, a game graph has the form $G = (V_0, V_1, E, \chi)$ with $\chi : E \to \{1, \ldots, d\}$. As before, if the owner of a position cannot move, the owner loses immediately. Otherwise, in an infinite game player i wins if the largest number q, which is seen infinitely often on the edges, satisfies $q \equiv i \bmod 2$. A parity game with vertex coloring χ can be transformed into a game with edge coloring χ' simply by defining $\chi'(e)$ by $\chi(u)$ if u is the source of e. For the other direction we introduce a smallest color 0, and we subdivide every edge $e = (u, v)$ into a path $u \to v_e \to v$ for a new vertex v_e. The old vertices are colored with 0 and the color of v_e is the color of e.   ◊

Remark 3. Reachability games can be encoded as parity games with two colors. Let $G = (V_0, V_1, E)$ be the game graph of a reachability game where (w.l.o.g.) it is player 0's objective to reach $R \subseteq V$. For all $v \in R$, we remove all outgoing edges. Then for all sinks v (which now includes all positions in R), we introduce a self-loop (v, v). After these two modifications, the resulting edge set is called E'. We let $\chi(v) = 2$ if $v \in R$; otherwise, we set $\chi(v) = 1$. The parity game $G' = (V_0, V_1, E', \chi)$ now has the following property: player 0 wins the reachability game (G, v) with target set R if and only if player 0 wins the parity game (G', v).   ◊

As noticed in Remark 3, we can eliminate all sinks in a parity game by introducing self-loops: let $G = (V_0, V_1, E, \chi)$ be a parity game with vertex coloring $\chi : V \to \{1, \ldots, d\}$. Let $S_i \subseteq V_i$ be the sinks belonging to player i. For every position $v \in S_0 \cup S_1$, we introduce a self-loop (v, v). The resulting edge set is called E'. Let $\chi' : V \to \{1, \ldots, \max\{2, d\}\}$ be a re-coloring of the vertices with

$$\chi'(v) = \begin{cases} i + 1 & \text{if } v \in S_i \text{ for } i \in \{0, 1\}, \\ \chi(v) & \text{otherwise.} \end{cases}$$

Then (G, v) and (G', v) for $G' = (V_0, V_1, E', \chi')$ have the same winner. The advantage is that the game graph G' is without sinks. However, this construction introduces new edges and for $d = 1$ it increases the number of colors, in general.

A long sequence of results culminated in the following theorem [3,8,12,13,18].

Theorem 2. *Parity games are positionally determined.*

Proof. Let $G = (V_0, V_1, E, \chi)$ be the game graph of a parity game with coloring $\chi : V \to \{1, \ldots, d\}$. We proceed by induction on d. If $d = 1$, then EVEN wins at all positions in $\mathrm{attr}_0(G, S_1)$ where S_1 are the sinks in V_1; all other positions are winning for ODD. Let now $d > 1$ and suppose that $d \equiv i \bmod 2$ for $i \in \{0, 1\}$. Let W_{1-i} be the support of a maximal $(1 - i)$-strategy and let $W_i = V \setminus W_{1-i}$. We need to show that there exists an i-strategy with support W_i. The sinks in V_i are all in W_{1-i}. On positions in $\mathrm{attr}_{1-i}(G, W_{1-i}) \setminus W_{1-i}$, player $1 - i$ can force the game to visit a position in W_{1-i} (see Proposition 2) and from there on, player $1 - i$ can follow the $(1 - i)$-strategy with support W_{1-i}. Therefore, $\mathrm{attr}_{1-i}(G, W_{1-i})$ is the support of a winning strategy and, by maximality of W_{1-i}, we have $W_{1-i} = \mathrm{attr}_{1-i}(G, W_{1-i})$. It follows that all outgoing edges of positions in $W_i \cap V_{1-i}$ lead to positions in W_i, and every position in $W_i \cap V_i$ has at least one outgoing edge to a position in W_i.

Let H be the subgraph of G induced by W_i, let $U_d = \{v \in W_i \mid \chi(v) = d\}$, let $A = \mathrm{attr}_i(H, U_d)$ and let G' be the subgraph of H induced by $W_i \setminus A$.

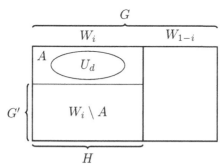

A $(1 - i)$-strategy with nonempty support W'_{1-i} on the game graph G' yields a $(1 - i)$-strategy with support $W_{1-i} \cup W'_{1-i}$ on G. Therefore, there is no nonempty $(1 - i)$-strategy on G'. By induction on the number of colors, there exists a maximal i-strategy σ' on G' with support $W_i \setminus A$. This leads to the following strategy for player i on positions in W_i within the game graph G:

- At positions in $U_d \cap V_i$, player i moves to a position in W_i.
- At positions in $(A \backslash U_d) \cap V_i$, player i moves according to the positional strategy for reaching U_d; see Proposition 2.
- At positions in $(W_i \backslash A) \cap V_i$, player i moves according to σ'.

The rules above define a positional strategy σ for player i with support W_i. To see that it is winning, consider any game α starting at a position in W_i which follows σ. Since player i never makes a move to W_{1-i} and since player $1-i$ can never make a move to W_{1-i}, all positions of α are in W_i. If α is finite, then it ends in a sink in V_{1-i} because there are no sinks in $V_i \cap W_i$; in particular, α is winning for player i in this case. We can therefore assume that α is infinite. If α enters A infinitely often, then α infinitely often visits a position in U_d. Therefore, the maximal color d is seen infinitely often; therefore, α is winning for player i. If, after some finite prefix, α stays in G', then α is winning for player i by choice of σ'. This shows that σ is an i-strategy. $\qquad\square$

Example 3. We consider the following parity game. Round vertices belong to EVEN, square vertices belong to ODD. The label x:n means that the name of the vertex is x and its color is n.

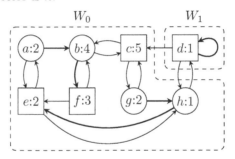

EVEN's winning region is $W_0 = \{a, b, c, e, f, g, h\}$ and ODD's winning region is $W_1 = \{d\}$. The respective winning strategies are indicated using thicker edges. We note that EVEN's winning strategy is not unique since the strategy's move (a, b) could be replaced by (a, e). $\qquad\Diamond$

Let the maximal color satisfy $d \equiv i \bmod 2$ for $i \in \{0, 1\}$. The proof of Theorem 2 shows that as soon as we know the winning positions of player $1 - i$, we can easily compute a winning strategy for player i. However, the proof implicitly also gives an algorithm for computing the winning positions W_{1-i} of player $1 - i$. Let $X \subseteq V$ be minimal such that

- X contains all sinks in V_i,
- $X = \mathrm{attr}_{1-i}(G, X)$, and
- (using the subgraph G' from the proof of Theorem 2) if W'_{1-i} are the winning positions of player $1 - i$ in the game G', then $W'_{1-i} \subseteq X$.

The support W_{1-i} of a maximal $(1 - i)$-strategy satisfies the above properties; therefore we have $X \subseteq W_{1-i}$. On the other hand, the proof of Theorem 2 gives a winning strategy for player i for all positions in $V \backslash X$. This yields $X = W_1$. In the next section, we consider this approach for solving finite parity games.

6 Zielonka's Algorithm for Parity Games

Let the number of positions V in G be finite and suppose that the largest color d satisfies $d \equiv i \bmod 2$ for $i \in \{0,1\}$. We can assume that there is at least one vertex with color d; otherwise, we decrease the dimension d. We initialize $W_{1-i} = \mathrm{attr}_{1-i}(G, S_i)$ where S_i are the sinks belonging to player i. Then we iterate the following steps until W_{1-i} does not increase anymore (i.e., until $W'_{1-i} = \emptyset$ or $W_{1-i} = V$):

1. $W_i \leftarrow V \setminus W_{1-i}$ and $H \leftarrow G[W_i]$
2. $U_d \leftarrow \{v \in W_i \mid \chi(v) = d\}$
3. $A \leftarrow \mathrm{attr}_i(H, U_d)$
4. $G' \leftarrow G[W_i \setminus A]$
5. Let W'_{1-i} be the winning positions of ODD in G'.
6. $W_{1-i} \leftarrow W_{1-i} \cup W'_{1-i}$
7. $W_{1-i} \leftarrow \mathrm{attr}_{1-i}(G, W_{1-i})$

Note that Step 5 consists of a recursive call for a game graph with fewer vertices (since there is at least one vertex $v \in V$ with $\chi(v) = d$) and colors $\{1, \ldots, d-1\}$. There is no recursive call if G' is empty.

After the algorithm terminates, the winning regions of the two players are W_i and W_{1-i}; note that the correctness of the algorithm was proven in the previous section. The above algorithm can also compute a $(1-i)$-strategy with support W_{1-i}: Initially, the strategy with support W_{1-i} is the strategy for winning a reachability game. If W_{1-i} is increased in Step 6, then we unite the two winning strategies (the strategy for W_{1-i} before the assignment and the strategy for W'_{1-i}). If W_{1-i} is increased in Step 7, then on the new positions we play according to the strategy for reaching the positions in W_{1-i} before this assignment.

The i-strategy with support W_i can be computed as follows: During the last iteration of the loop, we have $W'_{1-i} = \emptyset$; moreover, we can assume that the recursive call in Step 5 also returns an i-strategy σ' with support $W_i \setminus A$. As in the proof of Theorem 2, a winning strategy for player i is as follows: at position in U_d, player i makes some arbitrary move to a position in W_i; at positions in $A \setminus U_d$, player i moves according to the positional strategy for reaching U_d; and at positions in $W_0 \setminus A$, player i moves according to σ'. Without any significant additional effort, we can therefore assume that the above algorithm also computes the corresponding winning strategies. This approach for computing maximal positional winning strategies is known as *Zielonka's algorithm*.

Theorem 3. *Let G be a parity game with n vertices, m edges, and d colors. Then Zielonka's algorithm computes maximal winning strategies for both players in time $\mathcal{O}(n^{d-1}(n+m))$ and, thus, in time $\mathcal{O}(n^{d+1})$.*

Proof. Let $c \geq 1$ be a constant such that the initialization and one iteration of the loop when omitting the time for the recursive call in Step 5 takes time at most $c \cdot (n+m)$; see Proposition 3. Let $f(n,d) \cdot c \cdot (n+m)$ be the running time of the algorithm. It suffices to show that $f(n,1) \leq 1$ and $f(n,d) \leq 2n^{d-1}$ for

$d \geq 2$. This is true for $d = 1$ because there is no recursive call. Let now $d \geq 2$. The game graph G' is always smaller than G. Since the size of H decreases with every iteration, there are at most n iterations of the loop. Every recursive call in Step 5 uses at most $n - 1$ positions and $d - 1$ colors. Hence, the worst-case running time satisfies

$$f(n,d) \cdot c \cdot (n+m) \leq n \cdot \left(f(n-1, d-1) \cdot c \cdot (n+m) + c \cdot (n+m) \right)$$

Dividing by $c \cdot (n+m)$ yields

$$f(n,d) \leq n \cdot \left(f(n-1, d-1) + 1 \right) \tag{1}$$

For $d = 2$, we obtain $f(n,2) \leq n\left(f(n-1,1) + 1\right) \leq 2n = 2n^{d-1}$ because $f(n-1,1) \leq 1$. Let now $d > 2$. Using Eq. (1), we see that

$$
\begin{aligned}
f(n,d) &\leq n \cdot \left(2(n-1)^{d-2} + 1 \right) && \text{by induction hypothesis} \\
&\leq n \cdot \left(2(n-1)n^{d-3} + 1 \right) && \text{since } d \geq 3 \\
&= n \cdot \left(2n^{d-2} - 2n^{d-3} + 1 \right) \\
&\leq 2n^{d-1} && \text{since } -2n^{d-3} + 1 < 0
\end{aligned}
$$

The second part of the statement follows since $\mathcal{O}(n+m) \subseteq \mathcal{O}(n^2)$.   □

Example 4. Consider the following parity game with $2n$ vertices and 2 colors. EVEN's positions are $V_0 = \{a_1, \ldots, a_n\}$ and ODD's positions are $V_1 = \{b_1, \ldots, b_n\}$. All vertices in V_0 have the color 1 and all vertices in V_1 have the color 2. We have loops (a_i, a_i) and edges (b_i, a_i) for all i as well as edges (a_i, b_j) for all $i < j$. All positions are winning for ODD. The game graph for $n = 4$ is:

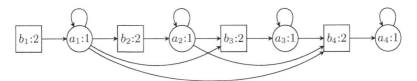

Initially, we have $W_1 = \emptyset$. In the first iteration of Zielonka's algorithm, we compute the 0-attractor of $U_2 = V_1$ which is $V \setminus \{a_n\}$. This computation uses a quadratic number of steps; see Proposition 3. Then the recursive call returns $W_1' = \{a_n\}$, after which we have $W_1 = \{a_n, b_n\}$ by computing the 1-attractor. The next iteration is similar, but with n decreased by 1. Since we have n iterations, this yields a cubic running time of Zielonka's algorithm. For $d = 2$, this shows that the bound of $\mathcal{O}(n^3)$ on the running time of Zielonka's algorithm is tight.   ◇

7   Lehtinen's Algorithm for Parity Games

The idea of Lehtinen's algorithm is to translate a given parity game into another parity game such that solutions of the new game yield solutions of the original game. Moreover, applying Zielonka's algorithm to the new parity game yields a quasi-polynomial running time $2^{\log^{\mathcal{O}(1)} n}$.

We need the following notions for graphs. A nonempty set of vertices $U \subseteq V$ is *strongly connected* if for all $u, v \in U$ there exists a path from u to v. Every singleton subset $\{v\} \subseteq V$ is strongly connected. A *strongly connected component* is a maximal strongly connected subset; i.e., U is a strongly connected component if there is no strongly connected subset U' with $U \subsetneq U' \subseteq V$. Every graph can be partitioned into strongly connected components; if U and U' are different strongly connected components, then there cannot exist paths both from U to U' and from U' to U. Therefore, by successively moving from one strongly connected component to another strongly connected component, one cannot visit the same strongly connected component twice. In particular, in a finite graph, there exist strongly connected components U such that one cannot reach any other strongly connected; in this case U is called *terminal*.

Let $G = (V_0, V_1, E, \chi)$ be the game graph of a parity game with vertices $V = V_0 \cup V_1$ and vertex coloring $\chi : V \to \{1, \ldots, d\}$. The r-register graph $R^r(G)$ of G is again a game graph, but with an edge coloring, see Remark 2. To avoid confusion, the vertices of $R^r(G)$ are called states. The states are the elements $(v, x, p) \in V \times \mathbb{N}^r \times \{s, t\}$ where $x = x_1 \cdots x_r$ satisfies $x_1 \leq \cdots \leq x_r$. States with $p = s$ are called *reset states*; states with $p = t$ are called *transition states*. All reset states belong to EVEN, every transition state (v, x, t) belongs to the owner of v. For every register $j \in \{1, \ldots, r\}$ and every reset state (v, x, s), there is an outgoing edge with label $reset(j)$. The target state is (v, y, t) with $y = (0, x_1, \ldots, x_{j-1}, x_{j+1}, \ldots, x_r)$. Formally, the label of the edge is not important it helps with reasoning about the game. If there is an outgoing edge at a transition state (v, x, t), then its target is a reset state (w, y, s) with $(v, w) \in E$ and $y_j = \max(\chi(w), x_j)$. The first kind of edges are called *resets* and the second kind of edges are called *transitions*. All paths alternate between resets and transitions. The color of all transitions is 0; the color of an edge with label $reset(j)$ is $2j$ if the value x_j of register j before the reset is even and $2j + 1$ if x_j is odd. The r-register game $R^r(G, v, x)$ is the parity game with initial state (v, x, s); its game graph is the subgraph of $R^r(G)$ induced by the states reachable from (v, x, s). For every game α in $R^r(G)$ starting at a state (u, x, p) there exists a *corresponding* game α_G in G starting at u. The game α_G is the sequence of first components at the transition states of α. Note that register games are not symmetric for the two players: Firstly, all reset states belong to EVEN. And secondly, resets of register j can have even and odd colors, but the odd color $2j + 1$ is larger than the corresponding even color $2j$. It is this second property which leads to the following lemma.

Lemma 3. *Let $r \geq 1$, let α be a game in $R^r(G)$ and let α_G be the corresponding game in G. If α_G is winning for ODD, then so is α.*

Proof. Let α_G be winning for ODD. The game α ends in the sink (v, x, t) if and only if α_G ends in the sink v. In particular, both sinks (v, x, t) and v then belong to the same player. Also note that reset states cannot be sinks. Since α_G is winning for ODD, we can assume that α is infinite (otherwise, α would end in a sink belonging to EVEN and therefore be winning for ODD, as desired).

Let q be the largest color which is seen infinitely often during the game α_G, and let j be the largest register such that EVEN infinitely often plays reset(j) in the game α. There is a point in α_G after which no color larger than q occurs. At the corresponding point in α, we can wait for j resets of register j. From then onwards, the value x_j of register j is at most q. In particular, whenever we then see the color q in α_G, the contents of register j is q, and it stays q at least until the next reset of register j. Therefore, there are infinitely many resets of register j when its value is q. Since α_G is winning for ODD, the number q is odd. We therefore infinitely often see the number $2j+1$ in the colors of α. Since all larger registers are reset only finitely often, $2j+1$ is the largest color of α which is seen infinitely often. Therefore, α is winning for ODD.   □

Lemma 4. *If* ODD *wins* (G, v), *then* ODD *wins* $R^r(G, v, x)$ *for all* $r \geq 1$ *and all* $x \in \mathbb{N}^r$.

Proof. If ODD wins (G, v), then there exists a positional strategy (V, F) such that ODD wins (G, v) by following this strategy. We adapt this strategy to $R^r(G)$: at a state (u, y, t) with $u \in V_1$, ODD moves to (u', y', s) with $(u, u') \in F$. It remains to show that this strategy is winning for ODD in the register game $R^r(G, v, x)$. Let α be a game starting at (v, x, s) and following the above strategy. The corresponding game α_G in G starts at v and follows the strategy (V, F). Therefore α_G is winning for ODD. By Lemma 3, ODD wins the game α.   □

Remark 4. Positional determinacy of parity games (Theorem 2) leads to the following consequence of Lemma 4: if EVEN wins $R^r(G, v, x)$ for some $r \geq 1$ and $x \in \mathbb{N}^r$, then EVEN wins (G, v). When following an analogous approach as above, then a direct proof for this consequence would need to translate a winning strategy for the register game $R^r(G, v, x)$ into a winning strategy for (G, v). However, even if EVEN's winning strategy for $R^r(G, v, x)$ is positional, the resulting strategy for (G, v) might not be positional because some different contents of the registers could lead to different moves at a given position in G.   ◊

For a weak converse of Lemma 4, we will use induction on the number of vertices. During this induction, smaller register games occur. Here, "smaller" either refers to the size of the corresponding game graph G or the number of registers. If G' is a subgraph of G, then $R^r(G')$ is a subgraph of $R^r(G)$. If $q \leq r$, then every positional strategy on $R^q(G)$ for EVEN defines a strategy on $R^r(G)$ in which EVEN never plays reset(j) for $j > q$.

During the proof of the following proposition, we will use a slightly different notion of a positional strategy. Instead of just the support, we assume that a positional strategy $\sigma : V \to V$ for player i is defined for all $v \in V_i$ which are not sinks (i.e., σ is also defined for the positions outside the support). Moreover, the proof will use defensive strategies. A strategy for EVEN in $R^r(G)$ is *defensive* if reset(r) is never played when the contents of register r is odd.

Proposition 4. *If* EVEN *wins* (G, v) *and* $|V| < 2^r$, *then* EVEN *wins* $R^r(G, v, x)$ *for all* $x \in \mathbb{N}^r$.

Proof. We assume without restriction that all vertices in G are reachable from v. We proceed by induction on $|V|$. First, suppose that $V = \{v\}$. If v is a sink, then it belongs to ODD because EVEN wins; in this case, after playing reset(1) at state (v, x, s), the game in $R^r(G)$ also ends in a sink belonging to ODD. If v is not a sink, then there is a self-loop and the color $\chi(v)$ is even (again because EVEN is wins). EVEN again always plays reset(1) and after the first reset (in which case the color depends on x), the color of all resets is 2. Since all other colors are 0, EVEN wins the register game. If $r = 1$, then $|V| = 1$ and this case was already considered. In the remainder of the proof, we can therefore assume that $r > 1$ and $|V| > 1$.

We fix a positional winning strategy for EVEN for (G, v). At transition states in the register game, EVEN always moves according to her strategy for G. We can remove all edges starting at EVEN's positions in G which are not part of the winning strategy. Since now, all reachable positions belonging to EVEN have exactly one outgoing edge, we can transfer ownership of these positions to ODD. In particular, now all transition states of $R^r(G, v, x)$ belong to ODD and the game alternates between EVEN's resets and ODD's transitions.

We show that EVEN can win $R^r(G, v, x)$ against every positional strategy of ODD. Let T be the transitions defining ODD's strategy. Consider is a strongly connected subgraph G' of G and let w be a vertex of G' such that (w, y, s) is a state of $R^r(G, v, x)$. Then $R^r(G', w, y)$ is a subgraph of $R^r(G, v, x)$. We say that a positional strategy of EVEN for $R^r(G', w, y)$ *is leaving* this subgraph if, starting at (w, y, s) in $R^r(G, v, x)$, alternating between EVEN's strategy for resets and ODD's strategy T for transitions eventually leads to a state outside $R^r(G', w, y)$.

As before for the graph G and EVEN's strategy, we can remove all transitions from the register game except for those in ODD's strategy T. We cannot transfer ownership because there might be sinks owned by ODD. However, there is never any choice to be made by ODD. EVEN, starting from (v, x, s), moves to some terminal strongly connected component H of $R^r(G, v, x)$; this means that there is no other strongly connected component which is reachable from H. In general, EVEN's strategy for reaching H is not defensive. The underlying positions (i.e., first components) of states in H form a strongly connected subgraph G' of G. If G' consists of a single sink, then this sink belongs to ODD (and, thus, EVEN also wins the corresponding register game). We can therefore assume that G' is not a sink. Since every position in G' lies on some non-trivial loop, the largest color d of G' is even. Since H is a terminal strongly connected component, all registers have only values which appear in G' (otherwise, EVEN could move to another strongly connected component by playing reset(r)). Next, EVEN goes to one of the vertices (w, y, s) such that $\chi(w) = d$. We now have $y = (d, \dots, d)$;

therefore, we can apply the following claim which then completes the proof of the proposition because H cannot be left.

Claim: Let G' be a strongly connected subgraph of G which is not a single sink. Let d be the largest color of the vertices of G'. Let w be a vertex of G'. Let $y = (y_1, \ldots, y_r)$ be such that $y_r \geq d$ and y_r is even, and $y_j \leq d$ for all $j < r$. Then EVEN has a defensive strategy for $R^r(G', w, y)$ which is either winning or which is leaving $R^r(G', w, y)$.

Proof of the Claim: The color d is even because EVEN wins (G, v). The proof is by induction on the number of vertices in G'. If G' contains a single vertex, then EVEN always plays reset(1) with color 2. This either yields an infinite game with the maximal infinite color being 2, or it ends in a sink belonging to ODD, or it leaves $R^r(G', w, y)$. In either case, the claim is true. Let now G' have at least two vertices. Let U_d consist of all vertices of G' with color d. Let $G_1, \ldots, G_k$ be the strongly connected components of $G' - U_d$. Some of the components might be sinks – even if G' does not have any sinks. If G_j has less than 2^{r-1} vertices, then the induction hypothesis in the proof of the proposition yields a winning strategy for the $(r-1)$-register game on G_j. Since G has less than 2^r vertices, at most one component has $\geq 2^{r-1}$ vertices. Let this component be G_1; (it might be that there is no such component, in which case we can simply assume that G_1 is never visited). It remains to give winning strategies for EVEN for register games on G_1 and on U_d. Suppose that we have such strategies, then EVEN always plays these winning strategies until ODD's strategy T forces her to move to

– a register game on another strongly component $G_1, \ldots, G_k$,
– a register game on U_d, or
– to leave $R^r(G', v, x)$.

In the first two cases, EVEN again applies the winning strategy of the corresponding register game. If the last case occurs, then the claim is true. Note that every path in G' from G_j to G_ℓ and back to G_j with $j \neq \ell$ visits U_d at some point before re-entering G_j.

Next, we describe the winning strategies for the register games on G_1 and on U_d. We will maintain the following invariants: Firstly, whenever we are leaving G_1, the contents of register r will either be even or less than d. And secondly, whenever we are leaving U_d, the contents of register r will be d. All other registers always have values $\leq d$. The components $G_2, \ldots, G_k$ do not affect these invariants because the colors are $\leq d$ and the strategies never play reset(r).

At reset states (u, y, s) with $u \in U_d$, EVEN plays reset(r) and moves to a transition state (u, y', t). When entering (u, y, s), the invariants ensure that the contents y_r of register r is an even number $\geq d$ and $y_j = d$ for all $j < r$. Therefore, the color of this reset edge is $2r$ and the value y'_r of register r after the reset is $y_{r-1} = d$ because $r \geq 2$.

It remains to consider the component G_1. EVEN plays reset($r - 1$) until all registers except for register r have a value which occurs in G_1 or until we are leaving G_1, whichever happens first. If we are leaving G_1, then all colors of the resets are $\leq 2r - 1$. Otherwise, the induction hypothesis in the proof of the claim yields a defensive winning strategy for the register game on G_1, and EVEN continues by following this strategy. Note that all resets in following a defensive strategy have colors $\leq 2r$. ODD's strategy T might force us to leave G_1 with a register configuration where the top register is smaller than d (and this value could even be over-written by another number smaller than d in one of the other components $G_2, \ldots, G_k$) but it will again be d when re-entering G_1 since we need to visit U_d before re-entering.

A game which follows EVEN's strategy and which does not leave G' can fall into one of two categories. The first category is that it infinitely often visits states (u, y, s) with $u \in U_d$. Then we have infinitely many resets with color $2r$ and all other resets have colors $\leq 2r$. Therefore, this game is winning for EVEN. The second category is that after some time, the game stays in one of the components G_j (i.e., all states (u, y, p) after some finite prefix have first components u in G_j). In this case, the game is winning because (after some finite prefix) it follows a strategy for G_j which is winning for EVEN. This completes the proof of the claim and, hence, the proof of the proposition. □

Theorem 4 (Lehtinen [9]). *Let G be a parity game with n vertices and let $r \geq 1$ such that $n < 2^r$. Then for every position v and every $x \in \mathbb{N}^r$, the games (G, v) and $R^r(G, v, x)$ have the same winner.*

Proof. If ODD wins (G, v), then ODD wins $R^r(G, v, x)$ by Lemma 4. If EVEN wins (G, v), then EVEN wins $R^r(G, v, x)$ by Proposition 4. The claim follows by Theorem 2. □

Remark 5. Lehtinen shows that there are parity games with n vertices such that EVEN wins at every vertex but she needs $\Omega(\log n)$ registers to win the corresponding register game [9, Lemma 4.4]. We revisit Lehtinen's example in terms of vertex colorings: We inductively construct a game graph G_r with $2^{r+1}-2$ vertices all belonging to ODD, with largest color $2r$, and such that there is exactly one position with color $2r$ and one with color $2r - 1$. EVEN wins (G_r, v) at all starting positions v but no register game $R^r(G_r, v, x)$. Moreover, EVEN wins $R^{r+1}(G_r, v, x)$ for all $v \in V$ and all $x \in \mathbb{N}^{r+1}$. We let R_1 be the following game graph with colors $\{1, 2\}$:

The graph G_r for $r > 1$ is constructed from two copies of G_{r-1} and two new vertices with colors $2r - 1$ and $2r$, respectively:

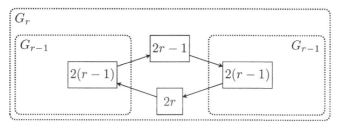

We briefly describe ODD's winning strategy for the r-register game in terms of the underlying graph. As long as EVEN only resets registers $\leq r-1$, ODD always stays within one of graphs G_{r-1}. After EVEN resets register r at least r times, ODD changes to the other copy of G_{r-1} via one of the vertices with color $2r-1$ or $2r$. EVEN wins the $(r+1)$-register game, basically by resetting register $j+1$ at positions with color $2j$ and register 1 at all other positions.   ◇

Theorem 5 (Calude, Jain, Khoussainov, Li, and Stephan [1]). *If G is a parity game with n vertices, then we can decide the winner of (G,v) in quasi-polynomial time $2^{\log^{\mathcal{O}(1)}(n)}$.*

Proof. Let the vertex coloring be $\chi : V \to \{1,\dots,d\}$. Let $r \geq 1$ be minimal such that $n < 2^r$. Then $r \in \mathcal{O}(\log n)$. By Theorem 4, it suffices to solve $R^r(G,v,\mathbf{0})$ for $\mathbf{0} = (0,\dots,0)$ in quasi-polynomial time to decide the winner of (G,v). The positions of $R^r(G,v,\mathbf{0})$ are all in $V \times \{0,\dots,d\}^r \times \{s,t\}$. In particular, there are at most $2n(d+1)^r$ positions in the register game with colors $\{0\}\cup\{2,\dots,2r+1\}$. We can solve this game using Zielonka's algorithm in time $n^{\mathcal{O}(r)}d^{\mathcal{O}(r^2)}$, see Remark 2. This yields a running time of $n^{\mathcal{O}(\log n)}d^{\mathcal{O}(\log^2 n)}$ since $r \in \mathcal{O}(\log n)$. We can assume that $d \leq n+1$ which yields a quasi-polynomial running time $n^{\mathcal{O}(\log^2 n)} = 2^{\mathcal{O}(\log^3(n))}$.   □

8   Conclusion

In this survey paper, we revisit Lehtinen's quasi-polynomial algorithm for solving parity games [9], and we provide all necessary preliminary results with full proofs. This includes the following topics:

– attractors and positional determinacy of reachability games,
– the computation of optimal winning strategies for reachability games,
– positional determinacy of parity games,
– an analysis of Zielonka's algorithm for solving parity games,
– and Lehtinen's register games.

Both determinacy results are proven for arbitrary game graphs; in particular, the graphs are allowed to be infinite. While reachability games can end after finitely many moves if the target set is reached, typical parity games have an infinite duration (except if they end in a sink). For a uniform treatment, we use a framework which includes both finite and infinite durations.

It would be interesting to have a tighter analysis of Zielonka's algorithm. Friedmann gives a game with a linear number of vertices and colors such that the running time of Zielonka's algorithm on this game takes time at least F_n for the n-th Fibonacci number [4]. There is still a significant gap between this lower bound and the upper bound in Sect. 6. Whether finite parity games can be solved in polynomial time is still the main open problem is this area.

References

1. Calude, C.S., Jain, S., Khoussainov, B., Li, W., Stephan, F.: Deciding parity games in quasipolynomial time. In: Hatami, H., McKenzie, P., King, V. (eds.) Proceedings of the STOC 2017, pp. 252–263. ACM (2017)
2. Cormen, T.H., Leiserson, C.E., Rivest, R.L., Stein, C.: Introduction to Algorithms, 4th edn. The MIT Press (2022). 1st edn. (1990)
3. Emerson, E., Jutla, C.: Tree automata, mu-calculus and determinacy. In: Proceedings of the FoCS 1991, pp. 368–377. IEEE Computer Society (1991)
4. Friedmann, O.: Recursive algorithm for parity games requires exponential time. RAIRO - Theor. Inform. Appl. **45**(4), 449–457 (2011)
5. Friedmann, O., Lange, M.: Solving parity games in practice. In: Liu, Z., Ravn, A.P. (eds.) ATVA 2009. LNCS, vol. 5799, pp. 182–196. Springer, Heidelberg (2009). https://doi.org/10.1007/978-3-642-04761-9_15
6. Gale, D., Stewart, F.M.: Infinite games with perfect information. In: Contributions to the Theory of Games. Annals of Mathematics Studies, vol. 2, no. 28, pp. 245–266. Princeton University Press, Princeton (1953)
7. Grädel, E., Thomas, W., Wilke, T. (eds.): Automata Logics, and Infinite Games. LNCS, vol. 2500. Springer, Heidelberg (2002). https://doi.org/10.1007/3-540-36387-4
8. Gurevich, Y., Harrington, L.: Trees, automata, and games. In: Lewis, H.R., Simons, B.B., Burkhard, W.A., Landweber, L.H. (eds.) Proceedings of the STOC 1982, pp. 60–65. ACM (1982)
9. Lehtinen, K.: A modal μ perspective on solving parity games in quasi-polynomial time. In: Dawar, A., Grädel, E. (eds.) Proceedings of the LICS 2018, pp. 639–648. ACM (2018)
10. Lehtinen, K., Parys, P., Schewe, S., Wojtczak, D.: A recursive approach to solving Parity Games in quasipolynomial time. Logical Methods Comput. Sci. **18** (2022)
11. Martin, D.A.: Borel determinacy. Ann. Math. (2) **102**(2), 363–371 (1975)
12. McNaughton, R.: Infinite games played on finite graphs. Ann. Pure Appl. Logic **65**(2), 149–184 (1993)
13. Mostowski, A.W.: Games with forbidden positions. Technical Report 78, University of Gdansk (1991)
14. Parys, P.: Parity games: Zielonka's algorithm in quasi-polynomial time. In: Rossmanith, P., Heggernes, P., Katoen, J. (eds.) Proceedings of the MFCS 2019. LIPIcs, vol. 138, pp. 10:1–10:13. Schloss Dagstuhl - Leibniz-Zentrum für Informatik (2019)
15. Rabin, M.O.: Decidability of second-order theories and automata on infinite trees. Trans. Am. Math. Soc. **141**, 1–35 (1969)
16. Thomas, W.: Languages, automata, and logic. In: Rozenberg, G., Salomaa, A. (eds.) Handbook of Formal Languages, pp. 389–455. Springer, Heidelberg (1997). https://doi.org/10.1007/978-3-642-59126-6_7
17. Dijk, T.: Oink: an implementation and evaluation of modern parity game solvers. In: Beyer, D., Huisman, M. (eds.) TACAS 2018. LNCS, vol. 10805, pp. 291–308. Springer, Cham (2018). https://doi.org/10.1007/978-3-319-89960-2_16
18. Zielonka, W.: Infinite games on finitely coloured graphs with applications to automata on infinite trees. Theor. Comput. Sci. **200**, 135–183 (1998)

Human-Cyber-Physical Automata
and Their Synthesis

Miaomiao Zhang[1](✉), Wanwei Liu[2], Xiaochen Tang[1], Bowen Du[3],
and Zhiming Liu[4,5](✉)

[1] School of Software Engineering, Tongji University, Shanghai, China
{miaomiao,xiaochen9697}@tongji.edu.cn
[2] College of Computer Science, National University of Defense Technology,
Changsha, China
wwliu@nudt.edu.cn
[3] Department of Computer Science, University of Warwick, Coventry, UK
B.Du@warwick.ac.uk
[4] School of Computer and Information Science, Southwest University,
Chongqing, China
zhimingliu88@swu.edu.cn
[5] School of Software, Northwest Polytechnical University, Xi'an, China
zliu@nwup.edu.cn

A cyber-physical system (CPS) is now well understood as an integration of hierarchical composition digital computing (or information processing) systems and physical systems [3,10,14]. The constituent components are CPSs too, and they are supposed to be heterogeneous, namely, they can be developed by different teams with different programming languages and technology platforms. These components are inherently distributed and run in concurrency. The underlying computational theory is the theory of *hybrid I/O automata* [17]. The widely appreciated model of system architecture is the layered components composition based on interface contracts [8,15,20], which supports interface based black-box orchestration, substitution, plug-and-play extension, and component-wise refinement by contract.

The advances in research on CPSs and increasing practice in their applications show the importance of the human in the loop of the CPS. This is because not all control tasks can be fully automated and control needs to switch between humans and machines, and there are social and ethical considerations. Having humans in the control loop introduces many potential problems for which we do not yet know the solutions. These problems are considered as potential causes of accidents in the two Boeing Max accidents which happened in October 2018 and March 2019 [11,12]. Therefore, extensions to CPSs with the consideration of human knowledge and behaviours, human-cyber and human-physical interactions and collaborations are proposed with the notion of *human-cyber-physical systems* (HCPSs) [16,19,21,22]. We computer scientists all clearly understand that the study and development of any newly emerged computing systems require

We acknowledge the support to this work by the projects NSFC under grants No. 62032019, 61972284 and 61872371.

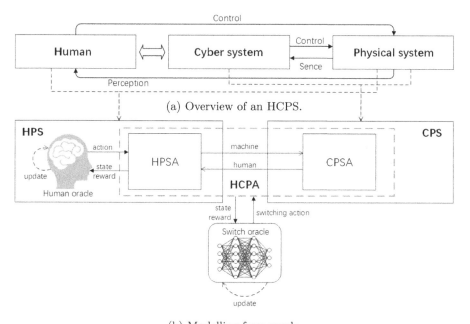

(a) Overview of an HCPS.

(b) Modelling framework.

Fig. 1. Overview of an HCPS and the modelling framework.

to establish its associated theory of computation. For example, we have the theory of automata (and Turing Machines [9]) for classical sequential computing, theory of I/O automata for concurrent and distributed computing [13], theory of timed automata [1,2,5] for real-time computing, probabilistic automata [18] for probabilistic computing, and hybrid I/O automata for CPSs (or hybrid systems). Therefore, Liu and Wang [16] strongly argue that there is an urgent need to develop a theory of *human-cyber-physical computing* or a theory of *human-cyber-physical automata* (HCPA). The reason for this need is from the fact that there does not exist a computational model which characterizes human knowledge and behaviours, the mechanisms of interactions between humans and machines, and between humans and the physical world. They further discuss methods of specification, design, and verification of HCPS, such as the model interface-contracts of human-cyber-physical components, which can only be developed on such an underlying theory of HCPA.

1   The Basic Model of HCPA

In this talk, we discuss our initial progress in our project on "Theory of Modelling and Software Defined Method for Human-Cyber-Physical Computing" which is supported by the Chinese Nature Science Foundation. We start with a simple and fundamental form of HCPSs[1], as shown in Fig. 1(a), consisting of three parts: a human model, a cyber system, and a physical system. In this model, the human and the cyber system jointly control the physical system. To do so, the human and the cyber system generate their own policies by sensing and analyzing the information of the physical system and then controlling the physical system in cooperation. In reality, a human can take the role of making control decisions and directly execute the control operation on the physical system or delegate the control operation to the cyber system. The model needs to consider that the human has the capability of automatic learning during the operation of the HCPS, and may make mistakes. The model of HCPA that we propose focuses on these characteristics of humans in an HCPS and the mechanism of control switching between the human and the cyber system. We give the formal definition of the basic models of HCPA we propose, which is shown in Fig. 1(b). It is important to note that we do not intend (we do not believe it is now theoretically feasible) to model generic human intelligence, but propose a modelling framework for representing the learning capability and process in an application-specific HCPS by machine learning model.

2   Synthesis of HCPS

Fig. 1(b) also illustrates the approach to constructing a model of HCPA. An HCPA of an HCPS is a composition of two automata, a *cyber-physical system automaton* (CPSA) and a *human-physical system automaton* (HPSA). The former characterizes the behaviour of the CPS in the HCPS according to given rules of state transitions, and the latter simulates behaviour of the human-physical system (HPS) in the HCPS and the behaviour of the physical system according to the control decisions made by the human. To characterize the learning ability of the human, we introduce a human oracle, which learns the interaction behaviour of the human with the physical system and updates and outputs human decisions. We further use another oracle which represents the control switching between the CPSA and the HPSA.

At any particular moment of time during its execution, an HCPA is in a state under the model of human control or the model of cyber control (also called machine control). A problem is that a human has learning capability and it can make mistakes in its decision making. This implies that the behaviour of performing control actions and state changes is probabilistic, and we cannot statically define the rules (or policies) in the process of human decision making and the conditions for switching from one mode to another. Furthermore, the requirements or properties required for analysis are in general probabilistic and can be specified by a logic formula, say in the linear temporal logic (LTL). We thus propose a synthesis method for automatic generation of the conditions for control mode switching and the policies to ensure that the HCPA satisfies a given objective with maximum probability. We use two Markov Decision Processes (MDPs) [4] to simulate the behaviours of the automata HPSA and CPSA,

---

[1] More humans, machines and physical systems are involved in a multi-layered HCPS.

respectively, and we extended the reinforcement learning algorithm of Bozkurt et al. [6] to implement the synthesis. We have evaluated our model and the method of synthesis with two case studies. The first is a grid-world motion planning case [6], and the second is a lunar landing case [7]. The results of our experiments show that the approach is effective in finding the policy that satisfies the given objective with maximum probability in an HCPA.

3   Concluding Remarks

In this talk, we propose research on the theory of computation for the new paradigm of human-cyber-physical computing. The grand goal is to support the design, development, operation, and maintenance of HCPSs, or the very closed notion of *cyber-physical-societal systems* (CPSSs). As the first step of the research, we assume an HCPS consists of a human-cyber system and a CPS in which a human operator and the cyber machine in the CPS jointly control the physical processes and define a basic model of human-cyber-physical automata (HCPA). An HCPA defines a composition of an automaton that models the behaviour of a human-physical system and an automaton that models a CPS. The model captures the key features that the human has learning and probabilistic behaviour, and provides abstractions for the interactions between the human and the cyber machines and between the human and the physical system. We also propose an approach to synthesize an HCPA to satisfy a given objective with maximum probability.

The basic model only assumes one human operator and one cyber machine in the system. The immediate further work includes the definition of compositions of a number of the HCPAs so as to form a multi-layered hierarchical HCPA. More future work includes the study of the properties, express power, and feasibility of implementation of this model. The development of a full theory of HCPA also involves fundamental and interdisciplinary research problems. For example, we can build the relation of different HCPA with different machine learning models so as to answer the question *if and when an HCPA is equivalent to a machine learning model*; and *how we can define an operational semantics of a program with the mixture of machine learning programs and traditional programs.*

Acknowledgments. We thank to our project colleagues Professor Wei Dong, Professor. Guanjun Liu and Dr. Hengjun Zhao for their comments. We express our thanks to Dr. Qiao Ke. She read the earlier version of the paper and provided good comments on the improvement of the paper.

References

1. Alur, R.: Timed automata. In: Halbwachs, N., Peled, D. (eds.) CAV 1999. LNCS, vol. 1633, pp. 8–22. Springer, Heidelberg (1999). https://doi.org/10.1007/3-540-48683-6_3
2. Alur, R., Dill, D.L.: A theory of timed automata. Theor. Comput. Sci. **126**(2), 183–235 (1994). https://doi.org/10.1016/0304-3975(94)90010-8

3. Baheti, R., Gill, H.: Cyber-physical systems. Impact Control Technol. **12**(1), 161–166 (2011)
4. Bellman, R.: A markovian decision process. J. Math. Mech. **6**(5), 679–684 (1957). http://www.jstor.org/stable/24900506
5. Bengtsson, J., Yi, W.: Timed automata: semantics, algorithms and tools. In: Desel, J., Reisig, W., Rozenberg, G. (eds.) ACPN 2003. LNCS, vol. 3098, pp. 87–124. Springer, Heidelberg (2004). https://doi.org/10.1007/978-3-540-27755-2_3
6. Bozkurt, A.K., Wang, Y., Zavlanos, M.M., Pajic, M.: Control synthesis from linear temporal logic specifications using model-free reinforcement learning. In: ICRA 2020, 31 May–31 August, Paris, France, 2020. pp. 10349–10355. IEEE (2020). https://doi.org/10.1109/ICRA40945.2020.9196796
7. Brockman, G., et al.: Openai gym. arXiv preprint arXiv:1606.01540 (2016)
8. Chen, X., Liu, Z.: Towards interface-driven design of evolving component-based architectures. In: Hinchey, M.G., Bowen, J.P., Olderog, E.-R. (eds.) Provably Correct Systems. NMSSE, pp. 121–148. Springer, Cham (2017). https://doi.org/10.1007/978-3-319-48628-4_6
9. Cole, C.: The universal turing machine: a half-century survey. Inf. Process. Manag. **32**(5), 640–641 (1996)
10. Derler, P., Lee, E.A., Sangiovanni-Vincentelli, A.L.: Modeling cyber-physical systems. Proc. IEEE **100**(1), 13–28 (2012). https://doi.org/10.1109/JPROC.2011.2160929
11. Herkert, J., Borenstein, J., Miller, K.W.: The Boeing 737 MAX: lessons for engineering ethics. Sci. Eng. Ethics **26**(6), 2957–2974 (2020). https://doi.org/10.1007/s11948-020-00252-y
12. Johnston, P., Harris, R.: The Boeing 737 max saga: lessons for software organizations. Softw. Qual. Prof. **21**(3), 4–12 (2019)
13. Lamport, L., Lynch, N.A.: Distributed computing: models and methods. In: van Leeuwen, J. (ed.) Handbook of Theoretical Computer Science, vol. B: Formal Models and Semantics, pp. 1157–1199. Elsevier and MIT Press (1990). https://doi.org/10.1016/b978-0-444-88074-1.50023-8
14. Lee, E.A.: Cyber physical systems: design challenges. In: 2008 11th IEEE International Symposium on Object and Component-Oriented Real-Time Distributed Computing (ISORC), pp. 363–369 (2008). https://doi.org/10.1109/ISORC.2008.25
15. Liu, Z., Bowen, J.P., Liu, B., Tyszberowicz, S., Zhang, T.: Software abstractions and human-cyber-physical systems architecture modelling. In: Bowen, J.P., Liu, Z., Zhang, Z. (eds.) SETSS 2019. LNCS, vol. 12154, pp. 159–219. Springer, Cham (2020). https://doi.org/10.1007/978-3-030-55089-9_5
16. Liu, Z., Wang, J.: Human-cyber-physical systems: concepts, challenges, and research opportunities. Front. Inf. Technol. Electron. Eng. **21**(11), 1535–1553 (2020). https://doi.org/10.1631/FITEE.2000537
17. Lynch, N.A., Segala, R., Vaandrager, F.W.: Hybrid I/O automata. Inf. Comput. **185**(1), 105–157 (2003). https://doi.org/10.1016/S0890-5401(03)00067-1
18. Rabin, M.O.: Probabilistic automata. Inf. Control. **6**(3), 230–245 (1963). https://doi.org/10.1016/S0019-9958(63)90290-0
19. Romero, D., Bernus, P., Noran, O., Stahre, J., Fast-Berglund, Å.: The operator 4.0: human cyber-physical systems & adaptive automation towards human-automation symbiosis work systems. In: Nääs, I., et al. (eds.) APMS 2016. IAICT, vol. 488, pp. 677–686. Springer, Cham (2016). https://doi.org/10.1007/978-3-319-51133-7_80

20. Sangiovanni-Vincentelli, A.L., Damm, W., Passerone, R.: Taming dr. frankenstein: contract-based design for cyber-physical systems. Eur. J. Control **18**(3), 217–238 (2012). https://doi.org/10.3166/ejc.18.217-238
21. Sowe, S.K., Simmon, E., Zettsu, K., de Vaulx, F.J., Bojanova, I.: Cyber-physical-human systems: putting people in the loop. IT Prof. **18**(1), 10–13 (2016). https://doi.org/10.1109/MITP.2016.14
22. Zhou, J., Zhou, Y., Wang, B., Zang, J.: Human-cyber-physical systems (hcpss) in the context of new-generation intelligent manufacturing. Engineering **5**(4), 624–636 (2019). https://doi.org/10.1016/j.eng.2019.07.015

A PO Characterisation of Reconfiguration

Yehia Abd Alrahman$^{(\boxtimes)}$(iD), Mauricio Martel(iD), and Nir Piterman(iD)

University of Gothenburg, Gothenburg, Sweden
{yehia.abd.alrahman,mauricio.martel,nir.piterman}@gu.se

Abstract. We consider partial order semantics of concurrent systems in which local reconfigurations may have global side effects. That is, local changes happening to an entity may block or unblock events relating to others, namely, events in which the entity does *not* participate. We show that partial order computations need to capture additional restrictions about event ordering, i.e., restrictions that arise from such reconfigurations. This introduces ambiguity where different partial orders represent exactly the same events with the same participants happening in different orders, thus defeating the purpose of using partial order semantics. To remove this ambiguity, we suggest an extension of partial orders called *glued partial orders*. We show that glued partial orders capture all possible forced reordering arising from said reconfigurations. Furthermore, we show that computations belonging to different glued partial orders are only different due to non-determinism. We consider channeled transition systems and Petri-nets with inhibiting arcs as examples.

1 Introduction

The most common way to represent computations is by considering linear sequences of events. When reasoning about concurrent systems, the linear order semantics of computation does not capture important information about participation in events and the interdependence of events. In order to capture this extra information in computations, instead of linear order, partial order semantics needs to be used. Existing approaches to partial order semantics (cf. *Process semantics* of Petri nets [18,21,23] and *Mazurkiewicz traces* of Zielonka automata [13,17,25]) proved useful in recovering information about the participants of events and (in)dependence of concurrent events.

In this paper, we are interested in concurrenct systems where events are affected by changes happening to non-participants. This situation, which we call in general *reconfiguration*, arises in two types of very different models of concucrrent systems: *Channeled Transition Systems* (CTS) [4,5][1] and *Petri net with inhibitor arcs* (PTI-nets) [9,12,16]. In the first, processes connect and disconnect

---

This work is funded by ERC consolidator grant D-SynMA (No. 772459) and Swedish research council grants: SynTM (No. 2020-03401) and grant (No. 2020-04963).

[1] CTS can be considered as a generalisation of Zielonka automata, supporting rich interactions alongside change of communication interfaces.

H. Seidl et al. (Eds.): ICTAC 2022, LNCS 13572, pp. 42–59, 2022.
https://doi.org/10.1007/978-3-031-17715-6_5

to channels during execution and by doing so disable and enable communications on these channels in which they ultimately do not participate. In the second, tokens enter and exit places that inhibit transitions and by doing so disable and enable said transitions without participating in the transitions themselves. In these two settings, dependencies among events emerge dynamically as side-effects of interaction, leading to difficulties in capturing these emergencies in partial-order semantics.

It is possible to suggest a partial order semantics of such types of systems. Indeed, we give a partial order semantics to both types of systems (cf. [15] for an alternative partial order semantics of PTI-nets). However, we recognise that reconfiguration induces another dimension of nondeterminism in these systems. Reconfiguration creates a situation where some events must be ordered with respect to *sequences of other events* dynamically during execution, and thus forcing interleaving in a non-trivial way. That is, from the point of an event, a sequence of other events is considered as a single block and can only happen before or after it.[2] Just like multiple linear sequences correspond to different interleavings arising from the same partial order, reconfigurations lead to multiple partial order computations corresponding to exactly the same events with exactly the same participants happening along a computation just in different orders.

To resolve that, we propose an extension of partial orders with additional objects called glue. Using these structures we can define semantics that characterises reconfiguration. Both reconfiguration points and their corresponding scheduling decisions are captured in a single structure, while preserving a *true-concurrent* execution of independent events.

Contributions. We show how to give partial order semantics to these two types of systems in a way that captures reconfigurations. We use a specialised version of partial orders, that we call *labelled partial orders* (LPO for short). We show how to construct an LPO representing the computations of a specific system. Such LPOs consider only the local views of individual processes/indistinguishable tokens and their interaction information. An LPO captures participation in events and the relations between events. In the spirit of Mazurkiewicz traces, the states of different processes/distinguishable tokens are (strictly) incomparable, that is there is no notion of a global state. This way we can easily single out finite sequences of computation steps where a process (or a group of processes)/tokens execute independently. We can also distinguish individual events from joint ones. As mentioned, despite the fact that an LPO may refer to reconfiguration points, it cannot fully characterise reconfiguration in a single structure. For this reason, we introduce *glued labeled partial orders* (g-LPO, for short), that is an extension of LPO with *glue* to separate a non-deterministic choice from

---

[2] Note that reconfiguration is an internal event, and is totally hidden from the perspective of an external observer [20] who may only observe message-/token-passing. Indeed, messages or tokens can only indicate the occurrence of exchange but cannot help with noticing that a reconfiguration has happened and what are the consequences of reconfiguration.

forced scheduling due to reconfiguration. We show that a g-LPO is sufficient to represent LPO computations that differ in scheduling due to reconfiguration. We also show that LPO computations belonging to different g-LPO(s) are different due to nondeterministic selection of independent events.

The paper is organised as follows: In Sect. 2, we informally present our partial order semantics and in Sect. 3, we introduce the necessary background. In Sect. 4, we provide the LPO semantics and in Sect. 5 we define the glued partial orders. In Sect. 6 we prove important results on g-LPO with respect to reconfiguration and nondeterminism. In Sect. 7 we present concluding remarks.

2   Labelled Partial Order Computations in a Nutshell

We use the CTS formalism to informally illustrate the LPO semantics under reconfiguration and the idea behind g-LPO. The example is kept simple to aid the reader, but our semantics can handle much more intricate cases where dependencies are nontrivial.

We consider the CTSs in Fig. 1(a-c) where each CTS $\mathcal{T}_i$ for $i \in \{1, 2, 3\}$ represents an individual agent and their parallel composition defines the system behaviour as we will explain shortly. A CTS $\mathcal{T}_i$ consists of a set of states and transitions. We will use the notation $\mathcal{T}_{i,k}$ to denote that agent $\mathcal{T}_i$ is currently in state k. A state is labelled with a dynamic listening function to define the set of channels that the agent is connected to, including a special nonblocking broadcast channel $\star$. All other channels are blocking multicast. An agent cannot disconnect from the broadcast channel. Each transition is labelled with a message of the form (v, r, ch) where v is the message contents, $r \in \{!, ?\}$ is the role of the transition either send ! or receive ?, and ch is a channel name.

The system behaviour is defined as follows: if there exists an agent with a send transition on a specific channel then for all other agents: In case of broadcast: the sender cannot be blocked and all agents who can supply a matching receive transition participate. In case of multicast: all agents who are listening to the channel must participate by supplying their matching receive transition or otherwise the sender is blocked. For instance, agent $\mathcal{T}_2$ can initially (i.e., in state $\mathcal{T}_{2,1}$) send the message $(v_2, !, d)$ and move to $\mathcal{T}_{2,2}$ and only agent $\mathcal{T}_3$ is initially listening to channel d in $\mathcal{T}_{3,1}$. Thus, $\mathcal{T}_3$ participates (and moves from $\mathcal{T}_{3,1}$ to $\mathcal{T}_{3,2}$) while $\mathcal{T}_1$ stays still as it cannot observe the communication. After the joint transition $\mathcal{T}_2$ starts listening to c (in $\mathcal{T}_{2,2}$) while $\mathcal{T}_3$ disconnects from d and starts listening to e (in $\mathcal{T}_{2,2}$).

Agents can reconfigure their interaction interfaces by updating their listening functions as in the previous example. The side effects of such reconfiguration may change the ordering of events at system level even though the reconfiguration happened internally. For instance, after sending message $(v_2, !, d)$, agent $\mathcal{T}_2$ starts listening to channel c (in state $\mathcal{T}_{2,2}$) but cannot supply a receive transition for this channel. Thus, agent $\mathcal{T}_1$ is now blocked until $\mathcal{T}_2$ exits state $\mathcal{T}_{2,2}$ and disconnects from c. That is, if $(v_2, !, d)$ happened before $(v_1, !, c)$ then $(v_1, !, c)$ may only happen after $(v_3, !, e)$. In other words, $(v_1, !, c)$ is now ordered with respect to the

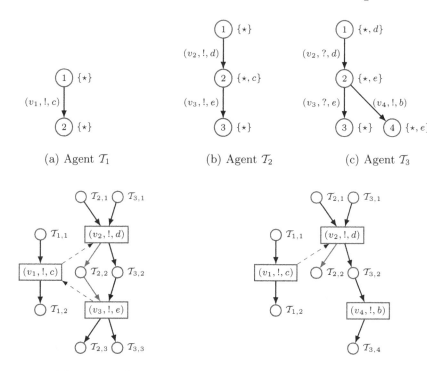

(a) Agent T_1 (b) Agent T_2 (c) Agent T_3

(d) Three LPO computations and two g-LPO computations

Fig. 1. Channel Transition System CTS

sequence $(v_2,!,d),(v_3,!,e)$. It should be noted that initially (from $T_{1,1}$ and $T_{2,1}$) there were no dependencies between $(v_1,!,c)$ and $(v_2,!,d)$, but such dependencies arose as side effects of internal reconfiguration of agent T_2.

Moreover, agent T_3 (from $T_{3,2}$) may inhibit the sending of message $(v_3,!,e)$ by nondeterministically choosing to send $(v_4,!,b)$ instead and moving to state $T_{3,4}$. Note that T_3 still listens to e (in $T_{3,4}$), but cannot supply a matching receive transition, and thus permanently blocks T_2 (in $T_{2,2}$).

By restricting attention to the interleavings, we have that $(v_1,!,c)$ considers both $(v_2,!,d)$ and $(v_3,!,e)$ as a single block, and their execution cannot be interrupted. Namely, the only viable interleavings (in case $(v_3,!,e)$ is scheduled later) are $(v_1,!,c),(v_2,!,d),(v_3,!,e)$ or $(v_2,!,d),(v_3,!,e),(v_1,!,c)$. Note that this is only from the point of view of $(v_1,!,c)$ and has no implications for other messages. This creates a forced interleaving in a non-trivial way due to the occurrence of non-observable reconfigurations that we cannot reason about from a global perspective. These dependencies among events emerge dynamically as side-effects of interaction, and thus put the correctness of partial order semantics at stake.

To handle this issue, we introduce a partial order semantics of computations under reconfiguration. We illustrate our LPO and g-LPO semantics in Fig. 1(d), which characterises all possible (maximal) computations of the composed system.

Here, we use the dashed arrow $--\rightarrow$ to indicate a happen before relation (or an interleaving order $\rightarrow_i$ as we will see later).

The two diagrams succinctly encode *three* possible LPOs: (i) the LPO obtained from Fig. 1(d) left structure with the dashed arrow from $(v_1, !, c)$ to $(v_2, !, d)$; (ii) the LPO obtained from Fig. 1(d) left structure with the dashed arrow from $(v_3, !, e)$ to $(v_1, !, c)$; and (iii) the LPO obtained from Fig. 1(d) right structure with the dashed arrow from $(v_1, !, c)$ to $(v_2, !, d)$.

LPOs (i) and (ii) agree that agent $\mathcal{T}_3$ (in state $\mathcal{T}_{3,2}$) nondeterministically chooses to send $(v_3, !, e)$ while in (iii) $\mathcal{T}_3$ nondeterministically chooses $(v_4, !, b)$. All LPOs capture information about interaction and interdependence among events. Indeed, in all cases we see that both states $\mathcal{T}_{2,1}$ and $\mathcal{T}_{3,1}$ synchronise through the transition $(v_2, !, d)$. States that are not strictly ordered with respect to a common transition are considered concurrent (or unordered). Thus, as in Mazurkiewicz traces there is no notion of a global state. Notice that LPOs (i) and (ii) differ only in the forced interleaving of $(v_1, !, c)$ with respect to the block $(v_2, !, d), (v_3, !, e)$.

Note that both LPOs (i) and (ii) have information both on reconfiguration and nondeterminism, but each individually cannot be used to distinguish the hidden reconfiguration. In fact, $(v_1, !, c) --\rightarrow (v_2, !, d)$ in (i) indicates that $(v_1, !, c)$ happened before a reconfiguration caused by $(v_2, !, d)$, and $(v_3, !, e) --\rightarrow (v_1, !, c)$ in (ii) indicates that $(v_1, !, c)$ happened after the reconfiguration. In (iii), due to the different nondeterminsitic choice, the only possible case we have to consider is that of $(v_1, !, c)$ happening before $(v_2, !, d)$.

This suggests that we can actually isolate reconfiguration from nondeterminism by using a more sophisticated structure than LPO, and thus expose the difference in a way that allows reasoning about these hidden events from a global perspective. For this reason, we define g-LPO computations, that are an extension of LPO with a notion of *glue*.

In this simple example, a g-LPO simply drops strict ordering of events with respect to each other (like $(v_1, !, c) --\rightarrow (v_2, !, d)$ or $(v_3, !, e) --\rightarrow (v_1, !, c)$), and instead assigns each event a (possibly empty) glue relation defining the *glued* elements from the point of view of that event. The glue relation is defined based on reconfiguration points in CTS, and on inhibitor arcs in Petri nets.

Consider now the structures in Fig. 1(d) without the dashed arrows and, now, with an explanation of the red arrows. These two structures are each a g-LPO. For the one on the left, since $\mathcal{T}_{2,2}$ inhibits $(v_1, !, c)$ all existing incoming and outgoing edges from $\mathcal{T}_{2,2}$ are glued to $\mathcal{T}_{2,2}$. Thus, $(v_1, !, c)$'s glue relation includes these edges (in red). All other transitions have empty glue relations because they are not inhibited. As they are not inhibited, their interdependence is well-captured statically based on their communication. Note that the glue relation is not required to be transitive and the glue only relates states and transitions. In the structure on the right of the figure, $(v_2, !, d)$ is glued only to $\mathcal{T}_{3,2}$. As $(v_4, !, b)$ is scheduled rather than $(v_3, !, e)$, then $\mathcal{T}_{2,2}$ remains as a maximal element.

As we show later, a single g-LPO can be used to characterise reconfiguration and separate it from other sources of nondeterminism in the system.

3 Preliminaries

3.1 Partial Orders and Labeled Partial Orders

We use a specialised form of partial orders to represent computations.

A *partial order* (PO, for short) is a binary relation $\leq$ over a set O that is reflexive, antisymmetric, and transitive. We use $a < b$ for $a \leq b$ and $a \neq b$. We use $a\#b$ for $a \not\leq b$ and $b \not\leq a$, i.e., a and b are incomparable.

A *labelled partial order* (LPO, for short) is $(O, \to_c, \to_i, \Sigma, \Upsilon, L)$, where $O = V \uplus E$ is a set of elements partitioned to nodes and edges, respectively, $\to_c$ and $\to_i$ are disjoint, anti-reflexive, anti-symmetric, and non-transitive *communication* and *interleaving* order relations over O. We have $\to_c \subseteq V \times E \cup E \times V$ and $\to_i \subseteq E \times E$. When $\to_i = \emptyset$ we omit it from the tuple. We denote $\to = \to_c \cup \to_i$. The relation $\leq$ is the reflexive and transitive closure of $\to$. We require that $\leq$ is a partial order. The labelling function $L : O \to \Sigma \cup \Upsilon$ satisfies $L(V) \subseteq \Sigma$ and $L(E) \subseteq \Upsilon$, where Σ is a node alphabet and Υ is an edge alphabet. Given an element $a \in O$ we write ${}^\bullet a$ for $\{b \mid b \to a\}$ and $a^\bullet$ for $\{b \mid a \to b\}$.

Intuitively, for CTS, elements in V relate to execution histories of individual agents and elements in E to communication events. Thus, a history belongs to an individual agent and a transition corresponds to either an individual computational step or a synchronisation point among multiple agents. The relation $\to_c$ captures participation in communication and the relation $\to_i$ captures order requirements.

For PTI-nets, elements in V correspond to a history of a token or multiple tokens with the same history and elements in E correspond to transitions. Similarly, $\to_c$ captures participation in transitions and $\to_i$ captures order.

3.2 Channelled Transition Systems (CTS)

We present Channeled Transition Systems [4,5]. A *Channelled Transition System* (CTS) is a tuple of the form $\mathcal{T} = \langle C, \Lambda, B, S, S_0, R, L, \mathrm{LS} \rangle$, where C is a set of channels, including the broadcast channel $(\star)$, Λ is a *state alphabet*, B is a *transition alphabet*, S is a set of states, $S_0 \subseteq S$ is a set of initial states, $R \subseteq S \times B \times S$ is a transition relation, $L : S \to \Lambda$ is a labelling function, and $\mathrm{LS} : S \to 2^C$ is a channel-listening function such that for every $s \in S$ we have $\star \in \mathrm{LS}(s)$. That is, a CTS is listening to the broadcast channel in every state. We assume that $B = B^+ \times \{!, ?\} \times C$, for some set B^+. That is, every transition labeled with some $b \in B$ is either a message send (!) or a message receive (?) on some channel $c \in C$. We write $B^!$ for $B^+ \times \{!\} \times C$ and $B^?$ for $B^+ \times \{?\} \times C$.

Given $(b^+, !, c) \in B$ we write $?(b^+, !, c)$ for $(b^+, ?, c)$ and $ch(b^+, -, c)$ for c. That is, $?(b)$ is the corresponding receive transition of a send transition b and $ch(b)$ is the channel of b.

For a receive transition $b = (b^+, ?, c)$ and a state $s \in S$ we write $s \to_b$ if $c \in \mathrm{LS}(s)$ and there is some s' such that $(s, b, s') \in R$. That is, s is listening on channel c and can participate, i.e., has an outgoing receive transition for b. We

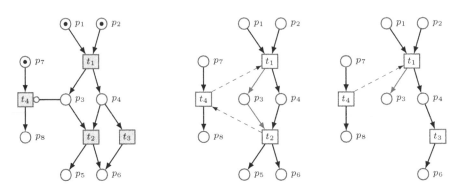

(a) Petri net with Inhibitor arcs   (b) Two possible g-LPO computations

Fig. 2. Petri net with inhibitor arcs

write $s \not\rightarrow_b$ if $c \in \text{LS}(s)$ and it is not the case that $s \rightarrow_b$. That is, s is listening on channel c and is not able to participate.

A *history* $h = s_0, \ldots, s_n$ is a finite sequence of states such that $s_0 \in S_0$ and for every $0 \leq i < n$ we have that $(s_i, b_i, s_{i+1}) \in R$ for some $b_i \in B$. The length of h is $n + 1$, denoted $|h|$. For convenience we generalise notations applying to states to apply to histories. For example, we write $c \in \text{LS}(h)$ when $c \in \text{LS}(s_n)$, $h \rightarrow_b$ when $s_n \rightarrow_b$ and $h \not\rightarrow_b$ for $s_n \not\rightarrow_b$. Similarly, if $h = s_0, \ldots, s_n$ and $h' = s_0, \ldots, s_n, s_{n+1}$ where $(s_n, b_n, s_{i+1}) \in R$, we write $(h, b_n, h') \in R$. Let $\mathbf{hist}(\mathcal{T})$ be the set of all histories of $\mathcal{T}$.

Consider a system $\mathcal{S} = \mathcal{T}_1 \parallel \cdots \parallel \mathcal{T}_n$ with n CTSs, where $\mathcal{T}_i = \langle C_i, \Lambda_i, B_i, S_i,$ $S_0^i, R_i, L_i, \text{LS}_i \rangle$ is a CTS. We denote $C = \bigcup_i C_i$, and $B = \bigcup_i B_i$ and $B^! = \bigcup_i B_i^!$. A global state of $\mathcal{S}$ is $S = \prod_i S_i$ and $S^0 = \prod_i S_0^i$ is the set of initial states. The global linear order transition relation $\Delta \subseteq S \times B^! \times S$ is defined as follows:

$$\Delta = \left\{ \begin{pmatrix} (s_1, \ldots, s_n), \\ (v, !, c), \\ (s_1', \ldots, s_n') \end{pmatrix} \middle| \begin{array}{l} \exists i \, . \, (s_i, (v, !, c), s_i') \in R_i \text{ and } \forall j \neq i \, . \\ (1) \ (s_j, (v, ?, c), s_j') \in R_j \text{ and } c \in \text{LS}_j(s_j) \text{ or} \\ (2) \ c \notin \text{LS}_j(s_j) \text{ and } s_j' = s_j \text{ or} \\ (3) \ c = \star, s_j' = s_j, \text{ and } \forall s'' \, . \, (s_j, (v, ?, c), s'') \notin R_j \end{array} \right\}$$

Intuitively, there exists one sender and potentially multiple receivers. Multicast channels are blocking, i.e., (1) all agents who are listening to the channel must be able to participate in the communication in order for a send to be possible; (2) agents that are not listening ignore the message. The broadcast channel is non-blocking and agents always listen to it, i.e., (1) if they can participate, each supplies a receive transition and receives the message; (3) if they cannot participate in a communication it still goes on without them.

3.3   Petri Nets with Inhibitor Arcs (PTI-nets)

We present Petri Nets with inhibitor arcs [9,12,16]. A Petri net N with inhibitor arcs is a bipartite directed graph $N = \langle P, T, F, I \rangle$, where P and T are the set of places and transitions such that $P \cap T = \emptyset$, $F : (P \times T) \cup (T \times P) \to \mathbb{N}$ is the flow relation, and $I \subseteq (P \times T)$ is the inhibiting relation. We write $(s, s') \in F$ for $F(s, s') > 0$. Without loss of generality, we restrict attention to Petri nets where all transitions have a non-empty preset and a non-empty post-set.

The configuration of a Petri net at a time instant is defined by a *marking*. Formally, let N be a Petri net with a set of places $P = \{p_1, \dots, p_k\}$. A marking is a function $m : P \to \mathbb{N}$, where $m(p_i)$ corresponds to the number of tokens in p_i, for $i = 1, \dots, k$. Functions can be added, subtracted, and compared in the usual way. We assume some initial marking m_0. For $p \in P$ let $\boldsymbol{p}$ be the function $\boldsymbol{p} : P \to \{0, 1\}$ such that $\boldsymbol{p}(p) = 1$ and $\boldsymbol{p}(p') = 0$ for every $p' \neq p$. Let M denote the set of all markings.

For a transition $t \in T$ we define the *pre-function* of t, denoted by ${}^\bullet t$, to be ${}^\bullet t(p) = F(p_i, t)$. Similarly, the *post-function* of t is $t^\bullet = F(t, p_i)$.

An inhibitor arc from a place to a transition means that the transition can only fire if no token is on that place. The inhibitor set of a transition t is the set $°t = \{p \in P \mid (p, t) \in I\}$, and represents the places to be "tested for absence" of tokens. That is, an inhibiting place allows to prevent the transition firing.

A transition t is enabled at m if for every p we have $m(p) \geq F(p, t)$ and all inhibitor places are empty, i.e., for every $p \in °t$ we have $m(p) = 0$. Note that if for some t and $p \in °t$ we have $(p, t) \in F$ then t can never fire, i.e., it is blocked.

The running example and the corresponding LPOs and g-LPOs can be modelled in PTI-Nets as in Fig. 2 where the multiplicities for all edges is 1. Intuitively, the inhibitor arc plays the role of a CTS state that listens to a message but does not supply a receive transition.[3]

4   LPO Semantics

In this section, we provide CTSs and PTI-nets with a labelled partial order semantics. The labelled partial order semantics of CTSs is novel while the one of Petri nets extends occurrence nets [18] with event-to-event connections that allow to capture reconfigurations.

4.1   Channelled Transition Systems (CTS)

Consider a system $\mathcal{S} = \mathcal{T}_1 \parallel \cdots \parallel \mathcal{T}_n$, where $\mathcal{T}_i = \langle C_i, \Lambda_i, B_i, S_i, S_0^i, R_i, L_i, \mathrm{LS}_i \rangle$. We denote $C = \bigcup_i C_i$, and $B = \bigcup_i B_i$.

Definition 1 (LPO-computation). *A computation of $\mathcal{S}$ is an LPO $(O, \to_c, \to_i, \Sigma, \Upsilon, L)$, where $V \subseteq \bigcup_i \boldsymbol{hist}(\mathcal{T}_i)$, $\Sigma = V$, $\to_c = \to_s \uplus \to_r$ is the disjoint union of the send and receive relations, $\Upsilon = \{(v, !, c) \in B\}$ are the set of message sends, and for $h \in V$ we have $L(h) = h$. In addition we require the following:*

C1. The edge e_ϵ such that $L(e_\epsilon) = (b, !, \star)$ is the unique minimal element according to $\leq$. For every i, we have $s_i^0 \in V$ and $e_\epsilon \to_r s_i^0$.

---

[3] A general translation of CTS to PTI-nets is quite involved and loses the distinction between channels and processes.

C2. *If $h \in V \cap \mathbf{hist}(\mathcal{T}_i)$ there is a unique $e \in E$ such that $e \to_c h$. If $|h| > 1$, there is also a unique $h' \in V \cap \mathbf{hist}(\mathcal{T}_i)$ such that $h' \to_c e$ and either $(h', L(e), h) \in R_i$ or $(h', ?(L(e)), h) \in R_i$.*

C3. *For every $h \in V$ there is at most one $e \in E$ such that $h \to_c e$.*
That is, h participates in at most one communication.

C4. *For every $e \in E \setminus \{e_\epsilon\}$ there is $I \subseteq [n]$ such that all the following hold:*
  (a) For every $i \in I$ we have $|{}^\bullet e \cap \mathbf{hist}(\mathcal{T}_i)| = 1$ and $|e^\bullet \cap \mathbf{hist}(\mathcal{T}_i)| = 1$.
    That is, for each agent that participates in a communication the edge connects exactly to one predecessor history and one successor history.
  (b) There is a unique $i \in I$ and $h, h' \in V \cap \mathbf{hist}(\mathcal{T}_i)$ such that $(h, L(e), h') \in R_i$ and $h \to_s e \to_s h'$ and for every $i' \in I \setminus \{i\}$ there are $h'', h''' \in V \cap \mathbf{hist}(\mathcal{T}_{i'})$ such that $(h'', ?(L(e)), h''') \in R_{i'}$ and $h'' \to_r e \to_r h'''$.
    That is, every communication has a unique sender and the rest are receivers. All these connections satisfy the respective agent transitions.
  (c) If $L(e) = (v, !, c)$ for $c \neq \star$ then for every $h \in V$ such that $c \in \mathrm{LS}(h)$ we have $h \leq e$ or $e \leq h$.
    That is, a communication on a multicast channel is ordered with respect to every history that listens to the same channel. Thus, the history either participates in the communication or happens before or after it.
  (d) If $L(e) = (v, !, \star)$ then for every $h \in V$ such that $h \to_{?(L(e))}$ we have $h \leq e$ or $e \leq h$.
    That is, a communication on the broadcast channel is ordered with respect to every history that could participate in the communication.

C5. *For every $e \neq e'$ such that $ch(e) = ch(e')$ we have $e \leq e'$ or $e' \leq e$.*
That is, all communications on the same channel are ordered.

C6. *If $e \to_i e'$ then there is some $h = s_0, \ldots, s_j$ and one of what follows holds:*
  (a) $ch(e) = ch(e')$.
  (b) $L(e') = (v, !, c)$ for $c \neq \star$, $h \to_c e$ and $ch(L(e')) \in \mathrm{LS}(h)$.
  (c) $L(e) = (v, !, c)$ for $c \neq \star$, $e' \to_c h$ and $ch(L(e')) \in \mathrm{LS}(h)$.
  (d) $L(e') = (v, !, \star)$, $h \to_c e$ and $h \to_{?(L(e'))}$.
  (e) $L(e) = (v, !, \star)$, $e' \to_c h$ and $h \to_{?(L(e))}$.
  That is, we only allow connections between two edges in order to capture the ordering in a single channel (a), to capture the order between multi-cast messages and histories that could be listening to them (b,c), or to capture the order between broadcasts and histories that could participate in them (d,e).

That is, a computation starts from a unique broadcast that initiates all the initial states of $\mathcal{T}_i$ for all i (C1). Every history has a unique communication that leads to it and (if it is not the initial state) the communication connects a unique previous history of the same agent according to the transition of the agent (C2). Every history participates in at most one communication (C3). For every transition there exists a set of agents participating in it (C4). Each agent participates in the communication exactly once (C4a), has one sender and all the rest are receivers (C4b), is ordered with respect to all places that could participate in it (C4c,d). Then, all communications on the same channel are ordered (C5). Interleaving (C4c,d and C5) is captured by interleaving relation. Communications on the same channel can be ordered (C6a). For a multicast, a history h that could participate in the multicast already participated in a communication (C6b), or the communication leading to h happens after the multicast (C6c). For a broadcast, a history h that could participate in the broadcast already participated in a communication (C6d), or the communication leading to h happens after the broadcast (C6e).

Note that an LPO computation relates histories of individual CTSs, and thus allows to draw relations among finite sequences of individual computation steps of one CTS (or a group of CTSs) with respect to others; Furthermore, a CTS is always listening to the broadcast channel, and thus, it becomes mandatory to order broadcast messages that enable/disable participation to each other.

We will use **comp**($\mathcal{S}$) to denote the set of LPO computations of $\mathcal{S}$.

4.2 Petri Nets with Inhibitor Arcs (PTI-nets)

We now define the LPO semantics of PTI-nets. We start with a definition of histories and then use them to define the vertices and edges of an LPO.

Definition 2 (History). *We define the set of histories of a net N by induction.*

We define a special transition t_ϵ such that $t_\epsilon{}^\bullet = m_0$. The pair $(\emptyset, t_\epsilon)$ is a t-history. Note that t_ϵ is not a transition in T.

For a place p, let $h = (S, t)$ be a t-history such that $t^\bullet(p) > 0$. Then we have $(h, p, t^\bullet(p))$ is a p-history. That is, given a t-history h ending in transition t, where p is in $t^\bullet$, then the combination of h, p, and the number of tokens that t puts in p form a p-history.

Consider a transition $t \in T$. A t-history is a pair (S, t), where $S = \{(h_1, i_1), \ldots, (h_n, i_n)\}$ is a multiset satisfying the following. For every j we have $h_j = (-, p, c_j)$ is a p-history, where $c_j \geq i_j$ and $^\bullet t = \sum_j i_j \cdot \mathbf{p}_j$. That is, the t-history identifies the p-histories from which t takes tokens and the number of occurrences of a p-history in the multiset is the number of tokens taken from it.

Let $\mathbf{hist}(N)$ be the set of all histories of N partitioned to $\mathbf{hist}_p(N)$ and $\mathbf{hist}_t(N)$ in the obvious way. Given a t-history $h = (S, t)$ and a p-history h' we write $h(h')$ for the number of appearances of h' in the multiset S.

We define the labelled partial order semantics of a PTI-net as follows.

Definition 3 (LPO-computation). *A computation of N is an LPO $(O, \rightarrow_c , \rightarrow_i, \Sigma, \Upsilon, L)$, where $V \subseteq \mathbf{hist}_p(N)$, $E \subseteq \mathbf{hist}_t(N)$, $\Sigma = P$, $\Upsilon = T$, for a p-history $v = (-, p, i)$ we have $L(v) = p$ and for a t-history (S, t) we have $L(e) = t$, and such that:*

N1. *The t-history $(\emptyset, t_\epsilon)$ is the unique minimal element according to $\leq$.*

N2. *For a p-history $v = (e, p, i) \in V$ we have $e \in E$ and e is the unique edge such that $e \rightarrow_c v$.*

N3. *For a p-history $v = (h, p, i) \in V$, let $e_1, \ldots, e_j$ be the t-histories such that $v \rightarrow_c e_j$. Then, for every k we have $e_k(v) > 0$ and $\sum_k e_k(v) \leq i$.*

   That is, v leads to t-histories that contain it with the multiplicity of v being respected.

N4. For every $e \in E$, where $e = (\{(v_1, i_1), \ldots, (v_n, i_n)\}, t)$, all the following hold:

  (a) $^\bullet e \cap V = \{v_1, \ldots, v_n\}$ and $e^\bullet \cap V = \{(e, p, t^\bullet(p)) \mid t^\bullet(p) > 0\}$.
    That is, the connections of a t-history respect the structure of the net.

  (b) For every $v = (h, p, i) \in V$ such that $p \in {}^\circ L(e)$ we have $e \leq v$ or, where $e_1, \ldots, e_j$ are all the edges such that $v \rightarrow_c e_k$, we have $\sum_k e_k(v) = i$ and for every k, $e_k < e$.
    That is, if a place inhibits a transition, then either the transition happens before the place is visited or all the tokens are taken from the place before the transition happens.

  (c) If $e \rightarrow_i e'$ then there is some v such that either (i) $v \rightarrow_c e$ and $(L(v), L(e')) \in I$ or (ii) $e' \rightarrow_c v$ and $(L(v), L(e)) \in I$.
    That is, we only allow connection between two t-histories to capture the forced interleaving due to inhibition.

That is, a computation starts from the dummy transition t_ϵ, which establishes the initial marking (N1) Every other transition is a t-history that connects the p-histories that it contains (N3) to those that contain it (N2). If a place inhibits a transition then either the transition happens before a token arrives to the place or after all tokens left that place (N4b). Namely, if p inhibits t then either t happens before the transition putting token in p or after the transitions taking the tokens from p (N4b). This is possible by adding direct interleaving dependencies ($\rightarrow_i$) between edges (N4c).

We will use **comp**(N) to denote the set of LPO computations of N.

5   Partial Order with Glue

We extend labeled partial orders with *glue*. Intuitively, two elements are glued from the point of view of another element if they both happen either before or after said element.

Definition 4 (Glue). *A* Glue *over a set O and a relation $\rightarrow_c \subseteq O \times O$ is a relation $R \subseteq \rightarrow_c$.*

Intuitively, a glue relation R over the set O and a relation $\rightarrow_c$ defines pairs of elements that are glued together.

Definition 5 (Glued LPO). *A* glued LPO *(g-LPO, for short) is* LPG $=$ $(P, \mathcal{G}, \mathcal{E})$, where $P = (O = V \uplus E, \rightarrow_c, \rightarrow_i, \Sigma, \Upsilon, L)$ *is an* LPO, $\mathcal{G} = \{G_1, \ldots, G_k\}$ *is a set of Glue relations over O and $\rightarrow_c$, and $\mathcal{E} : \Upsilon \hookrightarrow \mathcal{G}$ labels elements in E (with their edge labels) by glue relations.*

Definition 6 (g-LPO-refinement). *An* LPO LPO $= (O, \rightarrow_c, \rightarrow_i, \Sigma, \Upsilon, L)$ *where $O = V \uplus E$ refines a g-LPO* LPG $= (P_g, \mathcal{G}, \mathcal{E})$, *denoted* LPO $\preceq$ LPG, *where $P_g = (O, \rightarrow_c, \rightarrow_i^g \Sigma, \Upsilon, L)$ if the following conditions hold:*

  – *For every $e \in E$ and $(a, b) \in \mathcal{E}(L(e))$ we have $e \leq a$ or $b \leq e$.*

- $\to_i^g \subseteq \to_i$ and $(e, e') \in (\to_i \setminus \to_i^g)$ implies $(e', v) \in \mathcal{E}(L(e))$ or $(v, e) \in \mathcal{E}(L(e'))$ for some v.

That is, the two share the relation $\to_c$, the relation $\to_i^g$ is preserved and extended by extra interleaving to capture the glue. In order to respect the glue, an edge that is glued to a pair (a, b) must happen either before a or after b.

We show now that g-LPOs enable to remove parts of the interleaving order relation for both PTI-nets and CTSs. g-LPOs capture better reconfiguration by combining multiple orderings due to the same reconfiguration in the same g-LPO.

5.1 Glue Computations for CTSs

Consider a system $\mathcal{S} = \mathcal{T}_1 \parallel \cdots \parallel \mathcal{T}_n$, where $\mathcal{T}_i = \langle C_i, \Lambda_i, B_i, S_i, S_0^i, R_i, L_i, \mathrm{LS}_i \rangle$. We denote $C = \bigcup_i C_i$ and $B = \bigcup_i B_i$.

We now define a *g-computation* for CTS. The differences from the definition of LPO (Definition 1) are highlighted with a "$*$" (C4.(c-d) and C6.(b-e) are removed and $*$C7 is new).

Definition 7 (g-computation). *A g-computation of S is a g-LPO $(P, \mathcal{G}, \mathcal{E})$, where $P = (O, \to_i, \to_c, \Sigma, \Upsilon, L_V, L_E)$ and V, E, Σ, Υ, and L are as before, $\to_c = \to_s \uplus \to_r$, where:*

C1. *The edge e_ϵ such that $L(e_\epsilon) = (b, !, \star)$ is the unique minimal element according to $\le$. For every i, we have $s_i^0 \in V$ and $e_\epsilon \to_r s_i^0$.*

C2. *If $h \in V \cap \mathbf{hist}(\mathcal{T}_i)$ there is a unique $e \in E$ such that $e \to_c h$. If $|h| > 1$, there is also a unique $h' \in V$ such that $h' \to_c e$ and either $(h', L(e), h) \in R_i$ or $(h', ?(L(e)), h) \in R_i$.*

C3. *For every $h \in V$ there is at most one $e \in E$ such that $h \to_c e$.*

*C4. *For every $e \in E \setminus \{e_\epsilon\}$ there is $I \subseteq [n]$ such that all the following hold:*
   (a) *For every $i \in I$ we have $|{}^\bullet e \cap \mathbf{hist}(\mathcal{T}_i)| = 1$ and $|e^\bullet \cap \mathbf{hist}(\mathcal{T}_i)| = 1$.*
   (b) *There is a unique $i \in I$ and $h, h' \in V \cap \mathbf{hist}(\mathcal{T}_i)$ such that $(h, L(e), h') \in R_i$ and $h \to_s e \to_s h'$ and for every $i' \in I \setminus \{i\}$ there are $h'', h''' \in V \cap \mathbf{hist}(\mathcal{T}_{i'})$ such that $h'' \to_r e \to_r h'''$ and $(h'', ?(L(e)), h''') \in R_{i'}$.*

C5. *For every $e \ne e'$ such that $ch(e) = ch(e')$ we have $e \le e'$ or $e' \le e$.*

*C6. *If $e \to_i e'$ then the following holds:*
   (a) *$ch(e) = ch(e')$.*

*C7. *For every $(v, !, c) \in B$ then*

$$\mathcal{E}((v, !, c)) = \begin{aligned} &\{(h, e) \mid \text{for } c = \star,\ h \to_c e \text{ and } h \to_{?(v, !, c)}\} \cup \\ &\{(e, h) \mid \text{for } c = \star, e \to_c h \text{ and } h \to_{?(v, !, c)}\} \cup \\ &\{(h, e) \mid \text{for } c \ne \star,\ h \to_c e \text{ and } c \in \mathrm{LS}(h)\} \cup \\ &\{(e, h) \mid \text{for } c \ne \star, e \to_c h \text{ and } c \in \mathrm{LS}(h)\} \end{aligned}$$

We drop from the interleaving relation all order relations that correspond to reconfiguration and keep only those that correspond to the usage of a common resource. Furthermore, we assign each broadcast and multicast message with a glue relation. That is, for every broadcast b add all *existing* ingoing and outgoing messages of histories that may participate in m. The rationale is that if such histories can participate in a broadcast then they cannot be enabled independently from the broadcast as they would participate in it. For every multicast m add all *existing* ingoing and outgoing messages of histories that either block m or could participate in m. The rationale is that such histories cannot be independent from the multicast as they either block it or would participate in it. Note that $^*C7$ adds one glue for every multicast *channel* but one for every broadcast.

We use $\mathbf{comp}_g(\mathcal{S})$ to denote the set of g-computations of CTS $\mathcal{S}$ and show that it indeed captures the same notion of computation.

Theorem 1. *Given a CTS $\mathcal{T}$, $\mathbf{comp}(\mathcal{T}) = \{\pi \mid \pi \preceq \pi_g \wedge \pi_g \in \mathbf{comp}_g(\mathcal{T})\}$.*

5.2   Glue Computations for PTI-nets

Let $N = \langle P, T, F, I \rangle$ be a PTI-net and m_0 its initial marking. We now define a *g-computation*. The differences from the definition of LPO (Def. 3) are highlighted with a "$*$" (N4.(b-c) are removed and *N5 is new).

Definition 8 (g-computation). *A g-computation of N is a g-LPO $(P, \mathcal{G}, \mathcal{E})$, where $P = (O, \rightarrow_c, \Sigma, \Upsilon, L)$, the components V, E, Σ, Υ, and L are as for LPO, and the following holds.*

N1. *The t-history $(\emptyset, t_\epsilon)$ is the unique minimal element according to $\leq$.*

N2. *For a p-history $v = (e, p, i) \in V$ we have $e \in E$ and e is the unique edge such that $e \rightarrow_c v$.*

N3. *For a p-history $v = (h, p, i) \in V$, let $e_1, \ldots, e_j$ be the t-histories such that $v \rightarrow_c e_j$. Then, for every j we have $e_j(v) > 0$ and $\sum_j e_j(v) \leq i$.*
    That is, v leads to t-histories that contain it with the number of tokens in v being respected.

*N4. *For every $e \in E$, where $e = (\{(v_1, i_1), \ldots, (v_n, i_n)\}, t)$ the following holds:*
    *(a) $^\bullet e = \{v_1, \ldots, v_n\}$ *and* $e^\bullet = \{(e, p, t^\bullet(p)) \mid t^\bullet(p) > 0\}$.

*N5. *We define a predicate capturing that a place is left without tokens. For a p-history $v = (h, p, i)$, let $e_1, \ldots, e_j$ be the t-histories such that $v \rightarrow_c e_j$. If $\sum_j e_j(v) = i$ we write $f(v)$. Otherwise, it is the case that $\neg f(v)$.*
    For every $t \in T$ we have:

$$
\begin{aligned}
\mathcal{E}(t) \;=\; & \{(v, e) \mid v \rightarrow_c e \text{ and } (L(v), t) \in I\} & \cup \\
& \{(e, v) \mid e \rightarrow_c v \text{ and } (L(v), t) \in I\} & \cup \\
& \{(v, e) \mid \exists v' \,.\, (L(v'), t) \in I, \; \neg f(v'), \; v' \leq v, \text{ and } v \rightarrow_c e\} \cup \\
& \{(e, v) \mid \exists v' \,.\, (L(v'), t) \in I, \; \neg f(v'), v' \leq e, \text{ and } e \rightarrow_c v\}
\end{aligned}
$$

That is, for a transition t, add all existing *ingoing and outgoing transitions of places that inhibit t to t's glue. Moreover, if some place that inhibits t has some tokens left in it, then whatever happens after that place is glued as well.*

That is, we drop $\rightarrow_i$ and assign each inhibited transition with a glue relation.

We use $\mathbf{comp}_g(N)$ to denote the set of g-computations of Petri net N and show that it indeed captures the same notion of computation.

Theorem 2. *Given a PTI-net N, $\mathbf{comp}(N) = \{\pi \mid \pi \preceq \pi_g \wedge \pi_g \in \mathbf{comp}_g(N)\}$.*

6   Separating Choice and Forced Interleaving

We show that g-LPOs distinguish nondeterministic choice, which corresponds to different g-LPOs, and interleaving choices due to reconfiguration, which correspond to different ways to refer to glue. For both CTS and PTI-nets, we show that distinct g-LPOs contain different nondeterministic or order choices. Thus, we manage to define *one* structure that captures all possible interleavings and reconfigurations together.

6.1   Choice vs Reconfiguration-Forced Interleaving in CTSs

A choice that distinguishes two computations for a CTS is either (a) a situation where all the agents have exactly the same history and at least one agent participates in a different interaction or (b) communications on the same channel are ordered differentently. Note that as channels are global resources, the case that changing the order of communications on a channel does not have side effects is accidental. Indeed, such a change of order could have side effects and constitutes a different choice.

We show that every two distinct g-computations of the same CTS have a joint history of some agent that "sees the difference" or a channel that transfers messages in a different order. Difference for a history is either maximality in one and not the other or extension by different communications in the two g-computations.

Theorem 3. *Given a CTS T and two different g-LPOs $G_1, G_2 \in \mathbf{comp}_g(N)$ then one of the following holds:*

1. *For some agent i there exists a history h_i in both G_1 and G_2 such that either h_i is maximal in G_α and not maximal $G_{3-\alpha}$, where $\alpha \in \{1, 2\}$;*
2. *For some agent i there exists a history h_i in both G_1 and G_2 such that for the edges e_1 and e_2 such that $h_i \rightarrow_{c_1} e_1$ and $h_i \rightarrow_{c_2} e_2$ we have $L_1(e_1) \neq L_2(e_2)$;*
3. *or; There is a pair of agents i and i' and histories h_i and $h_{i'}$ in both G_1 and G_2 such that the order between the communications of i and i' is different in G_1 and G_2.*

Theorem 3 is not true for LPOs as shown by the LPOs and g-LPO of the CTS in Fig. 1. We note that by the proof of Theorem 1 all the LPOs that disagree only on forced interleavings are refined by the same g-LPO.

6.2   Choice vs Interleaving in PTI-nets

A choice that distinguishes two computations is a situation where a set of tokens have exactly the same history and they do a different exchange. We show that every two distinct g-computations of the same net have a set of tokens that "see the difference". That is, they participate in a different transition in the two g-computations. This includes the option of tokens in one g-computation participating in a transition and tokens in the other g-computation not continuing.

Theorem 4. *Given a Petri net P and two different g-LPOs $G_1, G_2 \in comp_g(N)$ then one of the following holds:*

1. *There is a node v_i in both G_1 and G_2 such that the number of tokens not taken from v_i in G_1 and G_2 is different.*
2. *There is a set of p-histories $v_1, \ldots, v_n$ in both G_1 and G_2 that participate in some transition t in G_α but not in $G_{3-\alpha}$, where $\alpha \in \{1, 2\}$.*

Note that item 2 includes the case where the transition t happens in both G_1 and G_2 but takes a different number of tokens from every node. This difference is significant as the nodes communicate via the identified transition and share the knowledge about the difference.

Theorem 4 is not true for LPOs. This is already shown by the very simple examples in Fig. 2(b). Indeed, in the two LPOs demonstrated by the dashed arcs in the figure, all sets of nodes participate in exactly the same transitions.

We note that by the proof of Theorem 2 all the LPOs that disagree only on forced interleavings are refined by the same g-LPO.

7   Concluding Remarks

We laid down the basis to reason about systems in which events are affected also by non-participants. We showed how to isolate forced interleaving decisions of the system due to such effects, and other decisions due to standard concurrent execution of independent events. This was shown for CTS [4,5] and PTI-nets [9,12], which cover a wide range of interaction capabilities from two different schools of concurrency. In particular, CTS capture channel communication and require order of events without flow of information (captured through the interleaving relation) while PTI-nets are unbounded and more general. We proposed, for both, a partial order semantics, named LPO, of computations under reconfiguration. An LPO supports event-to-event connections that allows to refer to reconfiguration points. Moreover, to fully characterise reconfiguration in a single structure, we proposed a glued LPO semantics, named g-LPO. The latter is able to fully isolate scheduling decisions due to reconfiguration from the ones due to standard concurrency. We show that any LPO computation is only a refinement of some g-LPO of the same system. Finally, we prove important results on g-LPO with respect to reconfiguration and nondeterminism.

Perspectives and Future Work: Capturing all possible interleavings in a single structure offers opportunities in terms of specification and verification. For example, using languages of linear sequences as a specification language for concurrent system requires some care. Indeed, languages that include certain interleavings of the same computation and exclude others are obviously inappropriate as specifications: there is no system that satisfies them. Invariability under interleaving *without reconfiguration* is easy to check using some representations of languages (deterministic automata) but harder using other representations (temporal logic). We do not know to characterise languages of linear sequences that capture all possible interleavings with reconfiguration. Thus, creating structures that capture precisely such behaviour is important for the definition of appropriate specification languages. Studying g-LPOs could give us insights into the properties of languages of linear sequences that are appropriate to specify concurrent systems with reconfigurations. We can exploit g-LPO semantics to define specifications over g-LPO computations (rather than linear sequences or LPOs).

Related Works: The prevalent approach to semantics of reconfigurable interactions is based on linear order semantics (cf. Pi-calculus [11,19], Mobile Ambients [10], Applied Pi-calculus [1], Psi-calculus [7,8], concurrent constraint programming [14,22], fusion calculus [24], the *AbC* calculus [2,3], RECIPE [4] etc.). This semantics cannot distinguish the different choices of the system from a global perspective. It hides information about interactions and possible interdependence among events. In fact, linear order semantics ignores the possible concurrency of events, which can be important e.g. for judging the temporal efficiency of the system [23]. Linear order semantics comes even shorter to capture information about reconfiguration from an external observer's point of view.

Partial order semantics (cf. *Process Semantics* of Petri nets [18,21,23] and *Mazurkiewicz traces* of Zielonka automata [13,17,25]), on the other hand, is able to refer to the interaction and event dependencies, but does not deal very well with reconfiguration. This is because the latter formalisms have fixed interaction structures, and thus the interdependence of events is defined structurally. Reconfiguration, on the other hand, enforces reordering of events dynamically in non-trivial ways, and thus makes defining correct partial order semantics very challenging. As shown in [15], some aspects of concurrency are almost impossible to tackle in either linear-order or partial-order causality-based models, and one of them is PTI-nets [12]. In fact, reconfiguration increases the expressive power of the formalism, e.g., adding inhibitor arcs to Petri nets makes them Turing Powerful [6]. However, this expressive power does not come without a cost. It prevents most analysis techniques for standard Petri nets [9].

Partial order semantics for PTI-nets are given in [16] and [15]. Much like our LPOs, they represent different forced interleavings *separately*. As they use occurrence nets they have many more ways to represent essentially the same computation due to symmetry between tokens. Relational Structures [15] add an additional "not later than" relation to partial orders. Their emphasis is on providing a general semantic framework for concurrent systems. Thus, relational structures handle issues like priority and error recovery, which we do not handle. However, they are not concerned with uniqueness of representation. So the two works serve different purposes and it would be interesting to investigate mutual extensions.

References

1. Abadi, M., Blanchet, B., Fournet, C.: The applied pi calculus: mobile values, new names, and secure communication. J. ACM **65**(1), 1:1–1:41 (2018). https://doi.org/10.1145/3127586
2. Abd Alrahman, Y., De Nicola, R., Loreti, M.: A calculus for collective-adaptive systems and its behavioural theory. Inf. Comput. **268** (2019). https://doi.org/10.1016/j.ic.2019.104457
3. Abd Alrahman, Y., De Nicola, R., Loreti, M.: Programming interactions in collective adaptive systems by relying on attribute-based communication. Sci. Comput. Program. **192**, 102428 (2020)
4. Abd Alrahman, Y., Perelli, G., Piterman, N.: Reconfigurable interaction for MAS modelling. In: Proceedings of the 19th International Conference on Autonomous Agents and Multiagent Systems, AAMAS 2020, Auckland, New Zealand, 9–13 May 2020, pp. 7–15. International Foundation for Autonomous Agents and Multiagent Systems (2020)
5. Abd Alrahman, Y., Piterman, N.: Modelling and verification of reconfigurable multi-agent systems. Auton. Agents Multi Agent Syst. **35**(2), 47 (2021)
6. Agerwala, T.: A complete model for representing the coordination of asynchronous processes. Technical Report, Johns Hopkins Univ., Baltimore, Md. (USA) (1974)
7. Bengtson, J., Johansson, M., Parrow, J., Victor, B.: Psi-calculi: a framework for mobile processes with nominal data and logic. Logical Meth. Comput. Sci. **7**(1) (2011). https://doi.org/10.2168/LMCS-7(1:11)2011
8. Borgström, J., et al.: Broadcast psi-calculi with an application to wireless protocols. Softw. Syst. Model. **14**(1), 201–216 (2015)
9. Busi, N.: Analysis issues in petri nets with inhibitor arcs. Theor. Comput. Sci. **275**(1–2), 127–177 (2002)
10. Cardelli, L., Gordon, A.D.: Mobile ambients. Electr. Notes Theor. Comput. Sci. **10**, 198–201 (1997). https://doi.org/10.1016/S1571-0661(05)80699-1
11. Ene, C., Muntean, T.: Expressiveness of point-to-point versus broadcast communications. In: Ciobanu, G., Păun, G. (eds.) FCT 1999. LNCS, vol. 1684, pp. 258–268. Springer, Heidelberg (1999). https://doi.org/10.1007/3-540-48321-7_21
12. Flynn, M.J., Agerwala, T.: Comments on capabilities, limitations and correctness of petri nets. In: Lipovski, G.J., Szygenda, S.A. (eds.) Proceedings of the 1st Annual Symposium on Computer Architecture, Gainesville, FL, USA, December 1973, pp. 81–86. ACM (1973). https://doi.org/10.1145/800123.803973
13. Genest, B., Gimbert, H., Muscholl, A., Walukiewicz, I.: Optimal Zielonka-type construction of deterministic asynchronous automata. In: Abramsky, S., Gavoille, C., Kirchner, C., Meyer auf der Heide, F., Spirakis, P.G. (eds.) ICALP 2010. LNCS, vol. 6199, pp. 52–63. Springer, Heidelberg (2010). https://doi.org/10.1007/978-3-642-14162-1_5
14. Gilbert, D.R., Palamidessi, C.: Concurrent constraint programming with process mobility. In: Computational Logic - CL 2000, First International Conference, London, UK, 24–28 July, 2000, Proceedings, pp. 463–477 (2000). https://doi.org/10.1007/3-540-44957-4_31

15. Janicki, R., Kleijn, J., Koutny, M., Mikulski, L.: Relational structures for concurrent behaviours. Theor. Comput. Sci. **862**, 174–192 (2021)
16. Kleijn, H.C.M., Koutny, M.: Process semantics of general inhibitor nets. Inf. Comput. **190**(1), 18–69 (2004)
17. Krishna, S., Muscholl, A.: A quadratic construction for Zielonka automata with acyclic communication structure. Theor. Comput. Sci. **503**, 109–114 (2013)
18. Meseguer, J., Montanari, U., Sassone, V.: On the semantics of petri nets. In: Cleaveland, W.R. (ed.) CONCUR 1992. LNCS, vol. 630, pp. 286–301. Springer, Heidelberg (1992). https://doi.org/10.1007/BFb0084798
19. Milner, R., Parrow, J., Walker, D.: A calculus of mobile processes, ii. Inf. Comput. **100**(1), 41–77 (1992)
20. Milner, R., Sangiorgi, D.: Barbed bisimulation. In: Kuich, W. (ed.) ICALP 1992. LNCS, vol. 623, pp. 685–695. Springer, Heidelberg (1992). https://doi.org/10.1007/3-540-55719-9_114
21. Petri, C.A., Reisig, W.: Petri net. Scholarpedia **3**(4), 6477 (2008)
22. Saraswat, V.A., Rinard, M.C.: Concurrent constraint programming. In: Conference Record of the Seventeenth Annual ACM Symposium on Principles of Programming Languages, San Francisco, California, USA, January 1990, pp. 232–245 (1990). https://doi.org/10.1145/96709.96733
23. Vogler, W.: Partial order semantics and read arcs. Theor. Comput. Sci. **286**(1), 33–63 (2002)
24. Wischik, L., Gardner, P.: Explicit fusions. Theor. Comput. Sci. **340**(3), 606–630 (2005)
25. Zielonka, W.: Notes on finite asynchronous automata. RAIRO Theor. Informatics Appl. **21**(2), 99–135 (1987)

Structural Rules and Algebraic Properties of Intersection Types

Sandra Alves[1]([✉]) and Mário Florido[2]

[1] DCC-FCUP & CRACS, Univ. Porto, Porto, Portugal
sandra@fc.up.pt
[2] DCC-FCUP & LIACC, Univ. Porto, Porto, Portugal

Abstract. In this paper we define several notions of term expansion, used to define terms with less sharing, but with the same computational properties of terms typable in an intersection type system. Expansion relates terms typed by associative, commutative and idempotent intersections with terms typed in the Curry type system and the relevant type system; terms typed by non-idempotent intersections with terms typed in the affine and linear type systems; and terms typed by non-idempotent and non-commutative intersections with terms typed in an ordered type system.

Keywords: Intersection types · Substructural type systems · Linearization

1 Introduction

In the Curry Type System [11,24] each assumption about the types of free variables may be used several times or not used at all. This can be achieved either by considering a set of type assumptions used in the type derivation, or a list of type assumptions and the existence of three structural rules in the type system: *exchange*, *weakening* and *contraction*. The *exchange* rule guarantees that the order in which we write variables in the basis is irrelevant. The second structural rule, *weakening*, indicates that we may safely add extra (unneeded) assumptions to the basis. The third structural rule, *contraction*, states that if a term is typed using two identical assumptions then it is also typed using a single assumption. This led to the definition of a *substructural type system* as type systems where the use of type assumptions is limited by the lack of one or more of the structural rules. Substructural type systems in general, have a precise relation (by the Curry-Howard correspondence) with substructural logics [34]. A substructural logic is a logic where also one or more of the structural rules do not hold. Examples of well-known substructural logics include linear logic [23]

Funded by National Funds through the Portuguese funding agency, FCT - Fundação para a Ciência e a Tecnologia, within projects LA/P/0063/2020 and FCT/UID/CEC/0027/2020.

H. Seidl et al. (Eds.): ICTAC 2022, LNCS 13572, pp. 60–77, 2022.
https://doi.org/10.1007/978-3-031-17715-6_6

and relevant logic [3]. A survey of prescriptive substructural type systems (a la Church) and its use to the control of memory resources can be found in [37]. Here we will use a descriptive view (á la Curry) of substructural type systems. Being restrictions to the Curry Type System, substructural type systems type less terms than the Curry Type System.

In the opposite direction we have Intersection Type Systems [6,9,10], which characterise exactly the set of strongly normalising terms. Applications of Intersection Type Systems in programming language theory cover a variety of diverse topics including the design of programming languages [35], program analysis [31], program synthesis [20], and extensions such as refinement and union types [15,16,21]. But the huge expressive power of intersection types comes with a price: problems such as type inference and inhabitation are undecidable in general [5,36].

In this paper we will address the following problem: to which extent can we approximate a term typed in the intersection type system by terms typable in a simpler type system, such as the Curry Type System or a substructural type system?

Let us look at the term $T \equiv (\lambda x.xx)I$, where I is the identity function $\lambda x.x$. This term has type $\alpha \rightarrow \alpha$, which does not involve intersections, although it is not typable in the Curry Type System nor in any substructural type system, because it has a non-typable subterm. The problem is the sharing of variable x in xx, where the two shared occurrences have non-unifiable types. Now notice that there is a term, $(\lambda x_1 x_2.x_1 x_2)II$, typable with the same type in the Curry Type System and several substructural type systems. This term uses less sharing than $(\lambda x.xx)I$ in the sense that each occurrence of a shared variable in $(\lambda x.xx)I$ corresponds to a distinct variable in $(\lambda x_1 x_2.x_1 x_2)II$.

A relation between terms typable by intersection types and versions with less sharing, and thus typable in a simpler type system, was made in [8], defining a translation from derivations in an intersection type system with associative (A), commutative (C) and idempotent (I) intersections, to terms typable in the Curry type system. Our ACI-expansion simplifies this translation using an inductive definition on the terms. In [25] Kfoury defined a relation with a linear calculus typed by an intersection type system where intersection was associative but neither commutative nor idempotent. Kfoury's calculus was the early stage of development of several lines of work including non-idempotent intersection types [7,14] and the linear polyadic calculus [27], and it also inspired and is related to our work. Main differences from our work are that Kfoury changed the calculus and we do not leave the λ-calculus. Also we consider different expansions for non-idempotent and non-commutative intersection types, which leads to different known substructural type systems. Several other works studied the link between non-idempotency and linearity [13,14,18,22,30]. Here we extend the work in [18] defining term expansion also for idempotent and non-commutative types. Another related line of research studied linear approximations of terms in the λ-calculus [17,27–29]. In [28] linear polyadic approximations by terms typed in several type systems, including some of the type systems considered in our paper, were defined by carefully designing an approximation theory based on category theory. However, the specification of these linear approximations is difficult to understand for experts and non-experts alike. Being more general and mathematically quite elegant, it is more complicated than the expansion operations defined here, requiring advanced notions from category theory. Surprisingly, it turns out that the essence of these approximations, when applied only to the four known substructural type systems, can be captured by a much simpler notion of expansion, which can be defined easily by induction. One contribution of our work is to recast the linear approximations when applied to the substructural type systems, and extend them to the ordered case, into a simpler mold and to disentangle its categorical construction of types from the properties actually needed by the expansion processes. We believe this leads to an approach that is better well suited for designers of type systems and programming languages. The present work borrows some inspiration from previous works on linearization of the λ-calculus [1,17,18,25,28] and aims to contribute to this line of research providing a simple uniform framework for addressing linearization related problems. Picking up on work in [18] here we extend the notion of term expansion to the Curry Type System and four substructural type systems: relevant, affine, linear and ordered type systems. Under this uniform framework we show that one can define terms with less sharing, but with the same computational properties of terms typable in an intersection type system. We will then show how we can tune the degree of sharing by choosing different algebraic properties of the intersection operator. A version of this paper with complete proofs can be found in [2].

2   Type Systems

The type systems used here are defined for the λ-calculus. We will first recall the *Curry Type System* [11,12] using a logic with explicit structural rules and lists of assumptions instead of the usual presentation without structural rules but using sets of assumptions. From now on, in the rest of the paper, terms of the λ-calculus are considered module α-equivalence and we assume that in a term M no variable is bound more than once and no variable occurs both free and bound in M. An infinite sequence of type-variables is assumed to be given. *Simple types* are expressions defined thus: (1) each type-variable is a simple type; (2) if σ and τ are simple types then $(\tau \rightarrow \sigma)$ is a simple type. Type-variables are denoted by α, β and arbitrary types are denoted by τ, σ. In both cases we may use or not number subscripts. Parentheses will often be omitted from types, assuming that the arrow is right associative. A finite list of pairs of the form $x : \tau$ (here called *assumptions*), where x is a term variable and τ is a simple type, is *consistent* if and only if the term variables are all distinct. A *basis* is a consistent finite list of pairs of assumptions. The "," operator appends a pair to the end of the list. The list (Γ_1, Γ_2) is the list that results from appending Γ_2 onto the end of Γ_1. We will use the notation $M : \sigma$ meaning that term M has type σ and $\Gamma \vdash M : \sigma$ to denote that $M : \sigma$ holds assuming the assumptions in the basis Γ.

The *Curry Type System* is defined by the following rules:

Axiom and **Structural Rules:**

$$x : \tau \vdash x : \tau \; (\textsf{ax})$$

$$\frac{\Gamma_1, \Gamma_2 \vdash M : \sigma}{\Gamma_1, x : \tau, \Gamma_2 \vdash M : \sigma} \; (\textsf{weak})$$

$$\frac{\Gamma_1, x : \tau_1, y : \tau_2, \Gamma_2 \vdash M : \sigma}{\Gamma_1, y : \tau_2, x : \tau_1, \Gamma_2 \vdash M : \sigma} \; (\textsf{ex})$$

$$\frac{\Gamma_1, x_1 : \tau, x_2 : \tau, \Gamma_2 \vdash M : \sigma}{\Gamma_1, x : \tau, \Gamma_2 \vdash [x/x_1, x/x_2]M : \sigma} \; (\textsf{ctr})$$

Logical Rules:

$$\frac{\Gamma, x : \tau_1 \vdash M : \tau_2}{\Gamma \vdash \lambda x.M : \tau_1 \rightarrow \tau_2} \; (\rightarrow \textsf{i})$$

$$\frac{\Gamma_1 \vdash M : \tau \rightarrow \sigma \qquad \Gamma_2 \vdash N : \tau}{\Gamma_1, \Gamma_2 \vdash MN : \sigma} \; (\rightarrow \textsf{e})$$

The Exchange rule (ex) guarantees that the order in which we write variables in the basis is irrelevant. Weakening (weak), indicates that we may safely add extra (unneeded) assumptions to the basis. Contraction (ctr), states that if a term is typed using two identical assumptions then it is also typed using a single assumption.

The lack of one or more of the structural rules leds to the definition of *substructural type systems*. There are four main substructural systems based in their logical counterparts: the *Relevant Type System* has only two structural rules (Exchange and Contraction); the *Affine Type System* has also two structural rules (Exchange and Weakening); the *Linear Type System* has only the Exchange structural rule; and finally, the *Ordered Type System* does not have any of the structural rules.

Relevant Types. In the *Relevant Type System* every assumption in the basis is used to type a term. This is guaranteed by not using the Weakening type rule. Thus the *Relevant Type System* corresponds to the Curry Type System without the Weakening rule.

Theorem 1. *If a term M is typed in the* Relevant Type System, *then M is a λI-term.*

This theorem shows that relevant types are related to the λI-*calculus*, a restriction to the λ-calulus where in every term M, for each subterm of form $\lambda x.N$ in M, x occurs free in N at least once.

Affine Types. In the *Affine Type System* there is no Contraction rule. This guarantees that function parameters are used at most once. Thus the *Affine Type System* corresponds to the Curry Type System without the Contraction rule. The following subset of λ-terms is related to the set of terms typed in the Affine Type System.

An *affine λ-term* is a λ-term M such that for each subterm of $\lambda x.N$ of M, x occurs free in N at most once and each free variable of M has just one occurrence free in M. The following theorems show that the set of terms typed in the *Affine Type System* is exactly the set of *affine terms*.

Theorem 2. *A term M is typed in the* Affine *Type System, if and only if M is an* Affine λ-*term*.

Linear Types. The *Linear Type System* corresponds to the implicational fragment of linear logic [23] confined with implication as its single connective. In the Linear Type System each assumption must be used exactly once. This means that if $\Gamma \vdash M : \tau$ is a valid typing in the Linear Type System, then each term variable in Γ occurs free exactly once in M. The Linear Type System does not have the Contraction rule, to guarantee that assumptions are used at most once, nor the Weakening rule, meaning that assumptions are used exactly once. We will follow the standard linear logic notation for functional linear types, written $\tau_1 \multimap \tau_2$. As expected, the set of terms typed in the Linear Type System is exactly the set of *linear terms*. A *linear λ-term* is a λ-term M such that for each subterm of $\lambda x.N$ of M, x occurs free in N exactly once and each free variable of M has just one occurrence free in M.

Theorem 3. *A term M is typed in the* Linear *Type System, if and only if M is a* linear λ-*term*.

Ordered Types. Many computational concepts are order sensitive (consider, for example, managing memory allocated on a stack). *Ordered Type Systems* provide a foundation for order sensitive computational problems. The central idea is that by avoiding the exchange rule, we are able to guarantee that program evaluation follows a pre-determined order. Ordered type systems are inspired by Lambek ordered logic [26] which has several applications to natural language processing. Ordered logic was further developed by Polakow and Pfenning [33].

The *Ordered Type System* has: no Contraction, thus it is linear; no Weakening, thus it is also a relevant system; and no Exchange, thus the order of use of assumptions matter.

Definition 1. *Let α range over an infinite set of type variables.* Ordered Types *are defined as $\tau ::= \alpha \mid \tau_1 \multimap_l \tau_2 \mid \tau_1 \multimap_r \tau_2$.*

The definition of the *Ordered Type System* follows:

Axiom:

$$\frac{}{x : \tau \vdash_o x : \tau} \ (\text{ax})$$

Logical Rules:

$$\frac{x : \tau_1, \Gamma \vdash_o M : \tau_2}{\Gamma \vdash_o \lambda x.M : \tau_1 \multimap_l \tau_2} \ (\to \text{i}_l) \qquad \frac{\Gamma, x : \tau_1 \vdash_o M : \tau_2}{\Gamma \vdash_o \lambda x.M : \tau_1 \multimap_r \tau_2} \ (\to \text{i}_r)$$

$$\frac{\Gamma_2 \vdash_o N : \tau \quad \Gamma_1 \vdash_o M : \tau \multimap_l \sigma}{\Gamma_2, \Gamma_1 \vdash_o MN : \sigma} \ (\to \text{e}_l) \qquad \frac{\Gamma_1 \vdash_o M : \tau \multimap_r \sigma \quad \Gamma_2 \vdash_o N : \tau}{\Gamma_1, \Gamma_2 \vdash_o MN : \sigma} \ (\to \text{e}_r)$$

Note that the different arrow types guide type derivations to guarantee that the order of assumptions is used consistently during typing. For example consider the term $(\lambda x.xz_2)z_1$. The two different typings $z_1 : \alpha \multimap_r \beta, z_2 : \alpha \vdash_o (\lambda x.xz_2)z_1 : \beta$ and $z_2 : \alpha, z_1 : \alpha \multimap_l \beta \vdash_o (\lambda x.xz_2)z_1 : \beta$ are valid. Note that if we change the order of the assumptions the typings are no longer valid, i.e. $z_2 : \alpha, z_1 : \alpha \multimap_r \beta \not\vdash_o (\lambda x.xz_2)z_1 : \beta$ and $z_1 : \alpha \multimap_l \beta, z_2 : \alpha \not\vdash_o (\lambda x.xz_2)z_1 : \beta$.

Intersection Types. Intersection types originate in the works of Barendregt, Coppo and Dezani [4,9] and give us a characterization of the strongly normalizable terms. Here we define an Intersection Type System where every type declared in the environment is used in the type derivation, a property which is going to be crucial in subsequent results.

Definition 2. *Let α range over an infinite set of type variables, and $n > 0$. Intersection types are defined thus $\sigma ::= \alpha \mid \sigma_1 \cap \cdots \cap \sigma_n \to \sigma$.*

Note that there is no empty intersection type (the ω type in Coppo-Dezani tradition). The original Coppo-Dezani Intersection Type System [9] considers intersection $\cap$ as an associative, commutative and idempotent operator. There are other works that consider non idempotent intersections [7,18,25]. To avoid ambiguities of notation we will use ACI-intersection to denote associative, commutative and idempotent intersections, AC-intersection to denote non-idempotent intersections and A-intersection to denote non-idempotent and non-commutative intersections. If we write only intersection we mean ACI-intersection. A *type environment* is a finite set of pairs of the form $x : \tau_1 \cap \cdots \cap \tau_n$, where x is a term variable, $\tau_1, \ldots, \tau_n$ are types, and the term variables are all distinct.

Definition 3. *Let Γ_1 and Γ_2 be two type environments. Then $\Gamma_1 \wedge \Gamma_2$ is the new environment where $x : \sigma \in \Gamma_1 \wedge \Gamma_2$ if and only if σ is defined thus:*

$$\sigma = \begin{cases} \sigma_1 \cap \sigma_2 & \text{if } x : \sigma_1 \in \Gamma_1 \text{ and } x : \sigma_2 \in \Gamma_2 \\ \sigma_1 & \text{if } x : \sigma_1 \in \Gamma_1 \text{ and } \neg \exists \sigma.x : \sigma \in \Gamma_2 \\ \sigma_2 & \text{if } x : \sigma_2 \in \Gamma_2 \text{ and } \neg \exists \sigma.x : \sigma \in \Gamma_1 \end{cases}$$

The *Intersection Type System* used here is defined thus:

$$\{x : \tau\} \vdash_\cap x : \tau \; (\mathbf{ax})$$

$$\frac{\Gamma \cup \{x : \tau_1 \cap \cdots \cap \tau_n\} \vdash_\cap M : \sigma}{\Gamma \vdash_\cap \lambda x.M : \tau_1 \cap \cdots \cap \tau_n \to \sigma} \; (\to \mathbf{i}) \qquad \frac{\Gamma \vdash_\cap M : \sigma \quad x \notin \mathbf{fv}(M)}{\Gamma \vdash_\cap \lambda x.M : \tau \to \sigma} \; (\to \mathbf{i_K})$$

$$\frac{\Gamma_0 \vdash_\cap M : \tau_1 \cap \cdots \cap \tau_m \to \sigma \qquad (\Gamma_i \vdash_\cap N : \tau_i)_{i=1\ldots m}}{\Gamma_0 \wedge \Gamma_1 \wedge \cdots \wedge \Gamma_m \vdash_\cap MN : \sigma} \; (\to \mathbf{e})$$

The two different $\to$ **i** rules are necessary because in this system if there is a derivation of $\Gamma \vdash M : \sigma$ and x does not occur free in M, then there is not a type declaration for x in Γ.

3   Term Expansion

We will now present the notion of *term expansion*, which generalises expansion as used in [18] to linearize the strongly normalizable terms. Expansion consists of replacing occurrences of variable in a term, typed with different types, by a new variable typed with the corresponding types. If x is expanded k times in $(\lambda x.M)N$ then N has to be copied k times. However if the expansion is inside N then M may be changed, because possible arguments of x may have to be copied. To define expansion we face one key problem: the expansion of MN is a term of the form $M_0N_1 \ldots N_k$ where M_0 is the expansion of M and $N_1 \ldots N_k$ are expansions of N. The problem is to find the right k. It is easy to determinate the number of new arguments when M is of the form $\lambda x.M'$ (just check how many fresh variables replace x), but if M is itself an application this information depends on expansions made inside M. This is where intersection types play a crucial role. If M has type $\tau_1 \cap \cdots \cap \tau_k \to \sigma$ in an intersection type system we know that MN will be expanded to a term of the form $M_0N_1 \ldots N_k$.

From Intersection Types to Simple Types: ACI-Expansion. In a previous work [18] we related terms typed by non-idempotent intersections with the affine λ-calculus. In this section we extend the results of [18] to relate terms typed by idempotent intersections with the Curry and the Relevant Type Systems. We will define the new notion of *ACI-expansion* of a λ-term. Let us first formalize the expansion of free variables. A *variable expansion* is an expression of the form $x : S$ where x is a variable and S is a set of pairs of the form $y : \tau$ where y is a variable and τ an intersection type. ($x : S$ should be read informally as "x expands to the variables in S"). An *expansion context* A is any finite set of variable expansions $A = \{x_1 : S_1, \ldots, x_n : S_n\}$ where the variables $\{x_1, \ldots, x_n\}$ are all different and the S_i are disjoint. We now define an operation that appends two expansion contexts.

Definition 4. *Let A_1 and A_2 be two expansion contexts. Then $A_1 \uplus A_2$ is a new context such that $x : S \in A_1 \uplus A_2$ if and only if*

$$
S = \begin{cases}
S_1 \cup S_2 & \text{if } x : S_1 \in A_1 \text{ and } x : S_2 \in A_2 \\
S_1 & \text{if } x : S_1 \in A_1 \text{ and } \neg \exists S.x : S \in A_2 \\
S_2 & \text{if } x : S_2 \in A_2 \text{ and } \neg \exists S.x : S \in A_1
\end{cases}
$$

From now on when we write $A \uplus \{x : S\}$ we assume that x does not occur in A. We are now able to formalize the notion of term expansion.

Definition 5. *Given a pair $M : \sigma$, where M is a term and σ an ACI-intersection type, a term N and an expansion context A we define here a relation $\mathcal{E}_I(M : \sigma) \lhd (N, A)$ called* ACI-expansion. *If A is empty we will sometimes omit it and write just $\mathcal{E}_I(M : \sigma) \lhd N$. Expansion is defined by:*

$$\mathcal{E}_I(x : \tau) \lhd (y, \{x : \{y : \tau\}\})$$
$$\text{if } x \neq y$$
$$\mathcal{E}_I(\lambda x.M : \tau_1 \cap \cdots \cap \tau_n \to \sigma) \lhd (\lambda x_1 \ldots x_n.M^*, A)$$
$$\text{if } x \text{ occurs in } M \text{ and}$$
$$\mathcal{E}_I(M : \sigma) \lhd (M^*, A \cup \{x : \{x_1 : \tau_1, \ldots, x_n : \tau_n\}\})$$
$$\mathcal{E}_I(\lambda x.M : \tau \to \sigma) \lhd (\lambda y.M^*, A)$$
$$\text{if } x \text{ does not occur in } M,$$
$$y \text{ is a fresh variable and}$$
$$\mathcal{E}_I(M : \sigma) \lhd (M^*, A)$$
$$\mathcal{E}_I(MN : \sigma) \lhd (M_0 N_1 \ldots N_k, A_0 \uplus A_1 \uplus \cdots \uplus A_k)$$
$$\text{if for some } k > 0 \text{ and } \tau_1, \ldots \tau_k,$$
$$\mathcal{E}_I(M : \tau_1 \cap \cdots \cap \tau_k \to \sigma) \lhd (M_0, A_0) \text{ and}$$
$$\mathcal{E}_I(N : \tau_i) \lhd (N_i, A_i), (1 \leq i \leq k)$$

From now on if $\mathcal{E}_I(M : \sigma) \lhd (N, A)$ we will refer to N as an expanded version of M.

We will now present an illustrating example. Let $I \equiv \lambda x.x$ and $M \equiv \lambda x.xx$. Let us show step by step how to calculate an expansion of $(MI : \alpha \to \alpha)$.

$\mathcal{E}_I(x : (\alpha \to \alpha) \to (\alpha \to \alpha)) \lhd (x_1, \{x : \{x_1 : (\alpha \to \alpha) \to (\alpha \to \alpha)\}\})$ and $\mathcal{E}_I(x : \alpha \to \alpha) \lhd (x_2, \{x : \{x_2 : \alpha \to \alpha\}\})$, thus $\mathcal{E}_I(xx : \alpha \to \alpha) \lhd (x_1 x_2, \{x : \{x_1 : (\alpha \to \alpha) \to (\alpha \to \alpha), x_2 : \alpha \to \alpha\}\})$ and $\mathcal{E}_I(\lambda x.xx : (((\alpha \to \alpha) \to (\alpha \to \alpha)) \cap (\alpha \to \alpha)) \to \alpha \to \alpha) \lhd \lambda x_1 x_2.x_1 x_2$. It easy to show that $\mathcal{E}_I(I : \alpha \to \alpha) \lhd I$ and $\mathcal{E}_I(I : (\alpha \to \alpha) \to (\alpha \to \alpha)) \lhd I$. Thus $\mathcal{E}_I(((\lambda x.xx)I) : \alpha \to \alpha) \lhd (\lambda x_1 x_2.x_1 x_2)II$. Note that if $\mathcal{E}_I(xx : \alpha \to \alpha) \lhd (x_1 x_2, \{x : \{x_1 : (\alpha \to \alpha) \to (\alpha \to \alpha), x_2 : \alpha \to \alpha\}\})$ it is also true that $\mathcal{E}_I(xx : \alpha \to \alpha) \lhd (x_1 x_2, \{x : \{x_2 : \alpha \to \alpha, x_1 : (\alpha \to \alpha) \to (\alpha \to \alpha)\}\})$, because $\{x_1 : (\alpha \to \alpha) \to (\alpha \to \alpha), x_2 : \alpha \to \alpha\}$ is a set and thus there is not a fixed order among its elements. Thus we also have $\mathcal{E}_I(\lambda x.xx : ((\alpha \to \alpha) \cap ((\alpha \to \alpha) \to (\alpha \to \alpha)))) \to \alpha \to \alpha) \lhd \lambda x_2 x_1.x_1 x_2$ and consequently $\mathcal{E}_I(((\lambda x.xx)I) : \alpha \to \alpha) \lhd (\lambda x_2 x_1.x_1 x_2)II$. Note that the result of ACI-expansion is a term typable in the Curry Type System, not necessarily linear. For example the expansion of $\lambda fx.f(fx)$ using type $(\alpha \to \alpha) \to \alpha \to \alpha$ is the term $\lambda f_1 x_1.f_1(f_1 x_1)$.

We now show that terms that we can expand are exactly the terms typable in an Intersection Type System i.e. the strongly normalizable terms. Let us first define two functions that transform expansion contexts into type environments and vice versa. Let Γ be a type environment and $\{x_1, \ldots, x_n\}$ be fresh term variables. Then $e(\Gamma)$ is the *expansion context* defined as $e(\Gamma) = \{x : \{x_1 : \tau_1, \ldots, x_n : \tau_n\} \mid x : \tau_1 \cap \cdots \cap \tau_n \in \Gamma\}$. Let A be an expansion context. Then $l(A)$ is the type environment defined as $l(A) = \{x : \tau_1 \cap \cdots \cap \tau_n \mid x : \{x_1 : \tau_1, \ldots, x_n : \tau_n\} \in A\}$.

Lemma 1. *Let Γ_1 and Γ_2 be type environments. Then $e(\Gamma_1) \uplus e(\Gamma_2) = e(\Gamma_1 \wedge \Gamma_2)$.*

Lemma 2. *Let A_1 and A_2 be two expansion contexts. Then $l(A_1) \wedge l(A_2) = l(A_1 \uplus A_2)$.*

We will now proceed with some auxiliary lemmas before presenting the main theorem.

Lemma 3. *Let* $\mathcal{E}_I(M : \sigma) \lhd (N, A \uplus \{x : \{x_1 : \tau_1, \ldots, x_k : \tau_k\}\})$. *Then the number of free occurrences of* x *in* M *is greater or equal than* k.

Theorem 4. *Let* M *be a* λ-*term such that there is an environment* Γ *and an intersection type* σ *such that* $\Gamma \vdash_\cap M : \sigma$. *Then there is a term* N *such that* $\mathcal{E}_I(M : \sigma) \lhd (N, e(\Gamma))$.

Lemma 4. *Let* M *be a* λ-*term such that there is an expansion context* A, *an intersection type* σ, *and a term* N *such that* $\mathcal{E}_I(M : \sigma) \lhd (N, A)$. *Then* $l(A) \vdash_\cap M : \sigma$.

Theorem 5. *Let* M *be a* λ-*term. Then* M *is strongly normalizable if and only if there are a term* N, *an expansion context* A *and a type* σ *such that* $\mathcal{E}_I(M : \sigma) \lhd (N, A)$.

ACI-Expansion and the Curry Type System. In [8] a translation from intersection types to simple types was given and used to show that derivations in an intersection type system with idempotent intersections can be transformed into terms typed in the Curry Type System. Here we show that our definition of ACI-expansion also preserves this translation. In fact, let $\mathcal{T}$ be the translation from intersection types to simple types defined in [8]. Then, if M is typable in the intersection type system with type σ, and $\mathcal{E}_I(M : \sigma) \lhd (N, A)$ then N is typable in the Curry Type System with type $\mathcal{T}(\sigma)$.

Definition 6. $\mathcal{T}$ *is a translation from intersection types to simple types defined by: 1)* $\mathcal{T}(\alpha) = \alpha$, *if* α *is a type variable; 2)* $\mathcal{T}((\tau_1 \cap \cdots \cap \tau_n) \to \sigma) = \mathcal{T}(\tau_1) \to \cdots \to \mathcal{T}(\tau_n) \to \mathcal{T}(\sigma)$.

$\mathcal{T}$ will be used later in the paper also for similar functions applied to linear and ordered types. Their use is clear in each context. The previous definition can be extended to expansion contexts:

Definition 7. *Let* $\mathcal{T}_e$ *be a translation from expansion contexts to bases defined as:* $\mathcal{T}_e(\emptyset) = \emptyset$ *and* $\mathcal{T}_e(A \cup \{x : \{x_1 : \tau_1, \ldots, x_n : \tau_n\}\}) = \mathcal{T}_e(A) \cup \{x_1 : \mathcal{T}(\tau_1), \ldots, x_n : \mathcal{T}(\tau_n)\}$.

Theorem 6. *Let* $\mathcal{E}_I(M : \sigma) \lhd (N, A)$. *Then* $\mathcal{T}_e(A) \vdash_C N : \mathcal{T}(\sigma)$, *where* $\vdash_C$ *stands for type derivation in the Curry Type System.*

Theorem 7. *Let* M *be a* λ-*term such that* $\Gamma \vdash_\cap M : \sigma$ *in the Intersection Type System. Then there is a basis* Γ_C *and a term* N *such that* $\Gamma_C \vdash_C N : \mathcal{T}(\sigma)$, *where* $\vdash_C$ *stands for type derivation in the Curry Type System.*

This theorem has, as a corollary, that if a term M is typable in the Intersection Type System with a simple type, then there is an expanded term with the same type derivable in the Curry Type System. Just notice that $\mathcal{T}(\sigma) = \sigma$ when σ is a simple type.

Weak Head Reduction. We will now show that ACI-expansion is preserved by a notion of reduction that is used in the implementation of functional programming languages: weak head reduction. This guarantees that the weak head normal form of a term M has an expanded version, which is a weak head normal form of an expanded version of M. We first present one lemma that is going to be used in the study of the preservation of expansion by reduction.

Lemma 5. Let $\mathcal{E}_I(M : \sigma) \lhd (M_0, A_0 \uplus \{x : \{x_1 : \tau_1, \ldots, x_k : \tau_k\}\})$ and $\mathcal{E}_I(N : \tau_i) \lhd (N_i, A_i)$ for $i \in \{1, \ldots, k\}$. Then $\mathcal{E}_I(M[N/x] : \sigma) \lhd (M_0[N_1/x_1, \ldots, N_k/x_k], A_0 \uplus \cdots \uplus A_k)$

Functional language compilers [32] consider only weak-head reduction and stop evaluation when a *weak-head normal form* (a constant or a λ-abstraction) is reached. Weak-head normal forms are sufficient because printable results only belong to basic domains. The following definition of weak head reduction appears in [19]: *Weak head reduction* $\underset{w}{\to}$ is defined by $(\lambda x.M)N \underset{w}{\to} M[N/x]$ and $MN \underset{w}{\to} M'N$ if $M \underset{w}{\to} M'$. We denote by $\underset{w}{\twoheadrightarrow}$ the reflexive and transitive closure of $\underset{w}{\to}$. Closed weak head normal forms are abstractions $\lambda x.M$.

We first define an inclusion relation between expansion contexts as follows:

Definition 8. Let A_1 and A_2 be two expansion contexts. $A_1 \sqsubseteq A_2$ if and only if $x : S_1 \in A_1 \Rightarrow x : S_2 \in A_2$ and $S_1 \subseteq S_2$.

We will now show that ACI-Expansion preserves weak head reduction in the sense that the following diagram commutes:

$$
\begin{array}{ccc}
M_1 & \overset{w}{\longrightarrow} & M_2 \\
\mathcal{E}_I \downarrow & & \downarrow \mathcal{E}_I \\
N_1 & \overset{w}{\longrightarrow} & N_2
\end{array}
$$

For this we need some auxiliary lemmas.

Lemma 6. Let $(\lambda x.M)N$ be a redex in the λ-calculus. Let $\mathcal{E}_I((\lambda x.M)N : \sigma) \lhd (N_1, A_1)$ Then there is a term N_2 such that $\mathcal{E}_I(M[N/x] : \sigma) \lhd (N_2, A_2)$, $A_2 \sqsubseteq A_1$ and $N_1 \underset{\beta}{\twoheadrightarrow} N_2$.

Theorem 8. Let $\mathcal{E}_I(M_1 : \sigma) \lhd (N_1, A_1)$ and $M_1 \underset{w}{\to} M_2$. Then there is a term N_2 such that $\mathcal{E}_I(M_2 : \sigma) \lhd (N_2, A_2)$, $N_1 \underset{w}{\twoheadrightarrow} N_2$ and $A_2 \sqsubseteq A_1$.

Definition 9. Let t and u be w-reductions starting, respectively, by M_0 and N_0:

$$
t : M_0 \underset{w}{\to} M_1 \underset{w}{\to} M_2 \underset{w}{\to} \cdots
$$

$$
u : N_0 \underset{w}{\twoheadrightarrow} N_1 \underset{w}{\twoheadrightarrow} N_2 \underset{w}{\twoheadrightarrow} \cdots
$$

We say that u is an expansion of t if there are expansion contexts $A_0, \ldots, A_k$ and a type σ such that $A_0 \sqsupseteq A_1 \sqsupseteq A_2 \sqsupseteq \cdots$ and $\mathcal{E}_I(M_i : \sigma) \lhd (N_i, A_i)$ for $i \geq 0$.

The following corollary of Theorem 8 makes explicit the simple fact that every finite w-reduction can be expanded. It holds trivially by successive applications of Theorem 8 to every w-reduction step in t.

Corollary 1 (of Theorem 8). *Every finite w-reduction t, can be expanded to another w-reduction (not necessarily unique).*

We saw that expansion is preserved by weak head reduction. This does not happen with β-reduction. In fact we may have $M_1 \underset{\beta}{\to} M_2$, $\mathcal{E}_I(M_1 : \sigma) \lhd (N_1, A_1)$ and there is not a type τ such that $\mathcal{E}_I(M_2 : \tau) \lhd (N_2, A_2)$ and $N_1 \underset{\beta}{\twoheadrightarrow} N_2$. Note that there is an expanded version, P, of M_2 (because M_1 is strongly normalizable thus M_2 is also strongly normalizable and thus, by Theorem 5, it has an expanded version). The point here is that $N_1 \underset{\beta}{\not\twoheadrightarrow} P$ for no expanded version P of M_2. To see this let $M_1 \equiv \lambda x.(\lambda y.z)xx$ and $M_2 \equiv \lambda x.zx$. We have $\lambda x.(\lambda y.z)xx \underset{\beta}{\to} \lambda x.zx$, $\mathcal{E}(\lambda x.(\lambda y.z)xx : \alpha_1 \cap \alpha_2 \to \beta) \lhd (\lambda x_1 x_2.(\lambda y_1.z_1)x_1 x_2, \{z : \{z_1 : \alpha_2 \to \beta\}\})$ and $\lambda x_1 x_2.(\lambda y_1.z_1)x_1 x_2 \underset{\beta}{\to} \lambda x_1 x_2.z_1 x_2$. Now note that, as x occurs in zx once, it follows from Lemma 3 that any expansion of $\lambda x.zx$ is of the form $\lambda x_1.M$ where M is one expansion of zx. Thus $\lambda x_1 x_2.z_1 x_2$ cannot be an expansion of $\lambda x.zx$ for any type. If preservation of expansion by β-reduction is not viewed as a goal by itself, then the lack of this property is not a problem, because it holds for a notion of reduction that is used in practice.

ACI-Expansion and the Relevant Type System. Here we will study ACI-expansion applied only to λI-terms. Note that it is the same relation, $\mathcal{E}_I$, defined in the previous section, but we now restrict its domain to the set of λI-terms. Thus the same symbol $\mathcal{E}_I$ will be used, overloaded, in this section to evoke this analogy.

The λI-calculus is a restriction of the λ-calculus where in terms of the form $\lambda x.M$, x occurs free in M. We now show that terms in the range of $\mathcal{E}_I$, when its domain is the λI-calculus, are typed in the Relevant Type System.

Theorem 9. *Let M be a λI-term such that $\mathcal{E}_I(M : \sigma) \lhd (N, A)$. Then $\mathcal{T}_e(A) \vdash_R N : \mathcal{T}(\sigma)$, where $\vdash_R$ stands for type derivation in the Relevant Type System.*

Theorem 10. *Let M be a λI-term such that $\Gamma \vdash_\cap M : \sigma$ in the Intersection Type System. Then there is a basis Γ_R and a term N such that $\Gamma_R \vdash_R N : \mathcal{T}(\sigma)$, where $\vdash_R$ stands for type derivation in the Relevant Type System.*

This theorem has, as a corollary, that if a λI-term M is typable in the Intersection Type System with a simple type, then there is an expanded term with the same type derivable in the Relevant Type System. Just notice that $\mathcal{T}(\sigma) = \sigma$ when σ is a Curry type.

Reduction. We now show that β-reduction is preserved by ACI-expansion for the λI-calculus, where erasing is not allowed. This means that for the λI-calculus the following diagram commutes:

$$M_1 \xrightarrow{\ \beta\ } M_2$$

$$\mathcal{E}_I \downarrow \qquad\qquad \downarrow \mathcal{E}_I$$

$$N_1 \xrightarrow[\beta]{\ } N_2$$

Lemma 7. *Let* $(\lambda x.M)N$ *be a redex in the* λI*-calculus. Let* $\mathcal{E}_I((\lambda x.M)N : \sigma) \lhd$ (N_1, A)*. Then there is a term* N_2 *such that* $\mathcal{E}_I(M[N/x] : \sigma) \lhd (N_2, A)$ *and* $N_1 \underset{\beta}{\twoheadrightarrow}$ N_2.

Theorem 11. *Let* M_1 *and* M_2 *be two terms in the* λI*-calculus. Let* $\mathcal{E}_I(M_1 : \sigma) \lhd$ (N_1, A) *and* $M_1 \underset{\beta}{\rightarrow} M_2$*. Then there is a term* N_2 *such that* $\mathcal{E}(M_2 : \sigma) \lhd (N_2, A)$ *and* $N_1 \underset{\beta}{\twoheadrightarrow} N_2$.

From Intersection Types to Linear Types: AC-Expansion. This expansion (AC) was first defined in [18] to linearize the strongly normalizable terms. AC-expansion relies on the use of non-idempotent intersection types, which give us a one-to-one relation between the number of types in an intersection and the number of occurrences of a formal parameter x in a function $\lambda x.M$. This means that expanded terms will be affine or linear terms (depending on the range of expansion). Thus the definition of AC-Expansion (which can be found in [18]) is similar to ACI-Expansion, using non idempotent intersections and the following different expansion rule for variables:

$$\mathcal{E}_C(x : \tau) \lhd (y, \{x : \{y : \tau\}\})$$
if x is a variable and y is a fresh variable

Proofs of theorems in this subsection about the relation between AC-expansion and Affine Types can be found in [18].

From now on, to stress that expanded versions are affine or linear, when we have $\mathcal{E}_C(M : \sigma) \lhd (N, A)$ we will refer to N as one linear version of M.

AC-Expansion and the Affine Type System

Definition 10. $\mathcal{T}$ *is a translation from intersection types to linear types defined by* $\mathcal{T}(\alpha) = \alpha$*, if* α *is a type variable and* $\mathcal{T}((\tau_1 \cap \cdots \cap \tau_n) \to \sigma) = \mathcal{T}(\tau_1) \multimap \cdots \multimap$ $\mathcal{T}(\tau_n) \multimap \mathcal{T}(\sigma)$.

Theorem 1. *Let* $\mathcal{E}_C(M : \sigma) \lhd (N, A)$*. Then* $\mathcal{T}_e(A) \vdash_A N : \mathcal{T}(\sigma)$*, where* $\vdash_A$ *stands for type derivation in the Affine Type System.*

Theorem 2. *Let* M *be a* λ*-term such that* $\Gamma \vdash_\cap M : \sigma$ *in the Intersection Type System. Then there is a basis* Γ_A *and a term* N *such that* $\Gamma_A \vdash_A N : \mathcal{T}(\sigma)$*, where* $\vdash_A$ *stands for type derivation in the Affine Type System.*

Weak-Head Reduction. AC-expansion is also preserved by weak head reduction. This guarantees that the weak head normal form of a term M has an expanded version, which is a weak head normal form of an expanded version of M. We first present one lemma that is going to be used in the study of the preservation of expansion by reduction.

Lemma 8. *Let* $\mathcal{E}_C(M : \sigma) \lhd (M_0, A_0 \uplus \{x : \{x_1 : \tau_1, \ldots, x_k : \tau_k\}\})$ *and* $\mathcal{E}_C(N : \tau_i) \lhd (N_i, A_i)$ *for* $i \in \{1, \ldots, k\}$. *Then*

$$\mathcal{E}_C(M[N/x] : \sigma) \lhd (M_0[N_1/x_1, \ldots, N_k/x_k], A_0 \uplus \cdots \uplus A_k)$$

AC-Expansion preserves weak head reduction, thus the following diagram commutes:

$$
\begin{array}{ccc}
M_1 & \xrightarrow{\ w\ } & M_2 \\
{\scriptstyle\mathcal{E}_C}\downarrow & & \downarrow{\scriptstyle\mathcal{E}_C} \\
N_1 & \xrightarrow{\ w\ } & N_2
\end{array}
$$

Theorem 3. *Let* $\mathcal{E}_C(M_1 : \sigma) \lhd (N_1, A_1)$ *and* $M_1 \xrightarrow{w} M_2$. *Then there is an affine term* N_2 *such that* $\mathcal{E}_C(M_2 : \sigma) \lhd (N_2, A_2)$, $N_1 \twoheadrightarrow_w N_2$ *and* $A_2 \sqsubseteq A_1$.

We saw that AC-expansion was preserved by weak head reduction. The same example used to prove that β-reduction is not preserved by ACI-expansion holds to show the lack of the same property for AC-expansion.

AC-Expansion and the Linear Type System. Here we will study AC-expansion applied only to λI-terms. Note that it is the same relation, $\mathcal{E}_C$, defined in the previous section, but we now restrict its domain to the set of λI-terms. Thus the same symbol $\mathcal{E}_C$ will be used overloaded.

We show that terms in the range of $\mathcal{E}_C$ when its domain is the λI-calculus are typed in the Linear Type System.

Theorem 12. *Let* M *be a* λI-*term such that* $\mathcal{E}_C(M : \sigma) \lhd (N, A)$. *Then* $\mathcal{T}_e(A) \vdash_L N : \mathcal{T}(\sigma)$, *where* $\vdash_L$ *stands for type derivation in the Linear Type System.*

Theorem 13. *Let* M *be a* λI-*term such that* $\Gamma \vdash_\cap M : \sigma$ *in the Intersection Type System. Then there is a basis* Γ_L *and a term* N *such that* $\Gamma_L \vdash_L N : \mathcal{T}(\sigma)$, *where* $\vdash_L$ *stands for type derivation in the Linear Type System.*

Reduction. We show that β-reduction is preserved by AC-expansion for the λI-calculus, where erasing is not allowed. This means that for the λI-calculus the following diagram commutes:

$$
\begin{array}{ccc}
M_1 & \xrightarrow{\ \beta\ } & M_2 \\
{\scriptstyle\mathcal{E}_C}\downarrow & & \downarrow{\scriptstyle\mathcal{E}_C} \\
N_1 & \xrightarrow{\ \beta\ } & N_2
\end{array}
$$

Lemma 9. *Let $(\lambda x.M)N$ be a redex in the λI-calculus. Let $\mathcal{E}_C((\lambda x.M)N : \sigma) \lhd$ (N_1, A) Then there is a linear term N_2 such that $\mathcal{E}_C(M[N/x] : \sigma) \lhd (N_2, A)$ and $N_1 \twoheadrightarrow_\beta N_2$.*

Theorem 14. *Let M_1 and M_2 be two terms in the λI-calculus. Let $\mathcal{E}_C(M_1 : \sigma) \lhd$ (N_1, A) and $M_1 \rightarrow_\beta M_2$. Then there is a term N_2 such that $\mathcal{E}_C(M_2 : \sigma) \lhd (N_2, A)$ and $N_1 \twoheadrightarrow_\beta N_2$.*

From Intersection Types to Ordered Types: Ordered Expansion. Here we define the new notion of *ordered expansion*, which relates terms typable by non-idempotent and non-commutative intersections with terms typable in the ordered type system. As order now matters, expansion contexts will be defined as lists.

Definition 11. *$\mathcal{T}$ is a translation from intersection types to ordered types defined by $\mathcal{T}(\alpha) = \alpha$, if α is a type variable and $\mathcal{T}((\tau_1 \cap \cdots \cap \tau_n) \rightarrow \sigma) = \mathcal{T}(\tau_1) \multimap_r \cdots \multimap_r \mathcal{T}(\tau_n) \multimap_r \mathcal{T}(\sigma)$.*

Definition 12. *A variable expansion is an expression of the form $x : S$ where x is a variable and S is a list of pairs of the form $y : \tau$ where y is a variable and τ an intersection type ($x : S$ should be read informally as "x expands to the variables in S").*

Definition 13. *An expansion context A is a finite list of variable expansions, $A = [x_1 : S_1, \ldots, x_n : S_n]$, where the variables $\{x_1, \ldots, x_n\}$ are all different and the S_i have no elements in common.*

We now define an operation that appends two expansion contexts.

Definition 14. *Let A_1 and A_2 be two expansion contexts. Then $A_1 + A_2$ is a new expansion context define inductively as:*

$$A_1 + A_2 = \begin{cases} A_1 & \text{if } A_2 = [\,] \\ (A_1', x : S_1, S_2, A_1'') + A_2' & \text{if } A_1 = A_1', x : S_1, A_1'' \text{ and } A_2 = x : S_2, A_2' \\ (A_1, x : S_2) + A_2' & \text{otherwise} \end{cases}$$

From now on when we write $A + [x : S]$ we assume that x does not occur in A. We are now able to formalize the notion of ordered expansion:

Definition 15 (Ordered Expansion). *The **ordered expansion** relation $\mathcal{E}_o(M : \sigma) \lhd (N^\tau, A)$ for M, N (pure) λ-terms, σ an intersection type and A an expansion context is inductively defined by:*

$$\mathscr{E}_o(x : \sigma) \lhd (y^\sigma, [x : [y : \sigma]]), y \text{ fresh}$$

$$\mathscr{E}_o(\lambda x.M : \sigma_1 \cap \cdots \cap \sigma_n \multimap \sigma) \lhd (\lambda y_1 \ldots y_n.M_0^{\sigma_1 \multimap_r \cdots \multimap_r \sigma_n \multimap_r \sigma}, A),$$

$$\text{if } x \in \mathbf{fv}(M) \text{ and}$$

$$\mathscr{E}_o(M : \sigma) \lhd (M_0^\sigma, A + [x : [x_1 : \sigma_1, \ldots, x_n : \sigma_n]])$$

$$\mathscr{E}_o(\lambda x.M : \sigma_1 \cap \cdots \cap \sigma_n \multimap \sigma) \lhd (\lambda x_1 \ldots x_n.M_0^{\sigma_1 \multimap_l \cdots \multimap_l \sigma_n \multimap_l \sigma}, A),$$

$$\text{if } x \in \mathbf{fv}(M) \text{ and}$$

$$\mathscr{E}_o(M : \sigma) \lhd (M_0^\sigma, [x : [x_n : \sigma_n, \ldots, x_1 : \sigma_1]] + A)$$

$$\mathscr{E}_o(MN : \sigma) \lhd ((M_0 N_1 \ldots N_m)^\sigma, A_0 + A_1 + \cdots + A_m),$$

$$\text{if for some } m > 0 \text{ and } \sigma_1, \ldots, \sigma_m$$

$$\mathscr{E}_o(M : \sigma_1 \cap \cdots \cap \sigma_m \multimap \sigma) \lhd (M_0^{\sigma_1 \multimap_r \cdots \multimap_r \sigma_m \multimap_r \sigma}, A_0)$$

$$\text{and } (\mathscr{E}_o(N : \sigma_i) \lhd (N_i^{\sigma_i}, A_i))_{i=1\ldots m}$$

$$\mathscr{E}_o(MN : \sigma) \lhd ((M_0 N_1 \ldots N_m)^\sigma, A_m + \cdots + A_1 + A_0),$$

$$\text{if for some } m > 0 \text{ and } \sigma_1, \ldots, \sigma_m$$

$$\mathscr{E}_o(M : \sigma_1 \cap \cdots \cap \sigma_m \multimap \sigma) \lhd (M_0^{\sigma_1 \multimap_l \cdots \multimap_l \sigma_m \multimap_l \sigma}, A_0)$$

$$\text{and } (\mathscr{E}_o(N : \sigma_i) \lhd (N_i^{\sigma_i}, A_i))_{i=1\ldots m}$$

Ordered Expansion and Ordered Types

Definition 16. *Let $\mathcal{T}_e$ be a translation from expansion contexts to bases defined as $\mathcal{T}_e(\epsilon) = \epsilon$ and $\mathcal{T}_e(A + [x : [x_1 : \tau_1, \ldots, x_n : \tau_n]]) = \mathcal{T}_e(A), x_1 : \tau_1, \ldots, x_n : \tau_n$.*

Theorem 15. *Let M be a λI-term. If $\mathscr{E}_o(M : \sigma) \lhd (N^{\mathcal{T}(\sigma)}, A)$, then $\mathcal{T}_e(A) \vdash_o N : \mathcal{T}(\sigma)$.*

We will now present an example illustrating Definition 15 and Theorem 15.

Example 1. Let $M \equiv (\lambda x.xz)z$. The ordered expansion of M is calculated step by step as:

$$\mathscr{E}_o((\lambda x.xz)z : \beta) = (((\lambda x_1.x_1 z_1) z_2)^\beta, [z : [z_2 : \alpha \to_r \beta, z_1 : \alpha]])$$
$$\mathscr{E}_o(\lambda x.xz : (\alpha \to \beta) \to \beta) = ((\lambda x_1.x_1 z_1)^{(\alpha \to_r \beta) \to_l \beta}, [z : [z_1 : \alpha]])$$
$$\mathscr{E}_o(xz : \beta) = ((x_1 z_1)^\beta, [x : [x_1 : \alpha \to_r \beta], z : [z_1 : \alpha]])$$
$$\mathscr{E}_o(x : \alpha \to_r \beta) = (x_1^{\alpha \to_r \beta}, [x : [x_1 : \alpha \to_r \beta]])$$
$$\mathscr{E}_o(z : \beta) = (z_1^\beta, [z : [z_1 : \beta]])$$
$$\mathscr{E}_o(z : \alpha \to \beta) = (z_2^{\alpha \to_r \beta}, [z : [z_2 : \alpha \to_r \beta]])$$

Theorem 15 guarantees that the expanded version of M is typable in the ordered type system (in this case with the same type). The corresponding type derivation follows:

$$\cfrac{\cfrac{\cfrac{[x_1 : \alpha \to_r \beta] \vdash_o x_1 : \alpha \to_r \beta \quad [z_1 : \alpha] \vdash_o z_1 : \beta}{[x_1 : \alpha \to_r \beta, z_1 : \alpha] \vdash_o x_1 z_1 : \beta}}{[z_1 : \alpha] \vdash_o (\lambda x_1.x_1 z_1) : (\alpha \to_r \beta) \to_l \beta} \quad [z_2 : \alpha \to_r \beta] \vdash_o z_2 : \alpha \to_r \beta}{[z_2 : \alpha \to_r \beta, z_1 : \alpha] \vdash_o (\lambda x_1.x_1 z_1) z_2) : \beta}$$

Reduction. As it happens with ACI-expansion and AC-expansion, ordered expansion is also preserved by β-reduction for λI-terms.

Lemma 10. *Let* $\mathscr{E}_o(M,\sigma) \lhd (N, A_1 + [x : [x_1 : \tau_1, \ldots, x_n : \tau_n]] + A_2)$, *then there exist n occurrences of x in M.*

Lemma 11. *Let* $\mathscr{E}_o(M,\sigma) \lhd (M_0^{\mathcal{T}(\sigma)}, A_0 + [x : [x_1 : \mathcal{T}(\tau_1), \ldots, x_n : \mathcal{T}(\tau_n)]] + A_{n+1})$ *and*

$$\left(\mathscr{E}_o(N,\tau_i) \lhd (N_i^{\mathcal{T}(\tau_i)}, A_i)\right)_{i=1\ldots n}$$

then $\mathscr{E}_o(M[N/x],\sigma) \lhd ((M_0[N_1/x_1, \ldots, N_n/x_n])^{\mathcal{T}(\sigma)}, A_0 +_{i=1\ldots n} A_i + A_{n+1})$.

Lemma 12. *Let* $(\lambda x.M)N$ *be a redex in the λI-calculus. Let* $\mathscr{E}_o((\lambda x.M)N : \sigma) \lhd (N_1^{\tau_1}, A)$. *Then there is a linear term N_2 and a type τ_2 such that* $\mathscr{E}_o(M[N/x] : \sigma) \lhd (N_2^{\tau_2}, A)$ *and* $N_1 \underset{\beta}{\twoheadrightarrow} N_2$.

Theorem 16. *Let M_1 and M_2 be two terms in the λI-calculus. Let* $\mathscr{E}_o(M_1 : \sigma) \lhd (N_1^{\tau_1}, A)$ *and* $M_1 \underset{\beta}{\twoheadrightarrow} M_2$. *Then there is a term N_2 and a type τ_2 such that* $\mathscr{E}_o(M_2 : \sigma) \lhd (N_2^{\tau_2}, A)$ *and* $N_1 \underset{\beta}{\twoheadrightarrow} N_2$.

4 Conclusions

This paper highlights a clear relation between algebraic properties of intersection types and the substructural rules: idempotent intersection is related with the contraction rule and commutative intersection with the exchange rule. The following table relates the algebraic properties of the intersection operator used in expansion with the different type systems obtained.

$\cap$	Source	Target	Preserves reductions
ACI	λ	Simple Types	Weak Head Reduction
ACI	λI	Relevant Types	β-reduction
AC	λ	Affine Types	Weak Head Reduction
AC	λI	Linear Types	β-reduction
A	λI	Ordered Types	β-reduction

References

1. Alves, S., Florido, M.: Weak linearization of the lambda calculus. Theor. Comput. Sci. **342**(1), 79–103 (2005)
2. Alves, S., Florido, M.: Structural rules and algebraic properties of intersection types. arXiv (2022)
3. Anderson, A.R., Belnap, N.: Entailment: The Logic of Relevance and Necessity, vol. I. Princeton University Press (1975)
4. Barendregt, H., Coppo, M., Dezani-Ciancaglini, M.: A filter lambda model and the completeness of type assignment. J. Symb. Log. **48**(4), 931–940 (1983)
5. Barendregt, H.P., Dekkers, W., Statman, R.: Lambda Calculus with Types. Perspectives in Logic. Cambridge University Press, Cambridge (2013)
6. Bono, V., Dezani-Ciancaglini, M.: A tale of intersection types. In: Proceedings of the 35th Annual ACM/IEEE Symposium on Logic in Computer Science, LICS 2020, pp. 7–20. Association for Computing Machinery, New York (2020)
7. Bucciarelli, A., Kesner, D., Ventura, D.: Non-idempotent intersection types for the lambda-calculus. Log. J. IGPL **25**(4), 431–464 (2017)
8. Bucciarelli, A., Lorenzis, S.D., Piperno, A., Salvo, I.: Some computational properties of intersection types. In: 14th Annual IEEE Symposium on Logic in Computer Science, pp. 109–118. IEEE Computer Society (1999)
9. Coppo, M., Dezani-Ciancaglini, M.: An extension of the basic functionality theory for the λ-calculus. Notre Dame J. Formal Log. **21**(4), 685–693 (1980)
10. Coppo, M., Dezani-Ciancaglini, M., Venneri, B.: Functional characters of solvable terms. Math. Log. Q. **27**(2–6), 45–58 (1981)
11. Curry, H.B.: Functionality in combinatory logic. Proc. Natl. Acad. Sci. **20**(11), 584–590 (1934)
12. Curry, H.B., Feys, R.: Combinatory Logic, vol. I. North-Holland (1958)
13. de Carvalho, D.: Intersection types for light affine lambda calculus. Electron. Notes Theor. Comput. Sci. **136**, 133–152 (2005)
14. de Carvalho, D.: Execution time of lambda-terms via denotational semantics and intersection types. CoRR, abs/0905.4251 (2009)
15. Dunfield, J.: Elaborating intersection and union types. In: ACM SIGPLAN International Conference on Functional Programming, ICFP 2012, Copenhagen, Denmark, 9–15 September 2012, pp. 17–28. ACM (2012)
16. Dunfield, J., Pfenning, F.: Type assignment for intersections and unions in call-by-value languages. In: Gordon, A.D. (ed.) FoSSaCS 2003. LNCS, vol. 2620, pp. 250–266. Springer, Heidelberg (2003). https://doi.org/10.1007/3-540-36576-1_16
17. Ehrhard, T., Regnier, L.: Uniformity and the Taylor expansion of ordinary lambda-terms. Theor. Comput. Sci. **403**(2–3), 347–372 (2008)
18. Florido, M., Damas, L.: Linearization of the lambda-calculus and its relation with intersection type systems. J. Funct. Program. **14**(5), 519–546 (2004)
19. Fradet, P.: Compilation of head and strong reduction. In: Sannella, D. (ed.) ESOP 1994. LNCS, vol. 788, pp. 211–224. Springer, Heidelberg (1994). https://doi.org/10.1007/3-540-57880-3_14
20. Frankle, J., Osera, P., Walker, D., Zdancewic, S.: Example-directed synthesis: a type-theoretic interpretation. In: Bodík, R., Majumdar, R. (eds.) Proceedings of the 43rd Annual ACM SIGPLAN-SIGACT Symposium on Principles of Programming Languages, POPL 2016, St. Petersburg, FL, USA, 20–22 January 2016. ACM (2016)

21. Freeman, T.S., Pfenning, F.: Refinement types for ML. In: Proceedings of the ACM SIGPLAN 1991 Conference on Programming Language Design and Implementation (PLDI), Toronto, Ontario, Canada, 26–28 June 1991, pp. 268–277. ACM (1991)
22. Gardner, P.: Discovering needed reductions using type theory. In: Hagiya, M., Mitchell, J.C. (eds.) TACS 1994. LNCS, vol. 789, pp. 555–574. Springer, Heidelberg (1994). https://doi.org/10.1007/3-540-57887-0_115
23. Girard, J.-Y.: Linear logic. Theor. Comput. Sci. **50**(1), 1–101 (1987)
24. Hindley, J.R.: Basic Simple Type Theory. Cambridge University Press, Cambridge (1997)
25. Kfoury, A.J.: A linearization of the lambda-calculus and consequences. J. Log. Comput. **10**(3), 411–436 (2000)
26. Lambek, J.: The mathematics of sentence structure. Am. Math. Mon. **65**(3), 154–170 (1958)
27. Mazza, D.: An infinitary affine lambda-calculus isomorphic to the full lambda-calculus. In: Proceedings of the 27th Annual IEEE Symposium on Logic in Computer Science, LICS 2012, Dubrovnik, Croatia, 25–28 June 2012, pp. 471–480. IEEE Computer Society (2012)
28. Mazza, D., Pellissier, L., Vial, P.: Polyadic approximations, fibrations and intersection types. Proc. ACM Program. Lang. **2**(POPL):6:1–6:28 (2018)
29. Melliès, P.-A., Tabareau, N., Tasson, C.: An explicit formula for the free exponential modality of linear logic. In: Albers, S., Marchetti-Spaccamela, A., Matias, Y., Nikoletseas, S., Thomas, W. (eds.) ICALP 2009. LNCS, vol. 5556, pp. 247–260. Springer, Heidelberg (2009). https://doi.org/10.1007/978-3-642-02930-1_21
30. Neergaard, P.M., Mairson, H.G.: Types, potency, and idempotency: why nonlinearity and amnesia make a type system work. In: Okasaki, C., Fisher, K. (eds.) Proceedings of the Ninth ACM SIGPLAN International Conference on Functional Programming, ICFP 2004, Snow Bird, UT, USA, 19–21 September 2004, pp. 138–149. ACM (2004)
31. Palsberg, J., Pavlopoulou, C.: From polyvariant flow information to intersection and union types. J. Funct. Program. **11**(3), 263–317 (2001)
32. Peyton Jones, S.L.: The Implementation of Functional Programming Languages. Prentice-Hall, Hoboken (1987)
33. Polakow, J., Pfenning, F.: Natural deduction for intuitionistic non-commutative linear logic. In: Girard, J.-Y. (ed.) TLCA 1999. LNCS, vol. 1581, pp. 295–309. Springer, Heidelberg (1999). https://doi.org/10.1007/3-540-48959-2_21
34. Restall, G.: An Introduction to Substructural Logics. Routledge, Milton Park (2000)
35. Reynolds, J.C.: Design of the Programming Language Forsythe, pp. 173–233. Birkhäuser Boston, Boston (1997)
36. Urzyczyn, P.: The emptiness problem for intersection types. In: Proceedings of the Ninth Annual Symposium on Logic in Computer Science (LICS 1994), Paris, France, 4–7 July 1994, pp. 300–309. IEEE Computer Society (1994)
37. Walker, D.: Substructural type systems. In: Advanced Topics in Types and Programming Languages, pp. 3–43. The MIT Press (2004)

Quantitative Weak Linearisation

Sandra Alves[1]([✉]) and Daniel Ventura[2]

[1] DCC-FCUP & CRACS, Univ. Porto, Porto, Portugal
sandra@fc.up.pt
[2] INF, Univ. Federal de Goiás, Goiânia, Brazil

Abstract. Weak linearisation was defined years ago through a static characterization of the intuitive notion of virtual redex, based on (legal) paths computed from the (syntactical) term tree. Weak-linear terms impose a linearity condition only on functions that are applied (consumed by reduction) and functions that are not applied (therefore persist in the term along any reduction) can be non-linear. This class of terms was shown to be strongly normalising with deciding typability in polynomial time. We revisit this notion through non-idempotent intersection types (also called quantitative types). By using an effective characterisation of minimal typings, based on the notion of tightness, we are able to distinguish between *"consumed"* and *"persistent"* term constructors, which allows us to define an expansion relation, between general λ-terms and weak-linear λ-terms, whilst preserving normal forms by reduction.

Keywords: Intersection types · Linearisation · Minimal typings

1 Introduction

The notion of linearisation of the λ-calculus, as a process of transforming (or simulating) non-linear terms into (or using) *"equivalent"* linear terms, was first introduced in [27], and has since been used as a transformation technique in different settings [19,20,31]. From the computational point of view, linear terms have nice properties: there are no infinite reduction sequences starting from linear terms, there is no duplication of terms upon function evaluation, and every linear term is typable in the simple type system [22] thus it is typable in polynomial time. Regarding implementation issues of linear programs, both inline expansion and updating of structures in place, can be done safely. Several abstract machines for functional calculi have been designed to take into account and optimise the computation in the case of linear functions (see for instance [5,28,30,33]). Linear functions are also naturally occurring in hardware compilation [19]. Circuits are static (i.e., they cannot be copied at run-time), so linear computations are more naturally compiled into hardware.

First author supported by National Funds through the Portuguese funding agency, FCT - Fundação para a Ciência e a Tecnologia, within project LA/P/0063/2020. Second author partially supported by CNPq Universal 430667/2016-7 grant.

H. Seidl et al. (Eds.): ICTAC 2022, LNCS 13572, pp. 78–95, 2022.
https://doi.org/10.1007/978-3-031-17715-6_7

In this paper we revisit the notion of weak-linearisation, as defined in [6], through a notion of expansion based on non-idempotent intersection types and the notion of minimal typings [1]. Non-idempotent intersections were independently introduced by Gardner [18] and Kfoury [27], and turned out to be crucial in several resource aware consumption investigations [2,3,7,9,12,24,26]. The foundation for resource aware reasoning dates back to Girard's seminal work on resource management in proof theory that lead to the definition of linear logic [21]. The quantitative feature of the non-idempotent intersections was highlighted in De Carvalho's thesis [16] where its relation with linear logic [21] and quantitative relational models has been deeply explored. In the intersection types discipline [14], objects are allowed to be typed with distinct types combined by means of an intersection operator. If this intersection operator ($\cap$) does not enjoy idempotency (that is, it distinguishes $\tau \cap \tau$ from τ), then besides providing qualitative information on how objects are used, it also gives quantitative information on how many times they are used. For that reason, these type systems are called (nowadays) quantitative type systems.

Kfoury [27], used non-idempotent intersections to define a linear λ-calculus and the notion of linearisation. Kfoury's linear calculus, denoted $\Lambda^\wedge$, came with a new notion of reduction, called $\beta^\wedge$. Linearisation was defined indirectly by means of the notion of *contraction*, such that well-formed terms of the new calculus were those for which there was a contracted term in the λ-calculus. The relation between linearisation and intersection types was further explored by Florido and Damas in [17], introducing a notion of expansion of terms in the λ-calculus into linear terms, such that, any term typable using intersection types [14] is related with a term typable using simple types [15]. In other words, any typable term can be expanded to a simply typable linear term. For instance, the term δI –where $\delta \equiv \lambda x.xx$ and $I \equiv \lambda x.x$– is typable in such an intersection type system and is related with term $(\lambda x_1 x_2.x_1 x_2) I I$, also said to be a linear expansion of the former. Expansion is preserved by weak-head reduction[1], in the sense that reduction commutes with expansion.

An operational notion of linearisation, called weak-linearisation, was defined by Alves and Florido [6], based on the notion of legal paths. Legal paths were introduced by Asperti and Laneve [8] as a characterisation based on paths of Lévy's redex families in the context of optimal reductions for the λ-calculus [29], providing a static characterisation of the intuitive notion of virtual redex. Weak linear λ-terms are strongly normalising, typable in polynomial time, and the transformation of general terms into weak linear terms was shown to preserve normal forms. A term t is weak linear if in any reduction sequence from t, when there is a contraction of a β-redex $(\lambda x.u)v$, then x occurs free in u at most once, therefore only functions that are applied to an argument in some reduction process are required to be linear. Although this class of terms is often called *affine*, whereas linear is used for terms $\lambda x.t$ where x occurs free exactly once in t, the definition of linear function used here follows [17,27]. Notice that the definition of weak linear term refers to all the abstractions $\lambda x.u$ that are

---

[1] A notion of reduction used in functional programming languages implementation, which does not evaluate inside values, *i.e.* under abstractions.

going to play the function part of a β-redex along the reduction of t, and legal paths were used to identify these virtual redexes. For example $t \equiv (\mathrm{I}\,\delta)k$ is not weak linear, since $(\delta\,k)$ is a redex in a reduction sequence from t, whereas $u \equiv ((\lambda xy.yx)\,\delta)k$ is weak-linear, since the only duplicating abstraction δ is never applied during (any) reduction from u. Note also that we require the capability to distinguish functions that are going to be applied, therefore "*consumed*" by (any) reduction, from the ones that are going to "*persist*" in the term. For example in $\delta\,\mathrm{I}$, only one of the copies of I is going to play the function part of a β-redex, whereas the other is going to remain in the normal form. This dichotomy of consumed/persistent terms has been highlighted in [25] for the $\lambda\mu$-calculus, and adapted to a pattern-calculus in [7], using a quantitative typing system extended with the notion of tight types. Tight-typings, which provide an effective characterisation of minimal typings, have been applied to the λ-calculus [1] to extract exact bounds for different evaluation strategies, and in particular for a maximal reduction strategy.

In this paper we combine the notion of expansion relation, as defined by Florido and Damas in [17], with the notion of tight types in a non-idempotent intersection type system following [1], and define a new expansion relation that captures the operational notion of weak-linearisation. We prove that expansion commutes with β-reduction and that expanded terms are weak-linear in the sense of [6], and therefore typable in polynomial time. Furthermore, because we base our expansion relation on a quantitative type system that characterises strong normalisation, we are able to show that all strong-normalising λ-terms can be simulated by a weak-linear λ-term, with the same β-normal form. This is a major breakthrough with respect to the approach based on legal paths [4,6], where such relation was left as a conjecture. Note that Kfoury also conjectured that strongly normalisable λ-terms are those that can be simulated by a corresponding well-formed term in $\Lambda^{\wedge}$ [27]. Additionally, using tight-types we are able to give a typing characterisation of expanded terms, by introducing a linear restriction of the typing system in [1], such that weak linear λ-terms are exactly the terms typed in this system.

Overview: The rest of the paper is structured as follows. In Sect. 2 we give some preliminary notions on the λ-calculus and discuss some properties of the non-deterministic maximal reduction strategy that we are using in this paper. In Sect. 3, we recall the non-idempotent type system for a maximal reduction strategy given in [1], together with some properties that we adapt to our non-deterministic strategy. Our expansion relation is developed in Sect. 4, where we prove its relation with our maximal reduction strategy. In Sect. 5, we give a typing characterisation of weak-linear terms, by means of a linear system with tight-typings. We discuss some related work in Sect. 6 and finally conclude and discuss future work in Sect. 7.

2   Terms and Reductions

We start by recalling some basic definitions on the λ-calculus. For a detailed reference see [10]. The **set of λ-terms**, denoted by Λ, is inductively defined by means of the following grammar: $t, u ::= x \mid \lambda x.t \mid t\,u$; here $x, y, z, w \ldots$ range over an infinite countable set of variables. The term x is called a *variable*, $\lambda x.t$ is an *abstraction* and tu is an *application*. We write $\mathtt{abs}(t)$, to denote that t is a term of the form $\lambda x.u$. The **size** $|t|$ of a term is defined by: $|x| = 0$; $|\lambda x.u| = 1 + |u|$ and $|uv| = |u| + |v| + 1$. **Free variables** of terms are defined as: $\mathtt{fv}(x) := \{x\}$, $\mathtt{fv}(\lambda x.t) := \mathtt{fv}(t) \setminus \{x\}$ and $\mathtt{fv}(tu) := \mathtt{fv}(t) \cup \mathtt{fv}(u)$.

Terms are considered modulo α-conversion, so that for example $\lambda xy.xz =_\alpha \lambda x'y'.x'z$, but $\lambda x.xz \neq_\alpha \lambda z.zz$. We use $t\{x/u\}$ to denote the **meta-level substitution** operation which replaces all the free occurrences of x in t by the term u. As usual, this operation is performed modulo α-conversion so that capture of free variables is avoided. Throughout the paper, whenever necessary, we will assume Barendregt's Variable Convention (BVC), regarding the use of free and bound variables (see [10]).

We now present an inductive definition of a non-deterministic maximal reduction strategy, denoted $\to_{\mathsf{nmx}}$, that is closely related to the deterministic maximal reduction strategy $\to_{\mathsf{mx}}$ in [1]. A maximal strategy computes the longest reduction sequence to a normal form, whenever such a reduction exists, obtaining an infinite reduction sequence otherwise. The $\to_{\mathsf{mx}}$ reduction strategy is based on a maximal strategy defined by [11] and further developed in [32]. This reduction was used in [32] to reason about strong normalisation, in [6] to prove strong normalization of weak-linear λ-terms and in [1] to reason about quantitative measures for reduction.

The $\to_{\mathsf{nmx}}$ **reduction strategy** on λ-terms is defined in Fig. 1. Superscript e in $\overset{e}{\to}_{\mathsf{nmx}}$ denotes the size of a term erased in reduction and is mostly omitted from notation throughout the paper. The definition of $\to_{\mathsf{nmx}}$ relies on the notion of **head-neutral normal forms**. An inductive definition of head-neutral normal forms, denoted by $t \in \mathcal{N}_{\mathsf{hd}}$, and (nmx)-**normal forms**, denoted by $t \in \mathcal{M}$, is given by the following grammars:

$$\mathcal{N}_{\mathsf{hd}} ::= x \mid \mathcal{N}_{\mathsf{hd}}\, \Lambda \qquad\qquad \mathcal{N} ::= x \mid \mathcal{N}\, \mathcal{M} \qquad\qquad \mathcal{M} ::= \mathcal{N} \mid \lambda x.\mathcal{M}$$

A term $t \in \mathcal{N}$ is called a neutral normal form. Note that $\mathcal{N} \subseteq \mathcal{N}_{\mathsf{hd}}$.
The **reflexive-transitive closure** of $\to_{\mathsf{nmx}}$, is defined by:

$$\frac{}{t \overset{0}{\to}_{\mathsf{nmx}}^{0} t} \qquad \frac{t \overset{r_1}{\to}_{\mathsf{nmx}} v \quad v \overset{r_2}{\to}_{\mathsf{nmx}}^{k} u}{t \overset{r_1+r_2}{\to}_{\mathsf{nmx}}^{k+1} u} \qquad \frac{t \overset{r}{\to}_{\mathsf{nmx}}^{k} u}{t \overset{r}{\to}_{\mathsf{nmx}}^{*} u}$$

The only difference between $\to_{\mathsf{mx}}$ and $\to_{\mathsf{nmx}}$ is that $\to_{\mathsf{mx}}$ last rule is defined with $t \in \mathcal{N}$, *i.e.* in a term of the form $xu_1 \ldots u_n$, while u_i will be reduced only when $xu_1 \ldots u_{i-1} \in \mathcal{N}$ in the former, *i.e.* $u_j \in \mathcal{M}$ for each $1 \leq j < i$, any u_i is reduced independently in the latter. For instance, let $t = x\,(\mathtt{I\,I})\,(\mathtt{I\,I})$, then t can only be $\to_{\mathsf{mx}}$-reduced to $x\,\mathtt{I}\,(\mathtt{I\,I})$ while it can also be $\to_{\mathsf{nmx}}$-reduced to $x\,(\mathtt{I\,I})\,\mathtt{I}$. Therefore, $\to_{\mathsf{mx}} \subseteq \to_{\mathsf{nmx}}$.

We establish some necessary properties about $\to_{\mathsf{nmx}}$ and normal forms.

$$\frac{x \in \mathbf{fv}(t)}{(\lambda x.t)u \xrightarrow{0}_{\mathsf{nmx}} t\{x/u\}} \quad \frac{u \xrightarrow{r}_{\mathsf{nmx}} u' \quad x \notin \mathbf{fv}(t)}{(\lambda x.t)u \xrightarrow{r}_{\mathsf{nmx}} (\lambda x.t)u'} \quad \frac{u \not\rightarrow_{\mathsf{nmx}} \quad x \notin \mathbf{fv}(t)}{(\lambda x.t)u \xrightarrow{|u|}_{\mathsf{nmx}} t}$$

$$\frac{t \xrightarrow{r}_{\mathsf{nmx}} t'}{\lambda x.t \xrightarrow{r}_{\mathsf{nmx}} \lambda x.t'} \quad \frac{\neg\mathbf{abs}(t) \quad t \xrightarrow{r}_{\mathsf{nmx}} t'}{tu \xrightarrow{r}_{\mathsf{nmx}} t'u} \quad \frac{t \in \mathcal{N}_{\mathsf{hd}} \quad u \xrightarrow{r}_{\mathsf{nmx}} u'}{tu \xrightarrow{r}_{\mathsf{nmx}} tu'}$$

Fig. 1. Non-deterministic maximal reduction strategy

Proposition 1. *Let t be a λ-term:*

1. *If $t \in \mathcal{N}_{\mathsf{hd}}$ then $\neg\mathbf{abs}(t)$. In particular, $t \in \mathcal{N}$ implies that $\neg\mathbf{abs}(t)$.*
2. *$t \in \mathcal{M}$ iff $t \not\rightarrow_{\mathsf{nmx}}$.*
3. *If $t \in \mathcal{N}_{\mathsf{hd}}$ and $t \rightarrow_{\mathsf{nmx}} t'$ then $t' \in \mathcal{N}_{\mathsf{hd}}$.*

Proof. 1. Follows directly from the definition of $\mathcal{N}_{\mathsf{hd}}$.
2. ($\Rightarrow$): By induction on $t \in \mathcal{M}$. ($\Leftarrow$): A a slightly stronger result is proved by induction on t : If $t \not\rightarrow_{\mathsf{nmx}}$ then $\neg\mathbf{abs}(t)$ implies $t \in \mathcal{N}$ otherwise $t \in \mathcal{M}$.
3. By induction on $t \in \mathcal{N}_{\mathsf{hd}}$.

We prove that $\rightarrow_{\mathsf{nmx}}$ has the diamond property (DP) thus is also maximal.

Lemma 1 (nmx-reduction has DP). *Let t be a term. If $u \underset{\mathsf{nmx}}{\overset{e'}{\longleftarrow}} t \xrightarrow{e}_{\mathsf{nmx}} v$, with $u \neq v$, then there is w s.t. $u \xrightarrow{e}_{\mathsf{nmx}} w \underset{\mathsf{nmx}}{\overset{e'}{\longleftarrow}} v$.*

Proof. By induction on t. We present the case for $t = t_1 t_2$ where $\neg\mathbf{abs}(t_1)$:

– If $t_1 \in \mathcal{N}$, in which case (by Proposition 1.2) $t_1 \not\rightarrow_{\mathsf{nmx}}$, then $u = t_1 u_2$ and $v = t_1 v_2$ where $u_2 \underset{\mathsf{nmx}}{\overset{e'}{\longleftarrow}} t_2 \xrightarrow{e}_{\mathsf{nmx}} v_2$. By the *i.h.* there is w_2 s.t. $u_2 \xrightarrow{e}_{\mathsf{nmx}} w_2 \underset{\mathsf{nmx}}{\overset{e'}{\longleftarrow}} v_2$. Therefore $u \xrightarrow{e}_{\mathsf{nmx}} w \underset{\mathsf{nmx}}{\overset{e'}{\longleftarrow}} v$ for $w = t_1 w_2$.
– If $t_1 \notin \mathcal{N}$, but $t_1 \in \mathcal{N}_{\mathsf{hd}}$ then there are two subcases:
  • If $u = u_1 t_2$ where $t_1 \xrightarrow{e'}_{\mathsf{nmx}} u_1$, then $u_1 \in \mathcal{N}_{\mathsf{hd}}$ (Proposition 1.3.) and there are two possibilities:
    * If $v = t_1 v_2$ where $t_2 \xrightarrow{e}_{\mathsf{nmx}} v_2$ then, for $w = u_1 v_2$ we have that $u \xrightarrow{e}_{\mathsf{nmx}} w \underset{\mathsf{nmx}}{\overset{e'}{\longleftarrow}} v$.
    * If $v = v_1 t_2$ where $t_1 \xrightarrow{e}_{\mathsf{nmx}} v_1$ then by the *i.h.* there is w_1 s.t. $u_1 \xrightarrow{e}_{\mathsf{nmx}} w_1 \underset{\mathsf{nmx}}{\overset{e'}{\longleftarrow}} v_1$. Since $v_1 \in \mathcal{N}_{\mathsf{hd}}$ (Proposition 1.3.), we have that $u \xrightarrow{e}_{\mathsf{nmx}} w \underset{\mathsf{nmx}}{\overset{e'}{\longleftarrow}} v$ for $w = w_1 t_2$.
  • If $u = t_1 u_2$ where $t_2 \xrightarrow{e'}_{\mathsf{nmx}} u_2$ then the cases are similar as above.
– If $t_1 \notin \mathcal{N}_{\mathsf{hd}}$ then $u = u_1 t_2$ and $v = v_1 t_2$ where $u_1 \underset{\mathsf{nmx}}{\overset{e'}{\longleftarrow}} t_1 \xrightarrow{e}_{\mathsf{nmx}} v_1$. By the *i.h.* there is w_1 s.t. $u_1 \xrightarrow{e}_{\mathsf{nmx}} w_1 \underset{\mathsf{nmx}}{\overset{e'}{\longleftarrow}} v_1$. If $\mathbf{abs}(u_1)$ then either $t_1 = (\lambda x.t_{11})t_{12}$ and $u_1 = t_{11}\{x/t_{12}\}$ or $t_1 = (\lambda x.t_{11})t_{12}$ and $u_1 = t_{11}$. In either case we would have that $u = v$. Then, the only diverging case is when $\neg\mathbf{abs}(u_1)$ and $\neg\mathbf{abs}(v_1)$, therefore $u \xrightarrow{e}_{\mathsf{nmx}} w \underset{\mathsf{nmx}}{\overset{e'}{\longleftarrow}} v$ for $w = w_1 t_2$.

Corollary 1. $\rightarrow_{\mathsf{nmx}}$ *is maximal.*

3   Types

In this section we recall the non-idempotent type system for a maximal reduction strategy given in [1], which we will refer to as $\mathcal{MX}$. This can be seen as an extension of Gardner's system [18], but in which tight types are used to identify persistent term constructors, that is constructors that are not going to be consumed by reduction. The **sets of types** ($\mathcal{T}$) and **multi-types** are given by the following grammars:

$$\textbf{(tight-types)}\ \texttt{t} :: = \bullet_{\mathcal{M}} \mid \bullet_{\mathcal{N}} \qquad \textbf{(types)} \qquad \sigma, \tau :: = \texttt{t} \mid \mathcal{A} \to \sigma$$
$$\textbf{(multi-types)} \quad \mathcal{A} :: = [\sigma_k]_{k \in K}$$

where $\texttt{t}$ denotes **tight-types**: the constants $\bullet_{\mathcal{M}}$ and $\bullet_{\mathcal{N}}$ denote the type of any term reducing to a term in $\mathcal{M}$ and $\mathcal{N}$, respectively. A multiset type (multi-types) is an unordered list of (not necessarily different) elements where K denotes a (possibly empty) finite set of indexes. We use $[\,]$ to denote the *empty* multiset. We write $|\mathcal{A}|$ to denote the number of elements of the multiset $\mathcal{A}$. For example $[\bullet_{\mathcal{N}}, [\bullet_{\mathcal{N}}] \to \bullet_{\mathcal{N}}, \bullet_{\mathcal{N}}]$ is a multi-type of 3 elements, representing the intersection type $\bullet_{\mathcal{N}} \cap ([\bullet_{\mathcal{N}}] \to \bullet_{\mathcal{N}}) \cap \bullet_{\mathcal{N}}$, where $\cap$ is an associative, commutative and non-idempotent intersection type constructor. We write $\sqcup$ to denote multiset union. As usual the arrow constructor is right-associative.

A **typing context** Γ is a map from variables to multi-types, such that only finitely many variables are not mapped to the empty multiset $[\,]$. We write $\text{dom}(\Gamma)$ to denote the domain of Γ, which is the set $\{x \mid \Gamma(x) \neq [\,]\}$. We may write $\Gamma \# \Delta$ if and only if $\text{dom}(\Gamma)$ and $\text{dom}(\Delta)$ are disjoint. Given typing contexts $\{\Gamma_k\}_{k \in K}$ we write $+_{k \in K} \Gamma_k$ for the context that maps x to $\sqcup_{k \in K} \Gamma_k(x)$. One particular case is $\Gamma + \Delta$. We sometimes write $\Gamma; \Delta$ instead of $\Gamma + \Delta$, when $\Gamma \# \Delta$, and we do not distinguish $\Gamma; x : [\,]$ from Γ. **Context inclusion relation** is defined by: $\Delta \subseteq \Gamma$ iff $\exists \Gamma', \Delta + \Gamma' = \Gamma$. The typing context $\Gamma \backslash\!\backslash x$ is defined by $(\Gamma \backslash\!\backslash x)(y) = \Gamma(y)$ if $y \neq x$ and $[\,]$ otherwise.

We write $\texttt{tight}(\sigma)$, if σ is of the form $\bullet_{\mathcal{M}}$ or $\bullet_{\mathcal{N}}$. We extend this notion to multi-types and typing contexts as expected, that is, $\texttt{tight}([\sigma_i]_{i \in I})$ if $\texttt{tight}(\sigma_i)$ for all $i \in I$, and $\texttt{tight}(\Gamma)$ if $\texttt{tight}(\Gamma(x))$, for all $x \in \text{dom}(\Gamma)$.

The typing assignment system $\mathcal{MX}$ is given in Fig. 2. Indexes in the pair (b, r) in a typing $\Gamma \vdash_{\text{mx}}^{(b,r)} t : \tau$ are related with the number of $\to_{\text{nmx}}$ steps and the size of corresponding normal form, respectively, (see Example 1) and will be mostly ommitted throughout the paper. We use $\Phi \triangleright \Gamma \vdash_{\text{mx}} t : \sigma$ (resp. $\Phi \triangleright \Gamma \vdash_{\text{mx}} t : \mathcal{A}$) to denote a **type derivation** ending with the sequent $\Gamma \vdash_{\text{mx}} t : \sigma$ (resp. $\Gamma \vdash_{\text{mx}} t : \mathcal{A}$). The size of a derivation Φ, denoted by $\texttt{sz}(\Phi)$, is the number of all typing rules but $\texttt{many}_{>0}$ and $\texttt{none}$ used in Φ. Note that rule ($\texttt{none}$) demands typability of the premise, not allowing arguments of erasing-functions to be untyped thus preventing divergent terms as arguments.

System $\mathcal{MX}$ is **relevant**: if $\Phi \triangleright \Gamma \vdash_{\text{mx}} t : \tau$ then $\text{dom}(\Gamma) = \text{fv}(t)$. In other words, no weakening is allowed in the typing system. Given a derivation $\Phi \triangleright \Gamma \vdash_{\text{mx}} t : \tau$, we say Φ is **garbage-tight** if $\texttt{tight}(\sigma)$ in every application of rule ($\texttt{none}$); and is **(maximal) tight**, denoted by $\texttt{tight}(\Phi)$, if it is garbage-tight,

$$\frac{}{x : [\tau] \vdash_{\mathsf{mx}}^{(0,0)} x : \tau} \ (\mathbf{ax})$$

$$\frac{\Gamma \vdash_{\mathsf{mx}}^{(b,r)} t : \tau}{\Gamma \backslash\!\backslash x \vdash_{\mathsf{mx}}^{(b+1,r)} \lambda x.t : \Gamma(x) \to \tau} \ (\mathbf{fun}_b) \qquad \frac{\Gamma \vdash_{\mathsf{mx}}^{(b,r)} t : \mathtt{t} \quad \mathtt{tight}(\Gamma(x))}{\Gamma \backslash\!\backslash x \vdash_{\mathsf{mx}}^{(b,r+1)} \lambda x.t : \bullet_{\mathcal{M}}} \ (\mathbf{fun}_r)$$

$$\frac{\Gamma \vdash_{\mathsf{mx}}^{(b,r)} t : \mathcal{A} \to \tau \quad \Delta \vdash_{\mathsf{mx}}^{(b',r')} u : \mathcal{A}}{\Gamma + \Delta \vdash_{\mathsf{mx}}^{(b+b'+1,r+r')} t\,u : \tau} \ (\mathbf{app}_b) \qquad \frac{\Gamma \vdash_{\mathsf{mx}}^{(b,r)} t : \bullet_{\mathcal{N}} \quad \Delta \vdash_{\mathsf{mx}}^{(b',r')} u : \mathtt{t}}{\Gamma + \Delta \vdash_{\mathsf{mx}}^{(b+b',r+r'+1)} t\,u : \bullet_{\mathcal{N}}} \ (\mathbf{app}_r^{lo})$$

$$\frac{(\Delta_k \vdash_{\mathsf{mx}}^{(b_k,r_k)} t : \sigma_k)_{k \in K} \quad |K| > 0}{+_{k \in K} \Delta_k \vdash_{\mathsf{mx}}^{(+_{k \in K} b_k, +_{k \in K} r_k)} t : [\sigma_k]_{k \in K}} \ (\mathbf{many}_{>0}) \qquad \frac{\Delta \vdash_{\mathsf{mx}}^{(b,r)} t : \sigma}{\Delta \vdash_{\mathsf{mx}}^{(b,r)} t : [\,]} \ (\mathbf{none})$$

Fig. 2. System $\mathcal{MX}$

$\mathtt{tight}(\Gamma)$ and $\mathtt{tight}(\tau)$. **Tightness** is the key notion in the typing system, in which persistent and consumable (term) constructors are discriminated. Such classification allows one to give precise measures on both number of steps and size of the corresponding normal form.

Example 1. Consider $t \equiv (\lambda x.x\mathtt{I}x)\Delta$, with $\mathtt{I} \equiv \lambda z.z$ and $\Delta \equiv \lambda y.yy$. Let $\mathcal{B} = [\underbrace{[[\bullet_{\mathcal{M}}] \to \bullet_{\mathcal{M}}] \to [\bullet_{\mathcal{M}}] \to \bullet_{\mathcal{M}}}_{\tau_1}, \underbrace{[\bullet_{\mathcal{M}}] \to \bullet_{\mathcal{M}}}_{\tau_2}]$ and $\mathcal{A} = [\bullet_{\mathcal{M}}, \mathcal{B} \to [\bullet_{\mathcal{M}}] \to \bullet_{\mathcal{M}}]$. Let Φ be:

$$\frac{\dfrac{\dfrac{}{x : [\bullet_{\mathcal{N}}] \vdash^{(0,0)} x : \bullet_{\mathcal{N}}} \quad \dfrac{}{x : [\bullet_{\mathcal{N}}] \vdash^{(0,0)} x : \bullet_{\mathcal{N}}}}{\dfrac{x : [\bullet_{\mathcal{N}}, \bullet_{\mathcal{N}}] \vdash^{(0,1)} xx : \bullet_{\mathcal{N}}}{\vdash^{(0,2)} \Delta : \bullet_{\mathcal{M}}}} \qquad \dfrac{\dfrac{\dfrac{}{x : [\tau_2] \vdash^{(0,0)} x : \tau_2}}{\dfrac{x : [\tau_1] \vdash^{(0,0)} x : \tau_1 \quad x : [\tau_2] \vdash^{(0,0)} x : [\tau_2]}{\dfrac{x : \mathcal{B} \vdash^{(1,0)} xx : [\bullet_{\mathcal{M}}] \to \bullet_{\mathcal{M}}}{\vdash^{(2,0)} \Delta : \mathcal{B} \to [\bullet_{\mathcal{M}}] \to \bullet_{\mathcal{M}}}}}}{\vdash^{(2,2)} \Delta : \mathcal{A}}$$

and $\Phi_{\mathtt{I}}$ be:

$$\frac{\dfrac{x : [\tau_2] \vdash^{(0,0)} x : \tau_2}{\vdash^{(1,0)} \mathtt{I} : \tau_1} \qquad \dfrac{y : [\bullet_{\mathcal{M}}] \vdash^{(0,0)} y : \bullet_{\mathcal{M}}}{\vdash^{(1,0)} \mathtt{I} : \tau_2}}{\vdash^{(2,0)} \mathtt{I} : \mathcal{B}}$$

We have the following tight derivation for t:

$$\frac{\dfrac{\dfrac{x : [\mathcal{B} \to [\bullet_{\mathcal{M}}] \to \bullet_{\mathcal{M}}] \vdash^{(0,0)} x : \mathcal{B} \to [\bullet_{\mathcal{M}}] \to \bullet_{\mathcal{M}} \quad (\Phi_{\mathtt{I}})_{(2,0)}}{x : [\mathcal{B} \to [\bullet_{\mathcal{M}}] \to \bullet_{\mathcal{M}}] \vdash^{(3,0)} x\mathtt{I} : [\bullet_{\mathcal{M}}] \to \bullet_{\mathcal{M}}} \quad \dfrac{x : [\bullet_{\mathcal{M}}] \vdash^{(0,0)} x : \bullet_{\mathcal{M}}}{x : [\bullet_{\mathcal{M}}] \vdash^{(0,0)} x : [\bullet_{\mathcal{M}}]}}{\dfrac{x : \mathcal{A} \vdash^{(4,0)} x\mathtt{I}x : \bullet_{\mathcal{M}}}{\vdash^{(5,0)} (\lambda x.x\mathtt{I}x) : \mathcal{A} \to \bullet_{\mathcal{M}}} \qquad \Phi_{(2,2)}}{\vdash^{(8,2)} (\lambda x.x\mathtt{I}x)\Delta : \bullet_{\mathcal{M}}}$$

Moreover, $t \to_{\mathsf{nmx}} \Delta\mathtt{I}\Delta \to_{\mathsf{nmx}} \mathtt{II}\Delta \to_{\mathsf{nmx}} \mathtt{I}\Delta \to_{\mathsf{nmx}} \Delta$. In other words, $t \to_{\mathsf{nmx}}$-normalization has $4 = 8/2$ steps with normal form $|\Delta| = 2$. Notice that the Δ copy typed with $\bullet_{\mathcal{M}}$ in Φ characterizes its abstraction constructor as persistent, not consumed during normalisation, *i.e.* its λ is not applied and, in this case, occurs in t's normal form.

We now recall some properties from [1] that are relevant to our work. Properties regarding normal forms[2], such as typability with a tight derivation, and (Anti) Substitution Lemmas do not depend on the reduction strategy and thus trivially holds in the current presentation. Below we present one of such properties, which play a role when considering nmx-reductions.

Lemma 2 (Tight spreading on neutral terms for $\mathcal{MX}$[1]). *If $t \in \mathcal{N}_{hd}$ and $\Phi \triangleright \Gamma \vdash_{mx} t : \tau$ s.t. $\mathtt{tight}(\Gamma)$ then $\mathtt{tight}(\tau)$.*

Proposition 2 (Quantitative Subject Reduction). *If $\Phi \triangleright \Gamma \vdash_{mx}^{(b,r)} t : \tau$ is tight and $t \xrightarrow{e}_{nmx} t'$ then there is a $\Gamma' \subseteq \Gamma$ and a tight derivation Φ' s.t. $\Gamma' \vdash_{mx}^{(b-2,r-e)} t' : \tau$.*

Proof. As in [1], the proof is by induction on $t \xrightarrow{e}_{nmx} t'$ of a stronger property: Let $t \xrightarrow{e}_{nmx} t'$, $\Phi \triangleright \Gamma \vdash_{mx}^{(b,r)} t : \tau$ garbage-tight, $\mathtt{tight}(\Gamma)$ and either $\mathtt{tight}(\tau)$ or $\neg\mathtt{abs}(t)$. Then there are a $\mathtt{tight}(\Gamma')$ s.t. $\Gamma' \subseteq \Gamma$ and a garbage-tight typing $\Phi' \triangleright \Gamma' \vdash_{mx}^{(b-2,r-e)} t' : \tau$. It is sufficient to analyse the only case in which reduction $\rightarrow_{nmx}$ differs from the deterministic strategy in [1]. Lemma 2 is used in this case, which holds for terms in $\mathcal{N}_{hd}$. Therefore, the proof steps are the same as in [1]. ∎

We can then establish the corresponding subject expansion property with a similar consideration regarding Lemma 2.

Proposition 3 (Quantitative Subject Expansion). *If $\Phi \triangleright \Gamma \vdash_{mx}^{(b,r)} t : \tau$ is tight and $t' \xrightarrow{e}_{nmx} t$ then there is a $\Gamma \subseteq \Gamma'$ and a tight derivation Φ' s.t. $\Gamma' \vdash_{mx}^{(b+2,r+e)} t' : \tau$.*

Given that (quantitative) subject reduction and expansion properties still hold for nmx-reduction, tight correctness and completeness is proved as in [1].

Theorem 1 (Tight Correctness for nmx). *Let $\Phi \triangleright \Gamma \vdash_{mx}^{(b,r)} t : \tau$ be a tight derivation. Then there is an integer e and a term $u \in \mathcal{M}$ s.t. $t \xrightarrow{e}_{nmx}^{b/2} u$ and $|u| + e = r$. Moreover, if $\tau = \bullet_{\mathcal{N}}$ then $u \in \mathcal{N}$.*

Theorem 2 (Tight Completeness for nmx). *If $t \xrightarrow{e}_{nmx}^{k} u$ with $u \in \mathcal{M}$, then there exists a tight typing $\Phi \triangleright \Gamma \vdash_{mx}^{(2k,|u|+e)} t : \tau$. Moreover, if $u \in \mathcal{N}$ then $\tau = \bullet_{\mathcal{N}}$, and if $\mathtt{abs}(u)$ then $\tau = \bullet_{\mathcal{M}}$.*

Remark that, by the correctness and completeness results, an abstraction typed with $\bullet_{\mathcal{M}}$ in a tight derivation is in fact persistent. In other words, it occurs either in the normal form –contributing with $|u|$– or in some normal form erased along the reduction –contributing with e in the corresponding step.

---

[2] Both deterministic and non-deterministic strategies have the same normal forms.

$$\mathscr{E}(x : \sigma) \lhd (y, \{x : [y : \sigma]\}), \; y \text{ fresh}$$

$$\mathscr{E}(x : \mathsf{t}) \lhd (x, \{x : [x : \mathsf{t}]\})$$

$$\mathscr{E}(\lambda x.t : [\tau_i]_{i=1\ldots n} \to \sigma) \lhd (\lambda x_1 \ldots x_n.t^*, A), \text{if for some } n > 0 \text{ and fresh } x_1, \ldots, x_n$$

$$\mathscr{E}(t : \sigma) \lhd (t^*, A; \{x : [x_1 : \tau_1, \ldots, x_n : \tau_n]\})$$

$$\mathscr{E}(\lambda x.t : [\,] \to \sigma) \lhd (\lambda x.t^*, A), \text{ if } x \notin \mathtt{fv}(t) \text{ and}$$

$$\mathscr{E}(t : \sigma) \lhd (t^*, A)$$

$$\mathscr{E}(\lambda x.t : \bullet_{\mathcal{M}}) \lhd (\lambda x.t^*, A), \text{if for some tight type } \mathsf{t} \text{ and } n \geq 0$$

$$\mathscr{E}(t : \mathsf{t}) \lhd (t^*, A; \{x : [x : \mathsf{t}_1, \ldots, x : \mathsf{t}_n]\})$$

$$\mathscr{E}(tu : \sigma) \lhd (t_0 u_1 \ldots u_m, +_{j=0\ldots m} A_j), \text{ if for some } m > 0 \text{ and } \tau_1, \ldots, \tau_m$$

$$\mathscr{E}(t : [\tau_j]_{j=1\ldots m} \to \sigma) \lhd (t_0, A_0) \text{ and } (\mathscr{E}(u : \tau_j) \lhd (u_j, A_j))_{j=1\ldots m}$$

$$\mathscr{E}(tu : \sigma) \lhd (t^* u^*, A_1 + A_2), \text{ if for some type } \tau$$

$$\mathscr{E}(t : [\,] \to \sigma) \lhd (t^*, A_1) \text{ and } \mathscr{E}(u : \tau) \lhd (u^*, A_2)$$

$$\mathscr{E}(tu : \bullet_{\mathcal{N}}) \lhd (t^* u^*, A_1 + A_2), \text{ if for some tight type } \mathsf{t}$$

$$\mathscr{E}(t : \bullet_{\mathcal{N}}) \lhd (t^*, A_1) \text{ and } \mathscr{E}(u : \mathsf{t}) \lhd (u^*, A_2)$$

Fig. 3. Expansion $\mathscr{E}$

4   Weak-Linearisation for Strongly Normalising Terms

In this section we present our expansion relation, following the relation by Florido and Damas [17]. The expansion relation $\mathscr{E}$, associates to a λ-term t typed with a non-idempotent type σ in $\mathcal{MX}$, an expanded (weak-linear) λ-term u and an expansion context A.

An **expansion context** A is a map from variables to multisets of the form $[y_1 : \sigma_1, \ldots, y_m : \sigma_m]$, where y_i is variable and σ_i is a type, and such that only finitely many variables are not mapped to the empty multiset $[\,]$. As for typing contexts, we define $\mathtt{dom}(A)$ to denote the domain of A, which is the set $\{x \mid A(x) \neq [\,]\}$. The notions of $+_{k \in K} A_k$, and $A_1; A_2$, are defined as in the case of typing contexts but taking multisets of pairs $x : \sigma$, instead of multisets of types. The **expansion** relation $\mathscr{E}(t : \sigma) \lhd (u, A)$ is inductively defined in Fig. 3.

Example 2. Considering $t \equiv (\lambda x.x \mathrm{I} x)\Delta$ from Example 1, with (tight) typing $\Psi \rhd \vdash_{\mathsf{mx}}^{(8,2)} (\lambda x.x \mathrm{I} x)\Delta : \bullet_{\mathcal{M}}$. See Fig. 4 for the complete expansion of t, where $A = [\bullet_{\mathcal{M}}, \mathcal{B} \to [\bullet_{\mathcal{M}}] \to \bullet_{\mathcal{M}}]$ and $\mathcal{B} = [[[\bullet_{\mathcal{M}}] \to \bullet_{\mathcal{M}}] \to [\bullet_{\mathcal{M}}] \to \bullet_{\mathcal{M}}, [\bullet_{\mathcal{M}}] \to \bullet_{\mathcal{M}}]$.

We now prove some basic properties on $\mathscr{E}$.

Lemma 3 (Basic properties of $\mathscr{E}$). *If $\mathscr{E}(t : \sigma) \lhd (u, A)$, then:*

1. *If $\neg\mathsf{abs}(t)$ then $\neg\mathsf{abs}(u)$.*
2. *If $t \in \mathcal{N}_{\mathsf{hd}}$ then $u \in \mathcal{N}_{\mathsf{hd}}$.*
3. *If $t \not\to_{\mathsf{nmx}}$ then $u \not\to_{\mathsf{nmx}}$.*

$\mathscr{E}((\lambda x.xIx)\Delta : \bullet_{\mathcal{M}}) \lhd ((\lambda x_3 x_4.x_3 II x_4)(\lambda x_1 x_2.x_1 x_2)(\lambda x.xx), \emptyset)$

$\quad \mathscr{E}(\lambda x.xIx : A \rightarrow \bullet_{\mathcal{M}}) \lhd (\lambda x_3 x_4.x_3 II x_4, \emptyset)$

$\quad\quad \mathscr{E}(xIx : \bullet_{\mathcal{M}}) \lhd (x_3 II x_4, \{x : [x_3 : \mathcal{B} \rightarrow [\bullet_{\mathcal{M}}] \rightarrow \bullet_{\mathcal{M}}, x_4 : \bullet_{\mathcal{M}}]\})$

$\quad\quad\quad \mathscr{E}(xI : [\bullet_{\mathcal{M}}] \rightarrow \bullet_{\mathcal{M}}) \lhd (x_3 II, \{x : [x_3 : \mathcal{B} \rightarrow [\bullet_{\mathcal{M}}] \rightarrow \bullet_{\mathcal{M}}]\})$

$\quad\quad\quad\quad \mathscr{E}(x : \mathcal{B} \rightarrow [\bullet_{\mathcal{M}}] \rightarrow \bullet_{\mathcal{M}}) \lhd (x_3, \{x : [x_3 : \mathcal{B} \rightarrow [\bullet_{\mathcal{M}}] \rightarrow \bullet_{\mathcal{M}}]\})$

$\quad\quad\quad\quad \mathscr{E}(I : [[\bullet_{\mathcal{M}}] \rightarrow \bullet_{\mathcal{M}}] \rightarrow [\bullet_{\mathcal{M}}] \rightarrow \bullet_{\mathcal{M}}) \lhd (\lambda x_5.x_5, \emptyset)$

$\quad\quad\quad\quad\quad \mathscr{E}(x : [\bullet_{\mathcal{M}}] \rightarrow \bullet_{\mathcal{M}}) \lhd (x_5, \{x : [x_5 : [\bullet_{\mathcal{M}}] \rightarrow \bullet_{\mathcal{M}}]\})$

$\quad\quad\quad\quad \mathscr{E}(I : [\bullet_{\mathcal{M}}] \rightarrow \bullet_{\mathcal{M}}) \lhd (\lambda x_6.x_6, \emptyset)$

$\quad\quad\quad\quad\quad \mathscr{E}(x : \bullet_{\mathcal{M}}) \lhd (x_6, \{x : [x_6 : \bullet_{\mathcal{M}}]\})$

$\quad\quad\quad \mathscr{E}(x : \bullet_{\mathcal{M}}) \lhd (x_4, \{x : [x_4 : \bullet_{\mathcal{M}}]\})$

$\quad \mathscr{E}(\lambda x.xx : \mathcal{B} \rightarrow [\bullet_{\mathcal{M}}] \rightarrow \bullet_{\mathcal{M}}) \lhd (\lambda x_1 x_2.x_1 x_2, \emptyset)$

$\quad\quad \mathscr{E}(xx : [\bullet_{\mathcal{M}}] \rightarrow \bullet_{\mathcal{M}}) \lhd (x_1 x_2, \{x : [x_1 : [[\bullet_{\mathcal{M}}] \rightarrow \bullet_{\mathcal{M}}] \rightarrow [\bullet_{\mathcal{M}}] \rightarrow \bullet_{\mathcal{M}}, x_2 : [\bullet_{\mathcal{M}}] \rightarrow \bullet_{\mathcal{M}}]\})$

$\quad\quad\quad \mathscr{E}(x : [[\bullet_{\mathcal{M}}] \rightarrow \bullet_{\mathcal{M}}] \rightarrow [\bullet_{\mathcal{M}}] \rightarrow \bullet_{\mathcal{M}}) \lhd (x_1, \{x : [x_1 : [[\bullet_{\mathcal{M}}] \rightarrow \bullet_{\mathcal{M}}] \rightarrow [\bullet_{\mathcal{M}}] \rightarrow \bullet_{\mathcal{M}}]\})$

$\quad\quad\quad \mathscr{E}(x : [\bullet_{\mathcal{M}}] \rightarrow \bullet_{\mathcal{M}}) \lhd (x_2, \{x : [x_2 : [\bullet_{\mathcal{M}}] \rightarrow \bullet_{\mathcal{M}}]\})$

$\quad \mathscr{E}(\lambda x.xx : \bullet_{\mathcal{M}}) \lhd (\lambda x.xx, \emptyset)$

$\quad\quad \mathscr{E}(xx : \bullet_{\mathcal{N}}) \lhd (xx, \{x : [x : \bullet_{\mathcal{N}}, x : \bullet_{\mathcal{N}}]\})$

$\quad\quad\quad \mathscr{E}(x : \bullet_{\mathcal{N}}) \lhd (x, \{x : [x : \bullet_{\mathcal{N}}]\})$

$\quad\quad\quad \mathscr{E}(x : \bullet_{\mathcal{N}}) \lhd (x, \{x : [x : \bullet_{\mathcal{N}}]\})$

Fig. 4. An expansion for $(\lambda x.xIx)\Delta : \bullet_{\mathcal{M}}$

Proof. 1. Follows by contraposition from the fact that the result of $\mathscr{E}$ is an abstraction only when the initial term was itself an abstraction.

2. By induction on $t \in \mathcal{N}_{\text{hd}}$.

3. It suffices to prove that if $\mathscr{E}(t : \sigma) \lhd (u, A)$, then $t \in \mathcal{M}$ implies $u \in \mathcal{M}$. A slightly stronger result is then proved by induction on t: (1) If $t \in \mathcal{N}$ then $u \in \mathcal{N}$; (2) If $t \in \mathcal{M}$ then $u \in \mathcal{M}$.

Let A be an expansion context. The **typing context associated to** A, denoted Γ_A, is defined by:

$$\Gamma_{\{x:[x:\mathbf{t}_1,\dots,x:\mathbf{t}_n]\}} = \{x : [\mathbf{t}_1, \dots, \mathbf{t}_n]\} \qquad \Gamma_{A+B} = \Gamma_A + \Gamma_B$$
$$\Gamma_{\{x:[x_1:\tau_1,\dots,x_n:\tau_n]\}} = \{x : [\tau_1, \dots, \tau_n]\}$$

We say that A is tight, denoted by $\text{tight}(A)$, if $\text{tight}(\Gamma_A)$.

Lemma 4. *If* $\mathscr{E}(t : \sigma) \lhd (t_1, A)$, *then* $\Phi \rhd \Gamma_A \vdash_{\text{mx}} t : \sigma$. *If* Φ *is (garbage-)tight then we say that the expansion is (garbage-)tight.*

Corollary 2. *If* $\mathscr{E}(t : \sigma) \lhd (t_1, A)$, *then* $x \in \text{dom}(A)$ *iff* $x \in \text{fv}(t)$.

Lemma 5. *If* $\Phi \rhd \Gamma \vdash_{\text{mx}} t : \sigma$ *then there are* u *and* A, *s.t.* $\mathscr{E}(t : \sigma) \lhd (u, A)$, *where* $\Gamma_A = \Gamma$.

Proof. By induction on Φ. We present the case for rule (fun_b): $\Gamma \backslash\!\backslash x \vdash_{\text{mx}} \lambda x.t : \Gamma(x) \rightarrow \tau$ follows from $\Gamma \vdash_{\text{mx}} t : \tau$. We have two cases:

- If $\Gamma(x) = [\tau_i]_{i=1\dots n}$, thus $\Gamma = \Gamma'; x : [\tau_i]_{i=1\dots n}$ then by the *i.h.*, there exists u and A, such that $\mathscr{E}(t : \tau) \lhd (u, A)$ with $\Gamma_A = \Gamma$. Then $A = A'; \{x : [x_1 :$

$\tau_1, \ldots, x_n : \tau_n]\}$, with some $x_1, \ldots, x_n$ fresh variables and $\Gamma_{A'} = \Gamma'$. From which we get $\mathscr{E}(\lambda x.t : [\tau_i]_{i=1\ldots n} \to \tau) \lhd (\lambda x_1 \ldots x_n.u, A')$, and $\Gamma_{A'} = \Gamma' = \Gamma \backslash\!\backslash x$ as required.

– If $\Gamma(x) = [\,]$, then by the *i.h.*, there exists u and A, such that $\mathscr{E}(t : \tau) \lhd (u, A)$ with $\Gamma_A = \Gamma$. Note that, by relevance of $\mathcal{MX}$, $x \notin \mathtt{fv}(t)$, therefore, $\mathscr{E}(\lambda x.t : [\,] \to \tau) \lhd (\lambda x.u, A)$, and $\Gamma_A = \Gamma$ as expected.

Lemma 6. *If $\mathscr{E}(t : \sigma) \lhd (t_0, A_0; \{x : [x_1 : \tau_1, \ldots, x_n : \tau_n]\})$, then x occurs n times in t.*

Lemma 7. *If $\mathscr{E}(t : \sigma) \lhd (t_0, A_0; \{x : [x_1 : \tau_1, \ldots, x_n : \tau_n]\})$ and $\mathscr{E}(u : \tau_i) \lhd (u_i, A_i)$ for $i = 1 \ldots n$ with $n > 0$, then $\mathscr{E}(t\{u/x\} : \sigma) \lhd (t_0\{u_1/x_1, \ldots, u_n/x_n\}, A_0 + A_1 + \cdots + A_n)$. Moreover, if premise expansions are garbage-tight then so is the resulting expansion.*

Proof. By induction on t. We present the case for $t = \lambda y.t'$ with its three subcases:

– $\mathscr{E}(\lambda y.t' : [\sigma_i]_{i=1\ldots m} \to \sigma) \lhd (\lambda y_1 \ldots y_m.t^*, A; \{x : [x_1 : \tau_1, \ldots, x_n : \tau_n]\})$, follows from $\mathscr{E}(t' : \sigma) \lhd (t^*, A; \{x : [x_1 : \tau_1, \ldots, x_n : \tau_n]\}; \{y : [y_1 : \sigma_1, \ldots, y_m : \sigma_m]\})$, with $y \in \mathtt{fv}(t')$ (which is guaranteed to be garbage-tight whenever the main expansion is, by Lemma 4). By the *i.h.* $\mathscr{E}(t'\{u/x\} : \sigma) \lhd (t^*\{u_1/x_1, \ldots, u_n/x_n\}, A + A_1 + \cdots + A_n; \{y : [y_1 : \sigma_1, \ldots, y_m : \sigma_m]\})^3$, from which follows $\mathscr{E}(\lambda y.t'\{u/x\} : [\sigma_i]_{i=1\ldots m} \to \sigma) \lhd (\lambda y_1 \ldots y_m.t^*\{u_1/x_1, \ldots, u_n/x_n\}, A + A_1 + \cdots + A_n)$.
– $\mathscr{E}(\lambda y.t' : [\,] \to \sigma) \lhd (\lambda y.t^*, A; \{x : [x_1 : \tau_1, \ldots, x_n : \tau_n]\})$, follows from $\mathscr{E}(t' : \sigma) \lhd (t^*, A; \{x : [x_1 : \tau_1, \ldots, x_n : \tau_n]\})$, with $y \notin \mathtt{fv}(t')$. By the *i.h.* $\mathscr{E}(t'\{u/x\} : \sigma) \lhd (t^*\{u_1/x_1, \ldots, u_n/x_n\}, A + A_1 + \cdots + A_n)$, from which follows $\mathscr{E}(\lambda y.t'\{u/x\} : [\,] \to \sigma) \lhd (\lambda y.t^*\{u_1/x_1, \ldots, u_n/x_n\}, A + A_1 + \cdots + A_n)^4$.
– $\mathscr{E}(\lambda y.t' : \bullet_{\mathcal{M}}) \lhd (\lambda y.t^*, A; \{x : [x_1 : \tau_1, \ldots, x_n : \tau_n]\})$, follows from $\mathscr{E}(t' : \mathtt{t}) \lhd (t^*, A; \{x : [x_1 : \tau_1, \ldots, x_n : \tau_n]\}; \{y : [y : \mathtt{t}_1, \ldots, y : \mathtt{t}_m]\})$. Then $\mathscr{E}(t'\{u/x\} : \mathtt{t}) \lhd (t^*\{u_1/x_1, \ldots, u_n/x_n\}, A + A_1 + \cdots + A_n; \{y : [y : \mathtt{t}_1, \ldots, y : \mathtt{t}_m]\})$ by the *i.h.*, from which follows $\mathscr{E}(\lambda y.t'\{u/x\} : \bullet_{\mathcal{M}}) \lhd (\lambda y.t^*\{u_1/x_1, \ldots, u_n/x_n\}, A + A_1 + \cdots + A_n)$.

Theorem 3. *Let $\mathscr{E}(t_1 : \mathtt{t}) \lhd (u_1, A_1)$ be a tight expansion and $t_1 \to_{\mathsf{nmx}} t_2$:*

1. *There is a term u_2 such that $\mathscr{E}(t_2 : \mathtt{t}) \lhd (u_2, A_2)$ is tight, $u_1 \to^*_{\mathsf{nmx}} u_2$ and $A_2 \subseteq A_1$.*
2. *If $\neg\mathtt{abs}(u_1)$ then for any $u' \neq u_2$ s.t. $u_1 \to^*_{\mathsf{nmx}} u_2 = u_1 \to^*_{\mathsf{nmx}} u' \to^*_{\mathsf{nmx}} u_2$, $\neg\mathtt{abs}(u')$.*

Proof. By induction on $t_1 \to_{\mathsf{nmx}} t_2$ we prove a stronger first statement: if $\mathscr{E}(t_1 : \sigma) \lhd (u_1, A_1)$ is garbage-tight, with $\mathtt{tight}(A_1)$ and either $\mathtt{tight}(\sigma)$ or $\neg\mathtt{abs}(t_1)$, and $t_1 \to_{\mathsf{nmx}} t_2$ then there is u_2 such that $\mathscr{E}(t_2 : \sigma) \lhd (u_2, A_2)$ is garbage-tight with $\mathtt{tight}(A_2)$, $A_2 \subseteq A_1$ and $u_1 \to^*_{\mathsf{nmx}} u_2$. We present the case $tu \to_{\mathsf{nmx}} tu'$, if $t \in \mathcal{N}_{\mathsf{hd}}$ and $u \to_{\mathsf{nmx}} u'$, with its three subcases:

---

[3] Note that $(A; \{y : [y_1 : \sigma_1, \ldots, y_m : \sigma_m]\}) + A_1 + \cdots + A_n = A + A_1 + \cdots + A_n; \{y : [y_1 : \sigma_1, \ldots, y_m : \sigma_m]\}$ since by BVC $y \notin \mathtt{fv}(u)$ thus $y \notin \mathtt{dom}(A_i)$ for each $1 \leq i \leq n$.
[4] $y \notin \mathtt{fv}(t')$ and by BVC $y \notin \mathtt{fv}(u)$ thus $y \notin \mathtt{fv}(t'\{u/x\})$.

- $\mathcal{E}(tu : \sigma) \lhd (t_0 u_1 \ldots u_m, +_{j=0\ldots m} A_j)$, if for some $m > 0$ and $\tau_1, \ldots, \tau_m$, there are garbage-tight expansions $\mathcal{E}(t : [\tau_j]_{j=1\ldots m} \to \sigma) \lhd (t_0, A_0)$ and $(\mathcal{E}(u : \tau_j) \lhd (u_j, A_j))_{j=1\ldots m}$ with $\mathtt{tight}(A_j), j = 0 \ldots m$. By the *i.h.* for each $j = 1 \ldots m$, $\mathcal{E}(u' : \tau_j) \lhd (u'_j, A'_j)$, a garbage-tight expansion with $\mathtt{tight}(A'_j)$, $A'_j \subseteq A_j$ and $u_j \to^*_{\mathsf{nmx}} u'_j$. Therefore, $\mathcal{E}(tu' : \sigma) \lhd (t_0 u'_1 \ldots u'_m, A_0 +_{j=1\ldots m} A'_j)$ is a garbage-tight expansion with $\mathtt{tight}(A_0 +_{j=1\ldots m} A'_j)$ and $A_0 +_{j=1\ldots m} A'_j \subseteq +_{j=0\ldots m} A_j$. By Lemma 3.2 we have $t_0 \in \mathcal{N}_{\mathsf{hd}}$ thus $t_0 u'_1 \ldots u'_i \in \mathcal{N}_{\mathsf{hd}}$ for any $1 \le i \le m$ and $t_0 u_1 \ldots u_m \to^*_{\mathsf{nmx}} t_0 u'_1 \ldots u_m \to_{\mathsf{nmx}} \cdots \to^*_{\mathsf{nmx}} t_0 u'_1 \ldots u'_m$.
- $\mathcal{E}(tu : \sigma) \lhd (t_0 u_1, A_0 + A_1)$, if for some tight τ_1, there are garbage-tight expansions $\mathcal{E}(t : [\,] \to \sigma) \lhd (t_0, A_0)$ and $\mathcal{E}(u : \tau_1) \lhd (u_1, A_1)$ with $\mathtt{tight}(A_i), i = 0, 1$. By the *i.h.*, $\mathcal{E}(u' : \tau_1) \lhd (u'_1, A'_1)$ is garbage-tight with $\mathtt{tight}(A'_1)$ and $A'_1 \subseteq A_1$ and $u_1 \to^*_{\mathsf{nmx}} u'_1$. Therefore, $\mathcal{E}(tu' : \sigma) \lhd (t_0 u'_1, A'_0 + A'_1)$ is a garbage-tight expansion with $\mathtt{tight}(A_0 + A'_1)$ and $A_0 + A'_1 \subseteq A_0 + A_1$. By Lemma 3.2 we have $t_0 \in \mathcal{N}_{\mathsf{hd}}$ thus $t_0 u_1 \to^*_{\mathsf{nmx}} t_0 u'_1$.
- $\mathcal{E}(tu : \bullet_\mathcal{N}) \lhd (t^* u^*, A_1 + A_2)$, if for some tight type $\mathtt{t}$ there are garbage-tight expansions $\mathcal{E}(t : \bullet_\mathcal{N}) \lhd (t^*, A_1)$ and $\mathcal{E}(u : \mathtt{t}) \lhd (u^*, A_2)$ with $\mathtt{tight}(A_1 + A_2)$. By the *i.h.*, $\mathcal{E}(u' : \mathtt{t}) \lhd (u'', A'_2)$ is a garbage-tight expansion with $\mathtt{tight}(A'_2)$, $A'_2 \subseteq A_2$ and $u^* \to^*_{\mathsf{nmx}} u''$. Therefore, $\mathcal{E}(tu' : \bullet_\mathcal{N}) \lhd (t^* u'', A_1 + A'_2)$ is a garbage-tight expansion with $\mathtt{tight}(A_1 + A'_2)$ and $A_1 + A'_2 \subseteq A_1 + A_2$. By Lemma 3.2 we have $t^* \in \mathcal{N}_{\mathsf{hd}}$ thus $t^* u^* \to^*_{\mathsf{nmx}} t^* u''$.

5   A Characterisation of Weak-Linear Terms

In this section we introduce System $\mathcal{WL}$, proving that a term is tight-expanded if and only if its expansion is tight-typable in $\mathcal{WL}$. Let $\mathcal{WL}$ be the typing system with linear types, i.e. with types as in $\mathcal{T}$ where multi-types are restricted to either empty or unitary multi-sets, i.e. with $|K| \le 1$. Recall that our notion of linear is what is often referred to as affine, but given the relation of this work with [27] and [17], we will continue to use their notion of linear function.

The typing assignment system $\mathcal{WL}$ is given by the rules in Fig. 5. System $\mathcal{WL}$ is a restriction of System $\mathcal{MX}$, i.e. if $\Gamma \vdash_{\mathsf{wl}}^{(b,r)} t : \tau$ then $\Gamma \vdash_{\mathsf{mx}}^{(b,r)} t : \tau$ where τ is linear. (Garbage-) tightness of derivations in $\mathcal{WL}$ thus have the same properties, allowing a characterisation of **weak-linear terms** as defined in [6]: A term t is weak linear if in any reduction sequence of t, when there is a contraction of a β-redex $(\lambda x.u)v$, then x occurs free in u at most once.

Theorem 4 (Characterisation of Weak-Linear Terms). *A term t is weak-linear iff t is tight-typable in system $\mathcal{WL}$.*

Proof. Let $\Phi \rhd \Gamma \vdash_{\mathsf{wl}}^{(b,r)} t : \tau$. By induction on Φ we prove that any abstraction $\lambda x.u$ in t where u has multiple free occurrences of x must be typed with rule $(\mathtt{fun}_r)$. Since Φ is also a tight derivation in $\mathcal{MX}$, by tight-correctness (Theorem 1) such abstraction is either in the corresponding $\to_{\mathsf{nmx}}$-normal form or is in a normal form erased along normalisation, i.e. is not applied in any step along the $\to_{\mathsf{nmx}}$-normalisation. On the other hand, tight typability of normal forms

$$\frac{}{x : [\tau] \vdash_{\mathsf{wl}}^{(0,0)} x : \tau} \ (\mathsf{ax}) \qquad \frac{\Delta \vdash_{\mathsf{wl}}^{(b,r)} t : \sigma}{\Delta \vdash_{\mathsf{wl}}^{(b,r)} t : [\sigma]} \ (\mathsf{one}) \qquad \frac{\Delta \vdash_{\mathsf{wl}}^{(b,r)} t : \sigma}{\Delta \vdash_{\mathsf{wl}}^{(b,r)} t : [\,]} \ (\mathsf{none})$$

$$\frac{\Gamma \vdash_{\mathsf{wl}}^{(b,r)} t : \tau \qquad |\Gamma(x)| \leq 1}{\Gamma \backslash\!\backslash x \vdash_{\mathsf{wl}}^{(b+1,r)} \lambda x.t : \Gamma(x) \to \tau} \ (\mathsf{fun}_a) \qquad \frac{\Gamma \vdash_{\mathsf{wl}}^{(b,r)} t : \mathsf{t} \qquad \mathsf{tight}(\Gamma(x))}{\Gamma \backslash\!\backslash x \vdash_{\mathsf{wl}}^{(b,r+1)} \lambda x.t : \bullet_{\mathcal{M}}} \ (\mathsf{fun}_r)$$

$$\frac{\Gamma \vdash_{\mathsf{wl}}^{(b,r)} t : \mathcal{A} \to \tau \qquad \Delta \vdash_{\mathsf{wl}}^{(b',r')} u : \mathcal{A}}{\Gamma + \Delta \vdash_{\mathsf{wl}}^{(b+b'+1,r+r')} t\,u : \tau} \ (\mathsf{app}_b) \qquad \frac{\Gamma \vdash_{\mathsf{wl}}^{(b,r)} t : \bullet_{\mathcal{N}} \qquad \Delta \vdash_{\mathsf{wl}}^{(b',r')} u : \mathsf{t}}{\Gamma + \Delta \vdash_{\mathsf{wl}}^{(b+b',r+r'+1)} t\,u : \bullet_{\mathcal{N}}} \ (\mathsf{app}_r^{lo})$$

Fig. 5. System $\mathcal{WL}$

(see [1]) is still true for system $\mathcal{WL}$. Therefore, by $\mathcal{WL}$-typability of terms in $\mathcal{M}$, tight-completeness (Theorem 2) and observing that for any reduction step of a weak-linear term the typing restriction in system $\mathcal{WL}$ is sufficient for a (quantitative) subject expansion in the system, any weak-linear t is typable in system $\mathcal{WL}$.

In order to establish a relation between typings in $\mathcal{MX}$ and in $\mathcal{WL}$, we introduce a type translation and a mapping from expansion contexts, similarly to [17].

Type translation $\mathsf{w}(-)$ is defined by:

$$\mathsf{w}(\mathsf{t}) = \mathsf{t} \qquad\qquad \mathsf{w}([\tau_j]_{j=1\ldots m}) = [\mathsf{w}(\tau_j)]_{j=1\ldots m}$$
$$\mathsf{w}([\,] \to \tau) = [\,] \to \mathsf{w}(\tau) \qquad \mathsf{w}([\sigma_i]_{i=1\ldots m} \to \tau) = [\mathsf{w}(\sigma_1)] \to \cdots \to [\mathsf{w}(\sigma_m)] \to \mathsf{w}(\tau)$$

Extension of $\mathsf{w}(-)$ to typing contexts is straightforward. **Expanded Context** Γ_A^e is defined for any expansion context A by:

$$\Gamma_{\{x:[x:\mathsf{t}_1,\ldots,x:\mathsf{t}_n]\}}^e = \{x : [\mathsf{t}_1,\ldots,\mathsf{t}_n]\} \qquad\qquad \Gamma_{A+B}^e = \Gamma_A^e + \Gamma_B^e$$
$$\Gamma_{\{x:[x_1:\tau_1,\ldots,x_n:\tau_n]\}}^e = \{x_1 : [\mathsf{w}(\tau_1)],\ldots,x_n : [\mathsf{w}(\tau_n)]\}$$

Example 3. Considering $t \equiv (\lambda x.xIx)\Delta$ from Example 1, with (tight) typing $\Psi \rhd \quad \vdash_{\mathsf{mx}}^{(8,2)} (\lambda x.xIx)\Delta \ : \ \bullet_{\mathcal{M}}$ and expanded term $t_0 \equiv (\lambda x_3 x_4.x_3 II x_4)(\lambda x_1 x_2.x_1 x_2)(\lambda x.xx)$ (see Fig. 4), we present the $\mathcal{WL}$ typing corresponding to its expansion steps:

Unexpanded copy of Δ given by $\mathscr{E}(\lambda x.xx : \bullet_{\mathcal{M}}) \lhd (\lambda x.xx, \emptyset)$ has a $\mathcal{WL}$ typing Φ no different from the corresponding $\mathcal{MX}$ typing:

$$\frac{\dfrac{}{x : [\bullet_{\mathcal{N}}] \vdash_{\mathsf{wl}}^{(0,0)} x : \bullet_{\mathcal{N}}} \qquad \dfrac{}{x : [\bullet_{\mathcal{N}}] \vdash_{\mathsf{wl}}^{(0,0)} x : \bullet_{\mathcal{N}}}}{\dfrac{x : [\bullet_{\mathcal{N}}, \bullet_{\mathcal{N}}] \vdash_{\mathsf{wl}}^{(0,1)} xx : \bullet_{\mathcal{N}}}{\vdash_{\mathsf{wl}}^{(0,2)} \lambda x.xx : \bullet_{\mathcal{M}}}}$$

On the other side, the expanded copy of Δ given by $\mathscr{E}(\lambda x.xx : \mathcal{B} \to [\bullet_{\mathcal{M}}] \to \bullet_{\mathcal{M}}) \lhd (\lambda x_1 x_2.x_1 x_2, \emptyset)$ for $\mathcal{B} = [[[\bullet_{\mathcal{M}}] \to \bullet_{\mathcal{M}}] \to [\bullet_{\mathcal{M}}] \to \bullet_{\mathcal{M}}, [\bullet_{\mathcal{M}}] \to \bullet_{\mathcal{M}}]$ has the corresponding $\mathcal{WL}$ typing Φ', for $\varphi_1 = [\bullet_{\mathcal{M}}] \to \bullet_{\mathcal{M}}$, of the form:

$$\cfrac{\cfrac{\cfrac{x_1 : [[\varphi_1] \to \varphi_1] \vdash_{\mathsf{wl}}^{(0,0)} x_1 : [\varphi_1] \to \varphi_1 \quad \cfrac{\quad}{x_2 : [\varphi_1] \vdash_{\mathsf{wl}}^{(0,0)} x_2 : [\varphi_1]}}{x_2 : [\varphi_1], x_1 : [[\varphi_1] \to \varphi_1] \vdash_{\mathsf{wl}}^{(1,0)} x_1 x_2 : \varphi_1}}{x_1 : [[\varphi_1] \to \varphi_1] \vdash_{\mathsf{wl}}^{(2,0)} \lambda x_2.x_1 x_2 : [\varphi_1] \to \varphi_1}}{\vdash_{\mathsf{wl}}^{(3,0)} \lambda x_1 x_2.x_1 x_2 : [[\varphi_1] \to \varphi_1] \to [\varphi_1] \to \varphi_1}$$

where $\mathsf{w}(\mathcal{B} \to [\bullet_{\mathcal{M}}] \to \bullet_{\mathcal{M}}) = \mathsf{w}([[\varphi_1] \to \varphi_1, \varphi_1] \to \varphi_1) = [[\varphi_1] \to \varphi_1] \to [\varphi_1] \to \varphi_1$.

Finally, given expansion $\mathcal{E}(\lambda x.x\mathrm{I}x : \mathcal{A} \to \bullet_{\mathcal{M}}) \lhd (\lambda x_3 x_4.x_3 \mathrm{II} x_4, \emptyset)$ for $\mathcal{A} = [\bullet_{\mathcal{M}}, \mathcal{B} \to [\bullet_{\mathcal{M}}] \to \bullet_{\mathcal{M}}]$, let $\varphi_2 = [\varphi_1] \to \varphi_1$ and $\varphi_3 = [\varphi_2] \to \varphi_2$. From $\mathcal{WL}$ typings $\Psi(\varphi_1)$ and $\Psi(\bullet_{\mathcal{M}})$:

$$\cfrac{\cfrac{\cfrac{\quad}{x_5 : [\varphi_1] \vdash_{\mathsf{wl}}^{(0,0)} x_5 : \varphi_1}}{\vdash_{\mathsf{wl}}^{(1,0)} \lambda x_5.x_5 : [\varphi_1] \to \varphi_1}}{\vdash_{\mathsf{wl}}^{(1,0)} \lambda x_5.x_5 : [[\varphi_1] \to \varphi_1]} \qquad \cfrac{\cfrac{\cfrac{\quad}{x_6 : [\bullet_{\mathcal{M}}] \vdash_{\mathsf{wl}}^{(0,0)} x_6 : \bullet_{\mathcal{M}}}}{\vdash_{\mathsf{wl}}^{(1,0)} \lambda x_6.x_6 : [\bullet_{\mathcal{M}}] \to \bullet_{\mathcal{M}}}}{\vdash_{\mathsf{wl}}^{(1,0)} \lambda x_6.x_6 : [[\bullet_{\mathcal{M}}] \to \bullet_{\mathcal{M}}]}$$

we have derivation Ψ' of the form:

$$\cfrac{\cfrac{\cfrac{\cfrac{x_3 : [\varphi_3] \vdash_{\mathsf{wl}}^{(0,0)} x_3 : \varphi_3 \quad \Psi(\varphi_1)}{x_3 : [\varphi_3] \vdash_{\mathsf{wl}}^{(2,0)} x_3 \mathrm{I} : \varphi_2} \quad \Psi(\bullet_{\mathcal{M}})}{x_3 : [\varphi_3] \vdash_{\mathsf{wl}}^{(4,0)} x_3 \mathrm{II} : \varphi_1} \quad \cfrac{x_4 : [\bullet_{\mathcal{M}}] \vdash_{\mathsf{wl}}^{(0,0)} x_4 : \bullet_{\mathcal{M}}}{x_4 : [\bullet_{\mathcal{M}}] \vdash_{\mathsf{wl}}^{(0,0)} x_4 : [\bullet_{\mathcal{M}}]}}{x_3 : [\varphi_3], x_4 : [\bullet_{\mathcal{M}}] \vdash_{\mathsf{wl}}^{(5,0)} x_3 \mathrm{II} x_4 : \bullet_{\mathcal{M}}}}{\cfrac{x_3 : [\varphi_3] \vdash_{\mathsf{wl}}^{(6,0)} \lambda x_4.x_3 \mathrm{II} x_4 : \varphi_1}{\vdash_{\mathsf{wl}}^{(7,0)} \lambda x_3 x_4.x_3 \mathrm{II} x_4 : [\varphi_3] \to \varphi_1}}$$

where $\mathsf{w}(\mathcal{A} \to \bullet_{\mathcal{M}}) = [\varphi_3] \to \varphi_1$. Then we get the (tight) typing $\Psi \rhd \vdash_{\mathsf{wl}}^{(12,2)} t_0 : \bullet_{\mathcal{M}}$.

We prove that any expanded term is typable in system $\mathcal{WL}$.

Lemma 8. *If $\mathcal{E}(t : \sigma) \lhd (t_1, A)$, then there is a derivation $\Psi \rhd \Gamma_A^e \vdash_{\mathsf{wl}}^{(b,r)} t_1 : \mathsf{w}(\sigma)$. Moreover, if the expansion is (garbage-)tight, so is Ψ.*

Proof. By induction on t. We present the case when $t = t'u'$:

- $\mathcal{E}(t'u' : \sigma) \lhd (t_0 u_1' \ldots u_m', B_0 + \cdots + B_m)$, if for some $m > 0$ and $\sigma_1, \ldots, \sigma_m$, $\mathcal{E}(t' : [\sigma_j]_{j=1\ldots m} \to \sigma) \lhd (t_0, B_0)$ and $\big(\mathcal{E}(u' : \sigma_j) \lhd (u_j', B_j)\big)_{j=1\ldots m}$. By *i.h.*, $\Gamma_{B_0}^e \vdash_{\mathsf{wl}}^{(b_0, r_0)} t_0 : [\mathsf{w}(\sigma_1)] \to \cdots \to [\mathsf{w}(\sigma_m)] \to \mathsf{w}(\sigma)$ and $\big(\Gamma_{B_j}^e \vdash_{\mathsf{wl}}^{(b_j, r_j)} u_j' : \mathsf{w}(\sigma_j)\big)_{j=1\ldots m}$. Therefore $+_{j=0\ldots m}\Gamma_{B_j}^e \vdash_{\mathsf{wl}}^{(m + j=0\ldots m \, b_j, \, + j=0\ldots m \, r_j)} t_0 u_1' \ldots u_m' : \mathsf{w}(\sigma)$ by m applications of rules (**one**) and (**app**), where $+_{j=0\ldots m}\Gamma_{B_j}^e = \Gamma_{+j=0\ldots m B_j}^e$.

- $\mathcal{E}(t'u' : \sigma) \lhd (t_0 u_1', B_0 + B_1)$, if $\mathcal{E}(t' : [\,] \to \sigma) \lhd (t_0, B_0)$ and $\mathcal{E}(u' : \tau) \lhd (u_1', B_1)$ for some type τ. By the *i.h.*, $\Gamma_{B_0}^e \vdash_{\mathsf{wl}}^{(b,r)} t_0 : [\,] \to \mathsf{w}(\sigma)$ and $\Gamma_{B_1}^e \vdash_{\mathsf{wl}}^{(b',r')} u_1' : \mathsf{w}(\tau)$. Therefore $\Gamma_{B_0}^e + \Gamma_{B_1}^e \vdash_{\mathsf{wl}}^{(b+b'+1, r+r')} t_0 u_1' : \mathsf{w}(\sigma)$ by rules (**none**) and (**app**$_b$), where $\Gamma_{B_0}^e + \Gamma_{B_1}^e = \Gamma_{B_0+B_1}^e$.

- $\mathscr{E}(t'u' : \bullet_{\mathcal{N}}) \lhd (t^*u^*, B_1 + B_2)$, follows from $\mathscr{E}(t' : \bullet_{\mathcal{N}}) \lhd (t^*, B_1)$ and $\mathscr{E}(u' : t) \lhd (u^*, B_2)$. By $i.h.$, $\Gamma^e_{B_1} \vdash^{(b,r)} t^* : \bullet_{\mathcal{N}}$ and $\Gamma^e_{B_2} \vdash^{(b',r')} u^* : t$. By rule (app^{lo}_r) we have $\Gamma^e_{B_1} + \Gamma^e_{B_2} \vdash^{(b+b',r+r'+1)} t^*u^* : \bullet_{\mathcal{N}}$, where $\Gamma^e_{B_1} + \Gamma^e_{B_2} = \Gamma^e_{B_1+B_2}$.

Theorem 5. *If $\mathscr{E}(t : \sigma) \lhd (t', A)$ is tight, then t' is weak-linear.*

Proof. Let $\mathscr{E}(t : \sigma) \lhd (t', A)$ be a tight expansion. By Lemma 8 there is a tight $\Phi \rhd \Gamma^e_A \vdash^{(b,r)}_{\mathsf{wl}} t' : \mathsf{w}(\sigma)$, then by Theorem 4 t' is weak-linear.

6   Related Works and Discussions

As we mentioned before, the notion of linearisation of the λ-calculus, was first introduced in [27]. Directly related to this notion is the use of linearisation in hardware compilation [19,20] for synthesising digital circuits, in which a notion of serialization is defined to deal with contraction in concurrent contexts, based on type information that indicates bounds for the usage of functions. Kfoury's linearisation is also closely related to the notion of affine approximations by Mazza et al. [31], which identifies distinct occurrences of variables that apply linearly to sequences of arguments. A λ-term admits a simply-typed affine approximation if and only if it has an intersection type (in a non-idempotent and non-commutative intersection type system).

Non-idempotent types are crucial in the notion of linearisation defined by Kfoury, similarly to what happens in our work. However the linearisation process defined in [27] was not presented as a direct encoding of λ-terms into terms of the new calculus. Furthermore, intersections in Kfoury's work are also non-commutative, which differs from our approach and has the effect of excluding valid expanded terms in the sense that they still provide an effective simulation of the initial term: for example $(\lambda x_1 x_2.x_1 x_2)II$ and $(\lambda x_1 x_2.x_2 x_1)II$ can both be considered valid expansions of the non-linear term $(\lambda x.xx)I$. This leads to one interesting open question regarding the relation between the two approaches.

Our notion of expansion is directly related to the notion of expansion defined by Florido and Damas [17], where non-idempotent intersections were also considered and the target language was the linear λ-calculus. One of the implications of the expansion relation in [17] is that, any term typable using intersection types, can be expanded to a term typable using simple types, similarly to what happens with affine approximations. Also, Bucciarelli et al. [13], have given a translation of intersection typing derivations into Curry typeable terms, that preserves β-reduction, since the target language is the simply typed λ-calculus. The expansion relation in [17] is not preserved by β-reduction, but it is preserved by weak-head reduction. Note that taking into account different algebraic properties of $\cap$, can lead to different expansion relations and different properties on preservation of reduction.

Our goal here is to have preservation of normal forms and our target is the weak linear λ-calculus, introduced in [6], in which the notion of linearity is an operational one: functions are required to be linear, if they are ever applied.

Redexes that are eventually contracted, which correspond to the notion of virtual redexes, are as paths in the initial term, deriving from Lévy's definition of labelled reduction [29]. In this work, unlike the approach by Kfoury, the λ-calculus is simulated by a proper *linear* subset of the calculus, rather than by a non-standard calculus. Weak linear terms have good properties: non-duplicating reduction, therefore strong normalisation; it is decidable to know if a λ-term is weak linear; and type inference for weak linear terms is both decidable and polynomial. Linearisation from standard λ-terms into weak linear terms was defined by computing legal paths [8] on the initial term, identifying virtual redexes. The linearisation procedure preserves β-normal forms, provided that paths are chosen in the right way. Furthermore, if the procedure terminates then it yields a weak linear λ-term. However, there is a conjecture regarding termination: the linearisation procedure is a total function for the strongly normalising λ-calculus. Note that a similar conjecture exists for Kfoury's linearisation.

Our expansion relies on a quantitative type system that was used in [1] to extract exact measures for a maximal reduction strategy, which is closely related to the reduction strategy used in this paper. Both typing system and strategy in [1] are annotated with measures, which are not relevant to our expansion process, but which are essential to prove some properties of our expansion. We also believe they can provide an appropriate framework to reason about quantitative aspects of the expansion relation.

In [6], weak linear λ-terms proved to be typable in polynomial time. This was achieved by the definition of a typing system, which we will refer to as $\mathcal{WA}$, and a corresponding type inference algorithm that proved to type any weak linear λ-term in polynomial time. System $\mathcal{WA}$ can be seen as a generalization of Hindley's system of simple types [22,23]. A tight version of system $\mathcal{WA}$, where tight types are used to type functions that are not applied, can be seen as an intermediate system between $\mathcal{WL}$ and $\mathcal{WA}$. Translations can be defined between the systems where tight-types, which can be seen as type constants with no particular meaning, can be replaced by an appropriate type, therefore typability in polynomial time is also a property of the class of terms obtained by our expansion relation.

7 Conclusions and Future Work

In this paper we have defined an expansion relation between strongly normalising λ-terms and weak linear λ-terms with the same normal form. This expansion relation relies on a quantitative typing system and on the notion of tight typings, which were also used to give an exact typing characterisation of the class of weak linear λ-terms. This work provided an answer to a conjecture that stated that all strongly normalising λ-terms can be encoded as weak linear λ-terms.

To guide our expansion we used a quantitative typing system that provides measures for reduction sequences as well as the size of corresponding normal forms. One interesting question that is left for future work is to investigate how the expansion process affects these measures. Due to its operational linearity, weak linear λ-terms reduce in linear time, but the size of the expanded terms can be exponential with respect to the size of the term. Our intuition is that this could potentially show a nice interplay between time and space in computation.

Another relevant question that is left for future work is the relation between the approach by Kfoury and our approach. As mentioned before, Kfoury relies on non-commutative intersection types, so there is possibly a class of weak linear terms corresponding to a unique expanded term in $\Lambda^\wedge$. Establishing a relation between the two approaches could also provide an answer to the conjecture in [27].

References

1. Accattoli, B., Graham-Lengrand, S., Kesner, D.: Tight typings and split bounds, fully developed. J. Funct. Program. **30**, e14 (2020)
2. Accattoli, B., Guerrieri, G.: Types of fireballs. In: Ryu, S. (ed.) APLAS 2018. LNCS, vol. 11275, pp. 45–66. Springer, Cham (2018). https://doi.org/10.1007/978-3-030-02768-1_3
3. Accattoli, B., Guerrieri, G., Leberle, M.: Types by need. In: Caires, L. (ed.) ESOP 2019. LNCS, vol. 11423, pp. 410–439. Springer, Cham (2019). https://doi.org/10.1007/978-3-030-17184-1_15
4. Alves, S.: Linearisation of the lambda calculus. Ph.D. thesis, University of Porto (2007)
5. Alves, S., Fernández, M., Florido, M., Mackie, I.: Linearity and recursion in a typed lambda-calculus. In: Proceedings of the 13th ACM SIGPLAN Symposium on Principles and Practices of Declarative Programming, pp. 173–182. ACM (2011)
6. Alves, S., Florido, M.: Weak linearization of the lambda calculus. Theor. Comput. Sci. **342**(1), 79–103 (2005)
7. Alves, S., Kesner, D., Ventura, D.: A quantitative understanding of pattern matching. In: 25th International Conference on Types for Proofs and Programs. LIPIcs, vol. 175, pp. 3:1–3:36. Schloss Dagstuhl (2019)
8. Asperti, A., Laneve, C.: Paths, computations and labels in the λ-calculus. Theor. Comput. Sci. **142**(2), 277–297 (1995)
9. Balabonski, T., Barenbaum, P., Bonelli, E., Kesner, D.: Foundations of strong call by need. Proc. ACM Program. Lang. **1**(ICFP), 20:1–20:29 (2017)
10. Barendregt, H.P.: The Lambda Calculus: Its Syntax and Semantics. Studies in Logic and the Foundation of Mathematics, vol. 103. North-Holland (1984)
11. Barendregt, H.P., Bergstra, J., Klop, J.W., Volken, H.: Degrees, reductions and representability in the lambda calculus. Technical Report Preprint no.22, University of Utrecht, Department of Mathematics (1976)
12. Bucciarelli, A., Kesner, D., Ventura, D.: Non-idempotent intersection types for the lambda-calculus. Log. J. IGPL **25**(4), 431–464 (2017)
13. Bucciarelli, A., Lorenzis, S.D., Piperno, A., Salvo, I.: Some computational properties of intersection types. In: 14th Annual IEEE Symposium on Logic in Computer Science, Trento, Italy, 2–5 July 1999, pp. 109–118 (1999)
14. Coppo, M., Dezani-Ciancaglini, M.: An extension of the basic functionality theory for the λ-calculus. Notre Dame J. Form. Log. **21**(4), 685–693 (1980)
15. Curry, H.B.: Functionality in combinatory logic. Proc. Natl. Acad. Sci. U.S.A. **20**, 584–590 (1934)

16. de Carvalho, D.: Sémantiques de la logique linéaire et temps de calcul. Ph.D. thesis, Université Aix-Marseille II (2007)
17. Florido, M., Damas, L.: Linearization of the lambda-calculus and its relation with intersection type systems. J. Funct. Program. **14**(5), 519–546 (2004)
18. Gardner, P.: Discovering needed reductions using type theory. In: Hagiya, M., Mitchell, J.C. (eds.) TACS 1994. LNCS, vol. 789, pp. 555–574. Springer, Heidelberg (1994). https://doi.org/10.1007/3-540-57887-0_115
19. Ghica, D.R.: Geometry of synthesis: a structured approach to VLSI design. In: Proceedings of the 34th ACM SIGPLAN-SIGACT Symposium on Principles of Programming Languages, pp. 363–375. ACM (2007)
20. Ghica, D.R., Smith, A.: Geometry of synthesis III: resource management through type inference. In: Proceedings of the 38th ACM SIGPLAN-SIGACT Symposium on Principles of Programming Languages, pp. 345–356. ACM (2011)
21. Girard, J.: Linear logic. Theor. Comput. Sci. **50**, 1–102 (1987)
22. Hindley, J.R.: The principal type-scheme of an object in combinatory logic. Trans. Am. Math. Soc. **146**, 29–60 (1969)
23. Hindley, J.R.: Basic Simple Type Theory. Cambridge University Press, Cambridge (1997)
24. Kesner, D., Ventura, D.: A resource aware semantics for a focused intuitionistic calculus. Math. Struct. Comput. Sci. **29**(1), 93–126 (2019)
25. Kesner, D., Vial, P.: Consuming and persistent types for classical logic. In: Proceedings of the 35th Annual ACM/IEEE Symposium on Logic in Computer Science, pp. 619–632. ACM (2020)
26. Kesner, D., Vial, P.: Non-idempotent types for classical calculi in natural deduction style. Log. Methods Comput. Sci. **16**(1) (2020)
27. Kfoury, A.: A linearization of the lambda-calculus and consequences. J. Log. Comput. **10**(3), 411–436 (2000)
28. Lafont, Y.: The linear abstract machine. Theor. Comput. Sci. **59**, 157–180 (1988)
29. Lévy, J.-J.: Réductions correctes et optimales dans le lambda-calcul. Ph.D. thesis, Éditeur inconnu (1978)
30. Mackie, I.: The geometry of interaction machine. In: Proceedings of the 22nd ACM SIGPLAN-SIGACT Symposium on Principles of Programming Languages, POPL 1995, pp. 198–208. ACM Press (1995)
31. Mazza, D., Pellissier, L., Vial, P.: Polyadic approximations, fibrations and intersection types. Proc. ACM Program. Lang. **2**(6), 1–28 (2018)
32. van Raamsdonk, F., Severi, P., Sørensen, M.H., Xi, H.: Perpetual reductions in lambda-calculus. Inf. Comput. **149**(2), 173–225 (1999)
33. Walker, D.: Substructural type systems. In: Advanced Topics in Types and Programming Languages, chapter 1, pp. 3–43. MIT Press, Cambridge (2005)

On the Formalization and Computational Complexity of Resilience Problems for Cyber-Physical Systems

Musab A. Alturki[1,2], Tajana Ban Kirigin[3(✉)], Max Kanovich[4],
Vivek Nigam[5,6], Andre Scedrov[7], and Carolyn Talcott[8]

[1] Runtime Verification Inc., Urbana, IL, USA
`musab.alturki@runtimeverification.com`
[2] KFUPM, Dhahran, Saudi Arabia
[3] Faculty of Mathematics, University of Rijeka, Rijeka, Croatia
`bank@math.uniri.hr`
[4] University College, London, UK
`m.kanovich@ucl.ac.uk`
[5] Federal University of Paraíba, João Pessoa, Brazil
`vivek@ci.ufpb.br`
[6] Munich Research Center, Huawei, Munich, Germany
[7] University of Pennsylvania, Philadelphia, USA
`scedrov@math.upenn.edu`
[8] SRI International, Menlo Park, USA
`clt@csl.sri.com`

Abstract. Cyber-Physical Systems (CPS) are used to perform complex, safety-critical missions autonomously. Examples include applications of autonomous vehicles and drones. Given the complexity of these systems, CPS must be able to adapt to possible changes during mission execution, such as regulatory updates or changes in mission objectives. This capability is informally referred to as resilience. We formalize the intuitive notion of resilience as a formal verification property using timed multiset rewriting. An important innovation in our formalization is the distinction between rules that are under the control of the CPS and those that are not. We also study the computational complexity of resilience problems. Although undecidable in general, we show that these problems are PSPACE-complete for a class of bounded systems, more precisely, balanced systems where the rules do not affect the number of facts of the configurations and where facts are of bounded size.

Keywords: Resilience · Planning · Formal methods · Verification · Multiset rewriting · Computational complexity

1 Introduction

Cyber-physical systems (CPS) are being deployed to perform complex, safety-critical tasks, often with limited or no human intervention and in disruptive or hostile environments. Autonomous vehicles [25], for example, are a topic of intense

H. Seidl et al. (Eds.): ICTAC 2022, LNCS 13572, pp. 96–113, 2022.
https://doi.org/10.1007/978-3-031-17715-6_8

debate among researchers, industry experts, and certification bodies, primarily due to safety concerns and the unpredictability of the environment in which they operate. The same is true for autonomous applications using unmanned aerial vehicles (UAVs) [22]. A key challenge is to ensure that these systems can perform their assigned mission even when faced with changes, such as faults and unexpected changes to the mission, such as changes in goals or changes in operational constraints. This ability to adapt is often referred to as *resilience*.

The main goal of this paper is to formalize the intuitive notion of resilience as a verification problem for CPS. We start from our previous work [13,14], in which we proposed a Timed Multiset Rewriting (MSR) framework suitable for specification and verification of CPSes. The work addressed properties without assuming changes and considered only task realization under nominal conditions, with fixed goals and fixed regulations and policies. A key challenge is the formalization of changes against which a CPS has to be resilient. This is accomplished by distinguishing between rules that are under the control of the system and rules that are not. The latter rules specify the changes in system conditions, e.g., mission objectives, to which the system may need to adapt. The main contributions of the paper to the formalization of resilience are:

1. Extension of Timed MSR to include update rules that model changes that occur during plan execution but are outside the control of the system itself, such as changes in regulations or system goals;
2. Formal definitions for resilience as verification problems for Timed MSR systems. Intuitively, a CPS is resilient to changes if it can always accomplish its missions, even if a bounded number of changes to the mission or system have occurred;
3. Study of the complexity of resilience problems. We show that for the class of balanced systems with facts of bounded size [12], the resilience problems are in PSPACE. The PSPACE hardness follows from the complexity of the planning problem [13].

We end this section with a discussion of related work. In Sect. 2 we motivate the study of resilience. Section 3 gives a short overview of the timed MSR used in Sect. 4 to specify systems and in Sect. 5 to define formal resilience properties. In Sect. 6 we investigate the complexity of verification problems. In Sect. 7 we conclude with a discussion of future work.

1.1   Related Work

There are many informal definitions of resilience [2,4–6,8–10,15,23,30]. In the broadest sense, resilience is "the ability of a system to adapt and respond to changes (both in the environment and internal)" [5]. NIST [24] provides a more precise definition of resilience: "The ability to anticipate, withstand, recover, and adapt to adverse conditions, stresses, attacks or compromises on systems that use or are enabled by cyber resources." The formalization of the concept of resilience proposed in this paper captures the essence of most formulations in the literature and distinguishes it from similar concepts such as robustness, recoverability, fault tolerance, reliability, etc. Robustness, for example, "is the strength, or the ability of elements, systems, and other units of analysis to withstand a given level of stress or demand without suffering degradation or loss of function" [6]. Therefore, the main difference between robustness and resilience is that robust systems do not suffer under changes in the conditions, while resilient systems may temporarily be affected, but are capable of recovering.

There have been several attempts in the literature to formally define resilience. However, these attempts tend to focus only on specific (sometimes narrow) interpretations of resilience that are relevant to the particular application domain being considered. For instance, in the context of faulty hardware or unreliable communication media, formalizations of resilience focus on formalizing the ability of the system to compute the correct values. For example, in [27], models of resilience are defined using predicate abstraction, where a program is annotated with state abstractions that over-approximate the effects of errors on computations. A similar approach is proposed in [19], where behaviors are encoded in the system states and resilience is defined as CTL/LTL properties. Again, the properties need to be specific to the system being analyzed, and are checked using explicit-state model checking. The notion of resilience these methods capture is very narrow and rigid.

In [11], resilience (and robustness) are defined formally as constrained optimization problems in the context of learning-enabled state estimation systems in the presence of an attack. The systems are modelled using a specialized form of labelled transition systems, and the resilience property is specified as the negation of a minimization objective to be achieved within a given threshold. This formalization is used to show that the complexity of the verification problem of resilience is NP-complete. The modelling approach presented, however, is specific to a class of labelled transition systems inspired by the requirements of the application domain, and it is not clear how it can be made applicable to a wider range of systems. Furthermore, the formalization of the property is rather coarse-grained. It does not allow distinguishing active attacks from changes in goals, or define execution traces that show operationally how a resilient system may lose functionality temporarily and then recover. A similar coarse-grained, optimization-based formalization of resilience against attacks, but in the context of software obfuscation, appeared earlier in [3].

In [16,17], resilience is formally specified as pre-condition and post-condition assertions in "Resilient Contracts" (RC), which are contracts from the contract-based design methodology whose assertions can be probabilistic and incomplete. The definition is given in the context of multi-UAV swarm control systems. Measures of deviation from the target objective of the swarm system are encoded in the system's transition system, and used to analyze recoverability at varying degrees of achievable deviations. Similar limitations to the ones explained above apply to the RC methodology.

Our interest in resilience has been renewed by a recent talk by Vardi [31] in which he emphasised that computer science needs to recognize the tradeoff between efficiency and resilience. As our simple example will illustrate, resilience is the ability of a system to bounce back, to respond to changes that affect its correct operation and goals.

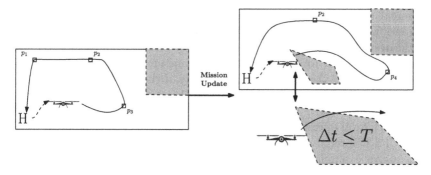

Fig. 1. Illustration of CPS resilience to mission change. Gray areas denote no-fly zones, boxes the points that the drone shall visit, and H the home base of the drone.

2 Motivating Example Involving Drones

Resilience is actively being pursued for the development of autonomous CPS (as described in the Introduction). We illustrate the concepts used in our definitions by considering unmanned aerial vehicles (UAV), also called drones. Consider a package delivery scenario [18]. The task of the UAV is to visit a set of locations to deliver packages while complying with the policies and constraints, specifying e.g., that all points of interest should be visited within a specified time period (or deadline); that an UAV may return to home base to recharge so that it does not run out of energy; that UAV shall not fly over no-fly zones, e.g., near airports; etc. There is no particular order in which locations should be visited. However, performance quality and capability may be affected by unforeseen events, external changes, or updates that include the following: i) regulatory changes, e.g., updates to drone flight altitude restrictions; ii) policy changes, e.g., limiting energy consumption; iii) task changes, e.g., change in points to be visited; iv) deadline for accomplishing the task. A resilient drone system should be able to respond to such events by adapting and completing the task according to the new policy.

Figure 1 illustrates a mission change. A drone started with the original mission to visit points p_1, p_2, and p_3 without flying over the grey area, which is a no-fly zone. During execution, the mission is updated, as depicted in the figure on the right. The points to visit are now p_2 and p_4, but with a newly established no-fly zone. Moreover, it may be the case that the system is not robust, i.e., that it cannot be avoided that the drone flies over the new no-fly zone.

To model resilience, some requirements may be associated to updates. For example, a drone mission update will also impose that the drone has at most T time units to leave a no-fly zone. According to the informal definitions described in Sect. 1.1, a resilient system of drones is able to adapt to such updates and still successfully execute the mission. In this example, the drone would be able to exit the no-fly zone within T time units, visit points p_2 and p_4 and return to home base without exhausting its energy.

Different resilience requirements may demand more or less powerful CPSes, e.g., drones with larger or smaller batteries, or more or fewer drones, which will affect the overall cost of CPS. For example, if the mission change shown in Fig. 1 places point p_4 too far from home base, the drone may not have enough battery capacity to complete the new mission. Similarly, if the drone is not fast enough, it may not be able to guarantee that it will leave the no-fly zone within the required time interval T. Therefore, it is important to determine during design time at which level of resilience a CPS is in relation to mission updates. A more resilient CPS will require more powerful capabilities and therefore higher costs.

The above example also illustrates the differences between resilience and reliability. Reliability (as in reliability engineering) addresses the problem of how often failures, typically in hardware, can occur and solutions to mitigate such failures, e.g., by introducing redundant hardware. In the example above, the drone system may be reliable but not resilient. For example, the drone may not be able to complete an updated mission even though there is no hardware failure, such as a motor that is not working properly. Therefore, it is not possible to directly use the rich literature on reliability to reason about the resilience of CPS.

3   Timed Multiset Rewriting

Assume a finite first-order typed alphabet, Σ, with variables, constants, function and predicate symbols. Terms and facts are constructed as usual (see [7]) by applying symbols of correct type (or sort). For instance, if P is a predicate of type $\tau_1 \times \tau_2 \times \cdots \times \tau_n \to o$, where o is the type for propositions, and $u_1, \ldots, u_n$ are terms of types $\tau_1, \ldots, \tau_n$, respectively, then $P(u_1, \ldots, u_n)$ is a *fact*. *Timestamped facts* are of the form $F@t$, where F is a fact and $t \in \mathbb{N}$ is a natural number called *timestamp*. There is a special predicate symbol *Time* with arity zero, which will be used to represent global time. A *configuration* is a multiset of ground timestamped facts, $\mathcal{S} = \{Time@t, F_1@t_1, \ldots, F_n@t_n\}$, with a single occurrence of a *Time* fact. Configurations are to be interpreted as states of the system. Configurations are modified by multiset rewrite rules, which can be interpreted as actions of the system. There is only one rule that modifies global time, *Tick*:

$$Time@T \longrightarrow Time@(T+1) \tag{1}$$

where T is a time variable. *Tick* rule advances global time, i.e., rewrites configuration $\{Time@t, F_1@t_1, \ldots, F_n@t_n\}$ to $\{Time@(t+1), F_1@t_1, \ldots, F_n@t_n\}$. For simplicity, in this work we consider discrete time. In our previous work [12], we proposed timed MSR systems with dense time. We believe that the proposed machinery for verifying resilience also applies to dense time, but this investigation is left for future work. The remaining rules are *instantaneous* as they do not modify global time, but may modify the remaining facts of configurations (those different from *Time*). Instantaneous rules have the form:

$$\begin{aligned} Time@T, \mathcal{W}, F_1@T_1', \ldots F_n@T_n' \mid \mathcal{C} \longrightarrow \\ Time@T, \mathcal{W}, Q_1@(T+D_1), \ldots Q_m@(T+D_m) \end{aligned} \tag{2}$$

where $D_1, \ldots, D_m$ are natural numbers, $\mathcal{W} = W_1@T_1, \ldots, W_n@T_n$ is a set of timestamped predicates possibly with variables, and $\mathcal{C}$ is the guard of the action which is a set of constraints involving the time variables appearing in the rule's pre-condition, i.e. the variables $T, T_1, \ldots, T_p, T'_1, \ldots, T'_n$. Constraints are of the form $T > T' \pm N$ and $T = T' \pm N$, where T and T' are time variables, and $N \in \mathbb{N}$ is a natural number. All variables in the guard of a rule appear in the rule's pre-condition. We use $T' \geq T' \pm N$ to denote the disjunction of $T > T' \pm N$ and $T = T' \pm N$. A rule $W \mid \mathcal{C} \longrightarrow W'$ can be applied on a configuration $\mathcal{S}$ if there is a ground substitution σ, such that $W\sigma \subseteq \mathcal{S}$ and $\mathcal{C}\sigma$ is true. The resulting configuration is $(\mathcal{S} \setminus W) \cup W'\sigma$. We write $\mathcal{S} \longrightarrow_r \mathcal{S}_1$ for the one-step relation where configuration $\mathcal{S}$ is rewritten to $\mathcal{S}_1$ using an instance of rule r.

A *trace* of timed MSR rules $\mathcal{A}$ starting from an initial configuration $\mathcal{S}_0$ is a sequence of configurations: $\mathcal{S}_0 \longrightarrow \mathcal{S}_1 \longrightarrow \mathcal{S}_2 \longrightarrow \cdots \longrightarrow \mathcal{S}_n$, such that for all $0 \leq i \leq n-1$, $\mathcal{S}_i \longrightarrow_{r_i} \mathcal{S}_{i+1}$ for some $r_i \in \mathcal{A}$.

Balanced Systems. Reachability problems for MSR systems are reduced to the existence of traces over given rules from some initial configuration to some specified configuration. Since reachability problems are undecidable in general [12], some restrictions are imposed in order to obtain decidability.[1] In particular, we use MSR systems with only *balanced* rules, i.e., rules for which the number of facts appearing in its pre-condition and in its post-condition is the same. Systems containing only balanced rules represent an important class of *balanced systems*, for which several reachability problems have been shown decidable [12]. Balanced systems are suitable, e.g., for modelling scenarios with a fixed amount of total memory. Balanced systems have the following important property [12]:

Proposition 1. *Let $\mathcal{R}$ be a set of balanced rules. Let $\mathcal{S}_0$ be a configuration with exactly m facts. Let $\mathcal{S}_0 \longrightarrow \cdots \longrightarrow \mathcal{S}_n$ be an arbitrary trace of rules $\mathcal{R}$ starting from $\mathcal{S}_0$. Then for all $0 \leq i \leq n$, $\mathcal{S}_i$ has exactly m facts. In particular, any trace without repetitions is of no more than exponential length. Moreover, the traces of exponential length may occur.*

Let $count_0$ denote exponential upper bound on the length of traces indicated in Proposition 1 stated above. In Sect. 6 we use the exponential upper bound $count_0$, to provide a termination for our NPSPACE procedures at least in $count_0$ steps.

Also, for some of our complexity results, we will assume an upper-bound on the size of facts, as in [12]. The size, $|F@t|$, of a timed fact $F@t$ is the total number of symbols in F, e.g., $|M(a, b, f(a, b))@t| = 6$.

4   Timed MSR for Resilient Systems

The proposed notion of resilience assumes two entities, a system and an external entity, such as the environment or regulatory authorities that mandate changes

---

[1] For a discussion on the form of rules and other conditions in the model that may affect complexity, see [12,13].

or updates to the policies that the system is supposed to comply with. We consider it "crital", i.e., unsatisfactory when the system does not adhere to such rules and guidelines. To model the two entities, we split the description of the whole scenario into a system part and a planning update part. Moreover, we consider different types of updates, including those that affect the goals of the system and those that regulate the expected behaviour of the system.

Definition 1 (Planning Configuration). *We assume a set of predicate symbols* $\Sigma_P = \Sigma_G \uplus \Sigma_C \uplus \Sigma_S \uplus \{\mathsf{Time}\}$ *consisting of four pairwise disjoint sets of predicates,* Σ_G, Σ_C, Σ_S *and* $\{\mathsf{Time}\}$. *Facts constructed using predicates from* Σ_G *are called* goal *facts, from* Σ_C critical *facts, and from* Σ_S system *facts. Facts constructed using predicates from* $\Sigma_C \cup \Sigma_G$ *are called* planning *facts. Configurations over* Σ_P *predicates are called* planning configurations.

For readability, we underline only planning predicates and refer to planning configurations as configurations for short.

Example 1. Predicates $\Sigma_G = \{\underline{\mathsf{Point}}, \underline{\mathsf{MinCov}}\}$, $\Sigma_C = \{\underline{\mathsf{MinBat}}, \underline{\mathsf{MinTimeToVisit}}\}$ and $\Sigma_S = \{\mathsf{Drone}, \mathsf{Visited}, \mathsf{NotVisited}, \mathsf{At}, \mathsf{BatStatus}, \mathsf{NumVisited}, \mathsf{Leq}\}$, allow the representation of information on visited points in the drone scenario with the following planning configuration:

$$\begin{aligned} \mathcal{S} = \{&\underline{\mathsf{Point}}(p(1,2))@0, \underline{\mathsf{Point}}(p(4,5))@0, \underline{\mathsf{MinBat}}(20)@0, \underline{\mathsf{MinCov}}(1)@0\} \cup \\ &\{\mathsf{Time}@4, \mathsf{Visited}(p(1,2))@2, \mathsf{At}(p(3,4))@4, \mathsf{BatStatus}(95)@4, \mathsf{NumVisited}(1)@4\} \end{aligned}$$

Remark 1. Note that the arithmetic comparisons in the MSR model are only used in time constraints, i.e., over time variables. However, we encode arithmetic conditions over non-timed variables using a binary system predicate Leq, denoting the "less or equal" relation. That is, in the (initial) planning configuration we include (persistent) facts Leq $(0,0)@0$, Leq $(0,1)@0$, Leq $(1,1)@0$, Leq $(0,2)@0$, Leq $(1,2)@0$, ..., for (N, M) such that $N \leq M$ up to some bound, and the $\mathsf{NLeq}(X, Y)$ facts for the remaining pairs (X, Y), for $X > Y$. The bound can be chosen to cover the numerical values of interest, such as the maximum resource values, the coordinates of the area of interest, etc.

The behaviour of the system is represented by traces of MSR rules. A system should achieve its goals while not violating certain regulations and policies, as well as restrictions related to the physical environment, such as distances and energy. This is modelled using the following concepts of goals and compliance.

Definition 2 (Critical/Goal Configurations). *A critical configuration specification* $\mathcal{CS}$ *(resp. goal* $\mathcal{GS}$*) is a set of pairs* $\{\langle \mathcal{S}_1, \mathcal{C}_1 \rangle, \ldots, \langle \mathcal{S}_n, \mathcal{C}_n \rangle\}$, *with each pair* $\langle \mathcal{S}_j, \mathcal{C}_j \rangle$ *being of the form* $\langle \{F_1@T_1, \ldots, F_p@T_{p_j}\}, \mathcal{C}_j \rangle$, *where* $T_1, \ldots, T_{p_j}$ *are time variables,* $F_1, \ldots, F_{p_j}$ *contains at least one critical fact (resp. goal fact), and* $\mathcal{C}_j$ *is a set of time constraints involving only variables* $T_1, \ldots, T_{p_j}$. *A configuration* $\mathcal{S}$ *is a critical configuration w.r.t.* $\mathcal{CS}$ *(resp. a goal configuration w.r.t.* $\mathcal{GS}$*) if for some* $1 \leq i \leq n$, *there is a grounding substitution,* σ, *such that* $\mathcal{S}_i\sigma \subseteq \mathcal{S}$ *and* $\mathcal{C}_i\sigma$ *evaluates to true.*

Example 2. Goal $\{\langle\{\mathsf{NumVisited}(N)@T_1, \underline{\mathsf{MinCov}}(r)@T_2, \mathsf{Leq}(r, N)@T_3\}, \emptyset\rangle\}$
denotes that the specified minimal number of points must be visited.
Critical configuration specification $\{\langle\{\mathsf{BatStatus}(E)@T_1, \underline{\mathsf{MinBat}}(m)@T_2, \mathsf{Leq}$
$(E, m)@T_3\}, \emptyset\rangle, \langle\{\mathsf{Time}@T, \mathsf{NotVisited}(P_1)@T_1, \underline{\mathsf{MinTimeToVisit}}(P_1, d)@T_2, T >$
$T_1+d\}\rangle\}$ denotes that the battery level should stay above the minimum allowed,
m, and that the points should be visited regularly, every d time units.

Definition 3 (Compliant Traces). *Given critical configuration specification*
$\mathcal{CS}$, *a trace* $\mathcal{T}$ *is* compliant *w.r.t.* $\mathcal{CS}$ *if* $\mathcal{T}$ *does not contain any critical configu-*
ration w.r.t. $\mathcal{CS}$.

Modelling Change. While system rules specify the behaviour of the system,
external influences that represent changes or updates that affect the system's
plan execution are modelled through update rules. All the rules used in our
models are either of the form (Eq. 1) or (Eq. 2).

Definition 4 (System Rules). *A system rule is either the Tick rule (Eq. 1)*
or a rule of form (Eq. 2) such that if a planning fact is involved, then it is a
permanent fact, i.e., it is not consumed by the rule.

Definition 5 (Update Rules). *Given a planning alphabet* Σ_P, *a goal* $\mathcal{GS}$ *and*
a critical configuration specification $\mathcal{CS}$, *an update rule is a rule of the form of*
Eq. (2) that is of one of the following type: a) System update rule (SUR) such
that if a planning fact is involved, then it is a permanent fact; b) Goal update
rule (GUR) that either consumes or creates at least one goal fact. If a critical
fact is involved, then it is a permanent fact; c) Critical update rule (CUR) that
either consumes or creates at least one critical fact. If a goal fact is involved,
then it is a permanent fact.

Intuitively, GUR and CUR model external influence on the system, such as
regulatory changes, additional tasks, etc., while SUR model changes in the system
that are not due to intentions of the system's agents, e.g., technical errors such
as a drone breaking down.

Example 3. The following GUR changes the location of the points that the drone
needs to visit by some given value d_G:

$$\mathsf{Time}@T, \underline{\mathsf{Point}}(X_1, X_2, X_3)@T_1, \mathsf{Visited}(X_1, X_2, X_3)@T_2, \mathsf{NumVisited}(Y + 1)@T_3 \longrightarrow$$
$$\mathsf{Time}@T, \underline{\mathsf{Point}}(X_1 + d_G, X_2, X_3)@T, \mathsf{NotVisited}(X_1 + d_G, X_2, X_3)@T, \mathsf{NumVisited}(Y)@T$$

The following CUR changes the minimal time between visits by some value d_C:
$$\mathsf{Time}@T, \underline{\mathsf{MinTimeToVisit}}(P)@T_1 \longrightarrow \mathsf{Time}@T, \underline{\mathsf{MinTimeToVisit}}(P + d_C)@T$$

Definition 6 (Planning Scenario). *A planning scenario is a tuple*
$(\mathcal{R}, \mathcal{GS}, \mathcal{CS}, \mathcal{E}, \mathcal{S}_0)$ *where* $\mathcal{R}$ *is a set of system rules,* $\mathcal{GS}$ *is a goal,* $\mathcal{CS}$ *is a crit-*
ical configuration specification, $\mathcal{E}$ *is a set of update rules, and* $\mathcal{S}_0$ *is an initial*
configuration.

Recoverability Conditions. We use auxiliary relations to distinguish resilience from similar properties such as robustness. Intuitively, recoverability relations specify quantitative aspects of resilience. Namely, a resilient system may not always withstand a suffered level of stress, but will recover from it in a satisfactory manner, as specified by the recoverability conditions.

Definition 7. *A recoverability condition δ is a binary relation over configurations. (We assume that recoverability conditions can be checked in poly-time.)*

Example 4. Recoverability conditions related to critical updates specify transitional policies before the system complies with the updated regulations and policies. For example, the time required for a system to recover from a critical situation may be bounded. After a CUR, which changes the allowed minimum battery level, the drone's energy level may be below the specified minimum. It should recharge within d time units, as specified by the following relation:

$$\{(\mathcal{S}_1, \mathcal{S}_2) \mid \mathsf{BatStatus}(B_1)@T_1 \in \mathcal{S}_1 \wedge$$
$$\{\underline{\mathsf{MinBat}(M_2)}@T_2, \mathsf{BatStatus}(B_2)@T_3, \mathsf{Leq}(M_2, B_2)@0\} \subseteq \mathcal{S}_2 \wedge T_3 - T_1 \leq d\}.$$

Example 5. Recoverability conditions related to goal updates specify how the new goal relates to the original goal. For example, a GUR may change the minimum number of points to visit. If the minimum coverage is increased, drones are given additional time d to complete the task, as specified by the relation:

$$\{(\mathcal{S}_1, \mathcal{S}_2) \mid \{\mathsf{Time}@T_0, \underline{\mathsf{MinCov}(C_1)}@T_1\} \subseteq \mathcal{S}_1 \wedge \mathsf{Leq}(C_1, C_2)@0 \wedge$$
$$\{\mathsf{NumVisited}(V_2)@T_2, \underline{\mathsf{MinCov}(C_2)}@T_3, \mathsf{Leq}(C_2, V_2)@0\} \subseteq \mathcal{S}_2 \wedge T_2 - T_0 \leq d\}.$$

5 Verification Problems

The first problem we consider is the planning problem (or the compliance problem) which consists in checking the existence of a compliant trace showing that a system can achieve the given goal considering the given critical configuration specifications, without any updates.

Definition 8 (Compliant Planning Scenario. Planning Problem). *A planning scenario $A = (\mathcal{R}, \mathcal{GS}, \mathcal{CS}, \mathcal{E}, \mathcal{S}_0)$ is compliant if there exists a trace τ using only $\mathcal{R}$ rules starting from $\mathcal{S}_0$ to a goal configuration w.r.t. $\mathcal{GS}$ that is compliant w.r.t. $\mathcal{CS}$. The planning problem consists in checking whether the given planning scenario is compliant.*

Resilience. In the next verification problems, we formalize resilience under the assumption that changes do not happen too often, i.e., a resilient system should handle a bounded number of updates. There are additional inputs to the problems w.r.t. the compliance problem from Definition 8. These inputs include the number of updates allowed and recoverability conditions (Definition 7).

The resilience problems defined below are considerably more intricate than the planning problem. First, the system must be able to find a good trace, i.e., a compliant trace that reaches a goal for the given initial specification. Moreover, at any point in this trace, any one of the update rules can be applied, changing either the goal, critical configurations, or the state of the system itself. The system should be able to handle such changes, recover within the specified conditions, and find a new good trace. There may be a series of updates, and the system should be able to handle any combination of such events. Hence, rather than just finding one good trace, as in the planning problem, the system must be able to create a set of good plans that ensures that the system can successfully adapt and reschedule after any sequence of updates.

The problems are defined recursively on the number of allowed updates.

Definition 9 (n-Resilience w.r.t. System Updates). *Given a natural number n, a planning scenario $A = (\mathcal{R}, \mathcal{GS}, \mathcal{CS}, \mathcal{E}, \mathcal{S}_0)$ is n-resilient w.r.t. system updates if*

1. *$n = 0$, then A is compliant (see Definition 3);*
2. *$n > 0$, then there exists a compliant trace τ from $\mathcal{S}_0$ to a goal configuration $\mathcal{S}_k$ using $\mathcal{R}$ such that if for any SUR $r \in \mathcal{E}$ applied on some configuration $\mathcal{S}_i$ in τ, where $\mathcal{S}_i \longrightarrow_r \mathcal{S}'_{i+1}$, there is a compliant trace $\tau' = \mathcal{S}'_{i+1} \longrightarrow \cdots \longrightarrow \mathcal{S}'_m$ using $\mathcal{R}$ such that*
   - *$\mathcal{S}'_m$ is a goal configuration;*
   - *the planning scenario $(\mathcal{R}, \mathcal{GS}, \mathcal{CS}, \mathcal{E}, \mathcal{S}'_{i+1})$ is $n - 1$-resilient w.r.t. system updates.*

Note that any update rule may be applied to any enabling configuration at any point in the trace. Following the change, a system should still be able to reach a goal. Moreover, by changing system facts, a system update should not affect compliance or otherwise the system will not be considered resilient. For example, in low temperatures battery consumption may increase, but resources should not fall to a critical level, i.e., below the minimum allowed. Similarly, if a drone malfunctions due to its electronic components being exposed to very high temperature, its performance may be degraded and the mission compromised.

The next resilience problem formalizes goal changes and involves a recoverability condition δ that relates the current goal and the new goal. A goal update changes the goals that the system must reach. Consequently, the system must provide a new trace that reaches the new goal within the conditions specified by δ, which relate the old to the new goal, and may refer to time, resources, etc. As with SUR, GUR should not compromise compliance, i.e., the newly scheduled trace should adhere at all times to the regulations and policies specified by $\mathcal{CS}$.

Definition 10 (δ, n-Resilience w.r.t. Goal Updates). *Given a recoverability condition δ and a natural number n, a planning scenario $A = (\mathcal{R}, \mathcal{GS}, \mathcal{CS}, \mathcal{E}, \mathcal{S}_0)$ is δ, n-resilient w.r.t. goal updates if*

1. *$n = 0$, then A is compliant (see Definition 3);*
2. *$n > 0$, then there exists a compliant trace τ from $\mathcal{S}_0$ to a goal configuration $\mathcal{S}_k$ using $\mathcal{R}$ such that if for any GUR $r \in \mathcal{E}$ applied on any configuration $\mathcal{S}_i$ in τ, where $\mathcal{S}_i \longrightarrow_r \mathcal{S}'_{i+1}$, there is a compliant trace $\tau' = \mathcal{S}'_{i+1} \longrightarrow \cdots \longrightarrow \mathcal{S}'_m$ using $\mathcal{R}$ such that*

- $\mathcal{S}'_m$ is a goal configuration;
- $\delta(\mathcal{S}_k, \mathcal{S}'_m)$;
- the planning scenario $(\mathcal{R}, \mathcal{GS}, \mathcal{CS}, \mathcal{E}, \mathcal{S}'_{i+1})$ is $\delta, n-1$-resilient w.r.t. goal updates.

Note that a resilient system should be able to reschedule a plan at any point and, following any of the possible updates, i.e., be ready for any update at any point in its current plan. Hence, checking for the resilience of a system involves checking the existence of multiple good traces obtained by applying the different update rules from the planning scenario at different points along its current plan. For example, if some additional points of interest need to be visited, the UAV system can be given some extra time to complete the extended mission. Regardless of when the GUR occurs during the original mission execution, a resilient UAV system should be able to adapt and perform the updated task.

Resilience to critical updates takes into account the fact that the system may find itself in a critical configuration due to a CUR. Hence, after a critical update, a "grace period" allows the system to adapt. This "grace period" is specified by the recoverability condition δ and is followed by a new compliant plan that takes into account the updated critical facts.

Definition 11 (δ, n-Resilience w.r.t. Critical Updates).
Given a recoverability condition δ and a natural number n, a planning scenario $A = (\mathcal{R}, \mathcal{GS}, \mathcal{CS}, \mathcal{E}, \mathcal{S}_0)$ is δ, n-resilient w.r.t. critical updates if

1. *$n = 0$, then A is compliant (see Definition 3);*
2. *$n > 0$, then there exists a compliant trace τ from $\mathcal{S}_0$ to a goal configuration using $\mathcal{R}$ such that if for any CUR $r \in \mathcal{E}$ applied on any configuration $\mathcal{S}_i$ in τ, where $\mathcal{S}_i \longrightarrow_r \mathcal{S}'_{i+1}$, there is a trace $\tau' = \mathcal{S}'_{i+1} \longrightarrow \cdots \longrightarrow \mathcal{S}'_m \longrightarrow \cdots \longrightarrow \mathcal{S}'_{m+p}$ using $\mathcal{R}$ such that*
   - *for each j, $m \leq j \leq m + p$, $\mathcal{S}'_j$ is not critical;*
   - *$\mathcal{S}'_{m+p}$ is a goal configuration;*
   - *$\delta(\mathcal{S}_i, \mathcal{S}'_m)$;*
   - *the planning scenario $(\mathcal{R}, \mathcal{GS}, \mathcal{CS}, \mathcal{E}, \mathcal{S}'_m)$ is $\delta, n-1$-resilient w.r.t. critical updates.*

Note that the subtrace $\mathcal{S}'_{i+1} \longrightarrow \cdots \longrightarrow \mathcal{S}'_m$ may not be compliant. This distinguishes the defined property of resilience from the general notion of robustness. Resilient systems may temporarily underperform because they are severely affected by changes, but are able to adapt to updated critical specifications and continue with a compliant plan $\mathcal{S}'_m \longrightarrow \cdots \longrightarrow \mathcal{S}'_{m+p}$.

For example, if no-fly zone restrictions are updated by a CUR at a certain stage of task execution. As shown in Fig. 1, it may not be possible for an UAV to avoid a newly declared no-fly zone, breaching the flight regulations. Hence, the system would reach a critical configuration. However, the recoverability conditions may specify the transition period during which the system must adapt to the new regulations. Thereafter, the resilient UAV system must comply with the new no-fly restrictions. Again, a resilient system should be able to adapt to any such update at any stage of task execution.

The most complicated verification problem involves all types of updates.

Definition 12 (δ_C, δ_G, n-**Resilience**). *Given recoverability conditions* δ_C, δ_G *and a natural number* n, *a planning scenario* $A = (\mathcal{R}, \mathcal{GS}, \mathcal{CS}, \mathcal{E}, \mathcal{S}_0)$ *is* δ_C, δ_G, n-*resilient if*

1. $n = 0$, *then* A *is compliant;*
2. $n > 0$, *then there exists a compliant trace* τ *from* $\mathcal{S}_0$ *to a goal configuration* $\mathcal{S}_k$ *using* $\mathcal{R}$, *such that if for any rule* $r \in \mathcal{E}$ *applied on any configuration* $\mathcal{S}_i$ *in* τ, *where* $\mathcal{S}_i \longrightarrow_r \mathcal{S}_{i+1}$, *there is a trace* τ' *using* $\mathcal{R}$, $\tau' = \mathcal{S}'_{i+1} \longrightarrow \cdots \longrightarrow$ $\mathcal{S}'_m \longrightarrow \cdots \longrightarrow \mathcal{S}'_{m+p}$, *such that*
   - *for each* j, $m \leq j \leq m + p$, $\mathcal{S}'_j$ *is not critical;*
   - $\mathcal{S}'_{m+p}$ *is a goal configuration;*
   - $\delta_C(\mathcal{S}_i, \mathcal{S}'_m)$;
   - $\delta_G(\mathcal{S}_k, \mathcal{S}'_{m+p})$;
   - *the planning scenario* $(\mathcal{R}, \mathcal{GS}, \mathcal{CS}, \mathcal{E}, \mathcal{S}'_m)$ *is* $\delta_C, \delta_G, n - 1$-*resilient.*

In the above resilience problems, goals and/or critical configurations may change during the trace since CUR and GUR change goal and critical facts. The system must keep pace with these updates, meet the new goals and satisfy the new requirements according to the given recoverability conditions.

Figure 1 illustrates a mission update involving both GUR and CUR, i.e., changes in the points to visit and in regulations involving no-fly zones.

Remark 2. Note that the δ_C, δ_G, n-resilience cannot be expressed directly as the combination of resilience w.r.t. system, goal and critical updates. Any combination of updates affects the original and updated missions that involve goals and critical specifications updated a multiple number of times. Note also that for $n = 0$, all the resilience problems reduce to the planning problem.

Remark 3. In problems involving critical updates, we assume that updates are not too frequent and/or that the system recovers reasonably efficiently. That is, another update does not occur until the system has recovered from the previous one. Namely, the last condition in Definitions 11 and 12 refers to resilience with a reduced number of updates, $n - 1$, and the planning scenario with a new initial configuration denoting the system after the "grace period".

Resilience problems check for the existence of a "good" trace that testifies the corresponding resilience property of a given planning scenario.

Definition 13 (Resilience Problems). δ_C, δ_G, n-resilience problem *(resp. n-resilience w.r.t. system updates, δ_G, n-resilience w.r.t. goal updates, δ_C, n-resilience w.r.t. critical updates) for a given planning scenario* $A = (\mathcal{R}, \mathcal{GS}, \mathcal{CS}, \mathcal{E}, \mathcal{S}_0)$, *recoverability conditions* δ_C, δ_G, *and a natural number* n, *is the problem of determining whether* A *is* δ_C, δ_G, n-resilient *(resp. n-resilient w.r.t. system updates, δ_G, n-resilient w.r.t. goal updates, δ_C, n-resilient w.r.t. critical updates).*

6   Computational Complexity Results

The PSPACE lower bound for the resilience problems can be inferred from the complexity of the planning problem [13]. The aim of this section is to design non-deterministic PSPACE procedures for the resilience problems from Sect. 5.

For the sake of perspicuity, we confine ourselves to the resilience problem in Definition 14 below, which is the main ingredient taken from the recursive definitions in Sect. 5. Recall, $\delta_G(\widehat{\mathcal{S}}, \mathcal{S}'_m)$ is supposed to relate the original goal $\widehat{\mathcal{S}}$ in the main trace τ and the 'new' goal $\mathcal{S}'_m$ in the particular reaction trace τ', the result of an update action.

Definition 14. *Given a planning scenario* $A = (\mathcal{R}, \mathcal{GS}, \mathcal{CS}, \mathcal{E}, \mathcal{S}_0)$ *and a recoverability condition* δ_G, *let* $\tau = \mathcal{S}_0 \longrightarrow \mathcal{S}_1 \longrightarrow \cdots \longrightarrow \mathcal{S}_i \longrightarrow \cdots \longrightarrow \widehat{\mathcal{S}}$ *be a compliant trace leading from an initial configuration* $\mathcal{S}_0$ *to a goal configuration,* $\widehat{\mathcal{S}}$. *We say that* τ *is a* resilient trace *against the update rules* $\mathcal{E}$ *and the recoverability condition* δ_G, *if for each update action caused by* $(r, \mathcal{S}_i)$, *where an update* $r \in \mathcal{E}$ *is applied to a configuration* $\mathcal{S}_i$ *in* τ, *with* $\mathcal{S}_i \longrightarrow_r \mathcal{S}'_{i+1}$, *the following holds: there is a compliant 'reaction' trace* $\tau' = \mathcal{S}'_{i+1} \longrightarrow \mathcal{S}'_{i+2} \longrightarrow \cdots \longrightarrow \cdots \longrightarrow \mathcal{S}'_m$, *from* $\mathcal{S}'_{i+1}$ *to a goal configuration* $\mathcal{S}'_m$ *such that, in addition,* $\delta_G(\widehat{\mathcal{S}}, \mathcal{S}'_m)$ *is valid.*

Remark 4. Intuitively, $\delta_G(\widehat{\mathcal{S}}, \mathcal{S}'_m)$ reads that $\mathcal{S}'_m$, the new goal configuration in the particular reaction trace τ', is accepted as an adapted version of $\widehat{\mathcal{S}}$, the original goal configuration in the main trace τ.

Remark 5. According to Definition 14, given an r, we have to investigate all pairs $(r, \mathcal{S}_i)$ so that $\mathcal{S}_i$ must be available at any position inside τ. One may initially believe that we need to store the whole trace τ, which, in principle, requires *exponential size*, please see Proposition 1 in Sect. 3.

Remark 6. As explained in Sect. 3, to obtain decidability of the resilience problems, we consider balanced systems with facts of bounded size. In addition, to obtain our complexity results, we assume that recoverability conditions are recognizable in time polynomial in the size of the system, see Definition 7.

Following Remarks 5 and 6, we can easily obtain the following result:

Proposition 2. *There exists an exponential space decision procedure that determines whether, for any given planning scenario* $A = (\mathcal{R}, \mathcal{GS}, \mathcal{CS}, \mathcal{E}, \mathcal{S}_0)$ *with a set of balanced rules* $\mathcal{R}$ *and an upper bound of size of facts, and a polynomial time recognizable recoverability condition* δ_G, *there exists a compliant trace* τ *leading from an initial configuration* $\mathcal{S}_0$ *to a goal configuration* $\widehat{\mathcal{S}}$, *such that* τ *is a resilient trace against the update rules and recoverability conditions in the sense of Definition 14.*

Resilience problems could, therefore, be reduced to compliance by generating a new compliance problem from the resilience problem. We note that while such a reduction is possible, it would result in an exponential increase of the size of the system. Notwithstanding previous points, we obtain Theorem 1, which provides a better upper bound.

Theorem 1. *There exists a PSPACE decision procedure that determines whether for any given planning scenario $A = (\mathcal{R}, \mathcal{GS}, \mathcal{CS}, \mathcal{E}, \mathcal{S}_0)$, with a set of balanced rules $\mathcal{R}$ and an upper bound of size of facts, and a polynomial time recognizable recoverability condition δ_G, there exists a compliant trace τ leading from an initial configuration $\mathcal{S}_0$ to a goal configuration $\widehat{\mathcal{S}}$, such that τ is a resilient trace against the update rules and recoverability conditions in the sense of Definition 14.*

Proof Sketch. The main idea of the proof is a dynamic execution step-by-step, not static. The following processes are run *in parallel*:

(a) The *main process*, to execute non-deterministically a main trace τ, step-by-step.
(b) For each update, $r \in \mathcal{E}$, a specific process to reschedule any branch τ' in accordance with recoverability conditions.

Recalling that NPSPACE equals PSPACE [26], we define a non-deterministic PSPACE procedure as follows: (Here, to exclude some cases, we will assume that no r is applied to the initial configuration $\mathcal{S}_0$.) By $count_0$ we denote exponential upper bound on the length of traces indicated in Proposition 1 in Sect. 3.
begin

- S is the configuration at the current step, $count$ is a counter to control termination, ok is a Boolean to control the success.
- Initially, $S := \mathcal{S}_0$, and $count := count_0$, and $ok := true$
- Choose non-deterministically a goal configuration, $\widehat{S}$. (We assume that the goal configurations are recognizable in polynomial time.) *The goal configuration $\widehat{S}$, defined at this initial step, is intended to be the correct goal configuration appeared at the final step of our trace τ developed by induction.*

repeat $count := count - 1$;

- If ok then, given the current S, **guess non-deterministically** a non-critical configuration $\widetilde{S}$ such that $S \longrightarrow_\rho \widetilde{S}$, for a regular system rule, ρ.
  We assume a polynomial number of system rules ρ, each executing in polynomial time, so we can check in polytime, if the set of such $\widetilde{S}$ is empty or not. **if** this set is empty, which means that we cannot continue our trace (deadlock) **then** reset $ok := false$; **else** reset $S := \widetilde{S}$;
  For each update, r, such that r is applied to the S at hand, with $S \longrightarrow_r S'$, if ok then we 'generate' the corresponding τ' as follows:
  - Here $\mathcal{H}$ stands for the configuration at the current step, $count'$ is a counter to control termination, ok is a Boolean to control the success.
  - Initially, $\mathcal{H} := S'$, and $count' := count_0$.
  - **while** $ok = true$, $count' > 0$, and it is not true that
    ($\mathcal{H}$ is a goal configuration, and $\delta_G(\widehat{S}, \mathcal{H})$)
    do $count' := count' - 1$.
    If ok then, given the current $\mathcal{H}$, **guess non-deterministically** a non-critical configuration $\widetilde{\mathcal{H}}$ such that $\mathcal{H} \longrightarrow_\rho \widetilde{\mathcal{H}}$, for a system rule, ρ.

       if such $\widetilde{\mathcal{H}}$ does not exist (deadlock) **then** reset $ok := false$; **else** reset $\mathcal{H} := \widetilde{\mathcal{H}}$;
       od

- $ok := false$ in the case where the current $\mathcal{H}$ is not a goal configuration or $\neg\delta_G(\widehat{\mathcal{S}}, \mathcal{H})$.

until $ok = false$, or $\mathcal{S} = \widehat{\mathcal{S}}$, or $count \leq 0$.
return "success" if $ok = true$, and the current $\mathcal{S}$ is a goal configuration such that $\mathcal{S} = \widehat{\mathcal{S}}$.
end of the procedure.

Lemma 1. *There is a non-deterministic branch terminated with "success" if and only if there is a compliant trace τ leading from an initial configuration $\mathcal{S}_0$ to a goal configuration, $\widehat{\mathcal{S}}$, such that τ is a resilient trace in the sense of Definition 14.*

Bringing all together, we conclude Theorem 1.   □

Remark 7. To verify that our NPSPACE procedure is correct, we play with two orthogonal paradigms in our constructions:

(a) "one r vs. exponentially many candidates $\mathcal{S}_i$ in a fixed τ";
    Within Definition 14, for a fixed r we likely deal with an exponential number of $\mathcal{S}_i$, candidates for a 'good' pair $(r, \mathcal{S}_i)$ to provide a compliant trace τ' leading from $\mathcal{S}'_{i+1}$ to a goal configuration, $\mathcal{S}'_m$.
(b) "one $\mathcal{S}$ at a moment vs. polynomially many candidates r";
    Within our procedure, at any moment we deal with a unique $\mathcal{S}$ and polynomial number of r's, candidates for a 'good' pair $(r, \mathcal{S})$ to initiate a compliant trace τ' leading from the corresponding $\mathcal{S}'$ to a goal configuration, $\widetilde{\mathcal{S}}$.

    Compliance/reachability problem is to prove that there exists a good trace τ such that a goal P is reachable. In resilience problems we are dealing with alternating quantifiers - the problem is to prove that there exists a good trace τ such that a goal P is reachable and that for all update rules applicable to arbitrary intermediate states in τ, there exists an adapted reaction trace such that for all update rules applicable to arbitrary intermediate states on each of the adapted traces, there exists a further adapted reaction trace, etc. etc. In addition to that, the algorithm has to provide, for instance, correlations between the new goals on one level and the old goals on another level. Only for a fixed number n of quantifier alternations we provide PSPACE complexity. If n is itself a part of the input, we get in fact PSPACE to the power of n.

7 Conclusions

Resilience is of great importance in today's civilization, from the Internet to logistics, finance, and environmental science, not excluding computer science. In this paper, we formalize resilience as a verification property of cyber-physical systems in a timed multiset rewriting framework. By distinguishing the rules that are under the control of CPS from those that are not, we use specific sets of traces involving changes and system recoverability to define a satisfactory system response to the new conditions. We study the complexity of resilience problems. Since the planning problem is undecidable in general [1], the resilience problems are undecidable in general. In case of systems with balanced transition rules and a bound on size of facts the PSPACE lower bound for the resilience problems follows from the PSPACE lower bound for the planning problem [13]. We note that many important cyber-physical systems are resource limited and can be naturally modelled using balanced transition rules.

In this paper, we show that the resilience problem is PSPACE-complete for the planning scenarios of Sects. 4 and 5. More precisely, we show PSPACE upper bound for a version of resilience that encapsulates resilience with respect to system updates and resilience with respect to goal updates. The case of resilience with respect to critical updates is more involved because in this case we also need to allow traces that are non-compliant during the grace periods following updates. We plan to consider the complexity of this case in the future.

We also plan to consider the time bounded versions of resilience problems and their complexity for the class of Progressing Time Systems [14]. Fragments of the formal model with lower complexity of some resilience properties may be identified. Finally, we are also investigating how to automate resilience checking. The Soft Agents (SA) framework has a builtin mechanism to model environmental perturbations such as faults, weather, or obstacles [18,20,28,29]. This mechanism corresponds to the use of rules not under the control of the system being considered and is thus well suited to modeling and analyzing resilience properties of cyber-physical systems such as those proposed in this paper. We plan to use SA to carry out a variety of experiments to better understand the practical aspects of checking resilience properties for different types of CPS. Some of the authors have recently proposed [21] the use of Rewriting Logic Modulo SMT for automating the generation of safety proofs for CPSes. We believe that this work can be extended so to generate resilience proofs based on the definitions proposed here. While the basic SA framework is well-suited to modeling the ability to achieve goals with acceptable outcomes, the Rewriting modulo STM approach allows us to consider recoverability issues.

We intend to study similar properties of CPSes and other complex systems, as well as compare formal definitions and computational complexities of these properties, including the realizability, survivability, recoverability, and reliability properties over infinite traces from our previous work [14]. Some of these properties could be interpreted using game theory. It would be interesting to compare our rewriting approach to the problems with the game-theoretic approach.

Acknowledgements. Ban Kirigin is supported in part by the Croatian Science Foundation under the project UIP-05-2017-9219. The work of Max Kanovich was partially supported by EPSRC Programme Grant EP/R006865/1: "Interface Reasoning for Interacting Systems (IRIS)." Scedrov was partially supported by the U. S. Office of Naval Research under award number N00014-20-1-2635. Talcott was partially supported by the U. S. Office of Naval Research under award numbers N00014-15-1-2202 and N00014-20-1-2644, and NRL grant N0017317-1-G002.

References

1. Aires Urquiza, A., et al.: Resource and timing aspects of security protocols. J. Comput. Secur. **29**(3), 299–340 (2021)
2. Allenby, B., Fink, J.: Toward inherently secure and resilient societies. Science **309**(5737), 1034–1036 (2005)
3. Banescu, S., Ochoa, M., Pretschner, A.: A framework for measuring software obfuscation resilience against automated attacks. In: 2015 IEEE/ACM 1st International Workshop on Software Protection, pp. 45–51 (2015)
4. Barker, K., Ramirez-Marquez, J.E., Rocco, C.M.: Resilience-based network component importance measures. Reliab. Eng. Syst. Saf. **117**, 89–97 (2013)
5. Bloomfield, R., et al.: Towards identifying and closing gaps in assurance of autonomous road vehicles-a collection of technical notes part 1. arXiv preprint arXiv:2003.00789 (2020)
6. Bruneau, M., et al.: A framework to quantitatively assess and enhance the seismic resilience of communities. Earthq. Spectra **19**(4), 733–752 (2003)
7. Enderton, H.B.: A Mathematical Introduction to Logic. Academic Press (1972)
8. Henry, D., Ramirez-Marquez, J.E.: Generic metrics and quantitative approaches for system resilience as a function of time. Reliab. Eng. Syst. Saf. **99**, 114–122 (2012)
9. Holling, C.S.: Resilience and stability of ecological systems. Annu. Rev. Ecol. Syst. **4**(1), 1–23 (1973)
10. Hosseini, S., Barker, K., Ramirez-Marquez, J.E.: A review of definitions and measures of system resilience. Reliab. Eng. Syst. Saf. **145**, 47–61 (2016)
11. Huang, W., et al.: Formal verification of robustness and resilience of learning-enabled state estimation systems for robotics (2020)
12. Kanovich, M., Ban Kirigin, T., Nigam, V., Scedrov, A., Talcott, C.L.: Time, computational complexity, and probability in the analysis of distance-bounding protocols. J. Comput. Secur. **25**(6), 585–630 (2017)
13. Kanovich, M., Ban Kirigin, T., Nigam, V., Scedrov, A., Talcott, C.L., Perovic, R.: A rewriting framework and logic for activities subject to regulations. Math. Struct. Comput. Sci. **27**(3), 332–375 (2017)
14. Kanovich, M., Kirigin, T.B., Nigam, V., Scedrov, A., Talcott, C.: On the complexity of verification of time-sensitive distributed systems. In: Dougherty, D., Meseguer, J., Mödersheim, S.A., Rowe, P. (eds.) Protocols, Strands, and Logic. LNCS, vol. 13066, pp. 251–275. Springer, Cham (2021). https://doi.org/10.1007/978-3-030-91631-2_14
15. Laprie, J.C.: From dependability to resilience. In: 38th IEEE/IFIP International Conference on Dependable Systems and Networks, pp. G8–G9. Citeseer (2008)
16. Madni, A.M., Erwin, D., Sievers, M.: Constructing models for systems resilience: challenges, concepts, and formal methods. Systems **8**(1) (2020)
17. Madni, A.M., Sievers, M.: Combining formal and probabilistic modeling in resilient systems design. Procedia Comput. Sci. **153**, 343–351 (2019). 17th Annual Conference on Systems Engineering Research (CSER)
18. Mason, I.A., Nigam, V., Talcott, C., Brito, A.: A framework for analyzing adaptive autonomous aerial vehicles. In: Cerone, A., Roveri, M. (eds.) SEFM 2017. LNCS, vol. 10729, pp. 406–422. Springer, Cham (2018). https://doi.org/10.1007/978-3-319-74781-1_28
19. Mouelhi, S., Laarouchi, M.E., Cancila, D., Chaouchi, H.: Predictive formal analysis of resilience in cyber-physical systems. IEEE Access **7**, 33741–33758 (2019)

20. Nigam, V., Kim, M., Mason, I., Talcott, C.: Detection and diagnosis of deviations in distributed systems of autonomous agents. Math. Struct. Comput. Sci. (2022)
21. Nigam, V., Talcott, C.: Automating safety proofs about cyber-physical systems using rewriting modulo SMT. In: Bae, K. (ed.) WRLA 2022. LNCS, vol. 13252, pp. 212–229. Springer, Cham (2022). https://doi.org/10.1007/978-3-031-12441-9_11
22. NIST: Autonomy levels for unmanned systems (ALFUS) framework. https://www.nist.gov/system/files/documents/el/isd/ks/NISTSP_1011_ver_1-1.pdf
23. Pregenzer, A.: Systems resilience: a new analytical framework for nuclear nonproliferation. Sandia National Laboratories, Albuquerque (2011)
24. Ross, R., Pillitteri, V., Graubart, R., Bodeau, D., McQuaid, R.: Developing cyber resilient systems: a systems security engineering approach. Technical report, National Institute of Standards and Technology (2019)
25. SAE: Recommended practice: taxonomy and definitions for terms related to driving automation systems for on-road motor vehicles. https://www.sae.org/standards/content/j3016_202104/
26. Savitch, W.J.: Relationship between nondeterministic and deterministic tape classes. J. Comput. Syst. Sci. **4**, 177–192 (1970)
27. Sharma, V.C., Haran, A., Rakamaric, Z., Gopalakrishnan, G.: Towards formal approaches to system resilience. In: 2013 IEEE 19th Pacific Rim International Symposium on Dependable Computing, pp. 41–50 (2013)
28. Talcott, C., Arbab, F., Yadav, M.: Soft agents: exploring soft constraints to model robust adaptive distributed cyber-physical agent systems. In: De Nicola, R., Hennicker, R. (eds.) Software, Services, and Systems. LNCS, vol. 8950, pp. 273–290. Springer, Cham (2015). https://doi.org/10.1007/978-3-319-15545-6_18
29. Talcott, C., Nigam, V., Arbab, F., Kappé, T.: Formal specification and analysis of robust adaptive distributed cyber-physical systems. In: Bernardo, M., De Nicola, R., Hillston, J. (eds.) SFM 2016. LNCS, vol. 9700, pp. 1–35. Springer, Cham (2016). https://doi.org/10.1007/978-3-319-34096-8_1
30. U.S. Department of Defense: Dictionary of military and associated terms. https://fas.org/irp/doddir/dod/jp1_02.pdf
31. Vardi, M.: Efficiency vs. resilience: what COVID-19 teaches computing. Commun. ACM **63**(5), 9 (2020)

Spatial and Timing Properties
in Highway Traffic

Christopher Bischopink$^{(\boxtimes)}$ and Ernst-Rüdiger Olderog

Department of Computing Science, University of Oldenburg, Oldenburg, Germany
{bischopink,olderog}@informatik.uni-oldenburg.de

Abstract. We introduce *Timed Multi-Lane Spatial Logic (TMLSL)*, a logic to express spatial and timing properties in highway traffic. For this purpose, we combine State-Clock Logic (SCL) and Multi-Lane Spatial Logic with Scopes (MLSLS), using MLSLS formulae as the propositions from which SCL formulae are built. SCL enables one to state through which phases a car has to pass when performing manoeuvres, like changing lanes. The phases themselves are described in the spatial logic MLSLS. Additionally, it is possible to express explicit timing constraints regarding the change of phases. Alongside the logic itself, we give a procedure to semi–decide whether there exists a run for a given traffic situation that satisfies a specification given in TMLSL.

Keywords: MLSL · Autonomous cars · Specifications · Timed automata · Spatio-temporal reasoning · Decidability

1 Introduction

The automation of car driving is advancing rapidly, ranging from advanced driver asssitance systems to (partially) autonomous cars. This poses the challenge to establish that these systems satisfy desirable behavioural properties. Regarding safety, it was observed in [1] that cars behave safely (avoid collisions) if at every moment they occupy disjoint spaces on the road. This led to the introduction of the Multi-Lane Spatial Logic (MLSL), where formulae are evaluated on *traffic snapshots* in an abstract road model. In addition to purely spatial properties like safety requirements, there is a need to express timing properties, e.g., whether a car has set its turn signal to prepare a desired lane change within a certain time bound. More generally, the question arises whether there exists a sequence of actions by the car that allows for such a lane change. While this question is easy to answer for some traffic snapshots (e.g., where each car has a free lane next to it and all cars drive at the same speed), it is much more complicated for others because in general one has to check whether the dynamical evolution of the system allows for the desired change. In this paper, we reason about the evolution of traffic snapshots as sequences of time-constrained phases.

This research was partially supported by the German Research Council (DFG) in the Research Training Group GRK 1765 SCARE.

H. Seidl et al. (Eds.): ICTAC 2022, LNCS 13572, pp. 114–131, 2022.
https://doi.org/10.1007/978-3-031-17715-6_9

Our contributions are the following. First, we introduce *Timed* MLSL to specify such evolutions. It is defined by combining State-Clock Logic (SCL) with MLSL with Scopes (MLSLS), a variant of MLSL with a decidable satisfaction problem. SCL enables one to state through which phases a car has to pass when performing a manoeuvre, like changing lanes. The phases themselves are specified in MLSLS. Second, we introduce and tackle the *Timed Satisfiability Problem*, describing whether a specification written in Timed MLSL is satisfiable from a given traffic snapshot onwards. A realistic restriction that we assume when answering this question is a maximum acceleration and speed of the cars.

Related Work. MLSL was introduced in [1] to reason about traffic situations in highway traffic. Since then, different extensions were proposed, such as [2], which extends MLSL to country roads. Both turn out to be undecidable [3,4], but decidable fragments were identified, like MLSLS [5]. The latest extension of MLSL was towards urban traffic [6] to handle complex intersections. These extensions allow for more complex topologies, including opening and ending of lanes in highway traffic. However, each of them lacks the possibility to explicitly express timing requirements. An exception is [3], where a branching time extension is considered. As a downside, it is only possible to express that formulae are invariant under certain intervals.

There are several other approaches considered for autonomous and partially autonomous traffic. Many of them, e.g. [7,8] concentrate on the part of establishing a safe (and optimal) adaptive cruise control for vehicles following each other. [8] used weighted and stochastic timed automata and games for specifying and games for solving the problem of generating a strategy for the cars to follow each other. We refrain from using an automata model directly to specify desirable properties, and prefer a textual specification language because it is closer to natural language and therefore should be easier to use. An approach that uses a textual specification language is [9], where the authors employ *Quantified Hybrid Programs* for the specification. In contrast to our approach, where the entire specification uses only spatial and temporal fragments, they included the dynamic behaviour of the system into the specification.

Structure of this Paper. Section 2 introduces the preliminaries of our approach: MLSL for the spatial fragment of the specification, and SCL for the timing fragment of the specification, as well as the *First-Order Theory of Real-Closed Fields* (FORCF). Section 3 introduces a combination of SCL and MLSLS called TMLSL and demonstrates its expressiveness using examples, before showing that this logic is at least semi-decidable in Sect. 4, translating the satisfiability problem to formulae of FORCF. Section 5 concludes the paper.

2   Preliminaries

First we recall the Multi-Lane Spatial Logic (with Scopes), consisting of the model (Sect. 2.1) to formalise real-world situations, the evolution of them

(Sect. 2.2) and the logic itself (Sect. 2.3) for expressing spatial properties on the models. This is followed by Sect. 2.4 that introduces State-Clock Logic for the timing aspect of highway traffic properties, and concludes with Sect. 2.5, where we briefly describe a decidable theory which we use to show that the Timed Satisfiability Problem is semi-decidable.

2.1   Abstract Model of Motorway Traffic

The model our work is based on is called a *Traffic Snapshot* [1]. It is defined over a set of lanes $\mathbb{L} = \{0, \ldots, n\}$ of an infinite length on which cars can claim and reserve spaces of finite extension (length). A *reservation* in this context is the actual space a car occupies (including its braking distance) when driving on one or (in case of a lane change) two lanes, whereas a *claim* represents the space a car would like to reserve in the future, which is the equivalent of setting the turn signal for that lane. Traffic snapshots abstract from real-world scenarios s.t. for every car from the set of car identifiers $\mathbb{I} = \{A, B, \ldots\}$, only its position, speed, acceleration, reservation and claims are known. Figure 1 shows the graphical representation of three traffic snapshots, where each of them has two lanes and two cars, both of them in lane one, with car A behind car B. The pentagon in front of the rectangle depicts the braking distance of the car. In the latter two traffic snapshots, car A is preparing for a lane change: it has set its turn signal to lane two, which is represented as a claim, shown as a dashed copy of its reserved space on lane one, to that lane.

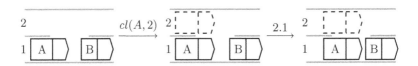

Fig. 1. A transition sequence including three traffic snapshots and two transitions.

Definition 1 (Traffic Snapshot).
A traffic snapshot is a tuple $TS = (res, clm, pos, spd, acc)$ with

- *$res/clm : \mathbb{I} \to \mathcal{P}(\mathbb{L})$, the lanes each car reserves/claims and*
- *$pos/spd/acc : \mathbb{I} \to \mathbb{R}$, the position/speed/acceleration of each car.*

We denote the set of all traffic snapshots as $\mathbb{TS}$.

In [3], *sanity conditions* are introduced that prohibit some undesirable models, e.g. where a car has reservations on two non-adjacent lanes. We do not focus on them here, as they can be expressed in the corresponding logic itself and are thus only a further part of a specification.

2.2   Evolution of a Traffic Snapshot

While a traffic snapshot describes a static situation at one point in time, this situation may evolve whenever the cars in the traffic snapshot execute actions. These actions can be the change of the acceleration or actions regarding the change of the lane. In MLSL, changes that occur at a traffic snapshot are modelled as *transitions*. We divide them into two types, one regarding the discrete dynamics and one regarding the continuous dynamics of the evolution. We refer to the first one as *discrete actions*. This type includes a car C claiming a lane n ($\mathsf{c}(C, n)$), withdrawing a claim ($\mathsf{wd\ c}(C)$), reserving a formerly claimed lane ($\mathsf{r}(C)$), and withdrawing all reservations except the one on lane n ($\mathsf{wd\ r}(C, n)$). In [1] a formal definition of these actions is given. The second type of actions regards the continuous evolution of the cars and thus the behaviour along the lanes. These transitions handle the change of a car's acceleration to some value a ($\mathsf{acc}(C, a)$) and the passing of t time units (t), where $\oplus$ is the overriding operator of Z [10]:

$$\mathcal{TS} \xrightarrow{t} \mathcal{TS}' \quad \Leftrightarrow \quad \mathcal{TS}' = (res, clm, pos', spd', acc)$$
$$\wedge \forall C \in \mathbb{I} : pos'(C) = pos(C) + spd(C) \cdot t + \frac{1}{2} acc(C) \cdot t^2$$
$$\wedge \forall C \in \mathbb{I} : spd'(C) = spd(C) + acc(C) \cdot t$$

$$\mathcal{TS} \xrightarrow{acc(C,a)} \mathcal{TS}' \quad \Leftrightarrow \quad \mathcal{TS}' = (res, clm, pos, spd, acc')$$
$$\wedge acc' = acc \oplus \{C \mapsto a\},$$

In what follows, we will often refer to *MLSL actions*, meaning the transitions just described, without the one regarding the passing of time. We denote this set of transitions that are possible to a certain traffic snapshot as *Act*.

Figure 1 illustrates the evolution of a traffic snapshot along a transitions sequence, where car A claims lane 2 and afterwards 2.1 time units pass, during which the two cars move along the lanes with their speeds and accelerations.

We can define timed words on the actions *Act*:

Definition 2 (Timed words on MLSL actions). *A* timed word *over the set of MLSL actions is an infinite sequence* $\varrho = \langle (\alpha_1, t_1), (\alpha_2, t_2), \dots \rangle$ *with* $\alpha_i \in Act$ *and* $\langle t_1, t_2, \dots \rangle$ *forming a real-time sequence, that is, a monotonically increasing sequence of time stamps.*

The term *time-stamped action sequence* is used as a synonym. We do not exclude Zeno behaviour here, it is indirectly excluded in Definition 7.

Next, we introduce the logic MLSL to reason about traffic snapshots. The semantics of MLSL in [1] considers the concept of a *view* to restrict the parts of the street a car has knowledge about. We only point out that a view is a tuple $V = (L, X, E)$, with L the lanes visible to the view's owner E, and X the finite extension (length of the road) visible to E. We do not further concentrate on this topic here and assume that our view is big enough that all formulae that may occur can be evaluated.

Additionally, a car's knowledge is limited through its sensors, which is formalised trough a *sensor function* and a car's *safety envelope*. A sensor function is a function $\Omega : \mathbb{I} \times \mathbb{TS} \to \mathbb{R}^{\geq 0}$ and returns a car's size plus its breaking distance in a traffic snapshot. The safety envelope then is the space car C occupies in a traffic snapshot TS, that is $s(C, TS, \Omega) = [pos(C), pos(C) + \Omega(C, TS)]$.

2.3   MLSL with Scopes

In [5], a variant of MLSL *with scopes* (MLSLS) is proposed. The idea is to restrict the formulae involving quantification or a free space to range over a finite domain CS of car identifiers only. This is done using a subset $cs \subseteq CVar$ (*scope*) of car variables. The authors showed that the satisfaction problem of MLSLS is, in contrast to pure MLSL, decidable. The syntax of MLSLS formulae is as follows:

Definition 3 (Syntax of MLSLS). *Given* $\gamma, \gamma' \in CVar, k \in \mathbb{R}$ *and* $cs \subseteq CVar$ *the syntax of MLSLS is given by*

$$\varphi ::= \gamma = \gamma' \mid \textit{free} \mid re(\gamma) \mid cl(\gamma) \mid l = k \mid \exists c.\varphi \mid \varphi_1 \frown \varphi_2 \mid \begin{matrix} \varphi_1 \\ \varphi_2 \end{matrix} \mid cs : \varphi,$$

and standard Boolean combinations of such formulae.

Atomic formulae are checks for equality of two car variables, *free* denoting free space on a lane, $re(\gamma)$ and $cl(\gamma)$ denoting a reservation and a claim of a car γ, respectively, and a check for equality of the length of a segment against some value k. Formulae can be combined by Boolean operations and quantification as well as two *chops*, that is, if one formula holds in front of another formula or if they hold on two neighbouring lanes. Also, the evaluation of formulae can be restricted to a certain scope (finite subset) cs of cars. We denote the set of all MLSLS formulae as Φ_{MLSLS}.

Formulae are called *well-scoped* if every formula containing the atom *free* or existential quantification has a scope and every scoped formula is followed by an existential quantification or the atom *free*. For the moment, we require that the scope of all formulae is the same.

Semantics. The semantics of a formula is evaluated with respect to a model M consisting of a traffic snapshot TS, a scope CS, the car's view V, and a valuation ν assigning values to variables. Intuitively, a formula holds on such a model if there is a partition of the visible excerpt of the traffic snapshots that corresponds to the vertical and horizontal chops of the formula into its subformulae. Then, these subformulae hold on the respective intervals if there are claims and reservations as required by the subformulae. A detailed, formal semantics can be found in [5].

We use some abbreviations to increase the readability. One of them is *true*, which is defined in a standard manner and another one is the *somewhere modality*

$\langle \varphi \rangle := true \frown \begin{pmatrix} true \\ \varphi \\ true \end{pmatrix} \frown true$, which expresses that, at some position in the model, the formula φ holds.

This abbreviation and the next examples use the horizontal ($\frown$) and vertical (stacked formula) chop operator. Both divide the view a traffic snapshot is evaluated on into two parts. In case of the horizontal chop, this means finding a "chopping" position along the lanes s.t. the first formula holds from the beginning of the view up to that position and the second formula holds from that position up to the end. The vertical chop operator, in contrast, searches for a border between two lanes to split the view at, with an analogous semantics.

Consider two example formulae. The first one is $\begin{pmatrix} cl(A) \frown free \\ re(A) \frown free \frown re(B) \end{pmatrix}$, specifying that car A has a claim on the lane next to its reservation, there is free space in front of both its claim and reservation, and there is another car B in front of it. The second one is $\{a, b\} : \neg \exists c. \langle cl(c) \rangle$, expressing that neither the car $\nu(a) = A$ nor $\nu(b) = B$ have a claim somewhere. On the second traffic snapshot depicted in Fig. 1, φ_1 holds, but φ_2 does not, as car A has a claim in it.

Additionally, in [11], the author shows that the question whether a formula φ holds globally through a given transition sequence ϱ starting in a model M, denoted $\varrho(M) \vDash_{seq} \Box \varphi$, is decidable, which we make use of later.

2.4 State-Clock Logic

Different logics have been proposed to deal with real–time requirements. We decided to use State–Clock Logic (SCL) [12]. It enables the specification of both the order in which phases need to be satisfied as well as explicit timing constraints in between these phases.

We start with the syntax of SCL:

Definition 4 (Syntax of SCL).

$$\psi ::= p \mid \psi_1 \vee \psi_2 \mid \neg \psi \mid \psi_1 \mathcal{U} \psi_2 \mid \psi_1 \mathcal{S} \psi_2 \mid \rhd_{\sim c} \psi \mid \lhd_{\sim c} \psi,$$

with $\sim \in \{<, \leq, =\geq, >\}$.

Here p ranges over a set Σ of propositional symbols, which are used to describe the phases. Apart from Boolean combinations and the usual temporal operators $\mathcal{U}$ (until) and $\mathcal{S}$ (since), there are two time dependent operators: $\rhd_{\sim c} \psi$ describes that the time until ψ holds for the next time must satisfy the constraint $\sim c$, and $\lhd_{\sim c} \psi$ handles the analogous case for the past. We use also some abbreviations, e.g. $\rhd_{[l,r)} \psi$ for $\rhd_{\geq l} \psi \wedge \rhd_{<r} \psi$.

Semantics. Unlike in many other temporal logics such as LTL [13], where formulae are evaluated on timed words, formulae of SCL are evaluated on timed sequences of states. This has a benefit when we e.g. specify some safety requirement that should hold throughout an evolution of a traffic snapshot. Using timed sequences of states ensures that it is indeed satisfied at all points in time, not just at the time points that a timed word considers. This is important, as some dangerous situation might be encountered between two observations. We now give a definition of timed sequences of states:

Definition 5 (Timed Sequences of states). *A Timed Sequence of States is a sequence* $m = \langle (s_0, I_0), (s_1, I_1), \dots \rangle$ *where* $s_i \subseteq \Sigma$ *and* I_i *is a real–valued non–empty interval. It is required that any two neighbouring intervals are adjacent and there is no Zeno behaviour, i.e. that time progresses beyond any bounds.*

SCL formulae are evaluated on such timed sequences of states. The semantics of boolean operators and $\mathcal{U}$ and $\mathcal{S}$ is as expected. The time-dependent operators $\triangleright_{\sim c} \psi$ ($\triangleleft_{\sim c} \psi$) are true when the time until (since) ψ holds (held) for the next (last) time complies to $\sim c$. For $\triangleright_{\sim c} \psi$, this means $t_j - t_i \vDash \sim c$, with t_j being the left border of the state where ψ holds for the next time and t_i the time point $\triangleright_{\sim c} \psi$ is evaluated at. For a detailed, formal definition of the semantics, we refer to [12]. There it is defined when an SCL formula φ holds in a timed sequence of states m at position i and at time $t \in I_i$, abbreviated $(m, i, t) \vDash \varphi$.

In [12], also a corresponding model of automata that accepts timed sequences of states, called *State-Clock Automata (SC Automata)*, is defined. We do not introduce them here, but mention that SC automata use two different types of clocks: one *history clock* x_p and one *prophecy clock* y_p for each proposition p used. The task of the history clock is as usual, it denotes the time since p held the last time, whereas y_p denotes the time until p holds for the next time.

2.5   First–Order Theory of Real–Closed Fields

In Sect. 4, we show that the Timed Satisfaction Problem can be expressed as formulae of the First-Order Theory of Real–Closed Fields (*FORCF*) [14]. We do not focus on that theory here, but would like to point out that it includes formulae of a first–order logic with a signature $\{0, 1, +, -, \cdot, \leq\}$. Quantification over the reals is as well possible as over finite domains. The satisfaction problem for FORCF–formulae is known to be decidable [14], with a double exponential complexity with respect to the length of the formula [15]. As an example consider the formula $\exists x \in \mathbb{R} : \forall c \in \mathbb{I} : y \leq \mathsf{pos}(c) + x$, asking if there exists a real-valued x s.t. for all cars c their position plus the value x is at least y.

3   Timed MLSL

The basic idea of our extension to deal with timing requirements for highway traffic is to use SCL based on MLSL(S) formulae as its set of propositions. Utilising SCL for this, we can express various kinds of desirable system properties. First, it is possible to specify that phases follow each other, e.g. a car has first a claim and then a reservation. Second, it is possible to express explicit timing requirements, e.g. how long such a state change is allowed to take. Additionally, the satisfiability problem of SCL (for uninterpreted propositions) is decidable. We start with the syntax of *Timed MLSL (TMLSL)*:

Definition 6. *TMLSL*

$$\varphi ::= p \mid \neg\varphi \mid \varphi_1 \vee \varphi_2 \mid \varphi_1 \mathcal{U} \varphi_2 \mid \varphi_1 \mathcal{S} \varphi_2 \mid \triangleright_{\sim c} \varphi \mid \triangleleft_{\sim c} \varphi$$

where $p \in \Phi_{MLSLS}$.

The only change to the standard definition of SCL is that we take MLSLS formulae instead of arbitrary propositional symbols.

Note. In contrast to our choice of using MLSLS formulae as propositions, one can argue that it would be a good idea to use MLSL actions instead. In this case, TMLSL would be combination of an *Event-Clock Logic* [16] over the set of MLSLS-actions. There are, however, some situations that can only be described using formulae rather than actions. Additionally, from a modelling perspective, one usually does not see the actual action taking place (e.g. accelerating) but senses only the effect, that is, the satisfaction of a formula (e.g. the distance between two cars more rapidly growing).

We give some examples of TMLSL formulae:

Example 1. (TMLSL Formulae).

$$\left\langle \langle re(\gamma) \rangle \wedge \neg \left\langle \begin{matrix} re(\gamma) \\ re(\gamma) \end{matrix} \right\rangle \right\rangle \mathcal{U} \langle cl(\gamma) \rangle \qquad\qquad \neg(true \,\, \mathcal{U} \, \langle re(\gamma) \wedge re(\gamma') \rangle) \quad (3)$$

$$(1)$$

$$cl(\gamma) \implies \triangleright_{[0,7)} \left\langle \begin{matrix} re(\gamma) \\ re(\gamma) \end{matrix} \right\rangle \qquad (2) \quad \triangleleft_{\geq 21} \langle cl(\gamma) \rangle \implies \triangleright_{[0,5)} \langle cl(\gamma) \rangle \quad (4)$$

Formula (1) specifies part of the phases an overtaking manoeuvre may need, in particular that a state where a car has only one reservation is followed by a state where it has a claim. Formula (2) specifies that having two reservations after having a claim takes less than 7 time units. Formula (3) specifies that two cars never have an overlap in their reservations (specifying the absence of collisions). Formula (4) specifies that a car has to claim a lane in less than 5 time units when the last claim occurred at least 21 time units ago. □

Semantics of TMLSL. The semantics of TMLSL formulae is, as for SCL, defined on timed sequences of states. The semantics of a formula of TMLSL is a direct combination of the SCL semantics with MLSLS propositions evaluated in their own semantics. We therefore restrain ourselves from showing the definition again and instead give a sequence satisfying the formulae (1) and (2) from Example 1:

Example 2 (Timed Sequence of States). Consider the (prefixes of a) timed sequences of states s_0 and s_1:

$$- \,\, s_0 = \langle (\{\langle re(A) \rangle\}, [0,2)), (\{\langle re(A) \rangle, \langle cl(A) \rangle\}, [2,4]), (\{\left\langle \begin{matrix} re(A) \\ re(A) \end{matrix} \right\rangle\}, (4,17]) \rangle$$

- $s_1 = \langle (\{\langle re(A)\rangle\}, [0, 4]), (\{\langle re(A)\rangle, \langle cl(A)\rangle\}, (4, 17]) \rangle$

Then s_0 satisfies the formulae (1) and (2) from Example 1 for $\gamma = A$ if extended appropriately, but s_1 does not, as A does not have two reservations at most 7 time units after it claimed a lane.

To reason about the satisfaction of TMLSL formulae with respect to traffic snapshots and actions, we lift the semantics to cover such cases:

Definition 7 (Semantics of TMLSL formulae on traffic snapshots) .

1. *A timed sequence of states m is a model of φ iff $(m, 0, 0) \vDash \varphi$, meaning that the initial state and time of m satisfy φ.*
2. *A timed word of MLSL actions ϱ and a traffic snapshot TS are a model of φ iff there exists a timed sequence of states $m = ((m_1, I_1), (m_2, I_2), \dots)$ that is a model of φ, where m contains only MLSLS propositions that φ is built from and that are successively valid during the evolution of TS according to ϱ, and the sets m_i consist of those propositions that are valid during I_i.*
3. *TS is a model of φ if there exists a timed word of MLSL actions ϱ such that ϱ and TS are a model of φ.*
4. *φ is satisfiable if there is a TS such that TS is a model of φ.*

We now provide a solution to the problem of finding suitable timed action sequences ϱ for point 3 and call it *Timed Satisfiability Problem* from TS on, TMLSL–SAT for short.

4   Semi–decision Procedure for TMLSL

We now tackle the TMLSL-SAT problem just defined: Given a model $M = (CS, TS, \Omega, V, \nu)$ and a specification φ, is there a sequence of actions for the cars to take s.t. these actions satisfy the specification φ? In answering this question, we respect some more constraints regarding the dynamic behaviour of the cars, namely an upper (acc_{max}) and lower (acc_{min}) bound on the acceleration, as well as a speed limit between 0 and a maximum speed (spd_{max}).

Remember that we define a behaviour that should hold through an infinite evolution of a traffic snapshot, so the sequence of actions we are searching for is infinite. Infinite sequences may not be encountered in reality, but ensure that we do not end up in a situation that is dangerous after a finite sequence. Luckily, the abstract model [1] uses infinite lanes and thus allows for infinite sequences.

The idea of SCL, which TMLSL is based on, is finding accepting loops/runs in a *Region Automaton*, which is a generalised Büchi automaton that accepts sequences that are models of the corresponding formula. As SCL formulae are built from uninterpreted propositions, it suffices for SCL to find a single loop which visits one state from each Büchi-set (generalised Büchi-acceptance condition) infinitely often. In case of TMLSL, where the propositions (i.e. MLSLS formulae) are interpreted, this does not suffice. The reason for this is that, given an initial model and a sequence of actions that satisfy the SCL-part of the formula, it can be the case that the cars cannot behave in a way that they are supposed to, e.g. reach certain points without accelerations beyond the specified physical bounds.

We solve this problem in two tiers: First, we generate the Region Automaton $\mathcal{R}(\varphi)$ [12,17] from the entire specification φ, which accepts runs that are *potential solutions*. These potential solutions dictate when the propositions need to be satisfied. The system however may not be able to behave in a way that the propositions (here MLSLS formulae) are indeed satisfied. As a consequence and second step, we check for each potential solution if the system can actually behave in a way that the propositions (MLSLS formulae) are satisfied. We formulate these checks as a FORCF-formula, which are decidable. Then, if the FORCF-formula is satisfiable, so is the specification φ and our potential solution is an actual one. If not, we proceed by checking whether the next (longer) potential solution is an actual solution, and so on. As we do not have a termination criterion yet, our approach yields only a semi-decision procedure.

Structure of the Formalisation. The definitions and theorems that follow have the following connection: Lemma 1 establishes that it is decidable what discrete actions need to be executed to satisfy a property. The remainder concentrates on the dynamic evolution of the system: Definition 8 states when two traffic snapshots are equivalent. We search for such equivalent traffic snapshots that occur along the potential solutions, as the actions between them are applicable infinitely often (Lemma 2). Searching for equivalent traffic snapshots requires the formalisation which traffic snapshots are reachable by the evolution between two regions in a potential solution (Definition 9) and along a potential solution (Definition 10). Whether such equivalent traffic snapshots are reachable in the evolution along a potential solution (with a maximum number of allowed steps in between) is decidable (Theorem 1). The question whether equivalent traffic snapshots (without a bound on the allowed steps) are possible and the infinitely often applicable part respects the specification is, due to a missing termination criterion, semi-decidable (Theorem 3).

Before proceeding with the formalisms needed to prove this claim, we first give a small running example that we will use throughout this section.

Example 3 (Region Automaton and initial Traffic Snapshot). Consider Fig. 2, where a traffic snapshot *TS* with initial values for the cars and a (simplified) region automaton $\mathcal{R}$ are depicted. The non-coloured states in $\mathcal{R}$ are placeholders for possibly more states that we are not interested in. Initially, car B is 15 units ahead of car A (ignoring size and braking distance of car A for simplicity). As also shown in the table, car B is driving pretty slow while car A is driving faster. We assume that in this example, the maximum speed cars can drive with is 13. The maximum positive acceleration force a car can apply is 5 and the maximum negative acceleration force is -10, as cars usually can decelerate stronger than accelerate.

The region automaton specifies that accepting runs of the systems are those where both l_1 and l_3 are visited infinitely often and it is therefore infinitely often the case that:

- The distance between the cars is equal to 15 ($\varphi_1 = \langle re(A) \frown free^{15} \frown re(B) \rangle$).
- The distance between the cars is equal to 21 ($\varphi_3 = \langle re(A) \frown free^{21} \frown re(B) \rangle$).

Including timing constrains that require the formulae to be satisfied alternately within 4 resp. 5 time units, the specification the region automaton is build from would include the TMLSL formulae $\varphi_1 \implies \triangleright_{=4} \varphi_3$ and $\varphi_3 \implies \triangleright_{=5} \varphi_1$. The formula $free^d$ stands for $free \wedge l = d$, describing a free space of length d. $\qquad \square$

While this property might not be the most sensible one, we can depict most of the following concepts using it and do so later.

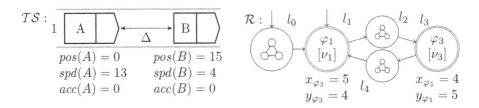

Fig. 2. A traffic snapshot TS including values for the position, speed and acceleration of both cars that we want to evolve in a way that it satisfies the specification translated into the region automaton $\mathcal{R}$. The two colours in $\mathcal{R}$ indicate different Büchi-sets that these (final) states belong to. The other two states summarise more states, which we do not depict for brevity. The constraints of the history clocks x_{φ_1}, x_{φ_3} and the prophecy clocks y_{φ_1}, y_{φ_3} are described below l_1 and l_3, the regions ν_0, ν_2, ν_4 are components of l_0, l_2, l_4, respectively.

In what follows, we assume that there is a region automaton $\mathcal{R}_\varphi$ for our specification φ, as the step of generating it is handled in [12]. A region $[\nu]$ can be described as a set of constraints that restrict the values of both history and prophecy clocks in this region, e.g. $c_1 < x < c_2$ or $x = c_1$ for a clock x and constants c_1 and c_2. We furthermore assume to have a finite sequence of regions $\pi = \langle [\nu_0], [\nu_1], \dots, [\nu_n] \rangle$, which has a suffix that can be repeated and visits each accepting state of $\mathcal{R}_\varphi$ infinitely often and is therefore a potential solution.

There are two steps we use π for: First, we check if discrete actions need to be executed from our initial traffic snapshot onwards. Second, we check the same regarding the dynamic actions. We handle the easier (first) part in Lemma 1 and afterwards focus on the more challenging second part.

Lemma 1 (Discrete Actions between Regions). *Given a sequence of regions $\pi = \langle [\nu_0], [\nu_1], \dots [\nu_n] \rangle$ and a traffic snapshot TS_0, it is decidable if there exist discrete actions that allow the traffic snapshot to evolve in a way that respects π.*

Proof (sketched). It is only possible to have one discrete action at a time in the MLSL model, so the difference between two adjacent regions can only be the result of one discrete action. One can apply every possible discrete action (which are finitely many as there are only finitely many cars and lanes in TS_0) to the corresponding first traffic snapshot and see if the result fits to the restrictions imposed by formulae of the next state, concerning only reservations and claims and ignoring the position of them along the lane. The time-stamps of the actions are the borders of the regions, as executing an action changes which MLSLS formulae are valid on the traffic snapshot and thus the state.   □

In Example 3 there are no discrete actions necessary or even possible between the regions $[\nu_1]$ and $[\nu_3]$, as we only have one lane.

Both the part on finding discrete actions as well as the part on dynamic actions have in common that we want to find actions that are applicable infinitely often. For this purpose, we formalise when two traffic snapshots are equivalent.

Definition 8 (Equivalent Traffic Snapshots). *Two traffic snapshots $TS = (res, clm, pos, spd, acc)$ and $TS' = (res, clm, pos', spd, acc)$ are called equivalent $(TS \equiv TS')$ iff there exists some $r \in \mathbb{R}$ s.t for all cars $c \in \mathbb{I} : pos'(c) = pos(c)+r$.*

Clearly, two equivalent traffic snapshots are indistinguishable by any MLSLS formulae, because the reservations and claims of all cars are on the same lanes in both of them and the distance between each two pair of cars is also the same. Furthermore, if a sequence of actions ϱ led from TS to TS' and $TS \equiv TS'$, ϱ can be applied infinitely often:

Lemma 2 (Infinite applicability). *A time-stamped action sequence ϱ starting in a traffic snapshot TS and ending in TS' with $TS \equiv TS'$ is applicable to TS infinitely often. Therefore, $TS \vDash \varphi$ iff $TS' \vDash \varphi$ for any MLSLS formula φ.*

Proof. By induction over ϱ.   □

Before focusing on the question whether potential solutions are actual solutions and formalising this question by FORCF–formulae, we mention problems that might occur and revisit the running example:

T1 Implicitly, we only consider sequences that start in initial states of $\mathcal{R}(\varphi)$, where the constraints are satisfied by the initial traffic snapshot.

T2 From $\pi = \langle [\nu_0], [\nu_1], \ldots [\nu_n] \rangle$ and TS_0, we need to find a time-stamped action sequence ϱ s.t. φ holds along ϱ from TS_0 onwards and has a part that is infinitely often applicable.

T3 Any two regions $[\nu]$ and $[\nu']$ in π can represent the start resp. end of the part of ϱ that is applicable infinitely often ...

T4 ... as long as this part respects the region automaton's acceptance condition.

T5 We still need to ensure that the dynamic evolution of the traffic snapshot does not violate the state it is supposed to be in.

T6 It may be necessary that some cars change their acceleration not only once but multiple times between two regions.

Example 3 (cont'd). There is one further simplification here to keep the example handy: we assume that car B's acceleration is constantly 0, so we search for actions regarding car A. Going through sequences of regions of increasing length we check whether there exists a sequence of actions that satisfies it. The sequences are $\pi_0 = \langle [\nu_1], \ldots, [\nu_3] \rangle$, $\pi_1 = \langle [\nu_0][\nu_1], \ldots, [\nu_3] \rangle$ and $\pi_2 = \langle [\nu_0][\nu_0][\nu_1], \ldots, [\nu_3] \rangle$. Additionally, we assume that we can stay in ν_0 for 1 time unit.

- π_0 (and any other sequence starting in $[\nu_1]/l_1$) cannot be a solution because it would require car A accelerate to -3.75 to have a distance of 21 to car B within 4 time units, which would result in a negative speed in l_3.
- π_1 cannot be a solution because reducing the speed to maintain a distance of 15 in 1 time unit would require to decelerate by -18, which is beyond our border on the possible deceleration force.
- π_2 is a solution, when car A makes one additional acceleration change in between l_1 and l_3. All values regarding this solution are given in Table 1.

We considered both initial states as their constraints are satisfied by TS. The sequence last considered gave the possibility to reach a traffic snapshot that is equivalent to a previous one, while staying in the same region. Thus, the last loop containing this state is applicable infinitely often and the sequence $[\nu_0][\nu_0]$ $([\nu_1][\nu_2][\nu_3][\nu_4])^\omega$ satisfies our specification from TS onwards. The corresponding sequence of timed actions is $\varrho = (acc(A, -10), 0), (acc(A, -1), 1),$ $(acc(A, 0.75), 3), (acc(A, 0.75), 7), (acc(A, -6), 11), (acc(A, 0.75), 12)$. □

The next definition defines which traffic snapshots are reachable with i possible acceleration changes (**T6**) per car and time bound t. It is used when formalising the evolution that can occur to a traffic snapshot within a single region:

Definition 9 (Step). *Given a traffic snapshot TS_0, the number i of allowed acceleration changes per car, an upper time bound t and a MLSLS-Formula φ_r to be satisfied, $step(TS_0, i, t, \varphi_r)$ is a traffic snapshot TS_n s.t.*

$$\exists a_{c,i} \exists t_{c,i} : TS_0 \xrightarrow{t_{A,1}} TS_1 \xrightarrow{acc(A, a_{A,1})} TS_2 \xrightarrow{t_{B,1}} TS_3 \xrightarrow{acc(B, a_{B,1})} \ldots \xrightarrow{t_{A,m}}$$

$$TS_{n-3} \xrightarrow{acc(A, a_{A,m})} TS_{n-2} \xrightarrow{t_{B,m}} TS_{n-1} \xrightarrow{acc(B, a_{B,m})} TS_n \wedge \varrho(TS_0) \models_{seq} \Box \varphi_r$$

$$\wedge \, \forall a_{c,i} : a_{c,i} \in [a_{min}, a_{max}] \wedge \forall c \in \mathbb{I} : \forall t_i \leq t : spd(c)_{@t_i} \in [0, spd_{max}]$$

with $a_{c,i}$ the acceleration of car c in step i, $\sum_{t_{c,i}} = t$, the overall time elapsed, $\varrho(TS_0)$ is the transition sequence $\varrho = \langle (acc_{A, a_{A,1}}, t_{A,1}), (acc_{B, a_{B,1}}, t_{B,1}), \ldots \rangle$ applied to TS_0 and $spd(c)_{@t_i}$ the speed of car c at time t_i.

The conjunct $\varrho(TS_0) \vDash_{seq} \Box\varphi_r$ was mentioned in Sect. 2.3 and is used to ensure that through the evolution along the transition sequence, each traffic snapshot still satisfies the MLSLS formula φ_r given by the corresponding region (**T5**). A detailed description of how one can formalise these actions by FORCF-formulae can be found in [11]. A formula we may want to be invariant under such a sequence, and thus would be part in every region, is that there is

Location	l_0	l_0	l_1	l_2	l_3	l_1
t	0	1	3	7	11	12
$pos(A)$	0	8	12	22	44	48
$pos(B)$	15	19	27	43	59	63
$spd(A)$	13	3	1	4	7	1
$acc(A)$	-10	-1	0.75	0.75	-6	0.75

Table 1. Possible evolution of TS along the accepting run π_3.

never an overlap in the reservation of two cars, specifying collision freedom.

Unwinding the MLSLS transitions in $step(TS_0, i, t, \varphi_r)$ and handling the traffic snapshot's functions in the points considered as variables, yields FORCF-formulae like the one given below, where the colours correspond to the respective parts in Definition 9. We ignore the handling of different lanes and claims and reservations on them as well as the sensor function here:

$\exists\, \mathsf{a}_{\mathsf{A},1}, \mathsf{a}_{\mathsf{B},1}, \mathsf{a}_{\mathsf{A},2}, \ldots \exists \mathsf{t}_{\mathsf{A},1}, \mathsf{t}_{\mathsf{B},1}, \mathsf{t}_{\mathsf{A},2}, \ldots \exists \mathsf{pos}_1(\mathsf{A}), \mathrm{pos}_2(\mathsf{A}), \ldots, \mathsf{pos}_i(\mathsf{B}), \mathsf{pos}_1(\mathsf{C}), \ldots$

$\exists\, \mathsf{spd}_1(\mathsf{A}), \mathrm{spd}_3(\mathsf{A}), \ldots, \mathsf{spd}_i(\mathsf{B}), \mathsf{spd}_1(\mathsf{C}), \cdots :$

$\mathsf{pos}_1(\mathsf{A}) = \mathsf{pos}_0(\mathsf{A}) + \mathsf{spd}_0(\mathsf{A}) \cdot \mathsf{t}_{\mathsf{A},1} + 0.5 \cdot \mathsf{t}_{\mathsf{A},1}{}^2 \cdot \mathsf{acc}_0(\mathsf{A})$

$\wedge\, \mathsf{pos}_3(\mathsf{A}) = \mathsf{pos}_1(\mathsf{A}) + \mathsf{spd}_1(\mathsf{A}) \cdot \mathsf{t}_{\mathsf{B},1} + 0.5 \cdot \mathsf{t}_{\mathsf{B},1}{}^2 \cdot \mathsf{a}_{\mathsf{A},1}$

$\wedge\, \mathsf{spd}_3(\mathsf{A}) = \mathsf{spd}_1(\mathsf{A}) + \mathsf{a}_{\mathsf{A},1} \cdot \mathsf{t}_{\mathsf{B},1} \wedge \cdots \wedge \mathsf{spd}_1(\mathsf{A}) = \mathsf{spd}_0(\mathsf{A}) + \mathsf{acc}_0(\mathsf{A}) \cdot \mathsf{t}_{\mathsf{A},1}$

$\wedge\, 0 \leq \mathsf{spd}_1(\mathsf{A}) \leq \mathsf{spd}_{\mathrm{max}} \wedge 0 \leq \mathsf{spd}_1(\mathsf{B}) \leq \mathsf{spd}_{\mathrm{max}} \wedge \ldots$

The next definition formalises the outcome of an evolution of a traffic snapshot along a sequence of regions rather than a single region, respecting that there might be discrete actions that took place in between the regions:

Definition 10 (Reach). *Given a sequence of regions* $\pi = \langle [\nu_0], [\nu_2], \ldots, [\nu_n] \rangle$, *a traffic snapshot* TS_0, *and the maximum number* j *of acceleration actions per car and step, we define* $reach(TS_0, \pi, j)$ *as a traffic snapshot* TS_n *s.t.*

$$step(TS_0, j, t_0, \varphi_0) \xrightarrow{\alpha_0} TS_1 \wedge step(TS_1, j, t_1, \varphi_1) \wedge \ldots$$

$$step(TS_{n-2}, j, t_i, \varphi_1) \xrightarrow{\alpha_i} TS_{n-1} \wedge step(TS_{n-1}, j, t_{i+1}, \varphi_2) = TS_n$$

where $\langle (\alpha_0, t_0), \ldots, (\alpha_i, t_i) \rangle$ *is a sequence of discrete actions and time stamps that need to be executed according to Lemma 1,* φ_i *the formula that needs to be satisfied in the regions* $[\nu_i]$ *and* t_i *is the time one is allowed to stay in* $[\nu_i]$.

Thus, *reach* defines all traffic snapshots that are reachable from a given traffic snapshot onwards and respect the constraints given by a sequence of regions and the constraints on the dynamics. For checking the satisfiability of our specification, we are interested in these traffic snapshots that are equivalent to a previous one and therefore restrict the outcome further, but first state that *reach* is correct:

Lemma 3 (Correctness of reach). *Given an initial and a final traffic snapshot TS resp. TS′ and a sequence of regions* $\pi = \langle [\nu_0], [\nu_2], \ldots, [\nu_i] \rangle$, *there exists a finite sequence of time-stamped actions* ϱ *s.t.* $TS \xrightarrow{\varrho} TS′$ *that respects the formulae imposed by* π, *that is, the TMLSL formula* φ *holds along* ϱ, *if and only if there exists a* $j \in \mathbb{N}$ *s.t.* $TS′ = reach(TS, \pi, j)$.

Proof. Due to Lemma 1, *reach* contains exactly the same discrete actions at the same times as ϱ. As ϱ is a finite sequence, there is an upper bound for the maximum number of acceleration actions in ϱ, so there exists a j. Then, *reach* quantifies over all possible combinations of acceleration and discrete actions that do not violate φ or the dynamic restrictions, so iff $TS \xrightarrow{\varrho} TS′$ then there exists a j s.t. $TS′ = reach(TS, \pi, j)$ holds. □

Theorem 1 (Decidability of reaching an equivalent traffic snapshot). *Given* $j \in \mathbb{N}$, *two traffic snapshots TS and TS′ and a sequence of regions* $\pi = \langle [\nu_0], [\nu_2], \ldots, [\nu_n] \rangle$, *it is decidable if* $TS′ \equiv reach(TS, \pi, j)$ *holds.*

Proof (sketched). After Definition 9, we sketched that *step* is expressible by FORCF–formulae. Handling the discrete actions in between can be achieved by extending the variables that respect the functions of the traffic snapshot tuple by a component regarding the possible lanes and the type of the occupation (reservation/claim). The result of this is again a FORCF–formula and thus decidable. □

With this, we can now check if there exist sequences of transitions that are infinitely often applicable to a traffic snapshot and respects the specification.

Definition 11 (Check). *For a sequence of regions* $\pi = \langle [\nu_0], [\nu_1], \ldots, [\nu_n] \rangle$ *and a traffic snapshot* TS_0, *we define* $check(TS_0, \pi)$ *as*

$$\bigvee_{i,j=0}^{n} (reach(TS_0, (\langle [\nu_0], \ldots, [\nu_i] \rangle), j) = TS \equiv reach(TS, \langle [\nu_{i+1}], \ldots, [\nu_n] \rangle, j)$$

$$\wedge \langle [\nu_0], \ldots, [\nu_i] \rangle \cdot \langle [\nu_i], \ldots, [\nu_k] \rangle^{\omega} \in L(\mathcal{R}(A_{\varphi})))$$

The disjunction over all i in the beginning ensures that we find the part of the sequence that generates equivalent traffic snapshots (**T3**) and thus there is an infinitely often applicable sequence of actions (**T2**). The disjunction over j is to respect that a car may need to change its acceleration more than once (**T6**). The second line ensures that the finite prefix concatenated with an infinite repetition of the part we have found is indeed in the language of $\mathcal{R}_{\varphi}$ (**T4**).

For Example 3, the correct instantiation of this predicate would be the one yielding $reach(TS_0, (\langle [\nu_0], [\nu_0], [\nu_0] \rangle), 1) \equiv reach(reach(TS_0, (\langle [\nu_0], [\nu_0], [\nu_0] \rangle), 1), \langle [\nu_1], [\nu_2], [\nu_3], [\nu_4] \rangle, 1)$ with the solution given previously and thus showing that the specification is satisfiable from TS_0 on.

Theorem 2 (Correctness of Check). *If there exists an* $n \in \mathbb{N}$ *s.t. for a traffic snapshot* TS_0 *and a sequence of regions* $\pi = \langle [\nu_0], \ldots, [\nu_n]] \rangle$, $check(TS_0, \pi)$ *is satisfied, then there exists an infinite transition sequence that satisfies the specified properties and respects the restrictions on both speed and acceleration.*

Proof (sketched). The disjunction over i ensures finding the part of the sequence that is applicable infinitely often. Due to Lemma 3, the remainder of the first line is true iff there exists a sequence of actions that leads to an equivalent traffic snapshot. Due to Lemma 2, this sequence is infinitely often applicable. The second line (Definition 11) is checking whether the infinite repetition of $\langle[\nu_{i+1}], \dots [\nu_n]\rangle$ complies to the language $L(\mathcal{R}_\varphi)$. □

By increasing the length of the sequences of regions and therefore the number of steps executed between two states, one can search for sequences that are long enough to allow for infinite applicability. As we do not have a criterion for deciding when to end this search, for now this only shows that TMLSL is semi–decidable:

Theorem 3 (Semi-Decidability of TMLSL–SAT).
The TMLSL–SAT Problem is semi–decidable.

5   Conclusion

Contribution. We combined SCL and MLSL(S) to form the logic TMLSL for expressing timing requirements in highway traffic and illustrated its usefulness on some examples. We showed how one can semi-decide whether a specification given in this logic together with an initial traffic snapshot is satisfiable. To this end, we used a prior approach [12] to find potential sequences of states that could satisfy the given specifications and afterwards check if the traffic situation can behave in a way that these states are actually reached in time.

Future Work. There are several possible directions of future work that we would like to point out. It would be nice to have tool support to check whether a specification is satisfiable from a given traffic snapshot onwards. An implementation of the procedure proposed here is under development, using Rust[1] for generating potential solutions and the tool iSAT [18] for checking them. The solution for the specification and traffic snapshot given in Example 3 was generated by iSAT. The number of locations of the region automaton is exponential in the length of the formula and checking the potential solutions is double exponential in the length of the FORCF-formula, who's length is linear in the length of the potential solution. Luckily, one can check multiple potential solutions at once.

At the moment, we assume global knowledge of the whole traffic snapshot. Further investigation deserves the question, under which conditions the autonomous vehicles can find a satisfying run for a traffic snapshot when they only have partial knowledge about their surrounding, e.g. only have knowledge about other cars' reservations, claims and positions within some range (view). In general, this should not be possible, as the satisfaction of a formulae might depend on the behaviour of another car that one is not aware of at the moment.

---

[1] https://www.rust-lang.org/.

To avoid such issues, *communication* between cars could be used. We therefore plan to use our approach in an *Runtime Enforcement* [19,20] setting: based on the specifications, for each car SC automata are synthesised that represent the satisfaction of their specification up to that time. Whenever a car wants to execute an action, it broadcasts this desire to all other cars, which then, with help of the SC automata, check whether this action might violate their specification in the (near) future. If so, the requested action is denied. Still, this might lead to problems if two cars compete for the same resource (segment of a lane) and announce their resp. actions too late. Therefore cars could repeat these procedure until they finally find a path that respects all cars specifications.

With a lower number of repetitions or communication delays, satisfaction of a specification might not be guaranteed. Still, it would be interesting to see how well the system performs, possibly with an implementation in an simulation environment. While taking this step towards more realistic assumptions, other assumptions might also be weakened, for example the assumption of perfect communication, e.g. that communication between two cars never fails.

References

1. Hilscher, M., Linker, S., Olderog, E.-R., Ravn, A.P.: An abstract model for proving safety of multi-lane traffic manoeuvres. In: Qin, S., Qiu, Z. (eds.) ICFEM 2011. LNCS, vol. 6991, pp. 404–419. Springer, Heidelberg (2011). https://doi.org/10.1007/978-3-642-24559-6_28

2. Hilscher, M., Linker, S., Olderog, E.-R.: Proving safety of traffic manoeuvres on country roads. In: Liu, Z., Woodcock, J., Zhu, H. (eds.) Theories of Programming and Formal Methods. LNCS, vol. 8051, pp. 196–212. Springer, Heidelberg (2013). https://doi.org/10.1007/978-3-642-39698-4_12

3. Linker, S., Hilscher, M.: Proof theory of a multi-lane spatial logic. In: Liu, Z., Woodcock, J., Zhu, H. (eds.) ICTAC 2013. LNCS, vol. 8049, pp. 231–248. Springer, Heidelberg (2013). https://doi.org/10.1007/978-3-642-39718-9_14

4. Ody, H.: Undecidability results for multi-lane spatial logic. In: Leucker, M., Rueda, C., Valencia, F.D. (eds.) ICTAC 2015. LNCS, vol. 9399, pp. 404–421. Springer, Cham (2015). https://doi.org/10.1007/978-3-319-25150-9_24

5. Fränzle, M., Hansen, M.R., Ody, H.: No need knowing numerous neighbours - towards a realizable interpretation of MLSL. In: Meyer, R., Platzer, A., Wehrheim, H. (eds.) Correct System Design. LNCS, vol. 9360, pp. 152–171. Springer, Cham (2015). https://doi.org/10.1007/978-3-319-23506-6_11

6. Hilscher, M., Schwammberger, M.: An abstract model for proving safety of autonomous urban traffic. In: Sampaio, A., Wang, F. (eds.) ICTAC 2016. LNCS, vol. 9965, pp. 274–292. Springer, Cham (2016). https://doi.org/10.1007/978-3-319-46750-4_16

7. Althoff, M., Maierhofer, S., Pek, C.: Provably-correct and comfortable adaptive cruise control. IEEE Trans. Intell. Veh. **6**, 159–174 (2021)

8. Larsen, K.G., Mikučionis, M., Taankvist, J.H.: Safe and optimal adaptive cruise control. In: Meyer, R., Platzer, A., Wehrheim, H. (eds.) Correct System Design. LNCS, vol. 9360, pp. 260–277. Springer, Cham (2015). https://doi.org/10.1007/978-3-319-23506-6_17

9. Loos, S.M., Platzer, A., Nistor, L.: Adaptive cruise control: hybrid, distributed, and now formally verified. In: Butler, M., Schulte, W. (eds.) FM 2011. LNCS, vol. 6664, pp. 42–56. Springer, Heidelberg (2011). https://doi.org/10.1007/978-3-642-21437-0_6

10. Woodcock, J., Davies, J.: Using Z: Specification, Refinement, and Proof. Prentice-Hall Inc, New Jersey (1996)

11. Ody, H.: Monitoring of traffic manoeuvres with imprecise information. Ph.D. thesis, University of Oldenburg, Germany (2020). https://oops.uni-oldenburg.de/4730

12. Raskin, J.-F., Schobbens, P.-Y.: State clock logic: a decidable real-time logic. In: Maler, O. (ed.) HART 1997. LNCS, vol. 1201, pp. 33–47. Springer, Heidelberg (1997). https://doi.org/10.1007/BFb0014711

13. Pnueli, A.: The temporal logic of programs. In: Proceedings of the 18th Annual Symposium on Foundations of Computer Science. In: SFCS 1977, USA, pp. 46–57. IEEE Computer Society (1977)

14. Tarski, A.: A decision method for elementary algebra and geometry. In: Caviness, B.F., Johnson, J.R. (eds.) Quantifier Elimination and Cylindrical Algebraic Decomposition. Texts and Monographs in Symbolic Computation, pp. 24–84. Springer, Vienna (1998). https://doi.org/10.1007/978-3-7091-9459-1_3

15. Bradley, A.R., Manna, Z.: The Calculus of Computation - Decision Procedures with Applications to Verification. Springer, Heidelberg (2007). https://doi.org/10.1007/978-3-540-74113-8

16. Raskin, J., Schobbens, P.: The logic of event clocks - decidability, complexity and expressiveness. J. Autom. Lang. Comb. **4**, 247–282 (1999)

17. Alur, R., Dill, D.L.: A theory of timed automata. Theor. Comput. Sci. **126**, 183–235 (1994)

18. Fränzle, M., Herde, C., Teige, T., Ratschan, S., Schubert, T.: Efficient solving of large non-linear arithmetic constraint systems with complex boolean structure. J. Satisf. Boolean Model. Comput. **1**, 209–236 (2007)

19. Schneider, F.B.: Enforceable security policies. ACM Trans. Inf. Syst. Secur. **3**, 30–50 (2000)

20. Falcone, Y.: You should better enforce than verify. In: Barringer, H., et al. (eds.) RV 2010. LNCS, vol. 6418, pp. 89–105. Springer, Heidelberg (2010). https://doi.org/10.1007/978-3-642-16612-9_9

Denotational and Algebraic Semantics for the CaIT Calculus

Ningning Chen and Huibiao Zhu[✉]

Shanghai Key Laboratory of Trustworthy Computing,
East China Normal University, Shanghai, China
hbzhu@sei.ecnu.edu.cn

Abstract. The Internet of Things (IoT) has been wildly used in various fields of our lives, such as health care, smart environment, transportation, etc. However, the existing research on IoT mainly concentrates on its practical applications, and there is still a lack of work on modelling and reasoning about IoT systems from the perspective of formal methods. Therefore, the Calculus of the Internet of Things (CaIT) has been proposed to model the interactions among components and verify the network deployment to ensure the quality and reliability of IoT systems. Unfortunately, the CaIT calculus can only support point-to-point communication, while broadcast communication is more common in IoT systems. Therefore, this paper updates the CaIT calculus by replacing its communication primitive with the broadcast. Based on the Unifying Theories of Programming (UTP), we further explore its denotational semantics and algebraic semantics, with a special focus on broadcast communication, actions with the timeout (e.g. input actions and migration actions), and channel restriction. To facilitate the algebraic exploration of parallel expansion laws, we further extend the CaIT calculus with a new concept called guarded choice, which allows us to transform each program into the guarded choice form.

Keywords: The CaIT calculus · IoT · UTP · Denotational semantics · Algebraic semantics

1 Introduction

Equipped with "Things" capable of sensing, processing, and communicating, smart devices in IoT systems can collect information from the Internet or the physical environment anytime, anywhere, and provide advanced services to end users. [1,2]. "Things" in IoT systems can be RFID tags that identify objects, sensors that capture changes in the environment, and actuators that provide information to the environment. With the increasing demand for applications and technologies of IoT, a variety of promising technologies (e.g. 5G, high speed, low latency networks, etc.) have been applied to the IoT paradigm. As a result, IoT is rapidly evolving towards IoT 2.0 to further meet the demands of a series of advanced technologies, such as machine learning, edge computing, and Industry 4.0 [3,4]. However, most of the existing studies on IoT are mainly focused on

H. Seidl et al. (Eds.): ICTAC 2022, LNCS 13572, pp. 132–150, 2022.
https://doi.org/10.1007/978-3-031-17715-6_10

its practical applications, and little work has been done to model interactions between components in IoT systems and to check IoT network deployments [5].

As a mathematics-based technique, the formal methods have been widely used to specify, verify, and analyze software and hardware systems, thereby ensuring the quality and reliability of systems. To the best of our knowledge, Lanese et al. have presented the first calculus for IoT named IoT-calculus, which aims to formalize a few fundamental characteristics of IoT systems: the partial topology of communications and the interaction between sensors, actuators, and computing processes [5]. Subsequently, Bodei et al. presented a secure untimed process calculus called IoT-LYSA, which employs static analysis technologies to track the sources and paths of IoT data and detect how they influence smart objects [6]. However, the above two calculi do not consider the effect of time on process actions. Thus, Lanotte et al. proposed the CaIT calculus with reduction semantics and a labeled transition system [7]. In contrast, the CaIT calculus can model discrete time behaviours with consistency and fairness properties by equipping process actions with timeouts. However, the CaIT calculus can only support point-to-point communication, rather than the more general broadcast communication. Thus, this paper refines the original CaIT calculus by replacing its point-to-point communication with broadcast communication [8].

The Unifying Theories of Programming (UTP) has been proposed by He and Hoare in 1998 [9], which has three methods to represent the semantics of a programing language: operational semantics [10], denotational semantics [11], and algebraic semantics [12]. The operational semantics of a programming language provides a complete set of individual steps to simulate the execution, which shows *how a program works* [10]. The denotational semantics gives meaning to a programming language from a purely mathematical point of view, which explains *what a program does* [11]. The algebraic semantics of a programming language includes a series of algebraic laws, which is well suited to the symbolic calculation of parameters and structures of an optimal design. The operational semantics of the CaIT calculus has been explored in [7]. This paper investigates the denotational and algebraic semantics of the CaIT calculus.

The main contributions of this paper are as follows:

- We enrich the CaIT calculus by replacing its point-to-point communication with broadcast communication.
- We explore the denotational semantics of the CaIT calculus, involving the basic commands, the guarded choice, the parallel composition, and channel restriction.
- We investigate the algebraic semantics of the CaIT calculus, especially channel restriction. By establishing the algebraic laws for the parallel composition of guarded choice components, we can describe any program as the guarded choice form.

The rest of this paper is organized as follows. In Sect. 2, we introduce the syntax of the CaIT calculus and the concept of guarded choice that is used to investigate the parallel expansion laws. In Sect. 3, we explore the denotational semantics of the CaIT calculus. In Sect. 4, we propose a set of algebraic laws for the CaIT calculus. The conclusion and future work are in Sect. 5.

2   The CaIT Calculus

In this section, we introduce the syntax of the CaIT calculus. To establish algebraic parallel expansion laws, we then give three kinds of guarded choices.

2.1   Syntax

Compared with the original CaIT calculus proposed in [7], we extend it by introducing more general broadcast communication and adding the migration operation to conveniently model node mobility. As shown in Table 1, the syntax of this calculus has a two-level structure: the first level illustrates the networks, and the second one models the processes. For greater clarity, the extensions have been bolded in Table 1.

Firstly, we define some functions for our exploration. Function $\mathbf{Rng}(c)$ is used to compute the transmission range of channel c. We can calculate the distance between locations l and l_1 with the function $\mathbf{Dis}(l, l_1)$. Two nodes at l and l_1 can communicate via channel c only if the distance between them is within the communication range of channel c, i.e., $\mathbf{Dis}(l, l_1) \leq \mathbf{Rng}(c)$. Otherwise, they cannot communicate via c.

Table 1. The syntax of CaIT calculus

Network			
	N, M	$::= \ 0$	Empty Network
		$\mid \quad M \| N$	Parallel Composition
		$\mid \quad (vc')M$	Channel Restriction
		$\mid \quad n[\Gamma \bowtie P]_l^u$	Node
Process			
	P, Q	$::= \ nil$	Termination
		$\mid \quad P \| Q$	Parallel Composition
		$\mid \quad [b]P, Q$	Conditional Choice
		$\mid \quad !\langle v \rangle^c; P$	**Output**
		$\mid \quad \rho; P$	Intra-node Action
		$\mid \quad \lfloor \pi; P \rfloor Q$	Action with Timeout
		$\mid \quad while \ b \ do \ P$	Iteration
	ρ	$::= \ \sigma$	Delay
		$\mid \quad s?y$	Reading Sensor
		$\mid \quad a!v$	Writing Actuator
	π	$::= \ ?(x)^c$	**Input**
		$\mid \quad move\_k$	**Migration**

Network Level:

(1) 0 stands for an empty network.
(2) $M\|N$ is the parallel composition.
(3) $(vc')M$ indicates that channel c' is private to the network M.

(4) $_n[\Gamma \bowtie P]_l^u$ denotes a network node, where n is the node ID, P is the process modelling the logic of this node, l records its current location, and Γ is its physical interface. The physical interface Γ can map the names of sensors and actuators to values. To ensure the security of nodes, each Γ is private for a node. Given node $_n[\Gamma \bowtie P]_l^u$, only the corresponding *controller process* P can read the values of sensors in Γ. Analogously, the values of actuators in Γ can be modified only by P. u is given to differentiate between stationary nodes (if $u = s$) and mobile nodes (if $u = m$).

Process Level:

(1) *nil* indicates this process terminates.

(2) $P\|Q$ stands for the parallel composition of processes P and Q.

(3) $[b]P, Q$ illustrates the conditional choice, where b has the form as $[w = w']$. If w is equal to w', process P works; otherwise, process Q.

(4) $!\langle v\rangle^c; P$ denotes that after sending the value v via c immediately, P runs.

(5) $\rho; P$ models intra-node actions, where $\rho \in \{\sigma, s?(y), a!v\}$. $\sigma; P$ means that process P starts executing after waiting for one time unit. A node can obtain a value from sensor s and assign it to variable y, denoted by $s?y; P$. Due to the execution of $a!v; P$, the value of the actuator a should be modified to the newly written value v, further leading to the update of Γ, i.e., $\Gamma' = \Gamma[v/\Gamma(a)]$.

(6) $\lfloor \pi; P \rfloor Q$ stands for some actions which execute with the timeout, where $\pi \in \{?(x)^c, \ move\_k\}$. For $\lfloor ?(x)^c; P \rfloor Q$, if a value can be received via channel c within one time unit, it continues as process P after that. Otherwise, Q runs after one time unit. $\lfloor move\_k; P \rfloor Q$ illustrates the node mobility. After delaying one time unit, if the node moves to the destination k successfully, this process terminates, and then P obtains the control at its new location k. Otherwise, Q starts at its original location after one time unit. $\pi; P$ indicates that process P begins only when action π has finished.

(7) *while b do P* is the iteration construct, where b is in the form $[w = w']$.

2.2 Guided Choice

To support our investigation of the algebraic parallel expansion laws, we extend the CaIT calculus with the following three types of guarded choices.

• Instantaneous Guarded Choice:

$$\mathbb{I}_{i \in I}\{g_i \to N_i\},$$

where, $g_i \in \{!\langle v\rangle^c@l, \ ?(x)^c@l, \ c.[v/x]@(l,l_1), \ s?y@l, \ a!v@l, \ move\_k@l, \ b_i\&\tau@l\}$.

The guard g_i is instantaneous, meaning that it executes without any time delay. $!\langle v\rangle^c@l$ indicates that a node at location l sends out the value v via channel c. And $c.[v/x]@(l,l_1)$ denotes that a node at l successfully sends v to another node at l_1 via c, where $[v/x]$ replaces the variable x with the received value v. $b_i\&\tau@l$ represents that a silent action occurs at location l if the Boolean expression

b_i is true, where the silent action does nothing and terminates immediately. For $(vc')M$, it should guarantee that communication actions (output actions or synchronous communication actions) that take place on c' are not visible outside of M. Thus, we conceal them by replacing them with $true\&\tau@l$.

- **Delay Guarded Choice:**

$$\#t \to N$$

The delay guarded choice denotes that the subsequent network N starts after delaying t time units, where t ranges from 0 to 1.

- **Hybrid Guarded Choice:**

$$\|_{i \in I}\{g_i \to N_i\}$$
$$\oplus \exists t' \in (0 \dots 1) \bullet \#t' \to N'$$
$$\oplus \#1 \to N''$$

The third type is the hybrid guarded choice, which has three branches combined by the notation $\oplus$, where $\oplus$ denotes the disjointness of timed behaviours.

3   Denotational Semantics

Here, we present the denotational semantics of the CaIT calculus based on UTP. We first introduce the semantics model and give healthiness conditions that each program must satisfy. We then discuss the denotational semantics of basic commands, guarded choices, the parallel composition, and channel restriction.

3.1   Semantic Model

Compared with the previous UTP theories [9], the CaIT calculus captures some vital characteristics of IoT systems, such as time constraints, communications, the node mobility, etc. To better describe its behaviours, we define the following observation tuple for this calculus.

$$(time, time', st, st', tr, tr')$$

(1) $time$ and $time'$ represent the start and end time points of an observation time interval, respectively. Δ is the time interval, where $\Delta = time' - time$.
(2) st and st' stand for the initial and final execution state of the program, respectively. For a program, it may have three types of execution states.

- ter : If a process terminates successfully, it runs into a ter state. "$st = ter$" means that the previous process terminates successfully, and the current process starts to execute. "$st' = ter$" denotes that the current process terminates successfully, and then the following process starts to work.
- $wait$: A process may be waiting to communicate with another process via a particular channel, as described by the $wait$ state. "$st = wait$" indicates that the previous process is in a $wait$ state. Thus, the current process cannot be executed. Similarly, "$st' = wait$" denotes that the current process reaches a $wait$ state. Therefore, the following process cannot be performed.

- div : When a process enters a div state and never terminates, its future behaviour becomes uncontrollable. $st = div$ means that the previous process diverges. Thus, the current process can never obtain control. $st' = div$ represents that the current process is uncontrolled. Thus, the next process never works.

(3) We introduce the notion of traces to record the communication behaviour of a process. We give a pair of variables tr and tr'. tr presents the initial trace of a process inherited from its predecessor. tr' is the final trace containing the contribution of the current process. $tr' - tr$ is the trace generated by the current process. $tr_1 \frown tr_2$ connects traces tr_1 and tr_2. A trace is a sequence of snapshots. The notation $\mathbf{head}(tr)$ stands for the first snapshot of trace tr. $\mathbf{tail}(tr)$ records the remainder after removing the first snapshot from trace tr. A snapshot is a quadruple formed by (t, l, o, f).

- t represents the time when the communication action occurs.
- l is the location of the node at which a communication action occurs.
- o means that a message is transmitted via a specific channel. The form of o is $c.v$, where c is the communication channel and v is the transmitted message. Further, we define the concepts $\mathbf{Chan}(o)$ and $\mathbf{Mess}(o)$ to obtain the communication channel and the transmitted message from o respectively, i.e., if $o = c.v$, then $\mathbf{Chan}(o) = c$ and $\mathbf{Mess}(o) = v$.
- To conveniently merge traces, we use the flag f to separate communication actions into two types. If $f = 1$, this action is an output action (e.g., $!\langle v \rangle^c$). Otherwise, $f = 2$ means that this is an input action (e.g., $?(x)^c$).

We introduce notations $\pi_i (i = 1, 2, 3, 4)$ to obtain the ith element of a snapshot, such as $\pi_1((t, l, o, f)) =_{df} t$.

3.2 Healthiness Conditions

Here, we give some healthiness conditions which every process must satisfy. **H1** indicates that traces cannot be shortened and time cannot go back. **H2** proposes the following two requirements. If the previous process runs into a $wait$ state, the current process cannot be activated. Thus, all values keep unchanged. Otherwise, the current process executes. As mentioned before, $st = div$ means that the behaviour of the previous process becomes unpredictable. Thus, the current process has never started and the initial values are unobservable. Therefore, **H3** should be satisfied.

(H1) $P = P \wedge \mathbf{Inv}(tr, time)$,
where, $\mathbf{Inv}(tr, time) =_{df} tr \preceq tr' \wedge time \preceq time'$, and $tr \preceq tr'$ denotes that sequence tr is a prefix of sequence tr'.

(H2) $P = \prod \lhd st = wait \rhd P$,
where, $P \lhd b \rhd Q =_{df} (b \wedge P) \vee (\neg b \wedge Q)$, $\prod =_{df} (st' = st) \wedge (time' = time) \wedge (tr' = tr)$.

(H3) $P = \mathbf{Inv}(tr, time) \lhd st = div \rhd P$

To present the denotational semantics for the CaIT calculus, we give the following definition for $\mathbf{H}(X)$, which not only caters to the above three healthiness conditions but is idempotent and monotonic.

$$\mathbf{H}(X) =_{df} \mathbf{Inv}(tr, time) \lhd st = div \rhd \left(\prod \lhd st = wait \rhd \left(X \wedge \mathbf{Inv}(tr, time) \right) \right)$$

3.3 Denotational Semantics of Basic Commands

In this subsection, we explore the denotational semantics of the basic commands. By defining $\mathbf{beh}(N)$, we depict the behaviour of a network N.

(1) Termination: *nil* represents a termination process, so that the execution state, termination time, and trace remain unchanged.

$$\mathbf{beh}(_n[\Gamma \bowtie nil]_l^u) =_{df} \mathbf{H}(st' = st \wedge time' = time \wedge tr' = tr)$$

(2) Sequential Composition: The behaviour of sequential composition is denoted by $N; M$, i.e., running N and M in sequence.

Definition 1. $N; M =_{df} \exists t, s, r \bullet N[t/time', s/st', r/tr'] \wedge M[t/time, s/st, r/tr]$

The denotational semantics of the sequential composition is given below:

$$\mathbf{beh}(N; M) =_{df} \mathbf{beh}(N); \mathbf{beh}(M)$$

(3) Delay: Given a delaying process $_n[\Gamma \bowtie \sigma; P]_l^u$, it denotes that process P starts to execute after one time unit.

$$\mathbf{beh}(_n[\Gamma \bowtie \sigma; P]_l^u) =_{df} \mathbf{beh}(\#1); \mathbf{beh}(_n[\Gamma \bowtie P]_l^u)$$

$\mathbf{beh}(\#t)$ describes the behaviour of waiting for t time units. $\Delta < t$ means that the process has not waited for t time units yet, thus it still needs to wait. In this case, its state and trace keep unchanged. The process stops waiting when $\Delta = t$, formed by $st' = ter$.

$$\mathbf{beh}(\#t) =_{df} \mathbf{H}\left((st' = wait \wedge \Delta < t \wedge tr' = tr) \vee (st' = ter \wedge \Delta = t \wedge tr' = tr)\right)$$

(4) Output: In $_n[\Gamma \bowtie !\langle v \rangle^c; P]_l^u$, the output command happens at the activeness time, modeled by $\mathbf{beh}(!\langle v \rangle^c@l)$. Then process P obtains the control.

$$\mathbf{beh}(_n[\Gamma \bowtie !\langle v \rangle^c; P]_l^u) =_{df} \left(\mathbf{beh}(!\langle v \rangle^c@l); \mathbf{beh}(_n[\Gamma \bowtie P]_l^u)\right)$$

We only need to add the outputting snapshot $(time', l, c.v, 1)$ to the end of the trace tr. The behaviour of $\mathbf{beh}(!\langle v \rangle^c@l)$ is as below.

$$\mathbf{beh}(!\langle v \rangle^c@l) =_{df} \mathbf{H}\left(st' = ter \wedge \Delta = 0 \wedge tr' = tr^{frown}\langle(time', l, c.v, 1)\rangle\right)$$

(5) Input: The semantics definition of an input command has three branches. The first branch (i.e., formula **(5.1)**) indicates that the input action happens at the triggering time. $\mathbf{beh}(?(m)^c@l)$ describes the behaviour of the input command, which means that node at location l receives a value m via channel c. The following behaviour is $\mathbf{beh}(_n[\Gamma \bowtie P[m/x]]_l^u)$. In the second branch (i.e., formula

(5.2)), the input command occurs after t' time units. The last branch (i.e., formula (5.3)) shows that this input command does not happen within one time unit. After delaying one time unit, the following behaviour is $\mathbf{beh}(_n[\Gamma \bowtie Q]_l^u)$. Here, $Type(c)$ denotes the type of messages transmitted in channel c.

$$\mathbf{beh}(_n[\Gamma \bowtie \lfloor ?(x)^c; P \rfloor Q]_l^u) =_{df}$$
$$\begin{pmatrix} \exists m \in Type(c) \bullet \mathbf{beh}(?(m)^c@l); \mathbf{beh}(_n[\Gamma \bowtie P[m/x]]_l^u) \vee & (5.1) \\ \exists t' \in (0\ldots 1) \bullet \mathbf{beh}(\#t'); \exists m \in Type(c) \bullet \mathbf{beh}(?(m)^c@l); & \\ \mathbf{beh}(_n[\Gamma \bowtie P[m/x]]_l^u) \vee & (5.2) \\ \mathbf{beh}(\#1); \mathbf{beh}(_n[\Gamma \bowtie Q]_l^u) & (5.3) \end{pmatrix}$$

Now, we describe the behaviour of $\mathbf{beh}(?(m)^c@l)$. The input action is instantaneous, thus, $\Delta = 0$. To record the input action, the snapshot $(time', l, c.m, 2)$ is added to the end of the trace.

$$\mathbf{beh}(?(m)^c@l) =_{df} \mathbf{H}\left(st' = ter \wedge \Delta = 0 \wedge tr' = tr^\frown \langle (time', l, c.m, 2) \rangle \right)$$

(6) Migration: We explore the denotational semantic of the moving command $\lfloor move\_k; P \rfloor Q$. Here, δ is the maximum distance that the node n can move within one time unit, which is set for the node in advance. For one time unit, the migration action is in a waiting state and its trace is unchanged. After one time unit, if it moves to the destination k successfully (i.e., $\mathbf{Dis}(k, l) \leq \delta$), a silent action $\mathbf{beh}(\tau@l)$ and a moving command $\mathbf{beh}(move\_k@l)$ happen sequentially, and the following behaviour is $\mathbf{beh}(_n[\Gamma \bowtie P]_k^m)$. Otherwise, a silent action $\mathbf{beh}(\tau@l)$ occurs, and then it continues as $\mathbf{beh}(_n[\Gamma \bowtie Q]_l^m)$.

$$\mathbf{beh}(_n[\Gamma \bowtie \lfloor move\_k; P \rfloor Q]_l^m) =_{df}$$
$$\left(\mathbf{beh}(\#1); \begin{pmatrix} \mathbf{beh}(\tau@l); \mathbf{beh}(move\_k@l); \mathbf{beh}(_n[\Gamma \bowtie P]_k^m) \\ \lhd Dis(l, k) \leq \delta \rhd \\ (\mathbf{beh}(\tau@l); \mathbf{beh}(_n[\Gamma \bowtie Q]_l^m)) \end{pmatrix} \right)$$

where, $\mathbf{beh}(move\_k@l) =_{df} \mathbf{H}\left(st' = ter \wedge \Delta = 0 \wedge tr' = tr \right)$,
$$\mathbf{beh}(\tau@l) =_{df} \mathbf{H}\left(st' = ter \wedge \Delta = 0 \wedge tr' = tr \right).$$

As mentioned before, traces are used to record the behaviour of communications. Thus, actions (i.e., the migration action) that do not involve communication need not be stored in traces.

(7) Reading Sensor: Now, we analyze the behaviour of reading a value from a sensor s, that is $\mathbf{beh}(s?\Gamma(s)@l))$. After that, the following behaviour is described by $\mathbf{beh}(_n[\Gamma \bowtie P[\Gamma(s)/y]]_l^u)$.

$$\mathbf{beh}(_n[\Gamma \bowtie s?y; P]_l^u) =_{df} \mathbf{beh}(s?\Gamma(s)@l); \mathbf{beh}(_n[\Gamma \bowtie P[\Gamma(s)/y]]_l^u)),$$
$$\text{where, } \mathbf{beh}(s?\Gamma(s)@l)) =_{df} \mathbf{H}\left(st' = ter \wedge \Delta = 0 \wedge tr' = tr \right).$$

(8) Writing Actuator: If the original value of actuator a (i.e., $\Gamma(a)$) is not the newly written value v, $\mathbf{beh}(\tau@l)$ and $\mathbf{beh}(a!v@l)$ perform orderly, and then process P is executed under the new interface Γ', where $\Gamma' = \Gamma[v/\Gamma(a)]$. Otherwise, P runs under Γ after $\mathbf{beh}(\tau@l)$.

$$\mathbf{beh}(_n[\Gamma \bowtie a!v; P]_l^u) =_{df} \left(\begin{array}{c} (\mathbf{beh}(\tau@l); \mathbf{beh}(a!v@l); \mathbf{beh}(_n[\Gamma' \bowtie P]_l^u)) \\ \triangleleft \Gamma(a) \neq v \triangleright (\mathbf{beh}(\tau@l); \mathbf{beh}(_n[\Gamma \bowtie P]_l^u)) \end{array} \right),$$

where, $\mathbf{beh}(a!v@l) =_{df} \mathbf{H}\left(st' = ter \wedge \Delta = 0 \wedge tr' = tr \right)$.

(9) Conditional: The behaviour of the condition choice is as follows.

$$\mathbf{beh}(_n[\Gamma \bowtie [b]P,Q]_l^u) =_{df} \left(\mathbf{beh}(_n[\Gamma \bowtie \tau; P]_l^u) \triangleleft b \triangleright \mathbf{beh}(_n[\Gamma \bowtie \tau; Q]_l^u) \right)$$

(10) Iteration: Referring to the traditional programming language, we give the denotational semantics of the iteration construct. F is a monotonic function mapping processes to processes. Based on the previously proposed healthy formulas, we give its the weakest fixed point, i.e., $\mu_{HF}F(X)$.

$$\mathbf{beh}(_n[\Gamma \bowtie while\ b\ do\ P]_l^u) =_{df} \mathbf{beh}(_n[\Gamma \bowtie \mu_{HF}X \bullet [b](P; X),nil]_l^u)$$

3.4   Denotational Semantics of Guarded Choice

There are three types of guarded choices. In this subsection, we give their denotational semantics.

- **Instantaneous Guard Choice:** $\mathbf{beh}(\|_{i \in I}\{g_i \rightarrow N_i\})$ indicates that an instantaneous action g_i is triggered, and the corresponding network N_i executes.

$$\mathbf{beh}(\|_{i \in I}\{g_i \rightarrow N_i\}) =_{df} \bigvee_{i \in I} \mathbf{beh}(g_i \rightarrow N_i)$$

where, $g_i \in \{!\langle v \rangle^c@l,\ ?(x)^c@l,\ c.[v/x]@(l,l_1),\ s?y@l,\ a!v@l,\ move\_k@l,\ b_i\&\tau@l\}$.

▲ If $g_i = c.[v/x]@(l,l_1)$, then
   $\mathbf{beh}(c.[v/x]@(l,l_1) \rightarrow N_i) =_{df} \mathbf{beh}(c.[v/x]@(l,l_1)); \mathbf{beh}(N_i[v/x])$,
   where, $\mathbf{beh}(c.[v/x]@(l,l_1)) =_{df} \mathbf{H}\left(st' = ter \wedge \Delta = 0 \wedge tr^\frown \langle (time', l, c.v, 1) \rangle \right)$.
   The instantaneous guard $c.[v/x]@(l,l_1)$ denotes that a node at l sends value v to another node at l_1 via channel c successfully, described as $\mathbf{beh}(c.[v/x]@(l,l_1))$. According to the characteristics of broadcast communication, the behaviour of broadcast communication actions can be simply described as broadcast output commands. Therefore, the snapshot $(time', l, c.v, 1)$ is added to the end of the trace tr.
   ▲ If $g_i = b_i\&\tau@l$, then $\mathbf{beh}(b_i\&\tau@l \rightarrow N_i) =_{df} b_i \wedge (\mathbf{beh}(\tau@l); \mathbf{beh}(N_i))$,
   where $beh(\tau@l)$ has been defined in Sect. 3.3 (6).
   The denotational semantics of other types of instantaneous guards can be established similarly.
- **Delay Guarded Choice:**

$$\mathbf{beh}(\#t \rightarrow N) =_{df} \mathbf{beh}(\#t); \mathbf{beh}(N)$$

For the delay guarded choice, it waits for the given time units, and then N gains the control. $\mathbf{beh}(\#t)$ has been given in Sect. 3.3 (3).

• **Hybrid Guarded Choice:**

$$G =_{df} \|_{i \in I} \{g_i \to N_i\}$$
$$\oplus \exists t' \in (0 \ldots 1) \bullet \#t' \to N'$$
$$\oplus \#1 \to N''$$

$\|_{i \in I} \{g_i \to N_i\}$ is the instantaneous guarded choice. $\exists t' \in (0 \ldots 1) \bullet \#t' \to N'$ has a delay guarded choice followed by the instantaneous guarded choice. $\#1 \to N''$ only contains the delay guarded choice.

$$\mathbf{beh}(G) =_{df} \begin{pmatrix} \bigvee_{i \in I} \mathbf{beh}(g_i \to N_i) \vee & (1) \\ \exists t' \in (0 \ldots 1) \bullet \mathbf{beh}(\#t'); \mathbf{beh}(N') \vee & (2) \\ \mathbf{beh}(\#1); \mathbf{beh}(N'') & (3) \end{pmatrix}$$

There are three branches corresponding to three cases that are progressive over time. In the first branch (*i.e.*, formula (1)), the instantaneous guard is triggered at the activation time of this process. The second branch (*i.e.*, formula (2)) denotes that the instantaneous guard is activated after waiting for t' time units. If the instantaneous guard cannot be triggered before one time unit, it is described by the third branch (*i.e.*, formula (3)). Obviously, the above three branches are disjoint.

3.5   Parallel Composition

In this subsection, we discuss the behaviour of two parallel networks. Here, a network may be a single node or the parallel composition of multiple nodes. The denotational of the parallel composition is presented below:

$$\mathbf{beh}(N_1 \| N_2) =_{df} \mathbf{beh}(N_1) \| \mathbf{beh}(N_2) =_{df}$$

$$\begin{pmatrix} \exists st_1, st_1', st_2, st_2', time_1, time_1', time_2, time_2', tr_1, tr_1', tr_2, tr_2' \bullet \\ \quad st_1 = st_2 = st \wedge time_1 = time_2 = time \wedge tr_1 = tr_2 = tr \wedge & (1) \\ \mathbf{beh}(N_1)[st_1, st_1', time_1, time_1', tr_1, tr_1'/st, st', time, time', tr, tr'] \wedge & (2) \\ \mathbf{beh}(N_2)[st_2, st_2', time_2, time_2', tr_2, tr_2'/st, st', time, time', tr, tr'] \wedge & (3) \\ Merge & (4) \end{pmatrix}$$

The first formula (i.e., formula (1)) means that the initial value of the state, time, and trace of the two parallel components are the same. The following two formulas (i.e., formulas (2) and (3)) show the independent behaviour of two components. In the last one (i.e., formula (4)), the predicate $Merge$ is used to merge states, termination time, and the traces (snapshot sequences) contributed by the two behavioral branches.

$$Merge =_{df} \begin{pmatrix} ((st_1' = ter \wedge st_2' = ter) \Rightarrow st' = ter) \wedge \\ ((st_1' = div \vee st_2' = div) \Rightarrow st' = div) \wedge \\ ((st_1' = wait \wedge st_2' \neq div) \vee (st_1' \neq div \wedge st_2' = wait) \Rightarrow st' = wait) \\ \wedge time' = max(time_1', time_2') \wedge \\ \exists trace \in (tr_1' - tr_1) \| (tr_2' - tr_2) \bullet tr' = tr\,\widehat{}\,trace \end{pmatrix}$$

If the final states of N_1 and N_2 are both *ter* states, the final state of $N_1\|N_2$ is *ter*. As long as one of them runs into a *div* state, the final state of $N_1\|N_2$ is *div*. If one of the two networks reaches a *wait* state, and the other is not in a *div* state, $N_1\|N_2$ is in a *wait* state. The termination time of the parallel composition is the maximum terminal time of N_1 and N_2.

Here, s and t represent the traces of N_1 and N_2, respectively. As mentioned before, a trace is a sequence of snapshots, and a snapshot is a quadruple (t, l, o, f). Next, we present some rules to merge traces. (**rule 1**) means that if both traces are empty (denoted by ϵ), the merged trace is still empty. (**rule 2**) indicates that the merged trace is not empty as long as one trace is not empty. (**rule 3**) denotes that the parallel composition of two traces is symmetrical.

- (**rule 1**) $\epsilon\|\epsilon =_{df} \{\epsilon\}$ • (**rule 2**) $s\|\epsilon =_{df} \{s\}$ • (**rule 3**) $s\|t =_{df} t\|s$

To emerge two nonempty traces, we propose the following notations to obtain the elements of their first snapshots (i.e., $\mathbf{head}(s)$ and $\mathbf{head}(t)$).

$$t_1 = \pi_1(\mathbf{head}(s)),\; l_1 = \pi_2(\mathbf{head}(s)),\; o_1 = \pi_3(\mathbf{head}(s)),\; f_1 = \pi_4(\mathbf{head}(s)),$$
$$t_2 = \pi_1(\mathbf{head}(t)),\; l_2 = \pi_2(\mathbf{head}(t)),\; o_2 = \pi_3(\mathbf{head}(t)),\; f_1 = \pi_4(\mathbf{head}(t)).$$

According to whether t_1 is equal to t_2, we discuss the following two cases: (1) $t_1 = t_2$ means that communication actions o_1 and o_2 happen at the same time, resolved by (**rule 4**). Before merging them, we take out communication channels and transmitted messages from o_1 and o_2, respectively.

$$c_1 = \mathbf{Chan}(o_1),\quad m_1 = \mathbf{Mess}(o_1),\quad c_2 = \mathbf{Chan}(o_2),\quad m_2 = \mathbf{Mess}(o_2).$$

- (**rule 4**) We describe the details of (**rule 4**) through the following steps:

▲ **Step 1:** If their channels are different (i.e., $c_1 \neq c_2$), we only need to append $\mathbf{head}(s)$ or $\mathbf{head}(t)$ into the end of the merged trace, described as T'. Otherwise, we go to **Step 2** for further inspection.

▲ **Step 2:** If $f_1 = 1 \vee f_2 = 1$ is true, it means that one of them is a sender, and another one is a receiver, then we go to **Step 3**. Otherwise, they are both receivers, and we go to **Step 7**.

▲ **Step 3:** If $f_1 = 1$ is true, it denotes that the node at l_1 is the sender, and another one at l_2 is a receiver, we go to **Step 4**. Otherwise, we go to **Step 6**.

▲ **Step 4:** If the communication condition (i.e., $\mathbf{Dis}(l_1, l_2) \leq \mathbf{Rng}(c)$) is satisfied, then we go to **Step 5**. Otherwise, we merge traces as T'.

▲ **Step 5:** Both o_1 and o_2 should have the same message, i.e., $m_1 = m_2$. If so, $\mathbf{head}(s)$ is added to the end of the merged trace. Otherwise, the merged trace is an empty set $\emptyset$.

▲ **Step 6:** We discuss the case in which the node at l_2 is the sender, which is similar to steps 4 and 5.

▲ **Step 7:** Now, we explore the case in which two nodes are both receivers. If o_1 and o_2 have the same message, (i.e., $m_1 = m_2$), we extend the merged trace with the snapshot $(t_1, \{l_1, l_2\}, o_1, 2)$. Otherwise, the merged trace is $\emptyset$.

$$s\|t =_{df} \left(\left(\left(\left(\begin{array}{c} \left((T_1 \lhd m_1 = m_2 \rhd \emptyset) \lhd \mathbf{Dis}(l_1, l_2) \leq \mathbf{Rng}(c_1) \rhd T'' \right) \\ \lhd f_1 = 1 \rhd \\ \left((T_2 \lhd m_1 = m_2 \rhd \emptyset) \lhd \mathbf{Dis}(l_1, l_2) \leq \mathbf{Rng}(c_1) \rhd T'' \right) \end{array} \right) \\ \lhd f_1 = 1 \vee f_2 = 1 \rhd \left(T_3 \lhd m_1 = m_2 \rhd \emptyset \right) \\ \lhd c_1 = c_2 \rhd T' \right) \right),$$

where,

$T' =_{df} \mathbf{head}(s)^\frown(\mathbf{tail}(s)\|t) \cup \mathbf{head}(t)^\frown(s\|\mathbf{tail}(t)), \quad T_1 =_{df} \mathbf{head}(s)^\frown(\mathbf{tail}(s)\|\mathbf{tail}(t)),$

$T_2 =_{df} \mathbf{head}(t)^\frown(\mathbf{tail}(s)\|\mathbf{tail}(t)), \qquad T_3 =_{df} \langle(t_1, \{l_1, l_2\}, o_1, 2)\rangle^\frown(\mathbf{tail}(s)\|\mathbf{tail}(t)).$

(2) If $t_1 \neq t_2$, o_1 and o_2 do not occur simultaneously, as shown in **(rule 5)**.
• **(rule 5)** If $t_1 < t_2$, o_1 happens before o_2. In this case, $head(s)$ is added to the end of the merged trace. Otherwise, $head(t)$ extends the merged trace.

$$s\|t =_{df} \begin{cases} \mathbf{head}(s)^\frown(\mathbf{tail}(s)\|t), & \text{if } t_1 < t_2. \\ \mathbf{head}(t)^\frown(s\|\mathbf{tail}(t)), & \text{if } t_1 > t_2. \end{cases}$$

3.6 Channel Restriction

As mentioned before, $(vc')M$ indicates that channel c' is private to the network M. Thus, sending messages via c' is invisible outside of M. Based on the above subsections of Sect. 3, we can obtain the denotational semantics of M. To further gain the denotational semantics of $(vc')M$, we need to remove the snapshots which record output actions and synchronous communication actions occurring on c' from the trace of M.

$$\mathbf{beh}((vc')M) =_{df} \left(\begin{array}{c} \mathbf{beh}(M)[\mathbf{Re}(tr' - tr, c')/tr' - tr, div/str'] \\ \lhd\mathbf{Diverge}(\mathbf{beh}(M), c')\rhd \\ \mathbf{beh}(M)[\mathbf{Re}(tr' - tr, c')/tr' - tr] \end{array} \right),$$

where, $\mathbf{Diverge}(\mathbf{beh}(M), c') =_{df} \forall n \bullet \exists t \bullet t = (tr' - tr) \wedge \#(t \upharpoonright c') > n.$

If the condition $\mathbf{Diverge}(\mathbf{beh}(M), c')$ is true, it means that the behaviour of M (i.e., $\mathbf{beh}(M)$) diverges due to the concealment of channel c'. In other words, $(vc')M$ may generate an infinite sequence of hidden actions (i.e., output actions and synchronous communication actions occurring on c'). Here, $tr' - tr$ is the trace generated by M. $t \upharpoonright c'$ represents a sub-trace of t that contains only the behaviour of the hidden actions, and $\#(t \upharpoonright c')$ is its length. The following function $\mathbf{Re}(s, c')$ removes the hidden actions involving c' from a trace s, where the predefinition function π_i gets the ith element from the first snapshot $\mathbf{head}(s)$ (Page 6) of trace s.

$$\mathbf{Re}(s, c') =_{df} \left(\left(\begin{array}{c} \mathbf{Re}(\mathbf{tail}(s), c') \\ \lhd\mathbf{Chan}(\pi_3(\mathbf{head}(s))) = c' \rhd (\mathbf{head}(s)^\frown\mathbf{Re}(\mathbf{tail}(s), c')) \\ \lhd\pi_4(\mathbf{head}(s)) = 1 \rhd (\mathbf{head}(s)^\frown\mathbf{Re}(\mathbf{tail}(s), c')) \end{array} \right) \right)$$

Example 1. Now, we give the following example to illustrate the CaIT calculus.

$$N = (vc)(N_1 \| N_2) \| N_3 \qquad N_1 =_{n_1} [\Gamma_1 \bowtie !\langle v_1 \rangle^c; \lfloor move\_l'_1; !\langle v_2 \rangle^{c'}; nil \rfloor nil]_{l_1}^m$$

$$N_2 =_{n_2} [\Gamma_2 \bowtie \lfloor ?(x)^c; nil \rfloor nil]_{l_2}^{u_2} \qquad N_3 =_{n_3} [\Gamma_3 \bowtie \sigma; \lfloor ?(y)^{c'}; nil \rfloor nil]_{l_3}^{u_3}$$

For simplicity, we assume that the activeness time of N is 0, and all communication and migration conditions on distance are satisfied. For example, $Dis(l_1, l_2) \leq Rng(c)$ at time 0. The channel c is private to nodes n_1 and n_2, but c' is shared by three nodes. Next, we explore the trace of N to show the usability of our denotational semantics.

(1) At time 0, node n_1 sends the value v_1 via c to n_2. After one time unit, n_1 moves to l'_1, and n_3 completes the delaying. After that, n_1 sends v_2 to n_2 at time 1. The traces of N_1, N_2, and N_3 are t, s, and w, respectively.

$$t = <(0, l_1, c.v_1, 1), (1, l'_1, c'.v_2, 1)>$$

$$s = <(0, l_2, c.v_1, 2)> \qquad w = <(1, l_3, c'.v_2, 2)>$$

(2) Then, we merge the t and s by using the rules of parallel compositions. In detail, the snapshots in the above two shaded areas are merged into one snapshot shown in the following shaded area.

$$t \| s = <(0, l_1, c.v_1, 1), (1, l'_1, c'.v_2, 1)>$$

(3) We conceal communication actions occurring on c to further obtain the trace T of $(vc)(N_1 \| N_2)$. Finally, we get the final trace of N by further merging w and T.

$$T = <(1, l'_1, c'.v_2, 1)>$$

(4) Finally, we get the final trace of N by further merging w and T.

$$T \| w = <(1, l'_1, c'.v_2, 1)>$$

4   Algebraic Semantics

4.1   Algebraic Laws of Basic Commands

We explore the algebraic laws of basic commands for the CaIT calculus. For **Input** and **Migration** commands, each one has two algebraic laws according to the different time intervals, i.e., their timers are 0 or greater than 0.

- **(Input0)** $_n[\Gamma \bowtie \lfloor ?(x)^c; P \rfloor^0 Q]_l^u =_n [\Gamma \bowtie Q]_l^u$

- **(Migration0)** $n[\Gamma \bowtie \lfloor move\_k; P\rfloor^0 Q]_l^m = \Big[\begin{cases} (Dis(l,k) \leq \delta)\&\tau@l \to move\_k@l \to \\ \quad n[\Gamma \bowtie P]_{k,\delta}^m, \\ \neg(Dis(l,k) \leq \delta)\&\tau@l \to_n [\Gamma \bowtie Q]_l^m \end{cases} \Big]$

- **(Delay)** $n[\Gamma \bowtie \sigma; P]_l^u = \#1 \to_n [\Gamma \bowtie P]_l^u$

- **(Input)** $n[\Gamma \bowtie \lfloor ?(x)^c; P\rfloor Q]_l^u = ?(x)^c@l \to_n [\Gamma \bowtie P]_l^u$

  $\qquad\qquad \oplus \exists t' \in (0\ldots 1) \bullet \#t' \to ?(x)^c@l \to_n [\Gamma \bowtie P]_l^u$

  $\qquad\qquad \oplus \#1 \to_n [\Gamma \bowtie Q]_l^u$

- **(Migration)** $n[\Gamma \bowtie \lfloor move\_k; P\rfloor Q]_l^m = \#1 \to_n [\Gamma \bowtie \lfloor move\_k; P\rfloor^0 Q]_l^m$

- **(Output)** $n[\Gamma \bowtie ! \langle v \rangle^c; P]_l^u = ! \langle v \rangle^c@l \to_n [\Gamma \bowtie P]_l^u$

- **(Reading Sensor)** $n[\Gamma \bowtie s?y; P]_l^u = s?y@l \to_n [\Gamma \bowtie P]_l^u$

- **(Writing Actuator)** $n[\Gamma \bowtie a!v; P]_l^u = \Big[\begin{cases} (\Gamma(a) \neq v)\&\tau@l \to a!v@l \to_n [\Gamma' \bowtie P]_l^u, \\ \neg(\Gamma(a) \neq v)\&\tau@l \to_n [\Gamma \bowtie P]_l^u \end{cases} \Big]$,

  where $\Gamma' = \Gamma[v/\Gamma(a)]$.

- **(Conditional)** $n[\Gamma \bowtie [b]P, Q]_l^u = \Big[\begin{cases} b\&\tau@l \to_n [\Gamma \bowtie P]_l^u, \\ \neg b\&\tau@l \to_n [\Gamma \bowtie Q]_l^u \end{cases} \Big]$

- **(Iteration)** $n[\Gamma \bowtie while\ b\ do\ P]_l^u = \Big[\begin{cases} b\&\tau@l \to_n [\Gamma \bowtie P; while\ b\ do\ P]_l^u, \\ \neg b\&\tau@l \to_n [\Gamma \bowtie nil]_l^u \end{cases} \Big]$

4.2   Algebraic Laws of Parallel Composition

Now, we explore the algebraic laws of the parallel composition. The empty network 0 is the identity of parallel composition, described by (**par-1**). The parallel composition of networks is symmetric and associative, as shown in (**par-2**) and (**par-3**).

- **(par-1)** $N\|0 = N = 0\|N$
- **(par-2)** $N\|M = M\|N$
- **(par-3)** $N\|(M\|R) = (N\|M)\|R$

Then we explore the algebraic laws of the parallel composition of guarded choices. In Sect. 2.2, we have proposed three types of guarded choices. Thus, there should be nine parallel expansion laws. Since the parallel composition is symmetric, we only give seven parallel expansion laws, as shown in Table 2.

Table 2. Parallel composition of two guarded choices

	Instantaneous	Delay	Hybrid
Instantaneous	(par-4-1), (par-4-2)	(par-5)	(par-6)
Delay		(par-7)	(par-8)
Hybrid			(par-9)

We first investigate the parallel composition of two instantaneous guarded components, shown in (**par-4-1**) and (**par-4-2**).

- **(par-4-1)** $N = \Big[_{i\in I}\{g_i \to N_i\} \qquad M = \Big[_{j\in J}\{h_j \to M_j\}$

  $N\|M = \Big[_{i\in I}\{g_i \to N_i\|M\}\Big[\Big[_{j\in J}\{h_j \to N\|M_j\}$

Here, we suppose that there are no communications between N and M. (**par-4-1**) shows the parallel composition of two instantaneous guarded choice components without communications. In this case, the first action of $N\|M$ is either g_i or h_j, and it converts into $N_i\|M$ or $N\|M_j$ correspondingly.

- (**par-4-2**) $N = N_1 \| N_2$ $N_1 = \|_{i \in I}\{g_i \rightarrow N_i\}$ $N_2 = \|_{w \in W}\{!\langle v_w \rangle^{c_w} @ l_w \rightarrow N'_w\}$

           $M = M_1 \| M_2$ $M_1 = \|_{j \in J}\{h_j \rightarrow M_j\}$ $M_2 = \|_{w \in W}\{?(x_w)^{c'_w} @ l'_w \rightarrow M'_w\}$

We assume that there are no communications between N_1 and M_1, and the communication condition (i.e., $c_w = c'_w \wedge \mathbf{Dis}(l_w, l'_w) \leq \mathbf{Rng}(c_w)$) is satisfied.

$$N\|M = \|_{i \in I}\{g_i \rightarrow N_i \| M\}$$
$$\| \|_{j \in J}\{h_j \rightarrow N \| M_j\}$$
$$\| \|_{w \in W}\{c_w \cdot [v_w / x_w] @ (l_w, l'_w) \rightarrow N'_w \| M'_w\}$$

There are three possibilities for the first action, i.e., g_i, h_j or communication action $c_w \cdot [v_w / x_w] @ (l_w, l'_w)$. Due to the features of broadcast communication, $c_w \cdot [v_w / x_w] @ (l_w, l'_w)$ can be seen as an output action continuing to communicate with other nodes.

- (**par-5**) $\|_{i \in I}\{g_i \rightarrow N_i\} \| \#t \rightarrow M = \|_{i \in I}\{g_i \rightarrow (N_i \| \#t \rightarrow M)\}$

Here, we discuss the parallel composition of the instantaneous guarded choice and the delay guarded choice. g_i is executed at the activation time, and then the process evolves as $N_i \| \#t \rightarrow M$.

- (**par-6**) $N = \|_{i \in I}\{g_i \rightarrow N_i\}$ $M = \|_{j \in J}\{h_j \rightarrow M_j\}$

                                        $\oplus \#t' \rightarrow M'$

                                        $\oplus \#1 \rightarrow M''$, for $t' \in (0 \dots 1)$.

           $N\|M = \|_{i \in I}\{g_i \rightarrow N_i\} \| \|_{j \in J}\{h_j \rightarrow M_j\}$

Here, we investigate the parallel composition of the instantaneous choice and the hybrid guarded choice. Clearly, the parallel composition is equal to the parallel composition of two instantaneous guarded choice components. We can obtain the final result based on the laws (i.e., (**par-4-1**) and (**par-4-2**)).

- (**par-7**) $N = \{\#t_1 \rightarrow N'\}$ $M = \{\#t_2 \rightarrow M'\}$

This is the parallel composition of two delay guarded choice components. N_1 and N_2 wait for t_1 and t_2 time units, respectively. Here, both t_1 and t_2 range from 0 to 1. There are three possibilities:

▲ If $t_1 < t_2$, then $N\|M = \#t_1 \rightarrow (N' \| (\#(t_2 - t_1) \rightarrow M'))$.

       N and M delay t_1 time units together, and then N turns into N'. But M still has to wait for $t_2 - t_1$ time units before converting into M'.

▲ If $t_1 = t_2$, then $N\|M = \#t_1 \rightarrow N' \| M'$.

▲ If $t_1 > t_2$, then $N\|M = \#t_2 \rightarrow (\#(t_1 - t_2) \rightarrow N' \| M')$.

- **(par-8)** $N = \|_{i \in I}\{g_i \to N_i\}$ $\qquad\qquad$ $M = \{\#t_1 \to M'\}$, for $t_1 \in [0 \dots 1]$.
  $\oplus \#t' \to N'$
  $\oplus \#1 \to N''$, for $t' \in (0 \dots 1)$.

Then, we analyze the parallel composition of the hybrid guarded choice and the delay guarded choice, which has the following two possibilities:

▲ If $t_1 < 1$, then $\ N\|M = \|_{i \in I}\{g_i \to N_i\|M\}$
$$\oplus \#t' \to (N'\|\#(t_1 - t') \to M')$$
$$\oplus \#t_1 \to N_1\|M', \text{ for } t' \in (0 \dots t_1),$$

where, $\quad N_1 = \|_{i \in I}\{g_i \to N_i\}$
$$\oplus \#t'' \to N'$$
$$\oplus \#(1 - t_1) \to N'', \text{ for } t'' \in (0 \dots 1 - t_1).$$

In this case, there are three alternative branches. In the first branch, g_i is triggered at the beginning time of the process. In the second one, g_i executes after waiting for t' time unit, and then this process is translated into $(N'\|\#(t_1 - t') \to M')$. For the last one, after t_1 time units, $N\|M$ evolves as $N_1\|M'$.

▲ If $t_1 = 1$, then $\ N\|M = \|_{i \in I}\{g_i \to N_i\|M\}$
$$\oplus \#t'' \to (N'\|\#(1 - t'') \to M')$$
$$\oplus \#1 \to N''\|M', \text{ for } t'' \in (0 \dots 1).$$

- **(par-9)** $N = \|_{i \in I}\{g_i \to N_i\}$ $\qquad\qquad$ $M = \|_{j \in J}\{h_j \to M_j\}$
  $\oplus \#t_1 \to \|_{i \in I}\{g_i \to N_i\}$ $\qquad\quad$ $\oplus \#t_2 \to \|_{j \in J}\{h_j \to M_j\}$
  $\oplus \#1 \to N'$, for $t_1 \in (0 \dots 1)$. $\qquad$ $\oplus \#1 \to M'$, for $t_2 \in (0 \dots 1)$.

The parallel composition of networks N and M is as below.

$$N\|M = \|_{i \in I}\{g_i \to N_i\} \ \| \ \|_{j \in J}\{h_j \to M_j\}$$
$$\oplus \#t' \to (\|_{i \in I}\{g_i \to (N_i\|M_1)\} \ \| \ \|_{j \in J}\{h_j \to (N_1\|M_j)\})$$
$$\oplus \#1 \to N' \ \| \ M', \text{ for } t' \in (0 \dots 1).$$

where, $N_1 = \|_{i \in I}\{g_i \to N_i\}$ $\qquad\qquad\qquad$ $M_1 = \|_{j \in J}\{h_j \to M_j\}$
$\quad \oplus \#t_1' \to \|_{i \in I}\{g_i \to N_i\}$ $\qquad\qquad\quad$ $\oplus \#t_2' \to \|_{j \in J}\{h_j \to M_j\}$
$\quad \oplus \#(1 - t') \to N',$ $\qquad\qquad\qquad\qquad$ $\oplus \#(1 - t') \to M',$
for $t_1', t_2' \in (0 \dots 1 - t')$.

In (**par-9**), we study the parallel composition of two hybrid guarded choice components with three branches. In the first branch, $N\|M$ equals $\|_{i \in I}\{g_i \to N_i\} \ \| \ \|_{j \in J}\{h_j \to M_j\}$ which has been analyzed in (**par-4-1**) and (**par-4-2**). The second branch means that an instantaneous action happens after t' time units, whose final results can be gained similar to the first case. In the third, no instantaneous action occurs before one time unit. After one time unit, $N\|M$ continues as $N'\|M'$.

- **(par-10)** According to the above laws, we find that any parallel program without restricted channels can be converted into the guarded choice form. To further describe the channel restriction (i.e., $(vc')M$), we give this law to replace output actions and synchronous communication actions happening in c' (i.e., $!\langle v \rangle^{c'} @l$ and $c'.[v/x]@(l, l_1)$) with the silent action $true\&\tau@l$, where l and l_1 are arbitrary locations in M.

▲ If $M = \|_{i \in I}\{g_i \rightarrow M_i\}$, then $(vc')M = \|_{i \in I}\{(vc')g_i \rightarrow (vc')M_i\}$.

▲ If $M = \#t \rightarrow M'$, then $(vc')M = \#t \rightarrow (vc')M'$.

▲ If $M = \|_{i \in I}\{g_i \rightarrow M_i\}$, then $(vc')M = \|_{i \in I}\{(vc')g_i \rightarrow (vc')M_i\}$

$\qquad \oplus \#t_1' \rightarrow M' \qquad\qquad\qquad\qquad \oplus \#t_1' \rightarrow (vc')M'$

$\qquad \oplus \#1 \rightarrow M'' \qquad\qquad\qquad\qquad \oplus \#1 \rightarrow (vc')M'',$

where, $(vc')g_i = \begin{cases} true\&(\tau@l), & \text{if } g_i \in \{!\langle v \rangle^{c'}@l, \ c'.[v/x]@(l, l_1)\}. \\ i, & \text{otherwise.} \end{cases}$

Example 2. Here, we continue to explore N mentioned in Example 1 (Page 12) to show the application of guarded choices and algebraic laws, where the first action of each parallel composition is represented in the shaded area.

(1.1) We get the first action of $N_1 \| N_2$ by using **(par-4-2)** and **(par-1)**.

$$N_1 \| N_2 = \boxed{c.v_1@(l_1, l_2)} \rightarrow N_1^1, \text{ where } N_1^1 =_{n_1} [\Gamma_1 \bowtie \lfloor move\_l_1'; !\langle v_2 \rangle^{c'}; nil \rfloor nil]_{l_1}^m.$$

(1.2) Then we can obtain the first action of $(vc)(N_1 \| N_2)$ by applying **(par-10)** to concealing the communication action happening on c.

$$(vc)(N_1 \| N_2) = \boxed{true\&(\tau@l_1)} \rightarrow (vc)N_1^1$$

(1.3) Now, we can know the first action of N (i.e., $(vc)(N_1 \| N_2) \| N_3$) with **(par-8)**.

$$(vc)(N_1 \| N_2) \| N_3 = \boxed{true\&(\tau@l_1)} \rightarrow (vc)N_1^1 \| N_3$$

(2) We further gain the first action () of $(vc)N_1^1 \| N_3$ according to **(par-7)** and **(par-5)**.

$$(vc)N_1^1 \| N_3 = \boxed{\#1} \rightarrow Dis(l_1, l_1') \leq \delta)\&\tau@l_1 \rightarrow move\_l_1'@l_1 \rightarrow (vc)N_1^2 \| N_3^1,$$

where, $(vc)N_1^2 \| N_3^1 = (vc)_{n_1}[\Gamma_1 \bowtie !\langle v_2 \rangle^{c'}; nil]_{l_1'}^m \|_{n_3} [\Gamma_3 \bowtie \lfloor ?(y)^{c'}; nil \rfloor nil]_{l_3}^{u_3}.$

(3) We use **(par-4-2)** and **(par-1)** to get the first action of $(vc)N_1^2 \| N_3^1$.

$$(vc)N_1^2 \| N_3^1 = \boxed{c'.v_2@(l_1', l_3)}$$

After the above steps, we can finally gain the guard choice form of N. It indicates that each program of the CaIT calculus can be converted into a guard choice form, even if the channel restriction is involved. In addition, it means that a parallel program can be sequentialized by using our algebraic laws.

5   Conclusion and Future Work

The CaIT calculus has been proposed to specify and verify IoT systems with discrete time, while it can only support point-to-point communication. In this paper, we have enhanced the CaIT calculus by introducing the more common broadcast communication. Furthermore, we explored its denotational and algebraic semantics based on the UTP framework, focusing on broadcast communication, actions with the timeout, and even channel restriction. To establish the parallel expansion laws, we have presented three types of guarded choices so that each program can be transformed into the guarded choice form.

In the future, we will study the deductive semantics of the CaIT calculus via Hoare Logic [13]. We will further explore the semantics linking theory of the CaIT calculus and try to implement it in suitable tools like Coq, Isabelle/HOL, PVS, etc.

Acknowledgements. This work was partly supported by the National Natural Science Foundation of China (Grant Nos. 62032024, 61872145), "Digital Silk Road" Shanghai International Joint Lab of Trustworthy Intelligent Software (Grant No. 22510750100), and the Dean's Fund of Shanghai Key Laboratory of Trustworthy Computing (East China Normal University).

References

1. Zhang, Y.: Technology framework of the Internet of Things and its application. Int. Conf. Electr. Control Eng. **2011**, 4109–4112 (2011)
2. Ashton, K.: That "Internet of Things" thing: in the real world things matter more than ideas. RFID J. (2009). http://www.rfidjournal.com/articles/view?4986
3. Gubbi, J., Buyya, R.: Internet of Things (IoT): a vision, architectural elements, and future directions. Future Gener. Comput. Syst. **29**(7), 1645–1660 (2013)
4. Miorandi, D., Sicari, S., De Pellegrini, F.: Internet of Things: vision, applications and research challenges. Ad Hoc Netw. **10**(7), 1497–1516 (2012)
5. Lanese, I., Bedogni, L., Di Felice M.: Internet of Things: a process calculus approach. In: SAC 2013, pp. 1339–1346 (2013)
6. Where do your IoT ingredients come from? COORDINATION 2016, pp. 35–50 (2016)
7. Lanotte, R., Merro, M.: A semantic theory of the Internet of Things. Inf. Comput. **259**(1), 72–101 (2018)
8. Singh, A., Ramakrishnan, C.R., Smolka, S.A.: A process calculus for mobile ad hoc networks. Sci. Comput. Program. **75**(6), 440–469 (2010)
9. Jifeng, H., Hoare, C.A.R.: Unifying Theories of Programming, pp.97–99. RelMiCS (1998)
10. Gordon, D.: Plotkin: a structural approach to operational semantics. J. Log. Algebraic Methods Program **60–61**, 17–139 (2004)
11. Stoy, J.E.: Foundations of denotational semantics. In: Bjøorner, D. (ed.) Abstract Software Specifications. LNCS, vol. 86, pp. 43–99. Springer, Heidelberg (1980). https://doi.org/10.1007/3-540-10007-5_35

12. Hennessy M.: Algebraic Theory of Processes. MIT Press Series in the Foundations of Computing, pp. I–VI, 1–270. MIT Press, Cambridge (1988). ISBN 978-0-262-08171-9

13. Apt, K.R., de Boer, F.S., Olderog E.R.: Verification of Sequential and Concurrent Programs. Texts in Computer Science, pp. i–xxiii, 1–502. Springer, Heidelberg (2009). ISBN 978-1-84882-744-8. https://doi.org/10.1007/978-1-84882-745-5

Reconciling Communication Delays and Negation

Luís Cruz-Filipe[1]([⊠])(ID), Graça Gaspar[2](ID), and Isabel Nunes[2](ID)

[1] Department of Mathematics and Computer Science,
University of Southern Denmark, Odense, Denmark
lcfilipe@gmail.com
[2] LASIGE, Department of Informatics, Faculty of Sciences,
University of Lisbon, Lisbon, Portugal
{mdgaspar,minunes}@fc.ul.pt

Abstract. Hypothetical continuous query answering over data streams was introduced as a way to anticipate answers to queries that depend on facts that may or may not happen in the future. Previous work has studied this problem for Temporal Datalog with negation and instantaneous communication, showing that hypothetical answers can be incrementally updated as new data arrives at the data stream.

In practice, individual communications take variable amounts of time, so data may arrive delayed and unordered. This motivates studying hypothetical continuous query answering in a setting with communication delays. The interaction between communication delays and negation is however problematic, and the existing approach is restricted to the positive fragment of the language. In this work we show how to remove this restriction by defining an appropriate operational semantics based on fixpoint theory, and showing that the relevant fixpoints can be computed in finite time by a carefully designed algorithm.

1 Introduction

The world of today is a constant stream of information, and the world of reasoning is no exception. Current reasoning systems are expected to receive data constantly (e.g., from sensors) and react to it in real time, continuously producing results in an online fashion. This task is known as *continuous query answering*.

One of the mainstream approaches to continuous query answering [7,15,34, 37,40] considers reasoners based on logic-programming style rules depending on facts that arrive through a *data stream* (an abstract conceptualization of the inflow of information), and applies logic-based methods to compute answers to those queries.

These approaches to continuous query answering all suffer from one drawback: they only produce output once something is guaranteed to be true. In some

---

Partially supported by FCT through the LASIGE Research Unit, ref. UIDB/00408/2020 and ref. UIDP/00408/2020.

H. Seidl et al. (Eds.): ICTAC 2022, LNCS 13572, pp. 151–169, 2022.
https://doi.org/10.1007/978-3-031-17715-6_11

applications – for example, if answers to queries correspond to system malfunctions – it is interesting to be able to have information about possibilities, rather than certainties, as this information can be used to foresee undesirable events. This observation led to the introduction of *hypothetical answers* to continuous queries [12]: answers that are consistent with (and even supported by) the information provided until now by the data stream, but that require additional future facts to be proven. Furthermore, for programs without negation, hypothetical answers can be computed by a polynomial online algorithm with an offline preprocessing step.

Most previous work on stream reasoning makes strong assumptions on the data stream – typically, that it is *ordered*: information about a given time point t is only produced after all information about previous points in time has been output. For a theoretical development, this is equivalent to assuming instantaneous communication (by disregarding the actual arrival time); in practice, such a constraint is not easy to implement, and may delay the whole system – as it requires waiting long enough to know that there can be no more information about time points previous to t lingering in the system [4,16,38].

Removing the assumption of an ordered data stream is tricky, since typical strategies for continuous query answering immediately break down. In the context of logical approaches to continuous query answering, the possibility of working with data that arrives out-of-order was considered in [13]. This work showed how hypothetical query answering could be addressed in a scenario with variable communication delays, but only for a language without negation – the strategy for addressing communication delays directly conflicted with the treatment of negation in [12]. Even with this restriction, the online step of the algorithm for computing hypothetical answers is no longer polynomial.

In the present work, we reconcile communication delays and negation. We show that it is possible to define an operational semantics for hypothetical continuous query answering by adapting previous definitions, accommodating for both communication delays and negation. This operational semantics is defined as the least fixpoint of a monotonic operator over a suitably defined bilattice [19], where the orders in each component reflect the two different ways in which negative information can affect hypothetical answers. The complexity stems mainly from the fact that default negation is non-monotonic, but hypothetical answers are by nature monotonic: we essentially work with Kleene's 3-valued logic, where answers to queries may be known to be true, known to be false, or unknown (as of yet). Our procedure for incrementally computing hypothetical answers in the presence of delays capitalizes on flexible strategies that deal with information as it arrives while acknowledging the possibility that older data may still arrive later on. The only requirement is that a limit is known to how delayed the information may be, which we argue is reasonable in many practical applications.

Structure. Section 2 revisits the syntax of Temporal Datalog [37] and the main ideas behind the formalism of hypothetical answers [13] in the presence of communication delays. Section 3 defines the declarative semantics of hypothetical answers for communication delays in the presence of negation. Section 4 is the bulk of our contribution, showing how an operational semantics for hypothetical answers can be defined by using a fixpoint construction. Section 5 presents the adapted online algorithm for computing this operational semantics under suitable assumptions. Section 6 discusses related work and concludes.

2   Background

This article builds heavily on previous work. In this section, we summarize the key concepts that are relevant for understanding our contribution.

2.1   Continuous Queries over Datastreams in Temporal Datalog

The language we work with is *Temporal Datalog* extended with negation, which is obtained from Datalog by adding the special temporal sort from [10]. Our formalism for writing continuous queries over datastreams closely follows that from [37], with only minor modifications.

Temporal Datalog extends Datalog [9] by allowing constants and variables to have two sorts: *object* or *temporal*. Sorts carry over to terms: an *object term* is either an object constant or an object variable, and a *time term* is either a natural number, a time variable, or an expression of the form $T + k$ where T is a time variable and k is an integer. Time constants are also called *timestamps*.

Predicates take exactly one temporal parameter, which is the last one. We define atoms, rules, facts and programs as usual, and assume rules to be safe: each variable in the head must occur in the body. A term, atom, rule, or program is *ground* if it contains no variables. In particular, all facts are ground. We write $\mathsf{var}(\alpha)$ for the set of variables occurring in an atom α, and extend this function homomorphically to rules and sets.

A predicate symbol is said to be *intensional* or IDB if it occurs in an atom in the head of a rule with non-empty body, and *extensional* or EDB if it is defined only through facts. This classification extends to atoms in the natural way.

Substitutions are functions mapping a finite set of variables to terms of the expected sort. Given a rule r and a substitution θ, the corresponding *instance* $r' = r\theta$ of r is obtained by simultaneously replacing every variable X in r by $\theta(X)$ and computing any additions of temporal constants.

A *temporal query* is a pair $\langle \Pi, Q \rangle$ where Π is a program and Q is an IDB atom in the language underlying Π. We do not require Q to be ground, and typically the temporal parameter is uninstantiated.[1] We thereafter refer to $\langle \Pi, Q \rangle$ as query Q (over Π).

A *dataset* is a family $D = \{D|_\tau \mid \tau \in \mathbb{N}\}$, where $D|_\tau$ contains the set of EDB facts delivered by a data stream at time point τ. Note that every fact in $D|_\tau$ has timestamp at most τ; facts with timestamp lower than τ correspond to communication delays. We call $D|_\tau$ the τ-*slice* of D, and define also the τ-history

---

[1] The most common exception is if Q represents a property that does not depend on time, where by convention the temporal parameter is instantiated to 0.

$D_\tau = \bigcup\{D|_{\tau'} \mid \tau' \leq \tau\}$. It follows that $D|_\tau = D_\tau \backslash D_{\tau-1}$ for every τ, and that D_τ also contains only facts whose temporal argument is at most τ. By convention, $D_{-1} = \emptyset$.

A substitution θ is an *answer* to query Q over Π and D if $\Pi \cup D \models Q\theta$.

We model communication delays by means of a function δ that maps each ground EDB atom in the language of Π to a natural number. The intuition is: if $\delta(P(t_1, \ldots, t_n)) = d$ and $P(t_1, \ldots, t_n) \in D|_\tau$, then $t_n \leq \tau \leq t_n + d$. We assume throughout this article that all datasets and delays satisfy this property. Function δ is extended to non-ground atoms by defining $\delta(P(t_1, \ldots, t_n))$ as the maximum of all $\delta(P(t'_1, \ldots, t'_n))$ such that $P(t'_1 \ldots, t'_n)$ is a ground instance of $P(t_1, \ldots, t_n)$, and to predicate symbols by $\delta(P) = \delta(P(X_1, \ldots, X_n))$. Furthermore, we assume that $\delta(P) < \infty$ for every predicate symbol P – this is trivially the case if the delay cannot depend on the timestamp, which is a reasonable assumption in many practical scenarios.

Example 1. The following program Π_E tracks activation of cooling measures in a set of wind turbines equipped with sensors, recording malfunctions and shutdowns, based on temperature readings $\mathsf{Temp}(\textit{Device}, \textit{Level}, \textit{Time})$.

$$\mathsf{Temp}(X, \mathsf{high}, T) \rightarrow \mathsf{Flag}(X, T)$$
$$\mathsf{Flag}(X, T) \wedge \mathsf{Flag}(X, T+1) \rightarrow \mathsf{Cool}(X, T+1)$$
$$\mathsf{Cool}(X, T) \wedge \mathsf{Flag}(X, T+1) \rightarrow \mathsf{Shdn}(X, T+1)$$
$$\neg\mathsf{Shdn}(X, T) \rightarrow \mathsf{OK}(X, T-2)$$

Two high temperature readings in a row should activate the cooling system on the corresponding turbine; if the temperature remains high, there has been a malfunction, and the turbine shuts down. If the turbine does not shutdown, then we can conclude that it was working properly two time steps previously.

Suppose that there are two turbines wt2 and wt4, and that we know that communications from turbine wt2 take at most 1 time units, while those from turbine wt4 can take up to 2. Then we have e.g. $\delta(\mathsf{Temp}(\mathsf{wt2}, \mathsf{high}, 2)) = 1$, $\delta(\mathsf{Temp}(\mathsf{wt4}, X, Y)) = 2$, and $\delta(\mathsf{Temp}) = 2$.   ◁

2.2 Hypothetical Answers to Continuous Queries

Hypothetical answers to continuous queries were introduced in [12] as a means to identify potential future answers to queries – substitutions that can become answers depending on data that may yet arrive, and in particular are compatible with the available information. Furthermore, if the dataset already contains facts without which a substitution would not be an answer, then we call the corresponding hypothetical answer *supported*. We present the definitions from [13], as the original work did not consider the possibility of communication delays. These definitions only apply to the positive fragment of the language; we extend them to include negation in Sect. 3.

Definition 1. *A* hypothetical answer *to query Q over Π and D_τ is a pair $\langle\theta, H\rangle$, where θ is a substitution and H is a finite set of ground EDB atoms (the hypotheses) such that:*

- $\mathsf{supp}(\theta) = \mathsf{var}(Q)$, *i.e., θ only changes variables that occur in Q;*
- *H only contains* future-possible *atoms for τ, i.e., atoms for which $\tau < t_n + \delta(P(t_1, \ldots, t_n))$;*
- *$\Pi \cup D_\tau \cup H \models Q\theta$;*
- *H is minimal with respect to set inclusion.*

If the minimal subset E of D_τ such that $\Pi \cup E \cup H \models Q\theta$ is non-empty, then $\langle\theta, H, E\rangle$ is a supported answer *to Q over Π and D_τ.*

Example 2. We illustrate these concepts with Example 1. Assume that $D|_0 = \{\mathsf{Temp}(\mathsf{wt2}, \mathsf{high}, 0)\}$ and $D|_1 = \emptyset$, and let $\theta = [X := \mathsf{wt2}, T := 2]$. Then

$$\langle\theta, \{\mathsf{Temp}(\mathsf{wt2}, \mathsf{high}, 1), \mathsf{Temp}(\mathsf{wt2}, \mathsf{high}, 2)\}\rangle$$

is a hypothetical answer to query $Q_E = \langle\Pi_E, \mathsf{Shdn}(X, T)\rangle$ over D_1, reflecting the intuition that $\mathsf{Temp}(\mathsf{wt2}, \mathsf{high}, 1)$ may still arrive in $D|_2$. This answer is supported by $\mathsf{Temp}(\mathsf{wt2}, \mathsf{high}, 0)$.   ◁

2.3   Operational Semantics

We begin by presenting the operational semantics for hypothetical answers by means of an online algorithm with pre-processing as defined in [13] – that is, without considering the possibility of negation. We assume the reader to have some familiarity with the operational semantics of logic programming.

Pre-processing. The pre-processing step applies SLD-resolution to the program and the query Q until it reaches a goal containing only EDB atoms, and returns a set P_Q containing a pair $\langle\theta, H\rangle$ for each successful derivation, where θ is the computed substitution for that derivation and H contains all the atoms in the leaf.

Pre-processing can be shown to terminate under some assumptions [12], which we do not discuss here. Soundness and completeness of pre-processing state that:

- if $\langle\theta, H\rangle \in P_Q$, then there exist a dataset D and substitution σ such that $Q\theta\sigma$ is ground, $H\theta \subseteq \bigcup D$ and $\theta\sigma$ is an answer to Q over Π and D;
- if σ is an answer to Q over Π and D, then there exists $\langle\theta, H\rangle \in P_Q$ such that $\sigma = \theta\rho$ for some ρ and $H\rho \subseteq \bigcup D$.

Example 3. In the context of Example 2, pre-processing query Q_E yields the singleton set

$$P_{Q_E} = \{\langle\emptyset, \{\mathsf{Temp}(X, \mathsf{high}, T), \mathsf{Temp}(X, \mathsf{high}, T+1), \mathsf{Temp}(X, \mathsf{high}, T+2)\}\rangle\}.$$

It is straightforward to check that this set has the properties stated above.   ◁

Online Step. The online part of the algorithm maintains a set of schematic hypothetical answers $\mathcal{S}_\tau$, where τ is the current timestamp, of the form $\langle \theta, E, H \rangle$, where E is a set of evidence.

Definition 2. *An atom $P(t_1, \ldots, t_n)$ is a* potentially future *atom wrt τ if either t_n contains a temporal variable or t_n is ground and $\tau < t_n + \delta(P(t_1, \ldots, t_n))$.*

This notion is an operational counterpart to the concept of future-possible atom, generalizing it to possibly non-ground atoms. In particular, any atom whose temporal parameter contains a variable is potentially future – intuitively, because it can be instantiated to a future timestamp.

Definition 3. *Let Γ and Δ be sets of atoms such that all atoms in Δ are ground. A substitution σ is a* local mgu *for Γ and Δ if, for every substitution θ such that $\Gamma\theta \cap \Delta = \Gamma\sigma \cap \Delta$, there exists another substitution ρ such that $\theta = \sigma\rho$.*

Local mgus were introduced to handle communication delays. Intuitively, a local mgu unifies a set of hypotheses with a subset of the datastream – leaving the possibility that some hypotheses may be instantiated at a later point in time. Local mgus can be computed by SLD-resolution [13].

Definition 4. *The set $\mathcal{S}_\tau$ of* schematic supported answers *for query Q at time τ is defined as follows.*

- $\mathcal{S}_{-1} = \{\langle \theta, \emptyset, H \rangle \mid \langle \theta, H \rangle \in \mathcal{P}_Q\}$.
- *If $\langle \theta, E, H \rangle \in \mathcal{S}_{\tau-1}$ and σ is a local mgu for H and $D|_\tau$ such that $H\sigma \backslash D|_\tau$ only contains potentially future atoms wrt τ, then $\langle \theta\sigma, E \cup E', H\sigma \backslash D|_\tau \rangle \in \mathcal{S}_\tau$, where $E' = H\sigma \cap D|_\tau$.*

This algorithm is sound and complete: the supported hypothetical answers at each time point τ are exactly the ground instantiations of the schematic answers computed at the same time point.

Example 4. We illustrate this mechanism in the setting of Example 2, where

$$\mathcal{P}_{Q_E} = \{\langle \emptyset, \underbrace{\{\mathsf{Temp}(X, \mathsf{high}, T), \mathsf{Temp}(X, \mathsf{high}, T+1), \mathsf{Temp}(X, \mathsf{high}, T+2)\}}_{H} \rangle\}.$$

We start by setting $\mathcal{S}_{-1} = \{\langle \emptyset, \emptyset, H \rangle\}$. Since $D|_0 = \{\mathsf{Temp}(\mathsf{wt2}, \mathsf{high}, 0)\}$, the local mgus for H and $D|_0$ are $\emptyset$ and $[X := \mathsf{wt2}, T := 0]$. Therefore,

$$\mathcal{S}_0 = \{\langle \emptyset, \emptyset, \{\mathsf{Temp}(X, \mathsf{high}, T), \mathsf{Temp}(X, \mathsf{high}, T+1), \mathsf{Temp}(X, \mathsf{high}, T+2)\} \rangle,$$
$$\langle [X := \mathsf{wt2}, T := 0], \{\mathsf{Temp}(\mathsf{wt2}, \mathsf{high}, 0)\}, \underbrace{\{\mathsf{Temp}(\mathsf{wt2}, \mathsf{high}, i) \mid i = 1, 2\}}_{H_0} \rangle\}.$$

Next, $D|_1 = \emptyset$, so the empty substitution is the only local mgu of H_0 and $D|_1$. Furthermore, H_0 only contains potentially future atoms wrt 1 because $\delta(\mathsf{Temp}(\mathsf{wt2}, X, Y)) = 1$. The same argument applies to $D|_1$ and H, so $\mathcal{S}_1 = \mathcal{S}_0$.

We now consider several possibilities for what happens to the schematic supported answer $\langle [X := \mathsf{wt2}, T := 0], \{\mathsf{Temp}(\mathsf{wt2}, \mathsf{high}, 0)\}, H_0 \rangle$ at time instant 2. Since H_0 is ground, the only local mgu of H_0 and $D|_2$ is $\emptyset$.

- If $\mathsf{Temp}(\mathsf{wt2}, \mathsf{high}, 1) \notin D|_2$, then $H_0 \backslash D|_2$ contains $\mathsf{Temp}(\mathsf{wt2}, \mathsf{high}, 1)$, which is not a potentially future atom wrt 2, and therefore this schematic supported answer is discarded.
- If $\mathsf{Temp}(\mathsf{wt2}, \mathsf{high}, 1) \in D|_2$ but $\mathsf{Temp}(\mathsf{wt2}, \mathsf{high}, 2) \notin D|_2$, then $H_0 \backslash D|_2 = \{\mathsf{Temp}(\mathsf{wt2}, \mathsf{high}, 2)\}$, which only contains potentially future atoms wrt 2, and therefore $\mathcal{S}_2$ contains the schematic supported answer

$$\langle [X := \mathsf{wt2}, T := 0], \{\mathsf{Temp}(\mathsf{wt2}, \mathsf{high}, i) \mid i = 0, 1\}, \{\mathsf{Temp}(\mathsf{wt2}, \mathsf{high}, 2)\} \rangle.$$

- Finally, if $\{\mathsf{Temp}(\mathsf{wt2}, \mathsf{high}, 1), \mathsf{Temp}(\mathsf{wt2}, \mathsf{high}, 2)\} \subseteq D|_2$, then $H_2 \backslash D|_2 = \emptyset$, and the system can output the answer $[X := \mathsf{wt2}, T := 0]$ to the original query. In this case, this answer (with no hypotheses) would be added to $\mathcal{S}_2$, and then trivially copied to all subsequent $\mathcal{S}_\tau$. ◁

2.4 Adding Negation

The original work on hypothetical answers [12] considers a language with negation (but without communication delays). We briefly recap the concepts that we reuse from that work, and summarize the intuitions that will reappear in the current development.

Pre-processing a program whose rule bodies can contain negative literals is a generalization of the previous construction. Negative literals are not allowed to be selected during the SLD-derivation, and as a consequence they may also appear in the leaves of derivations. For each such literal $\neg P(t_1, \ldots, t_n)$ a fresh auxiliary query $\langle \Pi, P(X_1, \ldots, X_n) \rangle$ is generated by replacing all terms with variables.[2] All generated queries are then in turn pre-processed, and may spawn additional auxiliary queries. The process is iterated until no fresh queries arise.

Example 5. Consider again the program from Example 1, where we now consider the query $Q_{OK} = \langle \Pi_E, \mathsf{OK}(X, T) \rangle$.

Pre-processing Q_{OK} yields $P_{Q_{OK}} = \{\langle \emptyset, \neg \mathsf{Shdn}(X, T + 2) \rangle\}$, generating the auxiliary query Q_E from Example 2. Pre-processing the latter is as in Example 3; in particular it generates no fresh auxiliary queries, so we are done. ◁

Given a set of literals A, we write A^+ for the subset of positive literals in A, and A^- for the set of negative literals in A.

The online step of the algorithm for the scenario without communication delays is presented in detail in [11]. We do not discuss it here, as it has to be adapted for the current setting. The relevant aspects are explained later (Sect. 5). Its termination is only proved for programs that are T-stratified.

Definition 5. *Let Π be a program and let $\Pi^\downarrow$ be the program obtained from P by grounding every rule in P and replacing every atom $P(t_1, \ldots, t_{n-1}, t)$ with $P_t(t_1, \ldots, t_{n-1})$. (So every predicate symbol P in Π generates a family of predicate symbols $\{P_n \mid n \in \mathbb{N}\}$ in $\Pi^\downarrow$.)*

Program Π is T-stratified if $\Pi^\downarrow$ is stratified (in the usual sense).

---

[2] See [11] for a discussion on alternative strategies for generating the auxiliary queries. The approach used here has the advantage that there is at most one query for each predicate symbol, which simplifies the presentation.

3   Declarative Semantics of Negation with Delays

To define a declarative semantics for hypothetical answers, we introduce the following data structure. We assume a fixed set of queries $Q = \{Q_i\}_{i \in I}$, obtained by pre-processing a particular query Q_0 over a program Π, and a τ-history D_τ.

Definition 6. *A datastream D is a possible extension of D_τ, $D \ni D_\tau$, if D's τ-history is exactly D_τ.*

In particular, any elements of D that do not appear in D_τ are necessarily future-possible wrt τ.

Definition 7. *A generalized hypothetical answer to Q over a τ-history D_τ is a family S of tuples $\langle Q, \theta, E, H \rangle$ where:*

- *$Q \in Q$;*
- *θ is a closed substitution ranging over the variables in Q;*
- *E and H are disjoint sets of EDB atoms and negated IDB atoms such that $E^+ \subseteq D_\tau$ and all elements of H^+ are future-possible wrt τ;*
- *for every $\langle Q, \theta, E, H \rangle \in S$ and $D \ni D_\tau$, (i) $\Pi \cup D \models E^-$ and (ii) if $\Pi \cup D \models H$, then $\Pi \cup D \models Q\theta$.*

This notion differs from hypothetical answers defined in previous work in two ways: it allows negated IDB atoms in hypotheses and evidence; and it is "flattened" in the sense that it contains tuples whose first component is the query they relate to, rather than being a family indexed on queries. These options simplify our development.

4   Operational Semantics of Negation with Delays

Our goal is to define (recursively) a sequence $\{S_n^{\downarrow}\}_{n \geq -1}$ such that $S_i^{\downarrow}$ is a generalized hypothetical answer to Q over D_i. In general, these sets are infinite – in the next section we discuss how to compute finite representations of them.

For every $Q \in Q$, we initialize $S_{-1}^{\downarrow}$ as follows: for each $\langle \theta, H \rangle \in P_Q$, $S_{-1}^{\downarrow}$ contains all tuples $\langle Q, \sigma|_Q, \emptyset, H\sigma \rangle$ where σ instantiates all free variables in H and Q, $\sigma = \theta\rho$ for some ρ, and $\sigma|_Q$ is the restriction of σ to the variables that appear in Q.

$S_{\tau+1}^{\downarrow}$ is defined in two steps. First, we update $S_\tau^{\downarrow}$ with the information from the dataset: we define an auxiliary generalized hypothetical answer $A_{\tau+1}$ containing all tuples $\langle Q, \theta, E \cup (H^+ \cap D|_{\tau+1}), H \backslash D|_{\tau+1} \rangle$ such that $\langle Q, \theta, E, H \rangle \in S_\tau^{\downarrow}$ for some $Q \in Q$ and $H^+ \backslash D|_{\tau+1}$ only contains future-possible atoms wrt $\tau + 1$.

The second step constructs $S_{\tau+1}^{\downarrow}$ by updating the sets of negative hypotheses and evidence in $A_{\tau+1}$. This is the first key contribution of this work, and the remainder of this section is dedicated to showing how it can be obtained as a fixpoint of a suitably defined operator.

4.1 The Evidence Lattice

As a first step, we construct a lattice over the set $\mathfrak{L}$ of all sets $\mathcal{X}$ of tuples $\langle Q, \theta, E, H \rangle$ where E and H are disjoint and such that (i) if $\langle Q, \theta, E, H \rangle \in \mathcal{X}$, then there exists $\langle Q, \theta, E', H' \rangle \in \mathcal{A}_{\tau+1}$ with $E \cup H = E' \cup H'$ and $E' \subseteq E$ and (ii) if $\langle Q, \theta, E, H \rangle$ and $\langle Q, \theta, E', H' \rangle$ are distinct elements of $\mathcal{X}$, then $E \cup H \neq E' \cup H'$. Throughout this and the next subsection we write simply $\mathcal{A}$ for $\mathcal{A}_{\tau+1}$, as this set is fixed.

Property (i) states that $\mathcal{X}$ corresponds to updating $\mathcal{A}$ with some learned evidence. Property (ii) states that this update is unique. Note that there is a one-to-one correspondence between elements of $\mathcal{A}$ and elements of $\mathcal{X}$; below, we refer to the "element of $\mathcal{A}$ generating" a tuple in $\mathcal{X}$.

Definition 8. *We define an order relation on $\mathfrak{L}$ as follows: $\mathcal{X} \sqsubseteq \mathcal{Y}$ if for every tuple $\langle Q, \theta, E, H \rangle \in \mathcal{X}$ there exists a tuple $\langle Q, \theta, E', H' \rangle \in \mathcal{Y}$ such that $E \cup H = E' \cup H'$ and $E \subseteq E'$.*

Intuitively, $\mathcal{X} \sqsubseteq \mathcal{Y}$ represents that hypothetical answers in $\mathcal{Y}$ are "closer to being proven" than those in $\mathcal{X}$.

Lemma 1. *The relation $\sqsubseteq$ is a partial order.*

Proof. Reflexivity and transitivity are straightforward.

For antisymmetry, assume that $\mathcal{X} \sqsubseteq \mathcal{Y} \sqsubseteq \mathcal{X}$, and pick $\langle Q, \theta, E, H \rangle \in \mathcal{X}$. Since $\mathcal{X} \sqsubseteq \mathcal{Y}$, there exists $\langle Q, \theta, E', H' \rangle \in \mathcal{Y}$ such that $E \cup H = E' \cup H'$ and $E \subseteq E'$. But since also $\mathcal{Y} \sqsubseteq \mathcal{X}$, there must also exist $\langle Q, \theta, E'', H'' \rangle \in \mathcal{X}$ such that $E' \cup H' = E'' \cup H''$ and $E' \subseteq E''$.

It then follows that $E \cup H = E'' \cup H''$, which by (ii) implies that $E = E''$. Therefore $E \subseteq E' \subseteq E$, so $E = E'$, and by disjointness also $H = H'$. So $\langle Q, \theta, E, H \rangle \in \mathcal{Y}$, whence $\mathcal{X} \subseteq \mathcal{Y}$.

A similar reasoning starting from a random element in $\mathcal{Y}$ establishes that $\mathcal{Y} \subseteq \mathcal{X}$, and therefore these two sets must be equal. $\square$

Lemma 2. *Every subset of $\mathfrak{L}$ has a least upper bound.*

Proof. Let $\mathfrak{D}$ be a subset of $\mathfrak{L}$. We claim that $\bigvee \mathfrak{D}$ is the set of all $\langle Q, \theta, E^\vee, H^\vee \rangle$ such that:

- $E^\vee = \bigcup \{E_i \mid \langle Q, \theta, E_i, H_i \rangle \in \bigcup \mathfrak{D}$ are generated by the same element of $\mathcal{A}\}$;
- $H^\vee = (E_S \cup H_S) \backslash E^\vee$ for the corresponding $\langle Q, \theta, E_S, H_S \rangle \in \mathcal{A}$.

Intuitively: for each hypothetical answer in $\mathcal{A}$, $\bigvee \mathfrak{D}$ contains the tuple that includes all evidence for $\langle Q, \theta \rangle$ that is in *some* element of $\mathfrak{D}$, and $H^\vee$ contains the remaining hypotheses.

Let $\mathcal{D} \in \mathfrak{D}$ and $\langle Q, \theta, E, H \rangle \in \mathcal{D}$. Since $\langle Q, \theta, E^\vee, H^\vee \rangle \in \bigvee \mathfrak{D}$ and $E \subseteq E^\vee$ by construction, $\mathcal{D} \sqsubseteq \bigvee \mathfrak{D}$. So $\bigvee \mathfrak{D}$ is an upper bound of $\mathfrak{D}$.

Now suppose that $\mathcal{Y}$ is an upper bound of $\mathfrak{D}$. We need to show that $\bigvee \mathfrak{D} \sqsubseteq \mathcal{Y}$. For this, choose $\langle Q, \theta, E^\vee, H^\vee \rangle \in \bigvee \mathfrak{D}$. For every $\langle Q, \theta, E, H \rangle \in \bigcup \mathfrak{D}$ that is generated by the same element of $\mathcal{A}$ as $\langle Q, \theta, E^\vee, H^\vee \rangle$, there must exist

$\langle Q, \theta, E', H' \rangle \in \mathcal{Y}$ such that $E' \cup H' = E \cup H$ and $E \subseteq E'$ (since $\mathcal{Y}$ is an upper bound of $\mathfrak{D}$). Furthermore, this element must be the same for all such tuples, since it is also generated by the same element of $\mathcal{A}$, and $\mathcal{Y}$ has only one element with this property. It follows that $E^{\vee} = \bigcup E \subseteq E'$. Since this holds for all elements of $\bigvee \mathfrak{D}$, we conclude that $\bigvee \mathfrak{D} \sqsubseteq \mathcal{Y}$, and therefore $\bigvee \mathfrak{D}$ is the least upper bound of $\mathfrak{D}$. $\qquad\square$

Corollary 1. $\mathfrak{L}$ *is a complete lattice, which we call the* evidence lattice.

4.2 The Negation Update Operator

The operator we consider is not defined over the evidence lattice, but over a bilattice of which $\mathfrak{L}$ is a projection.

Definition 9. *The set* $\mathbf{S}$ *contains all pairs* $\langle \mathcal{X}, \mathcal{Y} \rangle$ *where* $\mathcal{X} \subseteq \mathcal{A}$ *and* $\mathcal{Y} \sqsupseteq \mathcal{A}$. *We define an ordering over* $\mathbf{S}$ *by* $\langle \mathcal{X}, \mathcal{Y} \rangle \preceq \langle \mathcal{X}', \mathcal{Y}' \rangle$ *if* $\mathcal{X} \supseteq \mathcal{X}'$ *and* $\mathcal{Y} \sqsubseteq \mathcal{Y}'$.

Lemma 3. $\langle \mathbf{S}, \preceq \rangle$ *is a complete lattice.*

Proof. The result follows from the fact that both projections of $\mathbf{S}$ with the corresponding relations are complete lattices. $\qquad\square$

Definition 10. *The* negation update operator $R : \mathbf{S} \rightarrow \mathbf{S}$ *is defined as* $R(\mathcal{X}, \mathcal{Y}) = \langle R_1(\mathcal{X}, \mathcal{Y}), R_2(\mathcal{X}, \mathcal{Y}) \rangle$, *where:*

- $R_1(\mathcal{X}, \mathcal{Y})$ *is the result of removing from* $\mathcal{X}$ *the tuples* $\langle Q, \theta, E, H \rangle$ *for which there exists an element* $\langle Q', \theta', E', \emptyset \rangle \in \mathcal{Y}$ *such that* $\neg Q'\theta \in H$.
- $R_2(\mathcal{X}, \mathcal{Y})$ *is obtained from* $\mathcal{Y}$ *by replacing every tuple* $\langle Q, \theta, E, H \rangle$ *with the tuple* $\langle Q, \theta, E \cup P, H \backslash P \rangle$ *where* P *is the set of all* $\neg \alpha$ *such that there exists no tuple* $\langle Q', \theta', E', H' \rangle \in \mathcal{X}$ *with* $\alpha = Q'\theta'$.

Intuitively, R_1 removes tuples in $\mathcal{X}$ that include negative hypotheses disproven in $\mathcal{Y}$, while R_2 updates $\mathcal{Y}$ by moving negative facts to evidence if there is no hypothetical answer for them in $\mathcal{X}$. Keeping these two different updating mechanisms separate is essential to proving that we can reach a fixpoint.

Lemma 4. R *is monotonic.*

Proof. Assume that $\langle \mathcal{X}, \mathcal{Y} \rangle \preceq \langle \mathcal{X}', \mathcal{Y}' \rangle$, i.e., that $\mathcal{X} \supseteq \mathcal{X}'$ and $\mathcal{Y} \sqsubseteq \mathcal{Y}'$. We need to show that $R(\mathcal{X}, \mathcal{Y}) \preceq R(\mathcal{X}', \mathcal{Y}')$, i.e., that $R_1(\mathcal{X}, \mathcal{Y}) \supseteq R_1(\mathcal{X}', \mathcal{Y}')$ and $R_2(\mathcal{X}, \mathcal{Y}) \sqsubseteq R_2(\mathcal{X}', \mathcal{Y}')$.

For the first, observe that the result of R_1 is computed by removing some tuples from its first argument. Since $\mathcal{X} \supseteq \mathcal{X}'$, it suffices to show that any tuples removed from $\mathcal{X}$ are also removed from $\mathcal{X}'$. A tuple $\langle Q, \theta, E, H \rangle$ is removed from $\mathcal{X}$ if there exists $\langle Q', \theta', E', \emptyset \rangle \in \mathcal{Y}$ such that $\neg Q'\theta \in H$. Since $\mathcal{Y} \sqsubseteq \mathcal{Y}'$, there must be a tuple $\langle Q', \theta', E'', H'' \rangle \in \mathcal{Y}'$ such that $E'' \cup H'' = E' \cup \emptyset = E'$ and $H'' \subseteq \emptyset$. These conditions imply that $H'' = \emptyset$ and $E'' = E'$, i.e. $\langle Q', \theta', E', \emptyset \rangle \in \mathcal{Y}'$, and therefore $\langle Q, \theta, E, H \rangle$ is also removed from $\mathcal{X}'$ when computing $R_1(\mathcal{X}', \mathcal{Y}')$.

For the second, we note that the result of R_2 is computed by moving some literals from H to E in some tuples $\langle Q, \theta, E, H \rangle$ in its second argument. Since $\mathcal{Y} \sqsubseteq \mathcal{Y}'$, for each such tuple in $\mathcal{Y}$ there must be $\langle Q, \theta, E', H' \rangle$ such that $E \cup H = E' \cup H'$ and $E \subseteq E'$. The thesis can then be established by showing that any literals moved from H to E that are not already in E' will also be moved from H' to E'. Now, these literals are of the form $\neg \alpha$ and such that there exists no tuple $\langle Q^*, \theta^*, E^*, H^* \rangle \in \mathcal{X}$ with $\alpha = Q^* \theta^*$. Since $\mathcal{X} \supseteq \mathcal{X}'$, there can also be no such tuple in $\mathcal{X}'$, and therefore the same literal must also be moved from H' to E' when computing $R_2(\mathcal{X}', \mathcal{Y}')$, unless it already is in E' to start with.

Therefore R is a monotonic operator.   □

Corollary 2. *R has a least fixpoint.*

Proof. Consequence of the previous lemma and the Knaster–Tarski theorem. □

Let $\langle \mathcal{X}_0, \mathcal{Y}_0 \rangle$ be the least fixpoint of R, and define $\mathcal{S}^{\downarrow}_{\tau+1}$ as the set of tuples $\langle Q, \theta, E, H \rangle \in \mathcal{Y}_0$ for which there exists $\langle Q, \theta, E', H' \rangle \in \mathcal{X}_0$ with $E \cup H = E' \cup H'$. For convenience, we write simply $\mathcal{S}^{\downarrow}$ for $\mathcal{S}^{\downarrow}_{\tau+1}$ in the remainder of this section. Intuitively, $\mathcal{S}^{\downarrow}$ contains the tuples from $\mathcal{A}$ that remain in $\mathcal{X}_0$, with their sets of evidence updated as in $\mathcal{Y}_0$. In particular, (i) $\mathcal{S}^{\downarrow} \subseteq \mathcal{Y}_0$ and (ii) $\mathcal{X}_0 \sqsubseteq \mathcal{S}^{\downarrow}$. (Note however that $\mathcal{S}^{\downarrow} \notin \mathbf{S}$.)

Lemma 5. $\langle \mathcal{S}^{\downarrow}, \mathcal{S}^{\downarrow} \rangle$ *is a fixpoint of* R.

Proof. We need to show that $\langle \mathcal{S}^{\downarrow}, \mathcal{S}^{\downarrow} \rangle = R(\mathcal{S}^{\downarrow}, \mathcal{S}^{\downarrow})$, i.e. that $\mathcal{S}^{\downarrow} = R_i(\mathcal{S}^{\downarrow}, \mathcal{S}^{\downarrow})$ for $i = 1, 2$.

$R_1(\mathcal{S}^{\downarrow}, \mathcal{S}^{\downarrow})$ is obtained by removing from $\mathcal{S}^{\downarrow}$ the tuples $\langle Q, \theta, E, H \rangle$ for which there exists $\langle Q', \theta', E', \emptyset \rangle \in \mathcal{S}^{\downarrow}$ such that $\neg Q' \theta \in H$. But such a tuple $\langle Q', \theta', E', \emptyset \rangle$ would also be in $\mathcal{Y}_0$ by (i), and by (ii) this would imply that $R_1(\mathcal{X}_0, \mathcal{Y}_0) \neq \mathcal{X}_0$ (because it would lead to some tuple in $\mathcal{X}_0$ being removed by R_1), which contradicts $\langle \mathcal{X}_0, \mathcal{Y}_0 \rangle$ being a fixpoint of R.

$R_2(\mathcal{S}^{\downarrow}, \mathcal{S}^{\downarrow})$ is obtained by updating each tuple $\langle Q, \theta, E, H \rangle \in \mathcal{S}^{\downarrow}$ by moving literals of the form $\neg \alpha \in H$ to E if there exists no tuple $\langle Q', \theta', E', H' \rangle \in \mathcal{S}^{\downarrow}$ with $\alpha = Q' \theta'$. By (ii) this implies that no such tuple exists in $\mathcal{X}_0$ either (note that the condition does not impose restrictions on E' and H', so it does not matter that these sets may differ in the actual element of $\mathcal{X}_0$). By (i) any tuple updated in the computation of $R_2(\mathcal{S}^{\downarrow}, \mathcal{S}^{\downarrow})$ would therefore also be updated when computing $R_2(\mathcal{X}_0, \mathcal{Y}_0)$, which again would contradict $\langle \mathcal{X}_0, \mathcal{Y}_0 \rangle$ being a fixpoint of R.   □

It can also be shown that R is continuous, and therefore its least fixpoint is equal to $R^{\omega}(\mathcal{A}, \mathcal{A})$. However, this is immaterial for our presentation, and we skip the formal proof.

4.3   Soundness and Completeness

We begin this section with a simple lemma.

Lemma 6. *If* $\langle Q, \theta, E, H \rangle \in \mathcal{S}_\tau^\downarrow$ *or* $\langle Q, \theta, E, H \rangle \in \mathcal{A}_\tau$, *then* $E^+ \subseteq D_\tau$ *and every element of* H^+ *is future-possible wrt* τ.

Proof. Straightforward by induction on τ. $\square$

We now proceed to show that each $\mathcal{S}_\tau^\downarrow$ indeed is a generalized hypothetical answer to Q over D_τ. This is done by proving the following property by induction on τ:

Assume that $D \supseteq D_\tau$. Then $\langle Q, \theta, E, H \rangle \in \mathcal{S}_\tau^\downarrow$ with $H^+ \subseteq (D \backslash D_\tau)$ iff there exists a derivation $\mathcal{D}$ such that (i) $\mathcal{D}$ is an SLDNF-derivation proving that $\Pi \cup D \models Q\theta$ and (ii) $\mathcal{D}$ is an SLD$^\neg$-derivation proving that $\Pi \cup E \cup H \models Q\theta$ that uses all elements of $E \cup H$.   (∗)

By SLD$^\neg$-derivation we simply mean a (normal) SLD-derivation where negated atoms are treated by checking whether they appear as facts (in our case, in E^- or H^-). Derivation $\mathcal{D}$ "uses" a (negated) fact if that fact is unified in at least one step of $\mathcal{D}$.

For $\mathcal{S}_{-1}^\downarrow$, this property is a straightforward consequence of how pre-processing is defined; the interested reader can find a proof in [11].

The induction step proceeds in two parts. First, we show that the construction of the auxiliary set $\mathcal{A}_{\tau+1}$, obtained by updating the positive part of $\mathcal{S}_\tau^\downarrow$ with the information in $D|_{\tau+1}$, preserves property (∗).

Lemma 7. *If* $\mathcal{S}_\tau^\downarrow$ *satisfies* (∗), *then* $\mathcal{A}_{\tau+1}$ *satisfies* (∗).

Proof. Suppose that $D \supseteq D_{\tau+1}$. Then also $D \supseteq D_\tau$.

For the direct implication, assume that $\langle Q, \theta, E, H \rangle \in \mathcal{A}_{\tau+1}$ is such that $H^+ \subseteq D \backslash D_{\tau+1}$. By construction of $\mathcal{A}_{\tau+1}$, there exists $\langle Q, \theta, E', H' \rangle \in \mathcal{S}_\tau^\downarrow$ such that $E = E' \cup (H'^+ \cap D|_{\tau+1})$ and $H = H' \backslash D|_{\tau+1}$. Any elements in $H' \backslash H$ must be in $D|_{\tau+1}$, so $H' \subseteq D \backslash D_\tau$.

By hypothesis on $\mathcal{S}_\tau^\downarrow$, there exists a derivation $\mathcal{D}$ such that $\mathcal{D}$ is an SLDNF-derivation showing that $\Pi \cup D \models Q\theta$ and $\mathcal{D}$ is an SLD$^\neg$-derivation proving that $\Pi \cup E' \cup H' \models Q\theta$ that uses all elements of $E' \cup H'$. But $E' \cup H' = E \cup H$, so $\mathcal{D}$ is also an SLD$^\neg$-derivation proving that $\Pi \cup E \cup H \models Q\theta$ that uses all elements of $E \cup H$.

For the converse implication, let $\mathcal{D}$ be an SLDNF-derivation proving that $\Pi \cup D \models Q\theta$, and let F contain the set of elements of D that are used in $\mathcal{D}$ and all negative literals that appear in $\mathcal{D}$. Then $\mathcal{D}$ is also an SLD$^\neg$-derivation proving that $\Pi \cup F \models Q\theta$. By hypothesis on $\mathcal{S}_\tau^\downarrow$, there exists a tuple $\langle Q, \theta, E, H \rangle \in \mathcal{S}_\tau^\downarrow$ such that $H^+ \subseteq D \backslash D_\tau$ and $E \cup H = F$.

If $\langle Q, \theta, E, H \rangle \notin \mathcal{A}_{\tau+1}$, then $H^+ \backslash D_{\tau+1}$ contains some elements that are not future-possible wrt $\tau+1$; such elements cannot be in D, which is a contradiction (since they are in F, they are used in $\mathcal{D}$, but they cannot be unified with any element of $\Pi \cup D$).

Therefore $\mathcal{A}_{\tau+1}$ contains an element $\langle Q, \theta, E', H' \rangle$ with $E' = E \cup (H^+ \cap D|_{\tau+1})$, $H' = H \backslash D|_{\tau+1}$, and such that $H' \subseteq D \backslash D_{\tau+1}$. As a consequence, $E \cup H = E' \cup H' = F$, establishing the thesis. $\square$

Next, we show that $(*)$ is preserved in the construction of $\mathcal{S}^{\downarrow}_{\tau+1}$ from $\mathcal{A}_{\tau+1}$. We start with an auxiliary definition.

Definition 11. *For* $\langle \mathcal{X}, \mathcal{Y} \rangle \in \mathbf{S}$, *define* $\mathcal{X} \sqcap \mathcal{Y}$ *to be the set of tuples* $\langle Q, \theta, E, H \rangle \in \mathcal{Y}$ *for which there exists* $\langle Q, \theta, E', H' \rangle \in \mathcal{X}$ *with* $E \cup H = E' \cup H'$, $E^+ = (E')^+$ *and* $H^+ = (H')^+$.

In particular, $\mathcal{S}^{\downarrow}_{\tau+1} = \mathcal{X}_0 \sqcap \mathcal{Y}_0$, where $\langle \mathcal{X}_0, \mathcal{Y}_0 \rangle$ is the least fixpoint of R.

The proof uses transfinite induction. For simplicity, we again split it in several lemmas. Note that the base case is trivial, since the least element of $\mathbf{S}$ is $\langle \mathcal{A}_{\tau+1}, \mathcal{A}_{\tau+1} \rangle$ and trivially $\mathcal{A}_{\tau+1} \sqcap \mathcal{A}_{\tau+1} = \mathcal{A}_{\tau+1}$.

Lemma 8. *Let* $\langle \mathcal{X}, \mathcal{Y} \rangle \in \mathbf{S}$ *be such that: (i) if* $\langle Q, \theta, E, H \rangle \in \mathcal{X} \sqcap \mathcal{Y}$, *then* $E^+ \subseteq D_{\tau+1}$ *and (ii)* $\mathcal{X} \sqcap \mathcal{Y}$ *satisfies* $(*)$. *Then* $R_1(\mathcal{X}, \mathcal{Y}) \sqcap R_2(\mathcal{X}, \mathcal{Y})$ *satisfies* $(*)$.

Proof. Assume that $D \supseteq D_{\tau+1}$.

For the direct implication, choose $\langle Q, \theta, E, H \rangle \in R_1(\mathcal{X}, \mathcal{Y}) \sqcap R_2(\mathcal{X}, \mathcal{Y})$. In particular $\langle Q, \theta, E, H \rangle \in R_2(\mathcal{X}, \mathcal{Y})$, so there exists a tuple $\langle Q, \theta, E', H' \rangle \in \mathcal{X} \sqcap \mathcal{Y}$ such that $E \cup H = E' \cup H'$ and $(H')^+ = H^+$. The hypothesis on $\langle \mathcal{X}, \mathcal{Y} \rangle$ immediately establishes the thesis.

For the converse implication, assume that $\mathcal{D}$ is an SLDNF-derivation showing that $\Pi \cup D \models Q\theta$ and define F as before as the set of elements of D that are used in $\mathcal{D}$ together with all negative literals that appear in $\mathcal{D}$.

By hypothesis there exists a tuple $\langle Q, \theta, E, H \rangle \in \mathcal{X} \sqcap \mathcal{Y}$ such that $H^+ \subseteq (D \backslash D_{\tau+1})$ and $E \cup H = F$. By definition of $\sqcap$, there exists a tuple $\langle Q, \theta, E_X, H_X \rangle \in \mathcal{X}$ such that $E_X \cup H_X = E \cup H = F$, and $\langle Q, \theta, E, H \rangle \in \mathcal{Y}$. By definition of R_2, there is also a tuple $\langle Q, \theta, E_Y, H_Y \rangle \in R_2(\mathcal{X}, \mathcal{Y})$ such that $E_Y \cup H_Y = E \cup H = F$ and $H_Y^+ = H^+$. To establish the thesis, we only need to show that $\langle Q, \theta, E_X, H_X \rangle \in R_1(\mathcal{X}, \mathcal{Y})$.

Assume that this is not the case. Then there exists an element $\langle Q', \theta', E', \emptyset \rangle \in \mathcal{Y}$ with $\neg Q'\theta' \in H_X$. Since $\emptyset^+ \subseteq D \backslash D_{\tau+1}$ and $\langle \mathcal{X}, \mathcal{Y} \rangle$ satisfies $(*)$, there exists an SLDNF-derivation $\mathcal{D}'$ showing that $\Pi \cup D \models Q\theta'$, which contradicts the fact that $\mathcal{D}$ at some point must process the fact $\neg Q'\theta'$ by showing that no such derivation exists. □

Lemma 9. *Let* $\{\langle \mathcal{X}_i, \mathcal{Y}_i \rangle \mid i \in I\}$ *be a directed subset of* $\mathbf{S}$ *such that* $\mathcal{X}_i \sqcap \mathcal{Y}_i$ *satisfies* $(*)$ *for all* $i \in I$. *Let* $\langle \mathcal{X}, \mathcal{Y} \rangle = \bigvee \{\langle \mathcal{X}_i, \mathcal{Y}_i \rangle \mid i \in I\}$. *Then* $\mathcal{X} \sqcap \mathcal{Y}$ *satisfies* $(*)$.

Proof. Assume that $D \supseteq D_{\tau+1}$.

For the direct implication, pick $\langle Q, \theta, E, H \rangle \in \mathcal{X} \sqcap \mathcal{Y}$ with $H^+ \subseteq D \backslash D_{\tau+1}$. Then $\langle Q, \theta, E, H \rangle \in \mathcal{Y}_i$ for all i, and every $\mathcal{X}_i$ contains an element $\langle Q, \theta, E_i, H_i \rangle$ with $E_i \cup H_i = E \cup H$ and $E_i \subseteq E$. Applying the hypothesis for any i immediately establishes the thesis.

Conversely, let $\mathcal{D}$ be an SLDNF-derivation establishing $\Pi \cup D \models Q\theta$ and define F again as above. By hypothesis, for each i there must exist $\langle Q, \theta, E_i, H_i \rangle \in \mathcal{X}_i \sqcap \mathcal{Y}_i$ with $E_i \cup H_i = F$ and such that $H_i^+ \subseteq D \backslash D_{\tau+1}$. This means that $\langle Q, \theta, E_i, H_i \rangle \in \mathcal{X}_i$ for each i, and there exists $\langle Q, \theta, E_Y, H_Y \rangle$

such that, for every i, $E_Y \cup H_Y = E_i \cup H_i$ and $\langle Q, \theta, E_Y, H_Y \rangle \in \mathcal{Y}_i$. Then $\langle Q, \theta, E_Y, H_Y \rangle \in \mathcal{Y}$, and there is a tuple $\langle Q, \theta, E_X, H_X \rangle \in \bigvee \mathcal{X}_i$ such that $\langle Q, \theta, E_i, H_i \rangle \sqsupseteq \langle Q, \theta, E_X, H_X \rangle$. In particular, $E_X \cup H_X = E_i \cup H_i$ for all i, and therefore also $E_X \cup H_X = E_Y \cup H_Y$. Thus $\langle Q, \theta, E_X, H_X \rangle \in \mathcal{X} \sqcap \mathcal{Y}$, and since $E_X \cup H_X = F$ and $H_X^+ = H_i^+ \subseteq D \backslash D_{\tau+1}$ (for an arbitrary i) we can conclude that the thesis holds. $\square$

Corollary 3. *If $\mathcal{A}_{\tau+1}$ satisfies (∗), then $\mathcal{S}_{\tau+1}^{\downarrow}$ also satisfies (∗).*

Theorem 1. *If $\langle Q, \theta, E, H \rangle \in \mathcal{S}_{\tau}^{\downarrow}$, then $\langle Q, \theta, E, H \rangle$ is a generalized hypothetical answer to Q over D_{τ}.*

Proof. Let $\langle Q, \theta, E, H \rangle \in \mathcal{S}_{\tau}^{\downarrow}$. By construction, $Q \in \mathbf{Q}$ and θ is a closed substitution ranging over the variables in Q: these properties were guaranteed in the construction of $\mathcal{S}_{-1}^{\downarrow}$, and Q and θ are never changed afterwards. Furthermore, due to the way E and H are constructed and updated, they are necessarily disjoint and contain only EDB atoms and negated IDB atoms: this is true for $\mathcal{S}_{-1}^{\downarrow}$ by construction (where $E = \emptyset$), and all later updates are of the form "move an element from H to E", which preserves these properties.

E^+ and H^+ are only changed in the construction of $\mathcal{A}_{\tau}$, where elements are added to E^+ if they appear in $D|_{\tau}$ (so induction guarantees $E^+ \subseteq D_{\tau}$), and the tuple is only kept if all elements remaining in H^+ are future-possible wrt τ.

For the last point, we recall that $\mathcal{S}_{\tau}^{\downarrow}$ satisfies (∗). Assume that $D \supseteq D_{\tau}$.

To show that $\Pi \cup D \models E^-$, assume towards a contradiction that this is not the case, and choose an element $\neg\alpha \in E^-$ such that $\Pi \cup D \models \alpha$. Due to how pre-processing works, there exist a query Q' and a substitution θ' such that $\alpha = Q'\theta'$; furthermore, θ' is closed, and it can be assumed to range exactly over the variables in Q'. By completeness of SLDNF-resolution, there is an SLDNF-derivation $\mathcal{D}$ showing that $\Pi \cup D \models Q'\theta'$. Take F to be the elements of D that are used in $\mathcal{D}$ and all negative literals that appear in $\mathcal{D}$. Then $\mathcal{D}$ is again an SLD$^{\neg}$-derivation proving that $\Pi \cup F \models Q'\theta'$, whence $\mathcal{S}_{\tau}^{\downarrow}$ must contain a tuple $\langle Q', \theta', E', H' \rangle$ with $E' \cup H' = F$. But this contradicts the hypothesis that $\neg\alpha \in E^-$, since the only way to add elements to E^- is by application of R (specifically, R_2) when no such tuple exists, and the construction of $\mathcal{S}_{\tau}^{\downarrow}$ ensures that all tuples it contains ultimately originate from $\mathcal{S}_{-1}^{\downarrow}$.

Lastly, assume that $\Pi \cup D \models H$. Then $H^+ \subseteq (D \backslash D_{\tau})$, from which property (∗) ensures existence of an SLDNF-derivation $\mathcal{D}$ proving that $\Pi \cup D \models Q\theta$. $\square$

5   Computing the Operational Semantics

The operational semantics in the previous section is based on infinite sets, and can therefore not be directly implemented. In this section, we show that we can represent generalized hypothetical answers finitely and update them one timestamp at a time. We argue informally that our construction is correct.

We extend the algorithm from [13], which deals with communication delays in the positive fragment of our language (see Sect. 2.3), with the ideas from [11] for dealing with negation. The trick is to balance the amount of information in the schematic hypothetical answers computed online, so that the updating procedure terminates but negations are updated correctly.

We achieve this by: (i) ensuring that schematic hypothetical answers for every query that may need to be examined when updating negations are introduced, even if there is no evidence for them, and (ii) restricting the negated hypotheses that are updated to those whose timestamp is at most the current one. Furthermore, we assume that our program is T-stratified.

The algorithm is as follows. We initialize $\mathcal{S}_{-1}(Q) = \emptyset$ for every query Q.

1. *Define a set $\mathcal{B}_\tau$ updating $\mathcal{S}_{\tau-1}$ with information from the datastream.*
   (a) If $\langle \theta, H \rangle \in \mathcal{P}(Q)$ and σ is a non-empty local mgu for H and $D|_\tau$ such that $H\sigma\backslash D|_\tau$ only contains potentially future atoms wrt τ, then $\langle \theta\sigma, E \cup E', H\sigma\backslash D|_\tau \rangle \in \mathcal{B}_\tau(Q)$, where $E' = H\sigma \cap D|_\tau$.
   (b) If $\langle \theta, E, H \rangle \in \mathcal{S}_{\tau-1}(Q)$ and σ is a local mgu for H and $D|_\tau$ such that the set $H\sigma\backslash D|_\tau$ only contains potentially future atoms wrt τ, then $\langle \theta\sigma, E \cup E', H\sigma\backslash D|_\tau \rangle \in \mathcal{B}_\tau(Q)$, where $E' = H\sigma \cap D|_\tau$.
2. *Add answers to queries that might be examined when updating negations.*
   For each query $Q \in \mathbf{Q}$, let $\sigma = [T := \tau]$ with T the temporal variable in Q. If $\langle \theta, H \rangle \in \mathcal{P}_Q$ and every element of $H\sigma$ is either potentially future wrt τ or negated, then add $\langle \theta\sigma, \emptyset, H\sigma \rangle$ to $\mathcal{B}_\tau(Q)$.
3. *Process negated literals.*
   Fix a topological ordering of the stratification of $\Pi^\downarrow$. There is only a finite number of predicate symbols P_t such that Q_P has at least one schematic answer with $T\theta = t$ (where Q_P is the query on P and T is the temporal parameter in Q_P). For each of these P_t in order:
   (a) set $\ell = P(t_1,\ldots,t_n)$ and let $S(P_t)$ be the set of elements $\langle \theta, E, H \rangle$ in $\mathcal{S}_\tau(Q_P)$ such that $T\theta = t$;
   (b) if $S(P_t)$ contains a tuple $\langle \theta, E', \emptyset \rangle$, then: in each $\mathcal{B}_\tau(Q)$, replace every $\langle \sigma, E, H \rangle$ such that $\ell\sigma$ is unifiable with an element $h \in H^-$ with all possible $\langle \sigma\theta', E\theta', H\theta' \rangle$ such that θ' is a minimal substitution with the property that $\ell\theta$ is not unifiable with $h\theta'$;
   (c) for each $\langle \theta, E, H \rangle \in \mathcal{B}_\tau(Q)$ for some Q, if H^- contains an element h with predicate symbol P and timestamp $t \leq \tau$ and there is no tuple $\langle \theta', E', H' \rangle \in S(P_t)$ such that h and $\ell\theta'$ are unifiable, then remove $\neg h$ from H and add it to E.

Step (1) is essentially the update step from [13]. The use of local mgus ensures that no answers are lost even in presence of communication delays. Step (2), adapted from [11], guarantees that schematic hypothetical answers are added for any queries that may be evaluated when updating negated hypotheses – so their absence guarantees that they have been removed in a previous iteration. The sets $\mathcal{B}_\tau(Q)$ obtained at the end of this step correspond (modulo instantiation) to the subset of elements $\langle Q, \theta, E, H \rangle \in \mathcal{A}_\tau$ where either $E \neq \emptyset$ or $T\theta \leq \tau$. Step (3), also adapted from [11], updates negated hypotheses. The final result of this step again corresponds, modulo instantiation, to the subset of elements of $\mathcal{S}_\tau$ with the same property as above.

6   Related Work and Discussion

This work contributes to the field of stream reasoning, the task of conjunctively reasoning over streaming data and background knowledge [39].

Research advances on Complex Event Processors and Data Stream Management Systems [14], together with Knowledge Representation and the Semantic Web, all contributed to the several stream reasoning languages, systems and mechanisms proposed during the last decade [16].

Computing answers to a query over a data source that is continuously producing information requires techniques with some kind of *incremental evaluation*, in order to avoid reevaluating the query from scratch each time new information arrives. Efforts in this direction have capitalized on incremental algorithms based on seminaive evaluation [1,5,22,23,33], based on truth maintenance systems [6], or window oriented [20], among others. Being an incremental variant of SLD-resolution, our framework [12,13] fits naturally in the first class.

Hypothetical query answering over streams is broadly related to abduction in logic programming [17,24], namely to approaches that view negated atoms as hypotheses and relate them to contradiction avoidance [2,18]. In this sense, we apply an incremental form of data-driven abductive inference similar to [32], but with a different approach and in a different context. To our knowledge, hypothetical or abductive reasoning has not been previously applied to continuous query answering, although it has been applied to annotation of stream data [3].

Also incomplete databases include notions of possible and certain answers [25]. Here, possible answers are answers to a complete database D' that the incomplete database D can represent, while certain answers belong to all complete databases that D can represent. Libkin [30] explored an alternative way of looking at incomplete databases that dates back to Reiter [36], viewing a database as a logical theory. He explored the semantics of incompleteness independently of a particular data model, appealing to orderings to describe the degree of incompleteness of a database. Other authors [21,26,27,35] have also investigated ways to assign confidence levels to the information output to the user.

Most theoretical approaches to stream-processing systems commonly require input streams to be ordered. However, some approaches from the area of databases and event processing have developed techniques to deal with out-of-order data. An example is inserting special marks in the input stream (punctuations) to guide window processing [28], which assert a timestamp that is a lower bound for all future incoming values of an attribute. Another technique starts by the potential generation of out-of-order results, which are then ordered by using stackbased data structures and associated purge algorithms [29].

Other authors have considered languages using negation. Our definition of stratification is similar to the concept of temporal stratification from [41]. However, this notion requires the strata to be also ordered according to time; we make no such assumption in this work. A different notion of temporal stratification for stream reasoning is given in [7], but their framework also includes explicit temporal operators, making the whole formalization more complex.

References

1. Abiteboul, S., Hull, R., Vianu, V.: Foundations of Databases. Addison-Wesley, Boston (1995)
2. Alferes, J.J., Pereira, L.M: Reasoning with Logic Programming. LNCS, vol. 1111. Springer, Heidelberg (1996). https://doi.org/10.1007/3-540-61488-5
3. Alirezaie, M., Loutfi, A.: Automated reasoning using abduction for interpretation of medical signals. J. Biomed. Semant. **5**, 35 (2014)
4. Babcock, B., Babu, S., Datar, M., Motwani, R., Widom, J.: Models and issues in data stream systems. In: Popa, L., Abiteboul, S., Kolaitis, P.G. (eds.) Proceedings of the PODS, pp. 1–16. ACM (2002)
5. Barbieri, D.F., Braga, D., Ceri, S., Della Valle, E., Grossniklaus, M.: Incremental reasoning on streams and rich background knowledge. In: Aroyo, L., et al. (eds.) ESWC 2010. LNCS, vol. 6088, pp. 1–15. Springer, Heidelberg (2010). https://doi. org/10.1007/978-3-642-13486-9_1
6. Beck, H., Dao-Tran, M., Eiter, T.: Answer update for rule-based stream reasoning. In: Yang, Q., Wooldridge, M.J. (eds.) Proceedings of the IJCAI, pp. 2741–2747. AAAI Press (2015)
7. Beck, H., Dao-Tran, M., Eiter, T., Fink, M.: LARS: a logic-based framework for analyzing reasoning over streams. In: Bonet and Koenig [8], pp. 1431–1438 (2015)
8. Bonet, B., Koenig, S. (eds.): 29th AAAI Conference on Artificial Intelligence, AAAI 2015, Austin, TX, USA. AAAI Press (2015)
9. Ceri, S., Gottlob, G., Tanca, L.: What you always wanted to know about datalog (and never dared to ask). IEEE Trans. Knowl. Data Eng. **1**(1), 146–166 (1989)
10. Chomicki, J., Imielinski, T.: Temporal deductive databases and infinite objects. In: Edmondson-Yurkanan, C., Yannakakis, M. (eds.) Proceedings of the PODS, pp. 61–73. ACM (1988)
11. Cruz-Filipe, L., Gaspar, G., Nunes, I.: Hypothetical answers to continuous queries over data streams. CoRR abs/1905.09610 (2019). Submitted for publication
12. Cruz-Filipe, L., Gaspar, G., Nunes, I.: Hypothetical answers to continuous queries over data streams. In: Proceedings of the AAAI, pp. 2798–2805. AAAI Press (2020)
13. Cruz-Filipe, L., Gaspar, G., Nunes, I.: Can you answer while you wait? In: Proceedings of the FoIKS. LNCS. Springer (2022, to appear)
14. Cugola, G., Margara, A.: Processing flows of information: from data stream to complex event processing. ACM Comput. Surv. **44**(3), 1–62 (2012)
15. Dao-Tran, M., Eiter, T.: Streaming multi-context systems. In: Sierra, C. (ed.) Proceedings of the IJCAI, pp. 1000–1007. Ijcai.org (2017)
16. Dell'Aglio, D., Valle, E.D., van Harmelen, F., Bernstein, A.: Stream reasoning: a survey and outlook. Data Sci. **1**(1–2), 59–83 (2017)
17. Denecker, M., Kakas, A.: Abduction in logic programming. In: Kakas, A.C., Sadri, F. (eds.) Computational Logic: Logic Programming and Beyond. LNCS (LNAI), vol. 2407, pp. 402–436. Springer, Heidelberg (2002). https://doi.org/10.1007/3-540-45628-7_16
18. Dung, P.M.: Negations as hypotheses: an abductive foundation for logic programming. In: Furukawa, K. (ed.) Proceedings of the ICLP, pp. 3–17. MIT Press (1991)
19. Fitting, M.: Bilattices are nice things. In: Bolander, T., Hendricks, V., Pedersen, S.A. (eds.) Self-Reference, pp.53–77. CSLI Publications (2006)
20. Ghanem, T.M., Hammad, M.A., Mokbel, M.F., Aref, W.G., Elmagarmid, A.K.: Incremental evaluation of sliding-window queries over data streams. IEEE Trans. Knowl. Data Eng. **19**(1), 57–72 (2007)

21. Gray, A.J., Nutt, W., Williams, M.H.: Answering queries over incomplete data stream histories. IJWIS **3**(1/2), 41–60 (2007)
22. Gupta, A., Mumick, I.S., Subrahmanian, V.: Maintaining views incrementally. In: Buneman, P., Jajodia, S. (eds.) Proceedings of the SIGMOD, pp. 157–166. ACM Press (1993)
23. Hu, P., Motik, B., Horrocks, I.: Optimised maintenance of datalog materialisations. In: McIlraith and Weinberger [31], pp. 1871–1879 (2018)
24. Inoue, K.: Hypothetical reasoning in logic programs. J. Log. Program. **18**(3), 191–227 (1994)
25. Lipski Jr., W.: On semantic issues connected with incomplete information databases. ACM Trans. Database Syst. **4**(3), pp. 262–296 (1979)
26. Lang, W., Nehme, R.V., Robinson, E., Naughton, J.F.: Partial results in database systems. In: Dyreson, C.E., Li, F., Özsu, M.T. (eds.) Proceedings of the SIGMOD, pp. 1275–1286. ACM (2014)
27. de Leng, D., Heintz, F.: Approximate stream reasoning with metric temporal logic under uncertainty. In: Proceedings of the AAAI, pp. 2760–2767. AAAI Press (2019)
28. Li, J., Tufte, K., Shkapenyuk, V., Papadimos, V., Johnson, T., Maier, D.: Out-of-order processing: a new architecture for high-performance stream systems. Proc. VLDB Endow. **1**(1), 274–288 (2008)
29. Li, M., Liu, M., Ding, L., Rundensteiner, E.A., Mani, M.: Event stream processing with out-of-order data arrival. In: Proceedings of the ICDCS, p. 67. IEEE Computer Society (2007)
30. Libkin, L.: Incomplete data: what went wrong, and how to fix it. In: Hull, R., Grohe, M. (eds.) Proceedings of the PODS, pp. 1–13. ACM (2014)
31. McIlraith, S.A., Weinberger, K.Q. (eds.): 32nd AAAI Conference on Artificial Intelligence, AAAI 2018, New Orleans, LA, USA. AAAI Press (2018)
32. Meadows, B.L., Langley, P., Emery, M.J.: Seeing beyond shadows: incremental abductive reasoning for plan understanding. In: Proceedings of the PLAN. AAAI Workshops, vol. WS-13-13. AAAI (2013)
33. Motik, B., Nenov, Y., Piro, R.E.F., Horrocks, I.: Incremental update of datalog materialisation: the backward/forward algorithm. In: In: Bonet and Koenig [8], pp. 1560–1568 (2015)
34. Özçep, Ö.L., Möller, R., Neuenstadt, C.: A stream-temporal query language for ontology based data access. In: Lutz, C., Thielscher, M. (eds.) KI 2014. LNCS (LNAI), vol. 8736, pp. 183–194. Springer, Cham (2014). https://doi.org/10.1007/978-3-319-11206-0_18
35. Razniewski, S., Korn, F., Nutt, W., Srivastava, D.: Identifying the extent of completeness of query answers over partially complete databases. In: Sellis, T.K., Davidson, S.B., Ives, Z.G. (eds.) Proceedings of the SIGMOD, pp. 561–576. ACM (2015)
36. Reiter, R.: Towards a logical reconstruction of relational database theory. In: Brodie, M.L., Mylopoulos, J., Schmidt, J.W. (eds.) On Conceptual Modelling. Topics in Information Systems, pp. 191–238. Springer, New York (1984). https://doi.org/10.1007/978-1-4612-5196-5_8
37. Ronca, A., Kaminski, M., Grau, B.C., Motik, B., Horrocks, I.: Stream reasoning in temporal datalog. In: McIlraith, S.A., Weinberger, K.Q. (eds.) 32nd AAAI Conference on Artificial Intelligence, AAAI 2018, New Orleans, LA, USA, pp. 1941–1948 (2018)
38. Stonebraker, M., Çetintemel, U., Zdonik, S.B.: The 8 requirements of real-time stream processing. SIGMOD Rec. **34**(4), 42–47 (2005)

39. Valle, E.D., Ceri, S., van Harmelen, F., Fensel, D.: It's a streaming world! reasoning upon rapidly changing information. IEEE Intell. Syst. **24**(6), 83–89 (2009)
40. Zaniolo, C.: Logical foundations of continuous query languages for data streams. In: Barceló, P., Pichler, R. (eds.) Datalog 2.0 2012. LNCS, vol. 7494, pp. 177–189. Springer, Heidelberg (2012). https://doi.org/10.1007/978-3-642-32925-8_18
41. Zaniolo, C.: Expressing and supporting efficiently greedy algorithms as locally stratified logic programs. In: Vos, M.D., Eiter, T., Lierler, Y., Toni, F. (eds.) Technical Communications of ICLP. CEUR Workshop Proceedings, vol. 1433. CEUR-WS.org (2015)

A Combinatorial Study of Async/Await Processes

Matthieu Dien[1] , Antoine Genitrini[2] , and Frédéric Peschanski[2(✉)]

[1] Université de Caen – GREYC – CNRS UMR 6072, Caen, France
matthieu.dien@unicaen.fr
[2] Sorbonne Université – LIP6 – CNRS UMR 7606, Paris, France
{antoine.genitrini,frederic.peschanski}@lip6.fr

Abstract. In this paper we study families of async/await concurrent processes using techniques and tools from (enumerative) combinatorics and order theory. We consider the count of process executions as the primary measure of "complexity", which closely relates to the (in general, difficult) problem of counting linear extensions of partial orders. Interestingly, the control structures of async/await processes fall into the subclass of what we call the BIT-decomposable posets, providing an effective way to count executions in practice. We also show that async/await processes can be seen as generalizations of families of interval orders, a well-studied class of partial orders. Based on this combinatorial study, we define a variety of uniform random generation algorithms. We consider on the one side the generation of process structures, and on the other side the generation of execution paths – which is performed without requiring the explicit construction of the state-space.

Keywords: Async/await · Enumerative combinatorics · Uniform random generation

1 Introduction

Programming concurrent systems is a notoriously difficult task with various sources of complexity, among which *asynchronism* (the lack of a global clock), *non-determinism* (the existence of multiple distinct executions/outcomes) and *state explosion* (the exponential growth of such executions) appear to stand out. Various design patterns have been proposed to simplify the task at hand. *Bulk-synchronous parallelism* (BSP) [22] is such an example of a simplified architecture for (a limited form of) parallel computing. For asynchronous systems, the principle of *async/await* concurrency has emerged as a popular abstraction, based on the concepts of *promises* and/or *futures* [18] but with dedicated syntactic constructs. Widely used programming languages offer async/await abstractions, for example Javascript [8], Python [20] and others[1].

The main guiding idea of our research is that the complexity of synchronization patterns for concurrent processes is closely related to the relative difficulty of

---

[1] see https://en.wikipedia.org/wiki/Async/await.

H. Seidl et al. (Eds.): ICTAC 2022, LNCS 13572, pp. 170–187, 2022.
https://doi.org/10.1007/978-3-031-17715-6_12

counting process executions. For example, counting executions of series-parallel structures (such as in BSP) is easy (see e.g. [16]). At the other end of the spectrum, the lack of any obvious control structure makes counting executions akin to counting linear extensions of arbitrary posets, a ♯P-complete problem (cf. [4]).

In this paper, we consider the async/await processes as combinatorial objects – considering the execution count as their fundamental "measure" – and study them with the hopeful objective of corroborating the common belief that this would be a "simpler" concurrency model. As a starting point, we develop a minimal process calculus with not much more than the basic principles of async/await. One simple way to provide an interpretation for process behaviors is in the form of computation trees. With this interpretation, counting executions is easy: it is the number of distinct branches (thus leaves) of the trees. We propose an alternative representation of the control structure of processes as directed acyclic graphs (DAGs). The advantage of this representation is that it is exponentially more compact than the corresponding computation tree. And we can still count executions, although the task is now more complex. As a first contribution, we show that the corresponding structure falls into the subclass of what we call the BIT-decomposable posets. Based on our previous work [4], we obtain a way to formulate the counting problem as a compact multivariate integral which can be solved by a computer algebra system. This is discussed in Sect. 3. In Sect. 4, we establish interesting links between subclasses of async/await processes and the mathematical structures known as *interval orders*. In the last part of the paper (Sect. 5), we build on our combinatorial investigations to experiment uniform random generation algorithms. We discuss the generation of process structures as well as the generation of execution paths.

Related Work

Alternative combinatorial models of concurrency have been proposed in the literature, especially based on the *trace monoid* (see e.g. [1]). Closely related are the so-called *unfoldings* [9] which provides a compact representation of computation trees as occurrence nets (a subclass of Petri nets). However as discussed in [9] (e.g. page 29) the potentially exponential growth of the unfoldings is directly connected to the degree of synchronization exposed by the processes. The situation is similar in [3], which models synchronized automata as a product automaton of a size whose (exponential) growth is tightly connected to the number of required synchronizations. While the partial order representation we adopt is more restricted in terms of expressivity, it is less sensitive to the number of synchronizations and thus well-suited for "principled" synchronization models such as async/await. The counting of linear extensions of (unconstrained) partial orders is shown a ♯P-complete problem in [6]. This is also the case for posets of height 2 or dimension 2 [7]. Polynomial algorithms exist for series-parallel posets [16]. In [4] we introduce the class of BIT-decomposable processes together with a compact representation of the counting problem as a multivariate integral formula. While this does not directly yield a counting algorithm, computer algebra systems can be used for the numerical resolution. More generic algorithms

Listing 1.1. Async/await example in Javascript

```
function promise(arg) {
        return new Promise(resolve => {
                result = someComputation(arg);
                resolve(result)});
}

async function main() {
        // main program
        doThis();
        w1 = promise(1);
        w2 = promise(2)
        doThat();
        w3 = promise(3)
        result1 = await w1;
        use1(result1);
        result2and3 = await Promise.all([w2, w3]);
        use2and3(result2and3);
}
```

have been proposed in e.g. [14] (for sparse posets, with interesting applications in artificial intelligence) and [19] (based on a fast enumeration of linear extensions, not suitable for actual counting). In [4] we describe a linear extension sampler for BIT-decomposable processes, which we experiment on async/await processes in the present paper. An alternative approach is proposed in [13] which is based on a coupling from the past (MCMC) procedure. The advantage of this approach is that it can be applied on arbitrary posets, but its running time is aleatory. Other random generation methods have been proposed in e.g. [17] but, unlike our approach, they require in one way or another the explicit construction of the state-space of processes.

Interval orders [11] have been thoroughly studied in the literature, with the notable mention of [5] which provides a thorough study in the domain of enumerative combinatorics.

2   Async/Await Concurrency

In this section we present a very simple process calculus whose purpose is to capture the fundamental ingredients of async/await concurrency. Listing 1.1 shows a somewhat minimal Javascript example[2]. Putting aside the classical language features (function calls, assignments, etc.), we focus on the construct related to concurrency. First, the **async** keyword enables async/await concurrency in the scope of a function body (the function **main()** in the example). In our own

---

[2] A more complete and runnable version of the Javascript example is available online at the following address: https://jsfiddle.net/boah97dm/.

terminology, we will say that the body of such a function becomes a *control thread*. Such a control thread can perform three kinds of (concurrency-related) operations:

- perform basic atomic actions that have no further meaning than "something happened" as far as concurrency is concerned (in the example these are the doThis(), doThat() and use..() calls)
- spawn a new sub-process, called a *promise*, that will run asynchronously (this corresponds to the promise() calls in the example)
- await the completion of the spawned promises, based on a principle of *barrier synchronization* (in the example, the barriers are w1, w2 and w3). Note that a control thread may wait for multiple barriers at once, in an atomic manner (using Promise.all(...)).

Each promise is associated to a dedicated barrier, which it has to use to *signal* its termination to the control thread (in Listing 1.1, this is the role of the resolve() callback). The promises can also perform atomic actions and indeed be labeled async to become control threads themselves. In this case, we will say that the system has a *promise depth* greater than 1 (we will come back to this important characteristic later on).

Table 1. A calculus for async/await concurrency, and the definition of *promise depth*

$$
\begin{array}{llll}
\text{Process } P, Q & ::= & 0 & : \text{terminate the control thread} \\
& | & \alpha.P & : \text{perform action } \alpha \text{ and continue as process } P \\
& | & \nu(\omega)[Q].P & : \text{spawn promise } Q \text{ with barrier } \omega, \\
& & & \quad \text{and continue to run } P \text{ asynchronously} \\
& | & \overline{\omega} & : \text{signal on barrier } \omega \text{ (from a promise)} \\
& | & \langle \Omega \rangle.P & : \text{await all barriers in set } \Omega, \text{ and} \\
& & & \quad \text{after synchronization continue as } P
\end{array}
$$

$$
\left[
\begin{array}{l}
\text{depth}(0) = \text{depth}(\overline{\omega}) = 0 \\
\text{depth}(\alpha.P) = \text{depth}(\langle \Omega \rangle.P) = \text{depth}(P) \\
\text{depth}(\nu(\omega)[Q].P) = \max(\text{depth}(Q) + 1, \text{depth}(P))
\end{array}
\right.
$$

Table 1 presents the syntax of a process calculus that captures the features listed above, and nothing much beyond that. There is also the formal definition of the promise depth introduced previously. Using the proposed syntax, our example can be abstracted as follows:

$$
\text{this}.\nu(\omega_1)[\text{prom}_1.\overline{\omega_1}] \,.\nu(\omega_2)[\text{prom}_2.\overline{\omega_2}] \,.\text{that}.\nu(\omega_3)[\text{prom}_3.\overline{\omega_3}]
$$
$$
.\langle w_1 \rangle.\text{use}_1 \,.\langle w_2, w_3 \rangle.\text{use}_{2,3}.0
$$

Once the syntactic objects under study set, we have to give them a semantic interpretation. One way of explaining the behavior of processes is to pro-

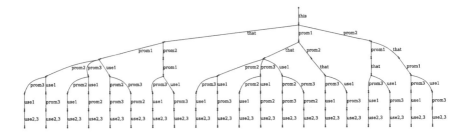

Fig. 1. A computation tree corresponding to the example of Listing 1.1

vide an operational semantics[3], which enables the construction of a first combinatorial object worth studying: what is colloquially called a *computation tree*. Figure 1 depicts the operational semantics of our example as a computation tree. Each directed edge in the tree corresponds to a possible labeled transition. For example, in the initial state only the atomic action labeled "this" is possible, which leads to a state from which three distinct transitions are possible: "that", "prom$_1$" and "prom$_2$" (the other actions being blocked by await constructs), and so on. Each possible *execution path* is depicted by a distinct branch in the tree. This representation has the interesting combinatorial characteristic of relating a structural notion of a size – the number of atomic actions to perform identified with the length of each path – to a corresponding semantic notion of a size – the number of execution paths identified with the number of leaves of the tree. In the example there are 20 distinct execution paths and each path has length 7. Most importantly, the number of leaves grows exponentially in the path length.

Table 2. Async/await processes: partial order semantics

$$[\![P]\!] = [\![P]\!]_{\circ_\top} \setminus \{\circ_\bot, \circ_\top\}$$
$$[\![0]\!]_x = \{x \mapsto \circ_\bot\}$$
$$[\![\alpha.P]\!]_x = [\![P]\!]_{\bullet_\alpha} \cup \{x \mapsto \bullet_\alpha\}$$
$$[\![\nu(\omega)[Q].P]\!]_{\bullet_u} = [\![\nu(\omega)[Q].P]\!]_{\circ_v} \cup \{\bullet_u \mapsto \circ_v\} \text{ with } \circ_v \text{ fresh}$$
$$[\![\nu(\omega)[Q].P]\!]_{\circ_v} = [\![Q]\!]_{\circ_v} \parallel_\omega [\![P]\!]_{\circ_v}$$
$$[\![\overline{\omega}]\!]_x = \{x \mapsto \circ_\omega\}$$
$$[\![\langle\Omega\rangle.P]\!]_{\bullet_u} = [\![\langle\Omega\rangle.P]\!]_{\circ_v} \cup \{\bullet_u \mapsto \circ_v\} \text{ with } \circ_v \text{ fresh}$$
$$[\![\langle\Omega\rangle.P]\!]_{\circ_v} = [\![P]\!]_{\circ_v} \cup \{\circ_\omega \mapsto \circ_v \mid \omega \in \Omega\}$$
$$\text{with } X_1 \parallel_\omega X_2 = \{x_1 \mapsto y_1 \in X_1 \mid y_1 \neq \circ_\omega\} \cup \{x_2 \mapsto y_2 \in X_2 \mid x_2 \neq \circ_\omega\}$$
$$\cup \{x \mapsto y \mid x \mapsto \circ_\omega \in X_1 \wedge \circ_\omega \mapsto y \in X_2\}$$

---

[3] In [4] we provide an operational semantics for a calculus of "barrier synchronization", which subsumes the async/await processes.

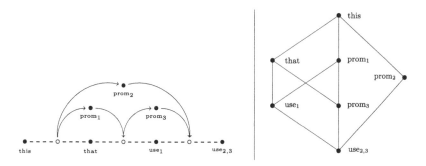

Fig. 2. The control graph (*chord process*, left) and the associated partial order (right) of the example of Listing 1.1

The main problem we are concerned with is the counting of possible execution paths of processes. With computation trees the solution is trivial since we only have to count the leaves of the tree. However, the construction of the tree itself suffers from combinatorial explosion, making this approach impractical. We thus adopt a more compact construction scheme, which is defined in Table 2. The idea is to interpret an async/await process as a directed acyclic graph (DAG) – namely its *control graph*. Figure 2 (left) depicts the result of the construction for our example process. In the constructed graph the nodes are *events* from two complementary kinds. The *white* nodes ∘ encode the control-structure of the processes, i.e. when processes are forked or when they synchronize. Each *black* node, denoted by $\bullet_\alpha$, encodes the occurrence of an atomic action α. The dashed line at the bottom corresponds to the control thread, and the *chords* above correspond to promises. This DAG has several good properties. First of all, its size is linear in the syntactic size of processes, hence there is no "explosion" involved at this step. Moreover, (intransitive) DAGs are tightly related to partially ordered sets (Posets) in that they correspond to their *transitive reduction*. In the computation tree of Fig. 1 only the labels of the atomic actions are considered. We can perform a similar abstraction on the control graph be removing the white nodes while maintaining the relations among the black ones.

Definition 1 (Partial orders of async/await processes).
Let P be an async/await process. We define: $\mathcal{PO}(P) = \{\alpha > \beta \mid \bullet_\alpha \mapsto \circ_u, \circ_u \mapsto \bullet_\beta \in [\![P]\!]\}^{refl\text{-}trans}$ *with, for a binary relation R,* $R^{refl\text{-}trans} = \bigcup_{n \geq 0} R^n$.

On the right of Fig. 2 the resulting poset is depicted using the most common representation as a Hasse diagram. There is an important connection between computation trees and such partial order semantics.

Theorem 1. *The number of transitions of an async/await process P, hence the number of leaves of its computation tree, corresponds to the number Ψ_P of linear extensions of $\mathcal{PO}(P)$*

Proof. This is a corollary of [4, Proposition 2.1], in which we consider a class of concurrent systems more general than that of async/await processes.   □

3 Partial Order Decomposition and the Counting Problem

We now investigate the problem of counting the execution paths of an async/await process P, based on the DAG representation $[\![P]\!]$ or, alternatively, its abstraction $\mathcal{PO}(P)$ as discussed in the previous section. The problem boils down to the counting of linear extensions in families of posets closely related to async/await processes[4].

Table 3. Series-parallel constructions and associated counting formulas (cf. [16]).

Series	$P \odot Q = (X_P \uplus X_Q, >_P \cup >_Q \cup (X_P \times X_Q))$	$\Psi_{P \odot Q} = \Psi_P \cdot \Psi_Q$
Parallel	$P \parallel Q = (X_P \uplus X_Q, >_P \cup >_Q)$	$\Psi_{P \parallel Q} = \binom{\lvert P\rvert + \lvert Q\rvert}{\lvert P\rvert} \cdot \Psi_P \cdot \Psi_Q$

$$\text{with } P = (X_P, >_P) \text{ and } Q = (X_Q, >_Q)$$

To our knowledge, there are very few (non-trivial) poset subclasses for which the counting problem can be said to be "easy". One remarkable example is that of *series-parallel* posets with dedicated and simple counting formulas, as described in Table 3. Async/await processes are not, in general, decomposable with only series and parallel operators. However, some of them *are* and, most importantly, one can often find series-parallel substructures in larger processes. This means that it is sometimes possible to use the series-parallel counting formulas, which we take advantage of in Sect. 5.

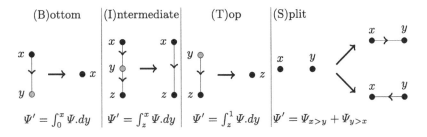

Fig. 3. BITS-decomposition and associated counting formula (from [4])

In [4] we define an alternative decomposing scheme for arbitrary partial orders. This so-called BITS-decomposition, summarized in Fig. 3, consists in applying "elimination rules" on the transitive reduction of a partial order, or equivalently on any intransitive DAG. The B-rule allows to remove a bottom node y, hence with in-degree 1 and out-degree 0. The T-rule is the complement for top nodes. The I-rule eliminates internal nodes with in and out degrees 1.

---

[4] We denote by $X_1 \uplus X_2$ the *disjoint sum* of the two sets X_1 and X_2.

Finally the S-rule consists in replacing two nodes x and y that are incomparable in the poset (they could both have parents or children in the DAG, which is not represented here), by two cases: first x is larger than y or the reverse y is larger than x. Obviously this rule induces a *split* requiring to consider then two distinct sub-orders. Most importantly, a symbolic formula Ψ for the linear extensions count (of the induced poset) can be constructed along the decomposition. Moreover, if one manages to only use the BIT-rules for decomposing a poset – which is then qualified as BIT-decomposable – then the formula we obtain is of a linear size. This does not mean that the counting problem itself becomes easy (in fact we conjecture it remains $\sharp P$-complete), however we get: (1) a concise way to formulate it, and (2) an effective way of computing the result using a computer algebra system.

One of the main result of the present paper follows.

Theorem 2. *The control graph $[\![P]\!]$ of an async/await processes P is BIT-decomposable.*

Proof (Proof sketch). The construction ensures that the black nodes have all in-degree and out-degree exactly one. Indeed, only white nodes can have in-degree or out-degree > 1 representing join or spawn events. The I-rule of the construction is thus powerful enough to remove the black nodes. Now, we consider the promises with maximal depth (i.e. promises not making further promises). Since such a promise cannot spawn a process, it has no white node except its fork and join events. Since we can remove its black nodes the promise itself can be removed, which means the out-degree of its fork node is reduced by one, and so is the in-degree of its join node. Hence, all promises of maximal depth can be removed by the BIT-rules. Once removed, their parent promises become of maximal depth, and by a simple inductive argument we conclude that the whole structure is decomposable. □

Here is an example of the counting formula generated thanks to the decomposition of the control graph of Fig. 2 (white nodes are labeled by w_1, w_2 and w_3 from left to right):

$$\int_0^1 \int_0^{w_1} \int_0^{w_2} \int_0^{w_3} \int_{w_1}^1 \int_{w_3}^{w_1} \int_{w_3}^{w_2} \int_{w_2}^{w_1} \int_{w_2}^{w_1} \int_{w_3}^{w_2} 1$$
$$d\text{use}_1 d\text{that} d\text{prom}_1 d\text{prom}_3 d\text{prom}_2 d\text{this} d\text{use}_{2,3} dw_3 dw_2 dw_1.$$

Once evaluated, this multivariate integral formula produces the value 24, which corresponds to the number of possible executions paths in the control graph. Note that this is more than the 20 possible execution branches of the computation tree of Fig. 1, since the white nodes are also taken into account and not just the atomic actions. If we consider the partial order $\mathcal{PO}(P)$ with all white nodes abstracted away, then BIT-decomposability is not guaranteed anymore. In the next section this is discussed more thoroughly but we can still consider the poset of (the right of) Fig. 2 as an illustration. The only node with input/output arity one is the node labeled "prom$_2$" and the other nodes have an arity > 1 even if "prom$_2$"

is deleted. Hence, this poset is *not* BIT-decomposable. However, luckily, it can be decomposed in series-parallel, as follows: this $\odot$ (((that $\|$ prom$_1$) $\odot$ (use$_1$ $\|$ prom$_3$)) $\|$ prom$_2$) $\odot$ use$_{2,3}$.

We can compute the number of linear extensions according to Table 3, which, schematically, gives:

$$1 \cdot ((\binom{2}{1} \cdot 1 \cdot 1) \cdot (\binom{2}{1} \cdot 1 \cdot 1) \| 1) \cdot 1 = (2 \cdot 2) \| 1 = \binom{4+1}{4} \cdot 4 \cdot 1 = 5 \cdot 4 = 20.$$

This is of course the number of leaves of the computation tree of Fig. 1.

4   Chord Processes, Interval Orders and Related Families

We now dig deeper into combinatorics questions. Our objective is to characterize relevant subclasses of async/await processes in a constructive way, following the principles of the *symbolic method* [12, part A]. The basic idea is to use generating functions to enumerate, symbolically, the constructed objects of a given size in the considered combinatorial class, and to derive an inductive equation (or less constrained, a functional equation) satisfied by such function. Most importantly, our ultimate goal is to relate such process subclasses to corresponding classes of partial orders. This imposes that we somewhat restrict the possibilities of constructing processes. In this section, we adopt the following constraints. First, we require that a promise spawned by a process performs exactly one atomic action at start-up time, which means that atomic actions and promises are somehow identified. Then, the promise may spawn one or several promises of greater depth, but ultimately it has to signal on its dedicated barrier. Moreover, we make sure that the number of white nodes is minimized in the control graphs. Because of its proximity to what is called a chord diagram elsewhere [21], the class we study in this section will be named *chord processes*.

Our first subclass of interest, named $\mathcal{S}_1$, considers chord processes with two further restrictions: (1) the *depth* of the process is one, and (2) there is no redundant promise. The first constraint means that there is exactly one control thread, thus promises cannot spawn further promises. For the second constraint, we consider two promises to be redundant if they are spawned and synchronized at the same time (i.e. they have the same origin and destination white nodes in the control graph). The class $\mathcal{S}_1$ corresponds to so-called *non-redundant* chord processes.

An example of a control graph of a process in the class $\mathcal{S}_1$ is depicted in Fig. 4 (left). We consider the size of such a process to be the number of black nodes in the control graph, hence here the size is 8. The abstraction from white nodes is essential to properly capture the order-theoretic nature of the construction. Note however that the white nodes are still part of the construction, only they do not participate in the size of the objects.

In order to explain the construction of the class $\mathcal{S}_1$ properly, we need to consider a slightly larger class, named $\mathcal{S}_1^+$, whose multivariate generating function

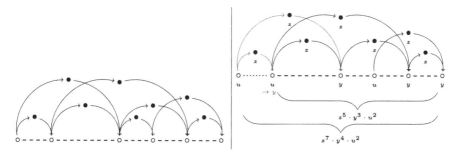

Fig. 4. (left) A process of class $\mathcal{S}_1$; (right) A process with monomial $z^5 y^3 u^2$, preceded by a new node u that spawns 2 promises (the new monomial is $z^7 y^4 u^2$).

can be written as follows:

$$S_1^+(z, y, u) = \sum_{n,k,\ell \geq 0} s_{n,k,\ell} \, z^n \, y^k \, u^\ell$$

We need no less than three parameters in this definition. First, the main parameter is z which represents the size of the objects[5]. The variable y is used to count the white nodes that can be simultaneous async and await events, while u counts the remaining white nodes that are "async only". In the definition above, the coefficient $s_{n,k,\ell}$ corresponds to the number of processes in the $\mathcal{S}_1^+$ class with n black nodes, k async and await white nodes, and ℓ "async only" nodes.

In the right part of Fig. 4, we illustrate how a larger process can be constructed from a smaller one while preserving the constraints of the considered combinatorial class $\mathcal{S}_1^+$. The process delimited by the "interior" brace is of size 5 (its number of black nodes), with $3 + 2$ white nodes. The "exterior" brace delimits a larger process consisting in prepending a "async only" (u) white node on the control thread, here with two non-redundant spawned promises[6]. This process increases the size by 2 because each promise performs an action, and we can see that a previously "async only" (u) white node now serves as an await and thus becomes a y node. Hence the larger process is characterized by the monomial $z^7 \cdot y^4 \cdot u^2$.

Summarizing all the possibilities of such incremental constructions, we now define more formally the combinatorial class $\mathcal{S}_1^+$ as follows.

Definition 2. *The generating function for the combinatorial class $\mathcal{S}_1^+$ is such that:*

$$S_1^+(z, y, u) = u + u \left(S_1^+(z, y + y \cdot z, u + y \cdot z) - S_1^+(z, y, u) \right). \tag{1}$$

---

[5] We remind the reader that generating function are formal *power series*, counting "things" through polynomial degrees.

[6] To be non-redundant from the same origin, the promises must have distinct destination white nodes.

The smallest process satisfying the equation is of size 0, consisting in just a single white node u (the first summand of the right-hand side of the equation). The basic principle to obtain a larger processes S' from a smaller process S is given by the second summand. This consists in adding a new white node of kind u at the beginning of the control thread (as illustrated on the right of Fig. 4), which corresponds to the u in factor in the equation. We then have to account for all the possibilities to connect this new "async" node with the rest of the process S with new promises. We consider each white node of S in turn. If it is a y node then either it stays the same, or it receives a new promise originating from the new u, hence becoming $y \cdot z$, the new z corresponding to the action of the spawned promise. If it is a u then either it is left untouched or it becomes a $y \cdot z$. In the construction, we force the new white node u to spawn at least one promise to the previous process, which is why we subtract the term $S_1^+(z, y, u)$ in the equation above, where no promise has been spawned.

Proposition 1. *Definition 2 is a sound and non-ambiguous construction.*

Proof. For the soundness part we need to prove that $\mathcal{S}_1^+$ effectively describes a combinatorial class. This means that for a given size n (the number of black nodes), there is a finite number of structures satisfying the equation of Definition 2. First, we identify the number of promises and the number of black nodes, thus there are exactly n promises for size n. The equation also enforces that each u or y node spawns at least one promise (except for the rightmost white node), so there are at most $n + 1$ such white nodes. Hence, for each such promise it remains in the worst case $n + 1$ white nodes as destination so a simple upper bound in the number of possibilities is $(n + 1)^n$. Thus, the number of admissible structures of size n is indeed finite.

The second important characteristics of a functional equation enumerating a combinatorial class is that it does not construct several times the same object (i.e. it is non-ambiguous). This is a fundamental characteristics because we use this functional equation to derive the number of objects of a given size. This property can be demonstrated by structural induction. For the base case, we consider the fact that there is a single minimal structure, namely $z^0 \cdot y^0 \cdot u^1$. And for the inductive case, if we suppose that a structure S has been constructed non-ambiguously then all the possible "one-step" larger structures S' are also obtained non-ambiguously through the equation of Definition 2. $\square$

The process class we are looking for is not directly $\mathcal{S}_1^+$ but a slightly restricted variant in which all the white nodes must be of the y kind, with the exception of the leftmost one of kind u. This accounts for our initial constraint that white nodes are minimized. Thus, the subsequence we consider is $(\cup_{k \geq 0} s_{n,k,1})_{n \in \mathbb{N}}$ in which only one parameter remains: the size n. We regroup all processes of size n regardless their number of white nodes. From this we obtain one of the main technical results of this paper.

Theorem 3. *The univariate generating function enumerating the processes from S_1 by their number of atomic actions is given by the explicit equation:*

$$S_1(z) = \frac{\partial S_1^+}{\partial u}(z, 1, 0) = 1 + \sum_{k \geq 1} \prod_{i=1}^{k} \left(1 - \frac{1}{(1+z)^i}\right).$$

The intuition here follows from Definition 2 taking into account the restriction to S_1 (having one white node), and abstracting away from the counting of the other white nodes. This explains the derivative on the left-hand side of the equation followed by the partial assignment $y \leftarrow 1; u \leftarrow 0$.

Proof. We are starting from Definition 2, but the exact enumeration for S_1, where only the actions are counted and the white nodes do not count anymore is such that in the processes enumerated by $S_1^+(z, y, u)$ only the last added white node u is not an await node (all other white nodes are thus been marked by y) and we do not care about the number of these white nodes. So the generating function for S_1 is given by $\frac{\partial S_1^+}{\partial u}(z, 1, 0)$. In fact, since we are interested in the monomials $\gamma \, z^n \, y^k \, u$, once differentiated according to u, they are not depending on u anymore, and then evaluating at $u = 0$ erases monomials where there still remains the u variable. Finally, letting $y = 1$, regroups together all monomials $\gamma' z^n$. Thus, with a partial differentiation in u:

$$\frac{\partial S_1^+}{\partial u}(z, y, u) = \frac{1}{(1+u)^2} \left(1 + S_1^+(z, y \cdot (1+z), u + y \cdot z)\right) + \frac{u}{1+u} \frac{\partial S_1^+}{\partial u}(z, y \cdot (1+z), u + y \cdot z).$$

Then by evaluating y at 1 and u at 0, it remains

$$\frac{\partial S_1^+}{\partial u}(z, 1, 0) = 1 + S_1^+(z, 1 + z, z).$$

Before going on, let us simplify Eq. (1) so that:

$$S_1^+(z, y, u) = \frac{u}{1+u} \left(1 + S_1^+(z, y + y \cdot z, u + y \cdot z)\right).$$

Now by injecting the latter equation we obtain

$$\frac{\partial S_1^+}{\partial u}(z, 1, 0) = 1 + \frac{z}{1+z} \left(1 + S_1^+(z, (1+z)^2, z + (1+z)z)\right).$$

By iterating this substitution we get:

$$\frac{\partial S_1^+}{\partial u}(z, 1, 0) = 1 + \sum_{k=0}^{n} \prod_{i=0}^{k} z \frac{(1+z)^0 + \cdots + (1+z)^i}{1 + (1+z)^0 z + \cdots + (1+z)^i z}$$

$$+ \prod_{i=0}^{n} z \frac{(1+z)^0 + \cdots + (1+z)^i}{1 + (1+z)^0 z + \cdots + (1+z)^i z}$$

$$\cdot S_1(z, (1+z)^{n+2}, (1+z)^0 z + \cdots + (1+z)^{n+1} z).$$

Letting n tending to infinity we finally get

$$\frac{\partial S_1^+}{\partial u}(z,1,0) = 1 + \sum_{k \geq 0} \prod_{i=0}^{k} z \frac{(1+z)^0 + \cdots + (1+z)^i}{1 + (1+z)^0 z + \cdots + (1+z)^i z} = 1 + \sum_{k \geq 0} \prod_{i=0}^{k} z \frac{\frac{1-(1+z)^{i+1}}{1-(1+z)}}{1 + z \frac{1-(1+z)^{i+1}}{1-(1+z)}}$$

$$= 1 + \sum_{k \geq 1} \prod_{i=1}^{k} \frac{(1+z)^i - 1}{(1+z)^i} = 1 + \sum_{k \geq 1} \prod_{i=1}^{k} \left(1 - \frac{1}{(1+z)^i}\right).$$

And the stated results are proved.   □

Based on this theorem, we can compute the counting sequence of S_1 processes. The first numbers from size 1 to 14 are as follows:

$$1, 1, 2, 5, 16, 61, 271, 1372, 7795, 49093, 339386, 2554596, 20794982, 182010945.$$

We think that this is a remarkable result since the sequence is in fact already known as OEIS A138265[7], which is the enumeration of rigid (unlabeled) interval orders [15]. Indeed, this class of partial order is characterized by the same functional equation, which establishes a one-to-one correspondence between the thoroughly studied class of interval orders [11] and the async/await processes. The interval orders are counted by the sequence of *Fishburn numbers* stored in OEIS A022493. The numbers of interval orders of sizes 1 to 14 are

$$1, 2, 5, 15, 53, 217, 1014, 5335, 31240, 201608, 1422074, 10886503, 89903100, 796713190.$$

It is interesting to see if we can define a class of async/await processes that exactly matches the interval orders. We of course consider the class S_1^+ as a starting point, since it corresponds to a restriction of interval orders. In fact, what distinguishes OEIS A138265 from OEIS A022493 is precisely the notion of redundant promise we introduced previously. We thus consider the subclass S_2 of the async/await processes, which corresponds to the class S_1 but allowing redundant promises.

Theorem 4. *We consider the class* S_2 *defined by the following equations:*

$$S_2(z) = \frac{\partial S_2^+}{\partial u}(z,1,0) \text{ with } S_2^+(z,y,u) = S_1^+\left(\frac{z}{1-z}, y, u\right).$$

The processes in S_2 *are in one-to-one correspondence with interval orders.*

Proof. Similarly to the previous results, we introduce an auxiliary class of processes, namely S_2^+, defined from S_1^+ (of Definition 2) but in which we allow to substitute each promise by a finite sequence of redundant promises. Thus the z in the definition becomes $z/(1-z)$ which is the closed formula for non-empty sequences (of z's). Now, from Theorem 3 and applying the substitution we obtain the equation:

$$\frac{\partial S_2^+}{\partial u}(z,1,0) = 1 + \sum_{k \geq 1} \prod_{i=1}^{k} \left(1 - (1-z)^i\right).$$

---

[7] Throughout this paper, a reference OEIS A··· points to an entry of Sloane's Online Encyclopedia of Integer Sequences www.oeis.org.

This equation exactly matches the generating function proposed in [5] to count the (unlabeled) interval orders.   □

As an interesting corollary, we remark that the bivariate generating functions $y\frac{\partial S_1^+}{\partial u}(z, y, 0)$ and $y\frac{\partial S_2^+}{\partial u}(z, y, 0)$ can be calculated easily from the previous theorems. These characterize the distributions of the number of white nodes in processes of a given size, which correspond to sequences already studied in the context of interval orders (respectively in OEIS A137252 and OEIS A137251). The concerned parameter of interval orders is called the *magnitude* [10]. There is a simple interpretation of the magnitude in terms of concurrency: this is the number of white nodes in the control thread of a chord process (respectively without or with redundant promises).

Once the connection with existing mathematical structures established, it is interesting to look for possible variations inspired by concurrency aspects. For now we considered chord processes of depth 1 and identified them with interval orders. It seems thus quite natural to investigate the process structures of depth > 1. The basic technical principle at work is the possibility to substitute subprocesses within processes through substitutions in the equations for the associated generating functions. For example, to construct S_2^+ from S_1^+ we substituted a promise by a sequence of promises. Accordingly, it seems possible to substitute a promise by a whole chord process. This way, from a subprocess of depth n we can construct a process of depth $n + 1$. In order to obtain a sound and non-ambiguous generalization of interval orders (of depth > 1), we must ensure that the elementary subprocesses are proper chord processes (hence "simple" interval orders). This leads to the following definition.

Definition 3. *The class S_3 of generalized interval orders is defined by the equation:*

$$S_3(z) = \frac{\partial S_3^+}{\partial u}(z, 1, 0)$$
$$\text{with } S_3^+(z, y, u) = \frac{u}{1+u}\left(1 + S_3^+\left(z, \frac{y}{1-z(1+S_3^+(z))}, u + y\frac{z(1+S_3^+(z))}{1-z(1+S_3^+(z))}\right)\right).$$

If compared to the previous equations, this definition is recursive so that whole sub-processes can be substituted.

Despite this extra complexity, it is still quite possible to enumerate efficiently the terms of the counting sequence. The number of processes in class S_3 from size 1 to 14 are

1, 3, 12, 56, 289, 1606, 9471, 58790, 382496, 2604284, 18564013, 138808595, 1092001289, 9070517772.

This sequence is not present yet in OEIS and will thus be submitted for contribution.

5   Uniform Random Generation: Experimental Study

In this section we present an experimentation of combinatorial algorithms directly connected to our study. Our objective is more to highlight the kinds of problem that can be solved in practice based on our combinatorial study, rather than a detailed description of the algorithms themselves. However, the whole source code of the experiment is available online in a complement repository[8] with detailed instructions.

Generating Structures. We investigate the generation of process structures using three complementary ways. First, there is the systematic enumeration of the structures by size. Since for each finite size we know that there is a finite number of possible structures, the second interesting way of generating a structure is through what is called *unranking*: construct the k-th structure of a given size n. Last but not least the generation of structures uniformly at random represents an interesting way to validate experimentally conjectures about said structures. In our case, this provides us a way to compare algorithms based on different techniques, without having too much of bias in the comparison.

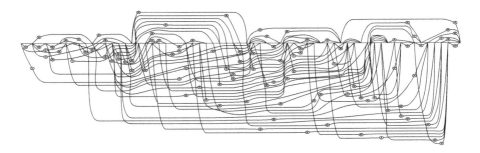

Fig. 5. The chord process corresponding to the unranking of ascent sequence of size $n = 100$ and rank $k = S_2[100]/2 - 1$

For all these needs, our starting point is [5] in which a constructive bijection between interval orders and *ascent sequences* is proposed. Quoting OEIS A022493:

> An ascent sequence is a sequence $[d(1), d(2), \ldots, d(n)]$ where $d(1) = 0$, $d(k) \geq 0$, and $d(k) \leq 1 + asc([d(1), d(2), \ldots, d(k-1)])$ where $asc(.)$ counts the ascents of its argument.

The enumeration of ascent sequences is easy, and moreover counting the number of such sequences of a given size n can be performed in polynomial time (in $O(n^3)$ arithmetic operations). This gives us first a quick way for unranking a sequence. Ascent sequences of a given length n can be recursively decomposed so the classical *recursive method* of [2] can be used to design a relatively efficient random sampler (in $O(n^2)$, once the complete counting of the number of structures until size n has been performed). The output of the sampler is an ascent sequence, i.e. a list of numbers, which we have to convert to an interval order

---

[8] cf. https://gitlab.com/ParComb/async-await-randgen.

exploiting the bijection of [5]. In a further step we can use the inverse of the construction of Table 2 to obtain a corresponding control graph, from which a process expression can be easily obtained. This way, we obtain a uniform random sampler for chord processes. As an illustration, in Fig. 5 we give an example of a generated chord process of size 100 from an unranked ascent sequence. More precisely, the sequence has rank $S_2[100]/2 - 1$ (where $S_2[100]$ is the number of sequences of size 100).

Uniform Random Generation of Execution Paths. Based on the algorithm described in [4], we now experiment the uniform random generation of execution paths of chord processes. The main interest of this algorithm is that it does not require the explicit construction of the state space of processes.

Table 4. Uniform random generation of execution paths.

Size	Rank	Nb. paths	Counting time (s)	Random gen. (avg. s)
10	81694	$\approx 8.0 \, e^5$	$4.1 \, e^{-4}$ s	$3.1 \, e^{-3}$ s
15	7122308736	$\approx 1.9 \, e^6$	$2.2 \, e^{-3}$ s	$4.5 \, e^{-3}$ s
20	230090562434702	$\approx 1.3 \, e^{13}$	$4.1 \, e^{-2}$ s	$2.3 \, e^{-2}$ s
25	113615274237648394333	$\approx 2.2 \, e^{17}$	1.5 s	$6.3 \, e^{-1}$ s
30	314109479073694330556823298	$\approx 2.2 \, e^{24}$	3.4 s	1.3 s

In Table 4 we provide the results of a preliminary benchmark of our random sampler for execution paths. The computer used for the experiments runs on GNU/Linux (Ubuntu 20.04), with a Intel Core i7-6700 CPU cadenced at 3.40GHz and 8Go of RAM. The input of the algorithm are random chord processes generated as explained previously. For each sampled process (described by its size and rank), we give the result of the counting procedure and the associated timing. And finally we generate 10 execution paths and provide the average generation time. While the implementation of the algorithm is at a very early stage of development, we think that the timing results show promising figures. Indeed, it is possible to generate execution paths uniformly at random in processes in a reasonable time, in the order of a few seconds in a size 30 process with quite a large state-space.

6   Conclusion and Future Work

The interpretation of concurrent systems as combinatorial objects is, we think, quite an insightful perspective. Our measure of the "complexity" of concurrent systems is that of counting execution paths. From this point of view, we show that thanks to BIT-decomposability the counting problem is in a way "simpler" for async/await processes than for arbitrary ones (in [4]). Complementary, interval orders can be seen as basic generators for async/await control paths, as suggested by our combinatorial investigation. While it is arguably a kind of a stretch, this correlates the practical experience that async/concurrency is a "simpler" form of concurrency, easier to deal with than less constrained forms. Taking this perspective upside-down, async/await processes can be seen as a generalization of interval orders, and are thus worth studying from a purely combinatorial point of view. Our section on experimenting with uniform random generation algorithms is mostly proposed as a proof of concept. We argue that there is an interest in developing analysis methods based on such building blocks. A strong argument in favor is that the algorithms can be applied directly on (the control graph of) processes without having to unfold the state-space.

References

1. Abbes, S., Mairesse, J.: Uniform generation in trace monoids. In: Italiano, G.F., Pighizzini, G., Sannella, D.T. (eds.) MFCS 2015. LNCS, vol. 9234, pp. 63–75. Springer, Heidelberg (2015). https://doi.org/10.1007/978-3-662-48057-1_5
2. Bychkov, A., Pogudin, G.: Optimal monomial quadratization for ODE systems. In: Flocchini, P., Moura, L. (eds.) IWOCA 2021. LNCS, vol. 12757, pp. 122–136. Springer, Cham (2021). https://doi.org/10.1007/978-3-030-79987-8_9
3. Basset, N., Mairesse, J., Soria, M.: Uniform sampling for networks of automata. In: Meyer, R., Nestmann, U. (eds.) CONCUR 2017, Berlin, Germany, 5–8 September 2017, LIPIcs, vol. 85, pp. 36:1–36:16 (2017)
4. Bodini, O., Dien, M., Genitrini, A., Peschanski, F.: Quantitative and algorithmic aspects of barrier synchronization in concurrency. Discret. Math. Theor. Comput. Sci. **22**(3), 1–36 (2021)
5. Bousquet-Mélou, M., Claesson, A., Dukes, M., Kitaev, S.: (2+2)-free posets, ascent sequences and pattern avoiding permutations. J. Comb. Theory, Ser. A **117**(7), 884–909 (2010)
6. Brightwell, G., Winkler, P.: Counting linear extensions is ♯p-complete. In: Proceedings of the Twenty-Third Annual ACM Symposium on Theory of Computing, STOC 1991, pp. 175–181. Association for Computing Machinery, New York (1991)
7. Dittmer, S., Pak, I.: Counting linear extensions of restricted posets. Electron. J. Comb. **27**(4), 4–48 (2020)
8. ECMA international: ECMAScript Language Specification, 9th edn. (2018)
9. Esparza, J., Heljanko, K.: Unfoldings. Springer, Heidleberg (2008). https://doi.org/10.1007/978-3-540-77426-6
10. Fishburn, P.C.: Interval lengths for interval orders: a minimization problem. Disc. Math. **47**, 63–82 (1983)
11. Fishburn, P.C.: Interval graphs and interval orders. Disc. Math. **55**(2), 135–149 (1985)
12. Flajolet, P., Sedgewick, R.: Analytic Combinatorics. Cambridge University Press, Cambridge (2009)
13. Huber, M.: Fast perfect sampling from linear extensions. Disc. Math. **306**(4), 420–428 (2006)
14. Kangas, K., Hankala, T., Niinimäki, T.M., Koivisto, M.: Counting linear extensions of sparse posets. In: IJCAI 2016. IJCAI/AAAI Press (2016)
15. Khamis, S.M.: Exact counting of unlabeled rigid interval posets regarding or disregarding height. Order **29**(3), 443–461 (2012)

16. Mörhing, R.H.: Algorithms and order (edited by ivan rival), chap. Computationally tractable classes of ordered sets, p. 127. Kluwer Academic Publishers (1987)
17. Oudinet, J., Denise, A., Gaudel, M.-C., Lassaigne, R., Peyronnet, S.: Uniform Monte-Carlo model checking. In: Giannakopoulou, D., Orejas, F. (eds.) FASE 2011. LNCS, vol. 6603, pp. 127–140. Springer, Heidelberg (2011). https://doi.org/10.1007/978-3-642-19811-3_10
18. Prasad, K., Patil, A., Miller, H.: Programming Models for Distributed Computing, chap. Futures and Promises (2017)
19. Pruesse, G., Ruskey, F.: Generating linear extensions fast. SIAM J. Comput. **23**(2), 373–386 (1994)
20. Selivanov, Y.: PEP 492 - Coroutines with async and await syntax. Python Org. (2015)
21. Stoimenow, A.: Enumeration of chord diagrams and an upper bound for vassiliev invariants. J. Knot Theory Ramifications **07**(01), 93–114 (1998)
22. Valiant, L.G.: A bridging model for parallel computation. Commun. ACM **33**(8), 103–111 (1990)

Unsatisfiability of Comparison-Based Non-malleability for Commitments

Denis Firsov[1,2]($\boxtimes$), Sven Laur[3], and Ekaterina Zhuchko[2,3]

[1] Guardtime, Tallinn, Estonia
denis.firsov@guardtime.com
[2] Tallinn University of Technology, Tallinn, Estonia
ekzhuc@ttu.ee
[3] Tartu University, Tartu, Estonia
swen@math.ut.ee

Abstract. There are two distinct formulations of non-malleability of commitments found in the literature: the comparison-based definition and the simulation-based definition. In this paper, we prove that the comparison-based definition is unsatisfiable by any realistic commitment scheme. Our proof is fully formalized in the EasyCrypt theorem prover.

Keywords: Cryptography · Commitments · Comparison-based · Non-malleability · Formal methods · EasyCrypt

1 Introduction

A commitment scheme is one of the fundamental primitives in cryptography. Intuitively, we can think of a commitment as a locked box containing a message. Only the sender who produced the commitment knows the secret opening key which can unlock the box and reveal the message. The sender can send this box to a receiver and then at a later stage give him the opening key to unlock it.

The most fundamental security properties of commitments are hiding and binding. We say that a commitment is hiding if an adversary is unable to see the message without the opening key (the box which contains the message should not be transparent). We say that a commitment is binding if, once the sender committed to a message and sent the commitment to the receiver, the sender cannot open the commitment to a different message (the box should not have any secret backdoors or double bottoms). But these properties do not prevent all of the attacks and most notably the "man-in-the-middle" attacks.

The *non-malleability* property aims to protect commitments against man-in-the-middle attacks. In such an attack, we have Mallory who is an active adversary between two parties: Alice and Bob. Let's assume that Alice sends a commitment c of a message m to Bob. However, all of their communication goes through the man-in-the-middle adversary Mallory who can modify the commitment or simply not deliver it. The goal of Mallory is to generate a commitment c' (based

© The Author(s), under exclusive license to Springer Nature Switzerland AG 2022
H. Seidl et al. (Eds.): ICTAC 2022, LNCS 13572, pp. 188–194, 2022.
https://doi.org/10.1007/978-3-031-17715-6_13

only on the commitment c) to another message m' which is non-trivially related to the original message m.[1] Later, for a successful attack, Mallory must generate an opening d' for commitment c' when it sees the Alice's opening d for commitment c.

A classical motivating example where non-malleability would be needed is that of a blind auction. Consider an auction where participants bid for an item by publishing commitments to their bids. At the end, bidders open their commitments and the highest bid wins. If the commitment scheme is malleable, an adversary could participate in the auction by posting for each of the other bids a commitment to a bid that is only one dollar higher. In this case, the adversary would have an unfair advantage. Moreover, the adversary has no need to learn the exact amounts that other bidders have placed. The goal of non-malleability definitions is to prevent these types of attacks.

There have been several attempts to formally define non-malleability of commitments. Most notably, Crescenzo et al. presented a simulation-based definition [1]. The main idea of their definition is to compare the success probability of an adversary and its simulator. The adversary sees a commitment c of a message m and must produce a commitment c' of a message m' which must be non-trivially related to m. At the same time, the simulator must also produce a message similarly related to m, but without seeing any of the derivatives of m (e.g., commitment on m). If the difference between success probabilities is negligible then the commitment scheme is considered simulation-based non-malleable.

Later, Laur et al. introduced a new formulation of non-malleability which is now known as *comparison-based definition* [3,5–7]. The goal of this definition is to phrase non-malleability without referring to a simulator. This was motivated by the fact that definitions formulated in terms of simulators are more complicated to falsify by presenting a specially programmed adversary.

The original intention of this paper was to analyze the comparison based non-malleability of commitments introduced by Laur et al. [5] and prove that it implies hiding and binding of the commitment scheme. However, after we started our formal analysis and specified the definition precisely in EasyCrypt, we were able to conjecture and then prove that the definition is unsatisfiable by any realistic commitment schemes, but is satisfiable by a completely non-binding "constant"-commitment scheme. Taking both discoveries into account we claim that the comparison-based non-malleability as defined by Laur et al. [5] is unfit for any practical and theoretical purposes.

Our result is formalized in the EasyCrypt theorem prover and the proof-scripts can be found in the supplementary material [2]. The results presented in this paper follow our formal EasyCrypt development. However, for the purpose of readability we present them in the standard mathematical notation.

---

[1] An example of a non-trivial relation could be that the message m' is the same as m except all occurrences of *"PAY TO: Alice"* are replaced with *"PAY TO: Mallory"*.

2   Comparison-Based Non-malleability

Definition 1 (Commitment Scheme). *A commitment scheme is a triple of efficient algorithms (Gen, Commit, Verify) where:*

- *Gen: is a distribution of public keys (also known as public parameters) of a commitment scheme.*
- *Commit(pk, m): is a distribution of commitment-opening pairs which is parameterized by a public key pk and a message m.*
- *Verify(pk, m, c, d): is a deterministic function which verifies the commitment c on the message m with respect to the opening key d.*

*The commitment scheme is **functional** iff all commitment-opening pairs produced by Commit(pk, m) verify on m:*

$$\forall\ c\ d\ pk\ m,\ pk \in Gen \wedge (c, d) \in Commit(pk, m) \implies Verify(pk, m, c, d) = 1.$$

(Here, $x \in D$ denotes that x is in support of distribution D.)

Let us give a formal definition of comparison-based non-malleability introduced by Laur et al. [5].

Definition 2 (Laur et al.). *A commitment scheme $C = (Gen, Commit, Verify)$ is **comparison-based non-malleable** iff for any efficient adversary A, the advantage $AdvC(C, A)$ is negligible, where*

$$AdvC(C, A) := |\mathsf{Pr}\,[r \leftarrow GN_0(C, A).main() : r = 1]$$
$$-\mathsf{Pr}\,[r \leftarrow GN_1(C, A).main() : r = 1]\,|.$$

```
1: module GN₀(C, A)                     1: module GN₁(C, A)
2:     proc main() = {                   2:     proc main() = {
3:         pk ←$ Gen                      3:         pk ←$ Gen
4:         M ← A.init(pk)                 4:         M ← A.init(pk)
5:         m ←$ M                         5:         m ←$ M;  n ←$ M
6:         (c, d) ←$ Commit(pk, m)        6:         (c, d) ←$ Commit(pk, m)
7:         (c', R) ← A.commit(c)          7:         (c', R) ← A.commit(c)
8:         (d', m') ← A.decommit(d)       8:         (d', m') ← A.decommit(d)
9:         v ← Verify(pk, m', c', d')     9:         v ← Verify(pk, m', c', d')
10:        return v ∧ R(m, m') ∧ c ≠ c'  10:        return v ∧ R(n, m') ∧ c ≠ c'
11:    }                                 11:    }
12: end                                  12: end
```

(For simplicity of presentation, in Definition 2 the adversary computes a single commitment c' while in the original definition of Laur et al. the adversary was allowed to return n commitments and $n + 1$-place relation R. In our EasyCrypt formalization, we work with the original definition, but in the paper we show the simplified version since this detail is irrelevant for the main unsatisfiability result.)

Both games are parameterized by a commitment scheme C and an adversary A. In the game GN_0, adversary A is given the public key pk and is asked to compute a message distribution $\mathcal{M}$. A message m is then sampled from $\mathcal{M}$ and a commitment-opening pair (c, d) is computed with respect to m. Next, adversary A is given the commitment c and asked to produce a commitment c' and a relation R. After that, A is given the opening d and asked to produce an opening-message pair (d', m). The adversary wins the game if the pair (c', d') is valid with respect to m', the relation R is satisfied by a pair (m, m') and A's commitment c' is different from c. The only difference in the game GN_1 is that a second message n is sampled from the message distribution (independently from m). The commitment-opening pair is still computed with respect to the message m, but the winning condition of GN_1 considers whether $R(n, m')$ holds (line 10).

The adversary's overall advantage is defined in terms of its ability to distinguish between games GN_0 and GN_1. In other words, A has to win one game and lose the other in order to increase the advantage. This means that to be successful, the adversary has to find the exact relation R which will hold given the pair (m, m') and will not hold given the pair (n, m'), or vice versa.

2.1   (Un)satisfiability of the Comparison-Based Definition

In this section, we show that Definition 2 is not satisfiable by any realistic[2] commitment scheme. More specifically, we construct a single adversary which can break the comparison-based non-malleability of any realistic commitment scheme with unacceptably high probability. Moreover, we also define a paradoxical and completely non-binding "constant"-commitment scheme which satisfies Definition 2. Taking both discoveries into consideration it must be sufficient to claim that the comparison-based non-malleability as defined by Laur et al. [5] is unfit for any practical and theoretical purposes.

Theorem 1. *For any functional commitment scheme $C = (\textit{Gen}, \textit{Commit}, \textit{Verify})$ the adversary A (see Fig. 1 for the definition) has the following comparison-based non-malleability advantage:*

$$AdvC(C, A) = \frac{1}{4} - \frac{1}{4} \cdot \Pr \left[\begin{array}{l} pk \xleftarrow{\$} \textit{Gen}; \ (c, d) \xleftarrow{\$} \textit{Commit}(pk, 0); \\ (c', d') \xleftarrow{\$} \textit{Commit}(pk, 0) : c = c' \end{array} \right].$$

(If commitments generated by Commit are sufficiently random then $AdvC(C, A)$ is not negligible.)

---

[2] We assume that in realistic schemes commitment values contain a sufficient amount of randomness.

Figure 1. Adversary for Comparison-Based Non-Malleability

```
1: fun R(m, m') := m = 0 ∧ m' = 0.      ▷ relation for which both messages must be 0
2:
3: module A
4:     var pk, c, c', d'
5:     proc init(pk) = {
6:         A.pk ← pk                     ▷ save the public key in the global variable
7:         return {0, 1}                 ▷ {0, 1} is a uniform distribution of bits
8:     }
9:     proc commit(c) = {
10:        A.c ← c                       ▷ the commitment is stored for the next phase
11:        (c', d') ←$ Commit(pk, 0)
12:        return (R, c')
13:    }
14:    proc decommit(d) = {
15:        if Verify(pk, 0, c, d) then
16:            return (d', 0)
17:        end if
18:        return ⊥                      ▷ denotes a pair which always fails the verification
19:    }
20: end
```

Proof. The adversary A is defined as follows (see Fig. 1): in the initialization phase, the adversary returns a uniform distribution of booleans. During the commit phase A receives the commitment c and generates a commitment-opening pair (c', d') on $m' = 0$. Moreover, the relation $R(m, m')$ is also fixed and will only hold true if $m = 0$ and $m' = 0$. During the "decommit" phase, A receives opening d and checks if it opens c with message $m = 0$. If so, A returns $(d', 0)$ as the opening-message pair. If the verification fails, the adversary intentionally loses the game (denoted by $\perp$).

In order to calculate the adversary's advantage we argue as follows:

$$\Pr\left[r \leftarrow GN_0(C, A).main() : r = 1\right] - \Pr\left[r \leftarrow GN_1(C, A).main() : r = 1\right]$$

$$\overset{(1)}{=} \left(\Pr\left[GN_0(A).main() : m = 0\right] - \Pr\left[GN_0(A).main() : m = 0, c = c'\right]\right)$$

$$- \left(\Pr\left[GN_1(A).main() : m = 0, n = 0\right] - \Pr\left[GN_1(A).main() : m = 0, n = 0, c = c'\right]\right)$$

$$\overset{(2)}{=} \frac{1}{2} - \Pr\left[GN_0(A).main() : m = 0, c = c'\right]$$

$$- \frac{1}{4} + \frac{1}{2} \cdot \Pr\left[GN_0(A).main() : m = 0, c = c'\right]$$

$$\overset{(3)}{=} \frac{1}{4} - \frac{1}{2} \cdot \Pr\left[\begin{array}{c} pk \overset{\$}{\leftarrow} Gen; \; \mathcal{M} \leftarrow A.init(pk); \; m \overset{\$}{\leftarrow} \mathcal{M}; \\ (c, d) \overset{\$}{\leftarrow} Commit(pk, m); \; (c', d') \overset{\$}{\leftarrow} Commit(pk, 0): \\ m = 0, c = c' \end{array}\right]$$

$$\overset{(4)}{=} \frac{1}{4} - \frac{1}{4} \cdot \Pr\left[\begin{array}{c} pk \overset{\$}{\leftarrow} Gen; \; (c, d) \overset{\$}{\leftarrow} Commit(pk, 0); \\ (c', d') \overset{\$}{\leftarrow} Commit(pk, 0) : c = c' \end{array}\right].$$

In step (1), we observe that for any functional scheme the commitment verification (i.e., $Verify(pk, 0, c', d') = 1$) is guaranteed to succeed. Also, we rewrite the winning probability in terms of an event complement to the $c \neq c'$ condition. In step (2), we can restate all the probabilities in relation to GN_0 by observing that n is independent from m and making explicit the probability of sampling $n = 0$ as a coefficient. In step (3), we compute the probabilities and inline the game GN_0. In step (4), we observe that the remaining probability expression is non-zero only when $m = 0$, so we can simplify the game further.

Observe that the following probability can be safely assumed to be negligible for any realistic commitment scheme which produces sufficiently random commitments:

$$\Pr \left[\begin{array}{c} pk \leftarrow Gen; \ (c,d) \xleftarrow{\$} Commit(pk,m); \\ (c',d') \xleftarrow{\$} Commit(pk,m) : c = c' \end{array} \right].$$

The reason why the adversary A is able to have a non-negligible advantage is because it could "intentionally lose" in the decommit phase. Once it receives the opening d, it can easily verify the content of the given commitment c and if verification fails, intentionally lose the game. Finally, we find it interesting that this analysis shows that the comparison-based definition cannot be instantiated with any realistic commitment scheme, but could be proved for some paradoxical schemes. Indeed, we can define the following "constant"-commitment scheme:

$$Gen := \{*\}$$
$$Commit(pk, m) := (*, m)$$
$$Verify(pk, m, c, d) := \textbf{if } m = d \textbf{ then } 1 \textbf{ else } 0$$

The public key and commitments are elements of a singleton set (denoted by $*$) and the opening of a commitment is a message itself. This commitment-scheme is functional, perfectly hiding, and completely non-binding. Moreover, since the winning condition $c \neq c'$ of GN_0 and GN_1 is never satisfied then we conclude that the above "constant"-commitment scheme is perfectly non-malleable according to Definition 2. This must be understood as another reason to abandon that definition of non-malleability.

3   Conclusions

The problem of inadequate definitions in cryptography is not new [4]. The errors in definitions may take many years to be discovered and the impact of these errors can range from a minimal nuisance to an actual threat that can be realised as an attack in the real world.

In our investigation, we were surprised to find the definition of comparison-based non-malleability unsatisfiable. The paper [5] radiates confidence of the authors that their definition is not only satisfiable, but that some constructions provide unreasonably high level of security. Moreover, the paper is well-cited with more than 200 citations to that date. However, according to our best knowledge, we are the first to spot the mistake. We attribute our discovery of unsatisfiability to the fact that our investigation was carried out in the formal setting of the

EasyCrypt theorem prover. Although the idea behind the proof is fairly simple, the formal derivation took considerable effort (the formalization is 600 loc).

Finally, this work stresses the need to provide higher assurance to the cryptographic security proofs. We believe that formal methods provide a solution which ensures rigor necessary for the mission critical systems.

In the future, we plan to investigate alternative definitions of comparison-based non-malleability.

Acknowledgments. This work was partially supported by the ESF-funded Estonian IT Academy research measure (project 2014-2020.4.05.19-0001), the ERDF-funded centre of excellence EXCITE (project 2014-2020.4.01.15-0018) and the Estonian Research Council grant no. PRG49.

References

1. Di Crescenzo, G., Katz, J., Ostrovsky, R., Smith, A.: Efficient and non-interactive non-malleable commitment. Cryptology ePrint Archive, Report 2001/032 (2001). https://ia.cr/2001/032
2. Firsov, D., Zhuchko, E., Laur, S.: Formal analysis of non-malleability for commitments in EasyCrypt (2022). https://github.com/dfirsov/comparison-based-non-malleabiltiy-unsat
3. Khalfaoui, S., Leneutre, J., Villard, A., Ma, J., Urien, P.: Security analysis of out-of-band device pairing protocols: a survey. Wirel. Commun. Mob. Comput. **2021**, 1–30 (2021)
4. Koblitz, N., Menezes, A.: Critical perspectives on provable security: fifteen years of "another look" papers. Adv. Math. Commun. **13**, 517–558 (2019)
5. Laur, S., Nyberg, K.: Efficient mutual data authentication using manually authenticated strings. In: Pointcheval, D., Mu, Y., Chen, K. (eds.) CANS 2006. LNCS, vol. 4301, pp. 90–107. Springer, Heidelberg (2006). https://doi.org/10.1007/11935070_6
6. Li, M., et al.: Secure ad-hoc trust initialization and key management in wireless body area networks. ACM Trans. Sensor Netw. **9**(2), 1–35 (2012)
7. Mirzadeh, S., Cruickshank, H., Tafazolli, R.: Secure device pairing: a survey. IEEE Commun. Surv. Tutor. **16**(1), 17–40 (2014)

Alternating Automatic Register Machines

Ziyuan Gao[1(✉)], Sanjay Jain[2(✉)], Zeyong Li[3(✉)], Ammar Fathin Sabili[2(✉)], and Frank Stephan[1,2(✉)]

[1] Department of Mathematics, National University of Singapore,
10 Lower Kent Ridge Road, S17, Singapore 119076, Republic of Singapore
`matgaoz@nus.edu.sg`
[2] School of Computing, National University of Singapore, 13 Computing Drive,
COM1, Singapore 117417, Republic of Singapore
{`sanjay,ammar,fstephan`}`@comp.nus.edu.sg`
[3] Centre for Quantum Technologies, National University of Singapore,
Block S15, 3 Science Drive 2, Singapore 117543, Singapore
`li.zeyong@u.nus.edu`

Abstract. This paper introduces and studies a new model of computation called an Alternating Automatic Register Machine (AARM). An AARM possesses the basic features of a conventional register machine and an alternating Turing machine, but can carry out computations using bounded automatic relations in a single step. One finding is that an AARM can recognise some NP-complete problems, including CNF-SAT (using a particular coding), in $\log^* n + \mathcal{O}(1)$ steps. On the other hand, if all problems in P can be solved by an AARM in $\mathcal{O}(\log^* n)$ rounds, then P $\subset$ PSPACE.

Furthermore, we study an even more computationally powerful machine, called a Polynomial-Size Padded Alternating Automatic Register Machine (PAARM), which allows the input to be padded with a polynomial-size string. It is shown that the polynomial hierarchy can be characterised as the languages that are recognised by a PAARM in $\log^* n + \mathcal{O}(1)$ steps. These results illustrate the power of alternation when combined with computations involving automatic relations, and uncover a finer gradation between known complexity classes.

Keywords: Theory of computation · Computational complexity · Automatic relation · Register machine · Nondeterministic complexity · Alternating complexity · Measures of computation time

1 Introduction

Automatic structures generalise the notion of regularity for languages to other mathematical objects such as functions, relations and groups, and were

Z. Gao (as RF) and S. Jain (as Co-PI), F. Stephan (as PI) have been supported by the Singapore Ministry of Education Academic Research Fund grant MOE2019-T2-2-121/R146-000-304-112. Furthermore, S. Jain is supported in part by NUS grants C252-000-087-001 and E-252-00-0021-01. Further support is acknowledged for the NUS tier 1 grants AcRF R146-000-337-114 (F. Stephan as PI) and R252-000-C17-114 (F. Stephan as PI).

H. Seidl et al. (Eds.): ICTAC 2022, LNCS 13572, pp. 195–211, 2022.
https://doi.org/10.1007/978-3-031-17715-6_14

discovered independently by Hodgson [10,11], Khoussainov and Nerode [14] as well as Blumensath and Grädel [1,2]. One of the original motivations for studying automaticity in general structures came from computable structure theory, in particular the problem of classifying the isomorphism types of computable structures and identifying isomorphism invariants. In computer science, automatic structures arise in the area of infinite state model checking; for example, Regular Model Checking, a symbolic framework for modelling and verifying infinite-state systems, can be expressed in Existential Second-Order Logic over automatic structures [17]. Although finite-state transducers are a somewhat more popular extension of ordinary finite-state automata for defining relations between sets of strings, there are several advantages of working with automatic relations, including the following: (1) in general, automatic relations enjoy better decidability properties than finite-state transducers; for example, equivalence between ordinary automata is decidable while this is not so for finite-state transducers; (2) automatic relations are closed under first-order definability [11,13,14] while finite-state transducers are not closed under certain simple operations such as intersection and complementation.

In this paper, we introduce a new model of computation, called an *Alternating Automatic Register Machine (AARM)*, that is analogous to an alternating Turing machine but may incorporate *bounded* automatic relations[1] into each computation step. The main motivation is to try to discover new interesting complexity classes defined via machines where automatic relations are taken as primitive steps, and use them to understand relationships between fundamental complexity classes such as P, PSPACE and NP. More powerful computational models are often obtained by giving the computing device more workspace or by allowing non-deterministic or *alternating* computations, where alternation is a well-known generalisation of non-determinism. We take up both approaches in this work, extending the notion of alternation to automatic relation computations. An AARM is similar to a conventional register machine in that it consists of a *register R* containing a string over a fixed alphabet at any point in time, and the contents of R may be updated in response to *instructions*. One novel feature of an AARM is that the contents of the register can be non-deterministically updated using an automatic relation. Specifically, an instruction J is an automatic relation. Executing the instruction, when the content of the register R is r, means that the contents of R is updated to any x in $\{x : (x,r) \in J\}$; if there is no such x, then the program halts. Each AARM contains two finite classes, denoted here as A and B, of instructions; during a computation, instructions are selected alternately from A and B and executed.

To further explain how a computation of an AARM is carried out, we first recall the notion of an *alternating Turing machine* as formulated by Chandra, Kozen and Stockmeyer [5]. As mentioned earlier, alternation is a generalisation

---

[1] Here an update relation is *bounded* if there is a constant such that each possible output is at most that constant longer than the longest input parameter; see Sect. 2. Since we only consider bounded automatic relations in this paper, such relations will occasionally be called "automatic relations".

of non-determinism, and it is useful for understanding the relationships between various complexity classes such as those in the polynomial hierarchy (PH). The computation of an alternating Turing machine can be viewed as a game in which two players – Anke and Boris – make moves (not necessarily strictly alternating) beginning in the start configuration of the machine with a given input w [8]. Anke and Boris move alternating with each having specific win configurations. A language L is in AAL$[f(n)]$ if there is an AARM such that, for each input x, one player can force a win in $f(|x|)$ many steps. Then x is in L if Anke can force the win. In general, we are for natural choices of f interested in the class AAL$[f(n) + \mathcal{O}(1)]$ and our results indicate that $f(n) = \log^* n$ is an important choice allowing interesting results; smaller functions f only lead to the class of regular languages. Furthermore, we found that the picture becomes much more interesting by allowing only such automatic relations which permit a player to choose between finitely many options. We call such automatic relations bounded and for each bounded automatic relation R there is a constant c such that $R(x, y)$ can only be satisfied if $|y| \le |x| + c$; here y is the value chosen by the player in dependence of a register content x. We also introduce and study Polynomial-Size Padded Bounded Alternating Automatic Register Machines (PAARMs), which allow a polynomial-size padding to the input of an AARM.

The idea of defining computing devices capable of performing single-step operations that are more sophisticated than the basic operations of Turing machines is not new. For example, Floyd and Knuth [7] studied *addition machines*, which are finite register machines that can carry out addition, subtraction and comparison as primitive steps. *Unlimited register machines*, introduced by Shepherdson and Sturgis [18], can copy the number in a register to any register in a single step. Bordihn, Fernau, Holzer, Manca and Martín-Vide [3] investigated another kind of language generating device called an *iterated sequential transducer*, whose complexity is usually measured by its number of states (or *state complexity*). More recently, Kutrib, Malcher, Mereghetti and Palano [15] proposed a variant of an iterated sequential transducer that performs length-preserving transductions on left-to-right sweeps. Automatic relations are more expressive than arithmetic operations such as addition or subtraction, and yet they are not too complex in that even one-tape linear-time Turing machines are computationally more powerful; for instance, the function that erases all leading 0's in any given binary word can be computed by a one-tape Turing machine in linear time but it is not automatic [20]. Despite the computational limits of automatic relations, we show in Theorem 6 below that the NP-complete Boolean satisfiability problem can be recognised by an AARM in $\log^* n + \mathcal{O}(1)$ steps, where n is the length of the formula. The results not only show a proof-of-concept for the use of automatic relations in models of computation, but also shed new light on the relationships between known complexity classes.

For an extended version of this paper that presents examples and additional basic results on AARMs and PAARMs, please refer to [9].

2   Preliminaries

Let Σ denote a finite alphabet. We consider set operations including union ($\cup$), concatenation ($\cdot$), Kleene star ($*$), intersection ($\cap$) and complement ($\neg$). Let Σ^* denote the set of all strings over Σ. A *language* is a set of strings. Let the empty string be denoted by ε. For a string $w \in \Sigma^*$, let $|w|$ denote the length of w and $w = w_1 w_2 ... w_{|w|}$ where $w_i \in \Sigma$ denotes the i-th symbol of w. Fix a special symbol $\#$ not in Σ. Let $x, y \in \Sigma^*$ such that $x = x_1 x_2 \ldots x_m$ and $y = y_1 y_2 \ldots y_n$. Let $x' = x'_1 x'_2 \ldots x'_r$ and $y' = y'_1 y'_2 \ldots y'_r$ where $r = \max(m, n)$, $x'_i = x_i$ if $i \leq m$ else $\#$, and $y'_i = y_i$ if $i \leq n$ else $\#$. Then, the *convolution* of x and y is a string over $(\Sigma \cup \{\#\}) \times (\Sigma \cup \{\#\})$, defined as $conv(x,y) = (x'_1, y'_1)(x'_2, y'_2) \ldots (x'_r, y'_r)$. A relation $J \subseteq X \times Y$ is *automatic* if the set $\{conv(x,y) : (x,y) \in J\}$ is regular, where the alphabet is $(\Sigma \cup \{\#\}) \times (\Sigma \cup \{\#\})$. Likewise, a function $f : X \to Y$ is *automatic* if the relation $\{(x, y) : x \in domain(f) \land y = f(x)\}$ is automatic [21]. An automatic relation J is *bounded* if $\exists$ constant c such that $\forall (x, y) \in J, \text{abs}(|y| - |x|) \leq c$. On the other hand, an unbounded automatic relation has no such restriction. The problem of determining satisfiability of any given Boolean formula in conjunctive normal form will be denoted by CNF-SAT. Automatic functions and relations have a particularly nice feature as shown in the following theorem.

Theorem 1 ([11,14]). *Every function or relation which is first-order definable from a finite number of automatic functions and relations is automatic, and the corresponding automaton can be effectively computed from the given automata.*

3   Alternating Automatic Register Machines

An *Alternating Automatic Register Machine* (AARM) consists of a *register R* and two finite sets A and B of *instructions*. A and B are not necessarily disjoint. Formally, we denote an AARM by M and represent it as a quadruple (Γ, Σ, A, B). (An equivalent model may allow for multiple registers.) At any point in time, the register contains a string, possibly empty, over a fixed alphabet Γ called the *register alphabet*. The current string in R is denoted by r. Initially, R contains an input string over Σ, an *input alphabet* with $\Sigma \subseteq \Gamma$. Strings over Σ will sometimes be called *words*. The contents of the register may be changed in response to an instruction. An instruction $J \subseteq \Gamma^* \times \Gamma^*$ is a bounded automatic relation; this changes the contents of R to some x such that $(x, r) \in J$ (if such an x exists). The instructions in A and B are labelled $I_1, I_2, \ldots$, (in no particular order and not necessarily distinct). A *configuration* is a triple (ℓ, w, r), where I_ℓ is the current instruction's label and $w, r \in \Gamma^*$. Instructions are generally nondeterministic, that is, there may be more than one way in which the string in R is changed from a given configuration in response to an instruction. A *computation history* of an AARM *with input w* for any $w \in \Sigma^*$ is a finite or infinite sequence $c_1, c_2, c_3, \ldots$ of configurations such that the following conditions hold. Let $c_i = (\ell_i, w_i, r_i)$ for all i.

- $r_1 = w$. We call c_1 the *initial configuration* of the computation history.
- For all i, $(w_i, r_i) \in I_{\ell_i}$. This means that I_{ℓ_i} can be carried out using the current register contents, changing the contents of R to w_i.
- Instructions executed at odd terms of the sequence belong to A, while those executed at even terms belong to B:

$$I_{\ell_i} \in \begin{cases} A \text{ if } i \text{ is odd;} \\ B \text{ if } i \text{ is even.} \end{cases}$$

- If c_{i+1} is defined, then $r_{i+1} = w_i$. In other words, the contents of R are (non-deterministically) updated according to the instruction and register contents of the previous configuration.
- Suppose i is odd (resp. even) and $c_i = (I_{\ell_i}, w_i, r_i)$ is defined. If there is some $I_\ell \in B$ (resp. $I_\ell \in A$) with $\{x : (x, w_i) \in I_\ell\}$ nonempty, then c_{i+1} is defined. In other words, the computation continues so long as it is possible to execute an instruction from the appropriate set, either A or B, at the current term.

We interpret a computation history of an AARM as a sequential game between two players, Anke and Boris, where Anke moves during odd turns and Boris moves during even turns. During Anke's turn, she must pick some instruction J from A such that $\{x : (x, r) \in J\}$ is nonempty and select some $w \in \{x : (x, r) \in J\}$; if no such instruction exists, then the game terminates. The contents of R are then changed to w at the start of the next turn. The moving rules for Boris are defined analogously, except that he must pick instructions only from B. Anke *wins* if the game terminates after a finite number of turns and she is the last player to execute an instruction; in other words, Boris is no longer able to carry out an instruction in B and the *length* of the game (or computation history), measured by the total number of turns up to and including the last turn, is odd. Boris wins the game if Anke does not win (this includes the case that Anke does not make any move). The AARM *accepts* a word w if Anke can move in such a way that she will always win a game with an initial configuration (ℓ, v, w) for some $I_\ell \in A$ and $v \in \Gamma^*$, regardless of how Boris moves. To state this acceptance condition more formally, one could define Anke's and Boris' *strategies* to be functions $\mathcal{A}$ and $\mathcal{B}$ respectively with $\mathcal{A} : (\mathbb{N} \times \Gamma^* \times \Gamma^*)^* \times \Gamma^* \mapsto A \times \Gamma^*$ and $\mathcal{B} : (\mathbb{N} \times \Gamma^* \times \Gamma^*)^* \times \Gamma^* \mapsto B \times \Gamma^*$, which map each segment of a computation history together with the current contents of R to a pair specifying an instruction as well as the new contents of R at the start of the next round according to the moving rules given earlier. The AARM accepts w if there is an $\mathcal{A}$ such that for every $\mathcal{B}$, there is a finite computation history $\langle c_1, \ldots, c_{2n+1} \rangle$ where

- $c_i = (\ell_i, w_i, r_i)$ for each i,
- $r_1 = w$,
- $\mathcal{A}((\langle c_i : i < 2j + 1 \rangle, r_{2j+1})) = (I_{\ell_{2j+1}}, w_{2j+1})$ for each $j \in \{0, \ldots, n\}$,
- $\mathcal{B}((\langle c_i : i < 2k \rangle, r_{2k})) = (I_{\ell_{2k}}, w_{2k})$ for each $k \in \{1, \ldots, n\}$;
- there is no move for B in c_{2n+1}, that is no instruction in B contains a pair of the form $(\cdot, w_{2n+1})$.

Here $\langle c_i : i < k \rangle$ denotes the sequence $\langle c_1, \ldots, c_{k-1} \rangle$, which is empty if $k \leq 1$. Such an $\mathcal{A}$ is called a *winning strategy for Anke with respect to* (M, w). Given a winning strategy $\mathcal{A}$ for Anke with respect to (M, w) and any strategy $\mathcal{B}$, the corresponding computation history of M with input w is unique and will be denoted by $\mathcal{H}(\mathcal{A}, \mathcal{B}, M, w)$. In most subsequent proofs, $\mathcal{A}$ and $\mathcal{B}$ will generally not be defined so formally. Set

$$L(M) := \{w \in \Sigma^* : M \text{ accepts } w\};$$

one says that M *recognises* $L(M)$. Note that a constant amount of extra state information can be stored in the register.

Definition 2 (Alternating Automatic Register Machine Complexity). *Let $M = (\Gamma, \Sigma, A, B)$ be an AARM and let $t \in \mathbb{N}_0$. For each $w \in \Sigma^*$, M accepts w in time t if Anke has a winning strategy $\mathcal{A}$ with respect to (M, w) such that for any strategy $\mathcal{B}$ played by Boris, the length of $\mathcal{H}(\mathcal{A}, \mathcal{B}, M, w)$ is not more than t. (As defined earlier, $\mathcal{H}(\mathcal{A}, \mathcal{B}, M, w)$ is the computation history of M with input w when $\mathcal{A}$ and $\mathcal{B}$ are applied.) An AARM decides a language L in $f(n)$ steps for a function f depending on the length n of the input if for all $x \in \{0, 1\}^n$, both players can enforce that the game terminates within $f(n)$ steps by playing optimally and one player has a winning strategy needing at most $f(n)$ moves and $x \in L$ if Anke is the player with the winning strategy. $AAL[f(n)]$ denotes the family of languages decided by AARMs that decide in time $f(n)$.*

It can be shown that AARMs recognise precisely the family of all recursively enumerable languages [9, Theorem 7], and that $AAL[\mathcal{O}(f(n))]$ is closed under the usual set-theoretic Boolean operations as well as the regular operations [9, Theorem 4].

We recall that an alternating Turing machine that decides in $\mathcal{O}(f(n))$ time can be simulated by a deterministic Turing machine using $\mathcal{O}(f(n))$ space. The following theorem gives a similar connection between the time complexity of AARMs and the space complexity of deterministic Turing machines.

Theorem 3. *For any f such that $f(n) \geq n$, $AAL[\mathcal{O}(f(n))] \subseteq DSPACE[\mathcal{O}((n + f(n))f(n))] = DSPACE[\mathcal{O}(f(n)^2)]$.*

Proof. Given an AARM M, there is a constant c such that each register update by an automatic relation used to define an instruction of M increases the length of the register's contents by at most c. Thus, after $\mathcal{O}(f(n))$ steps, the length of the register's contents is $\mathcal{O}(n + f(n))$. As implied by [4, Theorem 2.4], each computation of an automatic relation with an input of length $\mathcal{O}(n + f(n))$ can be simulated by a nondeterministic Turing machine in $\mathcal{O}(n + f(n))$ steps; this machine can then be converted to a deterministic space $\mathcal{O}(n + f(n))$ Turing machine. If M accepts an input w, then there are $\mathcal{O}(f(n))$ register updates by automatic relations when Anke applies a winning strategy, and so there is a deterministic Turing machine simulating M's computation with input w using space $\mathcal{O}((n + f(n))f(n))$. □

As a consequence, one obtains the following analogue of the equality between AP (classes of languages that are decided by alternating polynomial time Turing machines) and PSPACE.

Corollary 4. $\bigcup_k AAL[\mathcal{O}(n^k)] = PSPACE$.

Proof. The containment relation $AAL[\mathcal{O}(f(n))] \subseteq DSPACE[\mathcal{O}((n + f(n))f(n))]$ in Theorem 3 holds whether or not the condition $f(n) \geq n$ holds. Furthermore, the computation of an alternating Turing machine can be simulated using an AARM, where the transitions from existential (respectively, universal) states correspond to the instructions for Anke (respectively, Boris), and each computation step of the alternating Turing machine corresponds to a move by either player. Therefore PSPACE, which is equal to AP, is contained in $\bigcup_k AAL[n^k]$. $\square$

We come next to a somewhat surprising result: an AARM-program can recognise 3SAT using just $\log^* n + \mathcal{O}(1)$ steps. To prove the theorem, we give the following lemma, which illustrates most of the power of AARMs.

Lemma 5 (Log-Star Lemma). *Let* $u, v \in \Sigma^*$. *Let* $\#, \$ \notin \Sigma$. *Then both languages* $\{u'\$v' : u' \in \#^*u\#^*, v' \in \#^*v\#^*$ *and* $u = v\}$ *and* $\{u'\$v' : u' \in \#^*u\#^*, v' \in \#^*v\#^*$ *and* $u \neq v\}$ *are in* $AAL[\log^* n + \mathcal{O}(1)]$.

The Log-Star Lemma essentially states that a comparison of two substrings can be done by an AARM in $\log^* n + \mathcal{O}(1)$ time. This is done by ignoring the unnecessary symbols in the register by replacing them with $\#$'s and adding a separator ($\$$) between the two strings.

Proof. We now prove the Log-Star Lemma. The algorithm below recursively reduces the problem to smaller sizes of u, v in constant number of steps (the maximum of the length of u, v is reduced logarithmically in constant number of steps). For the base case, if size of u or v is bounded by a constant, then clearly both languages can be recognized in one step.

For larger size u, v, the algorithm/protocol works as follows. For ease of explanation, suppose Anke is trying to show that $u = v$ (case of Anke showing $u \neq v$ will be similar). Given input $s = u'\$v'$, player Anke will try to give each symbol except $\$$'s a mark $\in \{0, 1, 2, 3\}$ as follows:

1. For each $\#$ in u' and v', the mark of 3 will be given.
2. For the contiguous symbols of u, starting from the first symbol, the following infinite marking will be given (whitespaces are for the ease of readability and not part of marking):

   20 21 200 201 210 211 2000 2001 2010 2011 2100 2101 2110 2111 20000 $\cdots$

   Namely, a series of blocks of string in ascending length-lexicographical order. Let T be the so defined infinite sequence. Given a string $s = u'\$v'$, where $u' \in \#^*u\#^*$ and $v' \in \#^*v\#^*$ for some $u, v \in \Sigma^*$, each contiguous subsequence of u (resp. v) whose sequence of positions is equal to the sequence of positions of T of some string in $2\{0, 1\}^*$ such that the next symbol in T is 2 will be called a *block*. Each block starts with 2 followed by a binary string. Let k (≥ 2) be the maximum size of a block. Summing the lengths of the blocks of u gives that $(k - 2) \cdot 2^{k-1} + k \leq n$, and thus $k \leq \log n$.
3. For the contiguous symbols of v, the marking will be similar.

The marking is considered *valid* if all above rules are satisfied. This is an example of a *valid* marking of $S = $ "$\#foobar\#\#\$foobar\#\#$":

S	# f o o b a r # # \$ f o o b a r # #
Mark	3 2 0 2 1 2 0 3 3 \$ 2 0 2 1 2 0 3 3

If $u = v$ and the marking is *valid*, player Anke will guarantee that each symbol of u and v will be marked with exactly the same marking. However if $u \neq v$ and the marking is *valid*, either the length of u and v are different or there will be at least a single block which differs on at least one symbol between u and v. Therefore, player Boris can have the following choices of challenges:

1. Challenge that player Anke did not make a valid marking, or
2. $|u| \neq |v|$, or
3. the string in a specified block differs on at least one symbol between u and v.

Notice that $u = v$ if and only if player Boris could not successfully challenge player Anke. The first challenge will ensure that player Anke gave a valid marking. There are three possible cases of invalid marking:

(a) There is a $\#$ in u' or v' which is not given by a mark of 3. In this case, player Boris may point out its exact position. Here, player Boris needs 1 step.
(b) For u and v, the first block is not marked with "20". This can also be easily pointed out by player Boris. Here, player Boris needs 1 step.
(c) For u and v, a block is not followed by its successor. This can be pointed out by player Boris by checking two things: the length of the 'successor' block should be less than or equal to the length of the 'predecessor' block plus one, and the 'successor' block indeed should be the successor of the 'predecessor' block. Also, we note that the last block may be incomplete.
  (i) The length case can be checked by looking at how many symbols there are between the pair of 2's bordering each block. Let p and q be the length of 'predecessor' block and the 'successor' block respectively. In the case that the 'successor' block is not the last block (not incomplete), player Boris may challenge if $p \neq q$ and $p + 1 \neq q$. This can be done by marking both blocks with 1 separated by $\$$ and the rest with dummy symbols $\#$ and then doing the protocol for equality of the modified u and v recursively. As player Boris may try to find the 'short' challenge, player Boris will find the earliest block which has the issue and thus make sure that p is at most logarithmic in the maximum of the lengths of u and v. As q may be much larger than p, player Boris may limit the second block by taking at most $p + 2$ symbols.
  (ii) The successor case can be checked by the following observation. A successor of a binary string can be calculated by finding the last 0 symbol and flipping all digits from that position to the end while maintaining the previous digits. As an illustration, the successor of "10110̲0111" will

be "101101000" where the symbols are separated in 3 parts: the prefix which is the same, the last 0 digit, which is underlined, becoming 1; and all 1 digits on suffix becoming 0. Player Boris then may challenge the first part not to be equal or the last part not to be the same length or not all 1's by providing the position of the last 0 on the 'predecessor' block (or the last 1 on the 'successor' block, if any). Checking the equality of two strings can be done recursively, also similarly applied for checking the length. Notice a corner case of all 1's which has the successor consisting of 1 followed by 0's with the same length, which can be handled separately. Also notice that the 'successor' block may be incomplete if it is the last block, which can also be handled in a similar manner as above.

For the second challenge, player Boris can (assuming the marking is valid) check whether the last two blocks of u and v are equal. Again, player Boris may limit it for a 'short' challenge so the checking size is decreasing to its log. For the third challenge, player Boris will specify the two blocks on u and v (same block on both) which differ on at least one symbol between u and v. Again, same protocol will apply and the size is decreasing to its log. Furthermore, both the marking and selection of blocks are done in a single turn.

Thus, the above algorithm using one alternation of each of the players reduces the problem to logarithmic in the size of the maximum of the lengths of u and v. In particular, when the size of u and v are small enough, the checking will be done in constant number of steps. Thus, the complexity of the problem satisfies: $T(m_{k+1}) \leq T(\log m_k)$, where m_i denotes the maximum of the sizes of u and v at step i. As the lengths of u, v at each step are bounded by the length of the whole input string, the lemma follows. Note that either player can enforce that the algorithm runs in $\log^* n + \mathcal{O}(1)$ steps. The player makes the own markings always correct and challenges incorrect markings of the opponent at the first error so that the logarithmic size descent is guaranteed. Challenged correct markings always cause the size to go down once in a logarithmic scale. □

Theorem 6. *There is an NP-complete problem in $AAL[\log^* n + \mathcal{O}(1)]$.*

Proof. Consider any encoding of a SAT formula in conjunctive normal form such that after each variable occurrence there is a space for a symbol indicating the truth value of that variable. For example, literals may be represented as $+$ or $-$ followed by a variable name and then a space for the variable's truth value, clauses may be separated by semicolons, literals may be separated by commas and a dot represents the end of the formula. Anke sets a truth value for each variable occurrence in the formula and a dfa then checks whether or not between any two semicolons, before the first semicolon and after the last semicolon there is a true literal; if so, Boris can challenge that two identical variables received different truth values. It is now player Anke's job to prove that the two variables picked by Boris are different. By the Log-Star Lemma, this verification needs $\log^* n + \mathcal{O}(1)$ steps. Hence, CNF-SAT $\in$ AAL$[\log^* n + \mathcal{O}(1)]$. □

The Log-Star Lemma can also be applied, using a technique similar to that in the proof of Theorem 6, to show that for any $k \geq 3$, the NP-complete problem k-$COLOUR$ of deciding whether any given graph G is colourable with k colours belongs to $\text{AAL}[\log^* n + \mathcal{O}(1)]$. Using a suitable encoding of nodes, edges and colours as strings, Anke first nondeterministically assigns any one of k colours to each node and ensures that no two adjacent nodes are assigned the same colour; Boris then challenges Anke on whether there are two substrings of the current input that encode the same node but encode different colours.

The next theorem shows that the class $\text{AAL}[\log^* n + \mathcal{O}(1)]$ contains NLOGSPACE.

Theorem 7. $NLOGSPACE \subseteq AAL[\log^* n + \mathcal{O}(1)]$.

Proof. Consider an NLOGSPACE computation that takes time n^c. One creates a new variable consisting of $\sqrt{n}$ equal-sized blocks of length $\sqrt{n}$ (so the overall length is n) such that each block is used to store some configuration in the history so that constantly many alternating rounds between two players allow to check a LOGSPACE computation. Let s be the total number of steps on the input. Anke guesses for each block the following information:

- The overall number of steps needed, s;
- The block number;
- The rounded number of steps done in this block (approximately $\frac{s}{\sqrt{n}}$ steps);
- The total number of steps done until this block;
- The starting configuration at this block;
- The ending configuration at this block.

Furthermore, the number of variables needed is $2c$ plus a constant.

Boris can now challenge that some configuration is too long or that the number of digits is wrong or that the information at the end of one block does not coincide with the information at the start of another block or that initial and final configurations are not starting and ending configurations or select a block whose computation has to be checked in the next round, again by distributing the steps covered in this interval evenly onto $\sqrt{n}$ blocks in the next variable.

By $\mathcal{O}(c)$ iterations, the distance of steps between two neighbouring configurations becomes 1. Now Boris can select two pieces of information copied to check whether they are right or whether the LOGSPACE computation in the last step read the symbol correctly out of the input word and so on. These checks can all be done in $\log^* n + \mathcal{O}(1)$ steps.   □

As yet, we have no characterisation of those problems in NP which are in $\text{AAL}[\mathcal{O}(\log^* n)]$ and we think that for each such problem it might depend heavily on the way the problem is formatted. The reason is that it may be difficult to even prove whether or not P is contained in $\text{AAL}[\mathcal{O}(\log^* n)]$, due to the following proposition. We will later show that the class $\text{PAAL}[\log^* n + \mathcal{O}(1)]$ which is obtained from $\text{AAL}[\log^* n + \mathcal{O}(1)]$ by starting with one additional step which generates a variable of polynomially sized length coincides with the polynomial hierarchy (PH).

Proposition 8. *Assume that f is monotonically increasing and computed in PSPACE and there is a polynomial p with $f(n) \leq p(n)$ for all n. Then $AAL[f(n)] \subseteq DSPACE[\mathcal{O}(f(n) \cdot (f(n) + n)] \subseteq DSPACE[\mathcal{O}((n + f(n)) \cdot f(n))] \subseteq DSPACE[\mathcal{O}((n + p(n)) \cdot p(n))] \subset PSPACE$ and $P \subseteq AAL[f(n) + \mathcal{O}(1)]$ implies $P \subset PSPACE$.*

Proof. This result follows from Theorem 3 (the condition $f(n) \geq n$ is not necessary for the first inclusion relation to hold) and the space hierarchy theorem [19, Corollary 9.4]. □

4 Polynomial-Size Padded Alternating Automatic Register Machine

An AARM is constrained by the use of *bounded* automatic relations during each computation step. This is a real limitation: it can be shown that for any $f(n) = \Omega(\log \log n)$, the class of languages recognised in time $\mathcal{O}(f(n))$ by alternating automatic register machines that use *unbounded* automatic relations contains DSPACE $\left[\mathcal{O}(2^{2^{\mathcal{O}(f(n))}})\right]$ [16], and so by Theorem 3 and the space hierarchy theorem, this class properly contains $AAL[\mathcal{O}(f(n))]$. In fact, the exponential time hierarchy coincides with the class of languages recognised by AARMs using unbounded automatic relations in $\log^* n + \mathcal{O}(1)$ steps.

We study the effect of allowing a polynomial-size padding to the input of an Alternating Automatic Register Machine on its time complexity; this new model of computation will be called a Polynomial-Size Padded Bounded Alternating Automatic Register Machine (PAARM). The additional feature of a polynomial-size padding will sometimes be referred to informally as a "booster" step of the PAARM. Intuitively, padding the input before the start of a computation allows a larger amount of information to be packed into the register's contents during a computation history. We show two contrasting results: on the one hand, even a booster step does not allow an PAARM with time complexity $\mathcal{O}(1)$ to recognise non-regular languages; on the other hand, the class of languages recognised by PAARMs in time $\log^* n + \mathcal{O}(1)$ coincides with the polynomial hierarchy.

Formally, a *Polynomial-Size Padded Bounded Alternating Automatic Register Machine* (PAARM) M is represented as a quintuple $(\Gamma, \Sigma, A, B, p)$, where Γ is the register alphabet, Σ the input alphabet, A and B are two finite sets of instructions and p is a polynomial. As with an AARM, the register R initially contains an input string over Σ, and R's contents may be changed in response to an instruction, $J \subseteq \Gamma^* \times \Gamma^*$ which is a bounded automatic relation. A computation history of a PAARM with input w for any $w \in \Sigma^*$ is defined in the same way that was done for an AARM, except that the initial configuration is (ℓ, x, wv) for some $I_\ell \in A$, some $x, v \in \Gamma^*$, $(x, wv) \in I_\ell$, where $v = @^k$ for a special symbol $@ \in \Gamma - \Sigma$ and $k \geq p(|w|)$. Think of $@^k$ as padding of the input. Anke's and Boris' strategies, denoted by $\mathcal{A}$ and $\mathcal{B}$ respectively, are defined as before. For any $u \in \Gamma^*$, a winning strategy for Anke with respect to (M, u) is also defined as before. Given any $w \in \Sigma^*$, M accepts w if for every $v \in @^*$, with

$|v| \geq p(|w|)$, Anke has a winning strategy with respect to (M, wv). Similarly, M *rejects* w if for every $v \in @^*$, with $|v| \geq p(|w|)$, Boris has a winning strategy with respect to (M, wv). Note that the winning strategies need to be there for every long enough padding. If Anke and Boris do not satisfy the above properties, then (A, B) is not a valid pair.

Definition 9. (Polynomial-Size Padded Bounded Alternating Automatic Register Machine Complexity). *Let* $M = (\Gamma, \Sigma, A, B, p)$ *be a PAARM and let* $t \in \mathbb{N}_0$. *For each* $w \in \Sigma^*$, M *accepts* w *in time* t *if for every* $v = @^k$, *where* $k \geq p(|w|)$ *and* $@ \in \Gamma - \Sigma$, *Anke has a winning strategy* $\mathcal{A}$ *with respect to* (M, wv) *and for any strategy* $\mathcal{B}$ *played by Boris, the length of* $\mathcal{H}(\mathcal{A}, \mathcal{B}, M, wv)$ *is not more than* t. *For any function* f, $PAAL[f(n)]$ *is defined analogously to* $AAL[f(n)]$.

Remark 10. *Note that a PAARM-program can trivially simulate an AARM-program by ignoring the generated padding; thus* $AAL[\mathcal{O}(f(n))] \subseteq PAAL$ $[\mathcal{O}(f(n))]$. *On the other hand, to simulate a booster step, an AARM-program needs* $\mathcal{O}(p(n))$ *steps as each bounded automatic relation step can only increase the length by a constant.*

As with $AAL[\mathcal{O}(f(n))]$, the class $PAAL[\mathcal{O}(f(n))]$ is closed under the usual set-theoretic Boolean operations as well as regular operations [9, Theorem 16]. Our main result concerning PAARMs is a characterisation of the polynomial hierarchy as the class $PAAL[\log^* n + \mathcal{O}(1)]$.

Theorem 11. $PH = PAAL[\log^* n + \mathcal{O}(1)]$.

To help with the proof, we first extend the Log-Star Lemma as follows. Recall that a *configuration* (or *instantaneous description*) of a Turing Machine is represented by a string xqw, where q is the current state of the machine and x and w are strings over the tape alphabet, such that the current tape contents is xw and the current head location is the first symbol of w [12].

Lemma 12. *Checking the validity of a Turing Machine step, i.e., whether a configuration of Turing Machine follows another configuration (given as input, separated by a special separator symbol) can be done in* $AAL[\log^* n + \mathcal{O}(1)]$, *where* n *is the length of the shorter of the two configurations.*

Proof. Let the input be the two configurations of the Turing Machine, where the second configuration is supposedly the successive step of the first one and separated by a separator symbol. Now there are two things that need to be checked: (1) The configuration is "copied" correctly from the previous step. Note that a valid Turing Machine transition will change only the cell on the tape head and/or both of its neighbour; thus "copied" here means the rest of the tape content should be the same; (2) The local Turing step is correct.

For the first checking, the player who wants to verify, e.g. Anke, will give the infinite valid marking as used in the Log-Star Lemma. In addition, Anke also marks the position of the old tape head on the second configuration. Boris can then challenge the following: (a) The Log-Star Lemma marking is not valid; (b) The old tape head position is not marked correctly (in the intended position) on the second configuration; (c) The string in a specified block differs, but not the symbols around the tape head; (d) The length difference of the configuration is not bounded by a constant.

Challenge (a) can be done in $\log^* n + \mathcal{O}(1)$ steps; this follows from the Log-Star Lemma. Challenge (b) can also be done in $\log^* n + \mathcal{O}(1)$ steps where both players reduce the block to focus on that position, and finally check whether it is on the same position or not. Challenge (c) can also be done in $\log^* n + \mathcal{O}(1)$ steps; this follows again from the Log-Star Lemma. Note that if Boris falsely challenges that the different symbol is around the tape head, Anke can counter-challenge by pointing out that at least one of its neighbours is a tape head. For challenge (d), note that a valid Turing Machine transition will only increase the length by at most one. Thus, Boris can pinpoint the last character of the shorter configuration and also its pair on another configuration, then check whether the longer one is only increased by up to one in length. This again can be done in $\log^* n + \mathcal{O}(1)$ steps.

For the second checking about the correctness of the Turing step, it can be done in a constant number of checks as a finite automaton can check the computation and determine whether the Turing steps are locally correct, that is, each state is the successor state of the previous steps head position and the symbol to the left or right of the new head position is the symbol following from the transition to replace the old symbol and so on. Therefore, all-in-all the validity of a Turing Machine step can be checked in $\text{AAL}[\log^* n + \mathcal{O}(1)]$ steps. $\square$

Proof Sketch of Theorem 11. We first prove that $\text{PAAL}[\log^* n + \mathcal{O}(1)] \subseteq \text{PH}$. Define a binary function Tower recursively as follows:

$$\text{Tower}(0, c) = 1$$
$$\text{Tower}(d + 1, c) = 2^{c \cdot \text{Tower}(d,c)}.$$

We prove by induction that for each $c \geq 1$, there is a c' such that for all d, $\text{Tower}(d+c', 1) > \text{Tower}(d, c)$. When $c = 1$, $\text{Tower}(d, c)$ gives the usual definition of the tower function. In particular, when $c = 1$, one has $\text{Tower}(d + 1, c) > \text{Tower}(d, c)$ for all d, so the induction statement holds for all $c = 1$ and all d. Suppose that $c > 1$. Then there is some c' large enough so that $\text{Tower}(c', 1) > c^2 = c^2 \cdot \text{Tower}(0, c)$, and so the induction statement holds for $d = 0$. Assume by induction that $c > 1$ and that $\text{Tower}(c'' + d, 1) > c^2 \cdot \text{Tower}(d, c)$. Then $2^{\text{Tower}(c''+d,1)} > 2^{c^2 \cdot \text{Tower}(d,c)} \geq (2^{c \cdot \text{Tower}(d,c)})^c > c^2 \cdot 2^{c \cdot \text{Tower}(d,c)}$, and therefore $\text{Tower}(c'' + d + 1, 1) > c^2 \cdot \text{Tower}(d + 1, c)$. This completes the induction step.

Suppose that c is the number of states of the automaton M corresponding to the update function for the configuration of an AAL algorithm. Then the size of the dfa to recognise whether or not a player wins within k steps is at most $\text{Tower}(k + 3, c)$. We prove that a dfa of size $\text{Tower}(k + 2, c)$ recognises whether Anke (resp. Boris) wins within k steps when she (resp. Boris) starts. (We can similarly show that a dfa of size $\text{Tower}(k+2, c)$ recognises whether Boris (resp. Anke) wins within k steps when Anke (resp. Boris) starts, so the union of the two languages is recognised by a dfa of size at most $\text{Tower}(k+3,c)$.) Anke wins in one step on input x iff for some y such that M accepts $conv(y,x)$, for all y', M does not accept $conv(y',y)$; the latter condition can be checked with a dfa of size 2^{2^c}. She wins in zero steps on input x when Boris starts iff there is no y such that M accepts (y,x), which can be checked with a dfa of size 2^c. So a dfa of size $2^{c+2^c} \leq \text{Tower}(3,c)$ checks whether Anke wins within 1 step. Assume inductively that there is a dfa M_k of size $\text{Tower}(k+2,c)$ accepting x iff Anke wins within k steps on input x when Boris (resp. Anke) starts. Suppose it is Anke's turn to start and we need to check if she wins within $k+1$ steps. (A similar construction applies if it is Boris' turn.) Define an nfa N as follows. For each state p of M, make $\text{Tower}(k+2,c)$ states $(p,q_1),\ldots,(p,q_{\text{Tower}(k+2,c)})$, where $q_1,\ldots,q_{\text{Tower}(k+2,c)}$ are the states of M_k. Then each state (p,q) on input x goes to each state (p',q') such that in M, there is a string y such that p on $conv(y,x)$ goes to p' and in M_k, q on y goes to q'. The start state of N is (p_1,q_1), where p_1 and q_1 are the start states of M and M_k respectively, and the final states of N are states (p_f,q_f) such that p_f and q_f are final states of M and M_k respectively. Then N accepts x iff there is a string y such that M accepts (y,x) and Anke wins within k steps on input y when Boris starts. The nfa N, which is of size $c \cdot \text{Tower}(k+2,c)$, can then be converted into a dfa M' of size $2^{c\cdot\text{Tower}(k+2,c)} = \text{Tower}(k+3,c)$, as required. By the preceding result on the function Tower, $\text{Tower}(k+3,c)$ is bounded by $\text{Tower}(k+c',1)$ for some c'. Thus any language in $\text{PAAL}[\log^* n + \mathcal{O}(1)]$ is recognised in a constant number of alternating steps plus a predicate that can be computed by a dfa of size $\text{Tower}(\log^* n - 3, 1)$. This dfa can be computed in LOGSPACE since $\log^* n$ can be computed in logarithmic space. Then one constructs the dfa by determinizing out the last step until it reaches size $\log\log n$. This happens only when only constantly many steps are missing by the above tower result. These constantly many steps can be left as a formula with alternating quantifiers followed by a dfa computed in logarithmic space of size $\log\log n$. Thus the formula whether Anke wins is in PH. Similarly for the formula whether Boris wins and so the overall decision procedure is in PH.

For the proof that $\text{PH} \subseteq \text{PAAL}[\log^* n + \mathcal{O}(1)]$, we first note that PH can be defined with alternating Turing machines [6]. We define Σ_k^P to be the class of languages recognised by alternating Turing Machine in polynomial time where the machine alternates between existential and universal states k times starting with existential state. We also define Π_k^P similarly but starting with universal state. PH is then defined as the union of all Σ_k^P and Π_k^P for all $k \geq 0$. We now show $\Sigma_k^P \cup \Pi_k^P \subseteq \text{PAAL}[\log^* n + \mathcal{O}(1)]$ for any fixed constant k. As the alternating Turing Machine runs in polynomial time on each alternation, the full computation (i.e., sequence of configurations) in one single alternation can be captured non-deterministically in $p(m)$ Turing Machine steps, for some polynomial p (which we assume to be bigger than linear), where m is the length of the configuration at the start of the alternation. In a PAARM-program, Anke first invokes a booster step to have a string of length at least $p^k(n)$. After that, Boris and Anke will alternately guess the full computation of the algorithm of length $p(p^i(n))$, $i = 0, 1, \ldots$, in their respective alternation: Boris guesses the first $p(n)$ computations (the first alternation), Anke then guesses the next $p(p(n))$ computations on top of it (the second alternation), etc. In addition, they also mark the position of the read head and symbol it looks upon in each step. Ideally, the PAARM-program will take k alternating steps to complete the overall algorithm. Note that a PAARM can keep multiple variables in the register by using convolution, as long as the number of variables is a constant. Thus, we could store the k computations in k variables: $v_1, v_2, \cdots, v_k$. Now each player can have the following choices of challenges to what the other player did: (1) Copied some symbol wrongly from the input i.e. in v_1; (2) Two successive Turing Machine steps in the computation are not valid (at some v_i); (3) The last Turing Machine step on some computation (at some v_i) does not follow-up with the first Turing Machine step on the next computation (at v_{i+1}). All the above challenges can be done in $\log^* n + \mathcal{O}(1)$ steps by a slight modification of Lemma 12. In particular, the third challenge needs one to compare the first Turing Machine configuration of v_{i+1} and the last Turing Machine configuration v_i, which can be done in a way similar to the proof of Lemma 12. Thus, $\Sigma_k^P \cup \Pi_k^P \subseteq \text{PAAL}[\log^* n + \mathcal{O}(1)]$ for every fixed constant k, therefore $PH \subseteq \text{PAAL}[\log^* n + \mathcal{O}(1)]$. $\square$

Remark 13. *As $PAAL[\log^* n + \mathcal{O}(1)] = PH$, $PAAL[\log^* n + \mathcal{O}(1)]$ is closed under polynomial time Turing reducibility. Similarly one can show that $PAAL[\mathcal{O}(\log^* n)]$ is closed under polynomial time Turing reducibility. After Anke invokes the booster step, Boris will guess the accepting computation together with all of the oracle answers. Anke then can challenge Boris on either the validity of the computation (without challenging the oracle) or challenge one of the oracle answers. Both challenges can be done in the same fashion as in Theorem 11 but the latter needs one additional step to initiate the challenge of the oracle algorithm.*

In order to obtain the next corollary, we use the fact that the problem of deciding TQBF_f – the class of true quantified Boolean formulas with $\log^* n + f(n) + \mathcal{O}(1)$ alternations – does not belong to any fixed level of the polynomial hierarchy (PH) when PH does not collapse.

Corollary 14. *If PH does not collapse and f is a logspace computable increasing and unbounded function, then $AAL[\log^* n + f(n) + \mathcal{O}(1)] \not\subseteq PH$.*

Finally, we observe that if PH = PSPACE, then (i) by Theorem 11, PH = $\text{PAAL}[\mathcal{O}(\log^* n)]$ = PSPACE; (ii) by Proposition 8, P $\not\subseteq \text{AAL}[\mathcal{O}(\log^* n)]$; thus $\text{AAL}[\mathcal{O}(\log^* n)]$ would be properly contained in $\text{PAAL}[\mathcal{O}(\log^* n)]$.

Proposition 15. *If PH = PSPACE and f satisfies the precondition of Proposition 8, then $AAL[f(n)] \subset PAAL[\log^* n + \mathcal{O}(1)] = PSPACE$.*

Theorem 16. *If f is monotonically increasing and unbounded, then $AAL[\log^* n - f(n)] = REG$.*

Proof. Assume that there is an AARM such that for each word w there is either for Anke or for Boris a winning strategy of $\log^* n - f(n)$ steps. Then by the tower lemma, the resulting size of the dfa is $\mathcal{O}(\log \log n)$ for almost all n and input words of length n. Thus the combined two dfas have at most size $poly(\log \log n)$ and there is no word w on which not exactly one accepts in the given time. Now assume that for a given dfa of sufficient large n, there is a word w where neither player succeeds in $\log^* n - f(n)$ rounds, where the n is fixed. Due to the pumping lemma, on words of arbitrary length with this property, one can pump down these words until they have size below n. However, such short words with this property do not exist by assumption. Thus for this fixed n, all words of arbitrary length are accepted by computations of length $\log^* n - f(n)$. Thus the language is actually in AAL[$\mathcal{O}(1)$] and in REG. $\square$

The main results on complexity classes defined by AARMs are summed up in Fig. 1 while those on complexity classes defined by PAARMs are summed up in Fig. 2. For any function f, AAL[$f(n)$] denotes the class of languages recognised by an AARM in $f(n)$ time. An arrow is labelled with (a) reference(s) to the corresponding result(s) or definition(s) in the paper; folklore inclusions can be found in [12,19]. Results not stated in the present section are proven in [9]. Note that PSPACE $= \bigcup_k$ AAL[n^k] by Corollary 4.

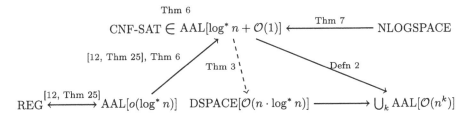

Fig. 1. Relationships between complexity classes/CNF-SAT. A solid arrow from X to Y means that X is a proper subset of Y. A double-headed solid arrow between X and Y means that X is equal to Y. If X is a subset of Y but it is not known whether they are equal sets, then the arrow is dashed.

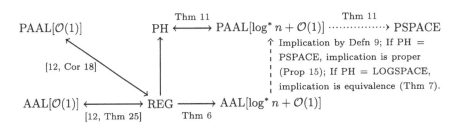

Fig. 2. Relationships between complexity classes.

References

1. Blumensath, A.: Automatic structures. Diploma thesis, RWTH Aachen University (1999)
2. Blumensath, A., Grädel, E.: Automatic structures. In: Proceedings of IEEE Symposium on Logic in Computer Science (LICS), pp. 51–62 (2000)
3. Bordihn, H., Fernau, H., Holzer, M., Manca, V., Martín-Vide, C.: Iterated sequential transducers as language generating devices. Theor. Comput. Sci. **369**, 67–81 (2006)
4. Case, J., Jain, S., Seah, S., Stephan, F.: Automatic functions, linear time and learning. Log. Methods Comput. Sci. 9(3), (2013)
5. Chandra, A., Kozen, D., Stockmeyer, L.: Alternation. J. Assoc. Comput. Mach. **28**(1), 114–133 (1981)
6. Chandra, A., Stockmeyer, L.: Alternation. In: 17th Annual Symposium on Foundations of Computer Science (FOCS 1976), pp. 98–108 (1976)
7. Floyd, R., Knuth, D.: Addition machines. SIAM J. Comput. **19**, 329–340 (1990)
8. Fürer, M.: Alternation and the Ackermann case of the decision problem. L'Enseignement Mathématique **II**(XXVII), 137–162 (1981)
9. Gao, Z., Jain, S., Li, Z., Sabili, A.F., Stephan, F.: Alternating automatic register machines. arXiv:2111.04254v5 [cs.CC] (2022). https://arxiv.org/pdf/2111.04254v5.pdf
10. Hodgson, B.R.: Théories décidables par automate fini. Ph.D. thesis, Université de Montréal (1976)
11. Hodgson, B.: Décidabilité par automate fini. Annales des sciences mathématiques du Québec **7**, 39–57 (1983)
12. Hopcroft, J., Ullman, J.: Introduction to Automata Theory, Languages, and Computation. Addison-Wesley, Maaschusetts (1979)
13. Khoussainov, B., Minnes, M.: Three lectures on automatic structures. In: Proceedings of Logic Colloquium 2007. Lecture Notes in Logic, vol. 35, pp. 132–176 (2010)
14. Khoussainov, B., Nerode, A.: Automatic presentations of structures. In: Leivant, D. (ed.) LCC 1994. LNCS, vol. 960, pp. 367–392. Springer, Heidelberg (1995). https://doi.org/10.1007/3-540-60178-3_93
15. Kutrib, M., Malcher, A., Mereghetti, C., Palano, B.: Deterministic and nondeterministic iterated uniform finite-state transducers: computational and descriptional power. In: Anselmo, M., Della Vedova, G., Manea, F., Pauly, A. (eds.) CiE 2020. LNCS, vol. 12098, pp. 87–99. Springer, Cham (2020). https://doi.org/10.1007/978-3-030-51466-2_8
16. Li, Z.: Complexity of linear languages and its closures and exploring automatic functions as models of computation. Undergraduate Research Opportunities Programme (UROP) Project Report, National University of Singapore, 2018/2019
17. Lin, A.W., Rümmer, P.: Regular model checking revisited. Technical report (2020)
18. Shepherdson, J.C., Sturgis, H.E.: Computability of recursive functions. J. Assoc. Comput. Mach. **10**, 217–255 (1963)
19. Sipser, M.: Introduction to the Theory of Computation, 3rd edn. Cengage Learning, Boston (2013)
20. Stephan, F.: Automatic structures - recent results and open questions. In: Third International Conference on Science and Engineering in Mathematics, Chemistry and Physics, vol. 622/1 (Paper 012013). J. Phys. Conf. Ser. (2015)
21. Stephan, F.: Methods and Theory of Automata and Languages. National University of Singapore, School of Computing (2016)

Functional Choreographic Programming

Luís Cruz-Filipe⬛, Eva Graversen$^{(\boxtimes)}$⬛, Lovro Lugović⬛, Fabrizio Montesi⬛,
and Marco Peressotti⬛

Department of Mathematics and Computer Science, University of Southern Denmark,
Odense, Denmark
`efgraversen@imada.sdu.dk`

Abstract. Choreographic programming is an emerging programming
paradigm for concurrent and distributed systems, where developers write
the communications that should be enacted and a compiler then automatically generates a distributed implementation.

Currently, the most advanced incarnation of the paradigm is Choral,
an object-oriented choreographic programming language that targets
Java.

Choral deviated significantly from known theories of choreographies,
and in particular introduced the possibility of expressing higher-order
choreographies that are fully distributed.

In this article, we introduce Chorλ, the first functional choreographic
programming language. It is also the first theory that explains the core
ideas of higher-order choreographic programming. We show that bridging
the gap between practice and theory requires developing a new evaluation strategy and typing discipline for λ terms that accounts for the
distributed nature of computation in choreographies.

Keywords: Choreographies · Concurrency · Lambda calculus · Type
systems

1   Introduction

Choreographies are coordination plans for concurrent and distributed systems,
which prescribe the communications that system participants should enact in
order to interact correctly with each other. They are widely used in industry,
especially for documentation [17,21,32]. Essentially, choreographies are structured compositions of communications. These are expressed using a variation of
the communication term from security protocol notation, Alice->Bob: M, which
reads "Alice communicates the message M to Bob" [27].

Choreographic programming is an emerging programming paradigm aimed
at producing correct-by-construction distributed implementations of choreographies [16,20,24]. In this paradigm, programs are choreographies in which communications are structured using standard control-flow constructs, e.g., conditionals. A compiler then *projects* a choreography onto each participant, creating
an executable program, which enacts the expected message passing behaviour.

Work partially supported by Villum Fonden, grant no. 29518.

Choreographies can be large in practice—some even over a hundred pages of text [28]. Thus, it is important to study how choreographies can be made *modular*, enabling the writing (preferably disciplined by types) of large choreographies as compositions of smaller, reusable ones. The state-of-the-art on modularity in choreographic programming is currently represented by Choral, an object-oriented choreographic programming language in which choreographies are compiled to Java libraries that applications can use as protocol implementations [15]. Choral is the first choreographic programming language powerful enough to support realistic, mainstream software development. In particular, it introduced higher-order composition to choreographic programming—the ability to define and invoke choreographies parameterised over other choreographies. Higher-order composition is essential to many practical scenarios, e.g. extensible protocols. An example (covered in Sect. 4.2) is the Extensible Authentication Protocol (EAP), a widely-employed link-layer protocol for the authentication of peers connecting to a network [31]. EAP is parametric over a list of authentication protocols, and therefore requires higher-order composition.

In Choral, data types are equipped with (possibly many) *roles*, which are abstractions of participants. This allows for writing object methods that involve multiple roles (choreographic methods). We illustrate with an example from [15].

Example 1 (Authentication protocol in Choral [15]). Consider a distributed authentication protocol in which a client (C) wishes to use its account at an identity provider (I) to access a service (S). Such a protocol can be implemented in Choral as follows.

```
class Authenticator@(S, C, I)
   { AuthResult@(C, S) authenticate(Credentials@C credentials){...} }
```

In the Choral code above, class Authenticator is distributed between the three roles S, C, and I. Method authenticate takes the credentials of C (to access its account) and returns the result of the authentication computed at I to C and S. The result AuthResult@(C, S) is a pair of session tokens, one located at C and the other at S (if the authentication fails, these will be empty). The interested reader can see how this example can be implemented in Chorλ in [6].   ◁

While Choral demonstrated the usefulness of higher-order choreographies, its development was driven by practice, and it is not grounded in any existing theory. In particular, the typing and semantics of higher-order choreographies is not formally understood yet. The current contribution aims at closing this gap.

This Article. We present the choreographic λ-calculus, Chorλ for short, a theory of choreographic programming that supports higher-order, modular composition.

Chorλ is the first choreographic programming model based on λ-calculus, which has two advantages. First, we can tap on a well-known foundation for higher-order programming. Second, it reveals that the key design features of

Choral work in the context of functional programming as well. In this way, Chorλ is also the first instance of *functional* choreographic programming.

Chorλ is expressive enough to serve as a model of the core features of Choral, which we illustrate by recreating some of the key examples given as motivation in the original presentation of Choral [15] (including remote computation, secure key exchange, and single sign-on) in our functional setting. We also model a more sophisticated scenario based on the Extensible Authentication Protocol (EAP). Our examples demonstrate that Chorλ allows for parameterising choreographies over different communication semantics, enabling protocol layering, a first for theory of choreographic programming.

To capture the essence of higher-order choreographies in the λ-calculus, we extend its syntax with features from choreographies and ambient calculi (Sect. 2.1) [3,25]. Namely, in Chorλ, data has explicit location and can be moved between roles using communication primitives. Another innovative feature is that the term for performing a communication is a function, and can therefore be composed with other terms as usual in functional programming.

We develop a typing discipline for Chorλ where types are located at roles (Sect. 2.2). The key novelty of our type system is that it tracks which roles are involved in which terms; this requires extending the standard connective for typing functions and a dedicated environment in typing judgements.

Another key contribution of this paper is a semantics for choreographies (Sect. 3) in Chorλ. Formulating an appropriate semantics has been particularly challenging, because there is no prior evaluation strategy for the λ-calculus that is suitable for functional choreographies. Since choreographies express distributed computation, theories of choreographic languages typically support out-of-order execution for subterms that can be evaluated at independent locations [2]. How to formulate the necessary inference rules is well-known in the imperative setting, but it has never been studied in others. This notion of out-of-order execution makes it possible to project the behaviour of each participant and get a correspondence between their behaviours and that of the choreography. This development is outside the scope of the current contribution; the interested reader can find the full discussion in the accompanying technical report [6].

Structure of the Paper. Chorλ, along with its typing, is presented in Sect. 2. Its semantics and key properties are discussed in Sect. 3. Examples of choreographies inspired by practice are given in Sect. 4. Related work is given in Sect. 5. Conclusions are presented in Sect. 6.

2   The Choreographic λ-calculus

In this section we introduce the Choreographic λ-calculus, Chorλ. This calculus extends the simply typed λ-calculus [5] with recursion, choreographic terms for communication, and roles.

Roles are independent participants in a system based on message passing. Terms in Chorλ are located at roles, to reflect distribution. For example, the value 5@Alice reads "the integer 5 at Alice". Terms are typed with novel data types that are annotated with roles. In this case, 5@Alice has the type Int@Alice, read "an integer at Alice".

Values can be moved from a role to another using a communication primitive. For example, the term $\textbf{com}_{\text{Alice,Bob}}$ 5@Alice represents the communication of the value 5 from Alice to Bob. This term evaluates to 5@Bob and has type Int@Bob.

2.1 Syntax

Definition 1. *The syntax of* Chorλ *is given by the following grammar*

$$M ::= V \mid f(\vec{R}) \mid M\ M \mid \textbf{case}\ M\ \textbf{of}\ \textbf{Inl}\ x \Rightarrow M;\ \textbf{Inr}\ x \Rightarrow M \mid \textbf{select}_{R,R}\ l\ M$$
$$V ::= x \mid \lambda x : T.M \mid \textbf{Inl}\ V \mid \textbf{Inr}\ V \mid \textbf{fst} \mid \textbf{snd} \mid \textbf{Pair}\ V\ V \mid ()@R \mid \textbf{com}_{R,R}$$
$$T ::= T \rightarrow_\rho T \mid T + T \mid T \times T \mid ()@R \mid t@\vec{R}$$

where M is a choreography, V is a value, T is a type, x is a variable, l is a label, f is a choreography name (or function name), R is a role, ρ is a set of roles, and t is a type variable.

Abstraction $\lambda x : T.M$, variable x and application MM are as in the standard (simply typed) λ-calculus, and pairs and sums are added in the standard way. For the sake of simplicity, constructors for sums (**Inl** and **Inr**) and products (**Pair**) are only allowed to take values as inputs, but this is only an apparent restriction: we can define, e.g., a function **inl** as $\lambda x : T.\textbf{Inl}\ x$ and then apply it to any choreography. Similarly, we can define the functions **inr** and **pair** (the latter for constructing pairs). We use these utility functions in our examples. Sums and products are deconstructed in the usual way, respectively by the **case** construct and by the **fst** and **snd** primitives.

The primitives $\textbf{com}_{S,R}$ and $\textbf{select}_{S,R}\ l\ M$ (where S and R are roles) come from choreographies and are the only primitives of Chorλ that introduce interaction between roles. The term $\textbf{com}_{S,R}$ is a *communication*: it acts as a function that takes a value at role S and returns the same value at role R. The standard choreographic primitive for synchronous communication Alice -> Bob: M is recovered as the function application $\textbf{com}_{\text{Alice,Bob}}\ M$. The term $\textbf{select}_{S,R}\ l\ M$ is a *selection*, where S informs R that it has selected the label l before continuing as M. Selections are needed for realisability: with this interaction, S communicates its internal choice to R so that both agree on their future behaviour. Labels are constants chosen from a fixed set (e.g., {left, right, start, stop, ... }).

Finally, $f(\vec{R})$ stands for a (choreographic) function f instantiated with the roles $\vec{R}$, which evaluates to the body of the function as given by an environment of definitions (a mapping from function names to choreographies). Function names are used to model recursion. In the typing and semantics of Chorλ, we use D to range over mappings of function names to choreographies. Within a choreography, there is no need to distinguish between roles that are statically fixed and role parameters: inside of a function definition, roles are parameters of the function; otherwise, roles are statically determined. All roles are treated in the same way by our theory.

To illustrate base values, we also have a term $()@R$ which denotes a unit value at the role R—other base values, like $5@R$ used in the examples above, can be easily included following the same approach. Values are not limited to one role in general; for example, **Pair** $()@S \ ()@R$ denotes a distributed pair where the first element resides at S and the second at R. We say a choreography (or value or type) is local to R if R is the only role mentioned in any subterm of the choreography, e.g., $\lambda x : ()@R.(\textbf{Pair} \ x \ ()@R)$ is a local function located at R.

Types in Chorλ record the distribution of values across roles: if role R occurs in the type given to V, then part of V will be located at R. Because a function may involve more roles besides those listed in the types of their input and output, the type of abstractions $T \to_\rho T'$ is annotated with a set of roles ρ denoting the roles that may participate in the computation of a function with that type besides those occurring in the input T or the output T'. We often omit this annotation if the set of additional roles is empty, writing $T \to T'$ instead of $T \to_\emptyset T'$. For example, if Alice wants to communicate an integer to Bob directly (without intermediaries), then she should use a choreography of type Int@Alice $\to$ Int@Bob; however, if the communication might go through a proxy, then she can use a choreography of type Int@Alice $\to_{\{Proxy\}}$ Int@Bob. This annotation is vital to the theory of projection, which is not presented in this paper.[1]

Aside from the annotations on arrows, our types resemble those of simply typed λ-calculus and serve the same primary purpose of keeping track of input and output of functions in order to prevent nonsensical choreographies. Consider the function $h = \lambda x : $ Int@Alice.$\textbf{com}_{Proxy,Bob} \ (\textbf{com}_{Alice,Proxy} \ x)$, which communicates an integer from Alice to Bob by passing through an intermediary Proxy and has the type Int@Alice $\to_{\{Proxy\}}$ Int@Bob. For any term M, the composition $h \ M$ makes sense if the evaluation of M returns something of the type expected by h, that is Int@Alice. The composition $h \ 5@$Alice makes sense, but $h \ 5@$Bob does not, because the argument is not at the role expected by h.

Types for sums and products are the usual ones. The type of units is annotated with the role where each unit is located; $()@R$ is the type of the unit value available (only) at role R. Recursive type variable $t@\vec{R}$ are annotated with the roles $\vec{R}$, instantiating the roles occurring in their definition (we discuss type definitions in Sect. 2.2).

Definition 2 (Roles of a type). *The roles of a type T, roles(T), are defined as follows.*

$$\text{roles}(t@\vec{R}) = \vec{R} \qquad\qquad \text{roles}(T \to_\rho T') = \text{roles}(T) \cup \text{roles}(T') \cup \rho$$
$$\text{roles}(()@R) = \{R\} \quad \text{roles}(T + T') = \text{roles}(T \times T') = \text{roles}(T) \cup \text{roles}(T')$$

In our examples we also assume the usual datatypes for integers (Int) and strings (String) together with their usual operations.

---

[1] The interested reader can find it in Fig. 6, in the appendix.

Example 2 (Remote Function). We can use Chorλ to define a small choreography, remFun(C, S) for a distributed computation in which a client, C sends an integer *val* to a server S where a function *fun* located at S is applied to *val* before the result gets returned to C.

$$\text{remFun}(C, S) = \lambda f : \text{Int@}S \to \text{Int@}S. \ \lambda v : \text{Int@}C. \ \textbf{com}_{S,C} \ (f \ (\textbf{com}_{C,S} \ v))$$

This choreography is parametrised on the roles S and C as well as the local function *fun* and value *val*.   ◁

Crucially, a choreographic term M may involve more roles than those listed in its type. For instance, the three choreographies $(()@R)$, $(\textbf{com}_{S,R} \ ()@S)$, and $(\textbf{com}_{P,R} \ (\textbf{com}_{S,P} \ ()@S))$ all have type $()@R$, but they implement different behaviours involving different roles. This yields a substitution principle for choreographies that makes them compositional, and will be important in establishing type preservation later.

A key concern of choreographic languages is knowledge of choice: the property that when a choreography chooses between alternative branches (as with our **case** primitive), all roles that need to behave differently in the branches are properly informed via appropriate selections [4]. We give an example of how selections should be used.

Example 3 (Remote Map). We now build on the remote function from Example 2 by using it to create a choreography remMap(C, S), where the server S applies a local function to not just one value received from the client C, but instead to each element of a list sent individually from C to S and then returned after the computation at S is complete.

remMap$(C, S) = \lambda f : \text{Int@}S \to \text{Int@}S. \ \lambda list : [\text{Int}]@C.$
   case *list* **of**
   Inl $x \Rightarrow \textbf{select}_{C,S}$ stop $()@C$;
   Inr $x \Rightarrow \textbf{select}_{C,S}$ go cons(C) (remFun(C, S) f (**fst** x)) (remMap(C, S) f (**snd** x))

Here, $[\text{Int}]@C$ is the recursive type satisfying $[\text{Int}]@C = ()@C + (\text{Int@}C \times [\text{Int}]@C)$, representing a list of integers and cons(C) is the usual list constructor located at C. In general, we write $[t]@(R_1, \ldots, R_n)$ to mean the recursive type satisfying

$$[t]@(R_1, \ldots, R_n) = (()@R_1 \times \cdots \times ()@R_n) + (t@(R_1, \ldots, R_n) \times [t]@(R_1, \ldots, R_n)).$$

When we introduce typing judgements later, we will show how to work with this kind of type equations.

The choreography uses selections so that S is informed about how it should behave (terminate or recur) depending on a local choice at C. This is essential if the choreography is to be implemented in a fully distributed way, since the information is initially available only at C. Notice how the **case** is evaluated on data at role C, so that role is the only one initially knowing which branch has been chosen. Each branch, however, starts with role C sending a label to role S. On the other hand, S must wait to receive a label from C to figure out whether it should terminate (label stop) or continue (label again): from its point of view, S is reactively handling a stream.   ◁

$$\dfrac{x : T \in \Gamma \quad \mathrm{roles}(T) \subseteq \Theta}{\Theta; \Sigma; \Gamma \vdash x : T} \ [\text{TVar}] \qquad \dfrac{\Theta; \Sigma; \Gamma \vdash N : T \to_\rho T' \quad \Theta; \Sigma; \Gamma \vdash M : T}{\Theta; \Sigma; \Gamma \vdash N\, M : T'} \ [\text{TApp}]$$

$$\dfrac{f(\vec{R'}) : T \in \Gamma \quad \vec{R} \subseteq \Theta \quad ||\vec{R}|| = ||\vec{R'}|| \quad \mathrm{distinct}(\vec{R})}{\Theta; \Sigma; \Gamma \vdash f(\vec{R}) : T[\vec{R'} := \vec{R}]} \ [\text{TDef}]$$

$$\dfrac{\Theta'; \Sigma; \Gamma, x : T \vdash M : T' \quad \rho \cup \mathrm{roles}(T) \cup \mathrm{roles}(T') = \Theta' \subseteq \Theta}{\Theta; \Sigma; \Gamma \vdash \lambda x : T.M : T \to_\rho T'} \ [\text{TAbs}]$$

$$\dfrac{\mathrm{roles}(T) = \{S\} \quad \{S, R\} \subseteq \Theta}{\Theta; \Sigma; \Gamma \vdash \mathbf{com}_{S,R} : T \to_\emptyset T[S := R]} \ [\text{TCom}] \qquad \dfrac{\Theta; \Sigma; \Gamma \vdash M : T \quad \{S, R\} \subseteq \Theta}{\Theta; \Sigma; \Gamma \vdash \mathbf{select}_{S,R}\ l\ M : T} \ [\text{TSel}]$$

$$\dfrac{\Theta; \Sigma; \Gamma \vdash M : t@\vec{R'} \quad t@\vec{R} =_\Sigma T \quad \vec{R'} \subseteq \Theta \quad ||\vec{R}|| = ||\vec{R'}|| \quad \mathrm{distinct}(\vec{R'})}{\Theta; \Sigma; \Gamma \vdash M : T[\vec{R} := \vec{R'}]} \ [\text{TEq}]$$

Fig. 1. Typing rules for Chorλ (representative selection).

Free and bound variables are defined as expected, noting that x and y are bound in **case** M **of Inl** $x \Rightarrow M'$; **Inr** $y \Rightarrow M''$. We write fv(M) for the set of free variables in term M. The formal definition can be found in [6]. We call a choreography closed if it has no free variables, and restrict our results to closed choreographies.

2.2   Typing

We now show how to type choreographies following the intuitions already given earlier. Typing judgements have the form $\Theta; \Sigma; \Gamma \vdash M : T$, where: Θ is the set of roles used for typing M; Σ is a set of type definitions parameterised on roles, i.e., expressions of the form $t@\vec{R} = T$ where the elements of $\vec{R}$ are distinct; and Γ is a typing environment, i.e. a list of assignments of variable names to their type ($x : T$) and of choreography names to the their set of bound roles and type ($f(\vec{R}) : T$). We require that a type variable t is defined at most once in Σ, that definitions are contractive [29], and that roles(T) = $\vec{R}$ for any $t@\vec{R} = T \in \Sigma$. We can use Σ to define common types such as Bool@R = ()@R + ()@R and the lists described in Example 3. We call $\Theta; \Sigma; \Gamma$ a typing context. Many of the rules resemble those for simply typed λ-calculus, but with roles added, and the additional requirements that only the roles in the type are used in the term being typed. We include some representative ones in Fig. 1 (the complete typing rules are given in [6]). We use the predicate distinct($\vec{R}$) to indicate that the elements of $\vec{R}$ are distinct and $||\vec{R}||$ to denote the number of elements of $\vec{R}$.

One novel part of our type system is the annotation ρ on the function type $T \to_\rho T'$, which, while not necessary for the results of this paper, ensures that the type of any value contains all the roles of that value. Rule TAbs uses Θ to ensure that ρ contains every additional role used in the function by requiring every role to be in Θ and restricting Θ to the roles of T, ρ, and T'.

Rules TVAR,TDEF,TABS exemplify how role checks are added to the standard typing rules for simply typed λ-calculus. Rule TCOM types communication actions, moving subterms that were placed at role S to role R (here $T[S := R]$ is the type expression obtained by replacing S with R). Note that the type of the value being communicated must be located entirely at S. Rule TSEL types selections as no-ops, only checking that the sender and receiver of the selection are legal roles. Rule TEQ allows rewriting a type according to Σ in order to mimic recursive types (see Example 3).

We also write $\Theta; \Sigma; \Gamma \vdash D$ to denote that a set of definitions D, mapping names to choreographies, is well-typed. Sets of definitions play a key role in the semantics of choreographies, and can be typed by the rule below.

$$\frac{\forall f(\vec{R}) \in \mathsf{domain}(D): \quad f(\vec{R}) : T \in \Gamma \quad \vec{R}; \Sigma; \Gamma \vdash D(f(\vec{R})) : T \quad \mathsf{distinct}(\vec{R})}{\Theta; \Sigma; \Gamma \vdash D}$$

Example 4. The set of definitions in Examples 2 and 3 can be typed in the typing context:

$$\Theta = \{C, S\} \qquad \Sigma = \{[\mathsf{Int}]@R = ()@R + (\mathsf{Int}@R \times [\mathsf{Int}]@R)\}$$

$$\Gamma = \left\{ \begin{array}{l} \mathsf{remFun}(C, S) : (\mathsf{Int}@S \to \mathsf{Int}@S) \to \mathsf{Int}@C \to \mathsf{Int}@C, \\ \mathsf{remMap}(C, S) : (\mathsf{Int}@S \to \mathsf{Int}@S) \to [\mathsf{Int}]@C \to [\mathsf{Int}]@C \end{array} \right\}$$

$\triangleleft$

3   Semantics of Chorλ

Chorλ comes with a reduction semantics that captures the essential ingredients of the calculi that inspired it: β- and ι-reduction from λ-calculus, and the usual reduction rules for communications and selections. Some representative rules are given in Fig. 2.

The key idea of our semantics is that terms at different roles can be evaluated independently, unless interaction is specified within the choreography. This kind of role-based out-of-order execution is typical for choreographic calculi [2], but we port it to λ-calculus here for the first time. In addition to functional choreographies having a different structure to imperative, out-of-order execution in higher-order choreographies is complicated by having actions where multiple roles are involved but no synchronisation happens, namely applications of values located at multiple roles such as choreographies and pairs with elements located at different roles.

The semantics are annotated with a label, ℓ, and a set of synchronising roles, **R**. The label is either λ, when an action is propagated out through a λ-term as in rule INABS, or τ otherwise. The set of synchronising roles is empty if no synchronisations are taking place. The purpose of the label and synchronising

$$\frac{}{\lambda x : T.M\ V \xrightarrow{\tau,\emptyset}_D M[x := V]} \text{[AppAbs]} \qquad \frac{M \xrightarrow{\ell,\mathbf{R}}_D M'}{\lambda x : T.M \xrightarrow{\lambda,\mathbf{R}}_D \lambda x : T.M'} \text{[InAbs]}$$

$$\frac{M \xrightarrow{\ell,\mathbf{R}}_D M' \quad \ell = \lambda \Rightarrow \mathbf{R} \cap \text{roles}(N) = \emptyset}{M\ N \xrightarrow{\tau,\mathbf{R}}_D M'\ N} \text{[App1]}$$

$$\frac{N \xrightarrow{\tau,\mathbf{R}}_D N'}{V\ N \xrightarrow{\tau,\mathbf{R}}_D V\ N'} \text{[App2]} \qquad \frac{N \xrightarrow{\tau,\mathbf{R}}_D N' \quad \mathbf{R} \cap \text{roles}(M) = \emptyset}{M\ N \xrightarrow{\tau,\mathbf{R}}_D M\ N'} \text{[App3]}$$

$$\frac{N \xrightarrow{\tau,\mathbf{R}}_D N'}{\mathsf{case}\ N\ \mathsf{of}\ \mathsf{Inl}\ x \Rightarrow M;\ \mathsf{Inr}\ x' \Rightarrow M' \xrightarrow{\tau,\mathbf{R}}_D \mathsf{case}\ N'\ \mathsf{of}\ \mathsf{Inl}\ x \Rightarrow M;\ \mathsf{Inr}\ x' \Rightarrow M'} \text{[Case]}$$

$$\frac{M_1 \xrightarrow{\ell,\mathbf{R}}_D M_1' \quad M_2 \xrightarrow{\ell,\mathbf{R}}_D M_2' \quad \mathbf{R} \cap \text{roles}(N) = \emptyset}{\mathsf{case}\ N\ \mathsf{of}\ \mathsf{Inl}\ x \Rightarrow M_1;\ \mathsf{Inr}\ x' \Rightarrow M_2 \xrightarrow{\ell,\mathbf{R}}_D \mathsf{case}\ N\ \mathsf{of}\ \mathsf{Inl}\ x \Rightarrow M_1';\ \mathsf{Inr}\ x' \Rightarrow M_2'} \text{[InCase]}$$

$$\frac{}{\mathsf{case}\ \mathsf{Inl}\ V\ \mathsf{of}\ \mathsf{Inl}\ x \Rightarrow M;\ \mathsf{Inr}\ x' \Rightarrow M' \xrightarrow{\tau,\emptyset}_D M[x := V]} \text{[CaseL]}$$

$$\frac{}{\mathsf{fst}\ \mathsf{Pair}\ V\ V' \xrightarrow{\tau,\emptyset}_D V} \text{[Proj1]} \qquad \frac{D(f(\vec{R'})) = M}{f(\vec{R}) \xrightarrow{\tau,\emptyset}_D M[\vec{R'} := \vec{R}]} \text{[Def]}$$

$$\frac{\text{fv}(V) = \emptyset}{\mathsf{com}_{S,R}\ V \xrightarrow{\tau,\{S,R\}}_D V[S := R]} \text{[Com]} \qquad \frac{}{\mathsf{select}_{S,R}\ l\ M \xrightarrow{\tau,\{S,R\}}_D M} \text{[Sel]}$$

$$\frac{M \xrightarrow{\ell,\mathbf{R}}_D M' \quad \mathbf{R} \cap \{S,R\} = \emptyset}{\mathsf{select}_{S,R}\ \ell\ M \xrightarrow{\ell,\mathbf{R}}_D \mathsf{select}_{S,R}\ \ell\ M'} \text{[InSel]} \qquad \frac{M \rightsquigarrow^* N \quad N \xrightarrow{\tau,\mathbf{R}}_D M'}{M \xrightarrow{\tau,\mathbf{R}}_D M'} \text{[Str]}$$

Fig. 2. Semantics of Chorλ.

roles is to ensure that synchronisations between the same roles occur in the expected order, the importance of which will become clear later.

Rules AppAbs, App1 and App2 implement a call-by-value λ-calculus. Rules Case and CaseL and its counterpart rule CaseR implement ι-reductions for sums, and likewise for rules Proj1 and Proj2 wrt pairs. The communication rule Com changes the associated role of a value, moving it from S to R, while the selection rule Sel implements selection as a no-op. Rule Def allows reductions to use choreographies defined in D.

In addition to the fairly standard λ-calculus semantics, we have some rules for out-of-order execution. These include rewriting terms as described in Fig. 3 and being able to propagate some transitions past an abstraction, case, and selection as in rules InAbs,InCase and InSel. We also have a "role-aware" variation of full β-reduction by using rule App3, the need for which is illustrated by Example 5. These rules serve the purpose of making our semantics decentralised, in the sense that actions at distinct roles can proceed independently.

$$\frac{x \notin \text{fv}(M')}{((\lambda x : T.M)\ N)\ M' \rightsquigarrow (\lambda x : T.(M\ M'))\ N}\ \text{[R-ABSR]}$$

$$\frac{x \notin \text{fv}(M')\quad \text{sroles}(M') \cap \text{roles}(N) = \emptyset}{M'\ ((\lambda x : T.M)\ N) \rightsquigarrow (\lambda x : T.(M'\ M))\ N}\ \text{[R-ABSL]}$$

$$\frac{x, x' \notin \text{fv}(M)}{\begin{array}{l}(\textbf{case}\ N\ \textbf{of}\ \textbf{Inl}\ x \Rightarrow M_1;\ \textbf{Inr}\ x' \Rightarrow M_2)\ M \rightsquigarrow\\ \qquad \textbf{case}\ N\ \textbf{of}\ \textbf{Inl}\ x \Rightarrow (M_1\ M);\ \textbf{Inr}\ x' \Rightarrow (M_2\ M)\end{array}}\ \text{[R-CASER]}$$

$$\frac{x, x' \notin \text{fv}(M)\quad \text{sroles}(M) \cap \text{roles}(N) = \emptyset}{\begin{array}{l}M\ (\textbf{case}\ N\ \textbf{of}\ \textbf{Inl}\ x \Rightarrow M_1;\ \textbf{Inr}\ x' \Rightarrow M_2) \rightsquigarrow\\ \qquad \textbf{case}\ N\ \textbf{of}\ \textbf{Inl}\ x \Rightarrow (M\ M_1);\ \textbf{Inr}\ x' \Rightarrow (M\ M_2)\end{array}}\ \text{[R-CASEL]}$$

$$\frac{}{(\textbf{select}_{S,R}\ l\ N)\ M \rightsquigarrow \textbf{select}_{S,R}\ l\ (N\ M)}\ \text{[R-SELR]}$$

$$\frac{\text{sroles}(M) \cap \text{roles}(N) = \emptyset}{M\ (\textbf{select}_{S,R}\ l\ N) \rightsquigarrow \textbf{select}_{S,R}\ l\ (M\ N)}\ \text{[R-SELL]}$$

Fig. 3. Rewriting of Chorλ.

Example 5. Consider the choreography $M = f(S)\ ((\lambda x : T@R.V@S)\ V'@R)$. (Note that we abuse notation when we write $V@S$ and $T@R$ to denote that V and T are located entirely at roles S and R, respectively, though this is not part of the syntax of Chorλ.) The choreography includes two independent roles, R and S, but the two never actually interact: the inner application involves an abstraction and an argument located only at R, so it should be evaluated independently of S. Likewise, $f(S)$ is located entirely at role S, so it should be evaluated independently of R.

Without rule APP3, M would be unable to evaluate the inner application before $f(S)$ finished running, which may be never if f diverges, breaking the assumption that roles execute in a decentralised way.   ◁

The rewriting rules are not standard for the λ-calculus, but they are not as strange as they first appear. Take, for example, rule R-ABSR; it simply states that if you have a function with two variables, $\lambda x : T.\lambda y : T'.M$, then x and y can be instantiated in any order as long as they each get the correct value. On the other hand, rule R-ABSL says that more of the computation can be pushed into an abstraction so long as it does not affect the order of synchronisations. The other rewriting rules work on similar principles, but dealing with conditionals and selections. These rules all work to ensure that while actions can be performed in different orders the result of the computation must remain the same before and after rewriting. In Example 6 we see why we need the rewriting rules in order to support the out-of-order executions necessary for the choreography to allow concurrent execution of computations located at different roles.

Example 6 (Rewriting). Consider the choreography with an abstraction at S inside an abstraction at R, $M = ((\lambda x : ()@R.\lambda x' : T@S.()@S)\ f(R))\ V@S$. As in Example 5, R and S each independently execute their part of the choreography. R evaluates $f(R)$ and then applies the result. Independently, S, executes the other application $\lambda x' : T@S.()@S\ V@S$. For M to be able to execute the application at S independently of R's actions, we need rule R-ABSR to get $\lambda x : T@S.()@S$ and $V@S$ next to each other by rewriting to $((\lambda x : ()@R.(\lambda x : T@S.()@S)\ V@S)\ f(R))$ and rule INABS to propagate the application of $(\lambda x : T@S.()@S)$ and $V@S$ past $\lambda x : ()@R$.   ◁

Some of the out-of-order-execution rules, specifically the ones pushing the left part of an application further in, have restrictions on them because we want to avoid there being more than one communication or synchronisation available at the same time on the same roles. This is because we need to ensure that communications and selections on a specific set of roles must always happen in the same order, as we otherwise get the problems illustrated by Example 7.

Example 7 (Communication order). Consider a choreography with two **com**$_{S,R}$ primitives, $M = (\lambda x : T@R.(\mathbf{com}_{S,R}\ V@S))\ (\mathbf{com}_{S,R}\ V'@S)$. This has a similar structure to $((\lambda x : ()@R.(\lambda x' : T@S.M)\ V@S)\ f(R))$ from Example 6, with part of the computation hidden behind an abstraction. However, while Example 6 needed to use rule INABS to allow the computation inside of the abstraction to execute before the computation outside, doing so would cause problems in $(\lambda x : T@R.(\mathbf{com}_{S,R}\ V@S))\ (\mathbf{com}_{S,R}\ V'@S)$.

Without going into the technical details, intuitively, the behaviour of M at R should be $(\lambda x : T.(\mathbf{recv}_S\ \bot))\ (\mathbf{recv}_S\ \bot)$ and the behaviour at S should be $(\lambda x : \bot.(\mathbf{send}_R\ V))\ (\mathbf{send}_R\ V')$ where $\mathbf{send}_R$ and $\mathbf{recv}_S$ are the obvious local actions implementing $\mathbf{com}_{S,R}$. In these behaviours, term $\bot$ denotes a part of the computation that takes place elsewhere.

It is common in choreographic programming, including in Choral, for the implementation of choreographies to assume that each pair of roles has one channel between them, which they use for all communications. In such a model, if the two communications can be performed in any order then S is currently able to send either V or V' and R is correspondingly able to receive either inside or outside the abstraction. Since S and R act independently, we have no guarantee that if S chooses to send V first R will also choose to use its left receive action or vice versa. This can create situations where S sending V synchronises with the right receive at R, creating a state not intended by the choreography.   ◁

We therefore restrict the out-of-order communications by restricting the synchronising names in rules INABS,APP1,APP3,INCASE and INSEL. To show that these rules restrict as intended, we have Proposition 1 stating that any reductions available at the same time must have different (or no) synchronisation roles.

Proposition 1. *Given a choreography M, if $M \xrightarrow{\ell,\mathbf{R}} M'$ and $M \xrightarrow{\ell',\mathbf{R}'} M''$ and there does not exist N such that $M' \rightsquigarrow^* N$, and $M'' \rightsquigarrow^* N$, then $\mathbf{R} \cap \mathbf{R}' = \emptyset$.*

Proof. The key here is that unless these transitions are either communications or selections, $\mathbf{R}$ and $\mathbf{R}'$ are empty. Once this is clear, the rest follows by induction on M. □

We use the label λ in rule INABS to restrict out-of-order communications, since we do not know which roles we need to restrict communication on in situations such as Example 7 until we reach the application, at which point the λ label becomes a τ again if it is allowed to propagate.

The restrictions on out-of-order communication in out-of-order execution rules force us to add similar restrictions in the rewriting rules, as illustrated by Example 8. For this purpose we use the concept of synchronisation roles.

Definition 3. *We define the set of synchronising roles of a choreography M, sroles(M), by recursion on the structure of M:*
sroles($\mathbf{com}_{S,R}$) = $\{S, R\}$, sroles($\mathbf{select}_{S,R}$ l M) = $\{S, R\} \cup$ sroles(M),
sroles($f(\vec{R})$) = $\vec{R}$, *and homomorphically on all other cases.*

Example 8. Consider a choreography with two communications between S and R, ($\mathbf{com}_{S,R}$ $V@S$) (($\lambda x : T@R.M$) ($\mathbf{com}_{S,R}$ $V'@S$)). Here, thanks to rule APP3 restricting on synchronisation roles, only the left $\mathbf{com}_{S,R}$ on V is available. If rule R-ABSL had no restriction on synchronisation roles, we could rewrite the choreography to ($\lambda x : T@R.(($\mathbf{com}_{S,R}$ $V@S$) M)) ($\mathbf{com}_{S,R}$ $V'@S$). This instead leaves the rightmost $\mathbf{com}_{S,R}$ on V' available. This means we have both communication available depending on whether we decide to rewrite and we have the same problem as in Example 7 of S potentially choosing to send V while R has rewritten and is expecting to receive the left $\mathbf{com}_{S,R}$. We therefore do not allow such a rewrite and use synchronisation roles to prevent it. ◁

We now show that closed choreographies remain closed under reductions.

Proposition 2. *Let M be a closed choreography. If $M \rightarrow_D M'$ then M' is closed.*

Proof. Straightforward from the semantics. □

A hallmark property of choreographies is that well-typed choreographies should continue to reduce until they reach a value. We split this result into two independent statements.

Theorem 1 (Progress). *Let M be a closed choreography and D a collection of named choreographies with all the necessary definitions for M. If there exists a typing context $\Theta; \Sigma; \Gamma$ such that $\Theta; \Sigma; \Gamma \vdash M : T$ and $\Theta; \Sigma; \Gamma \vdash D$, then either M is a value (and $M \nrightarrow_D$) or there exists a choreography M' such that $M \xrightarrow{\tau, \mathbf{R}}_D M'$.*

Proof. Follows by induction on the typing derivation of $\Theta; \Sigma; \Gamma \vdash M : T$. See details in [6]. □

Theorem 2 (Type Preservation). *Let M be a choreography and D a collection of named choreographies with all the necessary definitions for M. If there exists a typing context $\Theta; \Sigma; \Gamma$ such that $\Theta; \Sigma; \Gamma \vdash M : T$ and $\Theta; \Sigma; \Gamma \vdash D$, then $\Theta; \Sigma; \Gamma \vdash M' : T$ for any M' such that $M \xrightarrow{\ell, \mathbf{R}}_D M'$.*

Proof. Follows from induction on the derivation of $M \xrightarrow{\ell, \mathbf{R}}_D M'$. See details in [6]. □

Combining these results, we conclude that if M is a well-typed, closed, choreography, then either M is a value or M reduces to some well-typed, closed choreography M'. Since M' still satisfies the hypotheses of the above results, either it is a value or it can reduce.

4   Illustrative Examples

In this section, we illustrate the expressivity of Chorλ with some representative examples. Specifically, we use Chorλ to implement the Diffie-Hellman protocol for key exchange [14] and the Extensible Authentication Protocol [31]. The first is used in [15] to illustrate the expressiveness of Choral, and we show how it can be adapted to Chorλ's functional paradigm. The second example requires using higher-order composition of choreographies, as the choreography is parametrised on a list of authentication protocols. Chorλ is the first theory capable of modelling these choreographies as they are parametric on roles and include functions which are parametric on other choreographies and no previous formalism includes both these features.

4.1   Secure Communication

We write a choreography for the Diffie–Hellman key exchange protocol [14], which allows two roles to agree on a shared secret key without assuming secrecy of communications. As in Example 3, we use the primitive type Int.

To define this protocol, we use the local function $\mathsf{modPow}(R)$ of the type

$$\mathsf{modPow}(R) : \mathsf{Int}@R \to \mathsf{Int}@R \to \mathsf{Int}@R \to \mathsf{Int}@R$$

which computes powers with a given modulo. Like all local functions in Chorλ, $\mathsf{modPow}(R)$ is modelled by a choreography located entirely at one role. Given $\mathsf{modPow}(R)$, we can implement Diffie–Hellman as the following choreography:

$\mathsf{diffieHellman}(P, Q) =$
 $\lambda psk : \mathsf{Int}@P.\ \lambda qsk : \mathsf{Int}@Q.\ \lambda psg : \mathsf{Int}@P.$
 $\lambda qsg : \mathsf{Int}@Q.\ \lambda psp : \mathsf{Int}@P.\ \lambda qsp : \mathsf{Int}@Q.$
  $\mathbf{pair}\ (\mathsf{modPow}(P)\ psg\ (\mathbf{com}_{Q,P}\ (\mathsf{modPow}(Q)\ qsg\ qsk\ qsp))\ psp)$
   $(\mathsf{modPow}(Q)\ qsg\ (\mathbf{com}_{P,Q}\ (\mathsf{modPow}(P)\ psg\ psk\ psp))\ qsp)$

Given the individual secret keys (psk and qsk) and a previously publicly agreed upon shared prime modulus and base ($psg = qsg, psp = qsp$), the participants exchange their locally-computed public keys in order to arrive at a shared key that can be used to encrypt all further communication. This means diffieHellman(P, Q) has the type:

$$\mathsf{Int}@P \rightarrow \mathsf{Int}@Q \rightarrow \mathsf{Int}@P \rightarrow \mathsf{Int}@Q \rightarrow \mathsf{Int}@P \rightarrow \mathsf{Int}@Q \rightarrow \mathsf{Int}@P \times \mathsf{Int}@Q$$

and represents the shared key as a pair of equal keys, one for each participant.

Using the key exchange protocol, we can now build a reusable utility that allows us to achieve secure bidirectional communication between the parties, by encrypting and decrypting messages with the shared key at the appropriate endpoints. For this we assume two functions that allow us to encrypt and decrypt a String message with a given Int key:

$$\mathsf{enc}(R) : \mathsf{Int}@R \rightarrow \mathsf{String}@R \rightarrow \mathsf{String}@R$$
$$\mathsf{dec}(R) : \mathsf{Int}@R \rightarrow \mathsf{String}@R \rightarrow \mathsf{String}@R$$

The choreography then takes a shared key as its parameter and produces a pair of unidirectional channels that wrap the communication primitive with the necessary encryption based on the key:

makeSecureChannels(P, Q) = λkey : $\mathsf{Int}@P \times \mathsf{Int}@Q$.
    Pair (λval : $\mathsf{String}@P$. (dec(Q) (**snd** key) (**com**$_{P,Q}$ (enc(P) (**fst** key) val))))
        (λval : $\mathsf{String}@Q$. (dec(P) (**fst** key) (**com**$_{Q,P}$ (enc(Q) (**snd** key) val))))

The fact that this choreography returns a pair of channels can also be seen from its type:

$$(\mathsf{Int}@P \times \mathsf{Int}@Q) \rightarrow ((\mathsf{String}@P \rightarrow \mathsf{String}@Q) \times (\mathsf{String}@Q \rightarrow \mathsf{String}@P))$$

Using the channels is as easy as using **com** itself and amounts to a function application.

4.2   EAP

Finally, we turn to implementing the core of the Extensible Authentication Protocol (EAP) [31]. EAP is a widely-employed link-layer protocol that defines an authentication framework allowing a peer P to authenticate with a backend authentication server S, with the communication passing through an authenticator A that acts as an access point for the network.

The framework provides a core protocol parametrised over a set of authentication methods (either predefined or custom vendor-specific ones), modelled as individual choreographies with type AuthMethod@(P, A, S) = $\mathsf{String}@S \rightarrow_{\{P,A\}} \mathsf{Bool}@S$. For this reason, it is desirable that the core of the protocol be written in a way that doesn't assume any particular authentication method.

The eap(P, A, S) choreography does exactly that by leveraging higher-order composition of choreographies:

$\mathsf{eap}(P, A, S) = \lambda methods : [\mathsf{AuthMethod}]@(P, A, S).$
$\quad \mathsf{eapAuth}(P, A, S) \ (\mathsf{eapIdentity} \ \text{"auth request"}@S) \ methods$
$\mathsf{eapAuth}(P, A, S) = \lambda id : \mathsf{String}@S. \ \lambda methods : [\mathsf{AuthMethod}]@(P, A, S).$
$\quad$ **if** $\mathsf{empty}(P, A, S) \ methods$ **then**
$\qquad \mathsf{eapFailure}(P, A, S) \ \text{"try again later"}@S$
$\quad$ **else**
$\qquad$ **if** (**fst** $methods$) id **then**
$\qquad\quad$ **select**$_{S,P}$ ok (**select**$_{S,A}$ ok ($\mathsf{eapSuccess}(P, A, S)$ "welcome"$@S$))
$\qquad$ **else**
$\qquad\quad$ **select**$_{S,P}$ ko (**select**$_{S,A}$ ko ($\mathsf{eapAuth}(P, A, S)$ id (**snd** $methods$)))

For the sake of simplicity, we have left out the definitions of a couple of helper choreographies that are referenced in the example:

$$\mathsf{eapIdentity}(P, A, S) : \mathsf{String}@S \rightarrow_{\{P,A\}} \mathsf{String}@S$$
$$\mathsf{eapSuccess}(P, A, S) : \mathsf{String}@S \rightarrow (\mathsf{String}@P \times \mathsf{String}@A)$$
$$\mathsf{eapFailure}(P, A, S) : \mathsf{String}@S \rightarrow (\mathsf{String}@P \times \mathsf{String}@A)$$

$\mathsf{eap}(P, A, S)$ fetches the client's identity using $\mathsf{eapIdentity}(P, A, S)$, a function which exchanges the EAP packets and delivers the client's identity to the server.

Once the identity is known, $\mathsf{eapAuth}(P, A, S)$ is invoked in order to try the list of authentication methods until one succeeds, or the list is exhausted and authentication fails. EAP is parametric on a choreography, or in this case a list of choreographies, $methods$. We use the notation for lists in $[\mathsf{AuthMethod}]@(P, A, S)$ as described in Example 3, while the function $\mathsf{empty}(P, A, S)$ allows us to determine whether the list of methods is empty. Note that each authentication method can be an arbitrarily-complex choreography with its own communication structures that can involve all three involved roles, and implements a particular authentication method on top of EAP.

Finally, depending on the outcome of the authentication, an appropriate EAP packet is sent with either $\mathsf{eapSuccess}(P, A, S)$ or $\mathsf{eapFailure}(P, A, S)$ to indicate the result to the client.

5   Related Work

We already discussed much of the previous and related work on choreographic languages and choreographic programming in Sect. 1. In this section, we discuss relevant technical aspects in related work more in detail.

Chorλ is inspired by Choral [15], the first higher-order choreographic programming language. As we discussed in Sect. 1, Choral comes with no formal explanation of its semantics, typing, and guarantees. We have covered these in the present article, showing that it is possible to formulate semantics and types of higher-order choreographies that satisfy the expected properties (out-of-order execution with progress).

There exist theories of choreographies that support some form of higher-order composition, which are more restrictive than Choral and Chorλ [13,18]. In particular, they fall short of capturing distribution, both in terms of independent execution and data structures. In [13], the authors present a choreographic language for writing abstract specifications of system behaviour (as in multiparty session types [19]) that supports higher-order composition. Compared to Chorλ, the design of the language hampers decentralisation: entering a choreography requires that the programmer picks a role as central coordinator, which then orchestrates the other roles with multicasts. This coordination effectively acts as a barrier, so processes cannot really perform their own local computations independently of each other when higher-order composition is involved. After [13] and Choral [15], a theory of higher-order choreographic programming was proposed in [18]. While this theory supports computation at roles, it is even more centralised than [13]: every function application in a choreography requires that all processes go through a global barrier that involves the entire system. The global barrier is modelled as a middleware in the semantics of the language, and involves even processes that do not contribute at all to the function or its arguments.

Previous theories of choreographies organised their syntax in two layers: one for local computation and one for communication [1,2,8,10–12,18,22]. Chorλ has a very different and novel design, whereby a unified language addresses both areas. An important consequence of our unified approach is that Chorλ can express distributed data structures (e.g., pairs with elements located at different roles), which can be manipulated by independent local computations or in coordination by performing appropriate communications. This feature is crucial for our examples in Sect. 4 (and several examples in the original presentation of Choral in [15]).

Another related line of work is that on multitier programming and its progenitor calculus, Lambda 5 [26]. Similarly to Chorλ, Lambda 5 and multitier languages have data types with locations [33]. However, they are used very differently. In choreographic languages (thus Chorλ), programs have a "global" point of view and express how multiple roles interact with each other. By contrast, in multitier programming programs have the usual "local" point of view of a single role but they can nest (local) code that is supposed to be executed remotely. The reader interested in a detailed comparison of choreographic and multitier programming can consult [16], which presents algorithms for translating choreographies to multitier programs and vice versa.

6   Conclusion and Future Work

We have presented Chorλ, a new theory of choreographic programming that supports higher-order, modular choreographies. Chorλ is equipped with a type system that guarantees progress (Theorems 1 and 2). Unlike previous choreographic programming languages, Chorλ is based on the λ-calculus. It therefore inherits the simple syntax of λ terms and it is the first purely functional choreographic programming language. The semantics of Chorλ makes it the first theory of higher-order choreographies that is truly decentralised: processes can proceed independently unless the choreography specifies explicitly that they should interact.

We have demonstrated the usefulness of higher-order choreographies in Chorλ by modelling common protocols in Sect. 4. The examples on single sign-on with encrypted channels and EAP, in particular, are parametrised on choreographies and cannot be expressed in previous theories, either because of lack of higher-order composition or because the semantics is not satisfactory due to global synchronisations—which the original protocol specifications do not expect.

Future Work An obvious extension of Chorλ would be to add generic data types, which we did not include to keep the focus on choreographies. Since we use λ-calculus as foundation, we believe that this would be a straightforward import of known methods.

Other features that are interesting for Chorλ have been investigated in the context of first-order choreographic languages and represent future work. These include: channel-based communication [2], dynamic creation of roles [7], internal threads [1], group communication [9], availability-awareness [23], and runtime adaptation [12].

A more sophisticated extension would be to reify roles, that is, extending the syntax such that values can be roles that can be acted upon. This could, for example, enable dynamic topologies: choreographies where a process receives at runtime a role that it needs to interact with at a later time.

Another interesting line of future work would be to extend existing formalisations of choreographic languages with the features explored in this work [10, 11, 18, 30].

A   Single Sign-on Authentication

We now implement the single sign-on authentication protocol inspired by the OpenID specification [28], the Choral implementation of which we described in Example 1. We first implement the choreography in a parametric way that allows us to specify the means of communication, and then combine it with the secure communication from the previous example.

The protocol involves three roles with the client C wanting to authenticate with the server S via a third party identity provider I. If authentication succeeds, the client and the server both get a unique token from the identity provider.

We use the following local functions for working with user credentials

$$\mathsf{username}(R) : \mathsf{Credentials}@R \to \mathsf{String}@R$$
$$\mathsf{password}(R) : \mathsf{Credentials}@R \to \mathsf{String}@R$$
$$\mathsf{calcHash}(R) : \mathsf{String}@R \to \mathsf{String}@R \to \mathsf{String}@R$$

computing the username and password from a local type $\mathsf{Credentials}@R$ (which can be a pair, for example), and the hash of a string with a given salt. These are mainly used by the client.

In addition, we require functions for retrieving the salt, validating the hash, and creating a token for a given username, which are used by the identity provider:

$$\text{getSalt}(R) : \text{String}@R \to \text{String}@R$$
$$\text{check}(R) : \text{String}@R \to \text{String}@R \to \text{Bool}@R$$
$$\text{createToken}(R) : \text{String}@R \to \text{String}@R.$$

Given the above helper functions, the authentication protocol is as follows. Here we use if-then-else as syntactic sugar for **case**:

authenticate$(S, C, I) = \lambda credentials : \text{Credentials}@C.$
$\quad \lambda comcip : \text{String}@C \to \text{String}@I. \; \lambda comipc : \text{String}@I \to \text{String}@C.$
$\quad \lambda comips : \text{String}@I \to \text{String}@S.$
$\quad\quad ((\lambda user : \text{String}@I. \; (\lambda salt : \text{String}@C. \; (\lambda hash : \text{String}@I.$
$\quad\quad\quad$ **if** $\text{check}(I) \; user \; hash$ **then**
$\quad\quad\quad\quad$ **select**$_{I,C}$ ok (**select**$_{I,S}$ ok
$\quad\quad\quad\quad\quad (\lambda token : \text{String}@I. \; \textbf{inl} \; (\textbf{pair} \; (comipc \; token) \; (comips \; token)))$
$\quad\quad\quad\quad\quad (\text{createToken}(I) \; user))$
$\quad\quad\quad$ **else**
$\quad\quad\quad\quad$ **select**$_{I,C}$ ko (**select**$_{I,S}$ ko **inr** $()@I))$
$\quad\quad\quad (comcip \; (\text{calcHash}(C) \; salt \; (\text{password}(C) \; credentials))))$
$\quad\quad\quad (comipc \; (\text{getSalt}(I) \; user)))$
$\quad\quad (comcip \; (\text{username}(C) \; credentials)))$

As mentioned, the choreography is parametrised over three channels between the participants, allowing the communication to be customized (*comcip*, *comipc* and *comips*). The client first sends their username to the identity provider who replies with the appropriate salt. The client then calculates a salted hash of their password and sends it back to the identity provider. Finally, the identity provider validates the hash and either sends a token to both participants or returns a unit. The shared token is again represented using a pair of equal values, visible from the type of the choreography:

$$\text{Credentials}@C \to (\text{String}@C \to \text{String}@I) \to (\text{String}@I \to \text{String}@C)$$
$$\to (\text{String}@I \to \text{String}@S) \to ((\text{String}@C \times \text{String}@S) + ()@I)$$

We can now combine authenticate(S, C, I) and makeSecureChannels(P, Q) (from Sect. 4.1) to can obtain a choreography main(S, C, I) that carries out the authentication securely. Using makeSecureChannels(P, Q), the participants first establish secure channels backed by encryption keys derived using diffieHellman(P, Q). After the secure communication is in place, the participants can execute the authentication protocol specified by authenticate(S, C, I).

main$(S, C, I) =$
$\quad (\lambda k1 : \text{Int}@C \times \text{Int}@I. \; \lambda k2 : \text{Int}@I \times \text{Int}@S.$
$\quad\quad (\lambda c1 : (\text{String}@C \to \text{String}@I) \times (\text{String}@I \to \text{String}@C).$
$\quad\quad\quad \lambda c2 : (\text{String}@I \to \text{String}@S) \times (\text{String}@S \to \text{String}@I).$
$\quad\quad\quad\quad (\lambda t : (\text{String}@C \times \text{String}@S) + ()@I.$

```
case t of
    Inl x ⇒ "Authentication successful"@C
    Inr x ⇒ "Authentication failed"@C)
(authenticate(S, C, I) (fst c1) (snd c1) (fst c2)))
(makeSecureChannels(C, I) k1) (makeSecureChannels(I, S) k2))
(diffieHellman(C, I) csk ipsk csg ipsg csp ipsp)
(diffieHellman(I, S) ipsk ssk ipsg ssg ipsp ssp)
```

In this example, the client simply reports whether the authentication has succeeded with a value, which can be checked in a larger context. Or, alternatively, we could parameterise main over choreographic continuations to be invoked in case of success or failure.

We denote by Γ the set of typings we have given so far in this section. Then we can type $\{S, C, I\}; \emptyset; \Gamma \vdash \text{main}(S, C, I) : \text{String}@C$.

B   Full Definitions and Proofs

Definition 4 (Free Variables). *Given a choreography M, the free variables of M, $\text{fv}(M)$ are defined as:*

$$\text{fv}(N\ N') = \text{fv}(N) \cup \text{fv}(N') \qquad \text{fv}(\textbf{select}_{S,R}\ l\ M) = \text{fv}(M)$$
$$\text{fv}(x) = x \qquad\qquad\qquad \text{fv}(\lambda x : T.N) = \text{fv}(N) \setminus \{x\}$$
$$\text{fv}(()@R) = \emptyset \qquad\qquad\qquad \text{fv}(\textbf{com}_{S,R}) = \emptyset$$
$$\text{fv}(f) = \emptyset \qquad\qquad\qquad\quad \text{fv}(\textbf{Pair}\ V\ V') = \text{fv}(V) \cup \text{fv}(V')$$
$$\text{fv}(\textbf{case}\ N\ \textbf{of}\ \textbf{Inl}\ x \Rightarrow M; \textbf{Inr}\ y \Rightarrow M') = \text{fv}(N) \cup (\text{fv}(M) \setminus \{x\}) \cup (\text{fv}(M') \setminus \{y\})$$
$$\text{fv}(\textbf{fst}) = \text{fv}(\textbf{snd}) = \emptyset \qquad \text{fv}(\textbf{Inl}\ V) = \text{fv}(\textbf{Inr}\ V) = \text{fv}(V)$$

Definition 5 (Merging). *Given two behaviours B and B', $B \sqcup B'$ is defined as follows.*

$$B_1\ B_2 \sqcup B_1'\ B_2' = (B_1 \sqcup B_1')\ (B_2 \sqcup B_2')$$

$$\textbf{case}\ B_1\ \textbf{of}\ \textbf{Inl}\ x \Rightarrow B_2; \textbf{Inr}\ y \Rightarrow B_3 \sqcup \textbf{case}\ B_1'\ \textbf{of}\ \textbf{Inl}\ x \Rightarrow B_2'; \textbf{Inr}\ y \Rightarrow B_3' =$$
$$\textbf{case}\ (B_1 \sqcup B_1')\ \textbf{of}\ \textbf{Inl}\ x \Rightarrow (B_2 \sqcup B_2'); \textbf{Inr}\ y \Rightarrow (B_3 \sqcup B_3')$$

$$\oplus_R\ \ell\ B \sqcup \oplus_R\ \ell\ B' = \oplus_R\ \ell\ (B \sqcup B')$$

$$\&\{\ell_i : B_i\}_{i \in I} \sqcup \&\{\ell_j : B_j'\}_{j \in J} = \&\left(\{\ell_k : B_k \sqcup B_k'\}_{k \in I \cap J} \cup \{\ell_i : B_i\}_{i \in I \setminus J} \cup \{\ell_j : B_j'\}_{j \in J \setminus I}\right)$$

$$x \sqcup x = x \qquad \lambda x : T.B \sqcup \lambda x : T.B' = \lambda x : T.(B \sqcup B')$$

$$\textbf{fst} \sqcup \textbf{fst} = \textbf{fst} \qquad \textbf{snd} \sqcup \textbf{snd} = \textbf{snd}$$

$$\textbf{Inl}\ L \sqcup \textbf{Inl}\ L' = \textbf{Inl}\ (L \sqcup L') \qquad \textbf{Inr}\ L \sqcup \textbf{Inr}\ L' = \textbf{Inr}\ (L \sqcup L')$$

$$\textbf{Pair}\ L_1\ L_2 \sqcup \textbf{Pair}\ L_1'\ L_2' = \textbf{Pair}\ (L_1 \sqcup L_1')\ (L_2 \sqcup L_2') \qquad f \sqcup f = f$$

$$\textbf{recv}_R \sqcup \textbf{recv}_R = \textbf{recv}_R \qquad \textbf{send}_R \sqcup \textbf{send}_R = \textbf{send}_{send}R$$

$$\frac{\text{roles}(T \to_\rho T'); \Sigma; \Gamma, x : T \vdash M : T' \quad \text{roles}(T \to_\rho T') \subseteq \Theta}{\Theta; \Sigma; \Gamma \vdash \lambda x : T.M : T \to_\rho T'} \ [\text{TABS}]$$

$$\frac{x : T \in \Gamma \quad \text{roles}(T) \subseteq \Theta}{\Theta; \Sigma; \Gamma \vdash x : T} \ [\text{TVAR}] \qquad \frac{\Theta; \Sigma; \Gamma \vdash N : T \to_\rho T' \quad \Theta; \Sigma; \Gamma \vdash M : T}{\Theta; \Sigma; \Gamma \vdash N \ M : T'} \ [\text{TAPP}]$$

$$\frac{\Theta; \Sigma; \Gamma \vdash N : T_1 + T_2 \quad \Theta; \Sigma; \Gamma, x : T_1 \vdash M' : T \quad \Theta; \Sigma; \Gamma, x' : T_2 \vdash M'' : T}{\Theta; \Sigma; \Gamma \vdash \textbf{case } N \textbf{ of Inl } x \Rightarrow M'; \textbf{ Inr } x' \Rightarrow M'' : T} \ [\text{TCASE}]$$

$$\frac{\Theta; \Sigma; \Gamma \vdash M : T \quad S, R \in \Theta}{\Theta; \Sigma; \Gamma \vdash \textbf{select}_{S,R} \ l \ M : T} \ [\text{TSEL}]$$

$$\frac{f(\vec{R'}) : T \in \Gamma \quad \vec{R} \subseteq \Theta \quad ||\vec{R}|| = ||\vec{R'}|| \quad \text{distinct}(\vec{R})}{\Theta; \Sigma; \Gamma \vdash f(\vec{R}) : T[\vec{R'} := \vec{R}]} \ [\text{TDEF}]$$

$$\frac{R \in \Theta}{\Theta; \Sigma; \Gamma \vdash ()@R : ()@R} \ [\text{TUNIT}] \qquad \frac{S, R \in \Theta \quad \text{roles}(T) = S}{\Theta; \Sigma; \Gamma \vdash \textbf{com}_{S,R} : T \to_\emptyset T[S := R]} \ [\text{TCOM}]$$

$$\frac{\Theta; \Sigma; \Gamma \vdash V : T \quad \Theta; \Sigma; \Gamma \vdash V' : T'}{\Theta; \Sigma; \Gamma \vdash \textbf{Pair } V \ V' : (T \times T')} \ [\text{TPAIR}]$$

$$\frac{\text{roles}(T \times T') \subseteq \Theta}{\Theta; \Sigma; \Gamma \vdash \textbf{fst} : (T \times T') \to_\emptyset T} \ [\text{TPROJ1}] \qquad \frac{\text{roles}(T \times T') \subseteq \Theta}{\Theta; \Sigma; \Gamma \vdash \textbf{snd} : (T \times T') \to_\emptyset T'} \ [\text{TPROJ2}]$$

$$\frac{\Theta; \Sigma; \Gamma \vdash V : T \quad \text{roles}(T + T') \subseteq \Theta}{\Theta; \Sigma; \Gamma \vdash \textbf{Inl } V : (T + T')} \ [\text{TINL}] \qquad \frac{\Theta; \Sigma; \Gamma \vdash V : T' \quad \text{roles}(T + T') \subseteq \Theta}{\Theta; \Sigma; \Gamma \vdash \textbf{Inr } V : (T + T')} \ [\text{TINR}]$$

$$\frac{\Theta; \Sigma; \Gamma \vdash M : t@\vec{R} \quad t@\vec{R'} =_\Sigma T \quad ||\vec{R}|| = ||\vec{R'}|| \quad \text{distinct}(\vec{R})}{\Theta; \Sigma; \Gamma \vdash M : T[\vec{R'} := \vec{R}]} \ [\text{TEQ}]$$

$$\frac{\forall f(\vec{R}) \in \text{domain}(D) : \quad f(\vec{R}) : T \in \Gamma \quad \vec{R}; \Sigma; \Gamma \vdash D(f(\vec{R})) : T \quad \text{distinct}(\vec{R}) \quad \vec{R} \subseteq \Theta}{\Theta; \Sigma; \Gamma \vdash D} \ [\text{TDEFS}]$$

Fig. 4. Full set of typing rules for Chorλ.

$$\frac{}{\lambda x : T.M \ V \xrightarrow{\tau,\emptyset}_D M[x := V]} \text{[AppAbs]} \qquad \frac{M \xrightarrow{\ell,\mathbf{R}}_D M'}{\lambda x : T.M \xrightarrow{\lambda,\mathbf{R}}_D \lambda x : T.M'} \text{[InAbs]}$$

$$\frac{M \xrightarrow{\ell,\mathbf{R}}_D M' \quad \ell = \lambda \Rightarrow \mathbf{R} \cap \text{roles}(N) = \emptyset}{M \ N \xrightarrow{\tau,\mathbf{R}}_D M' \ N} \text{[App1]}$$

$$\frac{N \xrightarrow{\tau,\mathbf{R}}_D N'}{V \ N \xrightarrow{\tau,\mathbf{R}}_D V \ N'} \text{[App2]} \qquad \frac{N \xrightarrow{\tau,\mathbf{R}}_D N' \quad \mathbf{R} \cap \text{roles}(M) = \emptyset}{M \ N \xrightarrow{\tau,\mathbf{R}}_D M \ N'} \text{[App3]}$$

$$\frac{N \xrightarrow{\tau,\mathbf{R}}_D N'}{\text{case } N \text{ of Inl } x \Rightarrow M; \text{ Inr } x' \Rightarrow M' \xrightarrow{\tau,\mathbf{R}}_D \text{case } N' \text{ of Inl } x \Rightarrow M; \text{ Inr } x' \Rightarrow M'} \text{[Case]}$$

$$\frac{M_1 \xrightarrow{\ell,\mathbf{R}}_D M_1' \quad M_2 \xrightarrow{\ell,\mathbf{R}}_D M_2' \quad \mathbf{R} \cap \text{roles}(N) = \emptyset}{\text{case } N \text{ of Inl } x \Rightarrow M_1; \text{ Inr } x' \Rightarrow M_2 \xrightarrow{\ell,\mathbf{R}}_D \text{case } N \text{ of Inl } x \Rightarrow M_1'; \text{ Inr } x' \Rightarrow M_2'} \text{[InCase]}$$

$$\frac{}{\text{case Inl } V \text{ of Inl } x \Rightarrow M; \text{ Inr } x' \Rightarrow M' \xrightarrow{\tau,\emptyset}_D M[x := V]} \text{[CaseL]}$$

$$\frac{}{\text{case Inr } V \text{ of Inl } x \Rightarrow M; \text{ Inr } x' \Rightarrow M' \xrightarrow{\tau,\emptyset}_D M'[x' := V]} \text{[CaseR]}$$

$$\frac{}{\text{fst Pair } V \ V' \xrightarrow{\tau,\emptyset}_D V} \text{[Proj1]} \qquad \frac{}{\text{snd Pair } V \ V' \xrightarrow{\tau,\emptyset}_D V'} \text{[Proj2]}$$

$$\frac{D(f(\vec{R'})) = M}{f(\vec{R}) \xrightarrow{\tau,\emptyset}_D M[\vec{R'} := \vec{R}]} \text{[Def]}$$

$$\frac{\text{fv}(V) = \emptyset}{\text{com}_{S,R} \ V \xrightarrow{\tau,\{S,R\}}_D V[S := R]} \text{[Com]} \qquad \frac{}{\text{select}_{S,R} \ l \ M \xrightarrow{\tau,\{S,R\}}_D M} \text{[Sel]}$$

$$\frac{M \xrightarrow{\ell,\mathbf{R}}_D M' \quad \mathbf{R} \cap \{S,R\} = \emptyset}{\text{select}_{S,R} \ \ell \ M \xrightarrow{\ell,\mathbf{R}}_D \text{select}_{S,R} \ \ell \ M'} \text{[InSel]} \qquad \frac{M \rightsquigarrow^* N \quad N \xrightarrow{\tau,\mathbf{R}}_D N'}{M \xrightarrow{\tau,\mathbf{R}}_D M'} \text{[Str]}$$

Fig. 5. Semantics of Chorλ

Choreographies:

$$[\![M\ N]\!]_R = \begin{cases} [\![M]\!]_R\ [\![N]\!]_R & \text{if } R \in \mathsf{roles}(\mathsf{type}(M)) \text{ or } R \in \mathsf{roles}(M) \cap \mathsf{roles}(N) \\ \bot & \text{if } [\![M]\!]_R = [\![N]\!]_R = \bot \\ [\![M]\!]_R & \text{if } [\![N]\!]_R = \bot \\ [\![N]\!]_R & \text{otherwise} \end{cases}$$

$$[\![\lambda x : T.M]\!]_R = \begin{cases} \lambda x.\,[\![M]\!]_R & \text{if } R \in \mathsf{roles}(\mathsf{type}(x : T.M)) \\ \bot & \text{otherwise} \end{cases}$$

$$[\![\mathsf{case}\ M\ \mathsf{of}\ \mathsf{Inl}\ x \Rightarrow N;\ \mathsf{Inr}\ x' \Rightarrow N']\!]_R =$$

$$\begin{cases} \mathsf{case}\ [\![M]\!]_R\ \mathsf{of}\ \mathsf{Inl}\ x \Rightarrow [\![N]\!]_R;\ \mathsf{Inr}\ x' \Rightarrow [\![N']\!]_R & \text{if } R \in \mathsf{roles}(\mathsf{type}(M)) \\ \bot & \text{if } [\![M]\!]_R = [\![N]\!]_R = [\![N']\!]_R = \bot \\ [\![M]\!]_R & \text{if } [\![N]\!]_R = [\![N']\!]_R = \bot \\ [\![N]\!]_R \sqcup [\![N']\!]_R & \text{if } [\![M]\!]_R = \bot \\ (\lambda x'' : \bot.\,[\![N]\!]_R \sqcup [\![N']\!]_R)\ [\![M]\!]_R & \text{for some } x'' \notin \mathsf{fv}(N) \cup \mathsf{fv}(N') \\ & \text{otherwise} \end{cases}$$

$$[\![\mathsf{select}_{S,S'}\ \ell\ M]\!]_R = \begin{cases} \oplus_{S'}\ \ell\ [\![M]\!]_R & \text{if } R = S \neq S' \\ \&_S\{\ell : [\![M]\!]_R\} & \text{if } R = S' \neq S \\ [\![M]\!]_R & \text{otherwise} \end{cases}$$

$$[\![\mathsf{com}_{S,S'}]\!]_R = \begin{cases} \lambda x.x & \text{if } R = S = S' \\ \mathsf{send}_{S'} & \text{if } R = S \neq S' \\ \mathsf{recv}_S & \text{if } R = S' \neq S \\ \bot & \text{otherwise} \end{cases}$$

$$[\![()@S]\!]_R = \begin{cases} () & \text{if } S = R \\ \bot & \text{otherwise} \end{cases} \qquad [\![x]\!]_R = \begin{cases} x & \text{if } R \in \mathsf{roles}(\mathsf{type}(x)) \\ \bot & \text{otherwise} \end{cases}$$

$$[\![f(\vec{R})]\!]_R = \begin{cases} f_i(R_1, \ldots, R_{i-1}, R_{i+1}, \ldots, R_n) & \text{if } \vec{R} = R_1, \ldots, R_{i-1}, R, R_{i+1}, \ldots, R_n \\ \bot & \text{otherwise} \end{cases}$$

$$[\![\mathsf{Pair}\ V\ V']\!]_R = \begin{cases} \mathsf{Pair}\ [\![V]\!]_R\ [\![V']\!]_R & \text{if } R \in \mathsf{roles}(\mathsf{type}(V) \times \mathsf{type}(V')) \\ \bot & \text{otherwise} \end{cases}$$

$$[\![\mathsf{fst}]\!]_R = \begin{cases} \mathsf{fst} & \text{if } R \in \mathsf{roles}(\mathsf{type}(\mathsf{fst})) \\ \bot & \text{otherwise} \end{cases} \qquad [\![\mathsf{snd}]\!]_R = \begin{cases} \mathsf{snd} & \text{if } R \in \mathsf{roles}(\mathsf{type}(\mathsf{snd})) \\ \bot & \text{otherwise} \end{cases}$$

$$[\![\mathsf{Inl}\ V]\!]_R = \begin{cases} \mathsf{Inl}\ [\![V]\!]_R & \text{if } R \in \mathsf{roles}(\mathsf{type}(\mathsf{Inl}\ V)) \\ \bot & \text{otherwise} \end{cases} \qquad [\![\mathsf{Inr}\ V]\!]_R = \begin{cases} \mathsf{Inr}\ [\![V]\!]_R & \text{if } r \in \mathsf{roles}(\mathsf{type}(\mathsf{Inr}\ V)) \\ \bot & \text{otherwise} \end{cases}$$

Types:

$$[\![T \to_\rho T']\!]_R = \begin{cases} [\![T]\!]_R \to [\![T']\!]_R & \text{if } R \in \rho \cup \mathsf{roles}(T) \cup \mathsf{roles}(T') \\ \bot & \text{otherwise} \end{cases} \qquad [\![()@S]\!]_R = \begin{cases} () & \text{if } S = R \\ \bot & \text{otherwise} \end{cases}$$

$$[\![T \times T']\!]_R = \begin{cases} [\![T]\!]_R \times [\![T']\!]_R & \text{if } R \in \mathsf{roles}(T \times T') \\ \bot & \text{otherwise} \end{cases} \qquad [\![T + T']\!]_R = \begin{cases} [\![T]\!]_R + [\![T']\!]_R & \text{if } R \in \mathsf{roles}(T + T') \\ \bot & \text{otherwise} \end{cases}$$

$$[\![t@\vec{R}]\!]_R = \begin{cases} t_i & \text{if } \vec{R} = R_1, \ldots, R_{i-1}, R, R_{i+1}, \ldots, R_n \\ \bot & \text{otherwise} \end{cases}$$

Definitions:

$$[\![D]\!] = \{f_i(R_1, \ldots, R_{i-1}, R_{i+1}, \ldots, R_n) \mapsto [\![D(f(R_1, \ldots, R_n))]\!]_{R_i} \mid f(R_1, \ldots, R_n) \in \mathsf{domain}(D)\}\}$$

Fig. 6. Projecting Chorλ onto a role

C   Proof of Theorem 1

Proof (Proof of Theorem 1). We prove this by induction on the typing derivation of $\Theta; \Sigma; \Gamma \vdash M : T$. Most cases either M is a value, or the result follows from simple induction, we go through the rest.

- Assume we use rule TApp, so $M = N_1 N_2$, $\Theta; \Sigma; \Gamma \vdash N_1 : T' \to_\rho T$, and $\Theta; \Sigma; \Gamma \vdash N_2 : T'$. If N_1 or N_2 is not a value then the result follows from induction and using rule App1 or rule App2. Otherwise, we have four cases:
  - Assume $\Theta; \Sigma; \Gamma \vdash N_1 : T' \to_\rho T$ uses rule TAbs. Then the result follows using rule AppAbs.
  - Assume $\Theta; \Sigma; \Gamma \vdash N_1 : T' \to_\rho T$ uses rule TComTAbs. Then, since M is closed, the result follows by rule Com.
  - Assume $\Theta; \Sigma; \Gamma \vdash N_1 : T' \to_\rho T$ uses rule TProj1. Then, since M is closed and N_2 is a value, $N_2 = \textbf{Pair } V V'$, and consequently the result follows using rule Proj1.
  - Assume $\Theta; \Sigma; \Gamma \vdash N_1 : T' \to_\rho T$ uses rule TProj2. Then, since M is closed and N_2 is a value, $N_2 = \textbf{Pair } V V'$, and consequently the result follows using rule Proj2.
- Assume we use rule TCase, so $M = \textbf{case } N_1 \textbf{ of Inl } x \Rightarrow N_2; \textbf{Inr } x' \Rightarrow N_3$, $\Theta; \Sigma; \Gamma \vdash N_1 : T_1 + T_2$, $\Theta; \Sigma; \Gamma, x : T_1 \vdash N_2 : T$, and $\Theta; \Sigma; \Gamma, x' : T_2 \vdash N_3 : T$. Then if N_1 is not a value the result follows from induction and using rule Case. If N_1 is a value then, since M is closed, either $N_1 = \textbf{Inl } V$ or $N_1 = \textbf{Inr } V$, and the result follows by rule CaseL or rule CaseR respectively.
- Assume we use rule TSel so $M = \textbf{select}_{S,R} l N : T$, $\Theta; \Sigma; \Gamma \vdash N : T$, and $S, R \in \Theta$. Then the result follows from using rule Sel.
- Assume we use rule TDef and $M = f(\vec{R})$, $f(\vec{R}' : T' \in \Gamma$, $\vec{R} \subseteq \Theta$, $||\vec{R}|| = ||\vec{R}'||$, distinct$(\vec{R})$, and $T = T'[\vec{R}' := \vec{R}]$. Then the result follows from D containing f, $\Theta; \Sigma; \Gamma \vdash D$ and rule Def.

D   Proof of Theorem 2

Lemma 1. *Given a choreography, M, if $\Theta; \Sigma; \Gamma \vdash M$ then $\Theta \cup \Theta'; \Sigma; \Gamma \vdash M$*

Proof. Follows from the typing rules only ever discussing subsets of Θ.

Lemma 2 (Type preservation under rewriting). *Let M be a choreography. If there exists a typing context $\Theta; \Sigma; \Gamma$ such that $\Theta; \Sigma; \Gamma \vdash M : T$, then $\Theta; \Sigma; \Gamma \vdash M' : T$ for any M' such that $M \rightsquigarrow M'$.*

Proof. We prove this by case analysis of the the rewriting rules:

rule R-AbsR Then $M = ((\lambda x : T_1.N_1) N_2) N_3$, and from the typing rules we get that there exist T_2 and ρ such that $\Theta; \Sigma; \Gamma, x : T_1 \vdash N_1 : T_2 \to_\rho T$, $\Theta; \Sigma; \Gamma \vdash N_2 : T_1$, and $\Theta; \Sigma; \Gamma \vdash N_3 : T_2$, and $M' = (\lambda x : T_1.(N_1 N_3)) N_2$. The result follows from using rules TApp and TAbs and $x \notin \text{fv}(N_3)$.

rule R-AbsL Then $M = N_1 \ ((\lambda x : T_1.N_3) \ N_2)$, $\Theta; \Sigma; \Gamma, x : T_1 \vdash N_1 : T_2 \rightarrow_\rho T$, $\Theta; \Sigma; \Gamma \vdash N_2 : T_1$, and $\Theta; \Sigma; \Gamma \vdash N_3 : T_2$, and $M' = (\lambda x : T_1.(N_1 \ N_3)) \ N_2$. The result follows from using rules TApp and TAbs and $x \notin \mathrm{fv}(N_1)$.

rule R-CaseR Then $M = \mathbf{case} \ N_1 \ \mathbf{of} \ \mathsf{Inl} \ x \Rightarrow N_2; \mathsf{Inr} \ x' \Rightarrow N_3) \ N_4$, and from the typing rules we get that there exist T_1, T_2, T_3, and ρ such that $\Theta; \Sigma; \Gamma \vdash N_1 : T_1 + T_2$, $\Theta; \Sigma; \Gamma, x : T_1 \vdash N_2 : T_3 \rightarrow_\rho T$, $\Theta; \Sigma; \Gamma, x' : T_2 \vdash N_3 : T_3 \rightarrow_\rho T$, and $\Theta; \Sigma; \Gamma \vdash N_4 : T_3$, and $M' = \mathbf{case} \ N_1 \ \mathbf{of} \ \mathsf{Inl} \ x \Rightarrow N_2 \ N_4; \mathsf{Inr} \ x' \Rightarrow N_3 \ N_4)$. The result follows from using rules TCase and TAbs and $x, x' \notin \mathrm{fv}(N_4)$.

rule R-CaseL This case is similar to the previous.

rule R-SelR Then $M = N_1 \ (\mathbf{select}_{S,R} \ l \ N_2)$, and from the typing rules we get that there exist T', and ρ such that $\Theta; \Sigma; \Gamma \vdash N_1 : T' \rightarrow_\rho T$ and $\Theta; \Sigma; \Gamma \vdash N_2 : T'$, and $M' = \mathbf{select}_{S,R} \ l \ (N_1 \ N_2)$. The result follows from using rules TSel and TAbs.

rule R-SelL This case is similar to the previous.

Proof (Proof of Theorem 2). We prove this by induction on the derivation of $M \xrightarrow{\tau, \mathbf{R}}_D M'$. The cases for rules AppAbs,App1 and App2 are standard for simply-typed λ-calculus. And the cases for rules InAbs,App3,Case,InCase and InSel follow from simple induction. We go through the rest.

- Assume we use rule CaseL. Then we know that $M = \mathbf{case} \ \mathsf{Inl} \ V \ \mathbf{of} \ \mathsf{Inl} \ x \Rightarrow N_1; \mathsf{Inr} \ x' \Rightarrow N_2$, and from the typing rules we get that there exists T' such that $\Theta; \Sigma; \Gamma \vdash V : T'$ and $\Theta; \Sigma; \Gamma, x : T' \vdash N_1 : T$. Therefore, $\Theta; \Sigma; \Gamma \vdash N_1[x := V] : T$.
- Assume we use rule CaseR. This is similar to the previous case.
- Assume we use rule Proj1. Then we know $M = \mathbf{fst} \ \mathbf{Pair} \ V \ V'$, and from the typing rules we get that $\Theta; \Sigma; \Gamma \vdash V : T$.
- Assume we use rule Proj2. This is similar to the previous case.
- Assume we use rule Def. From the typing of M we get that there exists $f(\vec{R'}) : T \in \Gamma$ such that $||\vec{R}|| = ||\vec{R'}||$, $\vec{R} \subseteq \Theta$, and $\mathrm{distinct}(\vec{R'})$. From the typing of D we get that $\mathrm{distinct}(\vec{R'})$ and $\vec{R'}; \Sigma; \Gamma \vdash D(f(\vec{R'}))$. Therefore, by Theroem 1, we get $\Theta; \Sigma; \Gamma \vdash D(f(\vec{R'}))$.
- Assume we use rule Com. Then we know that $M = \mathbf{com}_{S,R} \ V$, $\mathrm{fv}(V) = \emptyset$, and there exists T' such that $\Theta; \Sigma; \Gamma \vdash V : T'$, $\mathrm{roles}(T') = \{S\}$, and $T = T'[S := R]$. We see from our typing rules that the only time we use roles not mentioned in the choreography in typing is when handling free variables. Therefore we get that $\Theta; \Sigma; \Gamma \vdash V[S := R] : T$.
- Assume we use rule Sel. Then we know that $M = \mathbf{select}_{S,R} \ l \ N$ and $\Theta; \Sigma; \Gamma \vdash N : T$. The result follows.
- Assume we use rule Str. Then the result follows from Lemma 2 and induction.

References

1. Carbone, M., Honda, K., Yoshida, N.: Structured communication-centered programming for web services. ACM Trans. Program. Lang. Syst. **34**(2), 8:1–8:78 (2012). https://doi.org/10.1145/2220365.2220367

2. Carbone, M., Montesi, F.: Deadlock-freedom-by-design: multiparty asynchronous global programming. In: Giacobazzi, R., Cousot, R. (eds.) Proceedings, POPL, pp. 263–274. ACM (2013). https://doi.org/10.1145/2429069.2429101

3. Cardelli, L., Gordon, A.D.: Mobile ambients. Theor. Comput. Sci. **240**(1), 177–213 (2000). https://doi.org/10.1016/S0304-3975(99)00231-5

4. Castagna, G., Dezani-Ciancaglini, M., Padovani, L.: On global types and multiparty sessions. In: Bruni, R., Dingel, J. (eds.) FMOODS/FORTE -2011. LNCS, vol. 6722, pp. 1–28. Springer, Heidelberg (2011). https://doi.org/10.1007/978-3-642-21461-5_1

5. Church, A.: A set of postulates for the foundation of logic. Ann. Math. **33**(2), 346–366 (1932). http://www.jstor.org/stable/1968337

6. Cruz-Filipe, L., Graversen, E., Lugovic, L., Montesi, F., Peressotti, M.: Functional choreographic programming. CoRR **abs/2111.03701** (2021). https://arxiv.org/abs/2111.03701

7. Cruz-Filipe, L., Montesi, F.: Procedural choreographic programming. In: Bouajjani, A., Silva, A. (eds.) FORTE 2017. LNCS, vol. 10321, pp. 92–107. Springer, Cham (2017). https://doi.org/10.1007/978-3-319-60225-7_7

8. Cruz-Filipe, L., Montesi, F.: A core model for choreographic programming. Theor. Comput. Sci. **802**, 38–66 (2020). https://doi.org/10.1016/j.tcs.2019.07.005

9. Cruz-Filipe, L., Montesi, F., Peressotti, M.: Communications in choreographies, revisited. In: Proceedings of the 33rd Annual ACM Symposium on Applied Computing, SAC 2018, Pau, France, 09–13 April 2018, pp. 1248–1255. ACM (2018). https://doi.org/10.1145/3167132.3167267

10. Cruz-Filipe, L., Montesi, F., Peressotti, M.: Certifying choreography compilation. In: Cerone, A., Ölveczky, P.C. (eds.) ICTAC 2021. LNCS, vol. 12819, pp. 115–133. Springer, Cham (2021). https://doi.org/10.1007/978-3-030-85315-0_8

11. Cruz-Filipe, L., Montesi, F., Peressotti, M.: Formalising a turing-complete choreographic language in coq. In: Cohen, L., Kaliszyk, C. (eds.) 12th International Conference on Interactive Theorem Proving, ITP 2021, Rome, Italy (Virtual Conference), 29 June–1 July 2021, LIPIcs, vol. 193, pp. 15:1–15:18. Schloss Dagstuhl - Leibniz-Zentrum für Informatik (2021). https://doi.org/10.4230/LIPIcs.ITP.2021.15

12. Dalla Preda, M., Gabbrielli, M., Giallorenzo, S., Lanese, I., Mauro, J.: Dynamic choreographies: theory and implementation. Log. Methods Comput. Sci. **13**(2) (2017). https://doi.org/10.23638/LMCS-13(2:1)2017

13. Demangeon, R., Honda, K.: Nested protocols in session types. In: Koutny, M., Ulidowski, I. (eds.) CONCUR 2012. LNCS, vol. 7454, pp. 272–286. Springer, Heidelberg (2012). https://doi.org/10.1007/978-3-642-32940-1_20

14. Diffie, W., Hellman, M.E.: New directions in cryptography. IEEE Trans. Inf. Theory **22**(6), 644–654 (1976). https://doi.org/10.1109/TIT.1976.1055638

15. Giallorenzo, S., Montesi, F., Peressotti, M.: Choreographies as objects. CoRR **abs/2005.09520** (2020). https://arxiv.org/abs/2005.09520

16. Giallorenzo, S., Montesi, F., Peressotti, M., Richter, D., Salvaneschi, G., Weisenburger, P.: Multiparty languages: the choreographic and multitier cases. In: 35th European Conference on Object-Oriented Programming, ECOOP 2021, Aarhus, Denmark (Virtual Conference), 12–17 July 2021, LIPIcs, Schloss Dagstuhl - Leibniz-Zentrum fuer Informatik (2021). to appear. https://fabriziomontesi.com/files/gmprsw21.pdf

17. Object Management Group: Business Process Model and Notation (2011). http://www.omg.org/spec/BPMN/2.0/ (2011)

18. Hirsch, A.K., Garg, D.: Pirouette: higher-order typed functional choreographies. Proc. ACM Program. Lang. **6**(POPL), 1–27 (2022). https://doi.org/10.1145/3498684

19. Honda, K., Yoshida, N., Carbone, M.: Multiparty asynchronous session types. J. ACM **63**(1), 9 (2016). https://doi.org/10.1145/2827695, also: POPL, pages 273–284, 2008

20. Hüttel, H., et al.: Foundations of session types and behavioural contracts. ACM Comput. Surv. **49**(1), 3:1–3:36 (2016). https://doi.org/10.1145/2873052

21. Intl. Telecommunication Union: Recommendation Z.120: Message Sequence Chart (1996)

22. Jongmans, S.-S., van den Bos, P.: A predicate transformer for choreographies. In: ESOP 2022. LNCS, vol. 13240, pp. 520–547. Springer, Cham (2022). https://doi.org/10.1007/978-3-030-99336-8_19

23. López, H.A., Nielson, F., Nielson, H.R.: Enforcing availability in failure-aware communicating systems. In: Albert, E., Lanese, I. (eds.) FORTE 2016. LNCS, vol. 9688, pp. 195–211. Springer, Cham (2016). https://doi.org/10.1007/978-3-319-39570-8_13

24. Montesi, F.: Choreographic Programming. Ph.D. Thesis, IT University of Copenhagen (2013)

25. Montesi, F.: Introduction to Choreographies. Cambridge University Press, Cambridge (2022)

26. Murphy VII, T., Crary, K., Harper, R., Pfenning, F.: A symmetric modal lambda calculus for distributed computing. In: 19th IEEE Symposium on Logic in Computer Science (LICS 2004), Turku, Finland, 14-17 July 2004, Proceedings, pp. 286–295. IEEE Computer Society (2004). https://doi.org/10.1109/LICS.2004.1319623

27. Needham, R.M., Schroeder, M.D.: Using encryption for authentication in large networks of computers. Commun. ACM **21**(12), 993–999 (1978). https://doi.org/10.1145/359657.359659

28. OpenID Foundation: OpenID Specification (2014). https://openid.net/developers/specs/

29. Pierce, B.C.: Types and Programming Languages. MIT Press, Cambridge (2002)

30. Pohjola, J.Å., Gómez-Londoño, A., Shaker, J., Norrish, M.: Kalas: A verified, end-to-end compiler for a choreographic language. In: Andronick, J., de Moura, L. (eds.) 13th International Conference on Interactive Theorem Proving, ITP 2022, Haifa, Israel, 7–10 August 2022, LIPIcs, vol. 237, pp. 27:1–27:18. Schloss Dagstuhl - Leibniz-Zentrum für Informatik (2022). https://doi.org/10.4230/LIPIcs.ITP.2022.27

31. Vollbrecht, J., Carlson, J.D., Blunk, L., Aboba, D.B.D., Levkowetz, H.: Extensible Authentication Protocol (EAP). RFC 3748 (2004). https://doi.org/10.17487/RFC3748, https://rfc-editor.org/rfc/rfc3748.txt

32. W3C: WS Choreography Description Language (2004). http://www.w3.org/TR/ws-cdl-10/

33. Weisenburger, P., Wirth, J., Salvaneschi, G.: A survey of multitier programming. ACM Comput. Surv. **53**(4), 81:1–81:35 (2020). https://doi.org/10.1145/3397495

A Model Checking Based Approach to Detect Safety-Critical Adversarial Examples on Autonomous Driving Systems

Zhen Huang[1], Bo Li[1], DeHui Du[1], and Qin Li[1,2](✉) 📷

[1] Shanghai Key Laboratory of Trustworthy Computing,
East China Normal University, Shanghai, China
qli@sei.ecnu.edu.cn
[2] Shanghai Institute of Intelligent Science and Technology,
Tongji University, Shanghai, China

Abstract. The safety of autonomous driving systems (ADS) with machine learning (ML) components is threatened by adversarial examples. The mainstream defending technique against such threats concerns the adversarial examples that make the ML model fail. However, such an adversarial example does not necessarily cause safety problems for the entire ADS. Therefore a method for detecting the adversarial examples that will lead the ADS to unsafe states will be helpful to improve the defending technique. This paper proposes an approach to detect such safety-critical adversarial examples in typical autonomous driving scenarios based on the model checking technique. The scenario of autonomous driving and the semantic effect of adversarial attacks on object detection is specified with the Network of Timed Automata model. The safety properties of ADS are specified and verified through the UPPAAL model checker to show whether the adversarial examples lead to safety problems. The result from the model checking can reveal the critical time interval of adversarial attacks that will lead to an unsafe state for a given scenario. The approach is demonstrated on a popular adversarial attack algorithm in a typical autonomous driving scenario. Its effectiveness is shown through a series of simulations on the CARLA platform.

Keywords: Autonomous driving · Model checking · Adversarial examples

1 Introduction

As a safety-critical system, the autonomous driving system (ADS) has received intensive concern from both academia and industry. The modern ADS incorporates deep learning models into its key modules such as perception, control and

This work is supported by NKRDP (2020AAA0107800) and STCSM (20DZ1100300).

even decision module. However, due to the statistical nature and poor interpretability of deep learning, the safety assurance for ADS becomes a grand challenge. Many types of research reveal a new kind of threat to deep learning models from adversarial attacks [8,12–19]. These inputs perturbed with slight disturbances can make the deep learning model return wrong results with high confidence. Since the disturbances are hardly recognized by humans or other measurements based on semantical features, these adversarial attacks are difficult to be detected in advance with conventional methods. A number of algorithms like U-DOS (Universal Dense Object Suppression) and a suite of adversarial objectness gradient attacks, coined as TOG, are proposed to generate adversarial examples (AE) for CNNs used in the perception module of ADS [1,7–11]. These AEs may make the CNN fail to recognize an incoming vehicle and consequently cause the decision module of ADS to take the wrong decision which leads to collision accidents. Adversarial training is one of the main defensive approaches against adversarial attacks. Its basic idea is to incorporate the generated adversarial examples into the training process to improve the robustness of the deep learning models.

However, the compromised deep learning model is only a component of the entire ADS, and not every adversarial input that causes the deep learning component to fail may cause real harm to the entire ADS. For instance, consider a scenario in which an autonomous vehicle is approaching the intersection, the adversarial attack that makes it mistakenly recognize the traffic light from yellow to red would not change its decision to brake. In contrast, the adversarial attack that makes it mistakenly recognize the traffic light from red to green would make it violates the safety regulation and may cause serious accidents. Therefore, the timing and targeting of safety property are essential factors for the adversarial examples. However, the existing algorithms for generating adversarial examples hardly consider such information. In this paper, we call an adversarial example a safety-critical adversarial example (SCAE) if it can lead to the violation of scenario-oriented safety-critical properties of ADS. In this sense, it is a promising research topic to reveal such SCAEs among common AEs and improve the adversarial training with these SCAEs other than common AEs.

In this paper, we propose a novel approach to defining and detecting SCAEs in the ADS context. The rough framework of this approach is shown in Fig. 1. A formal model is built for the autonomous driving scenarios in which safety-critical properties are specified with the temporal logic formula ϕ. A black-box model of the DNN preceptor is included in the system model as a component and therefore provides an interface for the external inputs from the environment. An AE x' is determined as a SCAE if the system model with input x' violates ϕ while it satisfies ϕ with the original input x. To validate the effectiveness of this approach, we employ the simulation platform CARLA to set the attacking scenario with the SCAEs we found with the model checker. The simulation results justify that SCAEs can lead the scenario to collision accidents, while common AEs committed randomly in the process can hardly succeed.

In summary, this paper contains the following contributions:

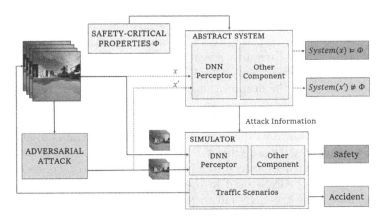

Fig. 1. The rough framework of the proposed method.

1. A formal definition for SCAEs is proposed in terms of the model checking notations. It relates the adversarial examples with the safety-critical properties of the entire system.
2. A novel model checking-based approach is proposed to detect SCAEs from a given autonomous driving scenario. For a particular AE generating algorithm, the approach can return the target and timing for the adversarial attack to ensure the violation of the safety-critical property, which allocates the corresponding SCAEs.
3. Experiments of our approach are conducted with the model checker UPPAAL and the simulation platform CARLA. From the simulation results, we can conclude that the SCAEs found by the model checker can cause collision accidents.

The rest of this paper is structured as follows: we give a brief introduction for model checking with the UPPAAL toolkit and the AE generating algorithms in Sect. 2. The formal definition of SCAE is given in Sect. 3. Section 4 gives the formal model of the autonomous driving scenario and shows how to detect SCAEs by verifying the safety-critical property. Section 5 shows the experimenting results of our approach on the simulation platform CARLA to justify its effectiveness. Section 6 concludes the paper and mentions future work.

2   Preliminaries

2.1   Model Checking with UPPAAL

UPPAAL [3,4] is a toolset for verification of real-time systems modelled as networks of extended timed automata. A timed automaton consists of a collection of locations connected by edges. Clock variables are the key features in timed automata to specify timing constraints. A location is defined on clock variables and bounded discrete variables satisfying an invariant. An edge defines a possible transition from one location to another subject to a guard condition, a synchronization action and a set of updating expressions.

Definition 1 (Timed Automata (TA)). *A timed automaton is a tuple* (L, l_0, V, A, E, I), *where* L *is a set of locations,* $l_0 \in L$ *is the initial location,* $V = C \cup D$ *is the set of variables consisting of clock variables in* C *and bounded discrete variables in* D, A *is a set of actions including internal* τ *action and synchronization actions,* $E \subseteq L \times A \times B(V) \times 2^V \times L$ *is a set of edges indicating transition relations between locations, and* $I : L \rightarrow B(V)$ *assigns invariants to locations.*

A TA network is a set of TA running in parallel and communicating with synchronization actions. Let $A_i = (L_i, l_0^i, V_i, A_i, E_i, I_i)$ with $i \in 1..n$ be n TAs in a TA network. Its semantics can be defined as $(S, s_0, \rightarrow)$ where $S = \{(\bar{L}, \bar{v}) | \bar{v} \models I(\bar{L})\}$ is a set of states consisting of the location vector $\bar{L} \in L_1 \times ... \times L_n$ and variable value vector $\bar{v}$ which is an evaluating function mapping all variables in the TA network to their values. s_0 is the initial state where every TA is in its initial location and every variable has its initial value. $\rightarrow \subseteq S \times (\mathbb{R}_{\geq 0} \cup A) \times S$ is the transition relation which contains delay transitions, internal action transitions and synchronization action transitions. Their semantics are defined as follows:

1. **Delay transition:** $(\bar{l}, \bar{v}) \xrightarrow{d} (\bar{l}, \bar{v} + d)$ if $\forall d' : 0 \leq d' \leq d \Rightarrow u + d' \in I(\bar{l})$, where $v + d$ maps every clock variable $x \in C_1 \cup ... \cup C_n$ to $v(x) + d$.
2. **Internal action transition:** $(\bar{l}, \bar{v}) \xrightarrow{a} (\bar{l}', \bar{v}')$ if there exists an edge $e_i = (l_i, a_i, g_i, u_i, l_i') \in E_i$ such that (1) a_i is not a synchronization action, (2)$\bar{v} \models g_i$, (3) $\bar{l}' = \bar{l}[l_i'/l_i]$, $\bar{v}' = u_i(\bar{v})$ and $\bar{v}' \models I(\bar{l}')$ where $I(\bar{l}') = \bigcap_i I_i(\bar{l}_i')$.
3. **Synchronization action transition:** $(\bar{l}, \bar{v}) \xrightarrow{c} (\bar{l}', \bar{v}')$ if there exists two edges $e_i = (l_i, a_i, g_i, u_i, l_i') \in E_i$ and $e_j = (l_j, a_j, g_j, u_j, l_j') \in E_j$ from two different TAs such that (1) $a_i = c!$ and $a_j = c?$ are synchronization actions with the same channel c, (2) $\bar{v} \models g_i \wedge g_j$, (3) $\bar{l}' = \bar{l}[l_i'/l_i, l_j'/l_j]$, $\bar{v}' = u_j(u_i(\bar{v}))$, and $\bar{v}' \models I(\bar{l}')$.

The UPPAAL supports parameterized TA templates. Let $A(Type\ x)$ be a parameterized TA templates with formal parameter x, we use the notation $A(v)$ to represent the TA model instantiated by actual parameter v. In this paper, we use parameters to instantiate the TA templates to adapt the model to different scenarios represented by input data streams.

A simple example of the TA network model in UPPAAL is shown in Fig. 2. The system contains two TAs *Env* and *Ctl* which communicate with each other through synchronization actions *e2c* and *c2e*. *period* is a constant representing the period of each cycle. Whenever receiving data from *Env*, the controller *Ctl* makes some computations and sends the feedback to the environment. The invariants on locations and guard conditions on edges ensure the cyclic behaviour of the system within the given fixed period. In the following part of this paper, the behaviour of the *Ctl* from location ready to do will be replaced by the dedicated

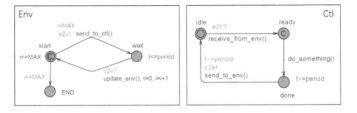

Fig. 2. An example of the UPPAAL model

processes specifying the corresponding components of the autonomous driving system.

The semantics model $(S, s_0, \rightarrow)$ yields a set of execution sequences $\langle s_0, s_1, ..., s_n \rangle$ where $s_i \in S$ and $s_i \rightarrow s_{i+1}$. The UPPAAL supports the verification of temporal properties specified with the following temporal operators $A\square, A\Diamond, E\square, E\Diamond$. Given a system model M and a state $s \in S$, we say

1. $M, s \models A\square p$ iff for any execution sequence $\pi = \langle s_0, s_1, ..., s_k \rangle$ of the system with $s_0 = s$, we have $M, \pi[i] \models p$ for any $i \in [0, k]$.
2. $M, s \models A\Diamond p$ iff for any execution sequence $\pi = \langle s_0, s_1, ..., s_k \rangle$ of the system with $s_0 = s$, we have $M, \pi[i] \models p$ for some $i \in [0, k]$.
3. $M, s \models E\square p$ iff $M, s \models \neg A\Diamond \neg p$.
4. $M, s \models E\Diamond p$ iff $M, s \models \neg A\square \neg p$.
5. $M \models p$ iff $M, s_0 \models p$.

A convention property $p \rightarrow q$ (p leads to q) means $A\square(p$ imply $A\Diamond q)$.

2.2   Adversarial Examples Generation Algorithm

Given a DNN model F and a data example x, an attacker can create an adversarial example of x by adding a perturbation δ, such that $F(x + \delta) \neq F(x)$ [2]. Generating adversarial examples can be interpreted as optimizing the example features toward adversarial objectives. The optimization objective can be generally parsed as follows:

$$\begin{cases} \min_\delta \|\delta\|_p \\ s.t. \ f(x + \delta) \in T \end{cases}$$

where T is an adversarial objective set by the attacker. $x + \delta$ produces an adversarial example x'. p is the distance metric, such as the L_0 norm measuring the percentage of the pixels that are changed, the L_2 norm computing the Euclidean distance, or the L_∞ norm denoting the maximum change to any pixel.

TOG and U-DOS are considered in this paper to attack object detectors to fail object detection in this paper. A suite of adversarial objectness gradient attacks, coined as TOG, can cause the deep object detection networks to suffer from untargeted random attacks or even targeted attacks with three types of specificity: (1) object-vanishing, (2) object-fabrication, and (3) object-mislabeling [20]. Universal Dense Object Suppression (U-DOS) algorithm can derive the universal adversarial perturbations against object detection and show that such perturbations with visual imperceptibility can lead the detectors to fail in finding any objects in most images [8].

3 The Safety-Critical Adversarial Examples

An intelligent system with ML components is generally a real-time system that interacts with the environment. Model checking tools can be used to model the system and its interactive environment. With the help of model checking technology, the information of the target and timing for adversarial attack can be obtained. The adversarial examples generated by the adversarial attack with the information can lead the system to an unsafe state.

We provide the following definition for such SCAEs:

Definition 2 (Safety-Critical Adversarial Examples). *Let $System(Type\ \&a)$ be a TA network model with a formal array parameter a. ϕ is a safety-critical property specified by timed temporal logic (TCTL) language. Let $x = \langle x_1, ..., x_n \rangle$ be an array representing an input data stream and $x' = \langle x'_1, ..., x'_n \rangle$ be another array with every its entry an adversarial example against the corresponding entry of x. We say x' is a safety-critical adversarial example against x, if*

1. *$System(x) \models \phi$ and*
2. *$System(x') \models \neg\phi$.*

Note that the SCAE can be a sequence of input data. A single adversarial example is usually not enough to violate the safety properties for ADS as long as it has chances to make proper amendments in consequent cycles. Therefore, a sustained attack is necessary to make real damage to the ADS. Our approach can check which timing and duration of a sustained adversarial attack can cause safety-critical problems in a given scenario. This kind of knowledge can then be used to develop a dedicated defensive mechanism for ADS in the future.

The following two sections will focus on the methodology to detect SCAEs and verify their validity according to 4 steps: (1) Modeling the ADS and its environment (such as traffic scenarios including road topology and other involved vehicles). (2) Characterize the safety properties of the system by TCTL, and run the UPPAAL model checker to locate the target and timing for adversarial attacks that can lead the system to unsafe states. (3) Combine the attack semantic information with current adversarial attack techniques to generate SCAEs. (4) Simulate the attacking scenarios with the SCAEs in the CARLA simulation platform to show the validity of SCAEs.

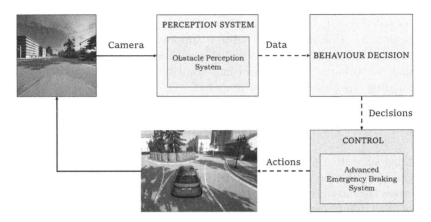

Fig. 3. A dedicated workflow of ADS.

4   Modelling the System and Detecting the SCAEs

This section will introduce the system modelling scheme in our approach. It is illustrated with a simplified autonomous driving scenario example where the autonomous vehicle recognizes another vehicle in an intersection and decides to brake to avoid the collision. We will model the behaviour of the autonomous vehicle in this simple scenario and find the SCAEs with the model checking technique. Other scenarios can be captured using extended models with similar modelling paradigms.

4.1   Abstract Model of ADS in UPPAAL

Figure 3 shows a dedicated workflow of ADS which only captures the typical autonomous decision-making scenario mentioned before. It contains the following modules. A camera-based perception module equipped with an obstacle perception algorithm based on DNN to detect surrounding obstacles (vehicles) from images captured by the camera. When the autonomous vehicle perceives obstacles nearby while driving, the Advanced Emergency Braking System (AEBS) determines whether there is a risk of collision with the obstacles. Once the AEBS calculates that the obstacles pose a threat to the autonomous vehicle, it will rapidly intervene and brake to avoid a collision.

As shown in Fig. 4, we model the above scenario with 8 time automata templates: (1) **EV**, namely environmental vehicle. (2) **EU**, namely environment update. (3) **IF**, namely interface module. (4) **OP**, namely obstacle perception module. (5) **BD**, namely behavior decision module. (6) **EB**, namely emergency braking module. (7) **CT**, namely synchronous controller. (8) **CD**, namely collision detection module. The system model can be divided into 3 components:

(1) the environment component contains **EV** to model the behaviours of environmental vehicles and **EU** to capture the updates of the environment state in every cycle. (2) the autonomous vehicle component consists of three internal modules **OP**, **BD**, **EB** and an interface module **IF**. The internal modules correspond to obstacle perception, behaviour decision and emergency braking modules in Fig. 3, while the interface module covers their interactions with the environment. (3) the synchronization component contains **CT** for coordinating the timing behaviours with a cyclic synchronization mechanism and **CD** for monitoring the safety property of the system at every cycle.

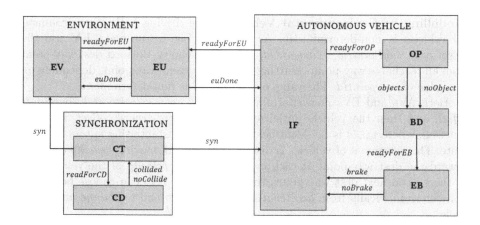

Fig. 4. The system model structure.

In this paper, we only present the modelling of **EV**, **EU**, **OP** and **IF** in detail due to the space limit. The full model can be found at https://github.com/Rruown/Formal-Model-of-Autonomous-Vehicle-in-UPPAAL.

The way-point model is used in this paper to model the traffic map, which can support multiple types of traffic scenarios (e.g. T-junction, crossroads). And actors considered are autonomous vehicles (AVs) and a number of environmental vehicles (EVs). EVs are born at a specified way-point and non-deterministically select the next way-point to drive on the traffic map, performing various behaviours (e.g. accelerate) at each cycle while driving. AV's driving path is initially specified using a set of way-points. Just by changing the way-point data, we can model a variety of different traffic scenarios.

The position of the vehicle is a point on 2D coordinates. The movement of the vehicle at each cycle is to add a 2D vector v, where the model of v is the velocity of the vehicle. In addition, a vector orthogonal is added to v to the vehicle's position, taking into account the vehicle width and driving offset. The driving trace of the vehicle at a cycle is abstracted as a rectangle in 2D coordinates.

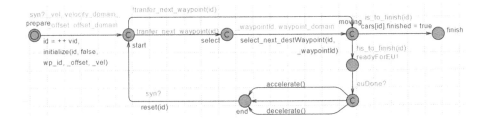

Fig. 5. Automata **EV** in UPPAAL

Modelling of Environmental Vehicles. The driving path of environmental vehicles is non-deterministic. As shown in Fig. 5, automata **EV** use the *select_next_wayPoint(id, _waypointId)* function to choose the next dest way-point from all reachable way-points starting from the current way-point, depending on the value of *waypointId*. The value of *waypointId* is non-deterministic.

Both AVs and EVs non-deterministically choose a *velocity* and *coordinate offset*, and then the vehicle initializes by *initialize(id, wp_id, offset, velocity)* function, where *wp_id* is the identification given by instantiating automata template. The movement of vehicles is discretely modelled, moving *velocity* distance toward the dest way-point at each cycle. When the *velocity* of the vehicle is 0 or there is no next dest way-point, the vehicle ends. EVs can choose behaviors non-deterministically from *acceleration*, *deceleration* and *unchange* after each cycle.

Modelling of Environment Update. The automata **EU**, as shown in Fig. 6, is responsible for the environment update of AVs and EVs. **EU** waits for all vehicles to be ready for environment update and then calls the *update* function to complete the environment update action including the movement of vehicle position.

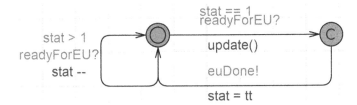

Fig. 6. Automata **EU** in UPPAAL

Modelling of Obstacle Perception Module. Different adversarial attack methods and neural network models may require different synchronous actions set to be defined. Modelling a system with neural network components can consider a neural network model as a black box, focusing only on its inputs and outputs. Define all the output of the model as output synchronization actions set. The model of the neural network accepts synchronization actions of the ground truth label and then non-deterministically sends a synchronization action back to the system. The adversarial attack method considered in this example is the object-vanish attack, so the input of the neural network can be ignored. The output synchronization actions are *objects* and *noObject* shown in Fig. 7, it literally means that the obstacle perception system has perceived objects and not perceived objects respectively.

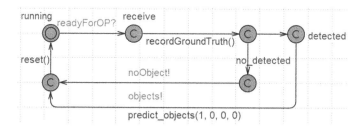

Fig. 7. Automata **OP** in UPPAAL

Modelling of Interface Module. The automata **IF**, as shown in Fig. 8, specifies a set of way-points as the driving path. At the end of each cycle, **IF** deliveries synchronization action *readyForOP* to **OP**. The **OP** returns its result of perception to behaviour decision module **BD**. Based on the result of perception, the **BD** will send synchronization action *readyForEB* to **EB** if it accepts a synchronization action *objects*. The **EB** calculates whether there is a risk of collision between the AV and EVs, and returns the results of the calculation to **IF**. If braking is required, the **IF** will brake by *emerge_brake()* function.

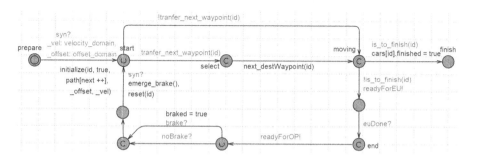

Fig. 8. Automata **IF** in UPPAAL

4.2   Locating the Target and Timing

We have discussed the modelling of the system and traffic scenarios in the previous section, and this section will continue to discuss how to detect SCAEs.

To guarantee that the model is valid, it must verify that ADS is safe under the condition that the obstacle perception system operates correctly. It can be informally described as *the AV will never collide with an environmental vehicle when the obstacle perception system always operates correctly*. Use the query language of UPPAAL to characterize it as:

$$(isOpNormal \land dist(av, ev) \geq D) \rightarrow !collision \tag{1}$$

where $isOpNormal$ is a global boolean variable, representing whether the obstacle perception system works normally; $collision$ is a global boolean variable, representing whether the AV has collided; av and ev are instances of **IF** and **EV** which represent the AV and environmental vehicle respectively; $dist(av, ev)$ function computes the relative distance between the AV and environmental vehicle, and D is the safety braking distance of the AEBS.

To successfully attack ADS, it is necessary to know when the obstacle perception system malfunctions will make the ADS unsafe. However, a single time point alone is insufficient to violate the safety properties for ADS, because the AEBS system's safety braking distance has an error distance of d_0, which gives it chances to make proper amendments in consequent cycles. Therefore, a valid time interval is needed for an adversarial attack on autonomous driving.

To obtain the above time interval, the scenarios are kept unchanged and verify the following properties:

$$!isOpNormal \land dist(av, ev) \leq d_1 \rightarrow collision \tag{2}$$

where d_1 is a parameter needing to be solved by querying the model in UPPAAL. It literally means as: *When the relative distance between the AV and an environmental vehicle is less than d_1, and the obstacle perception system fails, eventually the AV will collide*. The maximum value of d_1 that satisfies this property can be found with UPPAAL. A simple way is to initially set d_1 to 0 and find the largest d_1 in a gradually increasing manner. It means that keeping attacking until the time instant when $dist(av, ev) = d_1$ can guarantee the collision. Calculate manually in which cycle the relative distance between the autonomous vehicle and the environmental vehicle is less than or equal to d_1 by the vehicle's equation of motion and initial positions, and denote the cycle as t_1. The simulation platform can be used to verify whether the calculated d_1 corresponds to t_1.

Obviously, the attack is worthless when the relative distance between the vehicles is large enough. To lower the attack's cost, try to discover the earliest attack time. Another property can be characterised by UPPAAL's query language as follows:

$$!isOpNormal \land dist(av, ev) \geq d_2 \rightarrow !collision \tag{3}$$

where d_2 is a parameter needing to be solved by querying the model in UPPAAL. It literally means as: *When the relative distance between the AV and an environmental vehicle is greater than d_2, even if the obstacle perception system fails, the AV will never collide.* Find the minimum d_2 that satisfies this property. A simple way is to initially set d_2 to a larger value and gradually decrease the value to get the smallest d_2. If the attacking is conducted before the time instant when $dist(av, ev) = d_2$, it has no guarantee that the AV will collide. Denote the time point corresponding to d_2 as t_2. For the object vanishing attack discussed in this paper, $[0, t_2]$ is an invalid time interval.

The optimized valid time interval for safety-critical adversarial attack is $[t_2, t_1]$. A sustained object vanishing attack in this valid time interval will lead to vehicle collision.

5   Experimental Evaluation

To show that the SCAEs detected with the approach proposed in this paper are valid and feasible, we design a number of simulations using the CARLA simulator to show that SCAEs can actually lead AVs to collision accidents. The data of CARLA's scenarios map can be employed as a way-point map for the abstract model introduced in the Sect. 4. Besides, the scenarios of CARLA can generate original images which can be attacked by TOG or U-DOS with target and timing located in Sect. 4.2 to generate SCAEs. This experiment mainly explores the validity of the proposed method, so the time cost of an adversarial attack is ignored. The adversarial attack adopts an offline attack method which replaces the original images with SCAEs instead of an online adversarial attack.

We use CARLA 0.9.11 on a 16-core i7 desktop with 32 GB RAM and a single RTX 3080 GPU with 10 GB memory.

5.1   Experimental Setup

The system described in the Sect. 4.1 is implemented in CARLA. Data set KITTI [6] is used for training the Faster-RCNN [5] which is the obstacle perception to detect surrounding obstacles on the road. To simplify the experiment, we directly obtain the position of the obstacle from CARLA and then deliver it to the AEBS system for processing. In CARLA, the brake variable of the car is kept at 0.2, approximately 2.5 m/s^2 deceleration and the camera installed in AV capture 10 pictures per second.

5.2   Selection of Traffic Map

Two common traffic maps are mainly considered, as shown in Fig. 9, Fig. 10, which are selected from CARLA's *Town03* map.

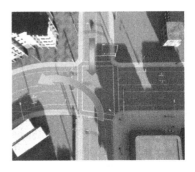

Fig. 9. Scenario 1.   **Fig. 10.** Scenario 2.

5.3 Quantitative Performance

The Safety-Critical Adversarial Examples Rate (SCAE rate) is defined as the ratio of adversarial examples, sampled from a time interval, as safety-critical adversarial examples.

$$SCAE\ rate = \frac{K}{\Sigma}$$

Specifically, the benign examples, which are sampled from CARLA within a time interval, are subjected to Σ adversarial attacks to yield Σ groups of adversarial examples, of which K groups are safety-critical adversarial examples.

5.4 Analysis of the Experiment

Table 1. Traffic scenarios in the experiment

Scenario	Velocity of vehicle	Sample size	Time	Traffic map
1	$v_{av} = 7$, $v_{ev} = 6$	14	69	Fig. 9
2	$v_{av} = 8$, $v_{ev} = 7$	17	57	Fig. 9
3	$v_{av} = 5$, $v_{ev} = 6$	14	50	Fig. 9
4	$v_{av} = 4$, $v_{ev} = 5$	19	68	Fig. 9
5	$v_{av} = 4$, $v_{ev} = 4$	16	91	Fig. 10
6	$v_{av} = 8$, $v_{ev} = 7$	30	24	Fig. 10
7	$v_{av} = 5$, $v_{ev} = 8$	25	56	Fig. 10

Optimized valid time interval is [**Time, Time+Sample Size - 1**].

The Table 1 gives brief information on all traffic scenarios in this experiment where v_{av} is the velocity of AV and v_{ev} is the velocity of NAV, and the optimized valid time interval for the safety-critical adversarial attack is given by **Time** and **Sample Size**. The initial positions of the vehicles are different for all scenarios.

Taking scenario 1 as an example, vehicles run according to the path shown in Fig. 9, and the velocities of AV and EV are 7 and 6 respectively. The valid time interval for the adversarial attack is $[69, 82]$. This paper will first show how to employ UPPAAL to locate the attack target and timing in the experimental scenario, and then compare the adversarial and original scenario in CARLA.

Locating the Target and Timing in UPPAAL. As introduced in Sect. 4.2, d_1 and d_2 are found by running property (2) and property (3). First, let $d_1 = 0$, then verify property (2). If property (2) is satisfied, set $d_1 + 1$ until property (2) is not satisfied. As shown in Fig. 11, a bigger $d_1 = 4$ has been computed, and the corresponding time point is 82 in CARLA. Similarly, shown in Fig. 12, let d_2 be the relative distance between the two vehicles' initial positions or even a bigger value like 50 and then verify the property (3). If the property (3) is satisfied, set $d_2 - 1$ until property (3) is not satisfied. So a smaller $d_2 = 8$ has been computed, and the corresponding time point is 69.

Fig. 11. d_1 solution example.   **Fig. 12.** d_2 solution example.

Comparison of Benign Examples and SCAEs. The benign examples are sampled from CARLA within the valid time interval $[69, 82]$ for the object-vanish attacks. The generated adversarial examples are SCAEs. The first row, as shown in Fig. 13, contains benign examples and their detection results. The second row contains SCAEs and their detection results. As we can see, the benign scenario is safe, but the adversarial scenario ends up colliding with other vehicles.

Correctness of Valid Time Interval. Let k_i denote the length of the optimized valid time interval of the ith scenario, and l_i denote the total time length of the ith scenario. $I_i = \{[j, j + k_i - 1] | 0 \le j \le l_i - k_i\}$ is a set of time intervals for scenario i. On the groups of benign examples sampled from CARLA in the time interval of I_i, we perform object vanishing attacks and simulate the results in CARLA to determine whether the vehicle collided. We tested 7 experimental scenarios based on two traffic scenarios with different vehicle initial positions and velocities. The experimental results are shown in Fig. 14. The red point represents the optimized time interval obtained by our proposed method. The success rate of adversarial attacks in the valid time intervals is above 98%. The mAP rate of the adversarial examples generated by TOG attacking Faster-RCNN is 1.4% [16]. The reason for the failure of the SCAEs is likely to be caused by the

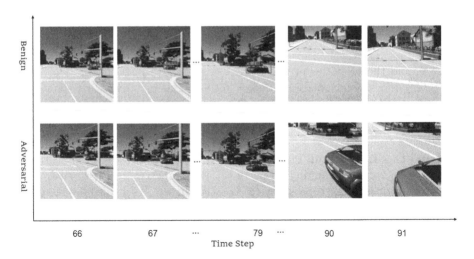

Fig. 13. The optimized valid time interval of scenario 1 is [69, 82].

adversarial attack algorithms. The results reveal that the time interval provided by our proposed method is indeed a valid time interval for a safety-critical adversarial attack, but there are also some valid time intervals around the red point obtained by our proposed method. Because the optimized valid time interval we found is an over-approximation of the minimal valid interval.

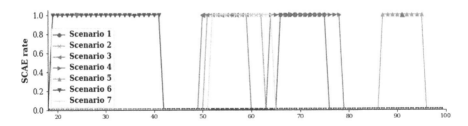

Fig. 14. There are seven scenarios in the figure, and a value on the x-axis represents a time interval starting from this value. For example, 70 on scenario 1 represents a time interval $[70, 70 + k_1 - 1]$.

6   Conclusion

In this paper, we propose a formal definition of SCAEs which can actually lead the ADS to an unsafe state. A novel approach based on a model checking technique is proposed to detect SACEs for a given autonomous driving scenario. Our approach can locate the target and timing for the adversarial attack that can ensure the violation of the safety-critical property. This kind of knowledge will be helpful to improve defending techniques. The experimental results obtained on the CARLA simulation platform reveal that the time interval provided by our method is indeed a valid time interval for safety-critical adversarial attacks, the success rate of adversarial attacks is above 98%. In the future, we intend to design a new adversarial example generation algorithm which embeds the knowledge obtained from the proposed method so that the AEs generated from this algorithm are indeed SCAEs.

References

1. Deng, Y., Zheng, X., Zhang, T., Chen, C., Lou, G., Kim, M.: An analysis of adversarial attacks and defenses on autonomous driving models. In: IEEE International Conference on Pervasive Computing and Communications (PerCom) 2020, pp. 1–10 (2020). https://doi.org/10.1109/PerCom45495.2020.9127389
2. Yuan, X., He, P., Zhu, Q., Li, X.: Adversarial examples: attacks and defenses for deep learning. IEEE Trans. Neural Netw. Learn. Syst. **30**(9), 25–2824 (2019). https://doi.org/10.1109/TNNLS.2018.2886017
3. Uppaal Home Page. http://www.uppaal.org/. Accessed 15 June 2020
4. Behrmann, G., David, A., Larsen, K.G.: A tutorial on UPPAAL. In: Bernardo, M., Corradini, F. (eds.) SFM-RT 2004. LNCS, vol. 3185, pp. 200–236. Springer, Heidelberg (2004). https://doi.org/10.1007/978-3-540-30080-9_7
5. https://github.com/chenyuntc/simple-faster-rcnn-pytorch
6. Geiger, A., Lenz, P., Urtasun, R.: Are we ready for autonomous driving? the kitti vision benchmark suite. In: 2012 IEEE Conference on Computer Vision and Pattern Recognition. IEEE (2012)
7. Chow, K.-H., et al.: Adversarial objectness gradient attacks in real-time object detection systems. In: 2020 Second IEEE International Conference on Trust, Privacy and Security in Intelligent Systems and Applications (TPS-ISA). IEEE, 2020
8. Li, D., Zhang, J., Huang, K.: Universal adversarial perturbations against object detection. Pattern Recogn. **110**, 107584 (2021)
9. Carlini, N., Wagner, D.: Towards evaluating the robustness of neural networks. In Proceedings of S&P, pp. 39–57. IEEE (2017)
10. Moosavi-Dezfooli, S.-M., Fawzi, A., Frossard, P.: Deepfool: a simple and accurate method to fool deep neural networks. In: Proceedings of CVPR, pp. 2574–2582. IEEE (2016)
11. Poursaeed, O., Katsman, I., Gao, B., Belongie, S.J.: Generative adversarial perturbations. In: Proceedings of CVPR, pp. 4422–4431. IEEE (2018)
12. Xie, C., Wang, J., Zhang, Z., Zhou, Y., Xie, L., Yuille, A.: Adversarial examples for semantic segmentation and object detection. In: IEEE International Conference on Computer Vision (ICCV) 2017, pp. 1378–1387 (2017). https://doi.org/10.1109/ICCV.2017.153
13. Wang, D., et al.: Daedalus: breaking nonmaximum suppression in object detection via adversarial examples. IEEE Trans. Cybern. (2020). https://doi.org/10.1109/TCYB.2020.3041481
14. Xiao, Y., Pun, C.-M., Liu, B.: Fooling deep neural detection networks with adaptive object-oriented adversarial perturbation. Pattern Recogn. **115**, 107903 (2021)

15. Zhang, H., Zhou, W., Li, H.: Contextual adversarial attacks for object detection. In: IEEE International Conference on Multimedia and Expo (ICME) 2020, pp. 1–6 (2020). https://doi.org/10.1109/ICME46284.2020.91025
16. Wang, Y., et al.: An adversarial attack on DNN-based black-box object detectors. J. Netw. Comput. Appl. **161**, 102634 (2020)
17. Wang, Y., et al.: Towards a physical-world adversarial patch for blinding object detection models. Inf. Sci. **556**, 459–471 (2021)
18. Shi, Z., et al.: Adversarial attacks on object detectors with limited perturbations. In: ICASSP 2021–2021 IEEE International Conference on Acoustics, Speech and Signal Processing (ICASSP), pp. 1375–1379 (2021) https://doi.org/10.1109/ICASSP39728.2021.9414125
19. Liao, Q., et al.: Transferable adversarial examples for anchor free object detection. In: IEEE International Conference on Multimedia and Expo (ICME) 2021, pp. 1–6 (2021). https://doi.org/10.1109/ICME51207.2021.9428301
20. Chow, K.-H., et al.: Adversarial objectness gradient attacks in real-time object detection systems. In: 2020 Second IEEE International Conference on Trust, Privacy and Security in Intelligent Systems and Applications (TPS-ISA) 2020, pp. 263–272 (2020). https://doi.org/10.1109/TPS-ISA50397.2020.00042

Ground Confluence and Strong Commutation Modulo Alpha-Equivalence in Nominal Rewriting

Kentaro Kikuchi[(✉)]

RIEC, Tohoku University, Sendai, Japan
kentaro.kikuchi@riec.tohoku.ac.jp

Abstract. Nominal rewriting was introduced as an extension of first-order term rewriting by a binding mechanism based on the nominal approach. A distinctive feature of nominal rewriting is that α-equivalence is not implicitly dealt with at the meta-level but explicitly dealt with at the object-level. In this paper, we introduce the notion of strong commutation modulo α-equivalence and give a sufficient condition for it. Using the condition, we present a new criterion for confluence modulo α-equivalence (on ground terms) of possibly non-terminating left-linear nominal rewriting systems.

1 Introduction

In languages with variable binding and variable names, α-equivalence needs to be treated. Usually α-equivalence is implicitly dealt with at the meta-level, but in the literature some authors seriously take it into account at the object-level (e.g. [6,20]). The nominal approach [5,13] is one of such studies, where variables that are possibly bound are called atoms. It deals with α-equivalence explicitly at the object-level, incorporating permutations and freshness constraints as basic ingredients.

Nominal rewriting [3,4] is a framework introduced as an extension of first-order term rewriting by a binding mechanism based on the nominal approach. It has a device to avoid accidental capture of free atoms on the way of rewriting, using the explicit α-equivalence and freshness constraints in rewrite rules.

Confluence is a fundamental property of rewriting systems that guarantees uniqueness of results of computation. Confluence of nominal rewriting systems has been discussed in [1,3,9,16,17]. Their aim is to provide confluence criteria for particular classes of nominal rewriting systems in the same way as discussed in the field of first-order term rewriting.

In the present paper, we study confluence of nominal rewriting systems that are defined by rewrite rules with atom-variables in the style of [10], where rewriting is performed only on ground nominal terms (so confluence properties discussed in this paper correspond to ground confluence etc. in terms of traditional nominal rewriting). In previous work [8], we have proved (ground) confluence

H. Seidl et al. (Eds.): ICTAC 2022, LNCS 13572, pp. 255–271, 2022.
https://doi.org/10.1007/978-3-031-17715-6_17

for this style of nominal rewriting systems whose rewrite rules have no overlaps which are computed using nominal unification with atom-variables [15]. In this paper, we present a sufficient condition for (ground) confluence of the same style of nominal rewriting systems possibly with overlaps of rewrite rules.

To discuss confluence in nominal rewriting, it is necessary to examine whether two terms can rewrite to α-equivalent terms. For doing this, we make use of suitable notions that are defined modulo an equivalence relation in terms of abstract reduction systems [11,12]. Such an approach was suggested in [20] (page 220). Precisely speaking, we present a sufficient condition for (ground) Church-Rosser modulo α-equivalence rather than confluence. The proof method using the sufficient condition can be seen as a generalisation of that for confluence of first-order term rewriting systems using the lemma of Hindley [6] and Rosen [14]. We will explain details of the methods in Sect. 3.

Contributions of the Paper. The contributions of the present paper are summarised as follows:

- We introduce the notion of strong commutation modulo α-equivalence and give a sufficient condition for it in left-linear uniform nominal rewriting systems. This notion has not been treated in [11,12] (in the case of a general equivalence relation $\sim$).
- Using the sufficient condition, we present a new criterion for Church-Rosser modulo α-equivalence (on ground nominal terms) of left-linear uniform nominal rewriting systems that are possibly non-terminating and may have overlaps of rewrite rules.

Organisation of the Paper. The present paper is organised as follows. In Sect. 2, we explain basic notions of nominal rewriting systems with atom-variables. In Sect. 3, we give a sufficient condition for strong commutation modulo α-equivalence, and use it to present a criterion for Church-Rosser modulo α-equivalence. In Sect. 4, we conclude with suggestions for further work.

2   Nominal Rewriting Systems with Atom-Variables

Nominal rewriting [3,4] is a framework that extends first-order term rewriting by a binding mechanism. In this section, we recall basic notions and notations concerning nominal rewriting systems with atom-variables [10]. For differences from the system of [3], see [8]. For simplicity, we treat a subset of the systems in [8,10].

2.1   Preliminaries

We fix a countably infinite set $\mathcal{X}$ of *variables* ranged over by $X, Y, \ldots$, a countably infinite set $\mathcal{A}$ of *atoms* ranged over by $a, b, \ldots$, and a countably infinite set $\mathcal{X}_A$ of *atom-variables* ranged over by $A, B, \ldots$. A *nominal signature* Σ is a set of *function symbols* ranged over by $f, g, \ldots$. Each $f \in \Sigma$ has a unique non-negative integer $arity(f)$. We assume that $\mathcal{X}$, $\mathcal{A}$, $\mathcal{X}_\mathcal{A}$ and Σ are pairwise disjoint. Unless otherwise stated, different meta-variables for objects in $\mathcal{X}$, $\mathcal{A}$, $\mathcal{X}_\mathcal{A}$ or Σ denote different objects.

The domain $dom(\phi)$ of a mapping $\phi : D \to E$ is defined as the set $\{d \in D \mid \phi(d) \neq d\}$ if $D \subseteq E$, and D otherwise. A mapping $\phi : D \to E$ is *finite* if its domain $dom(\phi)$ is a finite set.

Let $\bowtie$ be a binary relation. We write $\bowtie^=$ for the reflexive closure and $\bowtie^*$ for the reflexive transitive closure. If $\bowtie$ is written using $\to$, then the inverse $\bowtie^{-1}$ is written using $\leftarrow$. We use $\circ$ for the composition of two binary relations.

2.2 Ground Nominal Terms

In this subsection, we introduce the set of ground nominal terms, which we call NL_a following [8,10,15].

The set NL_a of *ground nominal terms*, or simply *ground terms*, is generated by the following grammar:

$$t, s ::= a \mid [a]t \mid f\langle t_1, \ldots, t_n \rangle$$

where $n = arity(f)$. Ground terms of the forms in the right-hand side are called, respectively, atoms, abstractions and function applications. We assume that function applications bind more strongly than abstractions. We abbreviate $f\langle \rangle$ as f, and refer to it as a *constant*. An abstraction $[a]t$ is intended to represent t with a bound. The set $FA(t)$ of *free* atoms occurring in t is defined as follows: $FA(a) = \{a\}$; $FA([a]t) = FA(t) \setminus \{a\}$; $FA(f\langle t_1, \ldots, t_n \rangle) = \bigcup_i FA(t_i)$.

Example 1. The nominal signature of the lambda calculus has two function symbols lam with $arity(\text{lam}) = 1$, and app with $arity(\text{app}) = 2$. The ground nominal term $\text{app}\langle \text{lam}\langle [a]\text{lam}\langle [b]\text{app}\langle b, a\rangle\rangle\rangle, b\rangle$ represents the lambda term $(\lambda a.\lambda b.ba)b$ in the usual notation. For this ground term t, we have $FA(t) = \{b\}$. □

A *swapping* is a pair of atoms, written $(a\ b)$. *Permutations* π are bijections on $\mathcal{A}$ such that $dom(\pi)$ is finite. Permutations are represented by lists of swappings applied in the right-to-left order. For example, $((b\ c)(a\ b))(a) = c$, $((b\ c)(a\ b))(b) = a$, $((b\ c)(a\ b))(c) = b$. The permutation action $\pi{\cdot}t$, which operates on terms extending a permutation on atoms, is defined as follows: $\pi{\cdot}a = \pi(a)$; $\pi{\cdot}([a]t) = [\pi{\cdot}a](\pi{\cdot}t)$; $\pi{\cdot}(f\langle t_1, \ldots, t_n \rangle) = f\langle \pi{\cdot}t_1, \ldots, \pi{\cdot}t_n \rangle$.

Positions are finite sequences of positive integers. The empty sequence is denoted by ε. The set $Pos(t)$ of positions in a ground term t is defined as follows: $Pos(a) = \{\varepsilon\}$; $Pos([a]t) = \{1p \mid p \in Pos(t)\} \cup \{\varepsilon\}$; $Pos(f\langle t_1, \ldots, t_n \rangle) = \bigcup_i \{ip \mid p \in Pos(t_i)\} \cup \{\varepsilon\}$. The subterm of t at a position $p \in Pos(t)$ is written as $t|_p$. For positions p and q, we say that p is deeper than q if there exists a position o such that $p = qo$. In that case, o is denoted by $p \setminus q$.

A *context* is a ground term in which a distinguished constant □ occurs. The ground term obtained from a context C by replacing each □ at positions p_i by ground terms t_i is written as $C[t_1, \ldots, t_n]_{p_1,\ldots,p_n}$ or simply $C[t_1, \ldots, t_n]$.

$$\frac{}{\vdash_{NL_a} a\#b} \qquad \frac{\vdash_{NL_a} a\#t_1 \quad \cdots \quad \vdash_{NL_a} a\#t_n}{\vdash_{NL_a} a\#f\langle t_1,\ldots,t_n\rangle}$$

$$\frac{}{\vdash_{NL_a} a\#[a]t} \qquad \frac{\vdash_{NL_a} a\#t}{\vdash_{NL_a} a\#[b]t}$$

Fig. 1. Rules for freshness relations on NL_a

$$\frac{}{\vdash_{NL_a} a \approx_\alpha a} \qquad \frac{\vdash_{NL_a} t_1 \approx_\alpha s_1 \quad \cdots \quad \vdash_{NL_a} t_n \approx_\alpha s_n}{\vdash_{NL_a} f\langle t_1,\ldots,t_n\rangle \approx_\alpha f\langle s_1,\ldots,s_n\rangle}$$

$$\frac{\vdash_{NL_a} t \approx_\alpha s}{\vdash_{NL_a} [a]t \approx_\alpha [a]s} \qquad \frac{\vdash_{NL_a} (a\ b)\cdot t \approx_\alpha s \quad \vdash_{NL_a} b\#t}{\vdash_{NL_a} [a]t \approx_\alpha [b]s}$$

Fig. 2. Rules for α-equivalence on NL_a

A pair $a\#t$ of an atom a and a ground term t is called a *freshness relation*. The rules in Fig. 1 define the validity of freshness relations. Note that the defined $\vdash_{NL_a} a\#t$ coincides with $a \notin FA(t)$.

The rules in Fig. 2 define the relation $\vdash_{NL_a} t \approx_\alpha s$. This is a congruence relation [3] and coincides with usual α-equivalence (i.e. the relation reached by renamings of bound atoms) [5]. The bottom-right rule in the figure is about the case where the ground terms t and s are abstracted by different atoms. In $(a\ b)\cdot t$, the free occurrences of a in t are replaced by b which is fresh in t under the right premise of the rule. We often write $t \approx_\alpha s$ for $\vdash_{NL_a} t \approx_\alpha s$.

The following properties are shown in [3,19].

Proposition 1. *1. $\vdash_{NL_a} a\#t$ if and only if $\vdash_{NL_a} \pi\cdot a\#\pi\cdot t$.*
2. $\vdash_{NL_a} t \approx_\alpha s$ if and only if $\vdash_{NL_a} \pi\cdot t \approx_\alpha \pi\cdot s$.
3. If $\vdash_{NL_a} a\#t$ and $\vdash_{NL_a} t \approx_\alpha s$ then $\vdash_{NL_a} a\#s$.

2.3   Nominal Term Expressions

Next we introduce the set of term expressions, which we call NL_{AX}. Each rewrite rule is defined using them to represent a schema of rules.

The set NL_{AX} of *nominal term expressions*, or simply *term expressions*, is generated by the following grammar:

$$e ::= A \mid X \mid [A]e \mid f\langle e_1,\ldots,e_n\rangle$$

where $n = arity(f)$. We write $Var_{\mathcal{X}}(e)$ and $Var_{\mathcal{X}_A}(e)$ for the sets of variables and atom-variables occurring in a term expression e, respectively. Also, we write $Var_{\mathcal{X},\mathcal{X}_A}(e)$ for $Var_{\mathcal{X}}(e) \cup Var_{\mathcal{X}_A}(e)$. A term expression e is *linear* if each variable $X \in Var_{\mathcal{X}}(e)$ occurs only once in e.

The set $Pos(e)$ of positions in a term expression e is defined similarly to that for a ground term (using atom-variables for atoms) with the additional clause that $Pos(X) = \{\varepsilon\}$. The subexpression of e at a position $p \in Pos(e)$ is written as $e|_p$. A position $p \in Pos(e)$ is called a *variable position* if $e|_p$ is a variable, and a *non-variable position* otherwise.

A *ground substitution* is a finite mapping that assigns ground terms to variables and atoms to atom-variables. We use σ, δ for ground substitutions. We write $\sigma_{\mathcal{X}}$ and $\sigma_{\mathcal{X}_A}$ for ground substitutions obtained from σ by restricting the domain to $dom(\sigma) \cap \mathcal{X}$ and $dom(\sigma) \cap \mathcal{X}_A$, respectively. When $Var_{\mathcal{X},\mathcal{X}_A}(e) \subseteq dom(\sigma)$, the application of σ on e is written as $e\sigma$ and called a *ground instance* of e. The application of σ simply replaces the variables X and atom-variables A occurring in e by $\sigma(X)$ and $\sigma(A)$, respectively, without considering capture of free atoms. Then we have $e\sigma \in NL_a$ for every ground instance $e\sigma$.

A pair $A\#e$ of an atom-variable A and a term expression e is called a *freshness constraint*. A finite set of freshness constraints is called a *freshness context*. For a freshness context ∇, we define $Var_{\mathcal{X},\mathcal{X}_A}(\nabla) = \bigcup_{A\#e \in \nabla}(\{A\} \cup Var_{\mathcal{X},\mathcal{X}_A}(e))$ and $\nabla\sigma = \{A\sigma\#e\sigma \mid A\#e \in \nabla\}$.

2.4   Nominal Rewriting Systems with Atom-Variables

Next we define nominal rewrite rules and nominal rewriting systems with atom-variables.

Definition 1. A *nominal rewrite rule with atom-variables*, or simply *rewrite rule*, is a triple of a freshness context ∇ and term expressions $l, r \in NL_{AX}$ such that $Var_{\mathcal{X},\mathcal{X}_A}(\nabla) \cup Var_{\mathcal{X},\mathcal{X}_A}(r) \subseteq Var_{\mathcal{X},\mathcal{X}_A}(l)$ and l is not a variable. We write $\nabla \vdash l \to r$ for a rewrite rule, and identify rewrite rules modulo renaming of variables and atom-variables. A rewrite rule $\nabla \vdash l \to r$ is *left-linear* if l is linear.

Definition 2 (Nominal rewriting system with atom-variables). A *nominal rewriting system with atom-variables* (NRS_{AX} for short) is a finite set of rewrite rules. An NRS_{AX} is *left-linear* if so are all its rewrite rules.

The following example of an NRS_{AX} corresponds to the system in Example 43 of [3] written in the style of traditional nominal rewriting. Note that the freshness constraint $A\#B$ in the rule (sub$_{\mathsf{lam}}$) below is used to mean that the atom-variables A and B should be instantiated by distinct atoms.

Example 2. We extend the nominal signature in Example 1 by a function symbol sub with $arity(\mathsf{sub}) = 2$. By $\mathsf{sub}\langle[a]t, s\rangle$, we represent an explicit substitution $t\langle a := s\rangle$. Then, an NRS_{AX} to perform β-reduction is defined by the rule (Beta):

$$\vdash \mathsf{app}\langle\mathsf{lam}\langle[A]X\rangle, Y\rangle \to \mathsf{sub}\langle[A]X, Y\rangle \quad \text{(Beta)}$$

together with an NRS_{AX} $\mathcal{R}_{\mathsf{sub}}$ to execute substitution:

$$\vdash \mathsf{sub}\langle[A]\mathsf{app}\langle X, Y\rangle, Z\rangle \to \mathsf{app}\langle\mathsf{sub}\langle[A]X, Z\rangle, \mathsf{sub}\langle[A]Y, Z\rangle\rangle \quad (\mathsf{sub_{app}})$$
$$\vdash \mathsf{sub}\langle[A]A, X\rangle \to X \quad (\mathsf{sub_{var}})$$
$$A\#X \vdash \mathsf{sub}\langle[A]X, Y\rangle \to X \quad (\mathsf{sub_{\epsilon}})$$
$$A\#B, B\#Y \vdash \mathsf{sub}\langle[A]\mathsf{lam}\langle[B]X\rangle, Y\rangle \to \mathsf{lam}\langle[B]\mathsf{sub}\langle[A]X, Y\rangle\rangle \quad (\mathsf{sub_{lam}})$$

In a standard notation, the system $\mathcal{R}_{\mathsf{sub}}$ is represented as follows:

$$
\begin{array}{rll}
\vdash & (XY)\langle A := Z\rangle \to (X\langle A := Z\rangle)(Y\langle A := Z\rangle) & (\mathsf{sub_{app}}) \\
\vdash & A\langle A := X\rangle \to X & (\mathsf{sub_{var}}) \\
A\#X \vdash & X\langle A := Y\rangle \to X & (\mathsf{sub_{\epsilon}}) \\
A\#B, B\#Y \vdash & (\lambda B.X)\langle A := Y\rangle \to \lambda B.(X\langle A := Y\rangle) & (\mathsf{sub_{lam}})
\end{array}
$$

$\square$

In the sequel, $\vdash_{NL_a}$ is extended to mean to hold for all members of the set in the right-hand side.

Definition 3 (Rewrite relation). Let $R = \nabla \vdash l \to r$ be a rewrite rule. For ground terms $s, t \in NL_a$, the *rewrite relation* is defined by

$$
s \to_{\langle R,p,\sigma\rangle} t \;\overset{\text{def}}{\Longleftrightarrow}\; \vdash_{NL_a} \nabla\sigma, \; s = C[s']_p, \; \vdash_{NL_a} s' \approx_\alpha l\sigma, \; t = C[r\sigma]_p
$$

Here the subterm s' of s is called the R-*redex*, or simply *redex* if R is understood. We write $s \overset{p}{\to}_R t$ if there exists σ such that $s \to_{\langle R,p,\sigma\rangle} t$. We write $s \to_R t$ if there exist p and σ such that $s \to_{\langle R,p,\sigma\rangle} t$. For an NRS_{AX} $\mathcal{R}$, we write $s \to_{\mathcal{R}} t$ if there exists $R \in \mathcal{R}$ such that $s \to_R t$.

An example of rewriting can be found in Example 4 of [8].

Lemma 1. *Let* $R = \nabla \vdash l \to r$ *be a rewrite rule, and let* s, t *be ground terms. If* $p \in Pos(s)$ *and* $s \overset{p}{\to}_R t$ *then* $\pi \cdot s \overset{p}{\to}_R \pi \cdot t$ *for every permutation* π.

Proof. This is proved in the same way as Lemma 2 of [8]. $\square$

2.5   Overlaps

The notion of overlap is useful for analysing confluence properties of rewriting systems. In the setting of the present paper, it can be defined using nominal unification with atom-variables [15]. Here we restrict the language of unification problems to NL_{AX}.

Definition 4 (Variable-atom nominal unification problem). Let Γ be a finite set of equations of the form $e_1 \approx e_2$ where e_1 and e_2 are term expressions, and let ∇ be a freshness context. Then the pair (Γ, ∇) is called a *variable-atom nominal unification problem* (*VANUP* for short).

Definition 5 (Solution of a VANUP). A ground substitution σ is a *solution* of a VANUP (Γ, ∇) if $\vdash_{NL_a} e_1\sigma \approx_\alpha e_2\sigma$ for every equation $e_1 \approx e_2 \in \Gamma$ and $\vdash_{NL_a} A\sigma\#e\sigma$ for every freshness constraint $A\#e \in \nabla$. A VANUP (Γ, ∇) is *solvable* if there exists a solution of (Γ, ∇).

Example 3. Consider the nominal signature of the lambda calculus in Example 1, and let P be the VANUP $(\{\mathtt{lam}\langle[A]\mathtt{app}\langle X, A\rangle\rangle \approx \mathtt{lam}\langle[B]Y\rangle\}, \{A\#X\})$. Then, the ground substitution $[A := a, B := b, X := c, Y := \mathtt{app}\langle c, b\rangle]$ is a solution of P. $\square$

Definition 6 (Overlap). Let $R_i = \nabla_i \vdash l_i \rightarrow r_i$ $(i = 1, 2)$ be rewrite rules. We assume without loss of generality that $Var_{\mathcal{X},\mathcal{X}_A}(l_1) \cap Var_{\mathcal{X},\mathcal{X}_A}(l_2) = \emptyset$. If the variable-atom nominal unification problem $(\{l_1 \approx l_2|_p\}, \nabla_1 \cup \nabla_2)$ is solvable for some non-variable position p of l_2, then we say that R_1 *overlaps* on R_2, and the situation is called an *overlap* of R_1 on R_2. If R_1 and R_2 are identical modulo renaming of variables and atom-variables, and $p = \varepsilon$, then the overlap is said to be *self-rooted*. An overlap that is not self-rooted is said to be *proper*.

Example 4. Let R_1 and R_2 be the rules (Eta) $A\#X \vdash \text{lam}\langle[A]\text{app}\langle X, A\rangle\rangle \rightarrow X$ and (Beta) $\vdash \text{app}\langle\text{lam}\langle[B]Y\rangle, Z\rangle \rightarrow \text{sub}\langle[B]Y, Z\rangle$, respectively. Then, R_1 overlaps on R_2, since the VANUP $(\{\text{lam}\langle[A]\text{app}\langle X, A\rangle\rangle \approx \text{app}\langle\text{lam}\langle[B]Y\rangle, Z\rangle|_1(= \text{lam}\langle[B]Y\rangle)\}, \{A\#X\})$ is solvable as seen in Example 3. This overlap is proper. □

Example 5. There exists a self-rooted overlap of the rule (Beta) on its renamed variant, since the VANUP $(\{\text{app}\langle\text{lam}\langle[A]X\rangle, Y\rangle \approx \text{app}\langle\text{lam}\langle[B]Z\rangle, W\rangle\}, \emptyset)$ is solvable by taking the ground substitution $[A := a, B := b, X := a, Y := c, Z := b, W := c]$ as a solution. □

Unlike in first-order term rewriting, self-rooted overlaps need to be analysed in the case of nominal rewriting (cf. [1,16]). We check the cases corresponding to self-rooted overlaps too in the sufficient conditions given in the next section.

2.6 Parallel Reduction

A key notion for proving confluence of left-linear rewriting systems is parallel reduction. Here we define it inductively, using grammatical contexts [8,16].

Definition 7. The *grammatical contexts*, ranged over by G, are the contexts defined by

$$G ::= a \mid [a]\square \mid f\langle\square_1, \ldots, \square_n\rangle$$

where $n = arity(f)$. For each rewrite rule R, the relation $\twoheadrightarrow_R$ is defined inductively by the following rules:

$$\frac{s \xrightarrow{\varepsilon}_R t}{s \twoheadrightarrow_R t} \text{ (B)} \qquad \frac{s_1 \twoheadrightarrow_R t_1 \quad \cdots \quad s_n \twoheadrightarrow_R t_n}{G[s_1, \ldots, s_n] \twoheadrightarrow_R G[t_1, \ldots, t_n]} \text{ (C)}$$

where n (≥ 0) depends on the form of G.

The following properties of parallel reduction hold.

Lemma 2. *1. $s \twoheadrightarrow_R s$.*
2. If $s \twoheadrightarrow_R t$ then $C[s] \twoheadrightarrow_R C[t]$.
3. If $s \rightarrow_{\langle R,p,\sigma\rangle} t$ then $s \twoheadrightarrow_R t$.
4. If $s \twoheadrightarrow_R t$ then $s \rightarrow_R^* t$.

Proof. 1. By induction on the structure of s.
2. By induction on the context C.
3. By 2 and the rule (B).
4. By induction on the derivation of $s \twoheadrightarrow_R t$.   □

3   Confluence Criteria by Strong Commutation

In this section, we present a proof method for confluence of left-linear NRS_{AX}'s using strong commutation modulo α-equivalence. First we review a basic proof method in rewriting systems with first-order rules. Then we introduce notions to discuss confluence in nominal rewriting, and give a criterion for NRS_{AX}'s.

3.1   Proof Method for Confluence by Strong Commutation

In this subsection, we survey the proof method for confluence by strong commutation. For first-order TRS's, the method is known, e.g. in [18]. Here we consider a restricted class of NRS_{AX}'s consisting only of first-order rules. Note however that the rewrite relation is still defined for ground nominal terms in NL_a.

Definition 8. An NRS_{AX} $\mathcal{R}$ is called a TRS_{AX} if for every $\nabla \vdash l \to r \in \mathcal{R}$, $\nabla = \emptyset$, and l and r are term expressions with neither atom-variables nor abstractions.

For a TRS_{AX}, we restrict the rewrite relation to the one with matching by identity instead of modulo α-equivalence (i.e. $s' = l\sigma$ instead of $\vdash_{NL_a} s' \approx_\alpha l\sigma$ in Definition 3).

Definition 9. Let $\mathcal{R}$ be a TRS_{AX}. $\to_\mathcal{R}$ is *confluent* if for all ground terms s and t, $s\ (\leftarrow^*_\mathcal{R} \circ \to^*_\mathcal{R})\ t$ implies $s\ (\to^*_\mathcal{R} \circ \leftarrow^*_\mathcal{R})\ t$.

The basic strategy in the proof method is to show commutation of any combination of two rules of the TRS_{AX}. We recall definitions and lemmas on commutation (cf. [2, pp. 31–33]).

Definition 10. Let R_1 and R_2 be rewrite rules of a TRS_{AX}.

1. $\to_{R_1}$ and $\to_{R_2}$ *commute* iff for all ground terms s_1 and s_2,
   if $s_1\ (\leftarrow^*_{R_1} \circ \to^*_{R_2})\ s_2$ then $s_1\ (\to^*_{R_2} \circ \leftarrow^*_{R_1})\ s_2$.
2. $\to_{R_1}$ *strongly commutes with* $\twoheadrightarrow_{R_2}$ iff for all ground terms s_1 and s_2,
   if $s_1\ (\leftarrow_{R_1} \circ \twoheadrightarrow_{R_2})\ s_2$ then $s_1\ (\twoheadrightarrow_{R_2} \circ \leftarrow^*_{R_1})\ s_2$.

By Hindley's results [6] and the properties shown in Lemma 2, we have the following.

Lemma 3. *If* $\to_{R_1}$ *strongly commutes with* $\twoheadrightarrow_{R_2}$ *then* $\to_{R_1}$ *and* $\to_{R_2}$ *commute.*

Lemma 4. *Let* $\mathcal{R}$ *be a* TRS_{AX}. *If* $\to_{R_i}$ *and* $\to_{R_j}$ *commute for every* $R_i, R_j \in \mathcal{R}$ *then* $\to_\mathcal{R}$ *is confluent.*

By Lemmas 3 and 4, to prove confluence of $\to_\mathcal{R}$, it is sufficient to show that for every combination of two rules $R_i, R_j \in \mathcal{R}$ (including the case $R_i = R_j$), $\to_{R_i}$ strongly commutes with $\twoheadrightarrow_{R_j}$, or $\to_{R_j}$ strongly commutes with $\twoheadrightarrow_{R_i}$.

Next we give conditions for strong commutation of $\to_{R_1}$ with $\twoheadrightarrow_{R_2}$.

Definition 11. Let R_1 and $R_2(= \vdash l_2 \to r_2)$ be rewrite rules of a TRS_{AX}. The conditions $\mathsf{sc}_1(R_1, R_2)$ and $\mathsf{sc}_2(R_1, R_2)$ are defined as follows:

$$\mathsf{sc}_1(R_1, R_2) \overset{\text{def}}{\iff} \text{If } s \overset{\varepsilon}{\to}_{R_1} s_1 \text{ and } s \twoheadrightarrow_{R_2} s_2 \text{ is derived with (C) as the last}$$
applied rule, then there exists t such that $s_1 \twoheadrightarrow_{R_2} t$ and $s_2 \to^*_{R_1} t$.

$$\mathsf{sc}_2(R_1, R_2) \overset{\text{def}}{\iff} \text{If } s \overset{p}{\to}_{R_1} s_1 \text{ and } s \overset{\varepsilon}{\to}_{R_2} s_2 \text{ where } p \text{ is a non-variable position}$$
of l_2, then there exists t such that $s_1 \twoheadrightarrow_{R_2} t$ and $s_2 \to^*_{R_1} t$.

Note that the conditional part of $\mathsf{sc}_2(R_1, R_2)$ arises only when R_1 overlaps on R_2.

The next lemma guarantees that $\mathsf{sc}_1(R_1, R_2)$ and $\mathsf{sc}_2(R_1, R_2)$ are a sufficient condition for strong commutation of $\to_{R_1}$ with $\twoheadrightarrow_{R_2}$. In Subsect. 3.3, we present a version of this lemma generalised to the case of NRS_{AX}.

Lemma 5. *Let R_1 and R_2 be left-linear rewrite rules of a TRS_{AX}. If the conditions $\mathsf{sc}_1(R_1, R_2)$ and $\mathsf{sc}_2(R_1, R_2)$ hold, then $\to_{R_1}$ strongly commutes with $\twoheadrightarrow_{R_2}$:*

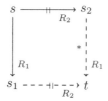

Proof. We prove by induction on the derivation of $s \twoheadrightarrow_{R_2} s_2$ that if $s \to_{R_1} s_1$ and $s \twoheadrightarrow_{R_2} s_2$ then there exists t such that $s_1 \twoheadrightarrow_{R_2} t$ and $s_2 \to^*_{R_1} t$.

– Suppose that the last part of the derivation of $s \twoheadrightarrow_{R_2} s_2$ has the form

$$\frac{u_1 \twoheadrightarrow_{R_2} v_1 \quad \cdots \quad u_n \twoheadrightarrow_{R_2} v_n}{G[u_1, \ldots, u_n] \twoheadrightarrow_{R_2} G[v_1, \ldots, v_n]} \text{ (C)}$$

- First we consider the case where the reduction $s \to_{R_1} s_1$ takes place in $G[u_1, \ldots, u_n]$ with $u_i \to_{R_1} u'_i$ for some $i \in \{1, \ldots, n\}$. Then by the induction hypothesis, there exists v'_i such that $u'_i \twoheadrightarrow_{R_2} v'_i$ and $v_i \to^*_{R_1} v'_i$. Hence by applying the rule (C), we have

$$s_1 = G[u_1, \ldots, u'_i, \ldots, u_n] \twoheadrightarrow_{R_2} G[v_1, \ldots, v'_i, \ldots, v_n]$$

Also, from $v_i \to^*_{R_1} v'_i$ we have

$$s_2 = G[v_1, \ldots, v_i, \ldots, v_n] \to^*_{R_1} G[v_1, \ldots, v'_i, \ldots, v_n]$$

Thus the claim follows by taking $t = G[v_1, \ldots, v'_i, \ldots, v_n]$.
- Next we consider the case where the redex of $s \to_{R_1} s_1$ is not in any u_i of $G[u_1, \ldots, u_n]$. Then we can assume that the R_1-redex is at the root (i.e. $s \overset{\varepsilon}{\to}_{R_1} s_1$). Hence the claim follows from the condition $\mathsf{sc}_1(R_1, R_2)$.

– Suppose that $s \twoheadrightarrow_{R_2} s_2$ is derived by the rule (B)

$$\frac{s \xrightarrow{\varepsilon}_{R_2} s_2}{s \twoheadrightarrow_{R_2} s_2} \text{ (B)}$$

where $R_2 = \vdash l_2 \rightarrow r_2$. Then by the definition of rewrite relation, there exists σ such that $s = l_2\sigma$ and $s_2 = r_2\sigma$.

- First we consider the case where the reduction $s \rightarrow_{R_1} s_1$ takes place in s with $X\sigma \rightarrow_{R_1} X\delta$ for some $X \in Var_{\mathcal{X}}(l_2)$, and $Y\sigma = Y\delta$ for all $Y(\neq X) \in Var_{\mathcal{X}}(l_2)$. Then by the left-linearity of R_2, we have $s_1 = l_2\delta \xrightarrow{\varepsilon}_{R_2} r_2\delta$, and so $s_1 \twoheadrightarrow_{R_2} r_2\delta$ by the rule (B). Also, we have $s_2 = r_2\sigma \rightarrow^*_{R_1} r_2\delta$. Hence the claim follows by taking $t = r_2\delta$.

- Otherwise, the reduction $s \rightarrow_{R_1} s_1$ takes place in s with $s \xrightarrow{p}_{R_1} s_1$ where p is a non-variable position of l_2. Then the claim follows from the condition $\mathsf{sc}_2(R_1, R_2)$.   □

By Lemmas 3, 4 and 5, we have the following theorem.

Theorem 1. *Let $\mathcal{R}$ be a left-linear TRS_{AX}. If for every $R_i, R_j \in \mathcal{R}$, $\mathsf{sc}_1(R_i, R_j)$ and $\mathsf{sc}_2(R_i, R_j)$, or $\mathsf{sc}_1(R_j, R_i)$ and $\mathsf{sc}_2(R_j, R_i)$, then $\rightarrow_{\mathcal{R}}$ is confluent.*

We give an example of application of the theorem.

Example 6. We extend the nominal signature in Example 1 by function symbols (constants) S and K. Consider the TRS_{AX} $\mathcal{R}_{\mathsf{CL}}$ consisting of the rewrite rules of combinatory logic (CL):

$$\begin{array}{ll} \vdash \mathsf{app}\langle\mathsf{app}\langle\mathsf{app}\langle\mathsf{S}, X\rangle, Y\rangle, Z\rangle \rightarrow \mathsf{app}\langle\mathsf{app}\langle X, Z\rangle, \mathsf{app}\langle Y, Z\rangle\rangle & \text{(S)} \\ \vdash \qquad\qquad \mathsf{app}\langle\mathsf{app}\langle\mathsf{K}, X\rangle, Y\rangle \rightarrow X & \text{(K)} \end{array}$$

We check the condition $\mathsf{sc}_1((\mathsf{S}), (\mathsf{K}))$. Suppose $\mathsf{app}\langle\mathsf{app}\langle\mathsf{app}\langle\mathsf{S}, u_1\rangle, u_2\rangle, u_3\rangle \xrightarrow{\varepsilon}_\mathsf{S} \mathsf{app}\langle\mathsf{app}\langle u_1, u_3\rangle, \mathsf{app}\langle u_2, u_3\rangle\rangle$ and $\mathsf{app}\langle\mathsf{app}\langle\mathsf{app}\langle\mathsf{S}, u_1\rangle, u_2\rangle, u_3\rangle \twoheadrightarrow_\mathsf{K} s_2$ with its last applied rule (C). Then the derivation of the latter must have the form

$$\frac{\dfrac{\overline{\mathsf{S} \twoheadrightarrow_\mathsf{K} \mathsf{S}} \text{ (C)} \quad \begin{array}{c}\vdots\ D_1\\ u_1 \twoheadrightarrow_\mathsf{K} v_1\end{array}}{\dfrac{\mathsf{app}\langle\mathsf{S}, u_1\rangle \twoheadrightarrow_\mathsf{K} \mathsf{app}\langle\mathsf{S}, v_1\rangle} \text{ (C)} \quad \begin{array}{c}\vdots\ D_2\\ u_2 \twoheadrightarrow_\mathsf{K} v_2\end{array}}{\dfrac{\mathsf{app}\langle\mathsf{app}\langle\mathsf{S}, u_1\rangle, u_2\rangle \twoheadrightarrow_\mathsf{K} \mathsf{app}\langle\mathsf{app}\langle\mathsf{S}, v_1\rangle, v_2\rangle} \text{ (C)} \quad \begin{array}{c}\vdots\ D_3\\ u_3 \twoheadrightarrow_\mathsf{K} v_3\end{array}}{\mathsf{app}\langle\mathsf{app}\langle\mathsf{app}\langle\mathsf{S}, u_1\rangle, u_2\rangle, u_3\rangle \twoheadrightarrow_\mathsf{K} \mathsf{app}\langle\mathsf{app}\langle\mathsf{app}\langle\mathsf{S}, v_1\rangle, v_2\rangle, v_3\rangle \ (= s_2)} \text{ (C)}$$

Hence we can construct a derivation of $\mathsf{app}\langle\mathsf{app}\langle u_1, u_3\rangle, \mathsf{app}\langle u_2, u_3\rangle\rangle \twoheadrightarrow_\mathsf{K}$ $\mathsf{app}\langle\mathsf{app}\langle v_1, v_3\rangle, \mathsf{app}\langle v_2, v_3\rangle\rangle$ from D_1, D_2 and D_3 by using the rule (C). We also have $s_2 = \mathsf{app}\langle\mathsf{app}\langle\mathsf{app}\langle\mathsf{S}, v_1\rangle, v_2\rangle, v_3\rangle \rightarrow_\mathsf{S} \mathsf{app}\langle\mathsf{app}\langle v_1, v_3\rangle, \mathsf{app}\langle v_2, v_3\rangle\rangle$, and so the condition $\mathsf{sc}_1((\mathsf{S}), (\mathsf{K}))$ is satisfied. On the other hand, it is seen that the condition $\mathsf{sc}_2((\mathsf{S}), (\mathsf{K}))$ is vacuously satisfied.

Next we consider the case where both rules are the rule (S). The condition $\mathsf{sc}_1((\mathsf{S}), (\mathsf{S}))$ can be checked similarly to the above case. For the condition

$\mathsf{sc}_2((\mathsf{S}),(\mathsf{S}))$, we only have to check the case where both redexes are at the root, and in that case the claim clearly holds.

The case where both rules are the rule (K) can be checked similarly. Therefore by Theorem 1, $\rightarrow_{\mathcal{R}_{\mathsf{CL}}} (= \rightarrow_{\mathsf{S}} \cup \rightarrow_{\mathsf{K}})$ is confluent. □

Note that ground terms here include countably many atoms (cf. Subsects. 2.1 and 2.2). By considering atoms as variables (rather than constants), we can see that confluence of a TRS_{AX} discussed above is an extension of confluence of the standard first-order TRS with the same function symbols and rewrite rules (so it is a property stronger than ground confluence of the first-order TRS). The TRS_{AX} $\mathcal{R}_{\mathsf{CL}}$ in Example 6 treats ground terms with atoms, and this is natural when considering an operator like λ^* (Definition 2.14 of [7]).

3.2 Confluence Properties in Nominal Rewriting

To discuss confluence in nominal rewriting, it is necessary to examine whether two terms can rewrite to the same term modulo α-equivalence. For doing this, we make use of suitable notions that are defined modulo an equivalence relation in terms of abstract reduction systems [11,12].

Definition 12. Let $\mathcal{R}$ be an NRS_{AX}.

1. $\rightarrow_{\mathcal{R}}$ is *confluent modulo* $\approx_\alpha$ iff for all ground terms s and t,
   if $s \ (\leftarrow^*_{\mathcal{R}} \circ \rightarrow^*_{\mathcal{R}}) \ t$ then $s \ (\rightarrow^*_{\mathcal{R}} \circ \approx_\alpha \circ \leftarrow^*_{\mathcal{R}}) \ t$.
2. $\rightarrow_{\mathcal{R}}$ is *Church-Rosser modulo* $\approx_\alpha$ iff for all ground terms s and t,
   if $s \ (\leftarrow_{\mathcal{R}} \cup \rightarrow_{\mathcal{R}} \cup \approx_\alpha)^* \ t$ then $s \ (\rightarrow^*_{\mathcal{R}} \circ \approx_\alpha \circ \leftarrow^*_{\mathcal{R}}) \ t$.

In general, Church-Rosser modulo an equivalence relation $\sim$ is a stronger property than confluence modulo $\sim$ [11]. So, in the rest of this section, we aim to give a sufficient condition for Church-Rosser modulo $\approx_\alpha$ of left-linear NRS_{AX}'s.

To this end, we restrict the class of NRS_{AX}'s further by (an adaptation of) the uniformity condition [3]. Intuitively, uniformity means that if an atom a is not free in s and s rewrites to t then a is not free in t.

Definition 13. A rewrite rule $\nabla \vdash l \rightarrow r$ is *uniform* if the following holds: for every atom a and every ground substitution σ such that $Var_{\mathcal{X},\mathcal{X}_A}(l) \subseteq dom(\sigma)$, if $\vdash_{NL_a} \nabla\sigma$ and $\vdash_{NL_a} a\#l\sigma$ then $\vdash_{NL_a} a\#r\sigma$. A rewriting system is *uniform* if so are all its rewrite rules.

For uniform rewrite rules, the following properties hold.

Lemma 6. *Suppose* $s \rightarrow_R t$ *for a uniform rewrite rule R. Then, for every atom a, if* $\vdash_{NL_a} a\#s$ *then* $\vdash_{NL_a} a\#t$.

Proof. This is proved in the same way as Proposition 2 of [8]. □

Definition 14. A relation $\rightarrow$ on ground terms is *strongly compatible with* $\approx_\alpha$ iff for all ground terms s and t, if $s \ (\approx_\alpha \circ \rightarrow) \ t$ then $s \ (\rightarrow^= \circ \approx_\alpha) \ t$.

Lemma 7. *If R is a uniform rewrite rule, then* $\rightarrow_R$ *is strongly compatible with* $\approx_\alpha$ *and* $\twoheadrightarrow_R$ *is strongly compatible with* $\approx_\alpha$.

Proof. This is proved in the same way as Lemmas 3 and 8 of [8]. □

3.3   A Sufficient Condition for Church-Rosser Modulo α-equivalence

Now we present a sufficient condition for Church-Rosser modulo $\approx_\alpha$ extending the sufficient condition for confluence in Theorem 1. First we introduce the notions of commutation and strong commutation modulo $\approx_\alpha$. The latter is not treated in [11,12] (in the case of a general equivalence relation $\sim$).

Definition 15. Let R_1 and R_2 be rewrite rules of an NRS_{AX}.

1. $\to_{R_1}$ and $\to_{R_2}$ *commute modulo* $\approx_\alpha$ iff for all ground terms s_1 and s_2,
   if $s_1 \, (\leftarrow^*_{R_1} \circ \to^*_{R_2}) \, s_2$ then $s_1 \, (\to^*_{R_2} \circ \approx_\alpha \circ \leftarrow^*_{R_1}) \, s_2$.
2. $\to_{R_1}$ *strongly commutes with* $\twoheadrightarrow_{R_2}$ *modulo* $\approx_\alpha$ iff for all ground terms s_1
   and s_2, if $s_1 \, (\leftarrow_{R_1} \circ \twoheadrightarrow_{R_2}) \, s_2$ then $s_1 \, (\twoheadrightarrow_{R_2} \circ \approx_\alpha \circ \leftarrow^*_{R_1}) \, s_2$.

The following lemmas are counterparts of Lemmas 3 and 4 in Subsect. 3.1.

Lemma 8. *If* $\to_{R_1}$ *strongly commutes with* $\twoheadrightarrow_{R_2}$ *modulo* $\approx_\alpha$, *and both* $\to_{R_1}$ *and* $\twoheadrightarrow_{R_2}$ *are strongly compatible with* $\approx_\alpha$, *then* $\to_{R_1}$ *and* $\to_{R_2}$ *commute modulo* $\approx_\alpha$.

Proof. First we consider the claim that for all ground terms s, s_1 and s_2, if $s_1 \leftarrow^*_{R_1} s \twoheadrightarrow_{R_2} s_2$ then there exist ground terms t_1 and t_2 such that $s_1 \twoheadrightarrow_{R_2} t_1 \approx_\alpha t_2 \leftarrow^*_{R_1} s_2$. This is proved by induction on the length of the steps of $s_1 \leftarrow^*_{R_1} s$.
Next we show that for all ground terms s, s_1 and s_2, if $s_1 \leftarrow^*_{R_1} s \twoheadrightarrow_{R_2} s_2$ then there exist ground terms t_1 and t_2 such that $s_1 \twoheadrightarrow^*_{R_2} t_1 \approx_\alpha t_2 \leftarrow^*_{R_1} s_2$. This is proved by induction on the length of the steps of $s \twoheadrightarrow^*_{R_2} s_2$. By Lemma 2, $\twoheadrightarrow^*_{R_2} = \to^*_{R_2}$, so we have that $\to_{R_1}$ and $\to_{R_2}$ commute modulo $\approx_\alpha$. $\quad\square$

Lemma 9. *Let* $\mathcal{R}$ *be a uniform* NRS_{AX}. *If* $\to_{R_i}$ *and* $\to_{R_j}$ *commute modulo* $\approx_\alpha$ *for every* $R_i, R_j \in \mathcal{R}$, *then* $\to_\mathcal{R}$ *is Church-Rosser modulo* $\approx_\alpha$.

Proof. By Lemma 7, $\to_{R_i}$ is strongly compatible with $\approx_\alpha$ for every $R_i \in \mathcal{R}$. Then the claim follows by Corollary 2.6.5 of [12]. $\quad\square$

Next we give conditions for strong commutation of $\to_{R_1}$ with $\twoheadrightarrow_{R_2}$ modulo $\approx_\alpha$.

Definition 16. Let R_1 and R_2 $(= \nabla \vdash l_2 \to r_2)$ be rewrite rules of an NRS_{AX}. The conditions $\mathsf{sc}_1(R_1, R_2, \approx_\alpha)$ and $\mathsf{sc}_2(R_1, R_2, \approx_\alpha)$ are defined as follows:

$\mathsf{sc}_1(R_1, R_2, \approx_\alpha) \xleftrightarrow{\text{def}}$ If $s \xrightarrow{\varepsilon}_{R_1} s_1$ and $s \twoheadrightarrow_{R_2} s_2$ is derived with (C) as the last applied rule, then there exist t_1 and t_2 such that $s_1 \twoheadrightarrow_{R_2} t_1$, $s_2 \to^*_{R_1} t_2$ and $t_1 \approx_\alpha t_2$.

$\mathsf{sc}_2(R_1, R_2, \approx_\alpha) \xleftrightarrow{\text{def}}$ If $s \xrightarrow{p}_{R_1} s_1$ and $s \xrightarrow{\varepsilon}_{R_2} s_2$ where p is a non-variable position of l_2, then there exist t_1 and t_2 such that $s_1 \twoheadrightarrow_{R_2} t_1$, $s_2 \to^*_{R_1} t_2$ and $t_1 \approx_\alpha t_2$.

Note that the conditional part of $\mathsf{sc}_2(R_1, R_2, \approx_\alpha)$ arises only when R_1 overlaps on R_2.

The next lemma guarantees that $\mathsf{sc}_1(R_1, R_2, \approx_\alpha)$ and $\mathsf{sc}_2(R_1, R_2, \approx_\alpha)$ are a sufficient condition for strong commutation of $\to_{R_1}$ with $\twoheadrightarrow_{R_2}$ modulo $\approx_\alpha$.

Lemma 10. *Let R_1 and R_2 be left-linear uniform rewrite rules of an NRS_{AX}. If the conditions $\mathsf{sc}_1(R_1, R_2, \approx_\alpha)$ and $\mathsf{sc}_2(R_1, R_2, \approx_\alpha)$ hold, then $\to_{R_1}$ strongly commutes with $\twoheadrightarrow_{R_2}$ modulo $\approx_\alpha$:*

$$
\begin{array}{ccc}
s & \overset{\twoheadrightarrow}{\underset{R_2}{\longrightarrow}} & s_2 \\
\Big\downarrow{\scriptstyle R_1} & & {\scriptstyle *}\Big\downarrow{\scriptstyle R_1} \\
s_1 & \dashrightarrow\twoheadrightarrow_{R_2} t_1 & \approx_\alpha t_2
\end{array}
$$

Proof. We prove by induction on the derivation of $s \twoheadrightarrow_{R_2} s_2$ that if $s \to_{R_1} s_1$ and $s \twoheadrightarrow_{R_2} s_2$ then there exist t_1 and t_2 such that $s_1 \twoheadrightarrow_{R_2} t_1$, $s_2 \to^*_{R_1} t_2$ and $t_1 \approx_\alpha t_2$.

– Suppose that the last part of the derivation of $s \twoheadrightarrow_{R_2} s_2$ has the form

$$
\frac{u_1 \twoheadrightarrow_{R_2} v_1 \quad \cdots \quad u_n \twoheadrightarrow_{R_2} v_n}{G[u_1, \ldots, u_n] \twoheadrightarrow_{R_2} G[v_1, \ldots, v_n]} \ (\mathsf{C})
$$

• First we consider the case where the reduction $s \to_{R_1} s_1$ takes place in $G[u_1, \ldots, u_n]$ with $u_i \to_{R_1} u'_i$ for some $i \in \{1, \ldots, n\}$. Then by the induction hypothesis, there exist v'_{i1} and v'_{i2} such that $u'_i \twoheadrightarrow_{R_2} v'_{i1}$, $v_i \to^*_{R_1} v'_{i2}$ and $v'_{i1} \approx_\alpha v'_{i2}$. Hence by applying the rule (C), we have

$$
s_1 = G[u_1, \ldots, u'_i, \ldots, u_n] \twoheadrightarrow_{R_2} G[v_1, \ldots, v'_{i1}, \ldots, v_n]
$$

Also, from $v_i \to^*_{R_1} v'_{i2}$ we have

$$
s_2 = G[v_1, \ldots, v_i, \ldots, v_n] \to^*_{R_1} G[v_1, \ldots, v'_{i2}, \ldots, v_n]
$$

Thus the claim follows by taking $t_1 = G[v_1, \ldots, v'_{i1}, \ldots, v_n]$ and $t_2 = G[v_1, \ldots, v'_{i2}, \ldots, v_n]$.

• Next we consider the case where the redex of $s \to_{R_1} s_1$ is not in any u_i of $G[u_1, \ldots, u_n]$. Then we can assume that the R_1-redex is at the root (i.e. $s \overset{\varepsilon}{\to}_{R_1} s_1$). Hence the claim follows from the condition $\mathsf{sc}_1(R_1, R_2, \approx_\alpha)$.

– Suppose that $s \twoheadrightarrow_{R_2} s_2$ is derived by the rule (B)

$$
\frac{s \overset{\varepsilon}{\to}_{R_2} s_2}{s \twoheadrightarrow_{R_2} s_2} \ (\mathsf{B})
$$

where $R_2 = \nabla \vdash l_2 \to r_2$. Then by the definition of rewrite relation, there exists σ such that $\vdash_{NL_a} \nabla\sigma$, $\vdash_{NL_a} s \approx_\alpha l_2\sigma$ and $s_2 = r_2\sigma$.

- First we consider the case where the reduction $s \xrightarrow{p}_{R_1} s_1$ takes place at a position p that is a variable position q of l_2 or deeper. Let $l_2|_q = X$. Then by Lemma 11 below, there exists δ such that $\vdash_{NL_a} s_1 \approx_\alpha l_2\delta$, $X\sigma \rightarrow_{R_1} X\delta$ and $Y\sigma = Y\delta$ for all $Y(\neq X) \in Var_\chi(l_2)$. Since we can see $\vdash_{NL_a} \nabla\delta$ using Lemma 6 (cf. Lemma 7(2) of [8]), we have $s_1 \xrightarrow{\varepsilon}_{R_2} r_2\delta$, and so $s_1 \twoheadrightarrow_{R_2} r_2\delta$ by the rule (B). Also, we have $s_2 = r_2\sigma \rightarrow^*_{R_1} r_2\delta$. Hence the claim follows by taking $t_1 = t_2 = r_2\delta$.
- Otherwise, the reduction $s \rightarrow_{R_1} s_1$ takes place in s with $s \xrightarrow{p}_{R_1} s_1$ where p is a non-variable position of l_2. Then the claim follows from the condition $\mathsf{sc}_2(R_1, R_2, \approx_\alpha)$. $\square$

Lemma 11. *Let R_1 and R_2 $(= \nabla \vdash l_2 \rightarrow r_2)$ be left-linear uniform rewrite rules of an NRS_{AX}. Suppose that σ is a ground substitution with $Var_{\chi, \chi_A}(l_2) \subseteq dom(\sigma)$ and $\vdash_{NL_a} \nabla\sigma$. Suppose also that a reduction $s \xrightarrow{p}_{R_1} s_1$ takes place at a position p that is a variable position q of l_2 or deeper, and $l_2|_q = X$. Then, for every position q' from ε to q, if $\vdash_{NL_a} s|_{q'} \approx_\alpha l_2|_{q'}\sigma$ then there exists δ such that $\vdash_{NL_a} s_1|_{q'} \approx_\alpha l_2|_{q'}\delta$, $X\sigma \rightarrow_{R_1} X\delta$, and $Y\sigma = Y\delta$ for all $Y(\neq X) \in Var_\chi(l_2)$.*

Proof. By induction on the length of $q \setminus q'$.

First we consider the case $q' = q$. Then $l_2|_{q'} = l_2|_q = X$. Suppose $\vdash_{NL_a} s|_{q'} \approx_\alpha l_2|_{q'}\sigma = X\sigma$. Since $s \xrightarrow{p}_{R_1} s_1$ with a deeper position p than q, we have $s|_q \rightarrow_{R_1} s_1|_q$. So by the strong compatibility of $\rightarrow_{R_1}$ (with $\rightarrow_{R_1}$ instead of $\rightarrow_{\overline{R_1}}$) there exists t such that $X\sigma \rightarrow_{R_1} t \approx_\alpha s_1|_q$. Hence we can take δ with $X\delta = t$ and $\vdash_{NL_a} s_1|_q \approx_\alpha X\delta = l_2|_q\delta$.

For the other cases, the proof is by case analysis according to the form of $l_2|_{q'}$. This is shown analogously to the case analysis in the proof of Lemma 10 of [8]. $\square$

By Lemmas 7, 8, 9 and 10, we have the following theorem.

Theorem 2. *Let $\mathcal{R}$ be a left-linear uniform NRS_{AX}. If for every $R_i, R_j \in \mathcal{R}$, $\mathsf{sc}_1(R_i, R_j, \approx_\alpha)$ and $\mathsf{sc}_2(R_i, R_j, \approx_\alpha)$, or $\mathsf{sc}_1(R_j, R_i, \approx_\alpha)$ and $\mathsf{sc}_2(R_j, R_i, \approx_\alpha)$ then $\rightarrow_\mathcal{R}$ is Church-Rosser modulo $\approx_\alpha$.*

In practice, if we know that R_1 does not overlap on R_2 and vice versa, we may use, instead of Lemma 8, Theorem 1 of [8] to show commutation modulo $\approx_\alpha$ of $\rightarrow_{R_1}$ and $\rightarrow_{R_2}$. So, to apply Theorem 2, we can concentrate on R_i and R_j such that there exists an overlap of R_i on R_j or R_j on R_i. Moreover, for $R_i = R_j$, we may skip checking the case $p = \varepsilon$ in $\mathsf{sc}_2(R_i, R_j, \approx_\alpha)$ when R_i is α-stable [16], so that we have only to check rules with proper overlaps when the NRS_{AX} is α-stable.

Definition 17 (α-stability). *A rewrite rule $R = \nabla \vdash l \rightarrow r$ is α-stable if $\vdash_{NL_a} s \approx_\alpha s'$, $s \rightarrow_{\langle R, \varepsilon, \sigma \rangle} t$ and $s' \rightarrow_{\langle R, \varepsilon, \sigma' \rangle} t'$ imply $\vdash_{NL_a} t \approx_\alpha t'$. An NRS_{AX} $\mathcal{R}$ is α-stable if so are all its rewrite rules.*

We demonstrate Theorem 2 on two examples.

Example 7. The NRS_{AX} $\mathcal{R}_{\mathsf{sub}}$ in Example 2 is left-linear, uniform and α-stable. In this NRS_{AX}, there are two pairs of rules that have proper overlaps: $((\mathsf{sub}_{\mathsf{app}}),$ $(\mathsf{sub}_\epsilon))$ and $((\mathsf{sub}_{\mathsf{lam}}),(\mathsf{sub}_\epsilon))$.

For the pair $((\mathsf{sub}_{\mathsf{app}}),(\mathsf{sub}_\epsilon))$, we first check the condition $\mathsf{sc}_1((\mathsf{sub}_{\mathsf{app}}),(\mathsf{sub}_\epsilon),$ $\approx_\alpha)$. Suppose $\mathsf{sub}\langle[a]\mathsf{app}\langle u_1, u_2\rangle, u_3\rangle \xrightarrow{\varepsilon}_{\mathsf{sub}_{\mathsf{app}}} \mathsf{app}\langle\mathsf{sub}\langle[a]u_1, u_3\rangle, \mathsf{sub}\langle[a]u_2, u_3\rangle\rangle$ and $\mathsf{sub}\langle[a]\mathsf{app}\langle u_1, u_2\rangle, u_3\rangle \twoheadrightarrow_{\mathsf{sub}_\epsilon} s_2$ with its last applied rule (C). Then the derivation of the latter must have the form

$$
\cfrac{\cfrac{\cfrac{\vdots\ D_1 \qquad\qquad \vdots\ D_2}{u_1 \twoheadrightarrow_{\mathsf{sub}_\epsilon} v_1 \qquad u_2 \twoheadrightarrow_{\mathsf{sub}_\epsilon} v_2}{\mathsf{app}\langle u_1, u_2\rangle \twoheadrightarrow_{\mathsf{sub}_\epsilon} \mathsf{app}\langle v_1, v_2\rangle}\ (\mathsf{C})}{[a]\mathsf{app}\langle u_1, u_2\rangle \twoheadrightarrow_{\mathsf{sub}_\epsilon} [a]\mathsf{app}\langle v_1, v_2\rangle}\ (\mathsf{C}) \qquad \cfrac{\vdots\ D_3}{u_3 \twoheadrightarrow_{\mathsf{sub}_\epsilon} v_3}}{\mathsf{sub}\langle[a]\mathsf{app}\langle u_1, u_2\rangle, u_3\rangle \twoheadrightarrow_{\mathsf{sub}_\epsilon} \mathsf{sub}\langle[a]\mathsf{app}\langle v_1, v_2\rangle, v_3\rangle\ (= s_2)}\ (\mathsf{C})
$$

Hence we can construct a derivation of $\mathsf{app}\langle\mathsf{sub}\langle[a]u_1, u_3\rangle, \mathsf{sub}\langle[a]u_2, u_3\rangle\rangle \twoheadrightarrow_{\mathsf{sub}_\epsilon}$ $\mathsf{app}\langle\mathsf{sub}\langle[a]v_1, v_3\rangle, \mathsf{sub}\langle[a]v_2, v_3\rangle\rangle$ from D_1, D_2 and D_3 by using the rule (C). We also have $s_2 = \mathsf{sub}\langle[a]\mathsf{app}\langle v_1, v_2\rangle, v_3\rangle \rightarrow_{\mathsf{sub}_{\mathsf{app}}} \mathsf{app}\langle\mathsf{sub}\langle[a]v_1, v_3\rangle, \mathsf{sub}\langle[a]v_2, v_3\rangle\rangle$, and so the condition $\mathsf{sc}_1((\mathsf{sub}_{\mathsf{app}}),(\mathsf{sub}_\epsilon))$ is satisfied.

Next we check the condition $\mathsf{sc}_2((\mathsf{sub}_{\mathsf{app}}),(\mathsf{sub}_\epsilon),\approx_\alpha)$. Suppose $\mathsf{sub}\langle[a]\mathsf{app}\langle u_1, u_2\rangle, u_3\rangle \xrightarrow{\varepsilon}_{\mathsf{sub}_{\mathsf{app}}} \mathsf{app}\langle\mathsf{sub}\langle[a]u_1, u_3\rangle, \mathsf{sub}\langle[a]u_2, u_3\rangle\rangle$ and $\mathsf{sub}\langle[a]\mathsf{app}\langle u_1, u_2\rangle, u_3\rangle$ $\xrightarrow{\varepsilon}_{\mathsf{sub}_\epsilon} \mathsf{app}\langle u_1, u_2\rangle\ (= s_2)$. From the latter, we see $\vdash_{NL_a} a\#u_1$ and $\vdash_{NL_a} a\#u_2$, and so we have $\mathsf{sub}\langle[a]u_1, u_3\rangle \rightarrow_{\mathsf{sub}_\epsilon} u_1$ and $\mathsf{sub}\langle[a]u_2, u_3\rangle \rightarrow_{\mathsf{sub}_\epsilon} u_2$. Hence we can construct a derivation of $\mathsf{app}\langle\mathsf{sub}\langle[a]u_1, u_3\rangle, \mathsf{sub}\langle[a]u_2, u_3\rangle\rangle \twoheadrightarrow_{\mathsf{sub}_\epsilon} \mathsf{app}\langle u_1, u_2\rangle$. Thus $\mathsf{sc}_2((\mathsf{sub}_{\mathsf{app}}),(\mathsf{sub}_\epsilon),\approx_\alpha)$ holds by taking $t_1 = t_2 = \mathsf{app}\langle u_1, u_2\rangle$.

For the other pair of rules with a proper overlap, we can analogously check $\mathsf{sc}_1((\mathsf{sub}_{\mathsf{lam}}),(\mathsf{sub}_\epsilon),\approx_\alpha)$ and $\mathsf{sc}_2((\mathsf{sub}_{\mathsf{lam}}),(\mathsf{sub}_\epsilon),\approx_\alpha)$.

Therefore by Theorem 2, we see that $\rightarrow_{\mathcal{R}_{\mathsf{sub}}}$ is Church-Rosser modulo $\approx_\alpha$. $\square$

Example 8. Consider the NRS_{AX} $\mathcal{R}_{\mathsf{subdup}}$ obtained from $\mathcal{R}_{\mathsf{sub}}$ in Example 2 by adding the following rewrite rule:

$$A\#Y \vdash \mathsf{sub}\langle[A]X, Y\rangle \rightarrow \mathsf{sub}\langle[A]\mathsf{sub}\langle[A]X, Y\rangle, Y\rangle \quad (\mathsf{sub}_{\mathsf{dup}})$$

This NRS_{AX} $\mathcal{R}_{\mathsf{subdup}}$ is left-linear, uniform and α-stable. Also we see that it is non-terminating due to the rule $(\mathsf{sub}_{\mathsf{dup}})$. By applying Theorem 2, we can show that $\rightarrow_{\mathcal{R}_{\mathsf{subdup}}}$ is Church-Rosser modulo $\approx_\alpha$. $\square$

4   Conclusion

We presented a sufficient condition for Church-Rosser modulo α-equivalence (on ground nominal terms) of left-linear uniform NRS_{AX}'s that may have overlaps of rewrite rules and may be non-terminating. This was achieved by introducing the notion of strong commutation modulo α-equivalence and giving a sufficient condition for it.

Currently, we are working on implementation of a tool that verifies sufficient conditions as developed in this paper. To compute overlaps in NRS_{AX}'s and extract useful information, it is necessary to construct an appropriate unification procedure for variable-atom nominal unification problems.

Acknowledgements. I am grateful to the anonymous referees for valuable comments. This work was partly supported by JSPS KAKENHI Grant Numbers JP19K11891 and JP20H04164.

References

1. Ayala-Rincón, M., Fernández, M., Gabbay, M.J., Rocha-Oliveira, A.C.: Checking overlaps of nominal rewriting rules. Electron. Notes Theor. Comput. Sci. **323**, 39–56 (2016)
2. Baader, F., Nipkow, T.: Term Rewriting and All That. Cambridge University Press, Cambridge (1998)
3. Fernández, M., Gabbay, M.J.: Nominal rewriting. Inform. Comput. **205**, 917–965 (2007)
4. Fernández, M., Gabbay, M.J., Mackie, I.: Nominal rewriting systems. In: Proceedings of the 6th PPDP, pp. 108–119. ACM (2004)
5. Gabbay, M.J., Pitts, A.M.: A new approach to abstract syntax with variable binding. Formal Aspects Comput. **13**, 341–363 (2002)
6. Hindley, J.R.: The church-rosser property and a result in combinatory logic. Ph.D. thesis, University of Newcastle-upon-Tyne (1964)
7. Hindley, J.R., Seldin, J.P.: Introduction to Combinators and Lambda-Calculus. Cambridge University Press, Cambridge (1986)
8. Kikuchi, K., Aoto, T.: Confluence and commutation for nominal rewriting systems with atom-variables. In: Fernández, M. (ed.) LOPSTR 2020. LNCS, vol. 12561, pp. 56–73. Springer, Cham (2021). https://doi.org/10.1007/978-3-030-68446-4_3
9. Kikuchi, K., Aoto, T., Toyama, Y.: Parallel closure theorem for left-linear nominal rewriting systems. In: Dixon, C., Finger, M. (eds.) FroCoS 2017. LNCS (LNAI), vol. 10483, pp. 115–131. Springer, Cham (2017). https://doi.org/10.1007/978-3-319-66167-4_7
10. Kutz, Y., Schmidt-Schauß, M.: Rewriting with generalized nominal unification. Math. Struct. Comput. Sci. **30**, 710–735 (2020)
11. Ohlebusch, E.: Church-Rosser theorems for abstract reduction modulo an equivalence relation. In: Nipkow, T. (ed.) RTA 1998. LNCS, vol. 1379, pp. 17–31. Springer, Heidelberg (1998). https://doi.org/10.1007/BFb0052358
12. Ohlebusch, E.: Advanced Topics in Term Rewriting. Springer, New York (2002). https://doi.org/10.1007/978-1-4757-3661-8
13. Pitts, A.M.: Nominal logic, a first order theory of names and binding. Inform. Comput. **186**, 165–193 (2003)
14. Rosen, B.: Tree-manipulating systems and Church-Rosser theorems. J. ACM **20**(1), 160–187 (1973)
15. Schmidt-Schauß, M., Sabel, D., Kutz, Y.D.K.: Nominal unification with atom-variables. J. Symb. Comput. **90**, 42–64 (2019)
16. Suzuki, T., Kikuchi, K., Aoto, T., Toyama, Y.: Confluence of orthogonal nominal rewriting systems revisited. In: Proceedings of the 26th RTA. LIPIcs, vol. 36, pp. 301–317 (2015)

17. Suzuki, T., Kikuchi, K., Aoto, T., Toyama, Y.: Critical pair analysis in nominal rewriting. In: Proceedings of the 7th SCSS. EPiC, vol. 39, pp. 156–168. EasyChair (2016)
18. Toyama, Y.: On the Church-Rosser property of term rewriting systems. Technical Report 17672, NTT ECL (1981). (in Japanese)
19. Urban, C., Pitts, A.M., Gabbay, M.J.: Nominal unification. Theoret. Comput. Sci. **323**, 473–497 (2004)
20. Vestergaard, R., Brotherston, J.: A formalised first-order confluence proof for the λ-calculus using one-sorted variable names. Inform. Comput. **183**, 212–244 (2003)

Local XOR Unification: Definitions, Algorithms and Application to Cryptography

Hai Lin$^{(\boxtimes)}$ and Christopher Lynch$^{(\boxtimes)}$

Clarkson University, Potsdam, NY 13699, USA
{hlin,clynch}@clarkson.edu

Abstract. Unification techniques have been proven to be useful for formal analysis of cryptographic systems. In this paper, we introduce a new unification problem called local XOR unification, motivated by formal analysis of security of modes of operation. The goal in local XOR unification is to find a substitution making two terms equivalent modulo the theory of exclusive-or, but each variable is only allowed to be mapped to a term from a given set of terms. We present two versions of the local XOR unification problem, and give algorithms to solve them, proving soundness, completeness and termination.

Keywords: Unification · Formal analysis of cryptography · Modes of operation

1 Introduction

In logic, unification is an algorithmic process of solving equations between symbolic expressions. The basic form of unification is syntactic unification, where both sides of each equation must be made exactly the same under some substitution. In equational unification, both sides of each equation can be the same under some substitution, modulo some background equational theory.

Equational unification has a number of successful applications in cryptography protocol verification [3,7,8]. This work is motivated by symbolic reasoning of cryptographic modes of operation [13,16]. The idea is that message blocks can be modelled symbolically as terms. In order to break security of modes of operation, an adversary needs to solve some certain unification problem. The unification problem is unification modulo the theory of exclusive-xor, together with some free function symbols. Another feature of the unification problem is that each variable is only allowed to be mapped to a term from a given set of terms. Intuitively, the set of terms associated with a variable (modelling some plaintext block) include everything that an adversary is able to compute when generating that plaintext block. We call this kind of unification problem *local*

The work is supported by NRL under contract N00173-19-1-G012.

H. Seidl et al. (Eds.): ICTAC 2022, LNCS 13572, pp. 272–289, 2022.
https://doi.org/10.1007/978-3-031-17715-6_18

XOR unification. We present two concrete versions of the local XOR unification problem. They are called *f-rooted local unification*, and *⊕-rooted local unification*. They can be used to analyze security of different cryptographic modes of operation. For *f*-rooted local unification, this paper gives a unification algorithm, which can find a subset of all the unifiers, called *minimal unifiers*. For ⊕-rooted local unification, this paper gives a unification algorithm, which can find all the unifiers. We prove the soundness, completeness and termination of both of those algorithms.

Formal methods have been used to analyze various cryptosystems, including cryptographic modes of operation, authenticated encryption schemes, signature schemes, garbled circuits, etc. [1,2,5,9,11,12,15]. In the literature, [15] is the closest to our work. In [15], a mode of operation is modelled as a directed acyclic graph. If a particular graph can be labeled while satisfying some constraints, then the corresponding mode of operation is secure. The method is sound, but incomplete. If a mode of operation is insecure, the method in [15] does not provide an explanation why it is insecure. In contrast, if a mode of operation is insecure, our algorithms produce unifiers, which explain why it is insecure.

The rest of this paper is organized as follows. Section 2 discusses some background that will be used in this paper. In Sect. 3, we introduce two concrete versions of the local XOR unification problem and discuss how they are related to security of modes of operation. In Sect. 4 and Sect. 5, we describe how these unification problems are solved. We conclude in Sect. 6.

2   Preliminaries

Terms can be built up from constants $(0, r_1, r_2, \ldots)$, variables, Boolean values, $\oplus$, $\times$, two unary function symbols f and h. $\times$ has a higher precedence than $\oplus$. We distinguish between two types of variables: *term variables* and *Boolean variables*. A term variable $(x, x_1, x_2, \ldots)$ can be instantiated by a term. A Boolean variable $(b, b_1, b_2, \ldots)$ can only be instantiated by a Boolean value $(0, 1)$. If a term t does not contain any variable, t is a *ground term*. If t does not contain any Boolean variables or Boolean values, we call it a *pure term*. Otherwise, we call it a *mixed term*. To be more precise, we can build up terms in the following way.

$term := constant \mid variable \mid f(term) \mid h(term) \mid term \oplus term \mid bool \times term$
$variable := term\_variable \mid Boolean\_variable$
$bool := Boolean\_variable \mid 0 \mid 1$

In the remainder of this paper, we assume that all terms are simplified to normal form by applying the following rules in R modulo AC(Associativity and Commutativity) of $\times$ and $\oplus$.

$$R = \{t \oplus t \rightarrow 0, t \oplus 0 \rightarrow t, 1 \times t \rightarrow t, 0 \times t \rightarrow 0, t \oplus t \oplus x \rightarrow x\}$$

We use a mixed term to represent a set of pure terms. For example, suppose that $mt = (b_1 \times r) \oplus (b_2 \times f(r))$, then mt represents the set of terms $T =$

$\{0, r, f(r), r \oplus f(r)\}$. The idea is that under all possible Boolean values for b_1 and b_2, mt is one of the pure terms in T after simplification. We will use this idea in Sect. 5.

A term t is an f-*rooted term* if t is of the form $f(t')$. Similarly, a $\times$-*rooted term* is of the form $co \times t$, where co is either a Boolean variable or a Boolean value, and t is a term. We call co the *coefficient* of $co \times t$. An $\oplus$-*rooted term* t is of the form $t_1 \oplus t_2 \oplus \ldots \oplus t_n$, where $t_1, \ldots, t_n$ are called *summands* of t. Let $T = \{t_1, t_2, \ldots, t_n\}$ be a set of terms, we use $\oplus T$ to denote $t_1 \oplus t_2 \oplus \ldots \oplus t_n$.

A *substitution* is a mapping assigning terms to variables. If a substitution σ is of the form $\{x_1 \mapsto t_1, x_2 \mapsto t_2, \ldots, x_n \mapsto t_n\}$, where $n > 0$, we can write it as $\sigma = \{x_1 \mapsto t_1\} \cup \Gamma$, where $\Gamma = \{x_2 \mapsto t_2, \ldots, x_n \mapsto t_n\}$. A *term substitution* maps term variables to terms. A *Boolean substitution* maps Boolean variables to Boolean values. We use $domain(\sigma)$ to denote the domain of a substitution σ. In this paper, we do not consider any substitution σ, where $domain(\sigma)$ contains both term variables and Boolean variables. We can apply a substitution σ to a term t in the straightforward way. If $x \in domain(\sigma)$, then replace each occurrence of x in t by $x\sigma$. Let $T = \{t_1, t_2, \ldots, t_n\}$ be a set of terms, σ be a substitution, then $T\sigma = \{t_1\sigma, t_2\sigma, \ldots, t_n\sigma\}$.

For simplicity, from now on, variables mean term variables, and substitutions mean term substitutions. We use $\sigma_1\sigma_2$ to denote the composition of two substitutions σ_1 and σ_2. We call $\sigma_1\sigma_2$ an *instance* of σ_1. For any term t, $t(\sigma_1\sigma_2) = (t\sigma_1)\sigma_2$. We use $\sigma \circ \tau$ to denote the composition of a substitution $\sigma = \{x_1 \mapsto t_1, x_2 \mapsto t_2, \ldots, x_n \mapsto t_n\}$ and a Boolean substitution τ. $\sigma \circ \tau = \{x_1 \mapsto t_1\tau, x_2 \mapsto t_2\tau, \ldots, x_n \mapsto t_n\tau\}$. So for any pure term t, $t(\sigma \circ \tau) = (t\sigma)\tau$. We use $\tau_1 \uplus \tau_2$ to denote the *consistent union* of two Boolean substitutions τ_1 and τ_2. This operation is undefined if there exists a Boolean variable b s.t. $b \in domain(\tau_1) \cap domain(\tau_2)$ and $b\tau_1 \neq b\tau_2$. Otherwise,

$$b(\tau_1 \uplus \tau_2) = \begin{cases} b\tau_1 & \text{if } x \in domain(\tau_1) \\ b\tau_2 & \text{otherwise} \end{cases}$$

Note that if $domain(\tau_1) \cap domain(\tau_2) = \emptyset$, then $\tau_1 \uplus \tau_2$ is exactly $\tau_1 \cup \tau_2$.

We use $t_1 =_\oplus t_2$ to denote that t_1 and t_2 have the same normal form w.r.t. R. Let eq be an equation of the form $t_1 \overset{?}{=} t_2$, where t_1 and t_2 are pure terms. σ is a unifier of eq if $t_1\sigma =_\oplus t_2\sigma$. Let eqs be a set of equations on pure terms, σ is a unifier of eqs if σ is a unifier of all the equations in eqs. The following definition defines a Complete Set of Unifiers (CSU) of a set of equations. The idea of CSU is that all unifiers can be obtained by instantiation. [14] shows how a finite complete set of unifiers can be computed.

Definition 1. *We use $CSU_\oplus(eqs)$ to denote the complete set of unifiers of eqs. $CSU_\oplus(eqs)$ is a set of substitutions s.t.*

- *If $\sigma \in CSU_\oplus(eqs)$, then σ is a unifier of eqs.*
- *If τ is a unifier of eqs, there exist $\sigma \in CSU_\oplus(eqs)$ s.t. $eqs\ \tau =_\oplus eqs\ \sigma\sigma'$ for some σ'.*

A *position* p is a sequence of positive integers. $len(p)$ denotes the length of the sequence p. λ denotes the empty sequence. Let p_1 and p_2 be two positions, p_1 is a *prefix* of p_2 if p_2 is of the form $p_1.i_1.i_2...i_n$, where i_j is a positive integer $(1 \le j \le n)$. p_1 is an *immediate prefix* of p_2 if p_2 is of the form $p_1.i$, where i is a positive integer. Let t be a term, and p be a position, we use $t|_p$ to denote the subterm of t at position p. For any term t, $t|_\lambda = t$. If g is a function symbol of arity n, then $g(t_1, t_2, \ldots, t_n)|_{i.i_1.i_2.\cdots.i_m} = t_i|_{i_1.i_2.\cdots.i_m}$. We use $t[s]_p$ to denote the term obtained by replacing in t the subterm at position p by term s. For example, $r_1 \oplus f(r_2)|_{2.1} = r_2$, $r_1 \oplus f(r_2)[x_1]_{2.1} = r_1 \oplus f(x_1)$. If t is a term, p is a position in t, σ is a substitution, then $(t|_p)\sigma = (t\sigma)|_p$.

3   Local XOR Unification

The goal of local XOR unification is to find a substitution making two terms equivalent modulo the theory of exclusive-or, but each variable is only allowed to be mapped to a term from a given set of terms. It is related to symbolic security of modes of operation [13,16]. The idea is that message blocks can be modelled symbolically as terms. Variables model plaintext blocks. Non-zero constants model blocks of random bits. "0" models a block of all 0's. f models a block cipher, h models a publicly computable cryptographic hash function.

In [13], a *symbolic history* H refers to messages exchanged between an adversary and an encryptor. At any point in time, the adversary knows all the messages that appear previously in the history. A term t is *computable* by the adversary when generating x if t can be built up from terms that appear earlier than x in H using functions that the adversary can compute (e.g. $\oplus$). A substitution σ is *computable* if for all $x \in domain(\sigma)$, $x\sigma$ is computable when generating x. A mode of operation is *symbolically secure* if, for any symbolic history H, and any computable substitution σ, there is no subset S of ciphertext blocks returned by the encryptor s.t. $\oplus S\sigma =_\oplus 0$. Obviously, if all the ciphertext blocks are either f-rooted or constants, a mode of operation is symbolically secure if, for any symbolic history H, and any computable substitution σ, there are no two ciphertext blocks t_1, t_2 returned by the encryptor s.t. $t_1\sigma =_\oplus t_2\sigma$. A mode of operation is *statically equivalent to random* if for every symbolic history H and every computable ground substitution σ, $H\sigma$ is statically equivalent to a frame H' in which each ciphertext block returned by the encryptor is replaced by a fresh constant (modelling a randomly generated block). In [13], it is shown that a mode is symbolically secure if and only if it is statically equivalent to random.

Intuitively, the adversary can use ciphertext blocks it has received previously from the encryptor to construct new plaintext blocks. Static equivalence to random may be thought of as the symbolic analog of IND$-CPA security [4]. In [13], the authors show that, in general, it is undecidable to check symbolic security of modes of operation. A sound and incomplete algorithm is given in [13]. Given a mode of operation, the algorithm somehow considers all possible symbolic histories of arbitrary length at the same time, and has two possible outputs: "secure" or "unknown". If the output is "secure", it means that the mode of operation is symbolically secure. If the output is "unknown", it means that the algorithm could not tell if the mode of operation is symbolically secure or insecure.

The work in this paper provides an alternative way of checking symbolic security. It keeps enumerating concrete symbolic histories, up to a fixed length, which can be set as a parameter. For each symbolic history, it checks if the XOR of some ciphertext blocks is 0 (under some constraint), by solving the local XOR unification problem. If so, the mode of operation is insecure, and the unifiers explain why it is insecure. Otherwise, we do not know if it is secure or insecure. Here are two examples of symbolic histories.

Example 1. *The following is the symbolic history of Cipher Block Chaining for 3 ciphertext blocks:*

$$H = [r, x_1, f(r \oplus x_1), x_2, f(f(r \oplus x_1) \oplus x_2)]$$

where x_1, x_2, x_3 model plaintext blocks, $r, f(r \oplus x_1), f(f(r \oplus x_1) \oplus x_2)$ model ciphertext blocks.

Note that all terms modelling ciphertext blocks are either constants or f-rooted terms. To check if Cipher Block Chaining is symbolically secure, we solve an f-rooted local unification problem, which will be introduced in Sect. 3.1.

Example 2. *The following is the symbolic history of Output Feedback Mode for 3 ciphertext blocks:*

$$H = [r, x_1, f(r) \oplus x_1, x_2, f(f(r)) \oplus x_2]$$

where x_1, x_2, x_3 model plaintext blocks, $r, f(r) \oplus x_1, f(f(r)) \oplus x_2$ model ciphertext blocks.

Note that all terms modelling ciphertext blocks are either constants or $\oplus$-rooted terms. To check if Output Feedback Mode is symbolically secure, we solve an $\oplus$-rooted local unification problem, which will be introduced in Sect. 3.2.

3.1 f-rooted Local Unification

In this section, we define f-rooted local unification. It can be used to check symbolic security of modes of operation, where ciphertext blocks are constants or f-rooted terms (e.g. Cipher Block Chaining, Propagating Cipher Block Chaining, Accumulated Block Cipher [10]).

Definition 2. *Let $\mathcal{M}$ be a mapping from variables to sets of pure terms. $\mathcal{M}$ is an f-mapping if*

- *For each variable $x \in domain(\mathcal{M})$, $0 \in \mathcal{M}(x)$.*
- *For each variable $x \in domain(\mathcal{M})$, if $t \in \mathcal{M}(x)$, then t is either a constant or an f-rooted term.*

To check symbolic security, let $\mathcal{M}$ map each variable x_i to 0 and all the terms that appear earlier than x_i in the symbolic history. Intuitively, $t \in \mathcal{M}(x_i)$ means that t is immediately available to the adversary. In Example 1, $\mathcal{M}(x_1) = \{0, r\}$, $\mathcal{M}(x_2) = \{0, r, f(r \oplus x_1)\}$.

Definition 3. *Let $\mathscr{M}$ be an f-mapping.*

- *If $t \in \mathscr{M}(x)$, then $t \prec_{\mathscr{M}_f} x$.*
- *If $t \prec_{\mathscr{M}_f} x$, then $h(t) \prec_{\mathscr{M}_f} x$.*
- *If $t_1 \prec_{\mathscr{M}_f} x$, $t_2 \prec_{\mathscr{M}_f} x$, ..., $t_n \prec_{\mathscr{M}_f} x$, then $t_1 \oplus t_2 \oplus \ldots \oplus t_n \prec_{\mathscr{M}_f} x$.*

$t \not\prec_{\mathscr{M}_f} x$ *if $t \prec_{\mathscr{M}_f} x$ does not hold.*

σ *is an admissible $\mathscr{M}_f$-substitution if, for each variable $x \in domain(\sigma)$, $x\sigma =_\oplus t\sigma$, for some $t \prec_{\mathscr{M}_f} x$.*

Intuitively, $t \prec_{\mathscr{M}_f} x$ means that the adversary can compute t when generating x, using terms in $\mathscr{M}(x)$ and some functions that the adversary can compute (e.g. $\oplus$ and h).

Definition 4. *Let $\mathscr{M}$ be an f-mapping, t_1, t_2 be two f-rooted pure terms. t_1 and t_2 are $\mathscr{M}_f$-unifiable if there exists some substitution σ such that*

- *σ is an admissible $\mathscr{M}_f$-substitution.*
- *$t_1\sigma =_\oplus t_2\sigma$.*

σ *is called a $\mathscr{M}_f$-unifier of t_1 and t_2. The problem of checking if t_1 and t_2 are $\mathscr{M}_f$-unifiable is called f-rooted local unification.*

In Example 1, $f(f(r \oplus x_1) \oplus x_2)$ and $f(r \oplus x_1)$ are $\mathscr{M}_f$-unifiable under the substitution $\{x_1 \mapsto r, x_2 \mapsto f(0)\}$. Thus, Cipher Block Chaining is not symbolically secure.

3.2   ⊕-rooted Local Unification

In this section, we define ⊕-rooted local unification. It can be used to check symbolic security of modes of operation, where ciphertext blocks are constants or ⊕-rooted terms (e.g. Cipher Feedback Mode, Output Feedback Mode). For technical reasons, we do not allow h (cryptographic hash functions) to be involved in ⊕-rooted local unification.

Definition 5. *Let $\mathscr{M}$ be a mapping from variables to sets of pure terms. $\mathscr{M}$ is an ⊕-mapping if*

- *For each variable $x_i \in domain(\mathscr{M})$, $0 \in \mathscr{M}(x_i)$.*
- *For each variable $x_i \in domain(\mathscr{M})$, if $t \in \mathscr{M}(x_i)$, then h does not occur in t.*

To check symbolic security, let $\mathscr{M}$ map each variable x to 0 and all the terms that appear earlier than x in the symbolic history. Intuitively, $t \in \mathscr{M}(x)$ means that t is immediately available to the adversary. In Example 2, $\mathscr{M}(x_1) = \{0, r\}$, $\mathscr{M}(x_2) = \{0, r, f(r) \oplus x_1\}$.

Definition 6. *Let $\mathscr{M}$ be an ⊕-mapping.*

- *If $t \in \mathscr{M}(x)$, then $t \prec_{\mathscr{M}_\oplus} x$.*
- *If $t_1 \prec_{\mathscr{M}_\oplus} x$, $t_2 \prec_{\mathscr{M}_\oplus} x$, ..., $t_n \prec_{\mathscr{M}_\oplus} x$, then $t_1 \oplus t_2 \oplus \ldots \oplus t_n \prec_{\mathscr{M}_\oplus} x$.*

$t \not\prec_{\mathcal{M}_\oplus} x$ if $t \prec_{\mathcal{M}_\oplus} x$ does not hold.

σ is an admissible $\mathcal{M}_\oplus$-substitution if, for each variable x in the domain of σ, $x\sigma =_\oplus t\sigma$, for some $t \prec_{\mathcal{M}_\oplus} x$.

Intuitively, $t \prec_{\mathcal{M}_\oplus} x$ means that the adversary can compute t when generating x, by taking the XOR of terms in $\mathcal{M}(x)$.

Definition 7. *Let $\mathcal{M}$ be an $\oplus$-mapping. $T = \{t_1, t_2, \ldots, t_n\}$, where h does not occur in T. A subset T' of T is $\mathcal{M}_\oplus$-unifiable with 0 if there exists some substitution σ such that*

- *σ is an admissible $\mathcal{M}_\oplus$-substitution.*
- *$\oplus(T'\sigma) =_\oplus 0$.*

σ is called a $\mathcal{M}_\oplus$-unifier of T'. The problem of checking if some subset T' of T is $\mathcal{M}_\oplus$-unifiable with 0 is called $\oplus$-rooted local unification.

In Example 2, no subset of $\{r, f(r) \oplus x_1, f(f(r)) \oplus x_2\}$ is $\mathcal{M}_\oplus$-unifiable with 0. This means that there is no attack for Output Feedback Mode, up to 3 ciphertext blocks.

4 Solving f-rooted Local Unification

4.1 Overview

In this section, we present an algorithm for solving f-rooted local unification. Given an f-mapping $\mathcal{M}$ and two pure f-rooted terms t_1 and t_2, the goal is to check if t_1 and t_2 are $\mathcal{M}_f$-unifiable. By Definitions 4 and 1, any $\mathcal{M}_f$-unifier of t_1 and t_2 must be an instance of some $\tau \in CSU_\oplus(t_1 \stackrel{?}{=} t_2)$. Therefore, we nondeterministically start from a substitution $\tau \in CSU_\oplus(t_1 \stackrel{?}{=} t_2)$, and keep applying the *Prev* rule and the *Cancel* rule, which will be defined later in this section. Eventually either no rule applies, or we get a $\mathcal{M}_f$-unifier of t_1 and t_2. We use Example 3 to motivate the *Prev* rule, and use Example 4 to motivate the *Cancel* rule. In this section, we only consider pure terms.

Example 3. *Suppose that we have the following mapping $\mathcal{M}$. We want to check if $f(x_1)$ and $f(h(x_2))$ are $\mathcal{M}_f$-unifiable.*
$\mathcal{M}(x_1) = \{0, r_1\}$
$\mathcal{M}(x_2) = \{0, r_1, r_2\}$

$CSU_\oplus(f(x_1) \stackrel{?}{=} f(h(x_2))) = \{\tau\}$, where $\tau = \{x_1 \mapsto h(x_2)\}$. τ is not a $\mathcal{M}_f$-unifier of $f(x_1)$ and $f(h(x_2))$, since $h(x_2) \not\prec_{\mathcal{M}_f} x_1$. By Definitions 4 and 1, any $\mathcal{M}_f$-unifier of $f(x_1)$ and $f(h(x_2))$ must be an instance of τ. So we need to instantiate τ using some substitution σ. We have the following two possible ways to find σ.

1. Let σ be the unifier of $h(x_2)$ and some t s.t. $t \prec_{\mathcal{M}_f} x_1$. But there are infinitely many such terms t, for instance $h(0), h(r_1), h(h(0)), h(h(r_1)), \ldots$.

2. Let σ be the unifier of x_2 and some t s.t. $t \in \mathcal{M}(x_1)$. By Definition 3, if $t \in \mathcal{M}(x_1)$, then $h(t) \prec_{\mathcal{M}_f} x_1$. This is better since $\mathcal{M}(x_1)$ is a finite set.

We take the second approach. σ can be either $\{x_2 \mapsto 0\}$ or $\{x_2 \mapsto r_1\}$. So we find two $\mathcal{M}_f$-unifiers of $f(x_1)$ and $f(h(x_2))$: $\tau_1 = \{x_1 \mapsto h(0), x_2 \mapsto 0\}$ and $\tau_2 = \{x_1 \mapsto h(r_1), x_2 \mapsto r_1\}$. Note that there are other $\mathcal{M}_f$-unifiers (e.g. $\tau_3 = \{x_1 \mapsto h(h(0)), x_2 \mapsto h(0)\}, \ldots$) that we cannot find. This is good enough for our application, since we just need one $\mathcal{M}_f$-unifier to conclude that a mode of operation is not symbolically secure. We call τ_1 and τ_2 minimal $\mathcal{M}_f$-unifiers, which will be defined later. Our algorithm can find all the minimal $\mathcal{M}_f$-unifiers.

Here is the idea for the *Prev* rule, which will be introduced later in this section. Suppose that we want to check if t_1 and t_2 are $\mathcal{M}_f$-unifiable, and suppose that τ is a unifier of t_1 and t_2, but not a $\mathcal{M}_f$-unifier. This means that τ is not an admissible $\mathcal{M}_f$-substitution. Therefore, there exists a variable x s.t. $x\tau \not\prec_{\mathcal{M}_f} x$. Suppose that $x\tau = h(t)$ for some t. It must be the case that $t \not\prec_{\mathcal{M}_f} x$, since the adversary knows how to compute h. Similarly, suppose that $x\tau = t' \oplus t''$, for some t' and t''. It must be the case that $t' \not\prec_{\mathcal{M}_f} x$ or $t'' \not\prec_{\mathcal{M}_f} x$, since the adversary knows how to compute $\oplus$. To "fix" τ so that τ is an admissible $\mathcal{M}_f$-substitution, we need to go below h and $\oplus$, until we hit a constant, an f-rooted term or a variable, to find the "root cause" why τ is not an admissible $\mathcal{M}_f$-substitution. We will define *innermost open position* to capture this idea. Intuitively, an innermost open position corresponds to a subterm, which is either a constant, an f-rooted term or a variable and is below h or $\oplus$. If an innermost open position is "bad" in the sense that it corresponds to a term t s.t. $t \not\prec_{\mathcal{M}_f} x$, then we can apply the *Prev* rule to unify it with some term in $\mathcal{M}(x)$.

Example 4. *Suppose that we have the following mapping $\mathcal{M}$. We want to check if $f(x_1)$ and $f(r_1 \oplus f(r_2) \oplus f(x_2))$ are $\mathcal{M}_f$-unifiable.*
$$\mathcal{M}(x_1) = \{0, r_1\}$$
$$\mathcal{M}(x_2) = \{0, r_1, r_2\}$$

$CSU_\oplus(f(x_1) \overset{?}{=} f(r_1 \oplus f(r_2) \oplus f(x_2))) = \{\tau\}$, where $\tau = \{x_1 \mapsto r_1 \oplus f(r_2) \oplus f(x_2)\}$. τ is not a $\mathcal{M}_f$-unifier of $f(x_1)$ and $f(r_1 \oplus f(r_2) \oplus f(x_2))$, since $f(r_2) \not\prec_{\mathcal{M}_f} x_1$ and $f(x_2) \not\prec_{\mathcal{M}_f} x_1$. In this case, we can use the *Cancel* rule, which will be introduced later in this section. We can instantiate τ by $\sigma = \{x_2 \mapsto r_2\}$, which is the unifier of $f(r_2)$ and $f(x_2)$. Then $\tau\sigma = \{x_1 \mapsto r_1, x_2 \mapsto r_2\}$ is a $\mathcal{M}_f$-unifier of $f(x_1)$ and $f(r_1 \oplus f(r_2) \oplus f(x_2))$. In general, we can use the *Cancel* rule to get rid of a "bad" subterm t_1 by unifying t_1 with some t_2, if t_1 and t_2 are both summands of the same $\oplus$-rooted term.

4.2 Algorithm for Solving f-rooted Local Unification

First we introduce the following notions of *open position* and *innermost open position*.

Definition 8. *An open position is of the form (t, p) where t is a term, p is a position, and for all prefix p' of p, $t|_{p'}$ is not an f-rooted term. (t, p) is an* *innermost open position if (t, p) is an open position, and $t|_p$ is a constant, a variable or an f-rooted term.*

An innermost open position (t, p) is extended from an open position (t, p') if p' is a prefix of p.

Example 5. Let $t = f(r_1) \oplus h(r_2)$.

(1) $(t, 1)$ is an innermost open position.
(2) $(t, 1.1)$ is not an open position, since $t|_1$ is an f-rooted term.
(3) $(t, 2)$ is an open position.
(4) $(t, 2.1)$ is an innermost open position.
(5) $(t, 2.1)$ is extended from $(t, 2)$.

Definition 9. Let $\mathcal{M}$ be an f-mapping, τ be a substitution. $(x\tau, p)$ is a bad open position in τ if for all $t' \prec_{\mathcal{M}_f} x$, $x\tau|_p \neq_\oplus t'\tau$.

$(x\tau, p)$ is a bad innermost open position in τ if $(x\tau, p)$ is both an innermost open position and a bad open position in τ.

The rules in Fig. 1 "fix" bad open positions by instantiating substitutions. The function f-ROOTED-UNIFY$(\mathcal{M}, t_1, t_2)$ in Algorithm 1 checks if two terms t_1 and t_2 are $\mathcal{M}_f$-unifiable.

Algorithm 1. Checking if t_1 and t_2 are $\mathcal{M}_f$-unifiable

---

1: **function** f-ROOTED-UNIFY$(\mathcal{M}, t_1, t_2)$
    // (1) $\mathcal{M}$ is an f-mapping. (2) t_1 and t_2 are two f-rooted terms.
2:    Nondeterministically choose a unifier τ from $CSU_\oplus(t_1 \overset{?}{=} t_2)$.
3:    $result \leftarrow FIX(\tau)$
4:    **if** $result = None$ **then**
5:        **return** $false$ //t_1 and t_2 are not $\mathcal{M}_f$-unifiable.
6:    **else**
7:        **return** $result$ //$result$ is a $\mathcal{M}_f$-unifier of t_1 and t_2.
8:    **end if**
9: **end function**
10:
11: **function** FIX(τ)
12:    **while** some rule is applicable to τ **do**
13:        $\tau \leftarrow Prev(\tau, \sigma)$ or $Cancel(\tau, \sigma)$.   //Nodeterministically apply a rule.
14:    **end while**
15:    **if** $\mathcal{M}_f$-ADMISSIBLE$(\mathcal{M}, \tau) = true$ **then**
16:        **return** τ.
17:    **else**
18:        **return** $None$.
19:    **end if**
20: **end function**

---

5 Solving $\oplus$-rooted Local Unification

5.1 Overview

In this section, we give an algorithm for solving $\oplus$-rooted local unification, which we introduced in Sect. 3.2. Given some $\oplus$-mapping $\mathcal{M}$ and a set of pure terms $\mathscr{C} = \{t_1, t_2, \ldots, t_n\}$, the goal is to check if any subset $\mathscr{C}'$ of $\mathscr{C}$ is $\mathcal{M}_\oplus$-*unifiable* with 0. We will use the following Example 6 as a running example:

$$\frac{\{x \mapsto t\} \cup \tau}{(\{x \mapsto t\} \cup \tau)\sigma} \; Prev$$

where (1) $x \in domain(\mathcal{M})$. (2) $\sigma \in CSU_\oplus(t|_p \overset{?}{=} t'\tau)$, where $t' \in \mathcal{M}(x)$, and (t,p) is a bad innermost open position in $\{x \mapsto t\} \cup \tau$.

$$\frac{\{x \mapsto t\} \cup \tau}{(\{x \mapsto t\} \cup \tau)\sigma} \; Cancel$$

where (1) $x \in domain(\mathcal{M})$. (2) $\sigma \in CSU_\oplus(t|_{p_1} \oplus t|_{p_2} \oplus \ldots \oplus t|_{p_n} \overset{?}{=} 0)$, where $\forall i \in \{1,2,\ldots,n\}$, (t,p_i) are open positions that share a common immediate prefix p, and $t|_p$ is an $\oplus$-rooted term. (3) $\exists i \in \{1,2,\ldots,n\}$ s.t. (t,p_i) is a bad open position in $\{x \mapsto t\} \cup \tau$.

Fig. 1. $\mathcal{R}_{fix}$ Note that we need condition (1) in both inference rules in $\mathcal{R}_{fix}$, since procedures for solving unification modulo exclusive-xor may generate new variables in general. We do not apply the $Prev$ rule or $Cancel$ rule on new variables.

Example 6. *Check if any subset $\mathscr{C}'$ of $\mathscr{C}$ is $\mathcal{M}_\oplus$-unifiable with 0, where:*
$\mathcal{M}(x_1) = \{0, r\}$.
$\mathcal{M}(x_2) = \{0, r, f(r \oplus x_1) \oplus x_1\}$.
$\mathscr{C} = \{r, f(r \oplus x_1) \oplus x_1, f(f(r \oplus x_1) \oplus x_2)\}$.

$\mathscr{C}$ is $\mathcal{M}_\oplus$-unifiable with 0, under $\{x_1 \mapsto r, x_2 \mapsto f(0)\}$. The key idea to solve this local unification problem is to represent the set of all possible $\mathcal{M}_\oplus$-substitutions compactly by introducing Boolean variables. The instantiations of those Boolean variables lead to concrete $\mathcal{M}_\oplus$-substitutions. To be more concrete:

1. In Example 6, all possible $\mathcal{M}_\oplus$-substitutions are represented compactly using the following term substitution:
   $\gamma^{\mathcal{M}} = \{x_1 \mapsto b_1 \times r, x_2 \mapsto b_2 \times r \oplus b_3 \times (f(r \oplus x_1) \oplus x_1)\}$, where b_1, b_2, b_3 are Boolean variables.
   $\gamma^{\mathcal{M}}$ can be composed with a Boolean substitution τ, where $domain(\tau) = \{b_1, b_2, b_3\}$. $\mathscr{C}'\sigma = 0$ if and only if $\mathscr{C}'\gamma^{\mathcal{M}}\tau = 0$. Therefore, our new goal is to find $\mathscr{C}'$ and τ s.t. $\mathscr{C}'\gamma^{\mathcal{M}}\tau = 0$. More details of this step is given in Sect. 5.2.
2. Conceptually, we can consider $\mathscr{C}\gamma^{\mathcal{M}}$ as the following matrix, where each row is a mixed term in $\mathscr{C}\gamma^{\mathcal{M}}$ and each column is a summand of a mixed term in $\mathscr{C}\gamma^{\mathcal{M}}$. The element at row i column j is 1 if column j is a summand of row i, and is 0 otherwise.

	$f(r\oplus x_1)\gamma^{\mathcal{M}}$	$x_1\gamma^{\mathcal{M}}$	$f(f(r\oplus x_1)\oplus x_2)\gamma^{\mathcal{M}}$	$r\gamma^{\mathcal{M}}$
$r\gamma^{\mathcal{M}}$	0	0	0	1
$(f(r\oplus x_1)\oplus x_1)\gamma^{\mathcal{M}}$	1	1	0	0
$f(f(r\oplus x_1)\oplus x_2)\gamma^{\mathcal{M}}$	0	0	1	0

Two mixed terms can possibly be unifiable under some Boolean substitution. This means that two columns of the above matrix may collapse into one under some Boolean substitution. For example, $\tau = \{b_1 \mapsto 1, b_2 \mapsto 1, b_3 \mapsto 1\}$ makes the 1st and the 3rd column both be $f(0)$, the 2nd and the 4th column both be r.

We can then get the following matrix. In Sect. 5.3.1, we present some inference rules for unifying two mixed terms.

$$
\begin{array}{c c}
 & \begin{array}{c c} f(0) & r \end{array} \\
\begin{array}{c}
r \\
f(0) \oplus r \\
f(0)
\end{array}
&
\begin{bmatrix}
0 & 1 \\
1 & 1 \\
1 & 0
\end{bmatrix}
\end{array}
$$

We can now combine (by taking the XOR of) all rows and get a row of all 0's. This means that we can take the XOR of all three terms and get 0. In Sect. 5.3.2, we present some inference rules for combining different rows and merging different columns of the matrices. To cut down the search space, we sort the columns of the matrices somehow and put restrictions on how rows should be combined. Similar to Gaussian Elimination, we combine two rows only if their leading rows are both non-zero. So in this example, we first combine the 2nd and the 3rd row, and then combine the result with the 1st row.

The matrix representation discussed above is for intuition only. Our algorithm deals with mixed terms, rather than matrices. In this section, variables mean term variables, substitutions mean term substitutions. We use $t, t_1, t_2, \ldots$ to denote pure terms, and use $mt, mt_1, mt_2, \ldots$ to denote mixed terms. $\sigma, \sigma_1, \sigma_2, \ldots$ denote term substitutions, $\tau, \tau_1, \tau_2, \ldots$ denote Boolean substitutions.

5.2   Handling Variables

In order to illustrate the idea of this step, let us consider Example 6. According to Definition 6, x_1 can only be instantiated by 0 or r. We denote this as $\{x_1 \mapsto b_1 \times r\}$, where b_1 is a Boolean variable. Similarly, $\{x_2 \mapsto b_2 \times r \oplus b_3 \times (f(r \oplus x_1) \oplus x_1)\}$, where b_2, b_3 are Boolean variables. We then instantiate x_1 and x_2 in $\mathscr{C}$ and get a set of mixed terms $\mathscr{C}_{mix} = \{r, f(r \oplus (b_1 \times r)) \oplus (b_1 \times r), f(f(r \oplus (b_1 \times r)) \oplus b_2 \times r \oplus b_3 \times (f(r \oplus (b_1 \times r)) \oplus (b_1 \times r)))\}$. Notice that there are no term variables in $\mathscr{C}_{mix}$. To formalize the above idea, we define the following operator: $\bullet$.

Definition 10. Let $T = \{t_1, t_2, \ldots, t_n\}$ be a set of terms, and $\vec{B} = \langle b_1, b_2, \ldots, b_n \rangle$ be a vector of Boolean variables, $T \bullet \vec{B}$ is defined to be $b_1 \times t_1 \oplus b_2 \times t_2 \oplus \ldots b_n \times t_n$. $T \bullet \vec{B}$ is called a linear combination of $t_1, t_2, \ldots, t_n$.

Given an $\oplus$-mapping $\mathscr{M}$ and a set of terms $\mathscr{C}$, our initial goal is to find a subset of terms in $\mathscr{C}$ s.t. their exclusive-or is 0 under some admissible $\mathscr{M}_\oplus$-substitution σ. REMOVE-TERM-VARIABLES($\mathscr{M}, \mathscr{C}$) in Algorithm 2 returns $(\gamma^{\mathscr{M}}, \mathscr{C}_{mix})$, where $\mathscr{C}_{mix} = \mathscr{C}\gamma^{\mathscr{M}}$. Now our new goal is to find a subset of terms in $\mathscr{C}_{mix}$ s.t. their exclusive-or is 0 under some Boolean substitution. The following lemma shows how $\gamma^{\mathscr{M}}$ is related to admissible $\mathscr{M}_\oplus$-substitutions.

Lemma 1. σ is an admissible $\mathscr{M}_\oplus$-substitution if and only if there exists a Boolean substitution τ s.t. $\gamma^{\mathscr{M}} \circ \tau = \sigma$.

Algorithm 2. remove term variables

1: **function** REMOVE-TERM-VARIABLES$(\mathcal{M}, \mathcal{C})$
2:     // Assume: $domain(\mathcal{M}) = \{x_1, x_2, \ldots, x_m\}$.
3:     $\gamma^{\mathcal{M}} \leftarrow \{x_1 \mapsto t_1', x_2 \mapsto t_2', \ldots, x_m \mapsto t_m'\}$, where $t_i' = \mathcal{M}(x_i) \bullet \vec{B_i}$, and $\vec{B_i}$ is a
    vector of fresh Boolean variables.
4:     $\mathcal{C}_{mix} \leftarrow \mathcal{C}\gamma^{\mathcal{M}}$.
5:     return $(\gamma^{\mathcal{M}}, \mathcal{C}_{mix})$
6: **end function**

5.3   Applying Inference Rules

Consider Example 6. REMOVE-TERM-VARIABLES$(\mathcal{M}, \mathcal{C})$ returns $(\gamma^{\mathcal{M}}, \mathcal{C}_{mix})$, where

$$\gamma^{\mathcal{M}} = \{x_1 \mapsto b_1 \times r, x_2 \mapsto b_2 \times r \oplus b_3 \times (f(r \oplus x_1) \oplus x_1)\}.$$
$$\mathcal{C}_{mix} = \{r, f(r \oplus (b_1 \times r)) \oplus (b_1 \times r), f(f(r \oplus (b_1 \times r)) \oplus b_2 \times r \oplus b_3 \times (f(r \oplus$$
$$(b_1 \times r)) \oplus (b_1 \times r)))\}$$

As we described in Sect. 5.1, $\mathcal{C}_{mix}$ can be considered conceptually as a matrix. In Sect. 5.3.1, we give an algorithm for checking if two mixed terms are unifiable under some Boolean substitution. In Sect. 5.3.2, we give inference rules for merging different columns and combining multiple rows of a matrix.

5.3.1   Unifying Two Mixed Terms

Definition 11. *Let eq be an equation $t_1 \overset{?}{=} t_2$ on mixed terms without term variables. eq is B-unifiable under some Boolean substitution τ if $t_1\tau =_{\oplus} t_2\tau$. We call τ a B-unifier of eq. Let eqs be a set of equations on mixed terms without term variables. eqs is B-unifiable under τ if each equation in eqs is B-unifiable under τ. We call τ a B-unifier of eqs.*

The function B-UNIFY(t_1, t_2) from Algorithm 3 checks if t_1 and t_2 are B-unifiable by nondeterministically applying the inference rules in $\mathcal{R}_{B-unif}$ (Fig. 2) to *states*. A *state* st is of the form $eqs|\tau$, where eqs is a set of equations on mixed terms and τ is a Boolean substitution. To check if two mixed terms t_1 and t_2 are B-unifiable, we start from the initial state: $\{t_1 \oplus t_2 \overset{?}{=} 0\}|\epsilon$, and we keep applying the inference rules in $\mathcal{R}_{B-unif}$ nondeterministically. Intuitively, the rules in $\mathcal{R}_{B-unif}$ list all possible ways that a mixed (sub)term can be simplified and eventually becomes 0. For example, *Duplicate$_r$* states that one way to simplify $b_1 \times r \oplus b_2 \times r$ is to make both b_1 and b_2 be 1, hence cancellation applies. By make inferences, eventually we reach either a final state or a stuck state. A *final state* is a state of the form $\emptyset|\tau$. A *stuck state* is a state of the form $eqs|\tau$, where $eqs \neq \emptyset$, and no rule applies. We call $st_1, st_2, \ldots$ a *trace* of t_1 and t_2 if st_1 is $\{t_1 \oplus t_2 \overset{?}{=} 0\}|\epsilon$, and $\forall i > 1$, st_i is the result of applying one of the inference rules to st_{i-1}.

In order to cut down the search space, we define the notion of $dep_f(t)$, where t is a mixed term without any term variables. If t is a ground term, $dep_f(t)$ is the singleton set containing the maximum number of nested f symbols in t. Or equivalently, $dep_f(t)$ is the singleton set containing the maximum number of f symbols among all root-to-leaf paths of the syntax tree of t. If t contains Boolean variables, $dep_f(t) = \bigcup_\tau dep_f(t\tau)$, where τ is a Boolean substitution and $t\tau$ is ground.

Algorithm 3. Check if two terms are B-unifiable

```
1: function B-UNIFY(t₁, t₂)
2:     /*Assume that t₁ and t₂ are mixed terms containing no term variables.*/
3:     st ← {t₁ =? t₂}|ε
4:     while st is not a final state or stuck state do
5:         Nondeterministically apply a rule in ℛ_{B−unif} to st
6:     end while
7:     if st is a final state of the form ∅|τ then
8:         return τ
9:     else
10:        return false
11:    end if
12: end function
```

$$\frac{\{0 \overset{?}{=} 0\} \cup \Gamma \mid \tau}{\Gamma \mid \tau} \quad Remove$$

$$\frac{\{b \times t_1 \oplus t_2 \overset{?}{=} 0\} \cup \Gamma \mid \tau}{(\{t_2 \overset{?}{=} 0\} \cup \Gamma)(\{b \mapsto 0\}) \mid \tau \cup \{b \mapsto 0\}} \quad Disappear$$

$$\frac{\{b_1 \times r \oplus b_2 \times r \oplus t \overset{?}{=} 0\} \cup \Gamma \mid \tau}{(\{t \overset{?}{=} 0\} \cup \Gamma)\tau' \mid \tau \cup \tau'} \quad Duplicate_r$$

where $\tau' = \{b_1 \mapsto 1, b_2 \mapsto 1\}$.

$$\frac{\{b_1 \times f(t_1) \oplus b_2 \times f(t_2) \oplus t_3 \overset{?}{=} 0\} \cup \Gamma \mid \tau}{(\{t_3 \overset{?}{=} 0, t_1 \oplus t_2 \overset{?}{=} 0\} \cup \Gamma)\tau' \mid \tau \cup \tau'} \quad Duplicate_f$$

where $\tau' = \{b_1 \mapsto 1, b_2 \mapsto 1\}$, $dep_f(t_1)$ and $dep_f(t_2)$ overlap.

Fig. 2. $\mathscr{R}_{B-unif}$

We write $dep_f(t) = [l, u]$ to denote that $dep_f(t)$ can be at least l and at most u. Note that two terms cannot possibly be B-unifiable unless their dep_f intervals overlap. Given a term t without any term variables, $dep_f(t)$ can be computed in the following way.

- $dep_f(r) = [0, 0]$, where r is a constant.
- $dep_f(b \times t) = [0, u]$, where $dep_f(t) = [l, u]$.
- $dep_f(f(t)) = [l + 1, u + 1]$, where $dep_f(t) = [l, u]$.
- $dep_f(t_1 \oplus t_2) = [0, max(u_1, u_2)]$, where $dep_f(t_1) = [l_1, u_1]$, $dep_f(t_2) = [l_2, u_2]$ and $dep_f(t_1)$ and $dep_f(t_2)$ overlap.
- $dep_f(t_1 \oplus t_2) = [max(l_1, l_2), max(u_1, u_2)]$, where $dep_f(t_1) = [l_1, u_1]$, $dep_f(t_2) = [l_2, u_2]$ and $dep_f(t_1)$ and $dep_f(t_2)$ do not overlap.

Example 7. $dep_f(b_1 \times r \oplus f(r)) = [1,1]$ $dep_f(r \oplus b_1 \times f(r)) = [0,1]$.

Example 8. *Check if* $t_1 = f(r \oplus (b_1 \times r))$ *and* $t_2 = f(f(r \oplus (b_1 \times r)) \oplus b_2 \times r \oplus b_3 \times (f(r \oplus (b_1 \times r)) \oplus (b_1 \times r)))$ *are B-unifiable.*

$$\{f(r \oplus (b_1 \times r)) \oplus f(f(r \oplus (b_1 \times r)) \oplus b_2 \times r \oplus b_3 \times (f(r \oplus (b_1 \times r)) \oplus (b_1 \times r))) \overset{?}{=} 0\}|\epsilon$$

$\xLongrightarrow{Duplicate_f} \{r \oplus (b_1 \times r) \oplus f(r \oplus (b_1 \times r)) \oplus b_2 \times r \oplus b_3 \times (f(r \oplus (b_1 \times r)) \oplus (b_1 \times r)) \overset{?}{=} 0\}|\epsilon$

$\xLongrightarrow{Duplicate_f} \{f(0) \oplus b_2 \times r \oplus b_3 \times f(0) \oplus b_3 \times r \overset{?}{=} 0\}|\{b_1 \mapsto 1\}$

$\xLongrightarrow{Duplicate_f} \{b_2 \times r \oplus r \overset{?}{=} 0\}|\{b_1 \mapsto 1, b_3 \mapsto 1\}$

$\xLongrightarrow{Duplicate_r} \{0 \overset{?}{=} 0\}|\{b_1 \mapsto 1, b_2 \mapsto 1, b_3 \mapsto 1\}$

$\xLongrightarrow{Remove} \emptyset|\{b_1 \mapsto 1, b_2 \mapsto 1, b_3 \mapsto 1\}$

So t_1 *and* t_2 *are B-unifiable under* $\{b_1 \mapsto 1, b_2 \mapsto 1, b_3 \mapsto 1\}$.

5.3.2   Saturation Procedure

Let $\mathscr{C}_{mix} = \{mt_1, mt_2, \ldots, mt_n\}$ be a set of mixed terms. Our goal is to take the XOR of a subset of terms in $\mathscr{C}_{mix}$, apply some Boolean substitution and get 0. Roughly speaking, we saturate $\mathscr{C}_{mix}$ using two rules: the *Combine* rule and the *Cancel* rule, which we will introduce later. The *Combine* rule allows us to take the XOR of two mixed terms mt_i, mt_j, and apply some Boolean substitution τ, provided that one summand of mt_i and another summand of mt_j are B-unifiable under τ. The *Cancel* rule allows us to take one mixed term mt_i and apply some Boolean substitution τ, provided that two summands of mt_i are B-unifiable under τ.

We keep track of some additional information along the way. We annotate each mixed term with a set of indices and a Boolean substitution. More formally, an *annotated mixed term* amt is of the form $mt[I; \tau]$, where mt is a mixed term, I is a set of indices and τ is a Boolean substitution. We need I and τ for the following reasons:

1. We maintain a crucial invariant during the saturation process, which is, if $mt[I; \tau]$ is generated, then $\oplus\{mt_i | i \in I\}\tau =_\oplus mt$. Intuitively, I and τ tell us how we can get mt.
2. If we have $mt_1[I_1; \tau_1]$ and $mt_2[I_2; \tau_2]$, where $I_1 \cap I_2 \neq \emptyset$, we do not take the XOR of mt_1 and mt_2, since it is not necessary to use a mixed term more than once.
3. If we have $mt_1[I_1; \tau_1]$ and $mt_2[I_2; \tau_2]$, where $\tau_1 \cup \tau_2$ is undefined, we do not take the XOR of mt_1 and mt_2, since τ_1 and τ_2 are inconsistent.

Let $MT = \{mt_1, mt_2, \ldots, mt_n\}$ be a set of mixed terms. We define $annotate(MT)$ to be $\{mt_1[\{1\}; \epsilon], mt_2[\{2\}; \epsilon], \ldots, mt_n[\{n\}; \epsilon]\}$. In Algorithm 4, ANNOTATE-AND-SATURATE(C_{mix}) first obtains $\mathscr{C}_{mix}^1$ by annotating $\mathscr{C}_{mix}$. It then saturates $\mathscr{C}_{mix}^1$ using the inference rules in $\mathscr{R}_{saturate}$ (Fig. 3), and obtains a sequence $\mathscr{C}_{mix}^1, \mathscr{C}_{mix}^2, \mathscr{C}_{mix}^3, \cdots$. $\forall i \geq 1$, $\mathscr{C}_{mix}^{i+1}$ is obtained from $\mathscr{C}_{mix}^i$ by nondeterministically making an inference and adding the result to $\mathscr{C}_{mix}^i$, if it is not already in $\mathscr{C}_{mix}^i$. $\mathscr{C}_{mix}^n$ is a saturation of $\mathscr{C}_{mix}^1$ if nothing new can be added to $\mathscr{C}_{mix}^n$.

We define an ordering on terms. Let mt_1 and mt_2 be two mixed terms. $mt_1 \prec mt_2$ if $dep_f(mt_1) = [l_1, h_1]$, $dep_f(mt_2) = [l_2, h_2]$ and $h_1 < l_2$. Let mt be a mixed term of the form $b_1 \times t_1 \oplus b_2 \times t_2 \oplus \ldots \oplus b_n \times t_n$. $b_i \times t_i$ is a maximal term in mt if there does not exist any $b_j \times t_j$ s.t. $b_i \times t_i \prec b_j \times t_j$. To cut down the search space, we require that both the *Combine* rule and the *Cancel* rule must be applied on maximal terms. We show that this requirement does not affect completeness.

Algorithm 4. annotate and saturate

1: **function** ANNOTATE-AND-SATURATE($\mathscr{C}_{mix}$)
2:    //Assume: $\mathscr{C}_{mix} = \{mt_1, mt_2, \ldots, mt_n\}$
3:    $\mathscr{C}_{mix}^1 \leftarrow annotate(\mathscr{C}_{mix})$
4:    Saturate $\mathscr{C}_{mix}^1$ using the *Combine* rule and *Cancel* rule.
5:    return $\mathscr{C}_{mix}^n$, which is the result of the saturation
6: **end function**

$$\frac{b_1 \times t_1 \oplus \Gamma_1[I_1; \tau_1] \quad b_2 \times t_2 \oplus \Gamma_2[I_2; \tau_2]}{(\Gamma_1 \oplus \Gamma_2)\tau_{123}[I_1 \cup I_2; \tau_{123}]} \; Combine$$

where
(1) $b_1 \times t_1$ is a maximal term in $b_1 \times t_1 \oplus \Gamma_1$, $b_2 \times t_2$ is a maximal term in $b_2 \times t_2 \oplus \Gamma_2$.
(2) $dep_f(b_1 \times t_1)$ and $dep_f(b_2 \times t_2)$ overlap.
(3) $I_1 \cap I_2 = \emptyset$.
(4) τ_3 is a B-unifier of $b_1 \times t_1$ and $b_2 \times t_2$, and $\tau_{123} = \tau_1 \uplus \tau_2 \uplus \tau_3$.

$$\frac{b_1 \times t_1 \oplus b_2 \times t_2 \oplus \Gamma[I; \tau_1]}{\Gamma\tau_{12}[I; \tau_{12}]} \; Cancel$$

where
(1) $b_1 \times t_1$ and $b_2 \times t_2$ are maximal terms in $t_1 \oplus t_2 \oplus \Gamma_2$
(2) τ_2 is a B-unifier of $b_1 \times t_1$ and $b_2 \times t_2$, and $\tau_{12} = \tau_1 \uplus \tau_2$.

Fig. 3. $\mathscr{R}_{saturate}$

Example 9. *Consider Example 6, where* $\mathscr{M}(x_1) = \{r\}$.
$\mathscr{M}(x_2) = \{r, f(r \oplus x_1) \oplus x_1\}$.
$\mathscr{C} = \{r, f(r \oplus x_1) \oplus x_1, f(f(r \oplus x_1) \oplus x_2)\}$.

REMOVE-TERM-VARIABLES($\mathscr{M}, \mathscr{C}$) *returns:*
$\gamma^{\mathscr{M}} = \{x_1 \mapsto b_1 \times r, x_2 \mapsto b_2 \times r \oplus b_3 \times (f(r \oplus x_1) \oplus x_1)\}$.
$\mathscr{C}_{mix} = \{r, f(r \oplus (b_1 \times r)) \oplus (b_1 \times r), f(f(r \oplus (b_1 \times r)) \oplus b_2 \times r \oplus b_3 \times (f(r \oplus (b_1 \times r)) \oplus (b_1 \times r)))\}$.

Here is what ANNOTATE-AND-SATURATE($\mathscr{C}_{mix}$) *does:*
$\mathscr{C}_{mix}^1 = annotate(\mathscr{C}_{mix}) = \{r[\{1\}; \epsilon], f(r \oplus (b_1 \times r)) \oplus (b_1 \times r)[\{2\}; \epsilon], f(f(r \oplus (b_1 \times r)) \oplus b_2 \times r \oplus b_3 \times (f(r \oplus (b_1 \times r)) \oplus (b_1 \times r)))[\{3\}; \epsilon]\}$.

As we showed in Example 8, $f(r \oplus (b_1 \times r))$ and $f(f(r \oplus (b_1 \times r)) \oplus b_2 \times r \oplus b_3 \times (f(r \oplus (b_1 \times r)) \oplus (b_1 \times r)))$ are unifiable under $\{b_1 \mapsto 1, b_2 \mapsto 1, b_3 \mapsto 1\}$. We can apply the Combine rule, and get:

$\mathscr{C}^2_{mix} = \{r[\{1\}; \epsilon], f(r \oplus (b_1 \times r)) \oplus (b_1 \times r)[\{2\}; \epsilon], f(f(r \oplus (b_1 \times r)) \oplus b_2 \times r \oplus b_3 \times (f(r \oplus (b_1 \times r)) \oplus (b_1 \times r)))[\{3\}; \epsilon], r[\{2, 3\}, \{b_1 \mapsto 1, b_2 \mapsto 1, b_3 \mapsto 1\}]\}$.

Obviously, r and r are unifiable. We can apply the Combine rule again, and get:

$\mathscr{C}^3_{mix} = \{r[\{1\}; \epsilon], f(r \oplus (b_1 \times r)) \oplus (b_1 \times r)[\{2\}; \epsilon], f(f(r \oplus (b_1 \times r)) \oplus b_2 \times r \oplus b_3 \times (f(r \oplus (b_1 \times r)) \oplus (b_1 \times r)))[\{3\}; \epsilon], r[\{2, 3\}, \{b_1 \mapsto 1, b_2 \mapsto 1, b_3 \mapsto 1\}], 0[\{1, 2, 3\}, \{b_1 \mapsto 1, b_2 \mapsto 1, b_3 \mapsto 1\}]\}$.

5.4 $\oplus$-rooted Local Unification Procedure

Algorithm 5 describes a function XOR-ROOTED-UNIFY for solving $\oplus$-rooted local unification.

Algorithm 5. Solving $\oplus$-rooted local unification

1: **function** XOR-ROOTED-UNIFY$(\mathscr{M}, \mathscr{C})$
2:     //Assume: (1) $\mathscr{M}$ is an $\oplus$-mapping. (2) $\mathscr{C} = \{t_1, t_2, \ldots, t_n\}$.
3:     $(\gamma^{\mathscr{M}}, \mathscr{C}_{mix}) \leftarrow$ REMOVE-TERM-VARIABLES$(\mathscr{M}, \mathscr{C})$
4:     $\mathscr{C}^n_{mix} \leftarrow$ ANNOTATE-AND-SATURATE$(\mathscr{C}_{mix})$
5:     $result \leftarrow \emptyset$
6:     **for all** annotated mixed term amt in $\mathscr{C}^n_{mix}$ **do**
7:         **if** amt is of the form $0[I; \tau]$ **then**
8:             $result \leftarrow result \cup (I, \gamma^{\mathscr{M}} \circ \tau)$ //$\{t_i | i \in I\}$ is $\mathscr{M}_{\oplus}$-unifiable with 0 under
                $\gamma^{\mathscr{M}} \circ \tau$
9:         **end if**
10:     **end for**
11:     **if** $result = \emptyset$ **then**
12:         **return** not $\mathscr{M}_{\oplus}$-unifiable
13:     **else**
14:         **return** $(\mathscr{M}_{\oplus}$-unifiable, $result)$
15:     **end if**
16: **end function**

Example 10. *Continuing with Example 9, we showed that $0[\{1, 2, 3\}; \{b_1 \mapsto 1, b_2 \mapsto 1, b_3 \mapsto 1\}] \in \mathscr{C}^3_{mix}$. The XOR of all three terms in $\mathscr{C}_{mix}$ is 0 under $\{b_1 \mapsto 1, b_2 \mapsto 1, b_3 \mapsto 1\}$.*

We can compose $\gamma^{\mathscr{M}} = \{x_1 \mapsto b_1 \times r, x_2 \mapsto b_2 \times r \oplus b_3 \times (f(r \oplus x_1) \oplus x_1)\}$ with $\{b_1 \mapsto 1, b_2 \mapsto 1, b_3 \mapsto 1\}$ and get an admissible $\mathscr{M}_{\oplus}$-substitution: $\sigma = \{x_1 \mapsto r, x_2 \mapsto f(0)\}$ s.t. $\oplus\{r, f(r \oplus x_1) \oplus x_1, f(f(r \oplus x_1) \oplus x_2)\}\sigma = 0$.

6   Conclusion

In this paper, we introduce a new unification problem, called local XOR unification, which is unification modulo the theory of exclusive-or with an additional restriction for variables. Local XOR unification can be used to analyze symbolic security of cryptographic modes of operation. We present two concrete versions of local XOR unification. f-rooted local unification can be used to analyze modes of operation including Cipher Block Chaining, Propagating Cipher Block Chaining, Accumulated Block Cipher, etc. $\oplus$-rooted local unification can be used to analyze modes of operation including Cipher Feedback Mode, Output Feedback Mode, etc. We give algorithms to solve both versions of local unification. The algorithms are implemented as part of the CryptoSolve tool[1]. Readers are referred to [6] for experimental results of local unification algorithms.

References

1. Akinyele, J.A., Green, M., Hohenberger, S.: Using SMT solvers to automate design tasks for encryption and signature schemes. In: Sadeghi, A., Gligor, V.D., Yung, M. (eds.) 2013 ACM SIGSAC Conference on Computer and Communications Security, CCS 2013, Berlin, Germany, 4–8 November 2013, pp. 399–410. ACM (2013)
2. Ambrona, M., Barthe, G., Schmidt, B.: Automated unbounded analysis of cryptographic constructions in the generic group model. In: Fischlin, M., Coron, J.-S. (eds.) EUROCRYPT 2016. LNCS, vol. 9666, pp. 822–851. Springer, Heidelberg (2016). https://doi.org/10.1007/978-3-662-49896-5_29
3. Anantharaman, S., Lin, H., Lynch, C., Narendran, P., Rusinowitch, M.: Cap unification: application to protocol security modulo homomorphic encryption. In: Feng, D., Basin, D.A., Liu, P. (eds.) Proceedings of the 5th ACM Symposium on Information, Computer and Communications Security, ASIACCS 2010, Beijing, China, 13–16 April 2010, pp. 192–203. ACM (2010). https://doi.org/10.1145/1755688.1755713
4. Bellare, M., Rogaway, P., Wagner, D.: The EAX Mode of operation. In: Roy, B., Meier, W. (eds.) FSE 2004. LNCS, vol. 3017, pp. 389–407. Springer, Heidelberg (2004). https://doi.org/10.1007/978-3-540-25937-4_25
5. Carmer, B., Rosulek, M.: Linicrypt: a model for practical cryptography. In: 36th Annual International Cryptology Conference, pp. 416–445 (2016)
6. Chichester, D., et al.: CryptoSolve: towards a tool for the symbolic analysis of cryptographic algorithms. In: 13th International Symposium on Games, Automata, Logics, and Formal Verification, Madrid, Spain (2022)
7. Erbatur, S., et al.: Asymmetric unification: a new unification paradigm for cryptographic protocol analysis. In: Bonacina, M.P. (ed.) CADE 2013. LNCS (LNAI), vol. 7898, pp. 231–248. Springer, Heidelberg (2013). https://doi.org/10.1007/978-3-642-38574-2_16
8. Escobar, S., et al.: Protocol analysis in Maude-NPA using unification modulo homomorphic encryption. In: Schneider-Kamp, P., Hanus, M. (eds.) Proceedings of the 13th International ACM SIGPLAN Conference on Principles and Practice of Declarative Programming, 20–22 July 2011, Odense, Denmark, pp. 65–76. ACM (2011). https://doi.org/10.1145/2003476.2003488
9. Hoang, V.T., Katz, J., Malozemof, A.J.: Automated analysis and synthesis of authenticated encryption schemes. In: Proceedings of the 22nd ACM SIGSAC Conference on Computer and Communications Security, pp. 84–95 (2015)
10. Knudsen, L.R. (ed.): Block chaining modes of operation. Department of Informatics, University of Bergen, Norway (2000)

---

[1] https://symcollab.github.io/CryptoSolve/.

11. Li, B., Micciancio, D.: Equational security proofs of oblivious transfer protocols. In: Abdalla, M., Dahab, R. (eds.) PKC 2018. LNCS, vol. 10769, pp. 527–553. Springer, Cham (2018). https://doi.org/10.1007/978-3-319-76578-5_18

12. Li, B., Micciancio, D.: Symbolic security of garbled circuits. In: 31st IEEE Computer Security Foundations Symposium, CSF 2018, Oxford, United Kingdom, 9–12 July 2018, pp. 147–161. IEEE Computer Society (2018)

13. Lin, H., et al.: Algorithmic problems in the symbolic approach to the verification of automatically synthesized cryptosystems. In: Konev, B., Reger, G. (eds.) FroCoS 2021. LNCS (LNAI), vol. 12941, pp. 253–270. Springer, Cham (2021). https://doi.org/10.1007/978-3-030-86205-3_14

14. Liu, Z., Lynch, C.: Efficient general unification for XOR with homomorphism. In: Bjørner, N., Sofronie-Stokkermans, V. (eds.) CADE 2011. LNCS (LNAI), vol. 6803, pp. 407–421. Springer, Heidelberg (2011). https://doi.org/10.1007/978-3-642-22438-6_31

15. Malozemoff, A.J., Katz, J., Green, M.D.: Automated analysis and synthesis of block-cipher modes of operation. In: Computer Security Foundations Symposium (CSF), pp. 140–152 (2014)

16. Meadows, C.: Moving the bar on computationally sound exclusive-or. In: Bertino, E., Shulman, H., Waidner, M. (eds.) ESORICS 2021. LNCS, vol. 12973, pp. 275–295. Springer, Cham (2021). https://doi.org/10.1007/978-3-030-88428-4_14

A Matching Logic Foundation for Alk

Alexandru-Ioan Lungu[(⊠)] and Dorel Lucanu

Alexandru Ioan Cuza University of Iași, Iași, Romania
lungualex00@gmail.com

Abstract. Alk is an educational platform designed to help in learning algorithms and acquiring algorithmic thinking. This paper describes how the semantics of Alk and the algorithm's properties can be formally described using matching logic such that the reasoning about algorithms, described as Alk programs, can be done in a uniform way. Challenges are coming from the specificity of the Alk Language: abstract descriptions for the values, no declarations for variable or for parameter types, and various algorithmic paradigms (e.g., non-deterministic algorithms). The main consequence of this approach is that we may use in a sound way the symbolic execution for proving algorithms' properties.

1 Introduction

Alk is an educational platform designated to help in learning algorithms and acquiring algorithmic thinking. It can be used for writing, executing, debugging, experimenting, and analyzing algorithms. Alk was designed based on the following principles:

1. *The syntax of the language should be as simple as possible, expressive, intuitive, and including the main algorithmic thinking structures.*
2. *The formal semantics of the language has to be given at an abstract level that should help the algorithmic thinking, the understanding of the execution of the algorithms, and to supply a computation model suitable for analysis.*
3. *The designed algorithms, or fragments of them, must be executable and tested in an easy and flexible way.*
4. *There are embedded tools of helping an user to evaluate the suitability of algorithms for various applications.*
5. *There exists support for a good algorithm understanding, and, consequently, for acquiring an algorithmic thinking.*
6. *There exists support for time/space efficiency analysis.*
7. *To allow the design and analysis of various kinds of algorithms (e.g., deterministic, non-deterministic, probabilistic).*

In this paper we address the items 2 and 4, and 5. We adhere to the idea that an explanation of an algorithm consists of a sequence of logical deductions, made according to certain rules, and ends with a conclusion. The Alk language was extended with annotations, inspired from program verification, to specify

© The Author(s), under exclusive license to Springer Nature Switzerland AG 2022
H. Seidl et al. (Eds.): ICTAC 2022, LNCS 13572, pp. 290–304, 2022.
https://doi.org/10.1007/978-3-031-17715-6_19

properties of the computed data structures. Based on these properties, we may deduce, for instance, if the algorithm is suitable for some purpose. These annotations are also useful in understanding better the algorithm and its behavioral properties. All these properties specified by annotations are proved based on the semantics of the language.

Matching logic ($\mathcal{ML}$) [8–10,23] was developed as a logical foundation of the K (https://kframework.org/), a semantic framework for defining programming languages and developing formal analysis tools for these languages. Matching logic is a simple but expressive logic, which subsumes many logics, calculi, and models used in program specification and program verification (e.g., first-order logic, separation logic, reachability logic). The first version of Alk language was written in K, but now Alk is an independent platform written in Java, which further includes an interpreter, debugger, symbolic execution engine, and analysis tools.

Contribution. In this paper we present the foundation of the Alk platform using the latest version of matching logic [8], which allows to describe in a uniform way both the semantics of the Alk language and the behavioral properties of the algorithms written in this language. We explain how the operational semantics of the Alk language is described in $\mathcal{ML}$ (Sect. 3.2), how the behavioral properties of the algorithms, like contracts and invariants, are expressed as matching logic patterns (Sect. 4), how these properties are derived from annotations (Sect. 5.1), and how the derived properties are proved using the symbolic execution (Sect. 5.2). Both the interpreter and the symbolic execution engine are directly derived from the semantics of the language, which ensures that the whole approach is sound (Theorem 1).

Structure of Paper. After the introduction, Sect. 2 illustrates a single, yet comprehensive, example of a nondeterministic algorithm executed both in a concrete environment and symbolically. Section 3 provides an insight into the Matching Logic that is further used to define the Alk semantics. Section 4 shows an advanced application of $\mathcal{ML}$ patterns in the context of algorithms behavioral properties. Finally, Sect. 5 displays a formal definition of the Alk specifications and symbolic execution using reachability patterns. In the end, Sect. 6 is an insight into the related work, while Sect. 7 includes some conclusions.

2   A Taste of Alk

The Alk language is simple, abstract, having a syntax similar to that used in textbooks. We use an example to see how the algorithms are described, tested, and analyzed in Alk.

Figure 1a) shows Floyd's nondeterministic algorithm for the n queens problem [13], written in Alk. The algorithm uses three arrays, a, b and c, which are counting the number of queens on a specific row or diagonal (primary or secondary), respectively. Comparing to the original algorithm, an additional array *cb* (chessboard) is used to store the position of each queen: $cb[col] = row$ means that the queen is set on the position (row, col) on the chess board. The goal is to have exactly n queens set on the n columns, such that for each row and column there is at most one queen (i.e., the queens are placed on the chessboard so that none attack each other). The algorithm uses the Alk statement choose...st... to non-deterministically choose a row with desired properties for each column. If no row is found, then the execution of the algorithm fails. Otherwise, the four arrays are accordingly updated.

Figure 1b) displays The Floyd's algorithm annotated with specifications for invariants, algorithm's preconditions and postconditions, in order to check some of its properties. Since for the analysis the type of variables is needed, Alk allows to use annotations for type specifications. For the same reason, the initialization of the arrays were replaced by their symbolic representation counterpart[1]. The size of the array *cb* is assumed zero, because the arrays in Alk have a variable size, which is updated during the execution of the algorithm [22]. The properties we want to check are described by the three invariants of the for statement.

The analysis engine provides a feedback on the validity of such statements: whether the invariants are preserved by the loop body, whether the postcondition holds for any input satisfying the precondition. Note that the focus is to investigate the algorithm properties and not to show that it correctly solves a problem specified as a pair (precondition, postcondition), i.e., the focus is not the correctness verification. Therefore, the Alk specifications are used to solely allow the user to check its own presumptions. This way, certain properties can be validated while the final goal is to increase the comprehension of the algorithm.

A user should expect this kind of algorithm designing process from Alk. A possible scenario is to first provide a version of the algorithm that can be executed in a concrete environment with various inputs. Afterwards, specifications can be added one by one to model the reasoning into the code. This way, Alk analysis engine can confirm that specific assumptions are correct, and the user can confirm its reasoning across the written algorithm.

Executing the algorithm from the left hand side using a concrete initial configuration of $n \mapsto 4$, it is very probable to get an output in the following form:

```
failure
Note that the executed algorithm is nondeterministic.
```

The probability to obtain a successful execution is very small. Alk interpreter allows the user to exhaustively execute a non-deterministic algorithm and in that case it could obtain all successful executions, which for this examples are the following two:

```
Note that the executed algorithm    Note that the executed algorithm
is nondeterministic.                is nondeterministic.
[1, 3, 0, 2]                        [2, 0, 3, 1]
success                             success
```

---

[1] In many cases, the information needed for analysis, e.g., the types of variables and the variables modified by an iterative statement, can be deduced by static analysis. Such a component is a work in progress, and it will be presented somewhere else.

``queens(n) {
    a = [0 | i from {1..n}];
    b = [0 | i from {1..2*n}];
    c = [0 | i from {1..2*n}];
    for (col = 0; col < n; ++col) {
        choose row from {0..n-1} s.t.
            a[row] == 0 &&
            b[row + col] == 0 &&
            c[n + (row-col)] == 0;
        a[row]++;
        b[row + col]++;
        c[n + (row-col)]++;
        cb[col] = row;
    }
    return cb;
}

print(queens(n));``` | ```queens(n)   1
@requires n : int   2
@requires 1 <= n   3
@ensures \result : array<int>   4
{   5
    @havoc a:array<int>, b:array<int>,   6
           c:array<int>, cb:array<int>;   7
    @assume a.size() == n;   8
    @assume forall i : int ::   9
        0 <= i && i < n ==> a[i] == 0;   10
    @assume cb.size() == 0;   11
    for (col = 0; col < n; ++col)   12
    @invariant 0 <= col && col <= n   13
    @invariant cb.size() == col;   14
    @invariant forall i : int ::   15
        0 <= i && i < n ==> a[i] <= 1   16
    @modifies col, a, cb, cb.size   17
    {   18
        choose row from {0..n-1} s.t.   19
            a[row] == 0 &&   20
            b[row + col] == 0 &&   21
            c[n + (row-col)] == 0;   22
        a[row]++;   23
        b[row + col]++;   24
        c[n + (row-col)]++;   25
        cb[col] = row;   26
    }   27
    return cb;   28
}   29``` |
| a) | b) |

Fig. 1. Examples of algorithm written in Alk

The goal of the analysis engine is to allow a more powerful introspective into the algorithm design. The user can add specific annotations like @requires, @ensures, @havoc, @invariant, @assume to link the algorithm to the reasoning process. In the example, using @requires and @ensures can provide the Alk interpreter a feedback upon how does the function work. Another insightful specification is @invariant, that allows the analysis engine to check if a reasoning regarding a repetitive statement is valid.

Note that the example shows a mean of partially analyzing the algorithm as it only checks that there is at most one queen on each row. This analysis process succeeds as long as the intermediary conditional steps (invariants) are valid.

Symbolically executing the algorithm using a supporting SMT solver provides the following output:

```
[13:15] Loop invariant was verified!
[14:15] Loop invariant was verified!
[15:15] Loop invariant was verified!
Successfully verified: queens
Note that the executed algorithm is nondeterministic.
```

A successfully analyzing execution is one that does not display any error regarding verification. The example output states that all three invariants could be verified and are valid. Also, the post-condition holds for any input presuming the pre-conditions, so the Alk interpreter states that queens could be successfully verified.

3   Matching Logic Semantics of the Alk Language

In this section we show how the semantics and the algorithm properties can be formally expressed as a matching logic theory.

3.1   A Short Introduction to Matching Logic

Matching Logic ($\mathcal{ML}$) [8–10,23] is a variant of first-order logic (FOL) with fixpoints that makes no distinction between functions and predicates. It uses instead symbols and application to uniformly build patterns that can represent static structures and logical constraints at the same time. Here we present $\mathcal{ML}$ only at intuitive level; we recommend [8,10,23] for the technical details and [11] for seeing how $\mathcal{ML}$ supplies a theoretical foundation for the K framework.

An $\mathcal{ML}$ *signature* is a triple (EV, SV, Σ), where EV is a set of *element variables* $x, y, \ldots$, SV is a set of *set variables* $X, Y, \ldots$, and Σ is a set of *constant symbols* (or *constants*). The set PATTERN of Σ-*patterns* is generated by the grammar below, where $x \in EV$, $X \in SV$, and $\sigma \in \Sigma$:

$$\varphi ::= x \mid X \mid \sigma \mid \varphi_1 \, \varphi_2 \mid \bot \mid \lceil \varphi \rceil \mid \varphi_1 \to \varphi_2 \mid \exists x.\varphi \mid \mu X.\varphi \text{ if } \varphi \text{ is positive in } X$$

A pattern φ is positive in X if all free occurrences of X in φ are under an even number of negations. The syntax of patterns is extended with the following derived constructs:

$$
\begin{array}{lll}
\top \equiv \neg\bot & \lfloor\varphi\rfloor \equiv \neg\lceil\neg\varphi\rceil & \varphi_1 \vee \varphi_2 \equiv \neg\varphi_1 \to \varphi_2 \\
\neg\varphi \equiv \varphi \to \bot & \varphi_1 = \varphi_2 \equiv \lfloor\varphi_1 \leftrightarrow \varphi_2\rfloor & \varphi_1 \wedge \varphi_2 \equiv \neg(\neg\varphi_1 \vee \neg\varphi_2) \\
\forall x.\varphi \equiv \neg\exists x.\neg\varphi & \varphi_1 \neq \varphi_2 \equiv \neg(\varphi_1 = \varphi_2) & \varphi_1 \leftrightarrow \varphi_2 \equiv (\varphi_1 \to \varphi_2) \wedge (\varphi_2 \to \varphi_1) \\
x \in \varphi \equiv \lceil x \wedge \varphi\rceil & \varphi \subseteq \varphi' \equiv \lfloor\varphi \to \varphi'\rfloor & \nu X.\varphi \equiv \neg\mu X.\neg\varphi[\neg X/X]
\end{array}
$$

Semantically, $\mathcal{ML}$ patterns are interpreted as the sets of elements that match them. An element variable x is matched by a singleton set $\{a\} \subseteq M$, a set of variables X is matched by a subset of M, where M is the carrier set. Symbols σ are interpreted as subsets, and, usually, the needed interpretation for them (e.g., functions, relations) is obtained by adding axioms. For instance, the axiom $\forall x.\exists y.\, f\, x = y$ constrains the interpretation of f to a functional one.

The pattern $\varphi_1\, \varphi_2$ is called *application* and its semantics is a function $M \times M \to \mathcal{P}(M)$, which is pointwise extended to $\mathcal{P}(M) \times \mathcal{P}(M) \to \mathcal{P}(M)$. By convention, the application is left associative. The applications are useful to build various structures or relations (see the above example).

The pattern $\lceil \varphi \rceil$ is called *definedness*[2]. It is a predicative pattern since it has a two value semantics: its evaluation is either the whole carrier set M, when the interpretation of φ is a non-empty set, or the empty set, otherwise. The interpretation of $\top$ is the set of all values and it can be seen as the *true* value, while that of $\bot$ is the empty set and it can be seen as the *false* value. The interpretation of the pattern $\exists x.\varphi$ is the union of the φ interpretations, when x ranges over M. In particular, the interpretation of $\exists x.x$ is always M. The binder μ is used for defining sets as least fixpoints. For instance, $\top_{Nat} \equiv \mu X.zero \vee succ\, X$ defines the set $\{zero, succ\, zero, succ\, succ\, zero, \ldots\}$ (which equal up to an isorphism to the set of natural numbers $\{0, 1, 2, \ldots\}$). Dually, with the binder ν we can define sets as greatest fixpoints. For instance, the pattern $\nu X.nil \vee cons\, \top_{Nat}\, X$ defines the set of finite or infinite lists of natural numbers. We may define in a similar way the set of finite or infinite executions of a program.

Sorts s and their inhabitants $\top_s$ can be specified using a sort name symbol s, a symbol for inhabitants inh, and the following notations: $\top_s \equiv inh\, s$, $\forall x:s.\varphi \equiv \forall x.\, x \in \top_s \to \varphi$, $\exists x:s.\varphi \equiv \exists x.\, x \in \top_s \wedge \varphi$, $\varphi:s \equiv \exists z:s.\varphi = z$, and $\neg_s\varphi \equiv \top_s \wedge \neg\varphi$. Such an example is the sort Nat and its inhabitants set $\top_{Nat}$ defined as above. Now, we can specify that $succ$ is a function over naturals: $\forall x:Nat.\,\exists y:Nat.\, succ\, x = y$. We may use $succ:Nat \to Nat$ to denote this axiom. A first-order term $f(t_1, \ldots, t_n)$, where $f:s_1 \times \cdots \times s_n \to s$, can be seen as a notation for the $\mathcal{ML}$ pattern $f\, t_1 \ldots t_n$, and therefore we use to call it *term pattern*.

3.2   Alk Semantics in Matching Logic Terms

Matching logic is a framework where the semantics of programming languages and the reasoning about programs can be done in a uniform way [11]. We use it here for the Alk language and the algorithms expressed in Alk.

Values as $\mathcal{ML}$ Theories. We consider a "builtin" matching logic theory VAL that specifies the Alk values. The theory VAL includes symbols and axioms for integers, floats, arrays, lists, maps, records, sets. Each such a type is specified by a set of symbols and a set of axioms. For instance, the integers are specified by the theory of natural numbers given as above, a symbol $-$, a sort name int, its inhabitants $\top_{int} = \top_{Nat} \vee \exists x:Nat.\, -x$, and its operations: e.g., the addition is specified by an axiom for signature, $+_{int}:int \times int \to int$, and a (an infinite) set of axioms of the form $-3 +_{int} 5 = 2$ saying how the symbol $+_{int}$ is applied over inhabitants, where $-3 +_{int} 5$ is a notation for $+_{int}\, -3\, 5$. Here we take the

---

[2] For convenience, we introduce it directly in the syntax of patterns but it can be axiomatised as in [23].

advantage that the values in the Alk language are given at an abstract level and such a theory is a perfect mean to specify them. At the implementation level, this builtin theory is given (via a translation) by a library (used by the concrete executions) or a SMT solver (used by the symbolic executions).

(Symbolic) Configurations as $\mathcal{ML}$ Patterns. Since the Alk values are given at an abstract level, a *concrete configuration* is a simple pair $\langle \kappa \rangle \langle \sigma \rangle$, where κ is the Alk code (algorithm) to be executed and σ is the current state. A *state* σ is a map from the algorithm variables to their values. For the sake of presentation, we do not make a distinction between local and global variables. We write $\langle \kappa \rightsquigarrow \ldots \rangle \langle \ldots \sigma \ldots \rangle$ when we want to emphasize the first piece κ of code to be evaluated/executed in the next step and the part σ of the state that is used in evaluating/executing κ.

The Alk code is represented by its abstract syntax tree (AST), which is a term pattern in $\mathcal{ML}$. E.g., an assignment x = x+2 is described by a term pattern of the form *assgn* x (*plus* x 2). Similarly, the states are described by term patterns and a configuration $\langle \kappa \rangle \langle \sigma \rangle$ is a notation for the term pattern $(\langle \rangle \kappa)(\langle \rangle \sigma)$, where $\langle \rangle$ is a symbol in Σ. Recall that the term patterns are evaluated to (matched by) singletons. A (full) symbolic configuration is a pattern of the form $\varphi \equiv \langle k \rangle \langle \sigma \rangle \wedge \phi$, where ϕ is the path condition. An example of symbolic configuration is $\langle x = x + 1 \rangle \langle x \mapsto \$x \rangle \wedge \$x >_{\text{int}} 3 = \text{true}$[3], where $\$x$ is a symbolic value, i.e., a matching logic variable. Substituting $\$x$ with a concrete value, let say 8, we obtain an instance, which is a concrete configuration: $\langle x = x + 1 \rangle \langle x \mapsto 8 \rangle$ (note that $8 >_{\text{int}} 3$ evaluates to true).

Remark 1. The versatility of matching logic allows to express the path condition ϕ in terms of program variables. In that case we may think $\langle k \rangle \langle \sigma \rangle \wedge \phi$ as being a short notation for $\langle k \rangle \langle \sigma \rangle \wedge \phi[\sigma]$, where $\phi[\sigma]$ denotes the conjunction $\phi \wedge (\bigwedge_{x \mapsto v \in \sigma} x = v)$. Let us see an example to understand how such a pattern is built: the symbolic configuration $\langle x = x + 1 \rangle \langle x \mapsto \$x \rangle \wedge x > 3$ is a notation (sugar syntax) for $\langle x = x + 1 \rangle \langle x \mapsto \$x \rangle \wedge x > 3 = \text{true} \wedge x = \$x$, which is equivalent to $\langle x = x + 1 \rangle \langle x \mapsto \$x \rangle \wedge \$x > 3 = \text{true}$. Since $\$x$ is a symbolic value of sort int, $\$x > 3$ is equivalent to $\$x >_{\text{int}} 3$, by the semantics of $>$.

Let *Cfg* denote the sort of all (concrete and symbolic) configurations. For *Cfg* we consider an initial semantics [7], so that the semantics of $\top_{Cfg}$ is the set of concrete configurations (which are term patterns as well). The fact that a concrete configuration γ is an instance of a symbolic configuration φ is simply expressed now by the pattern $\gamma \rightarrow \varphi$. Since γ is functional (i.e., matched by singletons), $\gamma \rightarrow \varphi$ is equivalent to $\gamma \in \varphi$ (or to $\gamma \subseteq \varphi$).

Semantics Rules as $\mathcal{ML}$ Patterns. In order to express transitions as patterns, a new symbol $\bullet$ is introduced such that $\bullet \gamma'$ is matched by all γ having γ' as successor, i.e., $\gamma \Rightarrow \gamma'$ [10]. Conversely, having $\bullet \gamma'$ defined, then a transition step $\gamma \Rightarrow \gamma'$ is expressed by the fact that the pattern $\gamma \rightarrow \bullet \gamma'$ is a semantic

---

[3] In order to make the the presentation more intuitive, we use the full syntax for configurations, instead of the AST notation.

consequence of the theory specifying $\bullet$. This notation is naturally extended to symbolic configurations: $\bullet\varphi' \equiv \exists\gamma'. \bullet\gamma' \wedge \gamma' \in \exists var(\varphi'). \varphi'$, i.e., $\bullet\varphi'$ is matched by all the configurations for that there exists a next configuration in φ'. An "all paths" version of it is $\circ\varphi' \equiv \neg\bullet\neg\varphi'$, i.e., $\circ\varphi'$ is matched by all configurations for which there is no next configurations not in φ'. In other words, $\circ\varphi'$ is matched by the configurations having no next configurations (i.e., they are final) and by the configurations for that all the next configurations match φ'.

The operational semantics of Alk is given by a set of patterns specifying transition steps. We exemplify this by giving the semantics of if and choose in the terms of matching logic:

$$\langle \text{if}\,(e)\,s_1\,\text{else}\,s_2 \leadsto \kappa\rangle\,\langle\sigma\rangle \wedge \neg e\!:\!Value \rightarrow \bullet\langle e \leadsto \text{if}\,(\_)\,s_1\,\text{else}\,s_2 \leadsto \kappa\rangle\,\langle\sigma\rangle$$

$$\langle v \leadsto \text{if}\,(\_)\,s_1\,\text{else}\,s_2 \leadsto \kappa\rangle\,\langle\sigma\rangle \wedge v\!:\!Value \rightarrow \bullet\langle \text{if}\,(v)\,s_1\,\text{else}\,s_2 \leadsto \kappa\rangle\,\langle\sigma\rangle$$

$$\langle \text{if}\,(b)\,s_1\,\text{else}\,s_2 \leadsto \kappa\rangle\,\langle\sigma\rangle \wedge b\!:\!\text{bool} \rightarrow \bullet\langle s_1 \leadsto \kappa\rangle\,\langle\sigma\rangle \wedge b = \text{true}$$

$$\vee$$

$$\bullet\langle s_2 \leadsto \kappa\rangle\,\langle\sigma\rangle \wedge b = \text{false}$$

$$\langle \text{choose}\,x\,\text{from}\,e \leadsto \kappa\rangle\,\langle\sigma\rangle \wedge \neg e\!:\!Value \rightarrow \bullet\langle e \leadsto \text{choose}\,x\,\text{from}\,\_\leadsto \kappa\rangle\,\langle\sigma\rangle$$

$$\langle v \leadsto \text{choose}\,x\,\text{from}\,\_\leadsto \kappa\rangle\,\langle\sigma\rangle \wedge v\!:\!Value \rightarrow \bullet\langle \text{choose}\,x\,\text{from}\,v \leadsto \kappa\rangle\,\langle\sigma\rangle$$

$$\langle \text{choose}\,x\,\text{from}\,v \leadsto \kappa\rangle\,\langle\sigma\rangle \wedge v\!:\!Value \rightarrow \bullet \exists x_0.\,\langle\kappa\rangle\,\langle\sigma[x \mapsto x_0]\rangle \wedge x_0 \in v$$

where *Value* is the sort for values, bool for the boolean values (we have $\top_{\text{bool}} \subseteq \top_{Value}$). The first two patterns correspond to the evaluation of the expression E and the third one is the case analysis on the obtained value. For a concrete execution only one member of the disjunction will be a consistent pattern (different from $\perp$). For a symbolic execution, B has a symbolic value and we will obtain two branches of the execution, one for each disjunction member. Actually, the third pattern can be replaced by two patterns (one for each disjunction member), and the semantics remains the same. Having the semantics of if, we may automatically obtain the semantics of while using the equivalence $\text{while}\,(e)\,s \equiv \text{if}\,(e)\,\{s\,\text{while}\,(e)\,s\}\,\text{else}\,\{\}$. The first two patterns giving the semantics of the nondeterministic statement choose are similar to those for if and the last one is self-explanatory.

Let ALKSEM be the matching logic theory including VAL, the specification of the configurations, and all the semantic rules.

A configuration $\langle\kappa\rangle\,\langle\sigma\rangle \wedge \phi$ and a semantic rule $\psi_1 \rightarrow \bullet\psi_2$ may produce an execution step $\langle\kappa\rangle\,\langle\sigma\rangle\wedge\phi\wedge\psi_1 \Rightarrow \psi_2\wedge\phi$ provided that ALKSEM $\models \varphi\wedge\psi_1 \neq \perp$. For instance, the configuration $\langle\text{choose}\,\text{y}\,\text{from}\,[\$a, \$b];\leadsto\text{sum}\,\text{+=}\,\text{y};\rangle\,\langle\text{y} \mapsto y_0\,\text{sum} \mapsto \$s\rangle \wedge \phi$ and the semantic rule for choose produce the following execution step:

$$\langle\text{choose}\,\text{y}\,\text{from}\,[\$a, \$b];\leadsto\text{sum}\,\text{+=}\,\text{y};\rangle\,\langle\text{y} \mapsto y_0\,\text{sum} \mapsto \$s\rangle \wedge \phi \wedge$$

$$\langle\text{choose}\,x\,\text{from}\,v \leadsto \kappa\rangle\,\langle\sigma\rangle \wedge v\!:\!Value$$

$$\Rightarrow$$

$$\exists x_0.\,\langle\kappa\rangle\,\langle\sigma[x \mapsto x_0]\rangle \wedge x_0 \in v \wedge \phi$$

which is equivalent to

$$\langle \text{choose y from } [\$a, \$b]; \leadsto \text{sum += y;} \rangle \langle L \mapsto \$\ell \text{ sum} \mapsto \$s \rangle \wedge \phi$$

$$\Rightarrow$$

$$\exists x_0. \langle \text{sum+ = y;} \rangle \langle y \mapsto x_0 \text{ sum} \mapsto \$s \rangle \wedge x_0 \in [\$a, \$b] \wedge \phi$$

using an unification algorithm [3]. This step can also supply a proof certificate [3, 6] for

$$\mathsf{ALKSEM} \models$$

$$\langle \text{choose y from L}; \leadsto \text{sum += y;} \rangle \langle L \mapsto \$\ell \text{ sum} \mapsto \$s \rangle \wedge \phi$$

$$\rightarrow$$

$$\bullet \exists x. \langle \text{sum += y;} \rangle \langle L \mapsto \$\ell \text{ sum} \mapsto \$s \text{ y} \mapsto x \rangle \wedge x \in \$\ell \wedge \phi$$

4   Behavioral Properties of Algorithms as $\mathcal{ML}$ Patterns

We introduce here examples of patterns that are matched by sets of executions of Alk algorithms. A simple one is well founded, $\mathsf{WF} \equiv \mu X : Cfg. \circ X \equiv \mu X. (\circ X \wedge X \subseteq Cfg)$, that is matched by any configuration with the property that there is no infinite executions starting from it. This definition become more intuitive if we unroll WF using pre-fixpoint inference rule (see, e.g., [8]): $\mathsf{WF} \equiv \mu X : Cfg. \circ X = \circ(\mu X : Cfg. \circ X) \equiv \circ\mathsf{WF} = \circ\circ\mathsf{WF} = \cdots$. We specify first when a configuration γ has no successors, i.e., it is final: $\gamma! \equiv \neg_{Cfg}(\exists x : Cfg. \gamma \rightarrow \bullet x) \equiv \forall x : Cfg. \gamma \wedge \bullet x = \bot$. In other words, γ is final iff it is not predecessor to any configuration. Then:

- from the definition of $\circ$, we know that all the final configurations match $\circ\mathsf{WF}$, i.e., $\mathsf{WF}_0 \equiv \exists x : Cfg. x \wedge x! \subseteq \circ\mathsf{WF} = \mathsf{WF}$;
- all the configurations having all their next configurations in WF_0 match $\circ\circ\mathsf{WF}$, i.e., $\mathsf{WF}_1 \equiv \circ\mathsf{WF}_0 \subseteq \circ\circ\mathsf{WF} = \mathsf{WF}$;
- all the configurations having all their next configurations in WF_1 match $\circ\circ\circ\mathsf{WF}$, i.e., $\mathsf{WF}_2 \equiv \circ\mathsf{WF}_1 \subseteq \circ\circ\circ\mathsf{WF} = \mathsf{WF}$;
- ...

WF is the smallest set satisfying the above properties since it is defined as a least fixpoint.

Its negation $\neg\mathsf{WF} \equiv \nu X. \bullet X$ is matched by any configuration for that there is an infinite execution starting from it. The following two patterns are inspired from temporal logic [10]:

eventually	$\diamond \Psi \equiv \mu X. \Psi \vee \bullet X$
weak eventually	$\diamond_w \Psi \equiv \nu X. \Psi \vee \bullet X$
weak always finally	$\square_w \Psi \equiv \nu X. \Psi \vee (\circ X \wedge \bullet \top)$

Unrolling eventually, using pre-fixpoint inference rule, we obtain $\diamond\Psi = \Psi \vee \bullet(\mu X. \Psi \vee \bullet X) \equiv \Psi \vee \bullet \diamond \Psi = \Psi \vee \bullet\Psi \vee \bullet\bullet \diamond \Psi = \cdots$, which says $\diamond\Psi$ is the smallest set including

- configurations matching $\mathsf{EV}_0 \equiv \Psi$,
- configurations matching $\mathsf{EV}_1 \equiv \bullet\mathsf{EV}_0 \equiv \bullet\Psi$,

- configurations matching $EV_2 \equiv \bullet EV_1 \equiv \bullet\bullet\Psi$,
- ...

i.e., is matched by the configurations for that there is a finite execution that reaches a configuration matching Ψ. Unrolling weak eventually, using post-fixpoint inference rule, we obtain $\Diamond_w\Psi = \Psi \vee \bullet(\nu X. \Psi \vee \bullet X) \equiv \Psi \vee \bullet \Diamond_w \Psi = \Psi \vee \bullet\Psi \vee \bullet\bullet \Diamond_w \Psi = \ldots = \diamond\Psi \vee \neg\mathsf{WF}$, which actually says that $\Diamond_w\Psi$ is matched by the configurations for that there is an execution that reaches a configuration matching Ψ or it is infinite. Unrolling weak always finally we obtain $\Box_w\Psi = \Psi \vee (\circ\,\Box_w\,\Psi \wedge \bullet\top) = \Psi \vee (\circ(\Psi \vee (\circ\,\Box_w\,\Psi \wedge \bullet\top)) \wedge \bullet\top) = \cdots$. Then:

- from the first unrolling we deduce that the configurations matching ψ match $\Box_w\Psi$ as well, i.e., $\psi \subseteq \Box_w\Psi$;
- since

$$\circ\Psi \vee \circ(\circ\,\Box_w\,\Psi \wedge \bullet\top) \subseteq \circ(\Psi \vee (\circ\,\Box_w\,\Psi \wedge \bullet\top)) \qquad \text{implies}$$
$$(\circ\Psi \wedge \bullet\top) \vee \circ(\circ\,\Box_w\,\Psi \wedge \bullet\top) \wedge \bullet\top \subseteq \circ(\Psi \vee (\circ\,\Box_w\,\Psi \wedge \bullet\top)) \wedge \bullet\top,$$

from the second unrolling we deduce the configurations
  * matching $\bullet\top$ (i.e., having next configurations) and
  * with all their next configurations matching ψ (i.e., matching $\circ\psi$)
  match $\Box_w\Psi$ as well (i.e., $(\circ\psi \wedge \bullet\top) \subseteq \Box_w\Psi$);
- ...

Since $\Box_w\Psi$ is defined as a greatest fixpoint, it is the biggest set satisfying the above properties, i.e., the infinite executions match $\Box_w\Psi$ as well.

An *one path reachability pattern* is a pattern of the form $\varphi \to \Diamond_w\Psi$ and express the following property: for all concrete configurations matching φ *there is an execution* that reaches a configuration matching Ψ or is infinite. An *all path reachability pattern* $\varphi \to \Box_w\Psi$ expresses the following property: for any concrete configuration γ matching φ, *any execution* starting from γ reaches a configuration matching Ψ or is infinite. Here are two simple examples of valid all path reachability patterns:

$$\langle \text{while (x > 0) x = x-1;} \rangle \langle x \mapsto \$x \rangle \wedge \$x > 3 \to \Box_w \langle \cdot \rangle \langle x \mapsto 0 \rangle$$
$$\langle \text{while (true) \{\}} \rangle \langle x \mapsto \$x \rangle \to \Box_w \langle \cdot \rangle \langle x \mapsto 0 \rangle$$

5   Implementation of the Verification Process

The reachability properties we want to check, called from now on *proof obligations*, have the form

$$\forall vs.\ \langle code \rangle\, \langle \sigma[vs/xs] \rangle \wedge \phi \to \Box_w \exists \sigma'.\ \langle . \rangle\, \langle \sigma' \rangle \wedge \psi$$

where vs is a list of symbolic values, xs a list of program variables of the same length as vs, and the rest of notations is as usual. The above pattern actually says that the execution of *code* starting in a initial state satisfying ϕ either is finite and reaches at the end a state satisfying ψ or it is infinite. This is similar to partial correctness if ϕ is the precondition and ψ is the postcondition.

5.1   Deriving Reachability Patterns from Annotations

In this section we show how proof obligations, expressed as reachability patterns, can be generated from annotations. We consider only the cases of algorithm contracts and of loop invariants.

Algorithm Contracts. If an algorithm is described as an Alk function, then we may specify a contract for it using the following syntax (which is very similar to the one used for verification):

```
f(ips out ops) uses igps modifies mgps
@requires φ
@ensures ψ
code
```

where ips is the list of the "call-by-value" (input) parameters, out ops the list of parameters defined outside the function, uses $igps$ the set of the global variables used in the function body and not modified, and modifies $mgps$ the list of global variable used and modified by the function body.

Such a contract generates the following proof obligation:

$$\forall ivs.\,\forall ovs.\,\forall igvs.\,\forall mgvs.\,\langle code \rangle \,\langle \sigma_f \rangle \wedge \phi[\sigma_f] \rightarrow \Box_w \exists \sigma'.\,\langle . \rangle \,\langle \sigma' \rangle \wedge \phi' \wedge (\phi' \rightarrow \psi_f[\sigma, \sigma'])$$

where

- $\sigma_f \equiv ips \mapsto ivs \wedge ops \mapsto ovs \wedge igps \mapsto igvs \wedge mgps \mapsto mgvs$ is the state that initializes all the parameters and the involved global variables with fresh symbolic values,
- $\psi_f[\sigma, \sigma'] \equiv \psi \wedge \left(\bigwedge_{x \mapsto v \in old(\sigma)} x = v \right) \wedge \left(\bigwedge_{x \mapsto v \in \sigma'} x = v \right)$ is the matching logic pattern generated from the postcondition ψ, the initial state σ and the final state σ', and
- $old(\sigma)$ is obtained from σ by renaming variables x by \old$(x)$.

Note that the precondition ϕ and the postcondition ψ are given using Alk program variables.

Loop Invariant. Loop invariants are also important in understanding the behavior of the algorithms. A loop invariant is specified in Alk language as usual:

```
while (E)
  @modifies bxs
  @invariant ψ
  body
```

and it generates the following proof obligation:

$$\forall bvs.\,\langle body \rangle \,\langle \sigma[bvs/bxs] \rangle \,\langle \phi \wedge \psi \wedge E \rangle \rightarrow \Box_w \exists \sigma'.\,\langle . \rangle \,\langle \sigma' \rangle \,\langle \psi \rangle$$

where bxs is the list of variables modified by $body$, bvs is a list of fresh symbolic values of the same size as bxs. The list of variables bxs can be computed by data-flow analysis or specified using the @modifies clause.

5.2   Proving Reachability Patterns by Symbolic Execution

In this section we show that the proof obligations, expressed as matching logic patterns and generated from the annotated algorithms, can be proved using symbolic execution.

We first consider three new statements @havoc xs;, @assert ψ;, and @assume ψ; with the following semantics:

$$\langle \text{@havoc } xs; \rightsquigarrow \kappa \rangle \langle \sigma \rangle \rightarrow \bullet \langle \kappa \rangle \langle \sigma[vs/xs] \rangle$$
$$\langle \text{@assert } \psi; \rightsquigarrow \kappa \rangle \langle \sigma \rangle \wedge \psi \rightarrow \bullet \langle \kappa \rangle \langle \sigma \rangle$$
$$\langle \text{@assume } \psi; \rightsquigarrow \kappa \rangle \langle \sigma \rangle \rightarrow \bullet \langle \kappa \rangle \langle \sigma \rangle \wedge \psi$$

where xs is a list of program variables, vs is a list of fresh symbolic variables of the same length as xs, and $\sigma[vs/xs]$ is σ, excepting the variables from xs that are mapped to their corresponding new symbolic values from vs. This kind of statements are used by almost all verification tools.

We also consider two new rules handling the use of the annotated Alk code. A call of a function with a contract @requires ϕ @ensures ψ no longer execute the function body statements, but it "executes" its contract:

$$\langle F(VS) \rightsquigarrow \kappa \rangle \langle \sigma \rangle \rightarrow \bullet \left\langle \begin{array}{l} \text{@assert } \phi; \\ \text{@havoc}(MGV, IGV, OP, \backslash result); \\ \text{@assume } \psi; \\ \backslash result \rightsquigarrow \kappa \end{array} \right\rangle \langle \sigma \rangle$$

The source of inspiration for this rule is circular coinduction, which allows the use of proving goals as axioms in a sound way [21,25]. Firstly, the precondition ϕ is checked using @assert, then the symbolic execution continues from a state where the variables which are to be changed in the function body are assigned to fresh symbolic values and constrained by the post-conditions ψ (using @assume). Similarly, a loop annotated with a loop invariant is symbolically executed using its proof obligation as axiom:

$$\left\langle \begin{array}{l} \text{while } (E) \\ \quad \text{@invariant } \psi; \\ \quad S \rightsquigarrow \kappa \end{array} \right\rangle \langle \sigma \rangle \rightarrow \bullet \left\langle \begin{array}{l} \text{@assert } \psi; \\ \text{@havoc}(MV); \\ \text{@assume } \psi \wedge \neg E; \rightsquigarrow \kappa \end{array} \right\rangle \langle \sigma \rangle$$

where MV is the set of variables modified by the loop body.

Let $PrOb(A)$ denote the proof obligations generated form the annotated algorithm A.

Theorem 1 (Soundness). *If for each*

$$\forall vs. \langle code \rangle \langle \sigma[vs/xs] \rangle \wedge \phi \rightarrow \Box_w \exists \sigma'. \langle . \rangle \langle \sigma' \rangle \wedge \psi$$

in $PrOb(A)$ we have

$$\left\langle \begin{array}{l} \text{@havoc } xs; \\ \text{@assume } \phi; \\ code \\ \text{@assert } \psi; \end{array} \right\rangle \langle \cdot \rangle \Rightarrow^\forall \langle \cdot \rangle \langle \_ \rangle$$

then ALKSEM $\models PrOb(A)$, *where* $c \Rightarrow^\forall c'$ *denotes all complete symbolic execution paths starting from* c *must end in* c'.

The proof of Theorem 1 is by circular induction [21]. Actually, the symbolic executions, all together, build a proof-tree.

5.3   Implementation

The current implementation of the Alk platform includes an interpreter, a debugger, a symbolic execution engine, and VS Code extension. The Alk interpreter allows the user to test the algorithms written in the Alk language. The symbolic execution engine is implemented based on the theoretical approach described in this paper.

An integration with Z3 [12] is done in order to allow the reasoning in theory VAL. The path conditions translated from the Alk syntax to Z3 are following the guidelines of non-native Z3 equivalences, especially for arrays. This is mainly because Alk enables abstract types and expressions which are too specific to trivially map into the Z3 models.

For example, consider that Alk allows built-in methods and operators for arrays (`size`), lists (`pushBack`, `popFront`, etc.) or sets (`insert`, union, etc.). These are modeled using "Extended Z3 Array" [22] in an uniform manner. Other challenges were faced when dealing with the dynamic resizing of arrays.

The patterns describing the semantics of the Alk language are implemented by rewriting as it is described in Sect. 3.2. Each symbolic execution step can be seen as a proof of an implication between the corresponding patterns. In the end, if all the symbolic executions are successfully terminated, the implications proved by them can be combined into a proof of the goal generated from annotations, using the methods described, e.g., in [21,25].

Further Work. The implementation reached a stable state in which complex conditions and even some well-known algorithms can be analysed within seconds. However, the implementation may require a better integration with supporting back-ends or verifiers like Boogie [19]. A data-flow analysis [17] for inferring information needed for analysis, like the type of variables, the variables modified by a loop, the initialization of the complex data structures, is also planned.

6   Related Work

Having a single formal framework for expressing the definition of a programming language and the properties of its programs was the leading idea of the K Framework project (https://kframework.org/). Matching logic was developed as a theoretical foundation for the K Framework and it includes several versions [8–10,23,24], reflecting the main progress steps. In this paper we used that described in [8,9]. The first version of Alk was written in K Framework (https://github.com/alk-language/k-semantics). The current version is written in Java, following the K and matching logic principles.

The idea of using assertions for expressing properties of algorithms/programs was introduced by Floyd [14] and Hoare [15]. In this paper we showed how these assertions can generate matching logic patterns, which are then checked by symbolic execution. The language used for assertions is the usual one used by program verifiers, e.g., Dafny [20], Boogie [19],Why3 [5], Frama-C [18], JML [16], Key [1], Verifast [26], etc. However, Alk uses a minimal set of annotations since the focus is the algorithm understanding and not full verification. The symbolic execution engine was developed using the approach presented in [4,21]. The main principles based on Alk was designed are presented in [2]. In this paper we supply the matching logic foundation of the Alk platform.

7 Conclusion

The Alk educational platform is envisioned as a base technology for algorithm design and reasoning. In order to reach this goal, it must be based on a simple, solid, and rigorous foundation. In this paper, we showed that the matching logic is the most suitable for this purpose. We showed that the Alk semantics, the behavioral properties of algorithms written in Alk, and the analyzing tools available, can be uniformly described within matching logic. The implementation of the platform was given following this approach.

Alk also allows describing probabilistic algorithms. In future, we intend to investigate if the matching logic can be used, or it needs to be extended in order to allow the analysis of this kind of algorithms.

References

1. Ahrendt, W., Beckert, B., Bubel, R., Hähnle, R., Schmitt, P.H., Ulbrich, M. (eds.): Deductive Software Verification - The KeY Book - From Theory to Practice. LNCS, vol. 10001. Springer, Cham (2016). https://doi.org/10.1007/978-3-319-49812-6
2. Alexandru-Ioan, L., Lucanu, D.: Supporting algorithm analysis with symbolic execution in ALK. In: Aït-Ameur, Y., Craciun, F. (eds.) TASE 2022. LNCS, vol. 13299, pp. 406–423. Springer, Cham (2022). https://doi.org/10.1007/978-3-031-10363-6_27
3. Arusoaie, A., Lucanu, D.: Unification in matching logic. In: ter Beek, M.H., McIver, A., Oliveira, J.N. (eds.) FM 2019. LNCS, vol. 11800, pp. 502–518. Springer, Cham (2019). https://doi.org/10.1007/978-3-030-30942-8_30
4. Arusoaie, A., Lucanu, D., Rusu, V.: A generic framework for symbolic execution. In: Erwig, M., Paige, R.F., Van Wyk, E. (eds.) SLE 2013. LNCS, vol. 8225, pp. 281–301. Springer, Cham (2013). https://doi.org/10.1007/978-3-319-02654-1_16
5. Bobot, F., Filliâtre, J.-C., Marché, C., Paskevich, A.: Let's verify this with why3. Int. J. Softw. Tools Technol. Transf. **17**(6), 709–727 (2015)
6. Chen, X., Lin, Z., Trinh, M.-T., Roşu, G.: Towards a trustworthy semantics-based language framework via proof generation. In: Silva, A., Leino, K.R.M. (eds.) CAV 2021. LNCS, vol. 12760, pp. 477–499. Springer, Cham (2021). https://doi.org/10.1007/978-3-030-81688-9_23
7. Chen, X., Lucanu, D., Roşu, G.: Initial algebra semantics in matching logic. Technical report, University of Illinois at Urbana-Champaign, July 2020. submitted. http://hdl.handle.net/2142/107781

8. Chen, X., Lucanu, D., Roşu, G.: Matching logic explained. J. Log. Algebr. Methods Program. **120**, 100638 (2021)
9. Chen, X., Roşu, G.: Applicative matching logic. Technical report, University of Illinois at Urbana-Champaign, July 2019. http://hdl.handle.net/2142/104616
10. Chen, X., Roşu, G.: Matching mu-logic. In: Proceedings of the 34th Annual ACM/IEEE Symposium on Logic in Computer Science (LICS 2019) (2019, to appear)
11. Chen, X., Rosu, G.: SETSS'19 lecture notes on K. In: Bowen, J., Liu, Z. (eds.) Engineering Trustworthy Software Systems. LNCS, Springer, Cham (2019)
12. de Moura, L., Bjørner, N.: Z3: an efficient SMT solver. In: Ramakrishnan, C.R., Rehof, J. (eds.) TACAS 2008. LNCS, vol. 4963, pp. 337–340. Springer, Heidelberg (2008). https://doi.org/10.1007/978-3-540-78800-3_24
13. Floyd, R.W.: Nondeterministic algorithms. J. ACM **14**(4), 636–644 (1967)
14. Floyd, R.W.: Assigning meanings to programs. In: Colburn, T.R., Fetzer, J.H., Rankin, T.L. (eds.) Program Verification. Studies in Cognitive Systems, vol. 14, pp. 65–81. Springer, Dordrecht (1993). https://doi.org/10.1007/978-94-011-1793-7_4
15. Hoare, C.A.R.: An axiomatic basis for computer programming. Commun. ACM **12**(10), 576–580 (1969)
16. Huisman, M., Ahrendt, W., Grahl, D., Hentschel, M.: Formal specification with the java modeling language. In: Ahrendt, W., Beckert, B., Bubel, R., Hahnle, R., Schmitt, P., Ulbrich, M. (eds.) Deductive Software Verification – The KeY Book. LNCS, vol. 10001, pp. 193–241. Springer, Cham (2016). https://doi.org/10.1007/978-3-319-49812-6_7
17. Khedker, U.P., Sanyal, A., Karkare, B.: Data Flow Analysis - Theory and Practice. CRC Press, Boca Raton (2009)
18. Kosmatov, N., Signoles, J.: Frama-C, A collaborative framework for C code verification: tutorial synopsis. In: Falcone, Y., Sánchez, C. (eds.) RV 2016. LNCS, vol. 10012, pp. 92–115. Springer, Cham (2016). https://doi.org/10.1007/978-3-319-46982-9_7
19. Leino, K.R.M.: This is boogie 2. manuscript KRML **178**(131), 9 (2008)
20. Leino, K.R.M.: Dafny: an automatic program verifier for functional correctness. In: Clarke, E.M., Voronkov, A. (eds.) LPAR 2010. LNCS (LNAI), vol. 6355, pp. 348–370. Springer, Heidelberg (2010). https://doi.org/10.1007/978-3-642-17511-4_20
21. Lucanu, D., Rusu, V., Arusoaie, A.: A generic framework for symbolic execution: a coinductive approach. J. Symb. Comput. **80**, 125–163 (2017)
22. Alexandru-Ioan, L.: Extended z3 array. In: 23th International Symposium on Symbolic and Numeric Algorithms for Scientific Computing (FROM Workshop), SYNASC 2021. IEEE (2021, to appear)
23. Roşu, G.: Matching logic. Log. Methods Comput. Sci. **13**(4), 1–61 (2017)
24. Roşu, G., Ellison, C., Schulte, W.: Matching logic: an alternative to Hoare/Floyd logic. In: Johnson, M., Pavlovic, D. (eds.) AMAST 2010. LNCS, vol. 6486, pp. 142–162. Springer, Heidelberg (2011). https://doi.org/10.1007/978-3-642-17796-5_9
25. Stefanescu, A., Ciobâcă, Ş., Mereuta, R., Moore, B.M., Serbanuta, T.-F., Rosu, G.: All-path reachability logic. Log. Methods Comput. Sci. **15**(2) (2019)
26. Vogels, F., Jacobs, B., Piessens, F.: Featherweight verifast. Log. Methods Comput. Sci. **11**(3) (2015)

A Type System with Subtyping
for WebAssembly's Stack Polymorphism

Dylan McDermott[1], Yasuaki Morita[1]([✉]), and Tarmo Uustalu[1,2]

[1] Department of Computer Science, Reykjavik University, Reykjavik, Iceland
{dylanm,yasuaki20,tarmo}@ru.is
[2] Department of Software Science, Tallinn University of Technology, Tallinn, Estonia

Abstract. We propose a new type system for WebAssembly. It is a refinement of the type system from the language specification and is based on type qualifiers and subtyping. In the WebAssembly specification, a typable instruction sequence gets many different types, depending in particular on whether it contains instructions such as **br** (unconditional branch) that are stack-polymorphic in an unusual way. But one cannot single out a canonical type for a typable instruction sequence satisfactorily. We introduce qualifiers on code types to distinguish between the two flavors of stack polymorphism that occur in WebAssembly and a subtyping relation on such qualified types. Our type system gives every typable instruction sequence a canonical type that is principal. We show that the new type system is in a precise relationship to the type system given in the WebAssembly specification. In addition, we describe a typed functional-style big-step semantics based on this new type system underpinned by an indexed graded monad and prove that it prevents stack-manipulation related runtime errors. We have formalized our type system, inference algorithm, and semantics in Agda.

1 Introduction

WebAssembly (Wasm) [10] is a statically typed, stack-oriented bytecode language. Wasm has been designed with a formal semantics [2]. Watt [15] formalized the type system, the type checker, the small-step semantics and a proof of type soundness in Isabelle. Later, Wasm 1.0 became a W3C Recommendation [14], and Huang [3] and Watt et al. [17] came with formalizations in Coq. As type soundness gives safety, Wasm's type system plays a significant role in its semantics.

A key feature of the type system of Wasm is that it tracks how the stack shape evolves in program execution. Stacks are typed by their shapes, which are lists of value types. A piece of code is typed by a pair of stack types, an argument type and a result type. In Wasm, most instructions are typed monomorphically with their (net) stack effect, i.e., types for the portions of stack they pop and push. Instructions for unconditional control transfer like **br** however are typed differently, polymorphically and in an unusual way. Instruction sequences are typed polymorphically (in particular one cannot read off from the type how

H. Seidl et al. (Eds.): ICTAC 2022, LNCS 13572, pp. 305–323, 2022.
https://doi.org/10.1007/978-3-031-17715-6_20

long a prefix of the initial stack is actually touched) and typing of instruction sequences involving **br** becomes subtle.

In this paper, we analyze the stack polymorphism of the type system of Wasm in detail on a minimalistic fragment of the language. We first introduce a type system (Dir) that uniformizes the typing of instructions and instruction sequences making both stack-polymorphic in an adequate sense. Dir stands in a precise relationship to the type system of the language specification (which we call Spec); in particular instruction sequences get exactly the same types. Then we refine this type system to another one (which we call Sub) that has subtyping and equips all instructions and instruction sequences, notably **br** and instruction sequences involving **br**, with canonical types in the form of principal types. We achieve this by introducing the distinction between ordinary ("univariate") stack polymorphism (in the type of the untouched suffix of the stack) from the unusual "bivariate" stack polymorphism of Wasm characteristic to **br** and instruction sequences involving it. The two type systems Dir and Sub have a different status: Dir is a minor variant of Spec, which we introduce as a first step toward Sub; Sub is the main type system of our interest. On top of Sub, we build a typed big-step operational semantics in which run-time errors cannot occur. We also define an untyped big-step semantics that agrees with this typed semantics on typed programs when invoked on initial stacks that the typed semantics accepts.

Our type system and type inference algorithm with their properties and the typed and untyped big-step semantics have been formalized in Agda; the development is available at https://github.com/moritayasuaki/wasm-types.

2   A Small Fragment of Wasm

For the sake of simplicity, we work with a minimalistic fragment of Wasm. The syntax of the language is given in Fig. 1. A piece of code in this language is either an instruction or an instruction sequence.

$$
\begin{array}{rll}
a, r, m, d, e \;\in\; \mathbb{N} & & \text{stack types (called result types in the spec.)} \\
t ::= a \to r & & \text{code types (called stack types in the spec.)} \\
\ell \;\in\; \mathbb{N} & & \text{label indices} \\
z \;\in\; \mathbb{Z}_{32} & & \text{32-bit integers} \\
uop ::= \textbf{eqz} \mid \ldots & & \text{unary numeric operations} \\
bop ::= \textbf{add} \mid \ldots & & \text{binary numeric operations} \\
i ::= \textbf{const}\; z \mid uop \mid bop & & \text{numeric instructions} \\
\quad\mid\; \textbf{block}_t\; is\; \textbf{end} \mid \textbf{loop}_t\; is\; \textbf{end} & & \text{block-like instructions} \\
\quad\mid\; \textbf{br\_if}\; \ell \mid \textbf{br}\; \ell & & \text{branch instructions} \\
is ::= \varepsilon \mid is\; i & & \text{instruction sequences} \\
c ::= i \mid is & & \text{code}
\end{array}
$$

Fig. 1. Syntax of reduced Wasm

Since our focus is on stack manipulation and typing thereof, we have left out all unrelated aspects of Wasm, even the linear memory; also we do not have functions. To keep the presentation as clean as possible, we do not even have multiple value types. Of Wasm's value types **i32**, **i64**, **f32**, **f64** etc., we have kept only one, **i32**. A stack type in Wasm is a list of value types. Since in our reduced language, there is just one value type, a stack type boils down to a natural number for the height of the stack. With this simplification, issues such as values of the wrong type in the stack and value-polymorphism (of, e.g., the **drop** instruction) disappear. Having just numbers as stack types is arguably a significant simplification. Still all phenomena we want to discuss are maintained; we have verified that the arguments in this paper scale to lists of value types as stack types by replacing the total order on natural numbers by the (prefix) partial order on lists. The possibility of value-type mismatch then leads to partiality of the central operations on stack types and code types that are total in this paper.

There are three main categories of instructions—numeric, block-like and branch instructions—, and execution of each instruction is defined in the same way as in [2,10]. A numeric instruction pops some arguments from the current local stack (the global stack or the local stack of the closest encompassing block-like instruction), performs the corresponding operation, and pushes the result.

A block-like instruction **block** or **loop** type-annotated with $a \rightarrow r$ pops a values ("arguments") from the current local stack, constructs its own local stack containing these arguments, and executes the inner instruction sequence on this new local stack as current. If this terminates normally, there must be r values ("results") left on this local stack. The local stack is then destroyed and the r values are pushed to the parent local stack, which becomes current.

The unconditional branch instruction **br** ℓ is a jump instruction targeting either the end or the beginning of the ℓ-th encompassing block-like instruction depending on whether it is a block or a loop. If the type annotation on this instruction is $a \rightarrow r$, then, before the jump, r resp. a values are popped from the current local stack, the local stacks of enclosing block-like instructions up to the jump target are emptied and destroyed, the local stack of the jump target is emptied and the r or a values are pushed to it, and it becomes current. The conditional branch instruction **br_if** ℓ behaves similarly except that it consumes the top of the current local stack as a condition.

Type System

Figure 2 shows the typing rules of our chosen subset of Wasm. This type system matches the Wasm specification, and we call this type system Spec.

Typing judgements for instructions i and instruction sequences is have similar forms $rs \vdash^I i : a \rightarrow r$ and $rs \vdash^S is : a \rightarrow r$ where the code type $a \rightarrow r$ describes in both cases in some way (which we will discuss in detail) the stack effect of i or is in terms of a pair of stack types: the shapes of the local stack before (a, for "arguments") and after (r, for "results") a possible execution. The typing context rs, which is a list of stack types, records the result resp. argument types

$$\frac{}{rs \vdash^{\mathsf{I}} \mathbf{const}\, z : 0 \to 1}\ \text{Const} \qquad \frac{}{rs \vdash^{\mathsf{I}} uop : 1 \to 1}\ \text{Uop} \qquad \frac{}{rs \vdash^{\mathsf{I}} bop : 2 \to 1}\ \text{Bop}$$

$$\frac{r :: rs \vdash^{\mathsf{S}} is : a \to r}{rs \vdash^{\mathsf{I}} \mathbf{block}_{a \to r}\, is\, \mathbf{end} : a \to r}\ \text{Block} \qquad \frac{a :: rs \vdash^{\mathsf{S}} is : a \to r}{rs \vdash^{\mathsf{I}} \mathbf{loop}_{a \to r}\, is\, \mathbf{end} : a \to r}\ \text{Loop}$$

$$\frac{rs \,!!\, \ell = r}{rs \vdash^{\mathsf{I}} \mathbf{br\_if}\, \ell : 1 + r \to r}\ \text{Br\_if} \qquad \frac{rs \,!!\, \ell = r}{rs \vdash^{\mathsf{I}} \mathbf{br}\, \ell : r + d \to e}\ \text{Br}$$

$$\frac{}{rs \vdash^{\mathsf{S}} \varepsilon : a \to a}\ \text{Empty} \qquad \frac{rs \vdash^{\mathsf{S}} is : a \to m + d \quad rs \vdash^{\mathsf{I}} i : m \to r}{rs \vdash^{\mathsf{S}} is\, i : a \to r + d}\ \text{Seq}$$

Fig. 2. Typing rules of type system Spec, following the specification of Wasm

of the **block** or **loop** instructions encompassing i or is, in the inside-out order. We write $rs \,!!\, \ell$ for the ℓ-th element of rs ($\ell < |rs|$).

In this type system, every instruction except for **br** gets a unique code type (if it gets one at all). For numeric instructions, the meaning of this type is clear: $a \to r$ reflects the numbers of arguments and results of the operation, the numbers of elements popped from and pushed onto the stack. The type of **br_if** ℓ according to the rule BR_IF also reflects the operational semantics: **br_if** ℓ pops the top of the stack as a condition and then pops $r (= rs \,!!\, \ell)$ next elements additionally if this condition is non-zero (true). The argument type of **br_if** ℓ is therefore $1 + r$. Although **br_if** ℓ terminates abnormally by a jump in this case (thereby not posing any requirement on the result type), the same r next elements remain on the stack if the condition is zero (false). Therefore, the result type must be r since the code type must cover both cases; in the false case, we have to pretend that $1 + r$ elements are popped and the r last of those are pushed back (even if in reality only one element is popped and none pushed). We postpone a discussion of **br** ℓ.

In contrast, every instruction sequence gets many code types. For instance, the empty sequence ε in EMPTY gets code types $a \to a$ for any natural number a. If we take 0 for a, then it becomes $0 \to 0$. This choice can be called the tightest because the empty sequence consumes and produces nothing on the stack. The rule also allows us to choose $a = 1$. It is natural to think of the empty sequence as the identity function on the stack. However, the type $1 \to 1$ no longer tells us that the value at the top of the stack remains unchanged. In such a sense, we would say $\varepsilon : 1 \to 1$ is a reasonable typing but loose in comparison to $\varepsilon : 0 \to 0$. Though the specification does not give a specific term for this phenomenon, we call it *univariate stack polymorphism*, or simply, *univariate polymorphism* (as opposed to bivariate polymorphism, discussed below).[1] Univariate polymorphism allows code types to be loosened by adding the *same* number to both the argument and result type corresponding to an untouched part of the local stack.

The premises of the typing rule SEQ for the sequencing $is\, i$ of is and i require the result type $m + d$ of is to be at least the argument type m of i. This rule

---

[1] We use the term 'stack polymorphism' in the sense of Morrisett et al. [6], viz. polymorphism of stack functions in the type of the untouched part of the stack.

can be intuitively motivated relying on univariate polymorphism of instructions (which Spec does not have, but which is semantically justified). First, we think of the type $m + d \rightarrow r + d$ as a loosened version of the type $m \rightarrow r$ of i, although no typing rules allow us to give i this type officially. Since this loosening has made the types at the middle equal (the result type of is and the argument type of i have both become $m + d$), we can consider that the argument type a of is and the result type $r + d$ of i form a type for the sequence $is\,i$.

We notice that an instruction i and the singleton instruction sequence i (i.e., $\varepsilon\,i$) are not treated the same way in Spec. For example, **const** 17 as an instruction only has type $0 \rightarrow 1$ in any context, but as an instruction sequence it has the type $d \rightarrow 1 + d$ for any d (since ε admits the type $d \rightarrow d$).

Bivariate Stack Polymorphism

Although **br** ℓ is operationally the same as (**const** 1) (**br_if** ℓ), it has different characteristics in the type system (which does not involve any constant propagation analysis). The rule BR assigns many types to the instruction **br** ℓ: the d and e in the conclusion are arbitrary natural numbers. This is a big difference from the other instructions, which all get at most one type. Although the Wasm specification takes *stack polymorphism* to mean only this phenomenon, we will refer to it more specifically as *bivariate stack polymorphism*, or simply *bivariate polymorphism*, since d and e are independent metavariables for stack types. The natural intuition "code type = local stack type before and after" is no longer useful, since an execution of **br** cannot terminate normally at "after"; the next instructions in an encompassing block-like instruction or the end of it are never reached. Thanks to bivariate polymorphism, it is possible to place any instruction immediately after **br**, and this instruction will be unreachable code. In [2], an example of the use of bivariate stack polymorphism in compilers is discussed.

Typing of unreachable code is quite subtle in this type system. For example, the following instruction sequence is not typable when $r = 0$ and is typable when $r \geq 1$, even though the instruction **const** 17 and the end of the **loop** are unreachable:

$$\text{block}_{0 \rightarrow 0}\ \text{loop}_{0 \rightarrow r}\ (\text{br}\ 1)\ (\text{const}\ 17)\ \text{end}\ (\text{br}\ 0)\ \text{end}$$

We notice that the design of Spec is uneven in that **br** and instruction sequences are stack-polymorphic, but instructions other than **br** are not. For consistency, they should all be stack-polymorphic. The rules for sequencing "fix" this discrepancy—or cover it up, depending on how one looks at this. In the next section, we introduce a variant type system Dir, which remedies this issue.

3   Type System **Dir** with "Direct" Sequential Composition

The typing rules of the type system Dir are given in Fig. 3. They give many types not only to **br**, but also to other single instructions. The typing rule in Dir loosens the type assigned to an instruction by Spec by adding any natural number d to both the argument and result types. For the bivariate polymorphic instruction **br**, the typing rule is as in Spec. In other words, Dir has stack polymorphism (univariate or bivariate) for all instructions. The rule for sequencing is "direct": it only admits the case where the result type of is and the argument type of i coincide. This is fine now since all instructions have become stack-polymorphic.

$$\frac{}{rs \vdash \text{const } z : d \to 1 + d}\ \text{CONST} \qquad \frac{}{rs \vdash uop : 1 + d \to 1 + d}\ \text{UOP} \qquad \frac{}{rs \vdash bop : 2 + d \to 1 + d}\ \text{BOP}$$

$$\frac{r :: rs \vdash is : a \to r}{rs \vdash \text{block}_{a \to r}\ is\ \text{end} : a + d \to r + d}\ \text{BLOCK} \qquad \frac{a :: rs \vdash is : a \to r}{rs \vdash \text{loop}_{a \to r}\ is\ \text{end} : a + d \to r + d}\ \text{LOOP}$$

$$\frac{rs\ !!\ \ell = r}{rs \vdash \text{br\_if } \ell : 1 + r + d \to r + d}\ \text{BR\_IF} \qquad \frac{rs\ !!\ \ell = r}{rs \vdash \text{br } \ell : r + d \to e}\ \text{BR}$$

$$\frac{}{rs \vdash \varepsilon : r \to r}\ \text{EMPTY} \qquad \frac{rs \vdash is : a \to m \quad rs \vdash i : m \to r}{rs \vdash is\ i : a \to r}\ \text{SEQ}$$

Fig. 3. Typing rules in the type system Dir

For single instructions, Dir gives more valid types than Spec does. For example, $rs \vdash \text{const } 17 : d \to 1 + d$ in Dir, but in Spec, only $rs \vdash^{\mathsf{I}} \text{const } 17 : 0 \to 1$ can be derived. (But also recall that Spec does derive $rs \vdash^{\mathsf{S}} \text{const } 17 : d \to 1 + d$: for instruction sequences the two type systems give the same types.)

For an instruction to have a type in Dir, it must be typable also in Spec, but the argument and result type may be smaller by some same d. An instruction sequence has exactly the same types in Dir and Spec.

Theorem 1 (Dir vs. Spec).

$$rs \vdash_{\mathsf{Dir}} i : a \to r \iff (\exists d, a', r'.\ a = a' + d \land r = r' + d \land rs \vdash^{\mathsf{I}}_{\mathsf{Spec}} i : a' \to r')$$

$$rs \vdash_{\mathsf{Dir}} is : a \to r \iff rs \vdash^{\mathsf{S}}_{\mathsf{Spec}} is : a \to r$$

Proof. ($\Longrightarrow$) By mutual induction on the derivation trees of $rs \vdash_{\mathsf{Dir}} i : a \to r$ and $rs \vdash_{\mathsf{Dir}} is : a \to r$.

($\Longleftarrow$) We replace the backwards implication of the statement for i with the equivalent property that

$$(\forall d.\ rs \vdash_{\mathsf{Dir}} i : a + d \to r + d) \Longleftarrow rs \vdash^{\mathsf{I}}_{\mathsf{Spec}} i : a \to r$$

and then proceed by mutual induction on the derivation trees of $rs \vdash_{\mathsf{Spec}} i : a \to r$ and $rs \vdash_{\mathsf{Spec}} is : a \to r$.

The type system Dir is free of some of the problems of Spec: both instructions and instruction sequences get all types they should reasonably get. However, there is no satisfactory canonical type among them in all cases. Instructions other than **br** and the empty sequence do have principal types under the (unstated, but conceivable) subtyping relation induced by the inequation $a \to r <:$

$$\frac{}{a \to_{\text{bi}} r <: a + d \to_q r + e} \text{ SUBT}_{\text{bi}} \qquad \frac{}{a \to_{\text{uni}} r <: a + d \to_{\text{uni}} r + d} \text{ SUBT}_{\text{uni}}$$

$$\frac{}{rs \vdash \text{const } z : 0 \to_{\text{uni}} 1} \text{ CONST} \qquad \frac{}{rs \vdash uop : 1 \to_{\text{uni}} 1} \text{ UOP} \qquad \frac{}{rs \vdash bop : 2 \to_{\text{uni}} 1} \text{ BOP}$$

$$\frac{r :: rs \vdash is : a \to_{\text{uni}} r}{rs \vdash \text{block}_{a \to r} \text{ is end} : a \to_{\text{uni}} r} \text{ BLOCK} \qquad \frac{a :: rs \vdash is : a \to_{\text{uni}} r}{rs \vdash \text{loop}_{a \to r} \text{ is end} : a \to_{\text{uni}} r} \text{ LOOP}$$

$$\frac{rs \,!!\, \ell = r}{rs \vdash \text{br\_if } \ell : 1 + r \to_{\text{uni}} r} \text{ BR\_IF} \qquad \frac{rs \,!!\, \ell = r}{rs \vdash \text{br } \ell : r \to_{\text{bi}} 0} \text{ BR}$$

$$\frac{}{rs \vdash \varepsilon : 0 \to_{\text{uni}} 0} \text{ EMPTY} \qquad \frac{rs \vdash is : a \to_q m \quad rs \vdash i : m \to_{q'} r}{rs \vdash is\, i : a \to_{q \sqcap q'} r} \text{ SEQ}$$

$$\frac{rs \vdash c : t' \quad t' <: t}{rs \vdash c : t} \text{ SUBS}$$

Fig. 4. Subtyping and typing rules in the type system Sub

$a + d \to r + d$, which can be justified by the fact that in Dir $rs \vdash c : a \to r$ implies $rs \vdash c : a + d \to r + d$ for any piece of code c. But **br** and general instruction sequences (specifically those containing **br**) do not have such principal types. We will now improve on this and introduce a type system Sub where even **br** and instruction sequences have principal types.

4 Type System **Sub** with Qualifiers and Subtyping

We introduce two qualifiers uni and bi (for "univariate" and "bivariate", using q as a typical metavariable for these qualifiers), and a partial order $\leq$ on them:

$$\overline{\text{bi} \leq q} \qquad \overline{\text{uni} \leq \text{uni}}$$

In the type system Sub code types have the form $a \to_q r$; the qualifier q specifies whether the code is univariately or bivariately stack-polymorphic. Code types are ordered by a subtyping relation $<:$, defined by the top two rules of Fig. 4.

The remainder of Fig. 4 consists of the typing rules of Sub. All instructions except **br** are assigned a uni-type by their typing rule; **br** gets a bi-type. This way, all single instructions including **br**, and the empty instruction sequence, get assigned their tightest type. The typing rule SEQ for sequencing is as in Dir, but the qualifier in the conclusion is the meet $\sqcap$ of the qualifiers in the premises. This operation is defined by uni $\sqcap$ uni = uni and $q \sqcap q' =$ bi otherwise. All looseness of typing is introduced by a subsumption rule SUBS that applies to both instructions and instruction sequences.

The uni-types assigned to a piece of code by Sub are precisely the types assigned by Dir.

Proposition 1 (Sub vs. Dir, take 1).

$$rs \vdash_{\text{Sub}} c : a \to_{\text{uni}} r \iff rs \vdash_{\text{Dir}} c : a \to r$$

Proof. ($\Longrightarrow$) By induction on the derivation of $rs \vdash_{\mathsf{Sub}} c : a \to_{\mathsf{uni}} r$ (by which we mean mutual induction on the derivation of $rs \vdash_{\mathsf{Sub}} c : a \to_{\mathsf{uni}} r$ for the two cases i and is of c).

($\Longleftarrow$) By induction on the derivation in $rs \vdash_{\mathsf{Dir}} c : a \to r$.

To also describe the bi-types of a piece of code in Sub in terms of its types in Dir, we first show a lemma about bi-types.

Lemma 1.

$$rs \vdash_{\mathsf{Dir}} c : a{+}d \to r \wedge rs \vdash_{\mathsf{Dir}} c : a \to r{+}e \wedge (d > 0 \vee e > 0) \implies rs \vdash_{\mathsf{Sub}} c : a \to_{\mathsf{bi}} r$$

Proof. By induction on c.

For a piece of code to acquire a particular type in Sub, all of its uni-supertypes must type it in Dir (and so also in Spec in the case of an instruction sequence).

Theorem 2 (Sub vs. Dir).

$$rs \vdash_{\mathsf{Sub}} c : a_0 \to_q r_0 \quad \Longleftrightarrow \quad (\forall a, r.\, a_0 \to_q r_0 <: a \to_{\mathsf{uni}} r \implies rs \vdash_{\mathsf{Dir}} c : a \to r)$$

Proof. From Proposition 1 and Lemma 1.

Type Inference

We define a type inference algorithm for Sub. We prove this algorithm computes a principal type for a given piece of code c for a given type context rs, provided it is typable in that context at all, i.e., type inference computes a derivable type which is a subtype of every other derivable type.

The algorithm is defined as a function infer recursive on c (i.e., mutually recursive on the two cases of c being an instruction or an instruction sequence) in Fig. 5; the algorithm traverses c once, from left to right (depth-first left-first). Maybe$X$ is the disjoint sum $1{+}X$, with coprojections Nothing and Just. For every instruction, and for the empty sequence, the inferred type is the type from the conclusion of the typing rule. This is not the case for sequencing. For numeric instructions and the empty sequence ε, their typing rules give them one type and this is the type inferred. For a given context, the types of **br** and **br_if** are also determined uniquely, but differently from all other instructions **br** gets a bi-type. The types of **block** and **loop** are determined by the annotation, but the instruction sequence inside may fail to admit this type. For this reason, infer is called recursively on this sequence to check its compatibility with the annotation.

The inferred type for a sequence $is\, i$ is defined by an operation $\oplus$ on qualified code types. Firstly, to satisfy the premises of the rule SEQ, the operation $\oplus$ needs to reconcile the middle stack types m and m' of the inferred types $a \to_q m$ and $m' \to_{q'} r$ of is and i. The unified middle type is actually $\max(m, m')$,

$$\text{infer } c \; rs : \text{Maybe } CodeType$$

$$
\begin{aligned}
\text{infer } (\textbf{const } z) \; rs &= \text{Just}(0 \to_{\text{uni}} 1) \\
\text{infer } uop \; rs &= \text{Just}(1 \to_{\text{uni}} 1) \\
\text{infer } bop \; rs &= \text{Just}(2 \to_{\text{uni}} 1) \\
\text{infer } (\textbf{block}_{a \to r} \; is \; \textbf{end}) \; rs &= \text{do } tis \leftarrow \text{infer } is \; (r :: rs) \\
&\quad \text{if } tis <: a \to_{\text{uni}} r \text{ then Just}(a \to_{\text{uni}} r) \text{ else Nothing} \\
\text{infer } (\textbf{loop}_{a \to r} \; is \; \textbf{end}) \; rs &= \text{do } tis \leftarrow \text{infer } is \; (a :: rs) \\
&\quad \text{if } tis <: a \to_{\text{uni}} r \text{ then Just}(a \to_{\text{uni}} r) \text{ else Nothing} \\
\text{infer } (\textbf{br\_if } \ell) \; rs &= \text{if } \ell < |rs| \text{ then Just}((1 + rs \, !! \, \ell) \to_{\text{uni}} (rs \, !! \, \ell)) \text{ else Nothing} \\
\text{infer } (\textbf{br } \ell) \; rs &= \text{if } \ell < |rs| \text{ then Just}((rs \, !! \, \ell) \to_{\text{bi}} 0) \text{ else Nothing} \\[4pt]
\text{infer } \varepsilon \; rs &= \text{Just}(0 \to_{\text{uni}} 0) \\
\text{infer } (is :: i) \; rs &= \text{do } tis \leftarrow \text{infer } is \; rs \\
&\quad ti \leftarrow \text{infer } i \; rs \\
&\quad \text{Just}(tis \oplus ti)
\end{aligned}
$$

Fig. 5. Type inference for Sub

whatever q and q' are.[2] But the possible invocations of SUBS differ depending on q and q'. For example, if we have $rs \vdash is : a \to_{\text{bi}} m$, then we can achieve $rs \vdash is : a \to_{\text{bi}} \max(m, m')$, but if we have $rs \vdash is : a \to_{\text{uni}} m$, then we only get $rs \vdash is : a + (\max(m, m') - m) \to_{\text{uni}} \max(m, m')$. As a result of exactly the same thing happening for $rs \vdash i : m' \to_q r$, the operation $\oplus$ can be defined uniformly in the four cases of q, q' using the "monus" operation $m \,\dot{-}\, m' = \max(m, m') - m$ and its qualified version $m \,\dot{-}_{\text{uni}}\, m' = m \,\dot{-}\, m'$, $m \,\dot{-}_{\text{bi}}\, m' = 0$. We define

$$(a \to_q m) \oplus (m' \to_{q'} r) = a + (m' \,\dot{-}_q\, m) \to_{q \sqcap q'} r + (m \,\dot{-}_{q'}\, m')$$

The algorithm is sound and complete, i.e., the algorithm infers a type for a piece of code precisely when it is typable, and the inferred type is principal (derivable and a subtype of any other derivable type).

Theorem 3 (Soundness of type inference of Sub).

$$\text{infer } c \; rs = \text{Just } t \implies rs \vdash c : t$$

Proof. By induction on c.

Theorem 4 (Completeness of type inference of Sub).

$$rs \vdash c : t \implies (\exists t_0.\ \text{infer } c \; rs = \text{Just } t_0 \wedge t_0 <: t)$$

Proof. By induction on the derivation of $rs \vdash c : t$.

---

[2] The intermediate type $\max(m, m')$ here is always defined just because we have one value type and stack types are natural numbers. If we consider multiple value types, the stack types m and m' are no longer natural numbers but lists of value types. In this setting, the unified middle type is defined only if one of m and m' is a prefix of the other; when this is not the case, the instruction sequence is not typable.

Pomonoid

The set of code types of Sub, together with its subtyping relation $<:$, the element $0 \to_{\text{uni}} 0$ and the operation $\oplus$ form a *pomonoid* (a partially ordered monoid). This pomonoid is a generalization for the qualified case of the *stack effect pomonoid* first considered as such by Pöial [9] (see also [13]) and studied earlier in algebra as the *polycyclic monoid* (the inverse envelope of a free monoid) by Nivat and Perrin [8] (modulo the fact that we have replaced lists of value types as stack types by natural numbers, which gives the *bicyclic monoid*).[3]

That we get a pomonoid is very reasonable: it is reflects the expectation that sequential composition of two pieces of code should be associative (up to semantic equivalence) and have the empty code as the unit, also that it should not matter whether subsumption is applied to one of the two pieces of code or to the composition. (Notice though that in Wasm we have no syntactic operation of composition of two sequences of instructions.) We have a reason to return to this pomonoid structure in the next section.

5 Typed Big-Step Semantics Based on Sub

We now demonstrate Sub in action by building on it a typed functional-style big-step semantics (a denotational semantics)[4] of simplified Wasm.

The denotation of a typing derivation of a piece of code is a function that takes

- a natural number as a bound on the number of backjumps that can be made within the loops that this piece of code is encompassed by [5]
- and a list of integers as an initial local stack,

runs the code and returns either

- nothing if the bound on the number of backjumps was exceeded,
- or a final local stack from normal termination (in the case of a bi-type, this is not a possibility),
- or a portion of stack to transfer to the branch target from abnormal termination from a jump to a label index.

---

[3] In the bicyclic monoid, the partial operation $\oplus$ is made total by adding a special zero element $\top$, the greatest in the partial order, for 'possible untypability'.

[4] For a discussion of the merits of functional-style rather than the usual relational-style big-step semantics in constructive programming theory, see e.g., [7].

[5] To avoid coinduction in the formalization of our constructive mathematical development, we make sure that all program executions terminate by limiting the number of backjumps—the only source of nontermination in simplified Wasm. This is poor man's domain theory that works well for our purposes; what we are using is a certain variation of Capretta's *delay monad* [1].

Denotations of derivable subtypings coerce between such functions.

The semantic function for code types is therefore defined by

$$[\![a \to_q r]\!] \, rs = \mathbb{N} \to \mathbb{Z}_{32}^a \to 1 + \mathsf{NT}_q(r) + \sum_{\ell < |rs|} \mathbb{Z}_{32}^{rs!!\ell}$$

where $\mathsf{NT}_{\mathsf{bi}}(r) = 0$ and $\mathsf{NT}_{\mathsf{uni}}(r) = \mathbb{Z}_{32}^r$ (NT for "normal termination"); here 0 stands for the empty set and $\sum$ for an indexed disjoint sum. We write Timeout, Norm and Jump for the coprojections of the ternary disjoint sum above.[6]

The semantic functions for derivable subtypings and type derivations are defined in Fig. 6; the latter is defined by structural recursion on the type derivation. The definitions use auxiliary functions $\mathsf{split}\, a : \mathbb{Z}_{32}^{a+d} \to \mathbb{Z}_{32}^a \times \mathbb{Z}_{32}^d$ that split a given local stack into two parts, with the first part containing the first a elements and the second containing the rest. The function $\mathsf{take}\, a : \mathbb{Z}_{32}^{a+d} \to \mathbb{Z}_{32}^a$ gives only the first part.

The denotation of a derivable subtyping $a \to_q r <: a + d \to_{q'} r + e$ is a higher-order function that takes a function f sending any stack of height a to a stack of height r if it terminates normally and returns a function sending a given stack stk of height $a + d$ to a stack of height $r + e$ if f applied to the first a elements of stk terminates normally. It is important to realize that, if $q = \mathsf{bi}$ (and $d \neq e$ in general), then normal termination (the case Norm stk') cannot happen. If $q = \mathsf{uni}$, then the last $d(= e)$ elements of stk that are split off from it before the first a elements are supplied to f are appended back to the result in this case.

Importantly, despite the fact that denotations $\left[\!\!\left[rs \vdash^{\pi} c : t \right]\!\!\right]$ are defined for type derivations (indicated by π) and not just for derivable typing judgements, any two derivations of the same typing judgement $rs \vdash c : t$ still acquire the same denotation. We prove this by relating the semantics to type inference: if there is a derivation of $rs \vdash c : t$, then, by completeness of type inference (Theorem 4), there exists a unique t_0 (depending only on c and rs) such that $\mathsf{infer}\; rs\; c = \mathsf{Just}\; t_0$ and $t_0 <: t$, and by soundness (Theorem 3) there is also a derivation of $rs \vdash c : t_0$. We relate the denotations of the derivations of $rs \vdash c : t$ and $rs \vdash c : t_0$.

Proposition 2 (Coherence of typed semantics). *If* $rs \vdash c : t$, *then*

$$\left[\!\!\left[rs \vdash^{\pi} c : t \right]\!\!\right] = [\![t_0 <: t]\!]\; rs \; \left[\!\!\left[rs \vdash^{\pi_0} c : t_0 \right]\!\!\right]$$

where the unique t_0 *such that* $\mathsf{infer}\; rs\; c = \mathsf{Just}\; t_0$ *is from Theorem 4 and* $rs \vdash^{\pi_0} c : t_0$ *is from Theorem 3. Hence any two derivations of* $rs \vdash c : t$ *have the same denotation.*

---

[6] Notice that $[\![a \to_{\mathsf{bi}} r]\!]$ does not really depend on r. This suggests that bi-types should perhaps not have a result type at all. Such a design is possible, we look at this in Sect. 6. The resulting type system accepts more programs but still provides safety.

$$[\![\, t <: t' \,]\!] \; rs : [\![t]\!] \; rs \to [\![t']\!] \; rs$$

$$[\![\, a \to_q r <: a + d \to_{q'} r + e \,]\!] \; f \; n \; stk = \mathsf{let} \; (astk, pstk) = \mathsf{split} \; a \; stk \; \mathsf{in} \; \mathsf{case} \; f \; n \; astk \; \mathsf{of}$$

$\qquad$ Timeout $\mapsto$ Timeout

$\qquad$ Norm $stk' \mapsto$ Norm$(stk' \mathbin{+\!\!+} pstk)$

$\qquad$ Jump$(\ell, stk') \mapsto$ Jump(ℓ, stk')

$$\left[\!\!\left[\, rs \overset{\pi}{\vdash} c : t \,\right]\!\!\right] : [\![t]\!] \; rs$$

$$\left[\!\!\left[\, \overline{rs \vdash \mathsf{const}\; z : 0 \to_{\mathsf{uni}} 1} \,\right]\!\!\right] \; n \; stk = \mathsf{Norm}(z :: stk)$$

$$\left[\!\!\left[\, \overline{rs \vdash uop : 1 \to_{\mathsf{uni}} 1} \,\right]\!\!\right] \; n \; (z :: stk) = \mathsf{Norm}([\![uop]\!]z :: stk)$$

$$\left[\!\!\left[\, \overline{rs \vdash bop : 2 \to_{\mathsf{uni}} 1} \,\right]\!\!\right] \; n \; (z_2 :: z_1 :: stk) = \mathsf{Norm}([\![bop]\!]z_1 z_2 :: stk)$$

$$\left[\!\!\left[\, \frac{r :: rs \vdash \overset{\pi}{is} : a \to r}{rs \vdash \mathsf{block}_{a \to r} \; is \; \mathsf{end} : a \to_{\mathsf{uni}} r} \,\right]\!\!\right] \; n \; stk = \mathsf{case} \left[\!\!\left[\, r :: rs \vdash \overset{\pi}{is} : a \to r \,\right]\!\!\right] \; n \; stk \; \mathsf{of}$$

$\qquad$ Timeout $\mapsto$ Timeout

$\qquad$ Norm $stk' \mapsto$ Norm stk'

$\qquad$ Jump$(0, stk') \mapsto$ Norm stk'

$\qquad$ Jump$(\ell + 1, stk') \mapsto$ Jump(ℓ, stk')

$$\left[\!\!\left[\, \pi' \left\{ \frac{a :: rs \vdash \overset{\pi}{is} : a \to r}{rs \vdash \mathsf{loop}_{a \to r} \; is \; \mathsf{end} : a \to_{\mathsf{uni}} r} \right. \,\right]\!\!\right] \; n \; stk = \mathsf{case} \left[\!\!\left[\, a :: rs \vdash \overset{\pi}{is} : a \to r \,\right]\!\!\right] \; n \; stk \; \mathsf{of}$$

$\qquad$ Timeout $\mapsto$ Timeout

$\qquad$ Norm $stk' \mapsto$ Norm stk'

$\qquad$ Jump$(0, stk') \mapsto$ if $n = 0$ then Timeout else $\left[\!\!\left[\, rs \vdash \mathsf{loop}_{a \to r} \; \overset{\pi'}{is} \; \mathsf{end} : a \to_{\mathsf{uni}} r \,\right]\!\!\right] \; (n - 1) \; stk'$

$\qquad$ Jump$(\ell + 1, stk') \mapsto$ Jump(ℓ, stk')

$$\left[\!\!\left[\, \overline{rs \vdash \mathsf{br} \; \ell : r \to_{\mathsf{bi}} 0} \,\right]\!\!\right] \; n \; stk = \mathsf{Jump}(\ell, \mathsf{take} \; (rs \mathbin{!!} \ell) \; stk)$$

$$\left[\!\!\left[\, \overline{rs \vdash \mathsf{br\_if} \; \ell : r \to_{\mathsf{uni}} 1 + r} \,\right]\!\!\right] \; n \; (z :: stk) = \mathsf{if} \; z \neq 0 \; \mathsf{then} \; \mathsf{Jump}(\ell, \mathsf{take} \; (rs \mathbin{!!} \ell) \; stk) \; \mathsf{else} \; \mathsf{Norm} \; stk$$

$$\left[\!\!\left[\, \overline{rs \vdash \varepsilon : 0 \to_{\mathsf{uni}} 0} \,\right]\!\!\right] \; n \; stk = \mathsf{Norm} \; stk$$

$$\left[\!\!\left[\, \frac{rs \vdash \overset{\pi}{is} : a \to_q m \quad rs \vdash \overset{\pi'}{i : m} \to_{q'} r}{rs \vdash is \; i : a \to_{q \sqcap q'} r} \,\right]\!\!\right] \; n \; stk = \mathsf{case} \left[\!\!\left[\, rs \vdash \overset{\pi}{is} : a \to_q m \,\right]\!\!\right] \; n \; stk \; \mathsf{of}$$

$\qquad$ Timeout $\mapsto$ Timeout

$\qquad$ Norm $stk' \mapsto \left[\!\!\left[\, rs \vdash \overset{\pi'}{i : m} \to_{q'} r \,\right]\!\!\right] \; n \; stk'$

$\qquad$ Jump$(\ell, stk') \mapsto$ Jump(ℓ, stk')

$$\left[\!\!\left[\, \frac{rs \overset{\pi}{\vdash} c : t \quad t <: t'}{rs \vdash c : t'} \,\right]\!\!\right] \; n = [\![\, t <: t' \,]\!]^{rs} \left(\left[\!\!\left[\, rs \overset{\pi}{\vdash} c : t \,\right]\!\!\right] \; n \right)$$

Fig. 6. Typed big-step semantics based on Sub

We also define an untyped semantics, which we relate to the typed semantics to characterize the safety the latter gives. In the untyped semantics, two kinds of runtime errors can occur in addition to exceeding the bound on backjumps: jumps too far out and stack underflow. The untyped semantics is defined in Fig. 7 where we write JumpOutside, StackUnderflow and Ok for the coprojections of the outer ternary disjoint sum and Timeout, Norm and Jump for those of the inner one.

We define two kinds of type erasure to relate the untyped semantics to the typed semantics. One is an injection from typed initial stacks (specific-length lists) to untyped initial stacks (arbitrary-length lists). The other is an injection from typed outcomes to untyped outcomes. Let erase_a be the inclusion $\mathbb{Z}_{32}^a \hookrightarrow \mathsf{List}\,\mathbb{Z}_{32}$ and $\mathsf{erase}_{rs,q,r}$ be the inclusion $1 + \mathsf{NT}_q(r) + \sum_{\ell < |rs|} \mathbb{Z}_{32}^{rs!!\ell} \hookrightarrow 1 + \mathsf{List}\,\mathbb{Z}_{32} + \mathbb{N} \times \mathsf{List}\,\mathbb{Z}_{32}$ (which hinges in particular on the inclusion $\mathbf{0} \hookrightarrow \mathsf{List}\,\mathbb{Z}_{32}$ in the case $q = \mathsf{bi}$). For every well-typed instruction sequence, the untyped denotation is identical to the type erasure of the typed denotation.

Theorem 5 (Untyped vs. typed semantics). *If* $rs \vdash c : a \to_q r$, *then*

$$(|c|)\ rs\ n\ (\mathsf{erase}_a\ stk) = \mathsf{Ok}(\mathsf{erase}_{rs,q,r}(\llbracket rs \vdash c : a \to_q r \rrbracket\ n\ stk))$$

for all n *and* $stk \in \mathbb{Z}_{32}^a$.

Proof. We prove that whenever $a \to_q r <: a' \to_{q'} r'$, we have

$$(|c|)\ rs\ n\ (\mathsf{erase}_{a'}\ stk)$$
$$= \mathsf{Ok}(\mathsf{erase}_{rs,q',r'}(\llbracket a \to_q r <: a' \to_{q'} r' \rrbracket\ rs\ \llbracket rs \vdash c : a \to_q r \rrbracket\ n\ stk))$$

for all $n \in \mathbb{N}$ and $stk \in \mathbb{Z}_{32}^{a'}$, by induction on the derivation of $rs \vdash c : a \to_q r$. The result follows because $\llbracket a \to_q r <: a \to_q r \rrbracket\ rs$ is the identity function. $\square$

In particular, Theorem 5 implies that no well-typed piece of code c can cause StackUnderflow or JumpOutside when run on a good initial stack stk.

Graded Monad

We further justify the denotational semantics of Sub by noting that underpinning it there is an indexed *graded monad* [4,5,11] (on the category of sets and functions). The indexed graded monad consists of sets of computations, indexed by stack types rs and graded by code types $a \to_q r$, and describes composition of functions from values to computations. It is a graded version of a combination of a state monad (for stack manipulation), an exception monad (for jumps) and the delay monad (to avoid nontermination).

Recall that the set of Sub's code types forms a pomonoid, with order $<:$, unit $0 \to_{\mathsf{uni}} 0$ and multiplication $\oplus$. The pomonoid structure is used in the types of the data of the indexed graded monad that we define in Fig. 8. For each context rs, code type $a \to_q r$, and set X, there is a set $T_{a \to_q r}^{rs} X$ of computations that produce values in the set X. The sets $T_{a \to_q r}^{rs} X$ are functorial in X in the

$$(\!|c|\!)\ rs : \mathbb{N} \to \mathsf{List}\,\mathbb{Z}_{32} \to 1 + 1 + (1 + \mathsf{List}\,\mathbb{Z}_{32} + \mathbb{N} \times \mathsf{List}\,\mathbb{Z}_{32})$$

$(\!|\mathbf{const}\ z|\!)\ rs\ n\ stk = \mathsf{Ok}(\mathsf{Norm}(z :: stk))$

$(\!|uop|\!)\ rs\ n\ stk = \text{case } stk \text{ of}$

$\qquad z :: stk' \mapsto \mathsf{Ok}(\mathsf{Norm}([\![uop]\!]z :: stk'))$

$\qquad \_ \mapsto \mathsf{StackUnderflow}$

$(\!|bop|\!)\ rs\ n\ stk = \text{case } stk \text{ of}$

$\qquad z_2 :: z_1 :: stk' \mapsto \mathsf{Ok}(\mathsf{Norm}([\![bop]\!]z_1 z_2 :: stk'))$

$\qquad \_ \mapsto \mathsf{StackUnderflow}$

$(\!|\mathbf{block}_{a \to r}\ is\ \mathbf{end}|\!)\ rs\ n\ stk = \text{if } a > |stk| \text{ then StackUnderflow else}$

$\text{let } (astk, pstk) = \mathsf{split}\ a\ stk \text{ in case } (\!|is|\!)\ (r :: rs)\ n\ astk \text{ of}$

$\qquad \mathsf{Timeout} \mapsto \mathsf{Ok}\ \mathsf{Timeout}$

$\qquad \mathsf{Norm}\ stk' \mapsto \mathsf{Ok}(\mathsf{Norm}(stk' + \!\!+ \ pstk))$

$\qquad \mathsf{Jump}(0, stk') \mapsto \mathsf{Ok}(\mathsf{Norm}(stk' + \!\!+ \ pstk))$

$\qquad \mathsf{Jump}(\ell + 1, stk') \mapsto \mathsf{Ok}(\mathsf{Jump}(\ell, stk'))$

$(\!|\mathbf{loop}_{a \to r}\ is\ \mathbf{end}|\!)\ rs\ n\ stk = \text{if } a > |stk| \text{ then StackUnderflow else}$

$\text{let } (astk, pstk) = \mathsf{split}\ a\ stk \text{ in case } (\!|is|\!)\ (a :: rs)\ n\ astk \text{ of}$

$\qquad \mathsf{Timeout} \mapsto \mathsf{Ok}\ \mathsf{Timeout}$

$\qquad \mathsf{Norm}\ stk' \mapsto \mathsf{Ok}(\mathsf{Norm}(stk' + \!\!+ \ pstk))$

$\qquad \mathsf{Jump}(0, stk') \mapsto \text{if } n = 0 \text{ then Ok Timeout else}$

$$(\!|\mathbf{loop}_{a \to r}\ is\ \mathbf{end}|\!)\ rs\ (n-1)\ (stk' + \!\!+ \ pstk)$$

$\qquad \mathsf{Jump}(\ell + 1, stk') \mapsto \mathsf{Ok}(\mathsf{Jump}(\ell, stk'))$

$(\!|\mathbf{br}\ \ell|\!)\ rs\ n\ stk = \text{if } \ell \geq |rs| \text{ then JumpOutside else}$

$\text{if } rs\ !!\ \ell > |stk| \text{ then StackUnderflow else}$

$\mathsf{Ok}(\mathsf{Jump}(\ell, \mathsf{take}\ (rs\ !!\ \ell)\ stk))$

$(\!|\mathbf{br\_if}\ \ell|\!)\ rs\ n\ stk = \text{case } stk \text{ of}$

$\qquad 0 :: stk' \mapsto \mathsf{Ok}(\mathsf{Norm}\ stk')$

$\qquad \_ :: stk' \mapsto \text{if } \ell \geq |rs| \text{ then JumpOutside else}$

$\qquad\qquad \text{if } rs\ !!\ \ell > |stk'| \text{ then StackUnderflow else}$

$\qquad\qquad \mathsf{Ok}(\mathsf{Jump}(\ell, \mathsf{take}\ (rs\ !!\ \ell)\ stk'))$

$\qquad \_ \mapsto \mathsf{StackUnderflow}$

$(\!|\varepsilon|\!)\ rs\ n\ stk = \mathsf{Ok}(\mathsf{Norm}\ stk)$

$(\!|is\ i|\!)\ rs\ n\ stk = \text{case } (\!|is|\!)\ rs\ n\ stk \text{ of}$

$\qquad \mathsf{Timeout} \mapsto \mathsf{Ok}\ \mathsf{Timeout}$

$\qquad \mathsf{Norm}\ stk' \mapsto (\!|i|\!)\ rs\ n\ stk'$

$\qquad \mathsf{Jump}(\ell, stk') \mapsto \mathsf{Ok}(\mathsf{Jump}(\ell, stk'))$

Fig. 7. Untyped big-step semantics

obvious way. The unit η_X of the graded monad sends each result $x \in X$ to the computation that immediately returns x, and the multiplication μ_X provides composition of functions from values to computations via flattening of computations of computations into computations. Finally, the coercion functions $T^{rs}_{t<:t'}$ provide subsumption.

$$T^{rs}_{a \to_q r} X = \mathbb{N} \to \mathbb{Z}^a_{32} \to 1 + X \times \mathsf{NT}_q(r) + \sum_{i < |rs|} \mathbb{Z}^{rs!!i}_{32}$$

$$\eta^{rs}_X : X \to T^{rs}_{0 \to_{uni} 0} X$$

$$\eta^{rs}_X \ x \ n \ stk = (x, \mathsf{Norm} \ stk)$$

$$\mu^{rs}_{t,t',X} : T^{rs}_t (T^{rs}_{t'} X) \to T^{rs}_{t \oplus t'} X$$

$\mu^{rs}_{a \to_q m, m' \to_{q'} r, X} \ f \ n \ stk = $ let $(astk, pstk) = $ split $a \ stk$ in case $f \ n \ astk$ of

  Timeout $\mapsto$ Timeout

  Norm$(f', stk') \mapsto$ let $(astk', pstk') = $ split $m' \ (stk' +\!\!+ pstk)$ in case $f' \ n \ astk'$ of

    Timeout $\mapsto$ Timeout

    Norm$(x', stk'') \mapsto$ Norm$(x', stk'' +\!\!+ pstk')$

    Jump$(\ell, stk'') \mapsto$ Jump(ℓ, stk'')

  Jump$(\ell, stk') \mapsto$ Jump(ℓ, stk')

$$T^{rs}_{t <: t', X} : T^{rs}_t X \to T^{rs}_{t'} X$$

$T^{rs}_{a \to_q r <: a+d \to_{q'} r+e, X} \ f \ n \ stk = $ let $(astk, pstk) = $ split $a \ stk$ in case $f \ n \ astk$ of

  Timeout $\mapsto$ Timeout

  Norm$(x, stk') \mapsto$ Norm$(x, stk' +\!\!+ pstk)$

  Jump$(\ell, stk') \mapsto$ Jump(ℓ, stk')

Fig. 8. Indexed graded monad T

This is indeed the structure that we use in the denotational semantics of Sub: the set $[\![a \to_q r]\!]^{rs}$ is just $1 \to T^{rs}_{a \to_q r} 1$, i.e., a special case of a general Kleisli map $X \to T^{rs}_{a \to_q r} Y$, while the denotations of ε, *is i* and subsumptions can be written using the unit, multiplication resp. coercion of the indexed graded monad.

6 An Improvement over Sub

The typed big-step semantics of Sect. 5 hints that there is no need for code types qualified with bi to have a result type since they type pieces of code that surely fail to terminate normally—as they surely jump.

This suggests that we can improve on Sub by dropping result types from bi-types. Indeed, we can work with types $a \to r$ for pieces of code that may terminate normally and types $a \to$ for pieces of code that surely do not. The subtyping and typing rules of this improved type system are in Fig. 9.

Notice that Sub' types more programs than Sub (and hence Spec). The instruction **block**$_{0 \to 0}$ (**br** 0) (**const** 17) **end**, for instance, is untypable in Sub, but typable with principal type $0 \to 0$ in Sub'.

Similarly to Sub, the type system Sub' enjoys principal types, with the principal type of a sequence given by an operation $\oplus'$.

$$\frac{}{a \to\ <: a + d \to}\ \text{SUBT}_{00} \qquad \frac{}{a \to\ <: a + d \to r + e}\ \text{SUBT}_{01} \qquad \frac{}{a \to r <: a + d \to r + d}\ \text{SUBT}_1$$

$$\frac{}{rs \vdash \mathbf{const}\ z : 0 \to 1}\ \text{CONST} \qquad \frac{}{rs \vdash uop : 1 \to 1}\ \text{UOP} \qquad \frac{}{rs \vdash bop : 2 \to 1}\ \text{BOP}$$

$$\frac{r :: rs \vdash is : a \to r}{rs \vdash \mathbf{block}_{a \to r}\ is\ \mathbf{end} : a \to r}\ \text{BLOCK} \qquad \frac{a :: rs \vdash is : a \to r}{rs \vdash \mathbf{loop}_{a \to r}\ is\ \mathbf{end} : a \to r}\ \text{LOOP}$$

$$\frac{rs\ !!\ \ell = r}{rs \vdash \mathbf{br\_if}\ \ell : 1 + r \to r}\ \text{BR\_IF} \qquad \frac{rs\ !!\ \ell = r}{rs \vdash \mathbf{br}\ \ell : r \to}\ \text{BR} \qquad \frac{}{rs \vdash \varepsilon : 0 \to 0}\ \text{EMPTY}$$

$$\frac{rs \vdash is : a \to \quad rs \vdash i : m \to}{rs \vdash is\,i : a \to}\ \text{SEQ}_{00} \qquad \frac{rs \vdash is : a \to \quad rs \vdash i : m \to r}{rs \vdash is\,i : a \to}\ \text{SEQ}_{01}$$

$$\frac{rs \vdash is : a \to m \quad rs \vdash i : m \to}{rs \vdash is\,i : a \to}\ \text{SEQ}_{10} \qquad \frac{rs \vdash is : a \to m \quad rs \vdash i : m \to r}{rs \vdash is\,i : a \to r}\ \text{SEQ}_{11}$$

$$\frac{rs \vdash c : t' \quad t' <: t}{rs \vdash c : t}\ \text{SUBS}$$

Fig. 9. Subtyping and typing rules of Sub'

The code types of Sub' with their subtyping relation $<:$, the type $0 \to 0$ and the type operation $\oplus'$ again form a pomonoid.[7] Moreover, there is an evident pomonoid homomorphism h from the pomonoid of code types of Sub, sending $a \to_{\mathsf{uni}} r$ to $a \to r$ and $a \to_{\mathsf{bi}} r$ to $a \to$. This function h has the properties that $t <: t'$ in Sub implies $h\ t <: h\ t'$ in Sub' and $rs \vdash c : t$ in Sub implies $rs \vdash c : h\ t$ in Sub', i.e., the subtyping and typing derivations in Sub translate into Sub'.

The type system Sub' admits a functional-style big-step semantics analogous to Sub in Sect. 5 and with the same property that the untyped denotations of typed programs agree with their typed denotations (in particular, they do not go wrong). In fact, the semantic functions for subtyping and typing derivations of Sub can be obtained by taking those for subtyping and typing derivations of Sub' and precomposing them with the translations from Sub to Sub'.

7 Conclusions and Future Work

We have shown two refinements of the type system of Wasm, explained on a minimal fragment of the language that only has the features of interest. Wasm's type system has the discrepancy that, while instruction sequences get assigned all valid types (for some definition of validity), instructions other than the exceptional **br** only get assigned their "tightest" (most informative) types. Thus instruction sequences are typed as one would expect from a *declarative* type system, but instructions are typed more in the spirit of a type inference *algorithm*. Our first type system Dir removes this discrepancy: both instructions and instruction sequences get all of their valid types, so Dir is properly declarative, one could say. Our second type system Sub improves on Dir by equipping all instructions and instruction sequences (specifically **br** and instruction sequences containing

---

[7] But with lists instead of natural numbers as stack types, normal associativity of $\oplus'$ is lost, as $((a_0 \to\ ) \oplus' (a \to m)) \oplus' (m' \to r) = (a_0 \to\ )$ while $(a \to m) \oplus' (m' \to r)$ is undefined when neither m nor m' is a prefix of the other. Totalizing $\oplus'$ with a zero greatest element $\top$ gives a skew pomonoid: associativity holds as an inequation.

br) with principal types. This is achieved by introducing a code type qualifier to specifically mark what we have here called bivariate stack polymorphism— an unusual form of stack polymorphism that only instructions and instruction sequences that surely fail to terminate normally enjoy.

We have argued that our type system design is systematic. Importantly, qualified code types form a pomonoid, leading to a denotational (functional big-step) semantics based on an indexed graded monad indexed by type contexts and graded by this pomonoid. This design demonstrates, in particular, that the Wasm type system may be considered to be too pedantic about surely non-returning programs. Such programs could be typed as a having no result type; then more programs would become typable without compromising safety, cf. system Sub' in Sect. 6. The systems Dir and Sub are (on purpose) conservative over the type system of the Wasm specification in that they type exactly the same programs. Sub has principal types because it has specifically marked types for surely non-returning programs. The type system of the specification does not record such information in types, but its type-checking algorithm calculates it nonetheless.[8]

Our semantics shows that Wasm, despite being profiled as low-level, is very well suited for big-step reasoning, thanks, of course, to the language having structured control in a form characteristic to high-level languages; small-step reasoning is not necessary. We should also highlight that continuation-passing is not necessary either; direct style is enough, one can use exceptions to describe the semantics of branching. Finally, the semantics is fully compositional also in regards to how the stack is treated: one only ever needs to talk about the local portion of the stack that the instruction or instruction sequence under analysis has access to; there is no need to pass around the global stack and information about which portion is owned by which parent block-like structure.

In future work, we will formally prove that the big-step semantics agrees with the small-step semantics from the specification. The big-step semantics readily suggests a design for a Hoare-style program logic that we will prove sound and complete wrt. the big-step semantics; adequacy for the small-step semantics will then be a corollary. (Cf. the work on a Hoare logic for Wasm by Watt et al. [16].) The short distance between big-step semantics and Hoare-style program logics is another good reason to work with big-step reasoning. Finally, we want to study some source-level stack-based program analyses, define them compositionally and show them correct wrt. the big-step semantics. (See for example [12].)

Acknowledgements. This work was supported by the Icelandic Research Fund grant no. 196323-053.

---

[8] One could argue that all of this is splitting hairs over typing code fragments that can be seen to be unreachable by a very simple analysis and that a good compiler from a higher-level language to Wasm should not produce this kind of unreachable code. The latter might be true, but a type system for Wasm must still handle all Wasm programs, in particular also programs containing this kind of unreachable code, in some adequate way, unless we declare these programs syntactically ill-formed.

References

1. Chapman, J., Uustalu, T., Veltri, N.: Quotienting the delay monad by weak bisimilarity. Math. Struct. Comput. Sci. **29**(1), 67–92 (2019). https://doi.org/10.1017/s0960129517000184
2. Haas, A., Rossberg, A., Schuff, D.L., Titzer, B.L., Holman, M., Gohman, D., Wagner, L., Zakai, A., Bastien, J.F.: Bringing the Web up to speed with WebAssembly. In: Proc. of 38th ACM SIGPLAN Conf. on Programming Language Design and Implementation, PLDI 2017, pp. 185–200. ACM Press, New York (2017). https://doi.org/10.1145/3062341.3062363
3. Huang, X.: A Mechanized Formalization of the WebAssembly Specification in Coq. Master's thesis, Rochester Institute of Technology (2019). https://www.cs.rit.edu/~mtf/student-resources/20191_huang_mscourse.pdf
4. Katsumata, S.: Parametric effect monads and semantics of effect systems. In: Proceedings of 41st ACM SIGPLAN-SIGACT Symposium on Principles of Programming Languages, POPL 2014, pp. 633–645. ACM Press, New York (2014). https://doi.org/10.1145/2535838.2535846
5. Melliès, P.A.: Parametric monads and enriched adjunctions. Manuscript (2012). https://www.irif.fr/~mellies/tensorial-logic/8-parametric-monads-and-enriched-adjunctions.pdf
6. Morrisett, G., Crary, K., Glew, N., Walker, D.: Stack-based typed assembly language. J. Funct. Program. **13**(5), 957–959 (2003). https://doi.org/10.1017/s0956796801004178
7. Nakata, K., Uustalu, T.: Trace-based coinductive operational semantics for While. In: Berghofer, S., Nipkow, T., Urban, C., Wenzel, M. (eds.) TPHOLs 2009. LNCS, vol. 5674, pp. 375–390. Springer, Heidelberg (2009). https://doi.org/10.1007/978-3-642-03359-9_26
8. Nivat, M., Perrot, J.F.: Une généralisation du monoïde bicyclique. Comptes Rendus Acad. Sci. Paris, Ser. A **271**, 824–827 (1970). https://gallica.bnf.fr/ark:/12148/bpt6k480299v/f830
9. Pöial, J.: Algebraic specification of stack-effects for Forth-programs. In: 1990 FORML Conference Proceedings, pp. 282–290. Forth Interest Group (1991). https://www.kodu.ee/~jpoial/teadus/EuroForth90_Algebraic.pdf
10. Rossberg, A.: WebAssembly core specification, version 1.1. Editor's Draft, 18 Dec. 2021 (2021). https://webassembly.github.io/spec/core/
11. Smirnov, A.: Graded monads and rings of polynomials. J. Math. Sci. **151**(3), 3032–3051 (2008). https://doi.org/10.1007/s10958-008-9013-7
12. Stiévenart, Q., De Roover, C.: Compositional information flow analysis for WebAssembly programs. In: Proceedings of IEEE 20th International Working Conference on Source Code Analysis and Manipulation, SCAM 2020, pp. 13–24. IEEE, Los Alamitos (2020). https://doi.org/10.1109/scam51674.2020.00007
13. Stoddart, B., Knaggs, P.J.: Type inference in stack based languages. Formal Aspects Comput. **5**(4), 289–298 (1993). https://doi.org/10.1007/bf01212404
14. W3C: WebAssembly core specification, version 1.0. W3C Recommendation, 5 Dec. 2019 (2019). https://www.w3.org/TR/wasm-core-1
15. Watt, C.: Mechanising and verifying the WebAssembly specification. In: Proceedings of 7th ACM SIGPLAN International Conference on Certified Programs and Proofs, CPP 2018, pp. 53–65. ACM Press, New York (2018). https://doi.org/10.1145/3167082

16. Watt, C., Maksimovic, P., Krishnaswami, N.R., Gardner, P.: A program logic for first-order encapsulated WebAssembly. In: Donaldson, A.F. (ed.) Proceedings of 33rd European Conference on Object-Oriented Programming, ECOOP 2019, Leibniz International Proceedings in Information, vol. 134, pp. 9:1–9:30. Dagstuhl Publishing, Saarbrücken/Wadern (2019). https://doi.org/10.4230/lipics.ecoop.2019.9
17. Watt, C., Rao, X., Pichon-Pharabod, J., Bodin, M., Gardner, P.: Two mechanisations of webassembly 1.0. In: Huisman, M., Păsăreanu, C., Zhan, N. (eds.) FM 2021. LNCS, vol. 13047, pp. 61–79. Springer, Cham (2021). https://doi.org/10.1007/978-3-030-90870-6_4

A Verified Implementation of B^+-Trees in Isabelle/HOL

Niels Mündler[1]([email]) and Tobias Nipkow[2]

[1] Department of Computer Science, ETH Zürich, Zurich, Switzerland
nmuendler@ethz.ch
[2] Department of Informatics, Technical University of Munich, Munich, Germany
https://in.tum.de/ nipkow/

Abstract. In this paper we present the verification of an imperative implementation of the ubiquitous B^+-tree data structure in the interactive theorem prover Isabelle/HOL. The implementation supports membership test, insertion and range queries with efficient binary search for intra-node navigation. The imperative implementation is verified in two steps: an abstract set interface is refined to an executable but inefficient purely functional implementation which is further refined to the efficient imperative implementation.

Keywords: Separation logic · Verification · Refinement

1 Introduction

B^+-trees form the basis of virtually all modern relational database management systems (RDBMS) and file systems. Even single-threaded databases are non-trivial to analyse and verify, especially machine-checked. Meanwhile it is important to verify various properties like functional correctness, termination and runtime, since RDBMS are ubiquitous and employed in critical contexts, like the banking sector and realtime systems. The only work in the literature on that topic that we are aware of is the work by Malecha *et al.* [10]. However, it lacks the commonly used range query operation, which returns a pointer to the lower bound of a given value in the tree and allows to iterate over all successive values. This operation is particulary challenging to verify as it requires to mix two usually strictly separated abstractions of the tree in order to reason about its correctness. We further generalize the implementation of node internal navigation. This allows to abstract away from its implementation and simplifies proofs. It further allows us to supply an implementation of efficient binary search, a practical and widespread runtime improvement as nodes usually have a size of several kilobytes. We provide a computer assisted proof in the interactive theorem prover Isabelle/HOL [13] for the functional correctness of an imperative implementation of the B^+-tree data-structure and present how we dealt with the resulting technical verification challenges.

© The Author(s), under exclusive license to Springer Nature Switzerland AG 2022
H. Seidl et al. (Eds.): ICTAC 2022, LNCS 13572, pp. 324–341, 2022.
https://doi.org/10.1007/978-3-031-17715-6_21

2   Contributions

In this work, we specify the B^+-tree data structure in the functional modeling language higher-order logic (HOL). The tree is proven to refine a finite set of linearly ordered elements. All proofs are machine-checked in the Isabelle/HOL framework. Within the framework, the functional specifications already yield automatic extraction of executable, but inefficient code.

The contributions of this work are as follows

- The first verification of genuine range queries, which require additional insight in refinement over iterating over the whole tree.
- The first efficient intra-node navigation based on binary rather than linear search.

The remainder of the paper is structured as follows. In Sect. 2.1, we present a brief overview on related work. The definition of B^+-tree and our approach is introduced in Sect. 3. In Sects. 4 and 5, we refine a functionally correct, abstract specification of point, insertion and range queries as well as iterators down to efficient imperative code. Finally, we present learned lessons and evaluate the results in Sect. 6.

The complete source code of the implementation referenced in this research is accessible via the Archive of Formal Proofs [11].

2.1   Related Work

There exist two pen and paper verifications of B^+-tree implementations via a rigorous formal approach. Fielding [5] uses gradual refinement of abstract implementations. Sexton and Thielecke [16] show how to use separation logic in the verification. These are more of a conceptual guideline on approaching a fully machine checked proof.

There are two machine checked proofs of imperative implementations. In the work of Ernst *et al.* [4], an imperative implementation is directly verified by combining interactive theorem proving in KIV [14] with shape analysis using TVLA [15]. The implementation lacks shared pointers between leaves. This simplifies the proofs about tree invariants. However, the tree therefore also lacks iterators over the leaves, and the authors present no straightforward solution to implement them. Moreover, by directly verifying an imperative version only, it is likely that small changes in the implementation will break larger parts of the proof.

Another direct proof on an imperative implementation was conducted by Malecha *et al.* [10], with the Ynot extension to the interactive theorem prover Coq. Both works use recursively defined shape predicates that describe formally how the nodes and pointers represent an abstract tree of finite height. The result is both a fairly abstract specification of a B^+-tree, that leaves some design decisions to the imperative implementation, and an imperative implementation that supports iterators.

Due to the success of this approach, we follow their example and define these predicates functionally. One example of the benefits of this approach is that we were able to derive finiteness and acyclicity only from the relation between imperative and functional specification. In contrast to previous work, the functional predicates describing the tree shape are kept completely separated from the imperative implementation, yielding more freedom for design choices within the imperative refinement. Both existing works rely on linear search for intra-node navigation, which we improve upon by providing binary search. We extend the extraction of an iterator by implementing an additional range query operation.

3   B$^+$-trees and Approach

The B$^+$-tree is a ubiquitous data structure to efficiently retrieve and manipulate indexed data stored on storage devices with slow memory access [3]. They are k-ary balanced search trees, where k is a free parameter. We specify them as implementing a set interface on elements of type $'a$, where the elements in the leaves comprise the content of an abstract set. The inner nodes contain separators. These have the same type $'a$ as the set content, but are only used to guide the recursive navigation through the tree by bounding the elements in the neighboring subtrees. Further the leaves usually contain pointers to the next leaf, allowing for efficient iterators and range queries. A more formal and detailed outline of B$^+$-trees can be found in Sect. 3.2.

The goal of this work is to define this data structure and implement and verify efficient heap-based imperative operations on them. For this purpose, we introduce a functional, algebraic definition and specify all invariants on this level that can naturally be expressed in the algebraic domain. It is important to note that this representation is not complete, as aliased pointers are left out on the algebraic level. However, important structural invariants, such as sortedness and balancedness can be verified.

In a second step an imperative definition is introduced, that takes care of the refinement of lists to arrays in the heap and introduces (potentially shared) pointers instead of algebraic structures. Using a refinement relationship, we can prove that an imperative refinement of the functional specification preserves the structural invariants of the imperative tree on the heap. The only remaining proof obligation on this level is to ensure the correct linking between leaf pointers.

The above outlined steps are performed via manual refinement in Imperative HOL [2]. We build on the library of verified imperative utilities provided by the Separation Logic Framework [9] and the verification of B-trees [11], namely list interfaces and partially filled arrays. The implementation is defined with respect to an abstract imperative operation for node-internal navigation. This means that within each node, we do not specify how the correct subtree for recursive queries is found, but only constrain some characteristics of the result. We provide one such operation that employs linear search, and one that conducts binary search. All imperative programs are shown to refine the functional specifications using the separation logic utilities from the Isabelle Refinement Framework by Lammich [8].

3.1   Notation

Isabelle/HOL conforms to everyday mathematical notation for the most part. For the benefit of the reader who is unfamiliar with Isabelle/HOL, we establish notation and in particular some essential datatypes together with their primitive operations that are specific to Isabelle/HOL. We write $t :: \, 'a$ to specify that the term t has the type $'a$ and $'a \Rightarrow 'b$ for the type of a total function from $'a$ to $'b$. The type for natural numbers is *nat*. Sets with elements of type $'a$ have the type $'a$ *set*. Analogously, we use $'a$ *list* to describe lists, which are constructed as the empty list $[]$ or with the infix constructor #, and are appended with the infix operator @. The function *concat* concatenates a list of lists. The function *set* converts a list into a set. For optional values, Isabelle/HOL offers the type *option* where a term *opt* :: $'a$ *option* is either *None* or *Some a* with $a :: \, 'a$.

3.2   Definitions

We first define an algebraic version of B+-trees as follows:

datatype $'a$ *bplustree* =
  Leaf ($'a$ *list*) |
  Node (($'a$ *bplustree* $\times$ $'a$) *list*) ($'a$ *bplustree*)

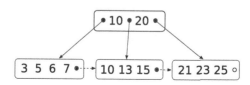

Fig. 1. Nodes contain several elements, the internal list/array structure is not depicted. The dotted lines represent links to following leaf nodes that are not present in the algebraic formulation.

Every node *Node* $[(t_1, a_1), ..., (t_n, a_n)] \, t_{n+1}$ contains an interleaved list of *keys* or *separators* a_i and *subtrees* t_i. We write as t_i the subtree to the left of a_i and t_{i+1} the subtree to the right of a_i. We refer to t_{n+1} as the *last* subtree. The leaves *Leaf* $[v_1, ..., v_n]$ contain a list of *values* v_i. The concatenation of lists of values of a tree t yields all elements contained in the tree. We refer to this list as *leaves* t. A B+-tree with the above structure must fulfill the invariants *balancedness*, *order* and *alignment*.

Balancedness requires that each path from the root to a leaf has the same length. In other words, the height of all trees in one level of the tree must be equal, where the height is the maximum path length to a leaf.

The *order* property ensures a minimum and maximum number of subtrees for each node. A B$^+$-tree is of order k, if each internal node has at least $k + 1$ subtrees and at most $2k + 1$. The root is required to have a minimum of 2 and a maximum of $2k + 1$ subtrees. We require that k be strictly positive, as for $k = 0$ the requirements on the tree root are contradictory.

Alignment means that keys are sorted with respect to separators: For a separator k and all keys l in the subtree to the left, $l < k$, and all keys r in the subtree to the right, $k \leq r$. (where $\leq$ and $<$ can be exchanged).

For the values within the leaves, *sortedness* is required explicitly. We require the even stronger fact that *leaves t* is sorted. This is a useful statement when arguing about the correctness of set operations.

3.3   Implementation Definitions

Proofs about the correctness of operations with respect to implementing an abtract set interface and preserving these invariants are only done on the abstract level, where they are much simpler and many implementation details can be disregarded. It will serve as a reference point for the efficient imperative implementation.

The more efficient executable implementation of B$^+$-trees is defined on the imperative level. Each imperative node contains non-null pointers (*ref*) rather than the algebraic subtree. We refine lists with partially filled arrays of capacity $2k$. A partially filled array (a, n) with capacity c is an array a of fixed size c. The array consists of the elements at indices 0 to $n-1$. Element accesses beyond index n are undefined. Unlike dynamic arrays, partially filled arrays are not expected to grow or shrink. Each imperative node contains the equivalent information to an abstract node. The only addition is that leaves now also contain a pointer to another leaf, which will form a linked list over all leaves in the tree. This was not implemented in the algebraic version as it requires pointer aliasing.

datatype *'a btnode* =
  Btleaf ('a pfarray) ('a btnode ref option) |
  Btnode (('a btnode ref option × 'a) pfarray) ('a btnode ref)

In order to use the algebraic data structure as a reference point, we introduce a refinement relation. The correctness of operations on the imperative node can then be shown by relating imperative input and output and to the abstract input and output of a correct abstract operation. In particular we want to show that if we assume R t t_i, where R is the refinement relation and t and t_i are the abstract and the imperative version of the same conceptual tree, R *o(t)* $o_i(t_i)$ should hold, where o_i is the imperative refinement of operation o. The relation is expressed as a separation logic formula that links an abstract tree to its imperative equivalent.

The notation for separation logic in Isabelle is quickly summarized in the list below.

– *emp* holds for the empty heap

- *true* and *false* hold for every and no heap respectively
- $\uparrow (P)$ holds if the heap is empty and predicate P holds
- $a \mapsto_r x$ holds if the heap at location a is reserved and contains value x
- $\exists_A x.\ P\ x$ holds if there exists some x such that Px holds on the heap.
- $P_1 * P_2$ denotes the separating conjunction and holds if each assertion P_1 and P_2 hold on non-overlapping parts of the heap
- *is_pfa* c *xs xsi* holds if *xsi* is a partially filled array with capacity c and $xs[i]$ $= xsi[i]$ holds for all $i \leq |xs| = |xsi|$.
- *list_assn* R *xs ys* holds if R $xs[i]$ $ys[i]$ holds for all $i \leq |xs| = |ys|$.

Separation Logic formulae express assertions that can be made about the state of the heap. They are therefore just called *assertion* in the following. The assertion P describes all heaps for which the formula P evaluates to *true*. The entailment $P \Longrightarrow_A Q$ holds iff Q holds in every heap in which P holds. For two assertions P and Q, $P = Q$ holds iff $P \Longrightarrow_A Q \wedge Q \Longrightarrow_A P$. For proving imperative code correct, assertions are used in the context of Hoare triples. We write $\langle P \rangle\ c\ \langle \lambda r.\ Q\ r \rangle$ if, for any heap where P holds, after executing imperative code c that returns value r, formula $Q\ r$ holds on the resulting heap. $\langle P \rangle\ c\ \langle \lambda r.\ Q\ r \rangle_t$ is a shorthand for $\langle P \rangle\ c\ \langle \lambda r.\ Q\ r * true \rangle$ More details can be found in the work of Lammich and Meis [9].

The assertion *bplustree_assn* expresses the refinement relation. It relates an algebraic tree (*bplustree*) and a non-null pointer to an imperative tree a (*btnode ref*), pinning its first leaf r and the first leaf of the next sibling z. The formal relation is shown in Fig. 2.

> **fun** *bplustree_assn* $::$ *nat* $\Rightarrow$ $'a$ *bplustree* $\Rightarrow$ $'a$ *btnode ref*
> $\Rightarrow$ $'a$ *btnode ref option* $\Rightarrow$ $'a$ *btnode ref option* **where**
> *bplustree_assn* k (*Node ts t*) $a\ r\ z = \exists_A$ *tsi ti tsi' rs.*
> $\quad a \mapsto_r$ *Btnode tsi ti*
> $\quad --$ Obtain list with array contents for folding *list_assn*
> $* $ *is_pfa* $(2*k)$ *tsi' tsi*
> $* \uparrow(length\ tsi' = length\ rs)$
> $\quad --$ Recursively apply the assertion to subtree pointers
> $*$ *list_assn* $((\lambda\ t\ (ti,r',z').\ bplustree\_assn\ k\ t\ (the\ ti)\ r'\ z') \times_a\ id\_assn)$ *ts* (
> $\quad --$ Pointers to left/right sibling are obtained by offset zipping
> $\quad zip\ (zip\ (map\ fst\ tsi')\ (zip\ (butlast\ (r\#rs))\ rs)))\ (map\ snd\ tsi')))$
> $*$ *bplustree_assn* k t *ti* (*last* $(r\#rs)$) z)
> $|$ *bplustree_assn* k (*Leaf xs*) $a\ r\ z = \exists_A$ *xsi fwd.*
> $\quad a \mapsto_r$ *Btleaf xsi fwd* $*$ *is_pfa* $(2*k)$ *xs xsi* $* \uparrow(fwd = z) * \uparrow(r = Some\ a)$

Fig. 2. The B$^+$-tree is specified by the split factor k, an abstract tree, a pointer to its root a, a pointer to its first leaf r and a pointer to the first leaf of the next sibling z. The pointers to first leaf and next first leaf are used to establish the linked leaves invariant.

The main structural relationship between abstract and imperative tree is established by linking abstract list and array via the *is_pfa* predicate. We then fold over the two lists using *list_assn*, which establishes a refinement relation for every pair of list elements.

In addition to the refinement of data structures, the first leaf r and next leaf z are used to express the structural invariant that the leaves are correctly linked. There is no abstract equivalent for the forwarding pointers in the leaves, therefore we only introduce and reason about their state on the imperative layer. The invariant is ensured by passing the first leaf of the right neighbor to each subtree. The pointer is passed recursively to the leaf node, where it is compared to the actual pointer of the leaf. All of this happens in the convoluted *list_assn*, by folding over the list of the leaf pointer list rs zipped with itself, offset by one. The linking property is required for the iterator on the tree in Sect. 5.1.

3.4   Node Internal Navigation

In order to define meaningful operations that navigate the node structure of the B$^+$-tree, we need to find a method that handles search within a node. Ernst *et al.* [4] and Malecha *et al.* [10] both use a linear search through the key and value lists. However, B$^+$-trees are supposed to have memory page sized nodes [3], which makes a linear search impractical.

We introduce a context (*locale* in Isabelle) in which we assume that we have access to a function that correctly navigates through the node internal structure. *Correct* in this context meaning that the selected subtree for recursive calls will lead to the element we are looking for. We call this function *split*, and define it only by its behavior. The specification for *split* is given in Fig. 3 (where $'b = 'a$ *bplustree* $\times$ $'a$). A corresponding function *split_list* is defined on the separator-only lists in the leaf nodes.

> **locale** *split_tree* =
>   **fixes** *split* :: $'b$ *list* $\Rightarrow$ $'a$ $\Rightarrow$ $'b$ *list* $\times$ $'b$ *list*
>   *split xs p* = (ls,rs) $\implies$ *xs* = *ls* @ *rs*
>   *split xs p* = $(ls@[(sub,sep)],rs)$; *sorted_less* (*separators xs*) $\implies$ *sep* $<$ *p*
>   *split xs p* = $(ls,(sub,sep)\#rs)$; *sorted_less* (*separators xs*) $\implies$ *p* $\leq$ *sep*

Fig. 3. Given a list of separator-subtree pairs and a search value x, the function should return the pair (s, t) such that, according to the structural invariant of the B$^+$-tree, t must contain x or will hold x after a correct insertion.

In the following sections, all operations are defined and verified based on *split* and *split_list*. When approaching imperative code extraction, we provide a binary search based imperative function, that refines *split*. Thus we obtain imperative code that makes use of an efficient binary search, without adding complexity to the proofs. The definition and implementation closely follows the approach described in detail in the verification of B-trees [11].

4   Set Operations

B+-trees refine sets on linearly ordered elements. For a tree t, the refined abstract set is computed as *set (leaves t)*. The set interface requires that there should be query, insertion and deletion operations o_t such that *set (leaves (o_t t)) = o (set (leaves t))*. Moreover, the invariants described in Sect. 3 can be assumed to hold for t and are required for o_t. We provide these operations and show their correctness on the functional layer first, then refine the operations further to the imperative layer. For point queries and insertion, we follow the implementation suggested by Bayer and McCreight [1].

4.1   Functional Point Query

For an inner node t and a searched value x, find the correct subtree s_t such that if a leaf of t contains x, a leaf of s_t must contain x. Then recurse on s_t. Inside the leaf node, we search directly in the list of values. We make use of the *split* and *isin_list* operation, as described in Sect. 3.4.

fun *isin::* '*a bplustree* $\Rightarrow$ '*a* $\Rightarrow$ *bool* **where**
    isin (Leaf ks) x = (isin_list x ks) |
    isin (Node ts t) x = (**case** *split ts x* **of**
        (_,(sub,sep)#rs) $\Rightarrow$ *isin sub x*
    | *(_,[])* $\Rightarrow$ *isin t x*
)

Since this function does not modify the tree involved at all, we only need to show that it returns the correct value.

theorem assumes *sorted_less (leaves t)* **and** *aligned l t u*
    shows *isin t x = (x* $\in$ *set (leaves t))*

In general, these proofs on the abstract level are based on yet another refinement relation suggested by Nipkow [12]. We say that the B+-tree t refines a sorted list of its leaf values, *leaves t*, the concatenated lists of values in leafs visited in in-order traversal of the tree. We argue that recursing into a specific subtree is equivalent to splitting this list at the correct position and searching in the correct sublist. The same approach was applicable for proving the correctnes of functional operations on B-trees [11].

The proofs on the functional level can therefore be made concise. We go on and define an imperative version of the operation that refines each step of the abstract operation to equivalent operations on the imperative tree.

4.2   Imperative Point Query

The imperative version of the point query is a partial function. Termination cannot be guaranteed anymore, at least without further assumptions. This is inevitable since the function would not terminate given cyclic trees. However, we will show that if the input refines an abstract tree, the function terminates and is correct. The imperative $isin_i$ refines each step of the abstract operation with an imperative equivalent. The result can be seen in Fig. 4.

```
partial_function (heap) isin_i :: 'a btnode ref ⇒ 'a ⇒  bool Heap where
  isin_i p x = do {
  node ← !p;
  (case node of
     Btleaf xs _ ⇒ isin_list_i x xs |
     Btnode ts t ⇒ do {
       i ← split_i ts x;
       tsl ← length ts;
       if i < tsl then do {
         s ← get ts i;
         let (sub,sep) = s in
           isin_i (the sub) x
       } else
           isin_i t x
     }
  )}
```

Fig. 4. The imperative refinement of the *isin* function. As a partial function, its termination is not guaranteed for all inputs. Additionally it implicitly makes use of the heap monad.

Again, we assume that $split_i$ performs the correct node internal search and refines an abstract *split*. Note how $split_i$ does not actually split the internal array, but rather returns the index of the pair that would have been returned by the abstract split function. The pattern matching against an empty list is replaced by comparing the index to the length of the list l. In case the last subtree should be recursed into, the whole list l is returned.

In order to show that the function returns the correct result, we show that it performs the same operation on the imperative tree as on the algebraic tree. This is expressed in Hoare triple notation and separation logic.

lemma assumes $k > 0$ **and** *root_order* $k\ t$ **and** *sorted_less* (*inorder* t)
  and *sorted_less* (*leaves* t) **shows**
  ⟨*bplustree_assn* $k\ t\ ti\ r\ z$⟩
    $isin_i\ ti\ x$
  ⟨$\lambda y.$ *bplustree_assn* $k\ t\ ti\ r\ z * \uparrow(isin\ t\ x = y)$⟩$_t$

The proof follows inductively on the structure of the abstract tree. Assuming structural soundness of the abstract tree refined by the pointer passed in, the returned value is equivalent to the return value of the abstract function. We must explicitly show that the tree on the heap still refines the same abstract tree after the operation, which was implicit on the abstract layer. It follows directly, since no operation in the imperative function modifies part of the tree.

4.3 Insertion and Deletion

The insertion operation and its proof of correctness largely line up with the one for point queries. But since insertion modifies the tree, we need to additionally show on the abstract level that the modified tree maintains the invariants of B$^+$-trees.

On the imperative layer, we show that the heap state after the operation refines the tree after the abstract insertion operation. It follows that the imperative operation also maintains the abstract invariants. Moreover, we need to show that the linked list among the leaf pointers is correctly maintained throughout the operation. This can only be shown on the imperative level as there is no abstract equivalent to the shared pointers.

lemma assumes $k > 0$ **and** *sorted_less* (*inorder t*)
  and *sorted_less* (*leaves t*) **and** *root_order k t* **shows**
  ⟨*bplustree_assn k t ti r z*⟩
  insert$_i$ k x ti
  ⟨$\lambda u.$ *bplustree_assn k* (*insert k x t*) *u r z*⟩$_t$

We provide a verified functional definition of deletion and a definition of an imperative refinement. Showing the correctness of the imperative version would largely follow the same pattern as the proof of the correctness of insertion. The focus of this work is not on basic tree operations, but on obtaining a (range) iterator view on the tree.

5 Range Operations

This section introduces both how the general iterator on the tree leaves is obtained and the technical challenges involved (Sect. 5.1) as well as how to obtain an iterator on a specific subset of elements efficiently (Sect. 5.2).

On the functional level, the forwarding leaf pointers in each leaf are not present, as this would require aliasing. Therefore, the abstract equivalent of an iterator is a concatenation of all leaf contents. When refining the operations, we will make use of the leaf pointers to obtain an efficient implementation.

5.1 Iterators

To obtain an iterator, recurse down the tree to obtain the first leaf. From there we follow leaf pointers until we reach the final leaf marked by a null forwarding pointer. From an assertion perspective the situation is more complex. Recall the refinement relation between abstract and implemented B$^+$-tree. It is important to find an explicit formulation of the linked list view on the leaf pointers. Meanwhile, we want to ensure that the complete tree does not change by iterating through the leaves. We cannot express an assertion about the linked list along the leaves and the assertion on the whole tree in two fully independent predicates as the memory described overlaps. Separation logic forces us to not make statements about the contents of any memory location twice.

We follow the approach of Malecha *et al.* [10] and try to find an equivalent formulation that separates the whole tree in a view on its inner nodes and the linked leaf node list. The central idea to separate the tree is to express that the linked leaf nodes refine *leaf_nodes t* and that the inner nodes refine *trunk t*, as depicted in Fig. 5. These are two independent parts of the heap and therefore the statements can be separated using the separating conjunction.

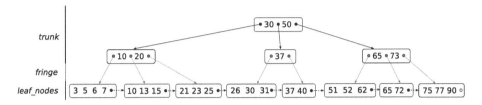

Fig. 5. In order to obtain separate assertions about the concatenated leaf list (*leaf_nodes*) and the internal nodes (*trunk*) of the tree, the structure is abstractly split along the pointers marked in red, the *fringe*. In order to be able to combine the *leaf_nodes* and the *trunk* together, the *fringe* has to be extracted and shared explicitly.

Formally, we define an assertion *trunk_assn* and *leaf_nodes_assn*. The former is the same as *bplustree_assn* (see Fig. 2), except that we remove all assertions about the content of the tree in the *Leaf* case. The latter is defined similar to a linked list refining a list of abstract tree leaf nodes, shown in Fig. 6. The list is refined by a pointer to the head of the list, which refines the head of the abstract list. Moreover, the imperative leaf contains a pointer to the next element in the list.

With these definitions, we can show that the heap describing the imperative tree may be split up into its leaves and the trunk.

lemma *bplustree_assn k t ti r z*
$\implies_A$ *leaf_nodes_assn k (leaf_nodes t) r z* $*$ *trunk_assn k t ti r z*

However, we cannot show that a structurally consistent, unchanged B$^+$-tree is still described by the combination of the two predicates. The reason is that we cannot express that the linked leaf nodes are precisely the leaf nodes on the lowest level of the trunk, depicted in red in Fig. 5.

The root of this problem is actually a feature of the refinement approach. When stating that a part of the heap refines some abstract data structure, we make no or little statements about concrete memory locations or pointers. This is useful, as it reduces the size of the specification and the proof obligations. In this case we need to find a way around it.

We need to specifically express that the leaf pointers, and not the abstract structure they refine, are precisely the same in the two statements.

In a second attempt, the sharing is made explicit. We extract from the whole tree the precise list of pointers to leaf nodes, the *fringe* in the correct order.

fun *leaf_nodes_assn* **where**
  leaf_nodes_assn k ((*Leaf xs*)#*lns*) (*Some r*) *z* =
  (∃_A *xsi fwd*.
      r ↦_r *Btleaf xsi fwd*
    * *is_pfa* (*2*k*) *xs xsi*
    * *leaf_nodes_assn k lns fwd z*
) |
  leaf_nodes_assn k [] *r z* = ↑(*r* = *z*) |
  leaf_nodes_assn _ _ _ _ = *false*

Fig. 6. The refinement relation for leaf nodes comprises the refinement of the node content as well as the recursive property of linking correctly to the next node.

Recursively, the fringe of a tree is the concatenation of all fringes in its subtrees. The resulting assertion, taking the fringe into account, can be seen in Fig. 7. As a convenient fact, this assertion is equivalent to Fig. 2.

lemma *bplustree_extract_fringe:*
  bplustree_assn k t ti r z = (∃_A*fringe. bplustree_assn_fringe k t ti r z fringe*)

Using the *fringe*, we can precisely state an equivalent separated assertion. We describe the trunk with the assertion *trunk_assn*, which is the same as *bplustree_assn_fringe*, except that the *Leaf* case is changed to only ↑ (*r* = *Some a* ∧ *fringe* = [*a*]). In addition, we extend the definition of *leaf_nodes_assn* to take the *fringe* pointers into account. We now require that the *fringe* of the trunk is precisely the list of pointers in the linked list refining *leaf_nodes*.

lemma *bplustree_view_split:*
  bplustree_assn_fringe k t ti r z fringe =
  leaf_nodes_assn k (*leaf_nodes t*) *r z fringe* * *trunk_assn k t ti r z fringe*

To obtain an iterator on the leaf nodes of the tree, we obtain the first leaf of the tree. By the formulation of the tree assertion, we can express the obtained result using the assertion about the complete tree.

lemma assumes *k* > *0* **and** *root_order k t* **shows**
  ⟨*bplustree_assn k t ti r z*⟩
  first_leaf ti
  ⟨λ*u. bplustree_assn k t ti r z* * ↑(*u* = *r*)⟩_t

On the result, we can apply lemmas *bplustree_extract_fringe* and *bplustree_view_split*. The transformed expression states that the result of *first_leaf ti* is a pointer to *leaf_nodes t*. The tree root *t* remains to refine *trunk t*.

From here, we could define an iterator over the leaf nodes along the fringe, refining the abstract list *leaf_nodes*. Our final goal is to iterate over the values within each array inside the nodes. We introduce a flattening iterator for this purpose. It takes an outer iterator over a data structure *a* that returns elements of type *b*, and inner iterator over the data structure *b* that returns elements of type *c*. It returns an iterator over data structure *a* that returns the concatenated

fun *bplustree_assn_fringe* **where**
    bplustree_assn_fringe k (*Leaf xs*) *a r z fringe* =
    $\exists_A$ *xsi fwd.*
        $a \mapsto_r$ *Btleaf xsi fwd*
    * *is_pfa* (*2∗k*) *xs xsi*
    * ↑(*fwd* = *z*)
    * ↑(*r* = *Some a*)
    −− In case of a singleton leaf, the leaf itself is the fringe of the tree
    * ↑(*fringe* = [*a*])
    |
    bplustree_assn_fringe k (*Node ts t*) *a r z fringe* =
    $\exists_A$ *tsi ti tsi' tsi'' rs fr_sep.*
        $a \mapsto_r$ *Btnode tsi ti*
    * *is_pfa* (*2∗k*) *tsi' tsi*
    * ↑(*length tsi'* = *length rs*)
    −− The fringe is decomposed into the fringe of each subtree
    * ↑(*concat fr_sep* = *fringe*)
    * ↑(*length fr_sep* = *length rs* + *1*)
    −− Folding over all subtrees as before, now passing each subfringe to subtrees
    * *list_assn* (
        (λ *t* (*ti,r',z',fr*). *bplustree_assn_fringe k t* (*the ti*) *r' z' fr*)
        $\times_a$ *id_assn*
) *ts* (*zip*
        (*zip* (*map fst tsi'*) (*zip* (*butlast* (*r#rs*)) (*zip rs* (*butlast fr_sep*))))
        (*map snd tsi'*)
)
    * *bplustree_assn_fringe k t ti* (*last* (*r#rs*)) (*last* (*rs@*[*z*])) (*last fr_sep*)

Fig. 7. An extended version of the B$^+$-tree assertion from Fig. 2 on imperative tree root *a*, first leaf *r*, first leaf of the next sibling *z* and leaf pointer list *fringe*. In order to be able to correctly relate leaf view and internal nodes, the shared pointers *fringe* are made explicit, without accessing their memory location.

list of elements of type *c*. The exact implementation of this iterator is left out as a technical detail.

The list iterator interface used is as defined by Lammich [7] and specifies the following function.

- An *init* function that returns the pointer to the head of the list.
- A *has_next* function that checks whether the current pointer is the null pointer.
- A *next* function that returns the the array in the current node and its forwarding pointer.
- Proofs that we can transform the *leaves_assn* statement into a leaf iterator statement and vice versa.

We implement such an iterator for the linked list of leaf nodes *leaf_nodes_iter* and combine it with the iterator over partially filled arrays using the flattening iterator to obtain the *leaves_iter*.

Finally, we want be able to express that the whole tree does not change throughout the iteration. For this, we need to keep track of both the leaf nodes assertion and the trunk assertion on *t*. The assertion describing the iterator therefore contains both. Most parameters to the iterator assertion are static, and express the context of the iterator, i.e. the full extent of the leaf nodes. The iterator state *it* itself is a pair of an iterator state for a partial array, the current position in that array and its size, and a pointer to the next leaf and the final leaf.

definition *bplustree_iter k t ti r vs it* $= \exists_A$ *fringe.*
  leaves_iter fringe k (leaf_nodes t) (leaves t) r vs it $*$
  trunk_assn k t ti r None fringe

Note how all notion of the explicitly shared fringe has disappeared from the client perspective as its existence is hidden within the definition of the tree iterator. We initialize the iterator using the *first_leaf* operation and obtain the singleton tree elements with the flattening iterator.

5.2 Range Queries

A common use case of B$^+$-trees is to obtain all values within a range [6]. We focus on the range bounded from below, *lrange t x* $= \{y \in set(t)|y \geq x\}$. From an implementation perspective, the operation is similar to the point query operation. On the leaf level, it returns a pointer to the reached leaf. This pointer is then interpreted as iterator over the remaining list of linked leaves. The range bounded from below comprises all values returned by the iterator. Due to the lack of a linked leaf list in the abstract tree, the abstract definition explicitly concatenates all values in the subtrees to the right of the reached node.

fun *lrange*:: *'a bplustree* $\Rightarrow$ *'a* $\Rightarrow$ *'a list* **where**
  lrange (Leaf ks) x $=$ *(lrange_list x ks)* |
  lrange (Node ts t) x $=$ (
    case *split ts x* **of** *(_,(sub,sep)#rs)* $\Rightarrow$ (
        lrange sub x @ (concat (map leaves rs)) @ leaves t
)
  | *(_,[])* $\Rightarrow$ *lrange t x*
)

As before, we assume that there exists a function *lrange_list* that obtains the *lrange* from a list of sorted values.

The verification of the imperative version turns out to be not as straightforward as expected, exactly due to this recursive step. The reason is that iterators can only be expressed on a complete tree, where the last leaf is explicitly a null pointer. The linked list of a subtree is however bounded by valid leaves, precisely the first leaf of the next subtree.

In order implement and verify a refinement of this function we therefore decide to implement an intermediate abstract function *leaf_nodes_lrange*. This function returns the leaf nodes comprising the *lrange* instead of their contents.

fun *leaf_nodes_lrange:: 'a bplustree ⇒ 'a ⇒ 'a bplustree list* **where**
  leaf_nodes_lrange (Leaf ks) x = [Leaf ks] |
  leaf_nodes_lrange (Node ts t) x = **case** *split ts x* **of**
    (_,(sub,sep)#rs) ⇒
      leaf_nodes_lrange sub x @ concat (map leaf_nodes rs) @ leaf_nodes t
    | (_,[]) ⇒ leaf_nodes_lrange t x

fun *concat_leaf_nodes_lrange* **where**
  concat_leaf_nodes_lrange t x = **case** *leaf_nodes_lrange t x* **of**
  (LNode ks)#list ⇒ lrange_list x ks @ concat (map leaves list)

We then show that the concatenation of the contents of the leaf nodes *concat_leaf_nodes_lrange t x = lrange t x*. On the imperative layer *leaf_nodes_lrange$_i$* can be obtained using only the *leaf_nodes* and *trunk* assertions as we never access the contents of the leaf nodes. We therefore avoid having to unfold any assertions about the structure of the leaf nodes. The function returns a pointer that splits the list of leaf nodes of the whole tree, terminated by the null pointer that marks the end of the complete tree. We transform the result into an iterator over the leaf nodes, as this pointer split notation aligns with the definition of *leaf_nodes_iter*. Finally we can transform this and the result of *lrange_list$_i$* to an iterator on the singleton leaf elements.

lemma assumes *k > 0* **and** *root_order k t*
  and *sorted_less (leaves t)* **and** *Laligned t u* **shows**
  ⟨bplustree_assn k t ti r None⟩
  concat_leaf_nodes_lrange$_i$ ti x
  ⟨bplustree_iter k t ti r (lrange t x)⟩$_t$

6   Conclusion

We were able to formally verify an imperative implementation of the ubiquitous B$^+$-tree data structure, featuring range queries and binary search.

6.1   Evaluation

The B$^+$-tree implemented by Ernst *et al.* [4] features point queries and insertion, however explicitly leaves out pointers within the leaves, which forbids the implementation of iterators. Our work is closer in nature to the B$^+$-tree implementation by Malecha *et al.* [10]. In addition to the functionality dealt with in their work, we extend the implementation with a missing Range iterator and supply a binary search within nodes. Our approach is modular, allowing for the substitution of parts of the implementation with even more specialized and sophisticated implementations.

Regarding the leaf iterator, we noticed that in the work of Malecha *et al.* there is no need to extract the fringe explicitly. The abstract leaves are defined such that they store the precise heap location of the refining node. In our proposed definition, the precise heap location is irrelevant in almost every situation and can be omitted. Only when splitting the tree we obtain the memory location of nodes explicitly, because these locations are needed to guarantee structual soundness of the whole tree. It is hard to quantify or evaluate which approach is more practical. From a theoretical view point we suggest that a less strict approach restricts the implementation space less and leaves more design decisions to the specification implementing developer.

With respect to the effort in lines of code and proof as depicted in Fig. 8, our approach is similar in effort to the approach by Malecha *et al.*. The numbers do not include the newly defined pure ML proof tactics. It includes the statistics for the additional binary search and range iterator, that make up around one thousand lines of proof each.

The comparison with Ernst *et al.* is difficult. Their research completely avoids the usage of linked leaf pointers, therefore also omitting iterators completely. The iterator verification makes up a signifant amount of the proof with at least one thousand lines of proof on its own. The leaf pointers also affect the verification of point and insertion queries due to the additional invariant on the imperative level. We conclude that the Isabelle/HOL framework provides a feature set such that verification of B^+-trees is both feasible and comparable in effort to using Ynot or KIV/TVLA. The strict separation of a functional and imperative implementation yields the challenge of making memory locations explicit

	Malecha *et al.*[10][+]	[4][d]	Our approach[+]
Functional code	360	-	413
Imperative code	510	1862	1093
Proofs	5190	350 + 510 + 2940[*]	8663
Timeframe (months)	?	> 6	6 + 6[**]

Fig. 8. Comparison of (unoptimized) Lines of Code and Proof and time investment in related mechanized B^+-tree verifications. All approaches are comparable in effort, taking into account implementation specifics. The marker [d] denotes that the implementation verifies deletion operations, whereas [+] denotes the implementation of iterators.
[*] The proof integrates TVLA and KIV, and hence comprises explicitly added rules for TVLA (the first number), user-invented theorems in KIV (the second number) and "interactions" with KIV (the second number). Interactions are i.e. choices of an induction variable, quantifier instantiation or application of correct lemmas. We hence interpret them as each one apply-Style command and hence one line of proof.
[**] 6 months include the preceding work on the verification of B-trees. As they share much of the functionality with B^+-trees but required their own specifics, the time spent on them cannot be accounted for 1:1.

where needed. On the other hand, it permits great freedom regarding the actual refinement on the imperative level.

6.2   Outlook

This research may serve as a template for the implementation of B^+-trees in Isabelle-LLVM. [7] At the beginning of this work, the code generator did not yet support recursive data structures, but this functionality was added recently.

As of now, the imperative implementation provided by this research was directly exported into executable imperative code in Haskell, SML and OCaml. It may thus find applications in the development of libraries where a verified implementation of a set interface is needed.

References

1. Bayer, R., McCreight, E.M.: Organization and maintenance of large ordered indices. Acta Informatica **1**, 173–189 (1972). https://doi.org/10.1007/BF00288683
2. Bulwahn, L., Krauss, A., Haftmann, F., Erkök, L., Matthews, J.: Imperative functional programming with Isabelle/HOL. In: Mohamed, O.A., Muñoz, C., Tahar, S. (eds.) TPHOLs 2008. LNCS, vol. 5170, pp. 134–149. Springer, Heidelberg (2008). https://doi.org/10.1007/978-3-540-71067-7_14
3. Comer, D.: The ubiquitous b-tree. ACM Comput. Surv. **11**(2), 121–137 (1979). https://doi.org/10.1145/356770.356776
4. Ernst, G., Schellhorn, G., Reif, W.: Verification of B^+ trees by integration of shape analysis and interactive theorem proving. Software & Systems Modeling **14**(1), 27–44 (2013). https://doi.org/10.1007/s10270-013-0320-1
5. Fielding, E.: The specification of abstract mappings and their implementation as b+ trees. Technical Report PRG18, OUCL (1980)
6. Graefe, G.: Modern b-tree techniques. Found. Trends Databases **3**(4), 203–402 (2011). https://doi.org/10.1561/1900000028
7. Lammich, P.: Generating verified LLVM from isabelle/hol. In: Harrison, J., O'Leary, J., Tolmach, A. (eds.) 10th International Conference on Interactive Theorem Proving, ITP 2019, Portland, OR, USA, 9–12 September 2019, vol. 141 of LIPIcs, pp. 22:1–22:19. Schloss Dagstuhl - Leibniz-Zentrum für Informatik (2019). https://doi.org/10.4230/LIPIcs.ITP.2019.22
8. Lammich, P.: Refinement to Imperative HOL. J. Autom. Reason. **62**(4), 481–503 (2017). https://doi.org/10.1007/s10817-017-9437-1
9. Lammich, P., Meis, R.: A separation logic framework for imperative HOL. Arch. Formal Proofs **2012** (2012). https://www.isa-afp.org/entries/Separation_Logic_Imperative_HOL.shtml
10. Malecha, J.G., Morrisett, G., Shinnar, A., Wisnesky, R.: Toward a verified relational database management system. In: Hermenegildo, M.V., Palsberg, J. (eds.) Proceedings of the 37th ACM SIGPLAN-SIGACT Symposium on Principles of Programming Languages, POPL 2010, Madrid, Spain, 17–23 January 2010, pp. 237–248. ACM (2010). https://doi.org/10.1145/1706299.1706329
11. Mündler, N.: A verified imperative implementation of B-trees. Arch. Formal Proofs **2021** (2021). https://www.isa-afp.org/entries/BTree.html

12. Nipkow, T.: Automatic functional correctness proofs for functional search trees. In: Blanchette, J.C., Merz, S. (eds.) ITP 2016. LNCS, vol. 9807, pp. 307–322. Springer, Cham (2016). https://doi.org/10.1007/978-3-319-43144-4_19

13. Nipkow, T., Klein, G.: Concrete Semantics. Springer, Cham (2014). https://doi.org/10.1007/978-3-319-10542-0

14. Reif, W., Schellhorn, G., Stenzel, K., Balser, M.: Structured specifications and interactive proofs with kiv. In: Automated Deduction - A Basis for Applications, vol. 2 (2000). https://doi.org/10.1007/978-94-017-0435-9_1

15. Sagiv, S., Reps, T.W., Wilhelm, R.: Parametric shape analysis via 3-valued logic. ACM Trans. Program. Lang. Syst. **24**(3), 217–298 (2002). https://doi.org/10.1145/514188.514190

16. Sexton, A.P., Thielecke, H.: Reasoning about B+ trees with operational semantics and separation logic. In: Bauer, A., Mislove, M.W. (eds.) Proceedings of the 24th Conference on the Mathematical Foundations of Programming Semantics, MFPS 2008, Philadelphia, PA, USA, 22–25 May 2008, vol. 218 of Electronic Notes in Theoretical Computer Science, pp. 355–369. Elsevier (2008). https://doi.org/10.1016/j.entcs.2008.10.021

Active Learning for Deterministic Bottom-Up Nominal Tree Automata

Rindo Nakanishi[1]([⊠]), Yoshiaki Takata[2], and Hiroyuki Seki[1]

[1] Graduate School of Informatics, Nagoya University,
Furo-cho, Chikusa, Nagoya 464-8601, Japan
rindo@sqlab.jp, seki@i.nagoya-u.ac.jp
[2] Graduate School of Engineering, Kochi University of Technology,
Tosayamada, Kami City, Kochi 782-8502, Japan
takata.yoshiaki@kochi-tech.ac.jp

Abstract. Nominal set plays a central role in a group-theoretic extension of finite automata to those over an infinite set of data values. Moerman et al. proposed an active learning algorithm for nominal word automata with the equality symmetry. In this paper, we introduce deterministic bottom-up nominal tree automata (DBNTA), which operate on trees whose nodes are labelled with elements of an orbit finite nominal set. We then prove a Myhill-Nerode theorem for the class of languages recognized by DBNTA and propose an active learning algorithm for DBNTA. The algorithm can deal with any data symmetry that admits least support, not restricted to the equality symmetry and/or the total order symmetry. To prove the termination of the algorithm, we define a partial order on nominal sets and show that there is no infinite chain of orbit finite nominal sets with respect to this partial order between any two orbit finite sets.

Keywords: Nominal tree automata · Active learning · Myhill-Nerode theorem

1 Introduction

Computational models such as finite automaton, pushdown automaton and context-free grammar provide a theoretical basis for automated technologies including model checking, testing and synthesis. Although the technologies have brought fruitful success, these models cannot directly deal with data values. However, if we add to a classical model the ability of processing data values, the resulting model easily becomes Turing machine-equivalent and the decidability needed for automated technologies is lost. Register automaton (RA) is an extension of finite automaton (FA) by adding registers for manipulating data values in a restricted way [12]. RA can compare an input data value with those stored in its registers to determine its behavior. RA inherits some of the good properties from FA including closure properties on language operations and the decidability of basic problems. For example, the membership and emptiness problems are

© The Author(s), under exclusive license to Springer Nature Switzerland AG 2022
H. Seidl et al. (Eds.): ICTAC 2022, LNCS 13572, pp. 342–359, 2022.
https://doi.org/10.1007/978-3-031-17715-6_22

decidable for RA and their complexities are extensively studied [12,15,20,23]. Similar extensions of other classical models have been proposed such as register tree automaton [10,13], register context-free grammar [6,24] and register pushdown automaton [18,25]. Logics on data words have also been proposed including LTL with the freeze quantifier [9] and two-variable first-order logic [2].

A common property of these models is that the behavior of an automaton (or a grammar) does not depend on data values themselves, but on the relationship (e.g., equality, total order) among data values. Assume that the comparison operator of RA is only equality check. Also assume that an RA A has one register to store the first data value of an input word and test whether the remaining data values are different from the data value in the register except the last one in the input, which should be the same as the first data value. Then, A accepts data words $2 \cdot 5 \cdot 6 \cdot 2$, $8 \cdot 1 \cdot 3 \cdot 8$, and so on. Note that the data word $8 \cdot 1 \cdot 3 \cdot 8$ can be obtained from $2 \cdot 5 \cdot 6 \cdot 2$ by the permutation that maps $2, 5$ and 6 to $8, 1$ and 3, respectively.

The above observation gives us a group-theoretic extension of FA [3]. Assume that we are given a countable set $\mathbb{D}$ of data values and a permutation group G on $\mathbb{D}$. To deal with data values in a restricted way, we use orbit finite sets instead of finite sets to represent both of an alphabet and a set of states. A set X is called a G-set if X is equipped with actions (or operations) having the group structure G. Let X be a G-set. The orbit of $x \in X$ is the set $\{x \cdot \pi \mid \pi \in G\}$. X is *orbit finite* if X is divided into a finite number of orbits. A set $C \subseteq \mathbb{D}$ is a *support* of $x \in X$ if any action π that acts as identity on C does not move x, i.e., maps x to x. X is *nominal* if every $x \in X$ has a finite support. Intuitively, X is nominal if for every $x \in X$, all the information on x can be represented by a finite subset of data values, which corresponds to the contents of registers. A nominal automaton over an orbit finite alphabet consists of an orbit finite nominal set of states and an (equivariant) transition relation on states.

Automated learning methods are incorporated into software verification and testing (see [7,14] for an overview). Two well-known applications are black-box checking [21] and compositional verification [8]. Among others, Angluin's L^* algorithm [1] is frequently used in these methods. The algorithm learns the minimum FA for an unknown regular language U by constructing an observation table. Rows and columns of the table are sample input strings and each entry of the table is 1 (accept) or 0 (reject). The algorithm expands the table based on answers from a teacher (oracle) of U for membership and equivalence queries until the teacher answers yes to an equivalence query. The correctness of L^* is guaranteed by the Myhill-Nerode theorem for regular languages. The L^* algorithm has been extended for register automata (e.g. [4,5]) and a learning tool RALib is implemented [5]. In RA, a state transition depends on the comparison among an input data value and those stored in the registers specified as the guard condition of an applied transition rule. Due to this feature of RA, an entry of an observation table is not just 0/1 but more complex information that represents the guard condition of a transition in RA (a symbolic decision tree in [5]), which makes the algorithm rather complicated. Moerman et al. proposed an L^*-style algorithm for nominal word automata [17]. Their algorithm recovers the simplicity of the original L^* algorithm by the abstract feature of nominal automaton, which is independent of a concrete representation of an automaton. However, the algorithm assumes the equality symmetry as the structure of the set of data values. Moreover, tree models that can manipulate data values are needed for the basis of XML document processing because an XML document usually contains data values associated with structural information represented by a tree [15,16]. For such applications, tree automata theory based on nominal sets should be developed.

In this paper, we define deterministic bottom-up nominal tree automata (DBNTA), which operate on trees whose nodes are labelled with elements of an orbit finite nominal set. We then prove a Myhill-Nerode theorem for the class of languages recognized by DBNTA and propose an active learning algorithm for DBNTA based on the theorem. The algorithm can deal with any data symmetry that admits least support, not restricted to the equality symmetry and/or the total order symmetry. To prove the termination of the algorithm, we define a partial order on nominal sets and show that there is no infinite chain of orbit finite nominal sets with respect to this partial order between any two orbit finite sets.

2   Preliminaries

2.1   Nominal Set

Let G be a group and X be a set. A group action of G on X is a function $\cdot : X \times G \to X$ satisfying

$$x \cdot e = x \qquad \text{and} \qquad x \cdot (\pi\sigma) = (x \cdot \pi) \cdot \sigma$$

for all $x \in X$ and $\pi, \sigma \in G$, where $e \in G$ is the neutral element of G and $\pi\sigma$ is the product of π and σ on G. We call a set with a group action of G a G-set.

We define the *orbit* of $x \in X$ as $Orbit(x) = \{x \cdot \pi \mid \pi \in G\} \subseteq X$. A G-set is uniquely partitioned into different orbits. A G-set consisting of one orbit is called a *single orbit* set, and a G-set consisting of a finite number of orbits is called an *orbit finite* set. We define an *alphabet* as an orbit finite set.

Let X be a G-set. $Y \subseteq X$ is called *equivariant* if $y \in Y \Rightarrow y \cdot \pi \in Y$ holds for all $\pi \in G$. Equivalently, this means that Y is a union of some orbits of X. In the same way, for G-sets X and Y, a binary relation $R \subseteq X \times Y$ is called equivariant if $(x, y) \in R \Rightarrow (x \cdot \pi, y \cdot \pi) \in R$ holds for all $\pi \in G$. An n-ary equivariant relation is defined in the same way for $n \geq 3$. If a binary relation $f \subseteq X \times Y$ is a function, f is equivariant if and only if $f(x \cdot \pi) = f(x) \cdot \pi$ holds for all $x \in X$ and $\pi \in G$.

Let $\mathbb{D}$ be a countable set of data values and G be a permutation group of $\mathbb{D}$, i.e., a subgroup of the symmetric group $\mathsf{Sym}(\mathbb{D})$ of $\mathbb{D}$. We call $(\mathbb{D}, G)$ a *data symmetry*. We show some examples of data symmetries. The equality symmetry is $(\mathbb{N}, \mathsf{Sym}(\mathbb{N}))$, where $\mathbb{N}$ is the set of natural numbers and $\mathsf{Sym}(\mathbb{N})$ is the group of all bijections on $\mathbb{N}$. The total order symmetry is $(\mathbb{Q}, G_<)$ where $\mathbb{Q}$ is the set of rational numbers and $G_<$ is the group of monotone bijections on $\mathbb{Q}$. The integer symmetry is $(\mathbb{Z}, G_{\mathbb{Z}})$ where $\mathbb{Z}$ is the set of integers and $G_{\mathbb{Z}}$ is the group of translations $i \mapsto i + c$ for $c \in \mathbb{Z}$.

Let $x \in X$ and $C \subseteq \mathbb{D}$. If for every $\pi \in G$,

$$(\forall c \in C.\ \pi(c) = c) \Rightarrow x \cdot \pi = x$$

holds, we say that C *supports* x or C is a *support* of x. That is, C supports x if every π which is the identity on C does not move x. A G-set is *nominal*, if every element of the set has a finite support. In any data symmetry $(\mathbb{D}, G)$, $\mathbb{D}$ itself is a nominal G-set because any element $d \in \mathbb{D}$ has a support $\{d\} \subseteq \mathbb{D}$. $\mathbb{D}^*$ is also nominal because any element $d_1 d_2 \cdots d_n \in \mathbb{D}^*$ has a support $\{d_1, d_2, \ldots, d_n\}$. On the other hand, $\mathbb{D}^\omega$, the set of infinite sequences over $\mathbb{D}$, is not nominal. In the following, we just call an alphabet that is nominal a *nominal alphabet*.

Let $C \subseteq \mathbb{D}$ be a support of $x \in X$. If all supports of x are supersets of C, C is the *least support* of x. For a data symmetry $(\mathbb{D}, G)$, if every element of every nominal G-set has a least support, the data symmetry *admits least support*.

It is shown in [11] that the equality symmetry and the total order symmetry admit least supports. (Also see [3, Corollaries 9.4 and 9.5].) In the integer symmetry, every $G_{\mathbb{Z}}$-set is nominal by the following reason. If a translation $i \mapsto i + c$ on $\mathbb{Z}$ does not move an integer $z \in \mathbb{Z}$, the translation must be the identity. Hence, any element x of any $G_{\mathbb{Z}}$-set is supported by a singleton set of an arbitrary integer. For the same reason, the integer symmetry does not admit least support.

For a function $f : X \to Y$ and a subset $Z \subseteq X$, we write the function whose domain is restricted to Z as $f|_Z$. For functions $f : X \to Y$ and $g : Y' \to Z$, we define $fg : X' \to Z$ as $fg(x) = g(f(x))$ where $X' = \{x \in X \mid f(x) \in Y'\}$.

Let $(\mathbb{D}, G)$ be a data symmetry that admits least support, $C \subseteq \mathbb{D}$ be a finite and fungible[1] set and $S \leq \mathsf{Sym}(C)$ be a permutation group on C. For injective functions u and v from C to $\mathbb{D}$ that extend to permutations from G (i.e., $u = \pi|_C$ and $v = \sigma|_C$ for some $\pi, \sigma \in G$), we define $u \equiv_S v$ if and only if $uv^{-1} \in S$ (which equivalently means $\tau u = v$ for some $\tau \in S$). It is easy to see that $\equiv_S$ is an equivalent relation, and thus $\equiv_S$ divides the set of all injections from C to $\mathbb{D}$ that extend to permutations from G into equivalent classes. The equivalent class of u defined by $\equiv_S$ is written as $[u]_S$. For these C and S, the G-set $[\![C, S]\!]$ is defined as the set of all equivalent classes defined by $\equiv_S$, i.e. $[\![C, S]\!] = \{[\pi|_C]_S \mid \pi \in G\}$, where the G-action is defined as $[u]_S \cdot \pi = [u\pi]_S$ for all $\pi \in G$. S is called a local symmetry. As we noted before, C corresponds to the set of (canonical) data values in the registers. By definition, an element of $[\![C, S]\!]$ is an equivalent class defined by $\equiv_S$ of an injection from C to $\mathbb{D}$ that extends to some permutation in G. As shown in the example in the introduction, an automaton cannot distinguish between C and the set of data values C' obtained

---

[1] A finite set $C \subseteq \mathbb{D}$ is *fungible* if for every $c \in C$ there exists a $\pi \in G$ such that $\pi(c) \neq c$ and $\pi(c') = c'$ for all $c' \in C \setminus \{c\}$. Fungibility is a technical condition guaranteeing that $[\![C, S]\!]$ is a single orbit nominal set, but it is not directly related to the paper.

from C by any injection from C to $\mathbb{D}$ which is consistent with G. Such an injection $u : C \to \mathbb{D}$ represents this change of data values in the registers from C to C', which is indistinguishable from the automaton.

Next, we describe an intuitive meaning of S. For example, if S consists of only the identity, it means that the order of registers is relevant. If $C = \{1, 2, 3\}$ and $S = \{id, a\}$ where id is the identity and a swaps 1 and 2, then S means that the order between the first and second values are irrelevant. Note that a standard register automaton corresponds to $S = \{id\}$.

The following two propositions guarantee that a single orbit nominal set and an equivariant function between them have finite representations.

Proposition 1 ([3, **Proposition 9.15**]).

1. $[\![C, S]\!]$ *is a single orbit nominal set.*
2. *Every single orbit nominal set is isomorphic to some* $[\![C, S]\!]$.

$[\![C, S]\!]$ is called a *support representation* of a single orbit nominal set. The following proposition can be shown by [3, Proposition 9.16].

Proposition 2. *Let* $X = [\![C, S]\!]$ *and* $Y = [\![D, T]\!]$ *be single orbit nominal sets. For every equivariant function* $f : X \to Y$, *there is an injection* u *from* D *to* C *satisfying* $uS \subseteq Tu$ *and* $f([\pi|_C]_S) = [u]_T \cdot \pi$, *for all* $\pi \in G$, *where* $uS = \{us \mid s \in S\}$ *and* $Tu = \{tu \mid t \in T\}$. *Conversely, for every injection* $u : D \to C$ *satisfying* $uS \subseteq Tu$, $f([\pi|_C]_S) = [u]_T \cdot \pi$ *is an equivariant function from* X *to* Y.

By Proposition 2, we can obtain a necessary and sufficient condition for two single orbit nominal sets to be isomorphic in terms of a bijection between supports.

Lemma 1. *Single orbit nominal sets* $[\![C, S]\!]$ *and* $[\![D, T]\!]$ *are isomorphic if and only if there exists a bijection* $u : D \to C$ *satisfying* $uS = Tu$ *that extends to a permutation from* G.

Proof. Assume that there exists a bijection $u : D \to C$ satisfying $uS = Tu$ that extends to a permutation from G. Then, we have $uS \subseteq Tu$ and $u^{-1}T \subseteq Su^{-1}$. By Proposition 2, we have two functions $f : [\![C, S]\!] \to [\![D, T]\!]$ and $g : [\![D, T]\!] \to [\![C, S]\!]$ such that

$$f([\pi|_C]_S) = [u]_T \cdot \pi$$
$$g([\sigma|_D]_T) = [u^{-1}]_S \cdot \sigma.$$

We show that g is the inverse of f. From the assumption on u, there is some $\rho \in G$ satisfying $\rho|_D = u$ (and $\rho^{-1}|_C = u^{-1}$). Thus, $f([\pi|_C]_S) = [u]_T \cdot \pi = [\rho|_D]_T \cdot \pi = [(\rho\pi)|_D]_T$. Substituting this into the definition of g yields $g([(\rho\pi)|_D]_T) = [u^{-1}]_S \cdot (\rho\pi) = [\rho^{-1}|_C]_S \cdot (\rho\pi) = [(\rho^{-1}\rho\pi)|_C]_S = [\pi|_C]_S$. We have $g(f([\pi|_C]_S)) = [\pi|_C]_S$, and thus g is the inverse of f. Therefore, $[\![C, S]\!]$ and $[\![D, T]\!]$ are isomorphic.

Conversely, assume that $[\![C, S]\!]$ and $[\![D, T]\!]$ are isomorphic, i.e., there exists some equivariant bijection f from $[\![C, S]\!]$ to $[\![D, T]\!]$. By Proposition 2, f can be written as $f([\pi|_C]_S) = [\sigma|_D]_T \cdot \pi$ for some $\sigma \in G$, such that there is an injection $u : D \to C$ satisfying $\sigma|_D = u$ and $uS \subseteq Tu$. Also by Proposition 2, f^{-1} can be written as $f^{-1}([\pi|_D]_T) = [\rho|_C]_S \cdot \pi$ for some $\rho \in G$, such that there is an injection $v : C \to D$ satisfying $\rho|_C = v$ and $vT \subseteq Sv$. From this, we can derive $f^{-1}([\sigma|_D]_T \cdot \pi) = f^{-1}([(\sigma\pi)|_D]) = [\rho|_C]_S \cdot (\sigma\pi)$. By $f([\pi|_C]_S) = [\sigma|_D]_T \cdot \pi$, we have $[\rho|_C]_S \cdot (\sigma\pi) = [\pi|_C]_S$, and hence $[\rho|_C]_S = [\pi|_C]_S \cdot (\sigma\pi)^{-1} = [(\sigma|_C)^{-1}]_S$. This means that $[v]_S = [u^{-1}]_S$. Thus, we have $vu \in S$. In the same way, we have $uv \in T$. By acting u on $vT \subseteq Sv$, we have $uvTu \subseteq uSvu$, and hence we have $Tu \subseteq uS$ by $vu \in S$ and $uv \in T$. By $uS \subseteq Tu$ and $Tu \subseteq uS$, $uS = Tu$.   □

Let X and Y be nominal sets. We define $Y \preceq X$ if and only if there is an equivariant surjection from a subset of X to Y. If $Y \preceq X$ and X and Y are not isomorphic, $Y \prec X$. We show that there is no infinite chain between two orbit finite nominal sets X and Y such that $Y \preceq X$. This property is used for proving the termination of the proposed learning algorithm. We start with X and Y being single orbits.

Lemma 2. *Let $(\mathbb{D}, G)$ be a data symmetry that admits least support. Then, for any two single orbit nominal sets X and Y such that $Y \prec X$, the length of any sequence of single orbit nominal sets $X_1, X_2, \ldots$ satisfying*

$$Y \prec X_1 \prec X_2 \prec \cdots \prec X$$

is finite.

Proof. By Proposition 1, it suffices to show the lemma for $X = [\![C, S]\!]$ and $Y = [\![D, T]\!]$. Assume $[\![D, T]\!] \prec [\![C, S]\!]$. By definition of $\prec$, there exists an equivariant surjective function from a subset of $[\![C, S]\!]$ to $[\![D, T]\!]$. The domain of this function is $[\![C, S]\!]$ because $[\![C, S]\!]$ and $[\![D, T]\!]$ are single orbit sets. Thus, by Proposition 2, there exists an injection $u : D \to C$ satisfying $uS \subseteq Tu$ that extends to a permutation from G. Because u is an injection, $|D| \leq |C|$ holds where $|D|$ is the number of elements of D. If $|D| < |C|$, no injections from D to C are bijections, and hence $[\![C, S]\!]$ and $[\![D, T]\!]$ are not isomorphic by Lemma 1. If $|D| = |C|$, then $uS \subsetneq Tu$ must hold because $[\![C, S]\!]$ and $[\![D, T]\!]$ are not isomorphic. Thus, we have $S < u^{-1}Tu$. This means that S is a proper subgroup of $u^{-1}Tu$ and thus $|S| < |T|$. Therefore, because C and D are finite sets and S and T are finite groups, the length of any sequence of single orbit nominal sets $X_1, X_2, \ldots$ satisfying

$$Y \prec X_1 \prec X_2 \prec \cdots \prec X$$

is finite.   □

Lemma 3. *Let $(\mathbb{D}, G)$ be a data symmetry that admits least support. Then, for any two orbit finite nominal sets X and Y, the length of any sequence of orbit finite nominal sets $X_1, X_2, \ldots$ satisfying*

$$Y \prec X_1 \prec X_2 \prec \cdots \prec X$$

is finite.

Proof. Any orbit finite nominal set is an union of a finite number of single orbit nominal sets. Hence, this lemma obviously holds by Lemma 2.   □

2.2   Data Tree

Let $(\mathbb{D}, G)$ be a data symmetry and A be an alphabet. We define an *m-ary data tree* (simply *tree*) over A as a function $t : Pos(t) \to A$ satisfying the following two conditions:

- $Pos(t) \subseteq \{1, \ldots, m\}^*$ is a non-empty finite set that is prefix-closed, and
- every $p \in Pos(t)$ has a non-negative integer $arity(p) \le m$ satisfying

$$pi \in Pos(t) \qquad \text{for all } i \in \{1, \ldots, arity(p)\},$$

where $p\,i$ is the concatenation of p and i. The set of all m-ary data trees over A is written as $Tree_m(A)$.

We define subtree $t|_p$ of t at $p \in Pos(t)$ as

- $Pos(t|_p) = \{q \in \{1, \ldots, m\}^* \mid pq \in Pos(t)\}$, and
- $t|_p(q) = t(pq)$ for all $q \in Pos(t|_p)$.

The set of all subtrees of t is written as $Subtree(t)$. To denote a tree, we will use term representation, which is recursively defined as follows. For $a \in A$ and terms $trm_1, \ldots, trm_k$ with $0 \le k \le m$, the term $a(trm_1, \ldots, trm_k)$ represents the tree t such that $arity(\varepsilon) = k$ and

$$t(p) = \begin{cases} a & \text{if } p = \varepsilon, \\ t_i(q) & \text{if } p = iq \end{cases} \quad \text{for } 1 \le i \le k,$$

where t_i is the tree represented by trm_i for $1 \le i \le k$.

The group action on $Tree_m(A)$ is defined as $t \cdot \pi = (a \cdot \pi)(t_1 \cdot \pi, \ldots, t_k \cdot \pi)$ for all $t \in Tree_m(A)$ and $\pi \in G$. $Tree_m(A)$ is a nominal set.

Let $x \notin A$ be a variable. A tree $t \in Tree_m(A \cup \{x\})$ is called a *context* of A if and only if there is exactly one $p \in Pos(t)$ satisfying $t(p) = x$ and $arity(p) = 0$. The set of all contexts of A is written as $Context_m(A)$. For $s \in Context_m(A)$ and $t \in (Tree_m(A) \cup Context_m(A))$, we define $s[t]$ as a tree with x in s replaced by t, i.e.,

$$s[t](p) = \begin{cases} s(p) & \text{if } p \in Pos(s) \text{ and } s(p) \ne x, \\ t(q) & \text{if } p = rq, s(r) = x \text{ and } q \in Pos(t). \end{cases}$$

For $S \subseteq Context_m(A)$ and $T \subseteq (Tree_m(A) \cup Context_m(A))$, we define $S[T] = \{s[t] \mid s \in S \text{ and } t \in T\}$. For all $\pi \in G$, we define $x \cdot \pi = x$.

Example 1. Let $c \in Context_m$ be a context of $\mathbb{N}$ such that $Pos(c) = \{\varepsilon, 1\}$, $c(\varepsilon) = 2$, $c(1) = x$. Let $t \in Tree_2(\mathbb{N})$ be a 2-ary tree over $\mathbb{N}$ such that $Pos(t) = \{\varepsilon, 1, 2\}$, $t(\varepsilon) = 3$, $t(1) = 1$, $t(2) = 5$. For c and t, $c[t]$ is the tree such that $Pos(c[t]) = \{\varepsilon, 1, 11, 12\}$, $c[t](\varepsilon) = 2$, $c[t](1) = 3$, $c[t](11) = 1$, $c[t](12) = 5$. Figure 1 illustrates c, t and $c[t]$. Term representations of c, t and $c[t]$ are $c = 2(x)$, $t = 3(1, 5)$ and $c[t] = 2(3(1, 5))$, respectively. The term representation of subtree $c[t]|_{12}$ of $c[t]$ at $12 \in Pos(c[t])$ is 5.

$$c = \begin{array}{c} 2 \\ | \\ x \end{array} \qquad t = \begin{array}{c} 3 \\ / \backslash \\ 1 \quad 5 \end{array} \qquad c[t] = \begin{array}{c} 2 \\ | \\ 3 \\ / \backslash \\ 1 \quad 5 \end{array}$$

Fig. 1. Data trees and a context over $\mathbb{N}$.

3 Deterministic Bottom-Up Nominal Tree Automata

Let $(\mathbb{D}, G)$ be a data symmetry and A be an alphabet. A *deterministic bottom-up tree automaton* (*G-DBTA*) over $Tree_m(A)$ is a triple $\mathcal{A} = (Q, F, \delta)$, where

- Q is a G-set of states,
- $F \subseteq Q$ is an equivariant set of accept states, and
- $\delta = (\delta_0, \ldots, \delta_m)$ is an $m + 1$-tuple of equivariant transition functions, where

$$\delta_0 : A \to Q,$$
$$\delta_k : A \times Q^k \to Q \quad \text{for } 1 \leq k \leq m.$$

We extend δ to the function on $Tree_m(A)$ by

$$\delta(a(t_1, \ldots, t_k)) = \begin{cases} \delta_k(a, \delta(t_1), \ldots, \delta(t_k)) & \text{if } k > 0, \\ \delta_0(a) & \text{if } k = 0. \end{cases}$$

A tree t is accepted by $\mathcal{A}$ if and only if $\delta(t) \in F$. We define $L(\mathcal{A}) = \{t \in Tree_m(A) \mid \delta(t) \in F\}$. We call $L \subseteq Tree_m(A)$ a *recognizable tree language* when there exists a G-DBTA $\mathcal{A}$ satisfying $L = L(\mathcal{A})$. A G-DBTA $\mathcal{A} = (Q, F, \delta)$ is *reachable* if for all $q \in Q$, there exists some $t \in Tree_m(A)$ such that $\delta(t) = q$. If A and Q are orbit finite nominal sets, then $\mathcal{A}$ is called a *deterministic bottom-up nominal tree automaton* (*G-DBNTA*). We call $L \subseteq Tree_m(A)$ a *recognizable nominal tree language* when there exists a G-DBNTA $\mathcal{A}$ satisfying $L = L(\mathcal{A})$.

Let $X \subseteq Tree_m(A)$ be a subset of trees. For a function $T : X \to \{0, 1\}$, a G-DBTA $\mathcal{A}$ is *consistent with* T if for all $t \in X$, $t \in L(\mathcal{A}) \Leftrightarrow T(t) = 1$.

Example 2. Let the set $\mathbb{N}$ of natural numbers be an alphabet and $(\mathbb{N}, \mathsf{Sym}(\mathbb{N}))$ be a data symmetry. Let $\mathcal{A} = (Q, F, \delta)$ be a G-DBTA over $Tree_2(\mathbb{N})$, where $Q = \mathbb{N} \cup \{accept, reject\}$, $F = \{accept\}$ and $\delta = (\delta_0, \delta_1, \delta_2)$ such that $\delta_0(d) = d$, $\delta_1(d, q) = reject$ and $\delta_2(d, q_1, q_2) = accept$ if $q_1 = q_2 = d$, *reject* otherwise. For all $\pi \in \mathsf{Sym}(\mathbb{N})$, we define $accept \cdot \pi = accept$ and $reject \cdot \pi = reject$. It is easy to see that all components of $\mathcal{A}$ are equivariant. The tree language recognized by $\mathcal{A}$ is $L(\mathcal{A}) = \{d(d, d) \mid d \in \mathbb{N}\}$.

4   Myhill-Nerode Theorem

Let $(\mathbb{D}, G)$ be a data symmetry that admits least support and A be a nominal alphabet. For $L \subseteq Tree_m(A)$, we define the binary relation $\approx_L$ over $Tree_m(A)$ as follows: $u \approx_L v$ if and only if

$$C[u] \in L \text{ iff } C[v] \in L \text{ for all } C \in Context_m(A).$$

It is easy to check that $\approx_L$ is an congruence relation on $Tree_m(A)$, i.e., $\approx_L$ is an equivalent relation that satisfies $a(u_1, \dots, u_k) \approx_L a(v_1, \dots, v_k)$ for all $a \in A$ and $u_1, \dots, u_k, v_1, \dots, v_k \in Tree_m(A)$ with $u_i \approx_L v_i$ for $0 \leq i \leq k$. We write the equivalent class of $t \in Tree_m(A)$ as $[t]$.

Lemma 4. *If $L \subseteq Tree_m(A)$ is equivariant, then $\approx_L$ is also equivariant.*

Proof. We show that $t \cdot \pi \approx_L t' \cdot \pi$ for all $\pi \in G$ and $t, t' \in Tree_m(A)$ such that $t \approx_L t'$. By the definition of $\approx_L$, $t \cdot \pi \approx_L t' \cdot \pi$ is equivalent to $C[t \cdot \pi] \in L$ iff $C[t' \cdot \pi] \in L$ for all $C \in Context_m(A)$. By the equivariance of L, this is equivalent to $C[t \cdot \pi] \cdot \pi^{-1} \in L$ iff $C[t' \cdot \pi] \cdot \pi^{-1} \in L$. By the definition of the group action on $Tree_m(A)$, this is equivalent to $(C \cdot \pi^{-1})[t] \in L$ iff $(C \cdot \pi^{-1})[t'] \in L$. We can prove this by $t \approx_L t'$. □

Lemma 5 ([3, **Lemma 3.5**]). *Let X be a G-set and $R \subseteq X \times X$ be an equivalence relation that is equivariant. Then the quotient X/R is a G-set, under the action $[x]_R \cdot \pi = [x \cdot \pi]_R$ of G, and the abstraction mapping $x \mapsto [x]_R : X \to X/R$ is an equivariant function.*

For $L \subseteq Tree_m(A)$, we define the *syntactic tree automaton* $\mathcal{A}_L = (Q_L, F_L, \delta_L)$ as

- $Q_L = Tree_m(A)/\approx_L$,
- $F_L = \{[t] \mid t \in L\}$ and
- $\delta_L = (\delta_{L,0}, \dots, \delta_{L,m})$ where $\delta_{L,0} : A \to Q_L$ and $\delta_{L,k} : A \times Q_L^k \to Q_L$ for $1 \leq k \leq m$ are defined as

$$\delta_{L,0}(a) = [a],$$
$$\delta_{L,k}(a, [u_1], \dots, [u_k]) = [a(u_1, \dots, u_k)].$$

Because $\approx_L$ is a congruence relation, δ_L is well-defined.

Lemma 6. *If $L \subseteq Tree_m(A)$ is equivariant, then the syntactic tree automaton $\mathcal{A}_L = (Q_L, F_L, \delta_L)$ is a reachable G-DBTA.*

Proof. Because L is equivariant, $\approx_L$ is also equivariant by Lemma 4. Thus, by Lemma 5, $Q_L = Tree_m(A)/\approx_L$ is a G-set. By the equivariance of L,

$$[t] \in F_L \Leftrightarrow t \in L \Leftrightarrow t \cdot \pi \in L \Leftrightarrow [t \cdot \pi] \in F_L \Leftrightarrow [t] \cdot \pi \in F_L.$$

Thus, F_L is equivariant. By $\delta_L(a, [u_1], \dots, [u_k]) \cdot \pi = [a(u_1, \dots, u_k)] \cdot \pi = [(a \cdot \pi)(u_1 \cdot \pi, \dots, u_k \cdot \pi)] = \delta_L(a \cdot \pi, [u_1 \cdot \pi], \dots, [u_k \cdot \pi]) = \delta_L(a \cdot \pi, [u_1] \cdot \pi, \dots, [u_k] \cdot \pi)$, δ_L is equivariant. Thus, $\mathcal{A}_L$ is a G-DBTA. $\mathcal{A}_L$ is apparently reachable. □

Let $\mathcal{A} = (Q, F, \delta)$ and $\mathcal{A}' = (Q', F', \delta')$ be G-DBTAs. An equivariant function $\varphi : P \to Q'$ for some $P \subseteq Q$ satisfying the following two conditions is called a *partial homomorphism* from $\mathcal{A}$ to $\mathcal{A}'$:

- $q \in F$ iff $\varphi(q) \in F'$ for all $q \in P$, and
- $\varphi(\delta(a, q_1, \ldots, q_k)) = \delta'(a, \varphi(q_1), \ldots, \varphi(q_k))$ for all $q_1, \ldots, q_k \in P$ $(0 \leq k \leq m)$ and $a \in A$.

When there exists a surjective partial homomorphism from a subset of Q to Q', we write $\mathcal{A}' \sqsubseteq \mathcal{A}$. If $P = Q$, then φ is called a *homomorphism* from $\mathcal{A}$ to $\mathcal{A}'$. It is easy to see that $L(\mathcal{A}) = L(\mathcal{A}')$ if there is a homomorphism φ from $\mathcal{A}$ to $\mathcal{A}'$. When φ is surjective, $\mathcal{A}'$ is called an *image* of $\mathcal{A}$. If $\mathcal{A}'$ is an image of $\mathcal{A}$ and the state set of $\mathcal{A}$ is orbit finite, the state set of $\mathcal{A}'$ is also orbit finite.

Lemma 7. *Let L be a recognizable tree language. The syntactic automaton A_L is an image of any reachable G-DBTA recognizing L.*

Proof. Let $\mathcal{A} = (Q, F, \delta)$ be a reachable G-DBTA recognizing L. We define $\varphi : Q \to Tree_m(A)/\approx_L$ as $\varphi(\delta(t)) = [t]$. The definition of φ is well-defined because $\mathcal{A}$ is reachable and $\delta(u) = \delta(v)$ implies $[u] = [v]$. It is easy to check that f is surjective. By the equivariance of δ,

$$\varphi(\delta(t) \cdot \pi) = \varphi(\delta(t \cdot \pi)) = [t \cdot \pi] = [t] \cdot \pi = \varphi(\delta(t)) \cdot \pi.$$

Thus, φ is equivariant. We have

$$\varphi(\delta(a(u_1, \ldots, u_k))) = [a(u_1, \ldots, u_k)]$$
$$= \delta_L(a, [u_1], \ldots, [u_k]) = \delta(a, \varphi(\delta(u_1)), \ldots, \varphi(\delta(u_k))).$$

We also have $\delta(t) \in F \Leftrightarrow t \in L \Leftrightarrow [t] \in F_L$. Therefore, φ is a homomorphism, and hence A_L is an image of $\mathcal{A}$. $\square$

Let $\mathcal{A} = (Q, F, \delta)$ be a reachable G-DBTA over $Tree_m(A)$. The equivariant function $t \mapsto \delta(t)$ from $Tree_m(A)$ to Q is surjective because $\mathcal{A}$ is reachable. If $C \subseteq \mathbb{D}$ supports t, then C also supports $\delta(t)$ because $t \cdot \pi = t$ implies $\delta(t) \cdot \pi = \delta(t \cdot \pi) = \delta(t)$ for all $\pi \in G$. Thus, Q is nominal because $Tree_m(A)$ is nominal.

Theorem 1. *Let $L \subseteq Tree_m(A)$ be an equivariant set. The following two conditions are equivalent:*

(1) $Tree_m(A)/\approx_L$ is orbit finite.
(2) L is recognized by a G-DBNTA.

Proof. (1) $\Rightarrow$ (2) can be easily proved by Lemma 6. Without loss of generality, assume that a given G-DBNTA is reachable. (2) $\Rightarrow$ (1) can be proved by Lemma 7. $\square$

5   Observation Table

In this and the next sections, we extend the L^*-style algorithm in [17] to DBNTA. For the extension from words to trees, we extend some notions given in [22], where another L^*-style algorithm is proposed to learn the set of derivation trees of an unknown context-free grammar without data values.

From now on, we assume a data symmetry $(\mathbb{D}, G)$ that admits least support and a nominal alphabet A. Let $B \subseteq Tree_m(A)$ and $C \subseteq Context_m(A)$. We say that B is *subtree-closed* if and only if for every $b \in B$, $Subtree(b) \subseteq B$ holds. We also say that C is *x-prefix-closed* on B if and only if every $c \in C \setminus \{x\}$ has some $c' \in C$ satisfying $c = c'[a(b_1, \ldots, b_{i-1}, x, b_i, \ldots, b_{k-1})]$ where $b_1, \ldots, b_{k-1} \in B$ and $a \in A$.

Definition 1. *Let U be an unknown recognizable nominal tree language. An observation table is a triple $(\mathcal{S}, \mathcal{E}, \mathcal{T})$, where*

- $\mathcal{S} \subseteq Tree_m(A)$ *is an equivariant orbit finite set that is subtree-closed and satisfies $A \subseteq \mathcal{S}$.*
- $Next(\mathcal{S}) = \{a(t_1, \ldots, t_k) \notin \mathcal{S} \mid a \in A, t_1, \ldots, t_k \in \mathcal{S}, 1 \le k \le m\}$,
- $\mathcal{E} \subseteq Context_m(A)$ *is an equivariant orbit finite set that is x-prefix-closed on $\mathcal{S}$, and*
- $\mathcal{T} : \mathcal{E}[\mathcal{S} \cup Next(\mathcal{S})] \to \{0, 1\}$ *is an equivariant function, where $\mathcal{T}(e[s]) = 1$ iff $e[s] \in U$ for all $e \in \mathcal{E}$ and $s \in \mathcal{S} \cup Next(\mathcal{S})$.*   □

We define the function $row_{(\mathcal{S}, \mathcal{E}, \mathcal{T})} : \mathcal{S} \cup Next(\mathcal{S}) \to 2^{\mathcal{E}}$ as $row_{(\mathcal{S}, \mathcal{E}, \mathcal{T})}(s) = \{e \in \mathcal{E} \mid \mathcal{T}(e[s]) = 1\}$. We abbreviate $row_{(\mathcal{S}, \mathcal{E}, \mathcal{T})}$ as row if $(\mathcal{S}, \mathcal{E}, \mathcal{T})$ is clear from the context. It is easy to see that row is equivariant. For $X \subseteq \mathcal{S} \cup Next(\mathcal{S})$, we define $row(X) = \{row(s) \mid s \in X\}$.

An observation table can be expressed by the table with rows labeled with the elements of $\mathcal{S} \cup Next(\mathcal{S})$ and columns labeled with the elements of $\mathcal{E}$ as shown in Fig. 2.

		$\mathcal{E}$
		e
$\mathcal{S}$	s	$\vdots$ $\cdots \quad \mathcal{T}(e[s])$
$Next(\mathcal{S})$		

Fig. 2. Observation table $(\mathcal{S}, \mathcal{E}, \mathcal{T})$

An observation table $(\mathcal{S}, \mathcal{E}, \mathcal{T})$ is *closed* if and only if for all $t \in Next(\mathcal{S})$, there exists some $s \in \mathcal{S}$ satisfying $row(t) = row(s)$. An observation table $(\mathcal{S}, \mathcal{E}, \mathcal{T})$ is *consistent* if and only if for every $s_1, s_2 \in \mathcal{S}$, $row(s_1) = row(s_2)$ implies

$$row(a(u_1, \ldots, u_{i-1}, s_1, u_i, \ldots, u_{k-1})) = row(a(u_1, \ldots, u_{i-1}, s_2, u_i, \ldots, u_{k-1}))$$

for all $a \in A, u_1, \ldots, u_{k-1} \in \mathcal{S}$ and $1 \le i \le k$.

Let $(\mathcal{S}, \mathcal{E}, \mathcal{T})$ be a closed and consistent observation table. We define the G-DBNTA $\mathcal{A}(\mathcal{S}, \mathcal{E}, \mathcal{T}) = (\tilde{Q}, \tilde{F}, \tilde{\delta})$ derived from $(\mathcal{S}, \mathcal{E}, \mathcal{T})$ as follows:

- $\tilde{Q} = row(\mathcal{S}) = \{row(s) \mid s \in \mathcal{S}\}$,
- $\tilde{F} = \{row(s) \mid s \in \mathcal{S}, \mathcal{T}(s) = 1\}$,
- $\tilde{\delta}_k(a, row(s_1), \ldots, row(s_k)) = row(a(s_1, \ldots, s_k))$ for $s_1, \ldots, s_k \in \mathcal{S}$.

It is easy to see that $\mathcal{A}(\mathcal{S}, \mathcal{E}, \mathcal{T})$ is well-defined: Let $s_1, s_2 \in \mathcal{S}$ be trees satisfying $row(s_1) = row(s_2)$. Because $\mathcal{E}$ is x-prefix-closed, $x \in \mathcal{E}$ holds. Thus, $\mathcal{T}(s_1) = \mathcal{T}(x[s_1])$ and $\mathcal{T}(s_2) = \mathcal{T}(x[s_2])$ are defined, and $\mathcal{T}(s_1) = \mathcal{T}(s_2)$, and so $\tilde{F}$ is well-defined. Because $(\mathcal{S}, \mathcal{E}, \mathcal{T})$ is consistent,

$$row(a(u_1, \ldots, u_{i-1}, s_1, u_i, \ldots, u_{k-1})) = row(a(u_1, \ldots, u_{i-1}, s_2, u_i, \ldots, u_{k-1}))$$

for all $a \in A, u_1, \ldots, u_{k-1} \in \mathcal{S}$ and $1 \le i \le k$. Moreover, because $(\mathcal{S}, \mathcal{E}, \mathcal{T})$ is closed, there is $s \in \mathcal{S}$ satisfying $row(s) = row(a(u_1, \ldots, u_{i-1}, s_1, u_i, \ldots, u_{k-1}))$. Therefore, $\tilde{\delta}$ is well-defined. Because $\mathcal{S}$ is an orbit finite nominal set and row is an equivarinat function, $\tilde{Q}(= row(\mathcal{S}))$ is also an orbit finite nominal set.

Lemma 8. *Let $(\mathcal{S}, \mathcal{E}, \mathcal{T})$ be a closed and consistent observation table. Then, $\mathcal{A}(\mathcal{S}, \mathcal{E}, \mathcal{T}) = (\tilde{Q}, \tilde{F}, \tilde{\delta})$ is consistent with $\mathcal{T}$.*

The proof is similar to the proof of Lemma 4.2 in [22].

Theorem 2. *For a (not necessarily closed and consistent) observation table $(\mathcal{S}, \mathcal{E}, \mathcal{T})$ and a G-DBNTA $\mathcal{A} = (Q, F, \delta)$ consistent with $\mathcal{T}$, $row(\mathcal{S}) \preceq Q$ holds.*

Proof. We show that the function $\delta(s) \mapsto row(s)$ is an equivariant surjection from $\{\delta(s) \mid s \in \mathcal{S}\} \subseteq Q$ to $row(\mathcal{S})$. This function is well-defined since

$$\delta(s_1) = \delta(s_2) \Rightarrow \forall e \in \mathcal{E}.\delta(e[s_1]) = \delta(e[s_2])$$
$$\Rightarrow \forall e \in \mathcal{E}.e[s_1] \in L(\mathcal{A}) \quad iff \quad e[s_2] \in L(\mathcal{A})$$
$$\Leftrightarrow \forall e \in \mathcal{E}.\mathcal{T}(e[s_1]) = \mathcal{T}(e[s_2])$$
$$\Leftrightarrow row(s_1) = row(s_2).$$

This function is also equivariant because $\delta(s) \cdot \pi = \delta(s \cdot \pi) \mapsto row(s \cdot \pi) = row(s) \cdot \pi$. Surjectivity is clear. Therefore, because there is an equivariant function from a subset of Q to $row(\mathcal{S})$, $row(\mathcal{S}) \preceq Q$ holds. □

If an observation table is closed and consistent, Theorem 2 can be lifted from a relation on states ($\preceq$) to a relation on automata ($\sqsubseteq$) as stated in the next lemma.

Lemma 9. *Let $(\mathcal{S}, \mathcal{E}, \mathcal{T})$ be a closed and consistent observation table. For every G-DBNTA $\mathcal{A}$ that is consistent with $\mathcal{T}$, $A(\mathcal{S}, \mathcal{E}, \mathcal{T}) \sqsubseteq \mathcal{A}$ holds.*

Proof. Let $A(\mathcal{S}, \mathcal{E}, \mathcal{T}) = (\tilde{Q}, \tilde{F}, \tilde{\delta})$ and $A = (Q, F, \delta)$. By the proof of Theorem 2, the function $\varphi : \delta(s) \mapsto row(s)$ from $\{\delta(s) \mid s \in \mathcal{S}\} \subseteq Q$ to $\tilde{Q}(= row(\mathcal{S}))$ is equivariant and surjective. By $\delta(s) \in F \Leftrightarrow \mathcal{T}(s) = 1 \Leftrightarrow row(s) \in \tilde{F} \Leftrightarrow \varphi(\delta(s)) \in \tilde{F}$ and $\varphi(\delta(a, \delta(s_1), \ldots, \delta(s_k))) = \varphi(\delta(a(s_1, \ldots, s_k))) = row(a(s_1, \ldots, s_k)) = \tilde{\delta}(a, row(s_1), \ldots, row(s_k)) = \tilde{\delta}(a, \varphi(\delta(s_1)), \ldots, \varphi(\delta(s_k)))$, φ is a partial homomorphism. □

By Lemmas 8 and 9, we have the following theorem.

Theorem 3. *Let $(\mathcal{S}, \mathcal{E}, \mathcal{T})$ be a closed and consistent observation table. $A(\mathcal{S}, \mathcal{E}, \mathcal{T})$ is consistent with $\mathcal{T}$, and for every G-DBNTA $\mathcal{A}$ that is consistent with $\mathcal{T}$, $A(\mathcal{S}, \mathcal{E}, \mathcal{T}) \sqsubseteq \mathcal{A}$ holds.*

6   Learning Algorithm

We show the proposed learning algorithm (Algorithm 1) in the following page. We will give a part of a run of Algorithm 1 on an example in Sect. 7. In Algorithm 1, we assume that the teacher answering queries is given as an oracle. In an application to the compositional verification, for example, the teacher is implemented as a model checker (see [8]).

Because $\mathcal{S}$ and $\mathcal{E}$ of an observation table $(\mathcal{S}, \mathcal{E}, \mathcal{T})$ can be infinite sets, we have to show that $(\mathcal{S}, \mathcal{E}, \mathcal{T})$ can be expressed by finite means and each step of Algorithm 1 runs in finite steps. We first show that $(\mathcal{S}, \mathcal{E}, \mathcal{T})$ has a finite description. Because $\mathcal{S}$ and $\mathcal{E}$ are orbit finite nominal sets, by Proposition 1, we can express $\mathcal{S}$ and $\mathcal{E}$ by support representations. By Proposition 2, we can express $\mathcal{T}$ by finite means because $\mathcal{T}$ consists of a finite number of equivariant functions whose domains and ranges are both single orbit nominal sets. In Algorithm 1, each orbit O is represented by any one element $s \in O$. Let us call s a representative of O.

Next, we show that each step of Algorithm 1 runs in finite steps. To check the closedness in line 10 of Algorithm 1, it suffices to check whether for each orbit O of $Next(\mathcal{S})$ and a representative s' of O, there is $s \in \mathcal{S}$ such that $row(s) = row(s')$. Finding $s \in \mathcal{S}$ satisfying $row(s) = row(s')$ is equivalent to finding $\pi \in G$ such that $row(s') = row(t \cdot \pi) (= row(t) \cdot \pi)$ for some representative $t \in \mathcal{S}$. Let $C, D \subseteq \mathbb{D}$ be the least supports of $row(s')$ and $row(t)$, respectively. The least support of $row(t) \cdot \pi$ is $D \cdot \pi$. Thus, if $row(s') = row(t \cdot \pi)$, then $C = D \cdot \pi$ must hold. Moreover, because D is the (least) support of $row(t)$, if $\pi_1|_D = \pi_2|_D$ then $row(t) \cdot \pi_1 = row(t) \cdot \pi_2$. Thus, we only have to check a finite number of π satisfying $C = D \cdot \pi$. To check the consistency in line 5 of Algorithm 1, it suffices to check the emptiness of

$$\{(s_1, s_2, a, e) \in \mathcal{S} \times \mathcal{S} \times A \times \mathcal{E} \mid row(s_1) = row(s_2) \text{ and for } \exists u_1, \ldots, u_{k-1} \in \mathcal{S},$$
$$\mathcal{T}(e[a(u_1, \ldots, u_{i-1}, s_1, u_i, \ldots, u_{k-1})]) \neq \mathcal{T}(e[a(u_1, \ldots, u_{i-1}, s_2, u_i, \ldots, u_{k-1})])\}.$$

Algorithm 1. Angluin-style algorithm for *G-DBNTA*

1: $\mathcal{S} := A, \mathcal{E} := \{x\}$;
2: Construct the initial observation table $(\mathcal{S}, \mathcal{E}, \mathcal{T})$ using membership queries;
3: **repeat**
4:     **while** $(\mathcal{S}, \mathcal{E}, \mathcal{T})$ is not closed or not consistent **do**
5:         **if** $(\mathcal{S}, \mathcal{E}, \mathcal{T})$ is not consistent **then**
6:             Find $s_1, s_2, u_1, \ldots, u_{k-1} \in \mathcal{S}, e \in \mathcal{E}, a \in A, i \in \mathbb{N}$ such that

$$row(s_1) = row(s_2) \text{ and}$$
$$T(e[a(u_1, \ldots, u_{i-1}, s_1, u_i, \ldots, u_k)]) \neq T(e[a(u_1, \ldots, u_{i-1}, s_2, u_i, \ldots, u_k)]);$$

7:             Add $Orbit(e[a(u_1, \ldots, u_{i-1}, x, u_i, \ldots, u_k)])$ to $\mathcal{E}$;
8:             Extend $\mathcal{T}$ to $\mathcal{E}[(\mathcal{S} \cup Next(\mathcal{S}))]$ using membership queries;
9:         **end if**
10:         **if** $(\mathcal{S}, \mathcal{E}, \mathcal{T})$ is not closed **then**
11:             Find $s' \in Next(\mathcal{S})$ such that $row(s') \neq row(s)$ for all $s \in \mathcal{S}$;
12:             Add $Orbit(s')$ to $\mathcal{S}$;
13:             Extend $\mathcal{T}$ to $\mathcal{E}[\mathcal{S} \cup Next(\mathcal{S})]$ using membership queries;
14:         **end if**
15:     **end while**
16:     Let $\mathcal{A} = \mathcal{A}(\mathcal{S}, \mathcal{E}, \mathcal{T})$;
17:     Construct the conjecture $\mathcal{A}$;
18:     **if** the Teacher replies *no* with a counter-example t **then**
19:         Add $Orbit(Subtree(t))$ to $\mathcal{S}$;
20:         Extend $\mathcal{T}$ to $\mathcal{E}[\mathcal{S} \cup Next(\mathcal{S})]$ using membership queries;
21:     **end if**
22: **until** the Teacher replies *yes* to the conjecture $\mathcal{A}$;
23: **return** $\mathcal{A}$;

$\mathcal{S} \times \mathcal{S} \times A \times \mathcal{E}$ is an orbit finite nominal set, and the above set is a union of some orbits of $\mathcal{S} \times \mathcal{S} \times A \times \mathcal{E}$. Thus, we can check the emptiness of the set, and if not, we can obtain representatives of the set.

Correctness Because Algorithm 1 uses an equivalence query, if it terminates, then it outputs the correct *G-DBNTA*.

    To prove the termination of Algorithm 1, we show the following two lemmas that guarantee that $row(\mathcal{S})$ strictly increases with respect to $\prec$ each time an observation table is extended.

Lemma 10. *If $(\mathcal{S}, \mathcal{E}, \mathcal{T})$ and $(\mathcal{S}', \mathcal{E}, \mathcal{T}')$ are observation tables such that $\mathcal{S} \subsetneq \mathcal{S}'$ and $T'(e[s]) = T(e[s])$ for all $e \in \mathcal{E}$ and $s \in \mathcal{S}$, then $row_{(\mathcal{S}, \mathcal{E}, \mathcal{T})}(\mathcal{S}) \prec row_{(\mathcal{S}', \mathcal{E}, \mathcal{T}')}(\mathcal{S}')$.*

Proof. The lemma obviously holds because if $\mathcal{S} \subsetneq \mathcal{S}'$, the number of orbits of $\mathcal{S}'$ is larger than that of $\mathcal{S}$.   □

Lemma 11. *If $(\mathcal{S}, \mathcal{E}, \mathcal{T})$ and $(\mathcal{S}, \mathcal{E}', \mathcal{T}')$ are observation tables such that $\mathcal{E} \subsetneq \mathcal{E}'$ and $T'(e[s]) = T(e[s])$ for all $e \in \mathcal{E}$ and $s \in \mathcal{S}$, then $row_{(\mathcal{S}, \mathcal{E}, \mathcal{T})}(\mathcal{S}) \prec row_{(\mathcal{S}, \mathcal{E}', \mathcal{T}')}(\mathcal{S})$.*

A proof of this lemma is given in the full version of this paper [19].

Termination and minimality. Let U be an unknown recognizable nominal tree language and $\mathcal{A}_U = (Q_U, F_U, \delta_U)$ be the syntactic tree automaton constructed from U. $\mathcal{A}_U$ is the minimum G-DBNTA recognizing U in the sence of Lemma 7. Let $(\mathcal{S}_0, \mathcal{E}_0, \mathcal{T}_0), (\mathcal{S}_1, \mathcal{E}_1, \mathcal{T}_1), (\mathcal{S}_2, \mathcal{E}_2, \mathcal{T}_2), \ldots$ be observation tables constructed by Algorithm 1 where $(\mathcal{S}_i, \mathcal{E}_i, \mathcal{T}_i)$ extends to $(\mathcal{S}_{i+1}, \mathcal{E}_{i+1}, \mathcal{T}_{i+1})$ for $i \geq 0$. Note that $\mathcal{A}_U$ is consistent with every $\mathcal{T}_i$ for $i \geq 0$. By Lemmas 10 and 11, $row(\mathcal{S}_0) \prec row(\mathcal{S}_1) \prec row(\mathcal{S}_2) \prec \cdots$. By Theorem 2, $row(\mathcal{S}_i) \preceq Q_U$ for $i \geq 0$. By Lemma 3, there is a non-negative integer n such that $row(\mathcal{S}_0) \prec row(\mathcal{S}_1) \prec \cdots \prec row(\mathcal{S}_n) = Q_U$. Thus, Algorithm 1 terminates in finite steps. By Lemma 9, $\mathcal{A}(\mathcal{S}_i, \mathcal{E}_i, \mathcal{T}_i) \sqsubseteq \mathcal{A}_U$ holds for every $i \geq 0$ such that $(\mathcal{S}_i, \mathcal{E}_i, \mathcal{T}_i)$ is closed and consistent, and hence, Algorithm 1 outputs the minimum G-DBNTA recognizing U when it terminates.

Running time analysis. When Algorithm 1 extends an observation table $(\mathcal{S}, \mathcal{E}, \mathcal{T})$, the number of orbits of $row(\mathcal{S})$ increases or some orbits of $row(\mathcal{S})$ extend. Extending an orbit $[\![C, S]\!]$ of $row(\mathcal{S})$ to $[\![D, T]\!]$ implies $|C| \leq |D|$. If $|C| = |D|$, then $T \leq uSu^{-1}$ must hold for some injection $u : D \to C$. By the standard theorem of finite groups, $|uSu^{-1}|(= |S|)$ can be divided by $|T|$. Therefore, we have the following theorem:

Theorem 4. *Let U be an unknown recognizable nominal tree language, $Q = [\![C_1, S_1]\!] \cup \cdots \cup [\![C_n, S_n]\!]$ be the set of states of the minimum G-DBNTA recognizing U, n be the number of orbits of Q and $m = \max\{|C_1|, \ldots, |C_n|\}$ be the largest cardinality of least supports of orbits of Q. Let $p_1, \ldots, p_k$ be prime numbers and $j_1, \ldots, j_k$ be positive integers such that $m! = p_1^{j_1} \cdot p_2^{j_2} \cdots \cdot p_k^{j_k}$. Observation tables are extended at most $O(nm(j_1 + \cdots + j_k))$ times.*

7   Example

Let $(\mathbb{N}, \mathsf{Sym}(\mathbb{N}))$ be the equality symmetry and $A = \mathbb{N}$ be an alphabet. Note that $(\mathbb{N}, \mathsf{Sym}(\mathbb{N}))$ admits least support and A is a single orbit nominal set. Let $U = Orbit(1) \cup Orbit(1(1)) \cup Orbit(1(1(1))) \subseteq Tree_2(A)$. We now show a part of a run of Algorithm 1 for U.

First, the elements of the initial observation table $(\mathcal{S}_0, \mathcal{E}_0, \mathcal{T}_0)$ shown in Table 1(a) are $\mathcal{S}_0 = Orbit(1) (= \mathbb{N})$, $\mathcal{E}_0 = \{x\}$, $Next(\mathcal{S}_0) = Orbit(1(1)) \cup Orbit(2(1)) \cup Orbit(1(1,1)) \cup Orbit(1(2,1)) \cup Orbit(1(1,2)) \cup Orbit(2(1,1))$, $\mathcal{T}_0(a) = \mathcal{T}_0(a(a)) = 1$ and $\mathcal{T}_0(a(b)) = \mathcal{T}_0(a(a,a)) = \mathcal{T}_0(a(b,a)) = \mathcal{T}_0(a(a,b)) = \mathcal{T}_0(a(b,b)) = 0$ for all $a, b \in A$ such that $a \neq b$. This observation table $(\mathcal{S}_0, \mathcal{E}_0, \mathcal{T}_0)$ is consistent but not closed because there is no $s \in \mathcal{S}_0$ such that $row(s) = row(2(1))$. Thus, Algorithm 1 adds $Orbit(2(1))$ to $\mathcal{S}_0$ and extends $\mathcal{T}_0$ using membership queries. We have the observation table $(\mathcal{S}_1, \mathcal{E}_1, \mathcal{T}_1)$ shown in Table 1(b) where

$$\mathcal{S}_1 = Orbit(1) \cup Orbit(2(1)), \quad \mathcal{E}_1 = \{x\},$$
$$Next(\mathcal{S}_1) = \{a(t) \notin \mathcal{S}_1 \mid a \in A, t \in \mathcal{S}_1\} \cup \{a(t_1, t_2) \notin \mathcal{S}_1 \mid a \in A, t_1, t_2 \in \mathcal{S}_1\}.$$

$(\mathcal{S}_1, \mathcal{E}_1, \mathcal{T}_1)$ is closed and consistent, and Algorithm 1 asks an equivalence query with G-DBNTA $\mathcal{A}(\mathcal{S}_1, \mathcal{E}_1, \mathcal{T}_1)$. $\mathcal{A}(\mathcal{S}_1, \mathcal{E}_1, \mathcal{T}_1)$ does not recognize U because $1(1(1)) \notin L(\mathcal{A}(\mathcal{S}_1, \mathcal{E}_1, \mathcal{T}_1)$. Thus, Algorithm 1 adds $Orbit(1(1(1)))$ to $\mathcal{S}_1$ if $1(1(1))$ is returned as a counterexample and extends $\mathcal{T}_1$ using membership queries. We have the observation table $(\mathcal{S}_2, \mathcal{E}_2, \mathcal{T}_2)$ shown in Table 1(c). $(\mathcal{S}_2, \mathcal{E}_2, \mathcal{T}_2)$ is closed but not consistent because despite $row(1) = row(1(1(1)))$, $row(1(1)) \neq row(1(1(1(1))))$. Thus, Algorithm 1 adds $Orbit(1(x))$ to $\mathcal{E}_2$ and extends $\mathcal{T}_2$ using membership queries, resulting in the observation table $(\mathcal{S}_3, \mathcal{E}_3, \mathcal{T}_3)$ shown in Table 1(d). Continuing these extensions, Algorithm 1 finally obtains an observation table $(\mathcal{S}_n, \mathcal{E}_n, \mathcal{T}_n)$ such that $\mathcal{A}(\mathcal{S}_n, \mathcal{E}_n, \mathcal{T}_n)$ recognizes U.

Table 1. An example run

Table 1(a)

	x
a	1
$a(a)$	1
$a(b)$	0
$a(a,a)$	0
$a(a,b)$	0
$a(b,a)$	0
$a(b,b)$	0

Table 1(b)

	x
a	1
$a(b)$	0
$a(a)$	1
$a(a,a)$	0
$a(a,b)$	0
$a(b,a)$	0
$a(b,b)$	0
$others$	0

Table 1(c)

	x
a	1
$a(b)$	0
$a(a(a))$	1
$a(a)$	1
$a(a,a)$	0
$a(a,b)$	0
$a(b,a)$	0
$a(b,b)$	0
$others$	0

Table 1(d)

	x	$c(x)$
a	1	$1\ (a = c)$ $0\ (a \neq c)$
$a(b)$	0	0
$a(a(a))$	1	0
$a(a)$	1	$1\ (a = c)$ $0\ (a \neq c)$
$a(a,a)$	0	0
$a(a,b)$	0	0
$a(b,a)$	0	0
$a(b,b)$	0	0
$others$	0	0

for all $a, b, c \in A$ satisfying $a \neq b$.

8   Conclusion

In this paper, we defined deterministic bottom-up nominal tree automata (DBNTA), which operate on trees whose nodes are labelled with elements of an orbit finite nominal set. We then proved a Myhill-Nerode theorem for the class of languages recognized by DBNTA and proposed an active learning algorithm for DBNTA based on the theorem. The algorithm can deal with any data symmetry that admits least support, not restricted to the equality symmetry and/or the total order symmetry.

Implementation and possible applications of the proposed learning algorithm are left as future work. For implementation, a concrete data structure for support representations of orbit finite sets in an observation table should be determined. Moreover, we are considering an application of the proposed algorithm to a compositional verification of a program that manipulates XML documents.

References

1. Angluin, D.: Learning regular sets from queries and counterexamples. Inf. Comput. **75**, 87–106 (1987)
2. Bojańczyk, M., David, C., Muscholl, A., Schwentick, T., Segoufin, L.: Two-variable logic on data words. ACM Trans. Comput. Log. **12**(4), 1–26, 27 (2011)
3. Bojańczyk, M., Klin, B., Lasota, S.: Automata theory in nominal sets. Log. Methods Comput. Sci. **10**(3:4), 1–44 (2014)
4. Bollig, B., Habermehl, P., Leucker, M., Monmege, B.: A fresh approach to learning register automata. In: Béal, M.-P., Carton, O. (eds.) DLT 2013. LNCS, vol. 7907, pp. 118–130. Springer, Heidelberg (2013). https://doi.org/10.1007/978-3-642-38771-5_12
5. Cassel, S., Howar, F., Jonsson, B., Steffen, B.: Active learning for extended finite state machines. Formal Aspects Comput. **28**(2), 233–263 (2016). https://doi.org/10.1007/s00165-016-0355-5
6. Cheng, E.Y.C., Kaminski, M.: Context-free languages over infinite alphabets. Acta Inform. **35**, 245–267 (1998)
7. Clarke, E.M., Grumberg, J.O., Kroening, D., Peled, D., Veith, H.: Model Checking, Second. Edition, Chapter 15: Verification with Automata Learning. The MIT Press, Cambridge (2018)
8. Cobleigh, J.M., Giannakopoulou, D., PǍsǍreanu, C.S.: Learning assumptions for compositional verification. In: Garavel, H., Hatcliff, J. (eds.) TACAS 2003. LNCS, vol. 2619, pp. 331–346. Springer, Heidelberg (2003). https://doi.org/10.1007/3-540-36577-X_24
9. Demri, S., Lazić, R.: LTL with the freeze quantifier and register automata. ACM Trans. Comput. Log. **10**(3), 1–30, 16 (2009)
10. Figueira, D., Segoufin, L.: Bottom-up automata on data trees and vertical XPath. In: 28th Symposium on Theoretical Aspects of Computer Science (STACS 2011), pp. 93–104 (2011)
11. Gabbay, M., Pitts, A.M.: A new approach to abstract syntax with variable binding. Formal Aspects Comput. **13**, 341–363 (2002)
12. Kaminski, M., Francez, N.: Finite-memory automata. Theor. Comput. Sci. **134**, 329–363 (1994)
13. Kaminski, M., Tan, T.: Tree automata over infinite alphabets. In: Avron, A., Dershowitz, N., Rabinovich, A. (eds.) Pillars of Computer Science. LNCS, vol. 4800, pp. 386–423. Springer, Heidelberg (2008). https://doi.org/10.1007/978-3-540-78127-1_21
14. Leucker, M.: Learning meets verification. In: de Boer, F.S., Bonsangue, M.M., Graf, S., de Roever, W.-P. (eds.) FMCO 2006. LNCS, vol. 4709, pp. 127–151. Springer, Heidelberg (2007). https://doi.org/10.1007/978-3-540-74792-5_6
15. Libkin, L., Tan, T., Vrgoč, D.: Regular expressions for data words. J. Comput. Syst. Sci. **81**(7), 1278–1297 (2015)
16. Libkin, L., Vrgoč, D.: Regular path queries on graphs with data. In: 15th International Conference on Database Theory (ICDT 2012), pp. 74–85
17. Moerman, J., Sammartino, M., Silva, A., Klin, B., Szynwelski, M.: Learning nominal automata. In: 44th ACM SIGPLAN Symposium on Principles of Programming Languages (POPL 2017), pp. 613–625 (2017)
18. Murawski, A.S., Ramsay, S.J., Tzevelekos, N.: Reachability in pushdown register automata. J. Comput. Syst. Sci. **87**, 58–83 (2017)

19. Nakanishi, R., Takata, Y., Seki, H.: Active learning for deterministic bottom-up nominal tree automata, arXiv preprint arXiv:2208.08319 (2022)
20. Neven, F., Schwentick, T., Vianu, V.: Finite state machines for strings over infinite alphabets. ACM Trans. Comput. Log. **5**(3), 403–435 (2004)
21. Peled, D., Vardi, M.Y., Yannakakis, M.: Black box checking. In: Wu, J., Chanson, S.T., Gao, Q. (eds.) Formal Methods for Protocol Engineering and Distributed Systems. IAICT, vol. 28, pp. 225–240. Springer, Boston, MA (1999). https://doi.org/10.1007/978-0-387-35578-8_13
22. Sakakibara, Y.: Learning context-free grammars from structural data in polynomial time. Theor. Comput. Sci. **76**, 223–242 (1990)
23. Sakamoto, H., Ikeda, D.: Intractability of decision problems for finite-memory automata. Theor. Comput. Sci. **231**, 297–308 (2000)
24. Senda, R., Takata, Y., Seki, H.: Complexity results on register context-free grammars and register tree automata. In: Fischer, B., Uustalu, T. (eds.) ICTAC 2018. LNCS, vol. 11187, pp. 415–434. Springer, Cham (2018). https://doi.org/10.1007/978-3-030-02508-3_22
25. Senda, R., Takata, Y., Seki, H.: Reactive synthesis from visibly register pushdown automata. In: Cerone, A., Ölveczky, P.C. (eds.) ICTAC 2021. LNCS, vol. 12819, pp. 334–353. Springer, Cham (2021). https://doi.org/10.1007/978-3-030-85315-0_19

Towards a User Interface Description Language Based on Bigraphs

Nicolas Nalpon[✉], Cyril Allignol[iD], and Celia Picard[iD]

ENAC, Toulouse University, Toulouse, France
{nicolas.nalpon,cyril.allignol,celia.picard}@enac.fr

Abstract. User interface description languages (UIDL) are high-level languages allowing to model user interfaces (UI). Their purpose is to ease the design of UIs. They are widely used, including to develop critical interactive systems. Nevertheless, the problem of verifying systems developed with UIDLs is barely addressed in the literature. The first step is to provide a formal semantics using an appropriate theory. We claim that the bigraphs theory is a good candidate theory. In this short paper, presenting a work in progress, we introduce the common features of UIDLs and show how bigraphs could be used to define UIDLs semantics and help with UI verification.

Keywords: User Interface Description Language · Graphical user interfaces · Formalisation · Bigraphs

1 Introduction

User interface description languages (UIDL) [10] are high-level languages allowing to model user interfaces (UI). Their purpose is to make the design of the UIs independent and avoid all the difficulties related to their programming such as spaghetti code due to callbacks [17] and the maintenance of an event loop.

Nowadays, UIDLs are widely used to design UIs for interactive systems, including critical systems [13,19]. This emphasizes the need of formal verification for the UIDLs [19], both on the language and program aspects e.g. formal semantics, verified compiler and properties verification on written programs. We focus on the UIDLs specialised on graphical user interfaces (GUI). These UIDLs allow to describe a scene graph and how it evolves over time according to user interactions. In safety-critical systems, the specifications of the GUIs expressed through the UIDLs need to be consistent during all the program lifetime. The purpose of this article is to present a new idea of formal foundations for UIDLs with the same objective. Generally, the formal aspect of UIDLs is little studied. This includes their semantics, except for a few works such as [9]. So, one of the first questions to tackle is the formalisation of their semantics.

The semantics of UIDLs specialised on GUIs description present two common features: the representation of the scene graph and the representation of the control flow. These features relate to the spatial and non-spatial aspects of the

© The Author(s), under exclusive license to Springer Nature Switzerland AG 2022
H. Seidl et al. (Eds.): ICTAC 2022, LNCS 13572, pp. 360–368, 2022.
https://doi.org/10.1007/978-3-031-17715-6_23

GUI and we need a suitable formalism to represent these aspects of the semantics. Bigraphs [16], a diagrammatic framework allowing to represent agents, their locality, their interactions and how they evolve over time, have the potential to represent appropriately these features and thus verify GUIs.

This short article, describing a work in progress, aims to motivate the use of the bigraphs theory to formalise and verify UIDLs semantics and UIs.

We first detail the definition and common mechanisms of the UIDLs in Sect. 2, before briefly presenting the bigraphs theory in Sect. 3. Then, in Sect. 4, we show on a QML example, how we can model the GUI mechanisms common to all UIDLs using the bigraphs theory. Furthermore, Sect. 5 gives a glimpse of how verification can be done on a bigraphs model. Finally, in Sect. 6, we give an overview of the existing work on GUIs verification and discuss the concrete benefit to use bigraphs to verify GUIs.

2 UIDLs

UIDLs are programming languages generally used to design UIs. Programming GUIs has been a tedious task for a long time: they had to be described by sequential code, and callbacks were used to handle events. These practices were criticised [14,17], in particular because of the causal relationships between the different program entities that were not clearly represented. UIDLs are the solution to this problem. Firstly, they make a clear distinction between the design of the UIs and the rest of the application to be developed. Secondly, they only focus on the design of the UIs and propose a suitable syntax to express graphical entities location and interactions (as QML signals and slots [8]).

UIDLs often express GUIs through a tree structure and interactions through special operators, variables affectation or scripting code. There are many UIDLs, but for illustration sake, here are some details about three of them: two popular UIDLs widely used in large projects, FXML and QML, and another one, smala, used to develop critical systems. A more detailed comparison of UIDLs based on XML syntax can be found in this survey [10]. FXML [5] based on Java, describes the graph scene through an XML syntax and represents interactions by variable affectation (bindings) or scripting code (event handler). QML [7], a UIDL based on C++ and Python, describes the interactions in the same way as FXML but JSON is favored to describe the graph scene. Lastly Smala [13], based on C++, uses a bracket syntax along with the graphical entities definition order to describe the scene graph and special operators to describe the interactions.

Despite the diversity of UIDLs, two features [20] are shared by all their semantics: 1) the representation of the graph scene, giving explicit information on the location of each graphical entity; 2) the interactions present in the GUI. To implement these features, UIDLs always provide the following kind of mechanisms: 1) an encapsulation mechanism, related to the scene graph criteria and allowing to create a hierarchy among the graphical entities; 2) event handlers and bindings (stream), allowing to handle GUIs interaction aspect. The hierarchy induced by the encapsulation and the entities dependencies induced by the event handlers and bindings can be respectively represented by a forest and a graph. This double graph structure is very similar to Milner's bigraphs one.

3   Bigraphs

Bigraphs [16] are a diagrammatic framework introduced by Robin Milner allowing to model systems that evolve over time and space. They consist of a set of entites (nodes) shared by two orthogonal graph structures. The place graph, which is a forest, represents the spatial aspect (by mean of nesting) of a system and the link graph, which is a hypergraph, represents the interactions (by means of hyperedges) present in the system.

3.1   Structural Aspect and Rewriting Rules

Bigraphs, illustrated by Fig. 1a and Fig. 1c, are composed of entities, to which we can associate a control (similar to a type), that in turn associates an arity (number of links we can connect) to the entity. For example, the control C in Fig. 1a has arity one and the controls A and B have arity zero. An entity has a fixed arity. Entities can be nested into other entities (place graph) and can be linked (through green hyperedges) to other entities (link graph). An entity that cannot contain another entity is called atomic and is a leaf in the place graph.

Special structures allow bigraphs to be built and decomposed compositionally as regions (dashed rectangle) and sites (grey rectangle). Regions are the root container of a bigraph. Sites abstract away a bigraph part. Sites contain an unspecified bigraph, even possibly the empty bigraph, contained in a region. So, it is possible to build a bigger bigraph by placing regions into sites. In the same way, the links allow composition by using names. For instance in Fig. 1b, the link tagged s can be connected to another link tagged s from another bigraph. Two types of link can be found in bigraphs: the open links, used to compose bigraphs, and the close one as in Fig. 1a

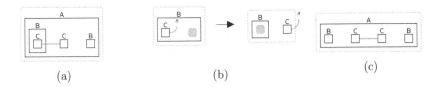

(a)   (b)   (c)

Fig. 1. (a) inital bigraph, (b) reaction rule and (c) bigraph after reaction

3.2   Bigraphical Reactive Systems (BRS)

A bigraph corresponds to a state of a system at a certain time. A BRS describes how bigraphs evolve over time using reaction rules, as shown in Fig. 1b. If the left hand side of a reaction rule is matched in a larger bigraph then we can replace the matched part by the right hand side of the rule. Figure 1b states that whenever a control B contains a control C we can rewrite it by removing C from B. Figure 1c is the result of applying the rule in Fig. 1b to the bigraph in Fig. 1a.

4 Representation of Mechanisms with Bigraphs

In this section, we present, using QML as an example, the graphical user interfaces mechanisms that most of UIDL specialised on GUI can express. The encapsulation in QML, is encoded via the type ITEM, inherited by all the graphical entities of the language, and is represented by records from the JSON syntax. About the event handler and the bindings, the former is encoded by the QML signals and slots and the latter by affectations of record fields. A bigraphical representation is provided for each mechanism, to give an idea on how bigraphs could model a GUI.

```
1  Rectangle {
2     width: 200
3     height: 200
4     color: "red"
5     signal mEvent()
6     Rectangle {
7        width: 100
8        height: parent.height
9        color: "blue"
10    }
11    Button {
12       onClicked:parent.mEvent()
13    }
14 }
```

(a) QML program example

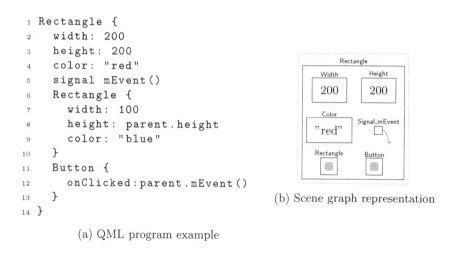

(b) Scene graph representation

Fig. 2. QML program example and its partial bigraph representation

4.1 Representation of the Scene Graph

The scene graph is an abstract representation of the program GUI and controls. Often, UIDLs are based on markup-languages (e.g. XML, JSON) because a tree structure is easily induced from their syntax and it also makes the UI design more intuitive for the developers [10]. Hence, reading the QML program from Fig. 2a, we understand that its scene graph root is the red rectangle and the root children are width:200, height:200, color: red, signal mEvent(), the blue rectangle and the button. Moreover, the induced tree gives information about the positioning of the entities on the actual interface. Since the blue rectangle and the button are children of the red rectangle, the GUI presents them on top of the red rectangle.

Figure 2b represents a part of the program scene graph. The nesting of bigraphs helps representing the hierarchical aspect of a GUI scene graph and therefore catching all the needed information.

4.2 GUI Interactions

UIDLs allow to describe interactions taking place in the GUI. For instance, two interactions are described in Fig. 2a. The first one, defined at line 8, relates the red rectangle height and the blue rectangle height and implies the update of the blue rectangle height each time the red rectangle height is updated. The second interaction, defined at line 12, relates the implicit `clicked` signal from the button and the signal `mEvent` defined at line 5. It implies that each time the `clicked` signal of the button is emitted (i.e. when the user clicks on the button) then the signal `myEvent` is also emitted.

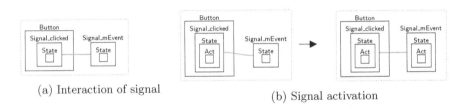

(a) Interaction of signal

(b) Signal activation

Fig. 3. QML Interactions

Generally, interactions are represented by links in a bigraph. Figure 3a, represents the interaction from Fig. 2a involving the signals. In this diagram, we define two linked entities corresponding to both the signals from the program. An entity State is nested into each signal, corresponding to its emission state i.e. emitted or not. The activation of a signal by another one can be represented by a reaction rule (Fig. 3b). This rule matches the signal Signal_clicked (implicit signal of the button) activated and linked to the signal mEvent. Then, it activates the signal mEvent by nesting an entity Act into its entity State.

4.3 Bigraphs Expressiveness

This section gives a glimpse of bigraphs expressiveness through two examples. The first case deals with an activation condition on entities. If an entity is encapsulated, then it can only be activated if its parent is activated. For instance, only the entities having their parent activated are rendered in a GUI. In other words, a GUI should never be in a state shown by Fig. 4. This property which defines semantics dynamic aspect can be covered by bigraphs thanks to reaction rules. It could be formalised by a rule similar to Fig. 6. Here, the bigraphs expressiveness allows to ensure parent activation (spatial aspect) and signal activation (non-spatial aspect). This is an original features of bigraphs compared to other process algebra theories.

The other case deals with types of entity activation. For instance, we could associate a type to the graphical entities and another one to the signal entities as shown in Fig. 5. This kind of typing eases the formalisation of the entities activation process. On the one hand, once activated, a graphical entity remains activated until the end of the program or until another entity deactivates it (depending on the UIDL expressive power). On the other hand, a signal entity, once emitted, is deactivated. Hence, bigraphs allow to define, via reaction rules, a general signal emission mechanism according to a typing defined on entities.

Fig. 4. Inconsistent GUI state   **Fig. 5.** Process type

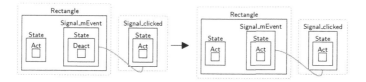

Fig. 6. Activation entity only if parent activated

5   Bigraphs Verification

Bigraphs develop a general theory which unifies and represents existing calculi for concurrent communication and mobility. One of the key benefits to formalise UI using bigraph is the possibility to check properties related by their spatial and communication aspects. Indeed, BigraphER [2] an open-source framework for working with bigraphs, allows a transition system, built from a BRS representing an UI states and update sequences, to be exported. The transition system can then be used by existing model checkers to check properties on the given UI. Here, the model checker PRISM [12], that allows specifying temporal properties in the PCTL specification language, is used to check properties. As our model is not probabilistic, we restrict ourselves to the non-probabilistic fragment. In the following, we show through a small example how bigraphs allow us to automatically check properties on UIs models.

5.1   Predicats

To check properties on the generated transition system we require labels on its states. In BigraphER, labels are defined as bigraph patterns $l = B$ that specify that a state should be labelled with l if there is a match of B in that state. In other words, you can think of these patterns as the left-hand-side of a reaction rule. For our analysis we specify two predicates : 1) *signal_clicked* that label states when `Signal_clicked` is activated and `Signal_mEvent` is not ; 2) *signal_mEvent* that label states when both `Signal_clicked` and `Signal_mEvent` are activated.

5.2   Properties Verification on UI

To show how properties can be checked on a given program we encode the example of Fig. 2a when the signal `signal_clicked` is triggered i.e. when the button has been clicked. Once the button is clicked, the signal `signal_clicked` is emitted then the rule from Fig. 3b is applied to the model to trigger the signal `signal_mEvent`. We can write a formula in PCTL ensuring that the signal `signal_mEvent` is really activated : A[*signal_clicked* $\implies$ F *signal_mEvent*].

This states that *forall* paths (A) if *signal_clicked* is activated then *eventually* (at some point in the future; F) *signal_mEvent* must be active.

This feature of bigraphs, can be useful for developers to check the soundness of the UI described. Indeed, the size of the UI makes the debugging much more harder [15] which can be eased my automatic verification. This feature could also be used to check that an UI satisfy semantics properties of the UIDL used.

6   Related and Future Work

This article gives a glimpse of the bigraphs theory, shows how it could be used to model common features of the semantics of GUI specialised UIDLs and how to automatically verify properties on the model. We provide [18] the formalisation of the example in Fig. 2a and a setup to run the verification from Fig. 4.

Currently, several works exist on the verification of UIs but none concerns UIDLs semantics. Verified react [1] is a project offering the possibility to check logic properties and explore state on react programs. Some work [4,6] exists on the framework Djnn/Smala addressing the verification of interactive and graphic properties by static analysis. Related to UIDLs, Interactive Cooperative Objects [19] (ICO) is a formalism aimed at describing UIs. It borrows concepts from the object-oriented approach (i.e. inheritance, encapsulation, dynamic instantiation) to describe the structural aspect of a system and uses a high-level Petri nets [11] to describe its dynamic aspect. To reason on this formalism, PetShop [3] will allow to simulate the model and all verification tools for Petri nets can be used.

Our purpose is more related to the programming language aspect. We aim to define a generic UIDL based on the bigraphs theory which covering all common features of GUI specialised UIDLs. The idea is to use this UIDL as an intermediate representation for other UIDLs. This would allow to model mobility and concurrent aspects of a GUI in a unique framework and enable the use of any tool relates to bigraphs, e.g. BigraphER, to formally verify the GUI.

References

1. Aitken, D.: Introducing verified react (2019). https://medium.com/imandra/introducing-verified-react-9c2ef03f821b
2. Archibald, B., Calder, M., Sevegnani, M.: Conditional bigraphs. In: Gadducci, F., Kehrer, T. (eds.) ICGT 2020. LNCS, vol. 12150, pp. 3–19. Springer, Cham (2020). https://doi.org/10.1007/978-3-030-51372-6_1
3. Barboni, E., et al.: Bridging the gap between a behavioural formal description technique and a user interface description language: enhancing ICO with a graphical user interface markup language. In: Science of Computer Programming, vol. 86, pp. 3–29 (2014). https://doi.org/10.1016/j.scico.2013.04.001. ISSN 01676423. https://linkinghub.elsevier.com/retrieve/pii/S0167642313000993. Accessed 17 June 2022
4. Béger, P.: Vérification formelle des propriétés graphiques des systémes informatiques interactifs, p. 195
5. Chappell, G., Hildebrandt, N.: Using FXML to create a user interface. English (2013). https://docs.oracle.com/javafx/2/get_started/fxml_tutorial.htm
6. Chatty, S., Magnaudet, M., Prun, D.: Verication of properties of interactive components from their executable code. In: Proceedings of the 7th ACM SIGCHI Symposium on Engineering Interactive Computing Systems. Duisburg Germany, pp. 276–285. ACM (2015). ISBN 978-1-4503-3646-8. https://doi.org/10.1145/2774225.2774848. Accessed 30 June 2022
7. Qt Company. QML Tutorial (2022). https://doc.qt.io/qt-5/qmltutorial.html
8. Qt Company. Signals & Slots (2022). https://doc.qt.io/qt6/signalsandslots.html
9. Calvary, G., de Wasseige, O., Faure, D., Vanderdonckt, J.: User interface eXtensible markup language SIG. In: Campos, P., Graham, N., Jorge, J., Nunes, N., Palanque, P., Winckler, M. (eds.) INTERACT 2011. LNCS, vol. 6949, pp. 693–695. Springer, Heidelberg (2011). https://doi.org/10.1007/978-3-642-23768-3_119
10. Garcia, J.G., et al.: A theoretical survey of user interface description languages: preliminary results. In: 2009 Latin American Web Congress. Merida, Yucatan, Mexico: IEEE, pp. 36–43 (2009). ISBN 978-0-7695-3856-3. http://ieeexplore.ieee.org/document/5341626/. Accessed 17 June 2022. https://doi.org/10.1109/LA-WEB.2009.40
11. Jensen, K., Rozenberg, G.: High-level Petri Nets: Theory and Application. Springer, Heidelberg (1991). https://doi.org/10.1007/978-3-642-84524-6
12. Kwiatkowska, M., Norman, G., Parker, D.: PRISM 4.0: verification of probabilistic real-time systems. In: Gopalakrishnan, G., Qadeer, S. (eds.) CAV 2011. LNCS, vol. 6806, pp. 585–591. Springer, Heidelberg (2011). https://doi.org/10.1007/978-3-642-22110-1_47
13. Magnaudet, M., et al., Smala, D.: A conceptual framework and a language for interaction-oriented programming. In: Proceedings of the ACM on Human-Computer Interaction 2. EICS, pp. 1–27 (2018). ISSN 2573-0142. https://dl.acm.org/doi/10.1145/3229094. Accessed on 29 June 2022
14. Maier, I., Rompf, T., Odersky, M.: Deprecating the observer pattern, p. 18 (2010)
15. Martin, A., Magnaudet, M., Conversy, S.: Causette: user-controlled rearrangement of causal constructs in a code editor. In: Proceedings of the 30th IEEE/ACM Conference on Program Comprehension (2022). https://halenac.archives-ouvertes.fr/hal-03659579. https://doi.org/10.1145/3524610.3527885
16. Milner, R.: The Space and Motion of Communicating Agents. Cambridge University Press, Cambridge (2009)

17. Myers, B.A.: Separating application code from toolkits: eliminating the spaghetti of call-backs. In: Proceedings of the 4th Annual ACM Symposium on User Interface Software and Technology - UIST 1991. Hilton Head, South Carolina, United States: ACM Press, pp. 211–220 (1991). ISBN 978-0-89791-451-2. http://portal.acm.org/citation.cfm?doid=120782.120805, https://doi.org/10.1145/120782.120805. Accessed 29 June 2022

18. Nalpon, N., Allignol, C., Picard, C.: Toward a User Interface Description Language based on bigraphs (model files, supplemental material) (2022). https://hal.archives-ouvertes.fr/hal-03754387

19. Navarre, D., et al.: ICOs: a model-based user interface description technique dedicated to interactive systems addressing usability, reliability and scalability. In: ACM Transactions on Computer-Human Interaction 16(4), pp. 1–56 (2009). ISSN 1073-0516, 1557-7325. https://dl.acm.org/doi/10.1145/1614390.1614393. Accessed 24 June 2022

20. Silva, C.E., Campos, J.C.: Can GUI implementation markup languages be used for modelling? In: Winckler, M., Forbrig, P., Bernhaupt, R. (eds.) HCSE 2012. LNCS, vol. 7623, pp. 112–129. Springer, Heidelberg (2012). https://doi.org/10.1007/978-3-642-34347-6_7

A Specification Logic for Programs in the Probabilistic Guarded Command Language

Raúl Pardo[1]([⊠]), Einar Broch Johnsen[2], Ina Schaefer[3], and Andrzej Wąsowski[1]

[1] IT University of Copenhagen, Copenhagen, Denmark
raup@itu.dk
[2] University of Oslo, Oslo, Norway
[3] Karlsruhe Institute of Technology, Karlsruhe, Germany

Abstract. The semantics of probabilistic languages has been extensively studied, but specification languages for their properties have received little attention. This paper introduces the probabilistic dynamic logic pDL, a specification logic for programs in the probabilistic guarded command language (pGCL) of McIver and Morgan. The proposed logic pDL can express both first-order state properties and probabilistic reachability properties, addressing both the non-deterministic and probabilistic choice operators of pGCL. In order to precisely explain the meaning of specifications, we formally define the satisfaction relation for pDL. Since pDL embeds pGCL programs in its box-modality operator, pDL satisfiability builds on a formal MDP semantics for pGCL programs. The satisfaction relation is modeled after PCTL, but extended from propositional to first-order setting of dynamic logic, and also embedding program fragments. We study basic properties of pDL, such as weakening and distribution, that can support reasoning systems. Finally, we demonstrate the use of pDL to reason about program behavior.

1 Introduction

This paper introduces a specification language for probabilistic programs. Probabilistic programming techniques and systems are becoming increasingly important not only for machine-learning applications but also for, e.g., random algorithms, symmetry breaking in distributed algorithms and in the modelling of fault tolerance. The semantics of probabilistic languages has been extensively studied, from Kozen's seminal work [1] to recent research [2–5], but specification languages for their properties have received little attention (but see, e.g., [6]).

The specification language we define in this paper is the probabilistic dynamic logic pDL, a specification logic for programs in the probabilistic guarded command language pGCL of McIver and Morgan [7]. This programming language combines the guarded command language of Dijkstra [8], in which the non-deterministic scheduling of threads is guarded by Boolean assertions, with state-dependent probabilistic choice. Whereas guarded commands can be seen as a core language for concurrent execution, pGCL can be seen as a core language for probabilistic and non-deterministic execution.

The proposed logic pDL can express both first-order state properties and reachability properties, addressing the non-deterministic as well as the probabilistic choice operators

ⓒ The Author(s), under exclusive license to Springer Nature Switzerland AG 2022
H. Seidl et al. (Eds.): ICTAC 2022, LNCS 13572, pp. 369–387, 2022.
https://doi.org/10.1007/978-3-031-17715-6_24

of pGCL. Technically, pDL is a probabilistic extension of (first-order) dynamic logic [9], a modal logic in which programs can occur within the modalities of logical formulae. The semantics of dynamic logic is defined as a Kripke-structure over the set of valuations of program variables. Dynamic logic allows reachability properties to be expressed for given (non-probabilistic) programs by means of modalities. The probabilistic extension pDL allows probabilistic reachability properties to be similarly expressed.

In order to precisely explain the meaning of specifications expressed in pDL, we formally define the semantics of this logic in terms of a satisfaction relation for pDL formulae (a model-theoretic semantics). The satisfaction relation is modeled after PCTL [10], but extended from a propositional to a first-order setting of dynamic logic, embedding program fragments in the modalities. Since pDL embeds pGCL programs in its formulae, the formalization of pDL satisfiability builds on a formal semantics for pGCL programs, which is defined by Markov Decision Processes (MDP) [11]. The formalization of pDL satisfiability allows us to study basic properties of specifications, such as weakening and distribution. Finally, we demonstrate how pDL can be used to specify and reason about program behavior. The main contributions of this paper are:

- The specification logic pDL to syntactically express probabilistic properties of stochastic non-deterministic programs written in pGCL;
- A model-theoretic semantics for pDL over a simple MDP semantics for pGCL programs; the satisfaction relation is modeled after PCTL, but extended from a propositional to a first-order setting of dynamic logics with embedded pGCL programs; and
- A study of basic properties of pDL and a demonstration of how pDL can be used to specify and reason about pGCL programs.

Our motivation for this work is ultimately to define a proof system which allows us to mechanically verify high-level properties for programs written in probabilistic programming languages. Dynamic logic has proven to be a particularly successful logic for such verification systems in the case of regular (non-probabilistic) programs; in particular, KeY [12], which is based on forward reasoning over DL formulae, has been used for breakthrough results such as the verification of the TimSort algorithm [13]. The specification language introduced in this paper constitutes a step in this direction, especially by embedding probabilistic programs into the modalities of the specification language. Further, the semantic properties of pDL form a semantic basis for proof rules, to be formalized, proven correct, and implemented in future work.

The proofs of the theorems below can be found in the extended version [14].

2   State of the Art

Verification of probabilistic algorithms has been addressed with abstract interpretation [15], symbolic execution [16], or probabilistic model checking [17]. Here, we focus on logical reasoning about probabilistic algorithms using dynamic logic. Existing dynamic logics for probabilistic programs are Kozen's PPDL and PrDL of Feldman and Harel. Kozen introduces probability by drawing variable values from distributions, while propositions are measurable real-valued functions [18]. The program semantics is purely probabilistic; PPDL does not include demonic choice. Probabilistic Dynamic Logic (PrDL) relies on the same notion of state, but introduces probabilistic transitions using a random choice operator [19]. Since neither PPDL nor PrDL include non-determinism, to reason about non-deterministic stochastic programs in a program logic we need a new specification language. We aim to develop a first-order dynamic logic for programs (PPDL was propositional) with demonic and probabilistic choice.

The main alternative for logical reasoning about probabilistic programs is the weakest pre-expectation calculus, proposed by McIver and Morgan for the probabilistic guarded command language (pGCL) [7]. The language contains explicit probabilistic and demonic choice. Program states are modeled by classical (non-probabilistic) variable assignments, and probabilities are introduced by an explicit probabilistic choice. Assertions are real-valued functions over program state capturing expectations, where a Boolean embedding is used to derive expectations from logical assertions. Reasoning in pGCL follows a backwards expectation transformer semantics. McIver and Morgan define an axiomatic semantics given by the weakest pre-expectation calculus over pGCL programs, but do not introduce an operational semantics for the language. Also they do not provide a specification language for pGCL assertions, i.e., real-valued functions, beyond the Boolean embedding (cf. [20]). In this work, we want to build on this tradition. However, we think there is a need for a specification language with classical model-theoretical semantics known from logics—a satisfaction semantics. Dynamic logics is a good basis for such a development, since it is strictly more expressive than Hoare logic and weakest precondition calculi—both can be embedded in dynamic logic [21]. In contrast to these calculi, dynamic logics are closed under logical operators such as first-order connectives and quantifiers; for example, program equivalence, relative to state formulae φ and ψ, can be expressed by the formula $\varphi \Rightarrow [s_1]\psi \iff \varphi \Rightarrow [s_2]\psi$.

As mentioned, the original pGCL lacked operational semantics. Since semantics is needed for a traditional definition of satisfaction in a modal logic, we propose to use the MDP semantics similar to the one of Gretz et al. [22], where post-expectations are rewards in final states. An alternative could be Kaminski's computation tree semantics [3], but we find it more complex and less standard for our purpose (deviating further from traditions of simpler logics like PCTL).

Termination analysis of probabilistic programs [2,23] considers probabilistic reachability properties. This and other directions of related work, such as separation logic for probabilistic programs [24], expected run-time analysis for probabilistic programs [25] and relational reasoning over probabilistic programs for sensitivity analysis [26], are orthogonal to the goal of defining a specification language for programs, and thus outside of scope of interest for this particular paper. Generally all these approaches rely on the backwards pre-expectation transformer semantics of McIver and Morgan [7].

3 Preliminaries

We review the basic semantic notions used in the main part of the paper.

Definition 1 (Markov Decision Process). *A Markov Decision Process (MDP) is a tuple $M = (State, Act, \mathbf{P})$ where (i) State is a countable set of states, (ii) Act is a count-*

able set of actions, (iii) $\mathbf{P}$: $State \times Act \rightharpoonup Dist(State)$ *is a partial transition probability function.*

Let σ denote the states and a the actions of an MDP. A state σ is *final* if no further transitions are possible from it, i.e. $(\sigma, a) \notin \text{dom}(\mathbf{P})$ for any a. A *path*, denoted $\overline{\sigma}$, is a sequence of states $\sigma_1, \ldots, \sigma_n$ such that σ_n is final and there are actions $a_1, \ldots, a_{n-1}$ such that $\mathbf{P}(\sigma_i, a_i)(\sigma_{i+1}) \geq 0$ for $1 \leq i < n$. Let $\text{final}(\overline{\sigma})$ denote the final state of a path $\overline{\sigma}$.

For a given state, the set of applicable actions of $\mathbf{P}$ defines the *demonic choices* between successor state distributions. A *positional policy* π is a function that maps states to actions, so π : $State \rightarrow Act$. We assume π to be consistent with $\mathbf{P}$, so $\mathbf{P}(\sigma, \pi(\sigma))$ is defined. Given a policy π, we define a transition relation $\rightarrow_\pi \subseteq State \times [0, 1] \times State$ on states that resolves all the demonic choices in $\mathbf{P}$ and write:

$$\sigma \xrightarrow{p}_\pi \sigma' \quad \text{iff} \quad \mathbf{P}(\sigma, \pi(\sigma))(\sigma') = p. \tag{1}$$

For a given policy π, we let $\xrightarrow{p}^*_\pi \subseteq State \times [0, 1] \times State$ denote the reflexive and transitive closure of the transition relation, and define the probability of a path $\overline{\sigma} = \sigma_1, \ldots, \sigma_n$ by

$$p = \text{Pr}(\overline{\sigma}) = 1 \cdot p_1 \cdots p_n \quad \text{where } \sigma_1 \xrightarrow{p_1}_\pi \cdots \xrightarrow{p_n}_\pi \sigma_n. \tag{2}$$

Thus, a path with no transitions consists of a single state σ, and $\text{Pr}(\sigma) = 1$. Let $\text{paths}_\pi(\sigma)$ denote the set of all paths with policy π from σ to final states.

In this paper we assume that MDPs (and the programs we derive them from) arrive at final states with probability 1 under all policies. This means that the logic pDL that we will be defining and interpreting over these MDPs can only talk about properties of almost surely terminating programs, so in general it cannot be used to reason about termination without adaptation. This is what corresponds to the notion of partial correctness in non-probabilistic proof systems.

An MDP may have an associated *reward function* r : $State \rightarrow [0, 1]$ that assigns a real value $r(\sigma)$ to any final state $\sigma \in State$. (In this paper we assume that rewards are zero everywhere but in the final states.) We define the *expectation* of the reward starting in a state σ as the greatest lower bound on the expected value of the reward over all policies; so the real valued function defined as

$$\mathbf{E}_\sigma(r) = \inf_\pi \mathbb{E}_{\sigma,\pi}(r) = \inf_\pi \sum_{\overline{\sigma} \in \text{paths}_\pi(\sigma)} \text{Pr}(\overline{\sigma})\, r(\text{final}(\overline{\sigma})) \;, \tag{3}$$

where $\mathbb{E}_{\sigma,\pi}(r)$ stands for the *expected value* of the random variable induced by the reward function under the given policy, known as the *expected reward*. Note that the expectation $\mathbf{E}_\sigma(r)$ always exists and it is well defined. First, for a given policy the expected value $\mathbb{E}_{\sigma,\pi}(r)$ is guaranteed to exist, as we only consider terminating executions and our reward functions are bounded, non-negative, and non-zero in final states only. The set of possible positional policies that we are minimizing over might be infinite, but the values we are minimizing over are bounded from below by zero, so the set of expected values has a well defined infimum. Finally, because the MDPs considered

$$v \ ::= \ \mathit{true} \mid \mathit{false} \mid 0 \mid 1 \mid \ldots$$
$$e \ ::= \ v \mid x \mid op \ e \mid e \ op \ e$$
$$op ::= \ + \mid - \mid * \mid / \mid > \mid == \mid \geq$$
$$s \ ::= \ s \sqcap s \mid s \ _e \oplus s \mid s; s \mid \mathsf{skip} \mid x := e \mid \mathsf{if} \ e \ \{s\} \ \mathsf{else} \ \{s\} \mid \mathsf{while} \ e \ \{s\}$$

Fig. 1. The syntax of the probabilistic guarded command language pGCL

here almost surely arrive at a final state, we do not need to condition the expectations on terminating paths to re-normalize probability distributions, which greatly simplifies the technical machinery.

To avoid confusing expectations and scalar values, we use bold font for expectations in the sequel. For instance, $\boldsymbol{p}$ represents an unknown expectation from the state space into $[0, 1]$, and $\boldsymbol{0}$ represents a constant expectation function, equal to zero everywhere.

We use characteristic functions to define rewards for the semantics of pGCL programs, consistently with McIver & Morgan [7]. For a formula φ in some logic with the corresponding satisfaction relation, a characteristic function $\llbracket \varphi \rrbracket$, also known as a Boolean embedding or an indicator function, assigns 1 to states satisfying φ and 0 otherwise. In this paper, models will be program states, and also states of an MDP. In general, characteristic functions can be replaced by arbitrary real-valued functions [3], but this is not needed to interpret logical specifications, so we leave this to future work.

Finally, given a formula φ that can be interpreted over a state space of an MDP, we define the truncation of a reward function $\boldsymbol{p}$ as the function $(\boldsymbol{p} \downarrow \varphi)(\sigma) = \boldsymbol{p}(\sigma) \cdot \llbracket \varphi \rrbracket(\sigma)$. The truncation of $\boldsymbol{p}$ to φ maintains the original value of $\boldsymbol{p}$ for states satisfying φ and gives zero otherwise. Note that $\boldsymbol{p} \downarrow \varphi$ remains a valid reward function if $\boldsymbol{p}$ was.

4 pGCL: A Probabilistic Guarded Command Language

The probabilistic guarded command language pGCL [7], extends Dijkstra's guarded command language [8] with probabilistic choice. Figure 1 gives the syntax of pGCL. We let x range over the set X of program variables, v over primitive values, and e over expressions Exp. Expressions e are constructed over program variables x and primitive values v by means of unary and binary operators op (including logical operators $\neg, \wedge, \vee$ and arithmetic operators $+, -, *, /$). Expressions are assumed to be well-formed.

Statements s include the non-deterministic (or demonic) choice $s_1 \sqcap s_2$ between the branches s_1 and s_2. We write $s \ _e \oplus s'$ for the probabilistic choice between the branches s and s'; if the expression e evaluates to a value p given the current values for the program variables, then s and s' have probability p and $1 - p$ of being selected, respectively. In many cases e will be a constant, but in general it can be an *expression over the state variables* (i.e., $e \in Exp$), so its semantics will be an real-valued function. Sequential composition, skip, assignment, if-then-else and while are standard (e.g., [8]).

The semantics of pGCL programs s is defined as an MDP $\mathcal{M}_s$ (cf. [22]), and its executions are captured by the partial transition probability function for a given policy π, which induces the relation $\xrightarrow{p}_\pi$ for some probability p, (Eq. (1)). A state σ of $\mathcal{M}_s$ is a pair of a *valuation* and a *program*, so $\sigma = \langle \varepsilon, s \rangle$ where the valuation ε is a mapping

$$\text{(ASSIGN)} \qquad \frac{}{\varepsilon' = \varepsilon[x \mapsto \varepsilon(e)]}$$

$$\langle \varepsilon, x := e \rangle \xrightarrow{1}_\pi \langle \varepsilon', \mathbf{skip} \rangle$$

$$\text{(PROBCHOICE1)} \qquad \frac{\varepsilon(e) = p \quad 0 \le p \le 1}{\langle \varepsilon, s_1 \,_e\oplus\, s_2 \rangle \xrightarrow{p}_\pi \langle \varepsilon, s_1 \rangle}$$

$$\text{(PROBCHOICE2)} \qquad \frac{\varepsilon(e) = p \quad 0 \le p \le 1}{\langle \varepsilon, s_1 \,_e\oplus\, s_2 \rangle \xrightarrow{1-p}_\pi \langle \varepsilon, s_2 \rangle}$$

$$\text{(DEMCHOICE)} \qquad \frac{i \in \{1,2\}}{\pi\langle \varepsilon, s_1 \sqcap s_2 \rangle = s_i}$$

$$\langle \varepsilon, s_1 \sqcap s_2 \rangle \xrightarrow{1}_\pi \langle \varepsilon', s_i \rangle$$

$$\text{(COMPOSITION1)} \qquad \frac{\langle \varepsilon, s_1 \rangle \xrightarrow{p}_\pi \langle \varepsilon', s_2 \rangle}{\langle \varepsilon, \mathbf{skip}; s_1 \rangle \xrightarrow{p}_\pi \langle \varepsilon', s_2 \rangle}$$

$$\text{(COMPOSITION2)} \qquad \frac{\langle \varepsilon, s_1 \rangle \xrightarrow{p}_\pi \langle \varepsilon', s_2 \rangle}{\langle \varepsilon, s_1; s \rangle \xrightarrow{p}_\pi \langle \varepsilon', s_2; s \rangle}$$

$$\text{(WHILE1)} \qquad \frac{\varepsilon(e) = \mathit{true}}{\langle \varepsilon, \mathbf{while}\ e\ \{s\} \rangle \xrightarrow{1}_\pi \langle \varepsilon, s; \mathbf{while}\ e\ \{s\} \rangle}$$

$$\text{(WHILE2)} \qquad \frac{\varepsilon(e) = \mathit{false}}{\langle \varepsilon, \mathbf{while}\ e\ \{s\} \rangle \xrightarrow{1}_\pi \langle \varepsilon, \mathbf{skip} \rangle}$$

$$\text{(IF1)} \qquad \frac{\varepsilon(e) = \mathit{true}}{\langle \varepsilon, \mathbf{if}\ e\ \{s_1\}\ \mathbf{else}\ \{s_2\} \rangle \xrightarrow{1}_\pi \langle \varepsilon, s_1 \rangle}$$

$$\text{(IF2)} \qquad \frac{\varepsilon(e) = \mathit{false}}{\langle \varepsilon, \mathbf{if}\ e\ \{s_1\}\ \mathbf{else}\ \{s_2\} \rangle \xrightarrow{1}_\pi \langle \varepsilon, s_2 \rangle}$$

Fig. 2. An MDP-semantics for pGCL.

from all the program variables in s to concrete values (sometimes we omit the program part, if it is unambiguous in the context). The state $\langle \varepsilon, s \rangle$ represents an *initial state* of the program s given some initial valuation ε and the state $\langle \varepsilon, \mathbf{skip} \rangle$ represents a *final state* in which the program has terminated with the valuation ε.

The rules defining the partial transition probability function for a given policy π are shown in Fig. 2. We denote by $\langle \varepsilon, s \rangle \xrightarrow{p}_\pi \langle \varepsilon', s' \rangle$ the transition from $\langle \varepsilon, s \rangle$ to $\langle \varepsilon', s' \rangle$ by action $\alpha = \pi(\langle \varepsilon, s \rangle)$, where p is the resulting probability. Note that for demonic choice, the policy π fixes the action choice between the distributions $0, 1$ and $1, 0$; for all other statements, there is already a single successor distribution. The transitive closure of this relation, denoted $\langle \varepsilon_0, s_0 \rangle \xrightarrow{p}{}^*_\pi \langle \varepsilon_n, s_n \rangle$, expresses that there is a sequence of zero or more such transitions from $\langle \varepsilon_0, s_0 \rangle$ to $\langle \varepsilon_n, s_n \rangle$ with corresponding actions $\alpha_i = \pi(\varepsilon_i, s_i)$ and probability p_i for $0 < i \le n$, such that $p = 1 \cdot p_1 \cdots p_n$.

Remark that the rules in Fig. 2 allow programs to get stuck, for instance if an expression e evaluates to a value outside $[0, 1]$ (PROBCHOICE). Since we are interested in partial correctness, we henceforth rule out such programs and only consider programs that successfully reduce to a single **skip** statement under all policies with probability 1.

5   Probabilistic Dynamic Logic

Formulae and Satisfiability. Given sets X of program variables and L of logical variables disjoint from X, let ATF denote the well-formed atomic formulae built using constants, program and logical variables. For every $l \in L$, let dom l denote the domain of l. We extend valuations to also map logical variables $l \in L$ to values in dom l and let $\varepsilon \models_{\text{ATF}} \varphi$ denote standard satisfaction, expressing that $\varphi \in \text{ATF}$ holds in valuation ε.

The formulae of probabilistic dynamic logic (pDL) are defined inductively as the smallest set generated by the following grammar:

$$\varphi \quad ::= \quad \mathsf{ATF} \mid \neg\varphi \mid \varphi_1 \wedge \varphi_2 \mid \forall l \cdot \varphi \mid [s]_p \, \varphi \qquad (4)$$

where φ ranges over pDL formulae, $l \in L$ over logical variables, s is a pGCL program with variables in X, and p is an expectation assigning values in $[0, 1]$ to initial states of the program s. The logical operators $\rightarrow$, $\vee$ and $\exists$ are derived in terms of $\neg$, $\wedge$ and $\forall$ as usual.

The last operator in Eq. (4) is known as the box-operator in dynamic logics, but now we give it a probabilistic interpretation along with the name "p-box." Given a pGCL program s, we write $[s]_p \, \varphi$ to express that the expectation that a formula φ holds after successfully executing s is at least p; i.e., the function p represents the expectation for φ in the current state of $\mathcal{M}_s$ using $[\![\varphi]\!]$ as the reward function (see Sect. 3). For the reader familiar with the CTL/PCTL terminology, the p-box formulae are path formulae, and all other formulae are state formulae.

We define semantics of *well-formed formulae* in pDL, so formulae with no free logical variables—all occurrences of logical variables are captured by a quantifier. The definition extends the standard satisfaction relation of dynamic logic [9] to the probabilistic case:

Definition 2 (Satisfaction of pDL Formulae). *Let φ be a well-formed pDL formula, π range over policies, $l \in L$, $p : State \rightarrow [0, 1]$ be an expectation lower bound, and ε be a valuation defined for all variables mentioned in φ. The* satisfiability *of a formula φ in a model ε, denoted $\varepsilon \models \varphi$, is defined inductively as follows:*

$$
\begin{array}{lll}
\varepsilon \models \varphi & \text{iff} & \varepsilon \models_{\mathsf{ATF}} \varphi \quad \text{for} \quad \varphi \in \mathsf{ATF} \\
\varepsilon \models \varphi_1 \wedge \varphi_2 & \text{iff} & \varepsilon \models \varphi_1 \quad \text{and} \quad \varepsilon \models \varphi_2 \\
\varepsilon \models \neg\varphi & \text{iff} & \text{not } \varepsilon \models \varphi \\
\varepsilon \models \forall l \cdot \varphi & \text{iff} & \varepsilon \models \varphi[l := v] \text{ for each } v \in \operatorname{dom} l \\
\varepsilon \models [s]_p \varphi & \text{iff} & p(\varepsilon) \leq \mathbf{E}_\varepsilon [\![\varphi]\!] \text{ where the expectation is taken in } \mathcal{M}_s
\end{array}
$$

For $\varphi \in \mathsf{ATF}$, $\models_{\mathsf{ATF}}$ can be used to check satisfaction just against the valuation of program variables since φ is well-formed. In the case of universal quantification, the substitution replaces logical variables with constants. The last case (p-box) is implicitly recursive, since the characteristic function $[\![\varphi]\!]$ refers to the satisfaction of φ in the final states of s.

The satisfaction of a p-box formula $[s]_p \, \varphi$ captures a lower bound on the probability of φ holding after the program s. Consequently, pDL supports specification and reasoning about probabilistic reachability properties in almost surely terminating programs.

It is convenient to omit the valuation ε from the satisfaction judgement, meaning that the judgement holds for all valuations (validity):

$$\models [s]_p \, \varphi \quad \text{iff} \quad \varepsilon \models [s]_p \, \varphi \quad \text{for all valuations } \varepsilon \qquad (5)$$

6   The P-Box Modality and Logical Connectives

We begin our investigation of pDL by exploring how the p-box operator interacts with different expectations and the other connectives of pDL.

In a proof system, weakening is useful to allow adjusting proven facts to a format of a syntactic proof rule. Since all operators of pDL, with the exception of p-box, behave like in first order logic, the usual qualitative weakening properties apply for these operators at the top-level. For instance, $\varphi_1 \wedge \varphi_2$ can be weakened to φ_1. These properties follow directly from Definition 2. The following proposition states the key properties for p-box:

Proposition 3 (Weakening). *Let ε stand for a valuation, $p, 0 \in State \rightarrow [0, 1]$ be expectation lower bounds, s a pGCL program, and $\varphi \in$ pDL. Then:*

1. *Universal lower bound: $\varepsilon \models [s]_0 \, \varphi$*
2. *Quantitative weakening: $\varepsilon \models [s]_{p_1} \, \varphi$ then $\varepsilon \models [s]_{p_2} \, \varphi$ if $p_2 \leq p_1$ everywhere*
3. *Weakening conjunctions: $\varepsilon \models [s]_p \, (\varphi_1 \wedge \varphi_2)$ then $\varepsilon \models [s]_p \, \varphi_i$ for $i = 1, 2$*
4. *Qualitative weakening: $\varepsilon \models [s]_p \, \varphi_1$ and $\models \varphi_1 \rightarrow \varphi_2$ then $\varepsilon \models [s]_p \, \varphi_2$.*

The first point states that there is a limit to the usefulness of weakening the expectation: if you cannot guarantee that the lower bound is positive, then you do not have any information at all. A zero lower-bound would hold for any property. The second property is a probabilistic variant of weakening, which follows directly from the last case of Definition 2; the lower bound on an expectation can always be lowered. The last two properties are the probabilistic counterparts of weakening in standard (non-probabilistic) dynamic logic; the third property is syntactic for conjunction, the last one is general.

When building proofs with pDL, the other direction of reasoning seems more useful: we would like to be able to derive a conjunction from two independently concluded facts. For state formulae, this holds naturally, like in first-order logic. For p-box formulae, we would like to use the expectations p_i of two formulae φ_i to draw conclusions about the expectation that their conjunction holds. It seems tempting to translate the intuitions from the Boolean lattice to real numbers, and to suggest that a minimum of the expectations for both formulae is a lower bound for their conjunction. To develop some intuition, let us first consider an incorrect proposal using the following counterexample:

Example 4. Consider the program ▓ , modeling a six-sided fair die:

$$\text{▓} \quad ::= \quad \text{x:=1} \,_{1/6} \oplus \, (\text{x:=2} \,_{1/5} \oplus \, (\text{x:=3} \,_{1/4} \oplus \, (\text{x:=4} \,_{1/3} \oplus \, (\text{x:=5} \,_{1/2} \oplus \, \text{x:=6})))) \quad (6)$$

Let 'odd' be an atomic formula stating that a value is odd, and 'prime' an atomic formula stating that it is prime. Since the die is fair, the expectations for each of these after ▓ are:

$$\models [\text{▓}]_{1/2} \, \text{odd}(x) \qquad \models [\text{▓}]_{1/2} \, \text{prime}(x) \qquad (7)$$

The minimum of the two expectations is a constant function which equals $1/2$ everywhere, but the expectation bound in $[s]_p(\text{odd}(x) \wedge \text{prime}(x))$ can be at most $1/3$ since only two outcomes ($x \mapsto 3$ and $x \mapsto 5$) satisfy both predicates. Effectively, even if $\varepsilon \models [s]_{p_1} \varphi_1$ and $\varepsilon \models [s]_{p_2} \varphi_2$ hold, we do not necessarily have $\varepsilon \models [s]_{\min(p_1,p_2)} \varphi_1 \wedge \varphi_2$. The reason is that the expectation bounds measure what is the lower bound on satisfaction of a property, but not where in the execution space this probability mass is placed. There is not enough information to see to what extent the two properties are overlapping.   □

Similarly, $p(\varepsilon) = p_1(\varepsilon)p_2(\varepsilon)$ is not a good candidate in Example 4, since it is only guaranteed to be a lower bound for a conjunction when φ_i are independent events. Unless $p_1 = p_2 = 1$, combining proven facts with conjunction (or disjunction) weakens the expectation:

Theorem 5. *Let ε be a valuation, $p, p_1, p_2 \in State \rightarrow [0,1]$ expectation lower bounds, s a pGCL program, and $\varphi_1, \varphi_2 \in$ pDL. Then:*

1. *p-box conjunction: if $\varepsilon \models [s]_{p_1} \varphi_1$ and $\varepsilon \models [s]_{p_2} \varphi_2$, then $\varepsilon \models [s]_p (\varphi_1 \wedge \varphi_2)$ where $p = \max(p_1 + p_2 - 1, 0)$ everywhere.*
2. *p-box disjunction: if $\varepsilon \models [s]_{p_1} \varphi_1$ or $\varepsilon \models [s]_{p_2} \varphi_2$, then $\varepsilon \models [s]_p (\varphi_1 \vee \varphi_2)$ where $p = \min(p_1, p_2)$ everywhere.*

Note the asymmetry between these cases: reasoning about conjunctions of low probability properties using Theorem 5.1 is inefficient, and quickly arrives at the lower bound expectation 0, which, as observed in Proposition 3, holds vacuously. If both properties have an expected probability lower than $1/2$, then pDL cannot really see (in a compositional manner) whether there is any chance that they can be satisfied simultaneously. In contrast, compositional reasoning about disjunctions makes sense both for low and high probability events. This is a consequence of using lower bounds on expectations. The bounds in Theorem 5 are consistent with prior work by Baier et al. on LTL verification of probabilistic systems [27].

The qualitative non-probabilistic specialization of Theorem 5.1 behaves reasonably: when φ_1 or φ_2 hold almost surely, then the theorem reduces to a familiar format:

$$\text{if } \varepsilon \models [s]_p \varphi_1 \text{ and } \varepsilon \models [s]_1 \varphi_2 \text{ then } \varepsilon \models [s]_p (\varphi_1 \wedge \varphi_2) \tag{8}$$

Theorem 6. *Let ε be a valuation, $p \in State \rightarrow [0,1]$ an expectation lower bound, s a pGCL program, and $\varphi \in$ pDL a well-formed formula.*

1. *If $\varepsilon \models [s]_p \forall l \cdot \varphi$ then $\varepsilon \models \forall l \cdot [s]_p \varphi$, but not the other way around in general.*
2. *If $\varepsilon \models \exists l \cdot [s]_p \varphi$ then $\varepsilon \models [s]_p \exists l \cdot \varphi$ but not the other way around in general.*

The essence of the above two properties lies in the fact that quantifiers in pDL only affect logical variables, programs cannot access logical variables, and we do not allow quantification over expectation variables.

In a deductive proof system, one works with abstract states, not just concrete states. A state abstraction can be introduced as a precondition, a pDL property that captures the essence of an abstraction, and is satisfied by all the abstracted states sharing the property. If an abstract property is a precondition for a proof, it is naturally introduced using implication. However, implication is unwieldy in an expectation calculus, so it is practical to be able to eliminate it in the proof machinery. The following theorem explains how a precondition can be folded into an expectation function:

Theorem 7 (Implication Elimination). *Let s be a* pGCL *program,* φ_i *be* pDL *formulae, and* p *a lower-bound function for expectations. Then:*

$$\models \varphi_1 \rightarrow ([s]_{\boldsymbol{p}} \varphi_2) \quad \textit{iff} \quad \models [s]_{\boldsymbol{p} \downarrow \varphi_1} \varphi_2$$

Note that we use validity naturally when working with abstract states, as the state is replaced by the precondition in the formula.

Finally, negation in pDL is difficult to push over boxes. This is due to non-determinism and the lower bound semantics of expectations it enforces. A p-box property expresses a lower bound on probability of a post-condition holding after a program. Naturally, a negation of a p-box property will express an *upper-bound* on a property, but pDL has no upper-bound modality first-class. We return to this problem in Sect. 8, where we discuss reasoning about upper-bounds in non-deterministic and in purely probabilistic programs.

7   Expectations for Program Constructs

This section investigates how expectations are transformed by pGCL program constructs, as opposed to logical constructs discussed above. We begin by looking at the composite statements, which build the structure of the underlying MDP. The probabilistic choice introduces a small expectation update, consistent with an expectation of a Bernoulli variable (item 1). The demonic choice (item 2), requires that both sides provide the same guarantee, which is consistent with worst-case reasoning.

Theorem 8 (Expectation and Choices). *Let* s_i *be programs,* φ *a PDL formula,* p_i *lower bound functions for expectations into* $[0, 1]$*, and* ε *a valuation of variables. Then:*

1. *If* $\varepsilon \models [s_1]_{p_1} \varphi$ *and* $\varepsilon \models [s_2]_{p_2} \varphi$ *then* $\varepsilon \models [s_1 {}_e\oplus s_2]_{p} \varphi$
   with $p = \varepsilon(e)p_1 + (1-\varepsilon(e))p_2$
2. $\varepsilon \models [s_1]_{p} \varphi$ *and* $\varepsilon \models [s_2]_{p} \varphi$ *if and only if* $\varepsilon \models [s_1 \sqcap s_2]_{p} \varphi$

Note that in the second case, demonic, we can always use weakening (Proposition 3.2) to equalize the left-hand-side expectation lower-bounds using a point-wise minimum, if the premises are established earlier for different lower bound functions.

Example 9. This example shows that a non-deterministic assignment is less informative than a probabilistic assignment. It shows that pDL can be used to make statements that compare programs directly in the formal system—one of its distinctive features in comparison with prior works (cf. Sect. 2). We check satisfaction of the following pDL formula for any expectation lower bound p:

$$\models \forall \delta \cdot \forall p \cdot 0 \leq p \leq 1 \rightarrow ([\mathsf{x:=0} \sqcap \mathsf{x:=1}]_p (x \geq \delta) \rightarrow [\mathsf{x:=0} \, {}_p\oplus \mathsf{x:=1}]_p (x \geq \delta)) \,.$$

For simplicity, we use the logical variable p directly in the rightmost program (this can easily be encoded as an additional assumption equating a fresh logical variable to a program variable). For the proof, we first simplify the formula using equivalence rewrites:

$$\models \forall \delta \cdot \forall p \cdot 0 \le p \le 1 \rightarrow ([\mathsf{x:=0} \sqcap \mathsf{x:=1}]_p \,(x \ge \delta) \rightarrow [\mathsf{x:=0}\,_p \oplus \mathsf{x:=1}]_p \,(x \ge \delta))$$

iff for ε, δ, p we have

$$\varepsilon \models 0 \le p \le 1 \rightarrow ([\mathsf{x:=0} \sqcap \mathsf{x:=1}]_p \,(x \ge \delta) \rightarrow [\mathsf{x:=0}\,_p \oplus \mathsf{x:=1}]_p \,(x \ge \delta)) \qquad \text{(Sect. 5, Definition 2 } \forall \text{)}$$

iff for ε, δ, p we have

$$\varepsilon \models \neg 0 \le p \le 1 \vee \neg [\mathsf{x:=0} \sqcap \mathsf{x:=1}]_p \,(x \ge \delta) \vee [\mathsf{x:=0}\,_p \oplus \mathsf{x:=1}]_p \,(x \ge \delta) \qquad \text{(syntactic sugar)}$$

iff for ε, δ, p we have

$$\neg 0 \le p \le 1 \vee \neg p(\varepsilon) \le \mathbf{E}_\varepsilon(x \ge \delta) \vee p(\varepsilon) \le \mathbf{E}_\varepsilon(x \ge \delta) \qquad \text{(Definition 2, the box)}$$

In the last line above the left expectation is taken in MDP $\mathcal{M}_{\mathsf{x:=0} \sqcap \mathsf{x:=1}}$ and the right one is taken in $\mathcal{M}_{\mathsf{x:=0}\,_p \oplus \mathsf{x:=1}}$.

Now the property is a disjunction of three cases. If the first or second disjunct hold the formula holds vacuously (the assumptions in the statement are violated). We focus on the last case, when the first two disjuncts are violated (so the assumptions hold). We need to show that the last disjunct holds. We split the reasoning in two cases:

1. $\delta \le 0$: Consider the right expectation $\mathbf{E}_\varepsilon(x \ge \delta)$. In the right program this expectation is equal to 1 because the formula always holds (both possible values of x are greater or equal to δ). Consequently, any expectation lower bound p is correct for this formula: $p(\varepsilon) \le \mathbf{E}_\varepsilon(x \ge \delta)$ in the right program.
2. $\delta > 0$: Consider the left expectation $\mathbf{E}_\varepsilon(x \ge \delta)$. By Eq. (3) this expectation is equal to zero (the policy that chooses the left branch in the program violates the property as $x = 0 < \delta$). Since $p(\varepsilon) \le \mathbf{E}_\varepsilon(x \ge \delta) = 0$, it must be that $p(\varepsilon) = 0$ in the left program. By the universal lower bound property (Proposition 3.1), all properties hold after any program with the expectation lower bound p, including the post-condition of the right program. $\qquad \square$

For any program logic, it is essential that we can reason about composition of consecutive statements; allowing the post-condition of one to be used as a pre-condition for the other. The following theorem demonstrates that sequencing in pGCL corresponds to composition of expectations in the MDP domain. It uses implication elimination (Theorem 7) to compute a post-condition for a sequence of programs. Crucially, the new lower bound is computed using an expectation operation in the MDP of the first program, using the lower-bound of the second program as a reward function. Here, the expectation operation acts as a way to explore the program graph and accumulate values in final states.

Theorem 10 (Expectation and Sequencing). *Let s_i be pGCL programs, φ_i be pDL formulae, ε be a valuation, and p an expectation lower bound function.*

$$\textit{If } \models \varphi_1 \rightarrow ([s_2]_p \, \varphi_2) \textit{ then } \varepsilon \models [s_1; s_2]_{\mathbf{E}_{\langle \varepsilon, s_1 \rangle}(p \downarrow \varphi_1)} \, \varphi_2 \ ,$$

where the expectation $\mathbf{E}_{\langle \varepsilon, s_1 \rangle}(p \downarrow \varphi_1)$ is taken in $\mathcal{M}_{s_1}$ with $p \downarrow \varphi_1$ as the reward function.

For a piece of intuition, note that the above theorem captures the basic step of a backwards reachability algorithm for MDPs, but expressed in pDL; it accumulates expectations backwards over s_1 from what is already known for s_2.

We now move to investigating how simple statements translate expectations:

Theorem 11 (Unfolding Simple Statements). *Let s be a pGCL program, φ a pDL formula, p a function into $[0, 1]$, a lower bound on expectations, and ε a valuation. Then*

1. $\varepsilon \models [\mathsf{skip}]_1 \varphi$ *iff* $\varepsilon \models \varphi$
2. $\varepsilon \models [s]_p \varphi$ *iff* $\varepsilon \models [\mathsf{skip}; s]_p \varphi$
3. $\varepsilon \models [\mathsf{x}\!:=\!e; s]_p \varphi$ *iff* $\varepsilon[x \mapsto \varepsilon(e)] \models [s]_p \varphi$

The case of if-conditions below is rather classic (Theorem 12.3). For any given state, we can evaluate the head condition and inherit the expectation from the selected branch. For this to work we assume that the atomic formulae (ATF) satisfaction semantics in pDL is consistent with the expression evaluation semantics in pGCL. The case of while loops is much more interesting—indeed a plethora of works have emerged recently on proposing sound reasoning rules for while loop invariants, post-conditions and termination (see Sect. 2). In this paper, we show the simplest possible reasoning rule for loops that performs a single unrolling, exactly along the operational semantics. Of course, we are confident that many other rules for reasoning about while loops (involving invariants, prefixes, or converging chains of probabilities) can also be proven sound in pDL—left as future work.

Theorem 12 (Unfolding Loops and Conditionals). *Let e be a program expression (also an atomic pDL formula over program variables in X), φ be a pDL atomic formula, s_i be pGCL programs, p an expectation lower bound function, and ε a valuation. Then:*

1. *If $\varepsilon \models e \wedge [s_1]_p \varphi$ then $\varepsilon \models [\mathsf{if}\ e\ \{\,s_1\,\}\ \mathsf{else}\ \{\,s_2\,\}]_p \varphi$*
2. *If $\varepsilon \models \neg e \wedge [s_2]_p \varphi$ then $\varepsilon \models [\mathsf{if}\ e\ \{\,s_1\,\}\ \mathsf{else}\ \{s_2\}]_p \varphi$*
3. *$\varepsilon \models [\mathsf{if}\ e\ \{s;\ \mathsf{while}\ e\ \{\,s\,\}\}\ \mathsf{else}\ \{\mathsf{skip}\}]_p \varphi$ iff $\varepsilon \models [\mathsf{while}\ e\ \{\,s\,\}]_p \varphi$*

8   Purely Probabilistic and Deterministic Programs

The main reason for the lower-bound expectation semantics in pDL (inherited from McIver & Morgan) is the presence of demonic choice in pGCL. With non-determinism in the language, calculating precise probabilities is not possible. However, this does not mean that pDL cannot be used to reason about upper-bounds. The following theorem explains:[1]

Theorem 13 (Joni's Theorem). *For a policy π, property φ, program s, and state ε: if $\varepsilon \models [s]_{p_1} \varphi$ and $\varepsilon \models [s]_{p_2} \neg \varphi$ then $\mathbb{E}_{\pi,\varepsilon}[\![\varphi]\!] \in [p_1, 1 - p_2]$.*

---

[1] The theorem is named as a tribute to the song *Both sides now* by Joni Mitchell.

The theorem means that for a purely probabilistic program derived by fixing a policy for a pGCL program s, the expected reward is bounded from below by the expectation of this reward in s, and from above by the expectation of its negation in s. The theorem follows directly from Eq. (3) and the negation case in Definition 2.

For deterministic programs, some surprising properties, follow from interaction of probability and logics. For instance, we can conclude a conjunction of *expectations* from an expectation of a disjunction.

Theorem 14. *Let s be a purely probabilistic pGCL program (a program that does not use the demonic choice), let ε stand for a valuation, $p \in State \rightarrow [0,1]$ be an expectation function, and $\varphi_i \in$ pDL properties. Then if $\varepsilon \models [s]_p (\varphi_1 \vee \varphi_2)$ then there exist p_1, p_2, $p_1 + p_2 \geq p$ everywhere, such that $\varepsilon \models [s]_{p_1} \varphi_1$ and $\varepsilon \models [s]_{p_2} \varphi_2$.*

Intuitively, the property holds, because each of the measure of the space of final states of the disjointed properties can be separated between the disjuncts. This separation would not be possible with non-determinism, as shown in the following counterexample.

Example 15. Consider the program $\circledS ::= x := H \sqcap x := T$. The following holds for any initial valuation ε:

$$\varepsilon \models [\circledS]_1 (x = H \vee x = T)$$

This happens because disjunction is weakening and a weaker property is harder to avoid, here impossible to avoid, for an adversary minimizing an expectation satisfaction. However, at the same time: $\varepsilon \models [\circledS]_0 (x = H)$ and $\varepsilon \models [\circledS]_0 (x = T)$ and $0 + 0 < 1$. Importantly, zero is the tightest expectation lower bound possible here. □

9   Program Analysis with pDL

In this section, we apply pDL to reason about two illustrative examples: the Monty Hall game (Sect. 9.1), and convergence of a Bernoulli random variable (Sect. 9.2).

9.1   Monty Hall Game

In this section, we use pDL to compute the probability of winning the *Monty Hall game*. In this game, a host presents 3 doors, one of which contains a prize and the others are empty, and a contestant must figure out the door behind which the prize is hidden. To this end, the host and contestant follow a peculiar sequence of steps. First, the location of the prize is non-deterministically selected by the host. Secondly, the contestant chooses a door. Then, the host opens an empty door from those that the contestant did not choose. Finally, the contestant is asked whether she would like to switch doors. We determine, using pDL, what option increases the chances of winning the prize (switching or not).

Listing 1.1 shows a pGCL program, Monty_Hall, modeling the behavior of host and contestant. There are 4 variables in this program: prize (door containing the prize), choice (door selected by the contestant), open (door opened by the host), switch (Boolean indicating whether the user switches in the last step). Note that the variable switch is undefined in the program. The value of switch encodes the strategy of the contestant, so its value will be part of a pDL specification that we study below. Line 1 models the hosts's non-deterministic choice of the door for the prize. Line 2 models the door choice of the contestant (uniformly over the 3 doors). Lines 3–6 model the selection of the door to open, from the non-selected doors by the contestant. Lines 7–10 model whether the contestant switches door or not. For clarity and to reduce the size of the program, in lines 6 and 8, we use a shortcut to compute the door to open and to switch, respectively. Note that for $x, y \in \{0, 1, 2\}$ the expression $z = (2x - y) \bmod 3$ simply returns $z \in \{0, 1, 2\}$ such that $z \neq x$ and $z \neq y$. Similarly, in line 4, the expressions $y = (x + 1) \bmod 3, z = (x + 2) \bmod 3$ ensure that $y \neq x, z \neq x$ and $y \neq z$. This shortcut computes the doors that the host may open when the contestant's choice (line 2) is the door with the prize.

Listing 1.1. Monty Hall Program (Monty_Hall)

```
1   prize := 0 ⊓ (prize := 1 ⊓ prize := 2);
2   choice := 0 1/3⊕ (choice:=1 1/2⊕ choice:=2);
3   if (prize = choice)
4       open := (prize+1)%3 ⊓ open := (prize+2)%3;
5   else
6       open := (2*prize-choice)%3;
7   if (switch)
8       choice := (2*choice-open)%3
9   else
10      skip
```

We use pDL to find out the probability of the contestant selecting the door with the prize. To this end, we check satisfaction of the following formula, and solve it for p.

$$\varepsilon[\mathit{switch} \mapsto \mathit{true}] \models [\texttt{Monty\_Hall}]_p(\mathit{choice} = \mathit{prize}). \tag{9}$$

First, we show that $p = \min(p_0, p_1, p_2)$ where each p_i is the probability for the different locations of the prize. Formally, we use Theorem 8.2 (twice) as follows

$$\varepsilon \models [\texttt{prize:=0;} \ldots]_{p_0}(\mathit{choice} = \mathit{prize}) \ \mathit{and}$$
$$\varepsilon \models [\texttt{prize:=1;} \ldots]_{p_1}(\mathit{choice} = \mathit{prize}) \ \mathit{and}$$
$$\varepsilon \models [\texttt{prize:=2;} \ldots]_{p_2}(\mathit{choice} = \mathit{prize}) \ \mathit{imply}$$
$$\varepsilon \models [\texttt{Monty\_Hall}]_{\min(p_0, p_1, p_2)}(\mathit{choice} = \mathit{prize})$$

For each p_i, we compute the probability for each branch of the probabilistic choice. To this end, we use Theorem 8.1 as follows:

$$\varepsilon \models [\texttt{choice:=0;} \ldots]_{p_{i0}}(\mathit{choice} = \mathit{prize}) \ \mathit{and}$$
$$\varepsilon \models [\texttt{(choice:=1}\,1/2\oplus\texttt{choice:=2);} \ldots]_{p_{i1}}(\mathit{choice} = \mathit{prize}) \ \mathit{imply}$$
$$\varepsilon \models [\texttt{choice:=0}\,1/3\oplus\texttt{(choice:=1}\,1/2\oplus\texttt{choice:=2);} \ldots]_{1/3 \cdot p_{i0} + 2/3 \cdot p_{i1}}(\mathit{choice} = \mathit{prize}).$$

and apply it again for p_{i1} to resolve the inner probabilistic choice:

$$\varepsilon \models [\text{choice:=1};\ldots]_{p_{i10}}(choice = prize) \quad and$$
$$\varepsilon \models [\text{choice:=2};\ldots]_{p_{i11}}(choice = prize), \ implies$$
$$\varepsilon \models [(\text{choice:=1}\ _{1/2}\oplus\ \text{choice:=2});\ldots]_{1/2\cdot p_{i10}+1/2\cdot p_{i11}}(choice = prize)$$

These steps show that $p_i = 1/3\cdot p_{i0} + 2/3\cdot 1/2\cdot p_{i10} + 2/3\cdot 1/2\cdot p_{i11}$ where p_{i0}, p_{i10} and p_{i11} are the probabilities for the paths with *choice* equals to 0, 1 and 2, respectively.

Let us focus on the case p_1. This is the case when the prize is behind door 1, $\varepsilon[prize \mapsto 1]$. In what follows, we explore the three possible branches of the probabilistic choice. Consider the case where the user chooses door 1, i.e., $\varepsilon[choice \mapsto 1]$ and

$$\varepsilon \models [\textbf{if } (\text{prize = choice}) \ \{s_1\} \ \textbf{else} \ \{s_1\};\ldots]_{p_{110}}(choice = prize)$$

where s_0 and s_1 correspond to lines 4 and 6 in Listing 1.1, respectively. Since $\varepsilon \models prize = choice$ holds and by Theorem 12.1 we derive that

$$\varepsilon \models [s_0;\ldots]_{p_{110}}(choice = prize).$$

Note that p_{110} remains unchanged. Statement s_1 contains a non-deterministic choice, so we apply Theorem 8.2 to derive $p_{110} = \min(p_{1100}, p_{1101})$ where each p_{110i} correspond to the cases where $\varepsilon[open \mapsto 2]$ and $\varepsilon[open \mapsto 0]$, respectively. Since $switch = true$ both branches execute line 8, and the probabilities remain the same (Theorem 12.1). A simple calculation shows that after executing line 8 $\varepsilon \not\models (prize = choice)$ for both cases. For instance, consider

$$\varepsilon[open \mapsto 0] \models [\text{choice := (2*choice-open)\%3}]_{p_{1100}}(prize = choice).$$

By Theorem 11.3 $\varepsilon[choice \mapsto (2*1-0)\%3 = 2]$, which results in $prize \neq choice$. By the universal lower bound rule (Proposition 3.1) we derive $p_{1100} = 0$. The same derivations show that $p_{1101} = 0$, and, consequently, $p_{110} = 0$.

The same reasoning shows that $prize = choice$ holds for the cases where $choice \neq 1$ in line 2, i.e., p_{i0} and p_{i11}—we omit the details as they are analogous to the steps above. In these cases, by Theorem 11.1 we derive that $p_{i0} = 1$ and $p_{i11} = 1$. Recall that $p_{110} = 0$ (see above), then we derive that $p_1 = 1/3\cdot 1 + 2/3\cdot 1/2\cdot 0 + 2/3\cdot 1/2\cdot 1$. Consequently, $p_1 = 1/3 + 1/3 = 2/3$. Analogous reasoning shows that all $p_i = 2/3$.

To summarize, the probability of choosing the door with the prize when switching is at most 2/3. In other words, we have proven that switching door maximizes the probability of winning the prize.

9.2 Convergence of a Bernoulli Random Variable

We use pDL to study the convergence of a program that estimates the expectation of a Bernoulli random variable. To this end, we compute the probability that an estimated expectation is above an error threshold $\delta > 0$. This type of analysis may be of practical value for verifying the implementation of estimators for statistical models.

Consider the following pGCL program for estimating the expected value of a Bernoulli random variable (Technically the program computes the number of successes out of n trials, and we will put the estimation into the post-condition):

Listing 1.2. Bernoulli Program (Bernoulli)

```
1   i := 0; c := 0;
2   while (i < n) {
3     s := 0 μ⊕ s := 1;
4     c := c + s;
5     i := i + 1
6   }
```

Intuitively, Bernoulli computes the average of n Bernoulli trials X_i with mean μ, i.e., $X = \sum_i X_i / n$. It is well-known that $E[X] = \mu$ (e.g., [28]). Each X_i can be seen as a sample or measurement to estimate μ. A common way to study convergence is to check the probability that the estimated mean X is within some distance $\delta > 0$ of μ, i.e., $\Pr(|X - \mu| > \delta)$. In Bernoulli, a sample X_i corresponds to the execution of the probabilistic choice $_\mu\oplus$ in line 3 of Listing 1.2. After running all loop iterations, variable c contains the sum of all the samples, i.e., $c = \sum_i X_i$. Thus, X is equivalent to c/n and the specification of convergence can be written as $\Pr(|c/n - \mu| > \delta)$. Note that this specification is independent of the implementation of the program. The same specification can be used for any program estimating μ—by simply replacing X with the term estimating μ in the program.

In pDL, we can study the convergence of this estimator by checking

$$\varepsilon \models [\texttt{Bernoulli}]_p (|c/n - \mu| > \delta)$$

for some value of $\mu \in [0, 1]$, $\delta > 0$ and $n \in \mathbb{N}$. Note that, since the program contains no non-determinism, $p = \Pr(|X - \mu| > \delta)$. We describe the reasoning to compute p.

First, note that the while-loop in Bernoulli is bounded. Therefore, we can replace it with a sequence of n iterations of the loop body. Let s_i denote the ith iteration of the loop (lines 3–4 in Listing 1.2). We omit for brevity the assignments in line 1 of Listing 1.2 and directly proceed with a state $\varepsilon[c \mapsto 0, i \mapsto 0]$. Consider the first iteration of the loop, i.e., $i = 0$. By Theorem 12.3 we can derive

$$\varepsilon \models [\texttt{if (0 < n) \{}s_0\texttt{; while (i < n) \{}s_1\texttt{\}\} else \{skip\}}]_p (|c/n - \mu| > \delta).$$

Assume $\varepsilon \models 0 < n$ holds, then by Theorem 12.1 we derive

$$\varepsilon \models [s_0\texttt{; while (i < n) \{}s_1\texttt{\}}]_p (|c/n - \mu| > \delta).$$

By applying the above rules repeatedly we can rewrite Bernoulli as

$$\varepsilon \models [s_0; \ldots; s_{n-1}; \texttt{skip}]_p (|c/n - \mu| > \delta)$$

with the **skip** added in the last iteration of the loop by Theorem 12.3 and 12.2.

Second, we compute the value of p for a possible path of Bernoulli. Consider the case when $c = 0$ after executing the program. That is,

$$\varepsilon \models [s_0; \ldots; s_{n-1}; \texttt{skip}]_p (c = 0).$$

This only happens for the path where the probabilistic choice is resolved as c:=0 for all loop iterations. Applying Theorem 10 we derive

$$\textit{If} \models (c = 0) \rightarrow [s_1; \ldots; s_{n-1}; \texttt{skip}]_{p'} (c = 0), \textit{ then}$$

$$\varepsilon \models [s_0; \ldots; s_{n-1}; \texttt{skip}]_{\mathbf{E}_\varepsilon p' \downarrow (c=0)} (c = 0).$$

Here $\mathbf{E}_\varepsilon$ is computed over $\mathcal{M}_{s_0}$ (cf. Theorem 10). For `Bernoulli`, this expectation is computed over the two paths resulting from the probabilistic choice in Listing 1.2, line 3. Since only the left branch satisfies $c = 0$ and it is executed with probability μ, then $\mathbf{E}_\varepsilon p' = \mu p'$. Applying this argument for each iteration of the loop we derive that $\varepsilon \models [s_0; \ldots; s_{n-1}; \mathbf{skip};]_p (c = 0)$ holds for $p = \mu^n$. Similarly, consider the case where $c = 1$ after running all iterations of the loop, due to the first iteration resulting in `c:=1` and the rest `c:=0`. Then, we apply Theorem 10 as follows

If $\models (c = 1) \rightarrow [s_1; \ldots; s_{n-1}; \mathbf{skip}]_{p'} (c = 1),$ *then*

$$\varepsilon \models [s_0; \ldots; s_{n-1}; \mathbf{skip}]_{\mathbf{E}_\varepsilon p' \downarrow (c=1)} (c = 1).$$

In this case, $\mathbf{E}_\varepsilon p' = (1-\mu)p'$, as the probability of $c = 1$ is $(1-\mu)$ (cf. Listing 1.2 line 3). Since, in this case, the remaining iterations of the loop result in `c:=0`, and from our reasoning above, we derive that $p' = \mu^{n-1}$. Hence, $p = (1 - \mu)\mu^{n-1}$. In general, by repeatedly applying these properties, we can derive that the probability of a path is $\mu^i(1 - \mu)^j$ where i is the number loop iterations resulting in `c:=0` and j the number of loop iterations resulting in `c:=1`.

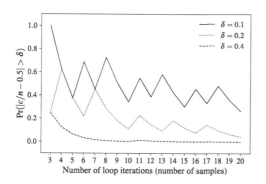

Fig. 3. Convergence of Bernoulli random variable with $\mu = 0.5$.

Now we return to our original problem $\varepsilon \models [\text{Bernoulli}]_p (|c/n - \mu| > \delta)$. Recall from Definition 2 that p is the sum of the probabilities over all the paths that satisfy the post-condition. `Bernoulli` has 2^n paths (two branches per loop iteration). Therefore, we conclude that $p = \sum_{i \in \Phi} \mu^{zeros(i)}(1 - \mu)^{ones(i)}$ where $zeros(\cdot), ones(\cdot)$ are functions returning the number of zeros and ones in the binary representation of the parameter, respectively, and $\Phi = \{i \in 2^n \mid |ones(i)/n - \mu| > \delta\}$ enumerates all paths in the program satisfying the post-condition. Note that the binary representation of $0, \ldots, 2^n$ conveniently captures each of the possible executions of `Bernoulli`.

The result above is useful to examine the convergence of `Bernoulli`. It allows us to evaluate the probability of convergence for increasing number of samples and different values of μ and δ. As an example, Fig. 3 shows the results for $\mu = 0.5$, $\delta \in \{0.1, 0.2, 0.4\}$ and up to $n = 20$ iterations of the loop. The dotted and dashed lines in the figure show that with 20 iterations the probability of having an error $\delta > 0.2$ is less than 5%. However, for an error $\delta > 0.1$ the probability increases to more than 20%.

10   Conclusion

This paper has proposed pDL, a specification language for probabilistic programs—the first dynamic logic for probabilistic programs written in pGCL. Like pGCL, pDL contains probabilistic and demonic choice. Unlike pGCL, it includes programs as first-order entities in specifications and allows forward reasoning capabilities as usual in dynamic logic. We have defined the model-theoretic semantics of pDL and shown basic properties of the newly introduced p-box modality. We demonstrated the reasoning capabilities on two well-known examples of probabilistic programs. In the future, we plan to develop a deductive proof system for pDL supported by tools for (semi-)automated reasoning about pGCL programs. Furthermore, the current definition of pDL gives no syntax to the expectations. Batz et al. propose a specification language for real-valued functions that is closed under the construction of weakest pre-expectations [20]; such a language could be used to express assertions for pGCL programs. It would be interesting to integrate these advances into pDL.

Acknowledgments. This work was supported by the Research Council of Norway via SIRIUS (project no. 237898).

References

1. Kozen, D.: Semantics of probabilistic programs. In: Proceedings 20th Annual Symposium on Foundations of Computer Science, IEEE Computer Society, 101–114 (1979)
2. Hark, M., Kaminski, B.L., Giesl, J., Katoen, J.: Aiming low is harder: induction for lower bounds in probabilistic program verification. In: Proceedings of ACM Programming Language, 4(POPL), pp. 37:1–37:28 (2020)
3. Kaminski, B.L.: Advanced weakest precondition calculi for probabilistic programs. PhD thesis, RWTH Aachen University, Germany (2019)
4. Stein, D., Staton, S.: Compositional semantics for probabilistic programs with exact conditioning. In: Proceedings on 36th Annual ACM/IEEE Symposium on Logic in Computer Science (LICS 2021), pp. 1–13 IEEE (2021)
5. Smolka, S., Kumar, P., Foster, N., Kozen, D., Silva, A.: Cantor meets Scott: semantic foundations for probabilistic networks. In: Castagna, G., Gordon, A.D., (eds.) Proceedings of the 44th ACM SIGPLAN Symposium on Principles of Programming Languages (POPL 2017), pp. 557–571. ACM (2017)
6. Batz, K., et al.: Foundations for entailment checking in quantitative separation logic. In: Sergey, I. (ed.) ESOP 2022. LNCS, vol. 13240, pp. 57–84. Springer, Cham (2022). https://doi.org/10.1007/978-3-030-99336-8_3
7. McIver, A., Morgan, C.: Abstraction, Refinement And Proof For Probabilistic Systems. Monographs in Computer Science. Springer, Cham (2005)
8. Dijkstra, E.W.: A discipline of programming. Prentice-Hall (1976)
9. Harel, D., Kozen, D., Tiuryn, J.: Dynamic Logic. Foundations of Computing, MIT Press, Cambridge (2000)
10. Hansson, H., Jonsson, B.: A logic for reasoning about time and reliability. Formal Aspects Comput. **6**(5), 512–535 (1994)
11. Puterman, M.L.: Markov Decision Processes. Wiley, Hoboken (2005)
12. Ahrendt, W., Beckert, B., Bubel, R., Hähnle, R., Schmitt, P.H., Ulbrich, M. (eds.): Deductive Software Verification - The KeY Book - From Theory to Practice. Lecture Notes in Computer Science, vol. 10001. Springer, Cham (2016)

13. de Gouw, S., Rot, J., de Boer, F.S., Bubel, R., Hähnle, R.: OpenJDK's Java.utils.Collection.sort() is broken: The good, the bad and the worst case. In: Kroening, D., Pasareanu, C.S., (eds.) Proceedings of 27th International Conference on Computer Aided Verification (CAV 2015), Lecture Notes in Computer Science, vol. 9206, pp. 273–289 Springer, Cham (2015)

14. Pardo, R., Johnsen, E.B., Schaefer, I., Wąsowski, A.: A specification logic for programs in the probabilistic guarded command language (extended version). ArXiv: https://arxiv.org/abs/2205.04822 (2022)

15. Cousot, P., Monerau, M.: Probabilistic abstract interpretation. In: Seidl, H. (ed.) ESOP 2012. LNCS, vol. 7211, pp. 169–193. Springer, Heidelberg (2012). https://doi.org/10.1007/978-3-642-28869-2_9

16. Filieri, A., Pasareanu, C.S., Visser, W.: Reliability analysis in symbolic pathfinder. In: 35th International Conference on Software Engineering (ICSE 2013). IEEE Computer Society, pp. 622–631 (2013)

17. Kwiatkowska, M.Z., Norman, G., Parker, D.: The PRISM benchmark suite. In: Ninth International Conference on Quantitative Evaluation of Systems (QEST 2012). IEEE Computer Society, pp. 203–204 (2012)

18. Kozen, D.: A probabilistic PDL. J. Comput. Syst. Sci. **30**(2), 162–178 (1985)

19. Feldman, Y.A., Harel, D.: A probabilistic dynamic logic. In: Proceedings of the 14th Annual ACM Symposium on Theory of Computing (STOC), pp. 181–195. ACM (1982)

20. Batz, K., Kaminski, B.L., Katoen, J., Matheja, C.: Relatively complete verification of probabilistic programs: an expressive language for expectation-based reasoning. Proc. ACM Program. Lang. **5**(POPL), 1–30 (2021)

21. Hähnle, R.: Dijkstra's legacy on program verification. In: Apt, K.R., Hoare, T., (eds.).: Edsger Wybe Dijkstra: His Life, Work, and Legacy. ACM / Morgan & Claypool, pp. 105–140 (2022)

22. Gretz, F., Katoen, J., McIver, A.: Operational versus weakest pre-expectation semantics for the probabilistic guarded command language. Perform. Eval. **73**, 110–132 (2014)

23. McIver, A., Morgan, C., Kaminski, B.L., Katoen, J.: A new proof rule for almost-sure termination. Proc. ACM Program. Lang. **2**(POPL), 33:1–33:28 (2018)

24. Batz, K., Kaminski, B.L., Katoen, J., Matheja, C., Noll, T.: Quantitative separation logic: a logic for reasoning about probabilistic pointer programs. Proc. ACM Program. Lang. **3**(POPL), 34:1–34:29 (2019)

25. Kaminski, B.L., Katoen, J.-P., Matheja, C., Olmedo, F.: Weakest precondition reasoning for expected run–times of probabilistic programs. In: Thiemann, P. (ed.) ESOP 2016. LNCS, vol. 9632, pp. 364–389. Springer, Heidelberg (2016). https://doi.org/10.1007/978-3-662-49498-1_15

26. Aguirre, A., Barthe, G., Hsu, J., Kaminski, B.L., Katoen, J., Matheja, C.: A pre-expectation calculus for probabilistic sensitivity. Proc. ACM Program. Lang. **5**(POPL), 1–28 (2021)

27. Baier, C., Kwiatkowska, M.Z., Norman, G.: Computing probability bounds for linear time formulas over concurrent probabilistic systems. Electron. Notes Theor. Comput. Sci. **22**, 29 (1999)

28. Dekking, F.M., Kraaikamp, C., Lopuhaä, H.P., Meester, L.E.: A Modern Introduction to Probability and Statistics: Understanding Why and How. STS, Springer, London (2005). https://doi.org/10.1007/1-84628-168-7

Card-Minimal Protocols for Symmetric Boolean Functions of More than Seven Inputs

Hayato Shikata[1](✉)[iD], Kodai Toyoda[1][iD], Daiki Miyahara[2,3][iD], and Takaaki Mizuki[1,3][iD]

[1] Tohoku University, Sendai, Japan
hayato.shikata.r3@dc.tohoku.ac.jp, mizuki+lncs@tohoku.ac.jp
[2] The University of Electro-Communications, Tokyo, Japan
[3] National Institute of Advanced Industrial Science and Technology, Tokyo, Japan

Abstract. Secure computations enable us to obtain the output value of a predetermined function while keeping its input values secret. Card-based cryptography realizes secure computations using a deck of physical cards. Because each input bit is typically encoded with two cards, an obvious lower bound on the number of required cards is $2n$ when securely computing an n-input Boolean function. Although card-based protocols often require helping cards (aside from $2n$ cards needed for input), there exist several protocols that require no helping card, namely, helping-card-free protocols. For example, there are helping-card-free protocols for several fundamental functions, such as the AND, XOR, and three-input majority functions. However, in general, it remains an open problem whether all Boolean functions have their helping-card-free protocols. In this study, we focus our attention on symmetric functions: Whereas the best known result is that any n-input symmetric function can be securely computed using two helping cards, we present a helping-card-free protocol for an arbitrary n-input symmetric function such that $n > 7$. Because much attention has been drawn to constructing card-based protocols using the minimum number of cards, our protocol, which is card-minimal, would be of interest to the research area of card-based cryptography.

Keywords: Card-based cryptography · Secure computation · Real-life hands-on cryptography · Symmetric function

1 Introduction

A *secure computation*, whose concept was first brought by Yao's seminal paper [38], enables us to obtain the output value of a predetermined function while keeping the input values secret. Various techniques for secure computations have been proposed so far (cf. [5]). While "computer-based (digital)" secure computations have been mainly studied and developed, "physical-tool-based" secure computations, such as using seals [27], balls [18], PEZ dispensers [1,3,28], flash

© The Author(s), under exclusive license to Springer Nature Switzerland AG 2022
H. Seidl et al. (Eds.): ICTAC 2022, LNCS 13572, pp. 388–406, 2022.
https://doi.org/10.1007/978-3-031-17715-6_25

lights [13], coins [12], and a deck of cards [20,21], have also been studied. Physical methods have a couple of advantages over computer-based methods; lay-people do not need to trust black boxes contained in computers and/or software, and the correctness and security of physical-tool based protocols tend to be easily understood without specialized knowledge. In this study, we focus on *card-based cryptography*, which uses a deck of physical cards to perform secure computations; refer to [9,10,25,34] for surveys.

1.1 What is Card-Based Cryptography?

Since Den Boer [4] invented the *five-card trick* in 1989, many *card-based cryptographic protocols* have been proposed. In these protocols, a one-bit value is usually encoded by a pair of cards ♣ and ♥, as follows:

$$\boxed{♣}\,\boxed{♥} = 0, \quad \boxed{♥}\,\boxed{♣} = 1. \tag{1}$$

According to Eq. (1), when two face-down cards $\boxed{?}\,\boxed{?}$ (whose face side is either $\boxed{♣}\,\boxed{♥}$ or $\boxed{♥}\,\boxed{♣}$) encode a bit $x \in \{0,1\}$, we call them a *commitment* to x, which is expressed as:

$$\underbrace{\boxed{?}\,\boxed{?}}_{x}.$$

A card-based cryptographic protocol, or simply a *protocol*, takes commitments as input to perform a secure computation. For example, the aforementioned five-card trick [4], which is a five-card protocol as the name suggests, takes commitments to $a, b \in \{0,1\}$ and one helping card $\boxed{♥}$ as input:

$$\underbrace{\boxed{?}\,\boxed{?}}_{a}\,\underbrace{\boxed{?}\,\boxed{?}}_{b}\,\boxed{♥}.$$

By applying some actions on the sequence of these five cards, such as rearranging, shuffling, and turning over cards, this protocol reveals only the value $a \wedge b$ of the AND function.

Another example is the *secure NOT computation*, which must be the simplest among all the existing protocols: Given a commitment to $x \in \{0,1\}$, switching the left and right cards of the commitment brings a commitment to its negation $\bar{x}$:

$$\underbrace{\overset{1}{\boxed{?}}\,\overset{2}{\boxed{?}}}_{x} \rightarrow \underbrace{\overset{2}{\boxed{?}}\,\overset{1}{\boxed{?}}}_{\bar{x}},$$

where we attach the numbers above to the cards for the sake of convenience, so as to display how the cards are rearranged.

1.2 Helping-Card-Free Protocols

One of the most attractive topics in card-based cryptography is to design *card-minimal* protocols that use the minimum number of cards. As most of the existing protocols follow the encoding rule (1) above (which is a "two-card-per-bit" encoding), this paper also focuses only on protocols whose inputs are given according to Eq. (1). Therefore, since a one-bit value is encoded by two cards, any protocol for an n-input Boolean function $f : \{0,1\}^n \to \{0,1\}$ uses at least $2n$ cards. That is, such a protocol takes n commitments to $x_1, x_2, \ldots, x_n \in \{0,1\}$,

$$\underbrace{\boxed{?}\boxed{?}}_{x_1}\underbrace{\boxed{?}\boxed{?}}_{x_2} \cdots \underbrace{\boxed{?}\boxed{?}}_{x_n}, \tag{2}$$

as input. If an n-input protocol does not use any (helping) card aside from the $2n$ cards for the input commitments as in Eq. (2), we call it a *helping-card-free* protocol. For example, the five-card trick [4] mentioned in Sect. 1.1 is not a helping-card-free protocol because it requires one helping card $\boxed{\heartsuit}$ to securely compute the AND function. Thus, a helping-card-free protocol for an n-input Boolean function f takes only $2n$ commitments (as in Eq. (2)) as input, and outputs only the value of $f(x_1, x_2, \ldots, x_n)$ after applying a series of actions such as shuffling and turning over cards. Note that any helping-card-free protocol is automatically a card-minimal protocol. This paper mainly deals with helping-card-free protocols (within the standard[1] computation model of card-based cryptography [24,25]).

To the best of our knowledge, the first helping-card-free protocol in history (other than the obvious NOT computation seen above) is the XOR protocol [26], invented in 2009, which securely computes the XOR function using only two commitments to $a, b \in \{0,1\}$:

$$\underbrace{\boxed{?}\boxed{?}}_{a}\underbrace{\boxed{?}\boxed{?}}_{b} \to \cdots \to \underbrace{\boxed{?}\boxed{?}}_{a \oplus b} .$$

Since the output of this protocol is a commitment to $a \oplus b$, the protocol can be repeated $n-1$ times to obtain a commitment to $x_1 \oplus x_2 \oplus \cdots \oplus x_n$ from n commitments to $x_1, x_2, \ldots, x_n$ (where we set $(a,b) = (x_1, x_2)$, $(a,b) = (x_1 \oplus x_2, x_3)$, and so on). Therefore, we immediately have a helping-card-free n-input XOR protocol.

Next came the AND protocol [23] proposed in 2012. This protocol does not produce a commitment to $a \wedge b$, but later in 2015, Koch et al. [11] constructed a helping-card-free AND protocol that outputs a commitment:

$$\underbrace{\boxed{?}\boxed{?}}_{a}\underbrace{\boxed{?}\boxed{?}}_{b} \to \cdots \to \underbrace{\boxed{?}\boxed{?}}_{a \wedge b} .$$

Since the output is a commitment, a helping-card-free n-input AND protocol can be constructed in a similar manner. Independently of this protocol, a helping-card-free n-input AND protocol was developed in 2016 [19]. Recently, a simpler helping-card-free 3-input AND protocol has also been devised [7].

As for functions other than AND and XOR, a helping-card-free protocol for the 3-input majority function has been constructed very recently [37]. Also, there

---

[1] There is another computation model where private actions are allowed, e.g. [2,14–17,29,32].

are helping-card-free protocols for the 3-input equality Boolean function (that outputs 1 when $x_1 = x_2 = x_3$ and 0 otherwise) [6,35].

Ruangwises and Itoh [33] designed a helping-card-free protocol for any function in the class of the so-called "doubly symmetric" Boolean functions. Note that an n-input Boolean function $f : \{0,1\}^n \to R$ with some set R as its range is said to be *symmetric* if for any i, j, $1 \le i, j \le n$, the following holds:

$$f(x_1, \ldots, x_i, \ldots, x_j, \ldots, x_n) = f(x_1, \ldots, x_j, \ldots, x_i, \ldots, x_n),$$

and that an n-input Boolean function $f : \{0,1\}^n \to R$ is said to be *doubly symmetric* if f is symmetric and the following holds:

$$f(x_1, x_2, \ldots, x_n) = f(\overline{x}_1, \overline{x}_2, \ldots, \overline{x}_n).$$

For example, the equality Boolean functions are doubly symmetric.

We have reviewed the existing helping-card-free protocols.

1.3   Contribution

As seen in Sect. 1.2, in the literature, we already have helping-card-free protocols for the limited classes of functions, such as the n-input AND and XOR functions and the doubly symmetric Boolean functions. Because the class of symmetric Boolean functions contains all these functions as well as many other important Boolean functions (such as threshold functions), a natural question is: Can one construct a helping-card-free protocol for any symmetric Boolean function?

As an upper bound on the number of required helping cards, in 2015, Nishida et al. [30] proved that two helping cards are sufficient for any n-input symmetric Boolean function $f : \{0,1\}^n \to \{0,1\}$ to be securely computed. Ruangwises and Itoh [33] extended the result to any range R, i.e., they constructed a two-helping-card protocol for any n-input symmetric Boolean function $f : \{0,1\}^n \to R$, where R is any set. Anyway, it is still open to determine whether one can obtain a protocol for any n-input symmetric Boolean function using fewer than two helping cards.

In this paper, we tackle this open problem. Namely, we aim to design a helping-card-free protocol for symmetric Boolean functions. Specifically, we will provide a generic construction of a helping-card-free protocol for an arbitrary n-input symmetric Boolean function $f : \{0,1\}^n \to \{0,1\}$ such that $n \ge 8$. Therefore, we give a partial answer to the open problem.

Our generic construction relies on the two novel sub-protocols, which will be presented in Sect. 3. The first sub-protocol transforms two commitments (to $a, b \in \{0,1\}$) into the result of their addition (namely, $a + b$) without any helping card; in addition, it produces one "free" card, which is very useful because such "free" cards can be used as helping cards in another protocol. Because the result of addition is obtained as an integer in a different encoding, the second sub-protocol transforms such an integer into commitments; in other words, it "binarizes" an integer. Making use of these two sub-protocols along with other existing protocols, we will design a generic protocol in Sect. 4. Before Sects. 3 and 4, we give some preliminaries in Sect. 2, and we conclude this paper in Sect. 5.

2   Preliminaries

In this section, we introduce a property of the symmetric functions and some of the existing protocols. Hereinafter, a symmetric Boolean function $f : \{0,1\}^n \to \{0,1\}$ is simply called a symmetric function.

2.1   Property of Symmetric Functions

Let $f : \{0,1\}^n \to \{0,1\}$ be a symmetric function, and let $x_i \in \{0,1\}$ for every i, $1 \leq i \leq n$. It is well-known that the value of $f(x_1, \ldots, x_n)$ depends only on the summation of the inputs, i.e., $\sum_{i=1}^n x_i$. That is, there exists a function $g : \{0,1,\ldots,n\} \to \{0,1\}$ such that

$$f(x_1, \ldots, x_n) = g\left(\sum_{i=1}^n x_i\right). \tag{3}$$

This implies that computing the summation $\sum_{i=1}^n x_i$ is one way for computing the symmetric function f.

2.2   Half Adder Protocol and Full Adder Protocol

A half-adder protocol is useful when computing the summation described in Sect. 2.1. The first card-based half-adder protocol was presented in 2013 [22]. After that, Nishida et al. [30] improved it by proposing a half-adder protocol with two helping cards:

$$\underbrace{\boxed{?}\boxed{?}}_{a}\underbrace{\boxed{?}\boxed{?}}_{b}\boxed{\clubsuit}\boxed{\heartsuit} \to \cdots \to \underbrace{\boxed{?}\boxed{?}}_{a \wedge b}\underbrace{\boxed{?}\boxed{?}}_{a \oplus b}\boxed{\clubsuit}\boxed{\heartsuit}.$$

A full-adder protocol using four helping cards was presented in 2013 [22]:

$$\underbrace{\boxed{?}\boxed{?}}_{a}\underbrace{\boxed{?}\boxed{?}}_{b}\underbrace{\boxed{?}\boxed{?}}_{c}\boxed{\clubsuit}\boxed{\heartsuit}\boxed{\clubsuit}\boxed{\heartsuit} \to \cdots \to \underbrace{\boxed{?}\boxed{?}}_{(a \wedge b) \vee (b \wedge c) \vee (c \wedge a)}\underbrace{\boxed{?}\boxed{?}}_{a \oplus b \oplus c}\boxed{\clubsuit}\boxed{\heartsuit}\boxed{\clubsuit}\boxed{\heartsuit}\boxed{\clubsuit}\boxed{\heartsuit}.$$

2.3   Protocol for Symmetric Functions with Two Helping Cards

In 2015, Nishida et al. [30] invented a protocol for any symmetric function using two helping cards (as mentioned in Sect. 1.3). Given n commitments and two helping cards,

$$\underbrace{\boxed{?}\boxed{?}}_{x_1}\underbrace{\boxed{?}\boxed{?}}_{x_2}\cdots\underbrace{\boxed{?}\boxed{?}}_{x_n}\boxed{\clubsuit}\boxed{\heartsuit},$$

their protocol produces a sequence of commitments that represents the binary representation of the summation,

$$\underbrace{\boxed{?}\boxed{?}\ \boxed{?}\boxed{?}\ \cdots\ \boxed{?}\boxed{?}}_{(\sum_{i=1}^n x_i)_2},$$

using the half-adder protocol introduced in Sect. 2.2; then, their protocol computes $g(\sum_{i=1}^{n} x_i)$ as in Eq. (3) using that sequence. Here, for a nonnegative integer $i \in \{0, 1, \ldots, \ell\}$, we denote the binary representation of i by $(i)_2$, which is represented as $\lceil \log_2(\ell + 1) \rceil$ commitments written as

$$\underbrace{\boxed{?}\boxed{?}\boxed{?}\boxed{?} \cdots \boxed{?}\boxed{?}}_{(i)_2}.$$

The range of the protocol above is $\{0, 1\}$, whereas Ruangwises and Itoh [33] constructed a protocol for a symmetric function $f : \{0, 1\}^n \to R$ with an arbitrary range R using two helping cards (as also mentioned in Sect. 1.3). Their protocol used the following ♣-*position* and ♡-*position* encodings (the ♣-pos. encoding and the ♡-pos. encoding for short, respectively). In the ♣-pos. encoding, for $k \geq 2$, one ♣ and $k - 1$ ♡s are used to represent an integer i ($0 \leq i \leq k - 1$) by placing ♣ at the $(i + 1)$-st position as follows:

$$\overset{1}{\boxed{♡}}\overset{2}{\boxed{♡}} \cdots \overset{i+1}{\boxed{♣}} \cdots \overset{k}{\boxed{♡}}.$$

In the following, we denote such a sequence of face-down cards by $E_k^{♣}(i)$, and write it as follows:

$$\underbrace{\boxed{?}\boxed{?}\boxed{?} \cdots \boxed{?}}_{E_k^{♣}(i)}.$$

The ♡-pos. encoding and $E_k^{♡}(i)$ are defined in the same way with the colors (i.e., suits) reversed.

2.4 Addition of Position Encodings

Ruangwises and Itoh [33] proposed the following method for adding two integers represented in the pos. encodings.[2]

1. Assume that we have $E_k^{♣}(a)$ and $E_k^{♡}(b)$ for two integers a, b. For convenience, we name each card as follows:

$$E_k^{♣}(a) : \underset{x_0\ x_1}{\boxed{?}\boxed{?}} \cdots \underset{x_{k-1}}{\boxed{?}}, \quad E_k^{♡}(b) : \underset{y_0\ y_1}{\boxed{?}\boxed{?}} \cdots \underset{y_{k-1}}{\boxed{?}}.$$

2. Rearrange the sequences as follows:

$$\underset{x_0}{\overset{y_{k-1}}{\boxed{?}}}\boxed{?} \quad \underset{x_1}{\overset{y_{k-2}}{\boxed{?}}}\boxed{?} \quad \cdots \quad \underset{x_{k-1}}{\overset{y_0}{\boxed{?}}}\boxed{?}.$$

3. Apply a *random 2-section cut* (also known as a pile-shifting shuffle [31]) to this sequence. Here, a random 2-section cut means to make each pair of cards into a single bundle and shuffle all the bundles cyclically. Thus, for a random number r, the sequence changes as follows:

$$\left[\underset{x_0}{\overset{y_{k-1}}{\boxed{?}}}\overset{y_{k-2}}{\boxed{?}} \underset{x_1}{\boxed{?}}\boxed{?} \cdots \underset{x_{k-1}}{\overset{y_0}{\boxed{?}}}\boxed{?}\right] \to \left[\underset{x_{0+r}}{\boxed{?}}\overset{y_{k-1-r}}{\boxed{?}} \underset{x_{1+r}}{\boxed{?}}\overset{y_{k-2-r}}{\boxed{?}} \cdots \underset{x_{k-1+r}}{\boxed{?}}\overset{y_{0-r}}{\boxed{?}}\right].$$

---

[2] This method is originated from the previous protocol [36] proposed by Shinagawa et al.

4. Rearrange them back to the first place as follows:

$$E_k^{\clubsuit}(a-r): \underbrace{\boxed{?}}_{x_{0+r}} \underbrace{\boxed{?}}_{x_{1+r}} \cdots \underbrace{\boxed{?}}_{x_{k-1+r}} \, , \quad E_k^{\heartsuit}(b+r): \underbrace{\boxed{?}}_{y_{0-r}} \underbrace{\boxed{?}}_{y_{1-r}} \cdots \underbrace{\boxed{?}}_{y_{k-1-r}} \, ,$$

where a is subtracted by the random number r and b is added by r.

5. Turn over $E_k^{\heartsuit}(b+r)$ and shift $E_k^{\clubsuit}(a-r)$ cyclically to the right by the revealed number, i.e., add $b+r$ to $a-r$; when revealing $E_k^{\heartsuit}(b+r)$, the value of b does not leak because a random value r was added to b:

$$E_k^{\clubsuit}(a-r): \underbrace{\boxed{?}}_{x_{0+r}} \underbrace{\boxed{?}}_{x_{1+r}} \cdots \underbrace{\boxed{?}}_{x_{k-1+r}} \;\rightarrow\; E_k^{\clubsuit}(a+b): \underbrace{\boxed{?}}_{x_{0-b}} \underbrace{\boxed{?}}_{x_{1-b}} \cdots \underbrace{\boxed{?}}_{x_{k-1-b}} \, .$$

This enables a secure computation of $(a-r)+(b+r)=a+b$ without leaking the values of a and b. That is, $E_k^{\clubsuit}(a+b)$ is obtained. Here, we did an addition of the $\clubsuit$-pos. encoding and the $\heartsuit$-pos. encoding, but other combinations are also feasible.

3   Building Blocks

Before describing our proposed protocol in the next section, we present two novel sub-protocols, which will be used in the proposed protocol as building blocks.

3.1   Addition of Two Commitments

To construct our proposed protocol, we first compute the summation of inputs as implied in Sect. 2.1. For this, we propose the following addition protocol to compute $a+b$ from commitments to $a, b \in \{0, 1\}$ without the need of any helping card[3]. That is, somewhat surprisingly, this novel sub-protocol is helping-card-free.

1. Apply a *random bisection cut* [26] (denoted by $[\cdots | \cdots]$) to the sequence of the commitments to a and b as follows:

$$\underbrace{\boxed{?}\boxed{?}}_{a}\underbrace{\boxed{?}\boxed{?}}_{b} \rightarrow [\,\boxed{?}\boxed{?}\,|\,\boxed{?}\boxed{?}\,] \rightarrow \boxed{?}\boxed{?}\boxed{?}\boxed{?}.$$

Here, a random bisection cut is to halve a sequence and shuffle the two halves randomly.

2. Shuffle the two cards in the middle as follows:

$$\boxed{?}\,[\,\boxed{?}\,|\,\boxed{?}\,]\,\boxed{?} \rightarrow \boxed{?}\boxed{?}\boxed{?}\boxed{?}.$$

---

[3] This protocol is inspired by the Mizuki–Kumamoto–Sone AND protocol [23]; the procedure is the same up to the middle.

3. Reveal the second card from the left; then, either ♣ or ♡ appears with a probability of $1/2$:

$$\boxed{?}\ \boxed{?}\ \boxed{?}\boxed{?}\ .$$
$$\uparrow$$
$$\text{Reveal}$$

(a) If ♣ appears, rearrange the sequence to obtain $a+b$ in the ♣-pos. encoding, i.e., $E_3^{\clubsuit}(a+b)$, as follows:

$$\overset{1\ 2\ 3\ 4}{\boxed{?}\boxed{\clubsuit}\boxed{?}\boxed{?}} \rightarrow \underset{E_3^{\clubsuit}(a+b)}{\overset{1\ 3\ 4\ 2}{\boxed{?}\boxed{?}\boxed{?}\boxed{\clubsuit}}}\ .$$

(b) If ♡ appears, rearrange the sequence to obtain $a+b$ in the ♡-pos. encoding, i.e., $E_3^{\heartsuit}(a+b)$, as follows:

$$\overset{1\ 2\ 3\ 4}{\boxed{?}\boxed{\heartsuit}\boxed{?}\boxed{?}} \rightarrow \underset{E_3^{\heartsuit}(a+b)}{\overset{4\ 3\ 1\ 2}{\boxed{?}\boxed{?}\boxed{?}\boxed{\heartsuit}}}\ .$$

We call this protocol the *helping-card-free two-commitment addition*. The correctness and security of this addition protocol can be proved by drawing the so-called KWH-tree [8,11]. We depict its KWH-tree in Fig. 1.

As seen above, we obtain either $E_3^{\clubsuit}(a+b)$ or $E_3^{\heartsuit}(a+b)$ (with a probability of $1/2$) as well as one free card from the commitments to a and b.

3.2 Binarization of Position Encoding

Our second novel sub-protocol is to "binarize" an integer in the position encoding. Let $0 \leq i \leq 3$; given $E_4^{\clubsuit}(i)$ and four helping cards, this sub-protocol produces commitments to $(i)_2$. (A protocol for $E_4^{\heartsuit}(i)$ can be constructed in a similar way.)

1. Turn the four helping cards face down (resulting in two commitments to 0 because of the encoding rule (1)):

$$\underset{E_4^{\clubsuit}(i)}{\underbrace{\boxed{?}\boxed{?}\boxed{?}\boxed{?}}}\ \boxed{\clubsuit}\boxed{\heartsuit}\boxed{\clubsuit}\boxed{\heartsuit} \rightarrow \underset{E_4^{\clubsuit}(2u+v)}{\underbrace{\boxed{?}\boxed{?}\boxed{?}\boxed{?}}}\ \underset{0}{\underbrace{\boxed{?}\boxed{?}}}\ \underset{0}{\underbrace{\boxed{?}\boxed{?}}}\ .$$

Here, we introduce $u, v \in \{0, 1\}$ such that $i = 2u + v$, i.e., u and v are the most and least significant bits of $(i)_2$, respectively.
2. Shuffle $E_4^{\clubsuit}(2u + v)$ and the middle commitment to 0 "synchronously" as follows.
(a) Rearrange the sequence as follows:

$$\underset{E_4^{\clubsuit}(2u+v)}{\underbrace{\overset{1\ 2\ 3\ 4}{\boxed{?}\boxed{?}\boxed{?}\boxed{?}}}}\ \underset{0}{\underbrace{\overset{5\ 6}{\boxed{?}\boxed{?}}}}\ \underset{0}{\underbrace{\overset{7\ 8}{\boxed{?}\boxed{?}}}} \rightarrow \underbrace{\overset{1\ 2\ 5}{\boxed{?}\boxed{?}\boxed{?}}}\ \underbrace{\overset{3\ 4\ 6}{\boxed{?}\boxed{?}\boxed{?}}}\ \underset{0}{\underbrace{\overset{7\ 8}{\boxed{?}\boxed{?}}}}\ .$$

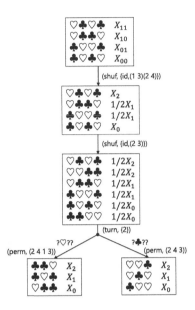

Fig. 1. KWH-tree of the helping-card-free two-commitment addition. Here, $X_0 = X_{00}$, $X_1 = X_{01} + X_{10}$, and $X_2 = X_{11}$.

(b) Apply a random bisection cut to the first six cards:

$$[\boxed{?}\boxed{?}\boxed{?}\,|\,\boxed{?}\boxed{?}\boxed{?}]\ \ \boxed{?}\boxed{?} \rightarrow \boxed{?}\boxed{?}\boxed{?}\boxed{?}\boxed{?}\boxed{?}\ \ \boxed{?}\boxed{?}.$$

(c) Rearrange the sequence as follows:

$$
\begin{array}{cc}
\overset{1\ 2\ 3\ 4\ 5\ 6}{\boxed{?}\boxed{?}\boxed{?}\boxed{?}\boxed{?}\boxed{?}} & \overset{7\ 8}{\boxed{?}\boxed{?}}
\end{array}
\rightarrow
\begin{array}{ccc}
\overset{1\ 2\ 4\ 5}{\boxed{?}\boxed{?}\boxed{?}\boxed{?}} & \overset{3\ 6}{\boxed{?}\boxed{?}} & \overset{7\ 8}{\boxed{?}\boxed{?}}
\end{array}.
$$
$$\underset{E_4^{\clubsuit}(2(u\oplus r_1)+v)}{}\quad\underset{r_1}{}\quad\underset{0}{}$$

Here, a random bit $r_1 \in \{0, 1\}$ is added to u and the middle commitment to 0 because of the random bisection cut in Step 2b.

3. Shuffle $E_4^{\clubsuit}((2u \oplus r_1) + v)$ and the right commitment to 0 "synchronously" as follows.

(a) Rearrange the sequence as follows:

$$
\begin{array}{ccc}
\overset{1\ 2\ 3\ 4}{\boxed{?}\boxed{?}\boxed{?}\boxed{?}} & \overset{5\ 6}{\boxed{?}\boxed{?}} & \overset{7\ 8}{\boxed{?}\boxed{?}}
\end{array}
\rightarrow
\begin{array}{cccc}
\overset{1\ 3\ 7}{\boxed{?}\boxed{?}\boxed{?}} & \overset{2\ 4\ 8}{\boxed{?}\boxed{?}\boxed{?}} & \overset{5\ 6}{\boxed{?}\boxed{?}}
\end{array}.
$$
$$\underset{E_4^{\clubsuit}(2(u\oplus r_1)+v)}{}\quad\underset{r_1}{}\quad\underset{0}{}\qquad\qquad\underset{r_1}{}$$

(b) Apply a random bisection cut to the first six cards:

$$[\boxed{?}\boxed{?}\boxed{?}\,|\,\boxed{?}\boxed{?}\boxed{?}]\ \ \boxed{?}\boxed{?} \rightarrow \boxed{?}\boxed{?}\boxed{?}\ \ \boxed{?}\boxed{?}\boxed{?}\ \ \boxed{?}\boxed{?}.$$

Table 1. How to swap commitments in Step 5 of the binarization protocol

Revealed seq.	Binary	Swapping
$E_4^{\clubsuit}(0)$	$(0,0)$	?? ??
$E_4^{\clubsuit}(1)$	$(0,1)$	?? ?? Swap
$E_4^{\clubsuit}(2)$	$(1,0)$	?? ?? Swap
$E_4^{\clubsuit}(3)$	$(1,1)$	?? ?? Swap Swap

(c) Rearrange the sequence as follows:

$$\underset{r_1}{\underbrace{\boxed{?}\boxed{?}\boxed{?}\boxed{?}\ \boxed{?}\boxed{?}\ \boxed{?}\boxed{?}}} \rightarrow \underset{E_4^{\clubsuit}(2(u\oplus r_1)+(v\oplus r_2))}{\underbrace{\boxed{?}\boxed{?}\boxed{?}\boxed{?}}}\ \underset{r_1}{\underbrace{\boxed{?}\boxed{?}}}\ \underset{r_2}{\underbrace{\boxed{?}\boxed{?}}}.$$

Here, a random bit $r_2 \in \{0,1\}$ is added to v and the right commitment to 0 because of applying the random bisection cut in Step 3b.

4. Reveal $E_4^{\clubsuit}(2(u \oplus r_1) + (v \oplus r_2))$:

$$\underset{\text{Reveal}}{\underbrace{\boxed{?}\boxed{?}\boxed{?}\boxed{?}}}\ \boxed{?}\boxed{?}\ \boxed{?}\boxed{?}.$$

5. From the revealed integer value in the previous step, obtain commitments to $(i)_2$ by swapping (or not swapping) the commitments to r_1 and r_2 as shown in Table 1: Consider commitments to the binary representation of the revealed integer value (i.e., the second column of the table); if we have 1 among the two-bit sequence, we swap the corresponding commitment; if we have 0, we do not swap the commitment. By rearranging the sequence in this way, we obtain

$$\underset{u}{\underbrace{\boxed{?}\boxed{?}}}\ \underset{v}{\underbrace{\boxed{?}\boxed{?}}},\ \text{i.e.,}\ \underset{(i)_2}{\underbrace{\boxed{?}\boxed{?}\ \boxed{?}\boxed{?}}}.$$

For example, if $E_4^{\clubsuit}(2)$ appears by revealing the sequence in Step 4 as

$$\underset{E_4^{\clubsuit}(2)}{\underbrace{\boxed{?}\boxed{?}\boxed{?}\boxed{?}}}\ \underset{r_1}{\underbrace{\boxed{?}\boxed{?}}}\ \underset{r_2}{\underbrace{\boxed{?}\boxed{?}}},$$

we swap the middle commitment to r_1, but do not swap the right commitment as follows:

$$\underset{E_4^{\clubsuit}(2)}{\underbrace{\boxed{?}\boxed{?}\boxed{?}\boxed{?}}}\ \underset{\text{Swap}}{\underbrace{\boxed{?}\boxed{?}}}\ \boxed{?}\boxed{?} \rightarrow \boxed{?}\boxed{?}\boxed{?}\boxed{?}\ \underset{(i)_2}{\underbrace{\boxed{?}\boxed{?}\ \boxed{?}\boxed{?}}}.$$

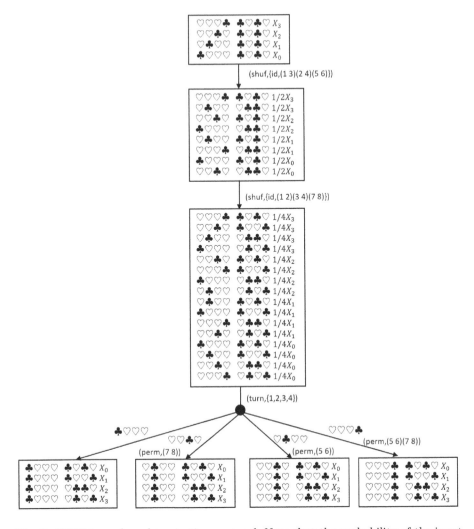

Fig. 2. KWH-tree of our binarization protocol. Note that the probability of the input sequence being $E_4^{\clubsuit}(i)$ is X_i.

The correctness and security of this protocol can be confirmed by drawing its KWH-tree depicted in Fig. 2. We believe that this sub-protocol is of independent interest.

4   Our Proposed Protocol

We are ready to describe our proposed protocol for securely computing any symmetric function $f : \{0,1\}^n \to \{0,1\}$ such that $n \geq 8$. Let us assume that

$n = 8$ for simplicity (the protocol can be easily extended to the case of $n \geq 9$). Thus, the input to the protocol is a sequence of 16 cards:

$$\boxed{?}\boxed{?}\;\boxed{?}\boxed{?}\;\boxed{?}\boxed{?}\;\boxed{?}\boxed{?}\;\boxed{?}\boxed{?}\;\boxed{?}\boxed{?}\;\boxed{?}\boxed{?}\;\boxed{?}\boxed{?}\;.$$
$$\;x_1\quad\; x_2\quad\; x_3\quad\; x_4\quad\; x_5\quad\; x_6\quad\; x_7\quad\; x_8$$

An overview of our protocol is as follows.

1. Add the inputs to obtain sequences of $x_1 + x_2 + x_7$, $x_3 + x_4$, and $x_5 + x_6 + x_8$ using our helping-card-free two-commitment addition proposed in Sect. 3.1 and the existing addition protocol introduced in Sect. 2.4 (Sect. 4.1).
2. Binarize the sequences obtained above using our binarization protocol proposed in Sect. 3.2 (Sect. 4.2).
3. Add the binarized sequences using the existing full-adder protocol introduced in Sect. 2.2 (Sect. 4.3).

4.1 Adding the Inputs

Computing $x_1 + x_2$. First, we obtain a sequence of $x_1 + x_2$ from the commitments to x_1 and x_2 using our helping-card-free two-commitment addition described in Sect. 3.1. For the sake of explanation, let us assume that the addition result is obtained in the ♣-pos. encoding, i.e., we obtain $E_3^{\clubsuit}(x_1 + x_2)$ without loss of generality. In this case, one free card ♣ is also obtained. In summary, the resulting sequence is as follows:

$$\boxed{?}\boxed{?}\boxed{?}\;\boxed{\clubsuit}\quad\boxed{?}\boxed{?}\quad\boxed{?}\boxed{?}\quad\cdots\quad\boxed{?}\boxed{?}\;.$$
$$\;E_3^{\clubsuit}(x_1+x_2)\qquad\quad x_3\qquad x_4\qquad\qquad x_8$$

Computing $x_3 + x_4$. We apply the helping-card-free two-commitment addition to obtain a sequence of $x_3 + x_4$. Here, we have two possible cases with a probability of $1/2$ as follows.

1. If the revealed card is ♡, the resulting sequence is as follows:

$$\boxed{?}\boxed{?}\boxed{?}\;\boxed{\clubsuit}\quad\boxed{?}\boxed{?}\boxed{?}\;\boxed{\heartsuit}\quad\boxed{?}\boxed{?}\quad\cdots\quad\boxed{?}\boxed{?}\;.$$
$$\;E_3^{\clubsuit}(x_1+x_2)\qquad E_3^{\heartsuit}(x_3+x_4)\qquad\; x_5\qquad\qquad x_8$$

2. If it is ♣, the resulting sequence is as follows:

$$\boxed{?}\boxed{?}\boxed{?}\;\boxed{\clubsuit}\quad\boxed{?}\boxed{?}\boxed{?}\;\boxed{\clubsuit}\quad\boxed{?}\boxed{?}\quad\cdots\quad\boxed{?}\boxed{?}\;.$$
$$\;E_3^{\clubsuit}(x_1+x_2)\qquad E_3^{\clubsuit}(x_3+x_4)\qquad\; x_5\qquad\qquad x_8$$

In the former case, we have ♣♡ as free cards. In the latter case, we have ♣♣ as free cards.

Computing x_5+x_6. For each of the two cases described in the previous paragraph, an addition is done as follows.

<u>Case 1</u>: We have free cards ♣♡.
We use the helping-card-free two-commitment addition for computing $x_5 + x_6$. Without loss of generality, let us assume that ♣ appears in this computation. Thus, the resulting sequence is as follows:

$$
\underbrace{\boxed{?}\boxed{?}\boxed{?}}_{E_3^{\clubsuit}(x_1+x_2)} \quad \underbrace{\boxed{?}\boxed{?}\boxed{?}}_{E_3^{\heartsuit}(x_3+x_4)} \quad \underbrace{\boxed{?}\boxed{?}\boxed{?}}_{E_3^{\clubsuit}(x_5+x_6)} \quad \boxed{♣}\boxed{♣}\boxed{♡} \quad \underbrace{\boxed{?}\boxed{?}}_{x_7} \quad \underbrace{\boxed{?}\boxed{?}}_{x_8} \ . \tag{4}
$$

<u>Case 2</u>: We have free cards ♣♣.
We want to acquire a free card ♡ (which is a different color from the current free cards) via the computation of $x_5 + x_6$. To achieve this, we use the existing addition protocol introduced in Sect. 2.4 to compute $x_5 + x_6$ while generating a ♡. Remember that the current sequence is:

$$
\underbrace{\boxed{?}\boxed{?}\boxed{?}}_{E_3^{\clubsuit}(x_1+x_2)} \quad \boxed{♣} \quad \underbrace{\boxed{?}\boxed{?}\boxed{?}}_{E_3^{\clubsuit}(x_3+x_4)} \quad \boxed{♣} \quad \underbrace{\boxed{?}\boxed{?}}_{x_5} \quad \cdots \quad \underbrace{\boxed{?}\boxed{?}}_{x_8} \ .
$$

Recall that the commitments to x_5 and x_6 are encoded by:

$$
\boxed{♣}\boxed{♡} = 0, \quad \boxed{♡}\boxed{♣} = 1.
$$

This can be viewed as representing an integer value at the position of ♣, i.e., $E_2^{\clubsuit}(x_5)$ or $E_2^{\clubsuit}(x_6)$. If we swap the two cards comprising each commitment, they are commitments to $\overline{x}_5$ and $\overline{x}_6$ and can be viewed as $E_2^{\heartsuit}(x_5)$ and $E_2^{\heartsuit}(x_6)$, respectively, because they represent values at the position of ♡. In this case, adding a ♣ to the rightmost does not change the value represented, resulting in $E_3^{\heartsuit}(x_5)$ and $E_3^{\heartsuit}(x_6)$. Based on this, we compute $x_5 + x_6$ as follows[4].

1. Place each of the two ♣s on the right of the commitments to $\overline{x}_5$ and $\overline{x}_6$ as follows:

$$
\underbrace{\boxed{?}\boxed{?}\boxed{♣}}_{\overline{x}_5} \quad \underbrace{\boxed{?}\boxed{?}\boxed{♣}}_{\overline{x}_6} \ .
$$

Then, turn over the face-up cards to have $E_3^{\heartsuit}(x_5)$ and $E_3^{\heartsuit}(x_6)$:

$$
\underbrace{\boxed{?}\boxed{?}\boxed{?}}_{E_3^{\heartsuit}(x_5)} \quad \underbrace{\boxed{?}\boxed{?}\boxed{?}}_{E_3^{\heartsuit}(x_6)} \ .
$$

---

[4] The idea of adding two pos. encodings of the same color was suggested by Kazumasa Shinagawa.

2. Apply the existing addition protocol introduced in Sect. 2.4 to the sequence to obtain $E_3^\heartsuit(x_5 + x_6)$:

$$\boxed{?|?|?}\ \boxed{?|?|?}\ \rightarrow\ \boxed{?|?|?}\ \boxed{\clubsuit|\clubsuit|\heartsuit}.$$
$$\underbrace{\qquad}_{E_3^\heartsuit(x_5)}\ \underbrace{\qquad}_{E_3^\heartsuit(x_6)}\qquad \underbrace{\qquad}_{E_3^\heartsuit(x_5+x_6)}$$

(Note that $\boxed{\clubsuit|\clubsuit|\heartsuit}$ appear as free cards because the three cards in the $\heartsuit$-pos. encoding are revealed.) In summary, the whole sequence is as follows:

$$\boxed{?|?|?}\quad \boxed{?|?|?}\quad \boxed{?|?|?}\ \boxed{\clubsuit|\clubsuit|\heartsuit}\ \boxed{?|?}\ \boxed{?|?}.\qquad (5)$$
$$\underbrace{\quad}_{E_3^\clubsuit(x_1+x_2)}\ \underbrace{\quad}_{E_3^\clubsuit(x_3+x_4)}\ \underbrace{\quad}_{E_3^\heartsuit(x_5+x_6)}\qquad\quad\ \underset{x_7}{}\quad\ \underset{x_8}{}$$

Thus, we have two possibilities of the current sequence (4) or (5). Hereinafter, we assume the sequence (5); the case for the sequence (4) will be easily handled just by exchanging "$x_3 + x_4$" and "$x_5 + x_6$" in the sequel.

Addition of $x_1 + x_2$ and x_7. As shown above, we have now three free cards $\boxed{\clubsuit|\clubsuit|\heartsuit}$[5]. Next, we add $E_3^\clubsuit(x_1+x_2)$ to the commitment to x_7 to obtain $E_4^\clubsuit(x_1 + x_2 + x_7)$ as follows.

1. Place the free card $\boxed{\heartsuit}$ on the right of $E_3^\clubsuit(x_1 + x_2)$ and place the two $\boxed{\clubsuit}$s on the right of the commitment to $\overline{x}_7$ as follows:

$$\boxed{?|?|?}\ \boxed{\heartsuit}\quad \boxed{?|?}\ \boxed{\clubsuit|\clubsuit}.$$
$$\underbrace{\qquad}_{E_3^\clubsuit(x_1+x_2)}\qquad \underbrace{\quad}_{\overline{x}_7}$$

Recall that the value of $x_1 + x_2$ is represented at the position of $\boxed{\clubsuit}$ in the sequence, and $\overline{x}_7$ is represented at the position of $\boxed{\heartsuit}$ in the commitment. Therefore, after turning over the face-up cards, each value is represented by the position encoding as follows:

$$\boxed{?|?|?|?}\ \boxed{?|?|?|?}.$$
$$\underbrace{\qquad}_{E_4^\clubsuit(x_1+x_2)}\ \underbrace{\qquad}_{E_4^\heartsuit(x_7)}$$

2. Apply the existing addition protocol introduced in Sect. 2.4:

$$\boxed{?|?|?|?}\ \boxed{?|?|?|?}\ \rightarrow\ \boxed{?|?|?|?}\ \boxed{\clubsuit|\clubsuit|\clubsuit|\heartsuit}.$$
$$\underbrace{\qquad}_{E_4^\clubsuit(x_1+x_2)}\ \underbrace{\qquad}_{E_4^\heartsuit(x_7)}\qquad \underbrace{\qquad}_{E_4^\clubsuit(x_1+x_2+x_7)}$$

In summary, the whole sequence is as follows:

$$\boxed{?|?|?|?}\quad \boxed{?|?|?}\quad \boxed{?|?|?}\ \boxed{\clubsuit|\clubsuit|\clubsuit|\heartsuit}\ \boxed{?|?}.$$
$$\underbrace{\qquad}_{E_4^\clubsuit(x_1+x_2+x_7)}\ \underbrace{\quad}_{E_3^\clubsuit(x_3+x_4)}\ \underbrace{\quad}_{E_3^\heartsuit(x_5+x_6)}\qquad\qquad\quad\ \underset{x_8}{}$$

---

[5] Generally, there are two cards of the same color and one card of the other color.

Addition of $x_5 + x_6$ and x_8 Now we have four free cards of three ♣s and one ♡. Using them, $E_3^\heartsuit(x_5 + x_6)$, and the commitment to x_8, we obtain $E_4^\heartsuit(x_5 + x_6 + x_8)$ in a similar way as in the above paragraph:

$$\underbrace{\boxed{?}\boxed{?}\boxed{?}\boxed{?}}_{E_4^\clubsuit(x_1+x_2+x_7)} \quad \underbrace{\boxed{?}\boxed{?}\boxed{?}}_{E_3^\clubsuit(x_3+x_4)} \quad \underbrace{\boxed{?}\boxed{?}\boxed{?}\boxed{?}}_{E_4^\heartsuit(x_5+x_6+x_8)} \quad \clubsuit\clubsuit\clubsuit\heartsuit\heartsuit.$$

4.2   Binarization

Up to now, we have at least four free cards of two ♣s and two ♡s. Using these, we binarize $E_4^\clubsuit(x_1 + x_2 + x_7)$ and $E_4^\heartsuit(x_5 + x_6 + x_8)$ by our binarization protocol proposed in Sect. 3.2.

After that, the resulting sequence is as follows:

$$\underbrace{\boxed{?}\boxed{?}\ \boxed{?}\boxed{?}}_{(x_1+x_2+x_7)_2} \quad \underbrace{\boxed{?}\boxed{?}\boxed{?}}_{E_3^\clubsuit(x_3+x_4)} \quad \underbrace{\boxed{?}\boxed{?}\ \boxed{?}\boxed{?}}_{(x_5+x_6+x_8)_2} \clubsuit\clubsuit\clubsuit\heartsuit\heartsuit.$$

4.3   Full Adder and Binarization

Full adder of $(x_1 + x_2 + x_7)_2$ and $(x_5 + x_6 + x_8)_2$. Using the existing full adder protocol introduced in Sect. 2.2, we add $(x_1 + x_2 + x_7)_2$ to $(x_5 + x_6 + x_8)_2$ with the free cards of two ♣s and two ♡s as follows:

$$\underbrace{\boxed{?}\boxed{?}\ \boxed{?}\boxed{?}}_{(x_1+x_2+x_7)_2} \underbrace{\boxed{?}\boxed{?}\ \boxed{?}\boxed{?}}_{(x_5+x_6+x_8)_2} \rightarrow \underbrace{\boxed{?}\boxed{?}\ \boxed{?}\boxed{?}\ \boxed{?}\boxed{?}}_{(x_1+x_2+x_5+x_6+x_7+x_8)_2} \clubsuit\heartsuit.$$

After that, the whole sequence is as follows:

$$\underbrace{\boxed{?}\boxed{?}\ \boxed{?}\boxed{?}\ \boxed{?}\boxed{?}}_{(x_1+x_2+x_5+x_6+x_7+x_8)_2} \quad \underbrace{\boxed{?}\boxed{?}\boxed{?}}_{E_3^\clubsuit(x_3+x_4)} \quad \clubsuit\clubsuit\clubsuit\clubsuit\heartsuit\heartsuit\heartsuit.$$

Binarization of $E_3^\clubsuit(x_3 + x_4)$ and Overall Addition. To obtain commitments to $(x_3 + x_4)_2$, we first place a ♡ on the right of $E_3^\clubsuit(x_3 + x_4)$ to obtain $E_4^\clubsuit(x_3 + x_4)$ as follows:

$$\underbrace{\boxed{?}\boxed{?}\boxed{?}}_{E_3^\clubsuit(x_3+x_4)} \heartsuit \rightarrow \underbrace{\boxed{?}\boxed{?}\boxed{?}\boxed{?}}_{E_4^\clubsuit(x_3+x_4)}.$$

To summarize the situation, we have

$$\underbrace{\boxed{?}\boxed{?}\ \boxed{?}\boxed{?}\ \boxed{?}\boxed{?}}_{(x_1+x_2+x_5+x_6+x_7+x_8)_2} \quad \underbrace{\boxed{?}\boxed{?}\boxed{?}\boxed{?}}_{E_4^\clubsuit(x_3+x_4)} \quad \clubsuit\clubsuit\clubsuit\clubsuit\heartsuit\heartsuit.$$

Then, we binarize $E_4^\clubsuit(x_3 + x_4)$ using our binarization protocol proposed in Sect. 3.2. Finally, we add $(x_3 + x_4)_2$ to $(x_1 + x_2 + x_5 + x_6 + x_7 + x_8)_2$ with the free cards using the existing full-adder protocol introduced in Sect. 2.2 as follows:

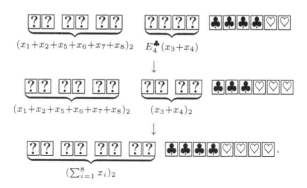

Now we have commitments to the summation of the inputs $\sum_{i=1}^{8} x_i$. From these commitments, we compute $g(\sum_{i=1}^{8} x_i)$ as in Eq. (3).

When $n \geq 9$, it suffices to add the remaining commitments to $x_9, x_{10}, \ldots, x_n$ to the summation $\sum_{i=1}^{8} x_i$ using the existing half-adder protocol because we have enough free cards.

5   Conclusion and Future Work

In this study, we proved that any n-input symmetric function such that $n \geq 8$ can be securely computed without the need of any helping cards. That is, we provided a helping-card-free protocol for any n-input symmetric function such that $n \geq 8$. Therefore, our protocol uses the minimum number of cards, i.e., it is card-minimal.

For the case of $n = 2$, the existing protocols [11,23,26] immediately imply that any 2-input symmetric function can be securely computed without any helping card. Therefore, the remaining open problem is to determine whether there exists a helping-card-free protocol for any n-input symmetric function such that $3 \leq n \leq 7$.

Acknowledgements. We thank the anonymous referees, whose comments have helped us improve the presentation of the paper. We thank Kazumasa Shinagawa for the idea of computing $x_5 + x_6$ for Case 2 in Sect. 4.1. This work was supported in part by JSPS KAKENHI Grant Number JP21K11881.

References

1. Abe, Y., Iwamoto, M., Ohta, K.: Efficient private PEZ protocols for symmetric functions. In: Hofheinz, D., Rosen, A. (eds.) Theory of Cryptography. LNCS, vol. 11891, pp. 372–392. Springer, Cham (2019). https://doi.org/10.1007/978-3-030-36030-6_15

2. Abe, Y., Nakai, T., Kuroki, Y., Suzuki, S., Koga, Y., Watanabe, Y., Iwamoto, M., Ohta, K.: Efficient card-based majority voting protocols. New Gener. Comput. 40, 173–198 (2022). https://doi.org/10.1007/s00354-022-00161-7

3. Balogh, J., Csirik, J.A., Ishai, Y., Kushilevitz, E.: Private computation using a PEZ dispenser. Theor. Comput. Sci. 306(1), 69–84 (2003). https://doi.org/10.1016/S0304-3975(03)00210-X

4. Boer, B.: More Efficient Match-Making and Satisfiability *The Five Card Trick*. In: Quisquater, J.-J., Vandewalle, J. (eds.) EUROCRYPT 1989. LNCS, vol. 434, pp. 208–217. Springer, Heidelberg (1990). https://doi.org/10.1007/3-540-46885-4_23

5. Evans, D., Kolesnikov, V., Rosulek, M.: A pragmatic introduction to secure multi-party computation. Foundations and Trends® in Privacy and Security 2(2–3), 70–246 (2018). https://doi.org/10.1561/3300000019

6. Heather, J., Schneider, S., Teague, V.: Cryptographic protocols with everyday objects. Formal Aspects of Computing **26**(1), 37–62 (2013). https://doi.org/10.1007/s00165-013-0274-7

7. Isuzugawa, R., Toyoda, K., Sasaki, Y., Miyahara, D., Mizuki, T.: A card-minimal three-input AND protocol using two shuffles. In: Chen, C.Y., Hon, W.K., Hung, L.J., Lee, C.W. (eds.) Computing and Combinatorics. LNCS, vol. 13025, pp. 668–679. Springer, Cham (2021). https://doi.org/10.1007/978-3-030-89543-3_55

8. Kastner, J., Koch, A., Walzer, S., Miyahara, D., Hayashi, Y., Mizuki, T., Sone, H.: The minimum number of cards in practical card-based protocols. In: Takagi, T., Peyrin, T. (eds.) Advances in Cryptology—ASIACRYPT 2017. LNCS, vol. 10626, pp. 126–155. Springer, Cham (2017). https://doi.org/10.1007/978-3-319-70700-6_5

9. Koch, A.: Cryptographic Protocols from Physical Assumptions. Ph.D. thesis, Karlsruhe Institute of Technology (2019). https://doi.org/10.5445/IR/1000097756

10. Koch, A.: The landscape of security from physical assumptions. In: IEEE Information Theory Workshop, pp. 1–6. IEEE, NY (2021). https://doi.org/10.1109/ITW48936.2021.9611501

11. Koch, A., Walzer, S., Härtel, K.: Card-based cryptographic protocols using a minimal number of cards. In: Iwata, T., Cheon, J.H. (eds.) Advances in Cryptology—ASIACRYPT 2015. LNCS, vol. 9452, pp. 783–807. Springer, Berlin, Heidelberg (2015). https://doi.org/10.1007/978-3-662-48797-6_32

12. Komano, Y., Mizuki, T.: Coin-based secure computations. Int. J. Inf. Secur. pp. 1–14 (2022). https://doi.org/10.1007/s10207-022-00585-8, in press

13. Lafourcade, P., Mizuki, T., Nagao, A., Shinagawa, K.: Light cryptography. In: Drevin, L., Theocharidou, M. (eds.) Information Security Education. Education in Proactive Information Security. IFIPAICT, vol. 557, pp. 89–101. Springer, Cham (2019). https://doi.org/10.1007/978-3-030-23451-5_7

14. Manabe, Y., Ono, H.: Card-based cryptographic protocols with a standard deck of cards using private operations. In: Cerone, A., Ölveczky, P.C. (eds.) Theoretical Aspects of Computing – ICTAC 2021. LNCS, vol. 12819, pp. 256–274. Springer, Cham (2021). https://doi.org/10.1007/978-3-030-85315-0_15

15. Manabe, Y., Ono, H.: Card-Based Cryptographic Protocols with a Standard Deck of Cards Using Private Operations. In: Cerone, A., Ölveczky, P.C. (eds.) ICTAC 2021. LNCS, vol. 12819, pp. 256–274. Springer, Cham (2021). https://doi.org/10.1007/978-3-030-85315-0_15

16. Manabe, Y., Ono, H.: Secure card-based cryptographic protocols using private operations against malicious players. In: Maimut, D., Oprina, A.G., Sauveron, D. (eds.) Innovative Security Solutions for Information Technology and Communications. LNCS, vol. 12596, pp. 55–70. Springer, Cham (2021). https://doi.org/10.1007/978-3-030-69255-1_5

17. Manabe, Y., Ono, H.: Card-based cryptographic protocols with malicious players using private operations. New Gener. Comput. 40, 67–93 (2022). https://doi.org/10.1007/s00354-021-00148-w

18. Miyahara, D., Komano, Y., Mizuki, T., Sone, H.: Cooking cryptographers: Secure multiparty computation based on balls and bags. In: Computer Security Foundations Symposium, pp. 1–16. IEEE, NY (2021). https://doi.org/10.1109/CSF51468.2021.00034

19. Mizuki, T.: Card-based protocols for securely computing the conjunction of multiple variables. Theor. Comput. Sci. 622(C), 34–44 (2016). https://doi.org/10.1016/j.tcs.2016.01.039

20. Mizuki, T.: Preface: Special issue on card-based cryptography. New Gener. Comput. 39, 1–2 (2021). https://doi.org/10.1007/s00354-021-00127-1

21. Mizuki, T.: Preface: Special issue on card-based cryptography 2. New Gener. Comput. 40, 47–48 (2022). https://doi.org/10.1007/s00354-022-00170-6

22. Mizuki, T., Asiedu, I.K., Sone, H.: Voting with a Logarithmic Number of Cards. In: Mauri, G., Dennunzio, A., Manzoni, L., Porreca, A.E. (eds.) UCNC 2013. LNCS, vol. 7956, pp. 162–173. Springer, Heidelberg (2013). https://doi.org/10.1007/978-3-642-39074-6_16

23. Mizuki, T., Kumamoto, M., Sone, H.: The Five-Card Trick Can Be Done with Four Cards. In: Wang, X., Sako, K. (eds.) ASIACRYPT 2012. LNCS, vol. 7658, pp. 598–606. Springer, Heidelberg (2012). https://doi.org/10.1007/978-3-642-34961-4_36

24. Mizuki, T., Shizuya, H.: A formalization of card-based cryptographic protocols via abstract machine. International Journal of Information Security 13(1), 15–23 (2013). https://doi.org/10.1007/s10207-013-0219-4

25. Mizuki, T., Shizuya, H.: Computational model of card-based cryptographic protocols and its applications. IEICE Trans. Fundam. E100.A(1), 3–11 (2017). https://doi.org/10.1587/transfun.E100.A.3

26. Mizuki, T., Sone, H.: Six-Card Secure AND and Four-Card Secure XOR. In: Deng, X., Hopcroft, J.E., Xue, J. (eds.) FAW 2009. LNCS, vol. 5598, pp. 358–369. Springer, Heidelberg (2009). https://doi.org/10.1007/978-3-642-02270-8_36

27. Moran, T., Naor, M.: Basing cryptographic protocols on tamper-evident seals. Theor. Comput. Sci. 411(10), 1283–1310 (2010). https://doi.org/10.1016/j.tcs.2009.10.023

28. Murata, S., Miyahara, D., Mizuki, T., Sone, H.: Public-PEZ cryptography. In: Susilo, W., Deng, R.H., Guo, F., Li, Y., Intan, R. (eds.) Information Security. LNCS, vol. 12472, pp. 59–74. Springer, Cham (2020). https://doi.org/10.1007/978-3-030-62974-8_4

29. Nakai, T., Misawa, Y., Tokushige, Y., Iwamoto, M., Ohta, K.: Secure computation for threshold functions with physical cards: Power of private permutations. New Gener. Comput. pp. 1–19 (2022). https://doi.org/10.1007/s00354-022-00153-7, in press

30. Nishida, T., Hayashi, Y., Mizuki, T., Sone, H.: Card-Based Protocols for Any Boolean Function. In: Jain, R., Jain, S., Stephan, F. (eds.) TAMC 2015. LNCS, vol. 9076, pp. 110–121. Springer, Cham (2015). https://doi.org/10.1007/978-3-319-17142-5_11

31. Nishimura, A., Hayashi, Y., Mizuki, T., Sone, H.: Pile-shifting scramble for card-based protocols. IEICE Trans. Fundam. 101(9), 1494–1502 (2018). https://doi.org/10.1587/transfun.E101.A.1494

32. Ono, H., Manabe, Y.: Card-based cryptographic logical computations using private operations. New Gener. Comput. 39(1), 19–40 (2021). https://doi.org/10.1007/s00354-020-00113-z

33. Ruangwises, S., Itoh, T.: Securely computing the n-variable equality function with 2n cards. Theor. Comput. Sci. 887, 99–110 (2021). https://doi.org/10.1016/j.tcs.2021.07.007

34. Shinagawa, K.: On the Construction of Easy to Perform Card-Based Protocols. Ph.D. thesis, Tokyo Institute of Technology (2020)

35. Shinagawa, K., Mizuki, T.: The six-card trick: Secure computation of three-inputequality. In: Lee, K. (ed.) Information Security and Cryptology. LNCS, vol. 11396,pp. 123–131. Springer, Cham (2019). https://doi.org/10.1007/978-3-030-12146-4_8

36. Shinagawa, K., Mizuki, T., Schuldt, J., Nuida, K., Kanayama, N., Nishide, T., Hanaoka, G., Okamoto, E.: Card-based protocols using regular polygon cards. IEICE Trans. Fundam. E100.A(9), 1900–1909 (2017). https://doi.org/10.1587/transfun.E100.A.1900

37. Toyoda, K., Miyahara, D., Mizuki, T.: Another use of the five-card trick: Card-minimal secure three-input majority function evaluation. In: Adhikari, A., Küsters, R., Preneel, B. (eds.) Progress in Cryptology - INDOCRYPT 2021. LNCS, vol. 13143, pp. 536–555. Springer, Cham (2021). https://doi.org/10.1007/978-3-030-92518-5_24

38. Yao, A.C.: Protocols for secure computations. In: Foundations of Computer Science. pp. 160–164. IEEE Computer Society, Washington, DC, USA (1982). https://doi.org/10.1109/SFCS.1982.88

Runners for Interleaving Algebraic Effects

Niels F. W. Voorneveld$^{(\boxtimes)}$

Tallinn University of Technology, Tallinn, Estonia
niels@cs.ioc.ee

Abstract. We study a model of interleaving concurrency for higher-order functional programs with algebraic effects, which can function as a basis for notions of behavioural equivalence of effectful programs within concurrent processes. Using the category of relations to describe nondeterministic functions, we model runs of programs using trace semantics. These traces have actions describing possible program-environment interactions. The functor of traces forms both a monad and a comonad in the category of relations, allowing us to describe programs as both active computations and passive background processes.

We adapt traditional concurrent interleaving semantics for traces as an operation in the category of relations, merging two traces into a set of interwoven traces. These semantics give rise to a runner for the monad, and in some cases form a monad-comonad interaction law. With this, we can simulate an environment of concurrent background processes, and describe the behaviour of a program within such an environment. This runner for interleaving concurrency is readily composable with runners for algebraic effects, allowing us to describe a wide variety of different concurrent effectful scenarios.

Keywords: Algebraic effects · Interleaving concurrency · Stateful runners · Trace semantics · Program equivalence

1 Introduction

Programs are rarely run in isolation. They are executed in a specific environment, using its resources and communicating to it. In the mean time, other programs may be executed in the same environment. How do programs behave in such circumstances where any line of communication with its environment may be interfered with by other background processes? In this paper, we aim to develop a model for describing the behaviour of higher-order functional effectful languages with such interfering background processes.

Interleaving Algebraic Effects. We study in particular programs with *algebraic effects* [23]. These express interactions with the environment in terms of algebraic operations. Each operation is a line of communication with the environment, awaiting a response from the environment and containing a continuation

Supported by the ESF funded Estonian IT Academy research measure (project 2014-2020.4.05.19-0001).

for each possible response. Programs are denoted by combinations of nested operations, which form elements in a *monad* of inductively generated trees [22].

The evaluation of such programs can be modelled by *stateful runners* [29], which consult a global state for *handling* the operations [24]. This gives us a way to find the result of a program, dependent on the initial state of the environment. These runners induce an algebraic theory of equations, relating trees when they are resolved in the same way in each possible state of the environment.

Complications arise when multiple effectful programs run in parallel, since the state of the environment may be changed in unpredictable ways. We investigate such situations using *interleaving concurrency*, which has been widely studied in different areas of computer science, including, but not limited to, labelled transition systems [14], bisimulation [21], and Petri nets [6].

We can apply traditional interleaving semantics, as studied in *communication processes* [4,5] and *actor semantics* [7], to our denotational trees. We work in the category of relations **Rel** (e.g. see [17]) and its subcategory of *total relations* **Rel$_+$**, which allow us to express nondeterministic functions. In both categories, we can transform our trees into collections of *traces* describing the branches of the tree, following ideas from *trace semantics* [12,28]. These traces will consist of a list of actions followed by either a result, or an exception. These exceptions are only included if there are nullary operations in the signature of effect operations, for instance an exception labelled ⊥ for describing divergence.

The interleaving semantics gives a *merge operator* [25] on the monad of traces T, merging two traces into a set of "merged" traces. This merge function, called the *parallel operator*, satisfies a variety of properties, like symmetry and associativity. It gives a binatural transformation if either there are no errors, or we limit ourselves to **Rel$_+$**. The parallel operator is however not preserved over program composition, which is necessary for the specification of a *congruent program equivalence* for functional languages. In order to establish preservation over program composition, we need to investigate a different perspective.

Congruent Program Equivalences. Program equivalences for programming languages are studied to answer the question: When can a program safely be replaced by another, without it affecting the behaviour of the entire system? A program equivalence is a relation on programs, which should provide a sufficient condition for guaranteeing this "safe replacement". Program equivalences with this feature are commonly called *congruences*.

Relators [16,27] are a common tool for defining notions of program equivalence. They lift relations on return values to relations on denotations of programs returning those values, following certain considerations of behaviour. They can be used to define a congruent notion of *applicative bisimilarity* [1] for effectful programs, as seen in paper [15]. Motivated by these applications, we use stateful runners to define relators with the right properties. Particularly, we need such relators to be preserved over program composition.

In order to recover preservation over program composition, we use a variant semantics of the parallel operator using *strongly focussed parallel operators*. This variant parallel operator nondeterministically chooses which program to focus on, whereafter that chosen program *has* to perform the next step. If that chosen program is done, the parallel operator is done, regardless of the state of the program we are currently not focussing on.

This models the situation where one program takes the lead, and the second program is considered as a background process, as part of the environment. To accommodate this shift in perspective, we use the interesting fact that the monad of traces T also forms a *comonad* in the category of relations, and comonads are commonly used to model notions of environment [30]. This construction is similar to the treatment of the exponential modality in linear logic as used in [8,9,20].

Contributions. One of the main contributions of this paper is the discovery that the focussed parallel operator satisfies the equations required by T-*residual monad-comonad interaction laws* [13] between T as a monad, and T as a comonad. If we leave out exceptions, this operation forms an interaction law in **Rel**. Regardless of the inclusion of exceptions, the operation induces a stateful runner which we call the *parallel runner* in the category of total relations **Rel$_+$**, where the denotation of the second program is part of the state of the environment.

Combining the parallel runner with runners for modelling algebraic effects, we get a runner for modelling effectful programs within environments of other effectful programs running in the background. The parallel runner implements a *program context* with a background process, e.g. Run P during Q where Q is considered as being run in the background. Importantly, Q is not necessarily evaluated completely, as it may continue to be evaluated after P is done.

The big motivation for this perspective is that runners readily specify relators with the right properties for inducing congruent notions of program equivalence for functional languages such as the untyped lambda calculus, following results from [15]. The final contribution is the development of state-dependent instances of such relators, which gives rise to a notion of equivalence dependent on the initial state of the environment, and which moreover allows for fine-tuning what aspects of the environment state are externally observable. Hence they are a powerful tool for verifying safety of effectful programs that are evaluated in parallel with other programs.

Paper Overview. We assume the reader is familiar with basic concepts from category theory, including but not limited to; natural transformations, monads and monoidal products. In Sect. 2 we look at the category of relations, and properties of tree monads used for modelling programs. In Sect. 3, we consider stateful runners on trees, and how to describe trees as collections of traces. Then, in Sect. 4, we study a variation on the interleaving concurrent operation, as an operation in the category of relations. Combining the above, we can construct runners for a variety of algebraic effects in concurrent environments, and we study how they induce state-dependent relators in Sect. 5 suitable for formulating program equivalences. We make some final observations in Sect. 6.

2   The Category of Total Relations

We will give a brief overview of some of the categorical concepts used in this paper. We use the category of relations **Rel** as a basis, which has as objects sets, and as morphisms relations between them. The space of morphisms from X to Y is denoted by $X \multimap Y$, and contains relations $\mathcal{R}$ relating elements from X to elements from Y. Such a relation can be given multiple representations:

1. a relation is a subset of $X \times Y$. This is used mainly in relational reasoning.
2. a relation is a set-theoretic function from X to the powerset $\mathcal{P}(Y)$, called a *nondeterministic function*. This is a common model for nondeterminism.

We write $x \mathcal{R} y$ to say $\mathcal{R}$ relates x to y, and $\mathcal{R}(x)$ for the set $\{y \in Y \mid x \mathcal{R} y\} \in \mathcal{P}(Y)$. The identity relation on X is denoted as $\mathcal{I}_X$, where $x \mathcal{I}_X x'$ if $x = x'$, and relation composition as $\mathcal{R}; \mathcal{S}$, where $x \mathcal{R}; \mathcal{S} z$ if there is a y such that $x \mathcal{R} y$ and $y \mathcal{S} z$. We write ι for the identity natural transformation, where $\iota_X = \mathcal{I}_X$.

We focus on two important properties a relation can have, which are satisfied by the identity relation, and preserved under composition.

- $\mathcal{R} : X \multimap Y$ is *total* if for any $x \in X$, there is a $y \in Y$ such that $x \mathcal{R} y$. In other words, for any $x \in X$, $\mathcal{R}(x)$ is non-empty.
- $\mathcal{R} : X \multimap Y$ is *thin* if for any $x \in X$ and $y, y' \in Y$, if $x \mathcal{R} y$ and $x \mathcal{R} y'$, then $y = y'$. In other words, for any $x \in X$, $\mathcal{R}(x)$ has at most on element.

Set-theoretic functions $f : X \to Y$ can be represented by total and thin relations between X and Y. This makes the category of sets **Set** the wide subcategory of **Rel** of total and thin relations. We denote the set of total relations from X to Y as $X \to Y$, and consider the wide subcategory of **Rel** of total relations **Rel$_+$**. Moreover, **Rel**, **Rel$_+$** are the Kleisli categories over respectively the powerset monad $\mathcal{P}$, and the non-empty powerset monad $\mathcal{P}_+$ in **Set**.

The Cartesian product $\times$ in **Set** can be lifted to a symmetric monoidal product in **Rel**, which sends sets X and Y to their Cartesian product $X \times Y$, and relations $\mathcal{R} : X \multimap X'$ and $\mathcal{S} : Y \multimap Y'$ to $(\mathcal{R} \times \mathcal{S}) : X \times Y \multimap X' \times Y'$, where $(x, y)(\mathcal{R} \times \mathcal{S})(x', y')$ if $x \mathcal{R} x'$ and $y \mathcal{S} y'$. Since it preserves totality, it also forms a symmetric monoidal product in **Rel$_+$**. We write γ for symmetry $\gamma_{X,Y} : X \times Y \multimap Y \times X$, and α for associativity $\alpha_{X,Y,Z} : (X \times Y) \times Z \multimap X \times (Y \times X)$.

The category **Rel** has a *dagger operation* $(-)^\dagger$ which sends morphisms $\mathcal{R} : X \multimap Y$ to $\mathcal{R}^\dagger : Y \multimap X$ defined as: $y \mathcal{R}^\dagger x$ if and only if $x \mathcal{R} y$. This satisfies the properties $(\mathcal{I}_X)^\dagger = \mathcal{I}_X$, $(\mathcal{R}; \mathcal{S})^\dagger = \mathcal{S}^\dagger; \mathcal{R}^\dagger$, and $((\mathcal{R})^\dagger)^\dagger = \mathcal{R}$. The dagger operation does not preserve totality or thinness, hence does not exist in **Set** and **Rel$_+$**.

We work in **Rel** and **Rel$_+$**, since it internalises the nondeterminism and we do not need keep track of the powerset monad $\mathcal{P}$ when composing functions. Instead, we need to check that the operations we define are *natural*.

Let **1** be the singleton set $\{*\}$. Consider two families of relations, $d_X : X \multimap \mathbf{1}$ and $c_X : X \multimap X \times X$ ranging over a set X, where $x \, d_X \, *$ and $x \, c_X \, (y, z)$ if $x = y = z$. Considered as functions, these respectively *delete* and *copy* elements. However, neither of the two are natural transformations in **Rel**. Specifically, d_X is only natural on total relations, hence natural in **Set** and **Rel**$_+$, but not **Rel**, and c_X is only natural on thin relations, hence natural in **Set** but not **Rel** and **Rel**$_+$.

So **Rel** is particularly restrictive in what it allows as natural transformations, since we can neither delete nor copy. **Rel**$_+$ however does allow us to delete and trim data. Though we will do most constructions in **Rel**, we shall keep track of those structures which are natural in **Rel**$_+$. We call a transformation *positively natural* if it is natural with respect to total relations. If a transformation is both positively natural and total, it is a natural transformation in **Rel**$_+$.

2.1   Trees as Monads and Comonads

We can define inductive data structures using *containers* to describe *signatures* of algebraic effect operations. A container S is a pair (O, ar) given by a set O of operations together with a function $ar : O \to$ **Set** associating an *arity* to each operation. We consider several examples of operations.

- We can model printing a message m on screen with an operation $\mathsf{output}(m)$ of arity $\mathbf{1} = \{*\}$. Each separate message has a separate operation.
- We can model reading an input from a user with an operation input whose arity has all possible responses the user can make.
- We can raise an exception or error using an operation $\mathsf{error}(m)$ of arity $\mathbf{0}$.
- We can model a choice (e.g. nondeterministic) with an operation of arity $\mathbf{2}$.

Given a container S, denote programs using such programs with S-trees.

Definition 1. *Given a container $S = (O, ar)$, the endofunctor in **Rel** of S-trees sends a set X to the set of trees $M_S X$ inductively defined by:*

- *leaf$(x) \in M_S X$ for any $x \in X$.*
- *node$(o)(c)$ for any $o \in O$ and $c : ar(o) \to M_S X$.*

and it sends a relation $\mathcal{R} : X \to Y$ to $M_S(\mathcal{R}) : M_S X \to M_S Y$, defined as:

- *leaf(x) $M_S(\mathcal{R})$ leaf(y) for any $x \in X$ and $y \in Y$ such that $x \mathcal{R} y$.*
- *node$(o)(c)$ $M_S(\mathcal{R})$ node$(o)(d)$ for any $o \in O$, $c : ar(o) \to M_S X$ and $d : ar(o) \to M_S Y$, such that $\forall i \in ar(o). c(i) M_S(\mathcal{R}) d(i)$.*

$M_S X$ as an endofunctor in **Set** is actually the *free monad* over the functor $F_S X = \Sigma_{o \in O}(X^{ar(o)})$. Hence M_S in **Rel** can be seen as a lifting of that free monad to the Kleisli category of $\mathcal{P}$, using a distributivity law of the free monad over $\mathcal{P}$.

M_S is a monad in **Rel**, since we can lift the monad structure from **Set**. The unit transformation $\eta_X^S : X \to M_S X$ is defined as $\eta_X^S(x) = \{leaf(x)\}$, and the multiplication relation $\mu_X^S : M_S M_S X \to M_S X$ is inductively defined as $\mu_X^S(leaf(t)) = \{t\}$ and $\mu_X^S(node(o)(c)) = \{node(o)(e) \in M_S X \mid \forall i \in ar(o), e(i) \in \mu_X^S(c(i))\}$. Both are natural transformations consisting solely of total and thin relations, which reflects the fact that they were lifted from the monad structure in **Set**.

Lemma 1. *Suppose (M, η, μ) is a monad in **Rel** with the additional property that for any relation $\mathcal{R} : X \multimap Y$, $(M(\mathcal{R}))^\dagger = M(\mathcal{R}^\dagger)$, then $(M, \eta^\dagger, \mu^\dagger)$ is a comonad in **Rel**.*

Indeed, M_S satisfies the property required in Lemma 1, so $(M_S, (\eta^S)^\dagger, (\mu^S)^\dagger)$ is a comonad. We give an alternative inductive definition for the comonadic operations. Let $\varepsilon_X^S : M_S X \multimap X$ and $\delta_X^S : M_S X \multimap M_S M_S X$ be inductively defined as:

- $\varepsilon_X^S(leaf(x)) = \{x\}$, and $\varepsilon_X^S(node(o)(c)) = \varnothing$.
- $\delta_X^S(leaf(x)) = \{leaf(leaf(x))\}$, and $\delta_X^S(node(o)(c)) = \{leaf(node(o)(c))\} \cup \{node(o)(d) \mid \forall i \in ar(o).\, c(i)\, \delta_X^S\, d(i)\}$.

Lemma 2. $\varepsilon_X^S = (\eta_X^S)^\dagger$ *and* $\delta_X^S = (\mu_X^S)^\dagger$, *hence* $(M_S, \varepsilon^S, \delta^S)$ *is a comonad.*

Now, ε is not total, hence it is not an operation in **Rel$_+$** and **Set**, though it is a natural transformation in **Rel**. On the other hand, δ is not thin, hence it is not an operation in **Set**, though it is a natural transformation in both **Rel** and **Rel$_+$**. Let us look at some additional properties which are satisfied:

Lemma 3. *The following four equations hold:*

- $\eta^S; \varepsilon^S = \iota$, $\delta^S; \mu^S = \iota(M_S)$, $\mu^S; \varepsilon^S = \varepsilon^S(\varepsilon^S)$,   *and* $\eta^S; \delta^S = \eta^S(\eta^S)$.

2.2   The Occasional Strength of Trees

Strength is an important property for monads when modelling programming languages. For example, it allows us to schedule the order of evaluation of programs. To define strength, consider the family of relations $\sigma_{X,Y}^S : X \times M_S Y \multimap M_S(X \times Y)$ over two set parameters X and Y, defined inductively as:

- $\sigma_{X,Y}^S(x, leaf(y)) = \{leaf(x, y)\}$.
- $\sigma_{X,Y}^S(x, node(o)(c)) = \{node(o)(d) \mid \forall i \in ar(o).\, d(i) \in \sigma_{X,Y}(x, c(i))\}$.

This is lifting the natural operation for strength of M_S as an endofunctor in **Set**, to a family of total and thin relations in **Rel**. This family is natural in Y, but not necessarily natural in X, due to previous observations related to copying and deleting. If the signature $S = (O, ar)$ has an operation $o \in O$ such that the set $ar(o)$ has more than one element, then σ^S is able to copy X. If the signature $S = (O, ar)$ has an operation $o \in O$ such that the set $ar(o) = \varnothing$, then σ^S is able to delete X. As a consequence, we have the following consequences:

1. σ^S is natural in **Rel** if and only if for each $o \in O$, $|ar(o)| = 1$.
2. σ^S is natural in **Rel$_+$** if and only if for each $o \in O$, $|ar(o)| \leq 1$.
3. σ^S is natural in **Set**, regardless of the signature.

Because of the above, we consider the following subclass of tree monads:

Definition 2. *Given sets A and E, which we respectively call actions and exceptions, we define the monad of (A, E)-traces as the monad of trees over the signature $(A + E, ar)$, where $ar(inl(a)) = \{*\}$ for any $a \in A$ (unary) and $ar(inr(e)) = \varnothing$ for any $e \in E$ (nullary). We denote this monad as $(T_{A,E}, \eta^{A,E}, \mu^{A,E})$.*

We may write $(a)t$ or $@t$ for $node(inl(a))(t)$, and $\langle e \rangle$ or $\diamondsuit$ for $node(inr(e))()$. Lastly, we may write $[x]$ for $leaf(x)$, hence using a different bracket type for each of the three possible constructors of the monad. Given a set X, the set $\mathsf{T}_{A,E}X$ is isomorphic to $A^* \times (X + E)$, where A^* is the set of lists over A. For example, the maybe monad can be given by $\mathsf{T}_{\varnothing,\{1\}}$. For any A and E, $\mathsf{T}_{A,E}$ is a strong monad in $\mathbf{Rel}_+$, and for any A, $\mathsf{T}_{A,\varnothing}$ is a strong monad and a comonad in $\mathbf{Rel}$.

Lemma 4. *For any signature S, and sets X and Y,*

- $(\eta_X^S \times \iota_Y); \sigma_{X,Y}^S = \eta_{X \times Y}^S$ *and* $(\mu_X^S \times \iota_Y); \sigma_{X,Y}^S = \sigma_{M_S X,Y}^S; M_S(\sigma_{X,Y}); \mu_{X \times Y}$.
- $\sigma_{X,Y}^S; \varepsilon_{X \times Y}^S = \varepsilon_X^S \times \iota_Y$ *and* $(\delta_X^S \times \iota_Y^S); \sigma_{M_S X,Y}^S; M_S(\sigma_{X,Y}^S) = \sigma_{X,Y}^S; \delta_{X \times Y}^S$.

We leave out subscripts and superscripts when they are obvious from context.

3 Nondeterministic Stateful Trace Runners

We model the behaviour of effectful programs by resolving algebraic effect operations by consulting some environmental state. This is done by stateful runners in the category of total relations $\mathbf{Rel}_+$. We shall first look at runners for trace monads, whereafter we shall see how they can be extended to runners on tree monads as well. Firstly, we look at runners in general, as they appear in [13, 29].

Definition 3. *Given a monoidal closed category with monads M and N, an N-residual runner on M is given by an object K and a natural transformation $\theta_X : MX \times K \to N(X \times K)$ such that:*

$$
\begin{array}{ccc}
X \times K & & \\
\eta_X^M \times K \downarrow \quad \searrow^{\eta_{X \times K}^N} & & \\
MX \times K \xrightarrow[\theta_X]{} N(X \times K) & &
\end{array}
\qquad
\begin{array}{ccc}
MMX \times K \xrightarrow{\theta_{MX}} N(MX \times K) \xrightarrow{N(\theta_X)} NN(X \times K) \\
\mu_X^M \times K \downarrow \qquad\qquad\qquad\qquad\qquad\qquad \downarrow \mu_{X \times K}^N \\
MX \times K \xrightarrow{\hspace{4cm}\theta_X\hspace{4cm}} N(X \times K)
\end{array}
$$

For instance, if M is a strong monad, then for each object K the strength transformation σ (with symmetry) forms an M-residual runner on M.

Definition 4. *Given sets A, E, A', E', a trace runner from (A, E) to (A', E') is a $\mathsf{T}_{A',E'}$-residual runner on $\mathsf{T}_{A,E}$ in $\mathbf{Rel}_+$.*

Lemma 5. *Trace runners from (A, E) to (A', E') are in 1-to-1 correspondence with triples consisting of a set K and two morphisms:*

- *a morphism $A \times K \to \mathsf{T}_{A',E'}K$ (or $A \times K \to A'^* \times (K + E')$),*
- *a morphism $E \times K \to \mathsf{T}_{A',E'}0$ (or $E \times K \to A'^* \times E'$).*

Proof. Given $f : A \times K \to \mathsf{T}_{A',E'}K$ and $g : E \times K \to \mathsf{T}_{A',E'}0$ we inductively define $\theta_X : \mathsf{T}_{A,E}X \times K \to \mathsf{T}_{A',E'}(X \times K)$ as:
$$\theta_X([x], k) = [x, k], \qquad \theta_X(@(t), k) = (\mathsf{T}_{A',E'}(\lambda v.\theta_X(t, v)); \mu^{A',E'})(f(a, k)),$$
$$\theta_X(\diamondsuit, k) = \mathsf{T}_{A',E'}()(g(e, k)).$$
Vice versa, given $\theta_X : \mathsf{T}_{A,E}X \times K \to \mathsf{T}_{A',E'}(X \times K)$, we define $f : A \times K \to \mathsf{T}_{A',E'}K$ as $\lambda(a, k).\theta_1(@[*], k)$ using the isomorphism $1 \times K \simeq K$, and we define $g : E \times K \to \mathsf{T}_{A',E'}0$ as $\lambda(e, k).\theta_0(\diamondsuit, k)$ using the isomorphism $0 \times K \simeq 0$.

We call the morphisms from Lemma 5 the *local functions* for the runner. In **Rel**, a runner can never raise an error when resolving an action. This severely restricts the examples we can model, and hence we focus on runners in **Rel**$_+$.

Following the theory on runners [29], we can compose them in the following way. Given a trace runner θ from (A_1, E_1) to (A_2, E_2) on state space K_1, and a trace runner ϕ from (A_2, E_2) from (A_3, E_3) on state space K_2, we can compose them into a trace runner $\theta \bullet \phi$ from (A_1, E_1) to (A_3, E_3) on state space $K_1 \times K_2$, given by $(\theta \bullet \phi)_X = (\theta_X \times \iota_{K_2}); \phi_{X \times K_1} : T_{A_1,E_1} X \times K_1 \times K_2 \rightarrow T_{A_3,E_3}(X \times K_1 \times K_2)$, using associativity of $\times$.

3.1   The Monad Morphism of Branches

Let us consider runners on trees as well.

Definition 5. *Given a container S and sets A and E, a tree runner from S to (A, E) is a $T_{A,E}$-residual runner on M_S in* **Rel**$_+$.

We can use trace runners to define runners on trees. This is done by defining an operation which takes a tree $M_S X$, and collects all the branches of the tree. We define the set of S-actions as the set $A(S) = \{(o, i) \mid o \in O, i \in ar(o)\}$, and the set of S-errors as $E(S) = \{o \in O \mid ar(o) = \varnothing\}$. The action (o, i) signifies the operation o being called, and the response i being given to the operation. Consider the family of operations $\beta_X^S : M_S X \rightarrow T_{A(S),E(S)} X$, defined by

- $\beta_X^S(leaf(x)) = \{leaf(x)\}$,
- $\beta_X^S(node(o)(c)) = \{(o, i)(t) \mid i \in ar(o), t \in \beta_X^S(c(i))\}$ if $ar(o)$ is non-empty,
- $\beta_X^S(node(o)(c)) = \{\langle o \rangle\}$ if $ar(o)$ is empty.

If S has any arity with more than one element, β_X^S is not natural in **Rel**. However, β_X^S is both total and natural in **Rel**$_+$.

Lemma 6. *In* **Rel**$_+$, β^S *forms a monad morphism from M_S to $T_{A(S),E(S)}$.*

As a direct consequence, we can transform a trace runner from $(A(S), E(S))$ to (A', E'), to a tree runner from S to (A', E').

3.2   Examples

We consider some examples using the maybe monad $T_{\varnothing,\{\bot\}} = (-)_\bot$ as residual. In each case, we specify the signature S, and define the runner on $T_{A(S),E(S)}$ by specifying its local functions (see Lemma 5).

Example 1. Consider a set of messages M, and for each $m \in M$ an output operation $\texttt{output}(m)$ of arity **1**. In this case, $A(S) = \{(\texttt{output}(m), *) \mid m \in M\} \simeq M$ and $E(S) = \varnothing$. A simple trace runner to consider is one that records all the outputs in a single list. We take as state space $K = M^*$, and define the runner with the local function $f : M \times M^* \rightarrow (M^*)_\bot$ using append $f(m, \tau) = \{m : \tau\}$.

Example 2. Consider a signature with a single input operation `input` of arity M, giving us $A(S) = \{(\texttt{input}, m) \mid m \in M\} \simeq M$ and $E(S) = \varnothing$. The runner consults some oracle of inputs, and verifies that the right response is made. As state space, we use $M^{\mathbb{N}}$, and the runner is given by the local function $f : M \times M^{\mathbb{N}} \rightharpoonup (M^{\mathbb{N}})_\perp$ where: $f(m, s) = \{\lambda n.s(n+1)\}$ if $s(0) = m$, and $\{\perp\}$ otherwise.

Example 3. We model global store over some global state M by taking as operations: for each $m \in M$ an operation $\texttt{update}(m)$ of arity **1**, and an operation $\texttt{lookup}$ of arity M. We simplify $A(S) = \{m!, m? \mid m \in M\}$ where $m! = (\texttt{update}(m), *)$ and $m? = (\texttt{lookup}, m)$. We define a runner over state space M with the local function $f : A(S) \times M \rightharpoonup M_\perp$ where: $f(m!, n) = \{m\}$, and $f(m?, n) = \{n\}$ if $m = n$, otherwise $\{\perp\}$.

Example 4. Consider a single choice operation `or` of arity $2 = \{0, 1\}$, hence our actions $A(S)$ are in bijection to **2**. Suppose `or` models some unbalanced nondeterministic choice, where the right choice only happens when some fee is paid, whereas the left choice is free. As state space we take $\mathbb{N}$, which tells us how many times we can pay the fee, and define the runner with the local function $f : \mathbf{2} \times \mathbb{N} \rightharpoonup \mathbb{N}_\perp$ where $f(0, n) = \{n\}$, $f(1, 0) = \{\perp\}$ and $f(1, n+1) = \{n\}$.

4   Interleaving Concurrency

Having established our main way of modelling effect behaviour in terms of runners, we now start looking at interleaving concurrency. We study a variation on the standard interleaving semantics, and use it to formulate a trace runners. This variation is necessary to ensure that the right properties hold, especially the unit equation for trace runners.

Definition 6. *The interleaving concurrency operations are three mutually inductive families of operations* $\mathbb{P}, \mathbb{L}, \mathbb{R} : TX \times TY \multimap T(X \times Y)$ *where:*

1. $\mathbb{P}(l, r) = \mathbb{L}(l, r) \cup \mathbb{R}(l, r)$.
2. $\mathbb{L}([x], r) = [x, \varepsilon(r)]$.
3. $\mathbb{L}(@l, r) = @\mathbb{P}(l, r)$.

4. $\mathbb{L}(\diamondsuit, r) = \diamondsuit$.

5. $\mathbb{R}(l, r) = T(\gamma)(\mathbb{L}(r, l))$.

We call $\mathbb{L}$ the *left-focussed parallel operator*, and $\mathbb{R}$ the *right-focussed parallel operator*. The main difference between the above semantics and traditional interleaving semantics (as e.g. in process algebra [4]) is in the treatment of the termination case. Here, $\mathbb{L}([x], r)$ will only give a result if r immediately terminates as well (is a leaf). If not, $\mathbb{L}([x], r) = \varnothing$. More traditionally, $\mathbb{L}([x], r)$ is taken to be $\sigma_{X,Y}(x, r)$. Despite this, we do have the following result:

Lemma 7. *The following equation holds:* $\mathbb{P}([x], r) = \sigma(x, r)$.

As a direct consequence, the map $\mathbb{P}$ does not change if we change the definition of $\mathbb{L}$ to give $\mathbb{L}([x], r) = \sigma(x, r)$ instead of $\mathbb{L}([x], r) = [x, \varepsilon(r)]$. We keep the formulation from Definition 7 for the following two reasons: 1) The left parallel operator $\mathbb{L}$ has a richer structure which allow us to formulate trace runners, and 2) this gives less duplicate results which makes it less cumbersome in formalisation efforts (less cases in set equality proofs). We make the following observations.

- $\mathbb{P}$ is total, $\mathbb{L}$ and $\mathbb{R}$ are not total if there is at least one action or exception.
- $\mathbb{P}$, $\mathbb{L}$ and $\mathbb{R}$ are positively natural over X and Y, hence $\mathbb{P}$ is natural in $\mathbf{Rel}_+$.
- If E is empty, then $\mathbb{P}$, $\mathbb{L}$ and $\mathbb{R}$ are natural in $\mathbf{Rel}$.

Lemma 8. $\mathbb{P}$ *is associative and symmetric, as it satisfies the equations:*

- $(\mathbb{P} \times \iota); \mathbb{P}; T(\alpha) = \alpha; (\iota \times \mathbb{P}); \mathbb{P},$
- $(\mathbb{L} \times \iota); \mathbb{L}; T(\alpha) = \alpha; (\iota \times \mathbb{P}); \mathbb{L},$
- $(\mathbb{R} \times \iota); \mathbb{L}; T(\alpha) = \alpha; (\iota \times \mathbb{L}); \mathbb{R},$
- $(\mathbb{P} \times \iota); \mathbb{R}; T(\alpha) = \alpha; (\iota \times \mathbb{R}); \mathbb{R}.$

- $\mathbb{P}; T(\gamma) = \gamma; \mathbb{P}.$
- $\mathbb{L}; T(\gamma) = \gamma; \mathbb{R}.$
- $\mathbb{R}; T(\gamma) = \gamma; \mathbb{L}.$

4.1 Monadic and Comonadic Properties

We will study how the interleaving transformations interact with both the monad and comonad structure of our monad T. First of all, consider the following.

Lemma 9. *The following equation and point-wise inclusion hold:*

$$
\begin{array}{ccc}
X \times Y = X \times Y & TTX \times TTY \xrightarrow{\mathbb{P}} T(TX \times TY) \xrightarrow{T\mathbb{P}} TT(X \times Y) \\
\eta \times \eta \downarrow \quad \downarrow \eta & \mu \times \mu \downarrow \quad |\cap \quad \downarrow \mu \\
TX \times TY \xrightarrow{\mathbb{P}} T(X \times Y) & TX \times TY \xrightarrow{\mathbb{P}} T(X \times Y)
\end{array}
$$

This shows that T is a monoidal monad in $\mathbf{Rel}_+$ in a *lax* sense. In relation to the comonad structure however, there is a stronger result.

Lemma 10. *The following two equations hold:*

$$
\begin{array}{ccc}
TX \times TY \xrightarrow{\mathbb{P}} T(X \times Y) & TX \times TY \xrightarrow{\quad\mathbb{P}\quad} T(X \times Y) \\
\varepsilon \times \varepsilon \downarrow \quad \downarrow \varepsilon & \delta \times \delta \downarrow \quad \downarrow \delta \\
X \times Y = X \times Y & TTX \times TTY \xrightarrow{\mathbb{P}} T(TX \times TY) \xrightarrow{T\mathbb{P}} TT(X \times Y)
\end{array}
$$

We could call T a monoidal comonad, though note that ε is not total. Hence T is only a monoidal comonad in $\mathbf{Rel}$ and only when $E = \varnothing$. Last but not least, we present equations which mix the monad and comonad structures.

Lemma 11. *The following two equations hold:*

$$
\begin{array}{ccc}
X \times Y = X \times Y & \iota \times \delta\,TTX \times TTY \xrightarrow{\mathbb{L}} T(TX \times TY) \xrightarrow{T\mathbb{L}} TT(X \times Y) \\
X \times TY \quad \downarrow \eta & TTX \times TY \quad \downarrow \mu \\
\eta \times \iota\,TX \times TY \xrightarrow{\mathbb{L}} T(X \times Y) & \mu \times \iota\,TX \times TY \xrightarrow{\quad\mathbb{L}\quad} T(X \times Y)
\end{array}
$$

Proof (Notes). The second equation can be shown by mutual induction with properties: 3. $\mathbb{P}(\mu(d), r) = \mu(T\mathbb{L}(\mathbb{P}(d, \delta(r))))$, 4a. $\mathbb{R}(\mu(d), r) \subseteq \mu(T\mathbb{L}(\mathbb{P}(d, \delta(r))))$, and 4b. $\mathbb{P}(\mu(d), r) \supseteq \mu(T\mathbb{L}(\mathbb{R}(d, \delta(r))))$. Property 3 can be directly shown using the other three properties, whereas those other properties can be proven by case analysis on the trace they focus on, using the induction hypothesis on Property 3.

The above result shows a strict preservation over program composition, and as a direct consequence, we can observe a connection to interaction laws [13].

Corollary 1. *If $E = \varnothing$, then in the category of relations $\mathbf{Rel}$, $\mathbb{L}$ forms a T-residual monad-comonad interaction law between T and T.*

4.2 The Parallel Runner

Following Lemma 11 and the theory developed in [13], we know that the following construction gives us a trace runner.

Definition 7. *For a set U and a trace monad T, the U-parallel runner is the trace runner $\rho_X^U : TX \times TU \rightarrow T(X \times TU)$ defined by $\rho_X^U = (\iota_{TX} \times \delta_U); \mathbb{L}$.*

This runner simulates running a program modelled by a set of traces from TX in parallel with some background process modelled by a set of traces from TU. This background process need not finish when the program finishes, and a remainder of its trace may carry over to continuations of the program.

The parallel runner goes hand in hand with the left-focussed parallel transformation $\mathbb{L}$, since the former is defined by the latter, and the latter can be retrieved from the former: $\mathbb{L}(l, r) = T(\iota \times \varepsilon)(\rho(l, r))$. Through Lemma 5, we can find the local definition of the parallel runner, given as follows:

- The morphism $A \times K \rightarrow TK$, where $K = TY$, sends (a, r) to $(a)\delta_U(r)$.
- The morphism $E \times K \rightarrow T\mathbf{0}$ sends (e, r) to $\langle e \rangle$.

As a culmination of previous results, we can observe some extra properties.

Lemma 12. *The following two equations hold, modulo associativity:*

- $(\rho_X^Y \times \iota_{TZ}); \rho_{X \times TY}^Z; T(\iota_X \times \gamma_{TY, TZ}) = (\iota_{TX} \times \gamma_{TY, TZ}); (\rho_X^Z \times \iota_{TY}); \rho_{X \times TZ}^Y,$
- $(\rho_X^Y \times \iota_{TZ}); \rho_{X \times TY}^Z; T(\iota_X \times \mathbb{P}_{Y,Z}) = (\iota_{TX} \times \mathbb{P}_{Y,Z}); \rho_X^{(Y \times Z)}.$

Definition 8. *The U-concurrent completion of a trace runner θ from (A, E) to (A', E') on state space K is the trace runner $\theta^{|U}$ from (A, E) to (A', E') on state space $T_{A,E}U \times K$ given by the composition $(\rho^U \bullet \theta)$.*

We commonly take the 1-concurrent completion of a trace runner, since our focus is on the program and not on the result of the background process. If we want to study the background process instead, we would shift focus and use the runner the other way around. Note that by Lemma 12, taking two concurrent completions is similar to taking one. In other words, running in parallel with two processes separately is, from the perspective of the program, the same as running in parallel with the merger of the two processes together.

5 Stateful Relational Reasoning

Consider a tree runner from S to (A, E). This runner induces a relation on trees over the signature S. In this section, we shall formulate such relations dependent on the state of the environment, and look at examples of such relations in scenarios of algebraic effects with concurrency.

5.1   Relators

When one wants to study the behaviour of programs denoted by a monad M, one may need tools to relate them. Given some notion of relatedness on values as a relation between two objects X and Y, we want to define a notion of relatedness between programs that produce these values; a relation between MX and MY. This can be done using a *relator* [16,27].

Definition 9. *Given a monad M in* **Set***, a* relator Γ *for M is a family of functions $\{\Gamma_{X,Y}\}_{X,Y}$ sending $\mathcal{R} \subseteq X \times Y$ to $\Gamma_{X,Y}(\mathcal{R}) \subseteq MX \times MY$ such that:*

Identity: $\mathcal{I}_{MX} \subseteq \Gamma_{X,X}(\mathcal{I}_X)$.
Composability: $\Gamma(\mathcal{S}); \Gamma(\mathcal{R}) \subseteq \Gamma(\mathcal{S}; \mathcal{R})$.
Order preservation: *If* $\mathcal{R} \subseteq \mathcal{S}$, *then* $\Gamma(\mathcal{R}) \subseteq \Gamma(\mathcal{S})$.
Naturality: *For $f : X \to Z$ and $g : Y \to W$, $M(f)(a)\, \Gamma(\mathcal{R})\, M(g)(b)$ holds if and only if $a\, \Gamma(\{(x,y) \mid f(x)\, \mathcal{R}\, g(y)\})\, b$.*

The lifting of M to **Rel** is an example of a relator, though the main examples we study in this paper are not of that form. There are two properties we would like a relator to satisfy in order for it to induce a congruent notion of equivalence.

Definition 10. *A relator Γ on a monad M is* monadic *if:*

Unit: *If $x\, \mathcal{R}\, y$ then $\eta_X^M(x)\, \Gamma(\mathcal{R})\, \eta_Y^M(y)$.*
Multiplication: *If $d\, \Gamma(\Gamma(\mathcal{R}))\, e$ then $\mu_X^M(d)\, \Gamma(\mathcal{R})\, \mu_Y^M(e)$.*

We shall focus on relators on tree monads (which include trace monads). In particular, the examples we have studied were formulated by runners to the exception monad $\mathsf{T}_{\varnothing,E}X \simeq X + E$. As such, we shall first look at relators there.

Example 5. Specifying a subset $V \subseteq E$ of detectable errors, we can define a relator Γ_V on $\mathsf{T}_{\varnothing,E}$ given by:

– $[x]\, \Gamma_V(\mathcal{R})\, [y]$ if $x\, \mathcal{R}\, y$, $\diamondsuit\, \Gamma_V(\mathcal{R})\, \diamondsuit$, $\diamondsuit\, \Gamma_V(\mathcal{R})\, t$ for any t if $e \notin V$.

A common sub-example is to take $E = \{\bot\}$ and $V = \varnothing$, in which case we get the standard relator $\Gamma_{\{\bot\}}$ on the maybe monad. This makes the $\bot$ exception not observable by the relator, which is useful in such cases where we model programs with undecidable termination, and non-termination is marked by $\bot$.

To deal with nondeterminism, we use a relator from the literature (e.g. [15]).

Definition 11. *We define a monadic relator $\overline{\mathcal{P}_+}$ on the monad $\mathcal{P}_+(-)$, where: $V\, \overline{\mathcal{P}_+}(\mathcal{R})\, W$ if for any $x \in V$, there is a $y \in W$ such that $x\, \mathcal{R}\, y$.*

A tree runner from S to (A, E) gives an $\mathcal{P}_+\mathsf{T}_{A,E}$-residual runner on M_S in **Set**. Hence it gives a natural transformation $\theta_X : \mathsf{M}_S X \times K \to \mathcal{P}_+\mathsf{T}_{A,E}(X \times K)$. We shall use this runner to define a relator on M_S. As base, we shall specify a relator Γ on $\mathsf{T}_{A,E}$, and compose it with the relator $\overline{\mathcal{P}_+}$ on $\mathcal{P}_+$, creating a relator on $\mathcal{P}_+\mathsf{T}_{A,E}$ which we denote by $\Gamma^{\mathcal{P}_+}$. In order for $\Gamma^{\mathcal{P}_+}$ to be monadic, we need the following distributivity property on Γ using a *distributivity law*[1] $d : \mathsf{T}\mathcal{P}_+ \to \mathcal{P}_+\mathsf{T}$:

---

[1] A distributivity law satisfies some equations with respect to the monad structure, as specified in [3].

P_+-**Distributivity:** If $t\,\Gamma(\overline{P_+}(\mathcal{R}))\,r$ then $d_X(t)\,\overline{P_+}(\Gamma(\mathcal{R}))\,d_Y(r)$.

Example 5 satisfies the distributivity property, and the proof of this necessarily uses the fact that P_+X does not include the empty set. The following relator is defined using runners, and is monadic as we shall see in Lemma 13.

Definition 12. *Suppose given a tree runner θ from S to (A, E) and a relator Γ on $T_{A,E}$. The* global θ-relator Γ^θ *is the relator on M_S given by:*

$$a\,\Gamma^\theta(\mathcal{R})\,b \quad \Longleftrightarrow \quad \forall k \in K.\, \theta_X(a, k)\,\Gamma^{P_+}(\mathcal{R} \times \mathcal{I}_K)\,\theta_Y(b, k)$$

Example 6. In case of $A = \varnothing$ and $V \subseteq E$, a $\Gamma_V^\theta(\mathcal{R})\,b$ holds if for any $k \in K$,

- If $[x, u] \in \theta_X(a, k)$, then there is a result $[y, u] \in \theta_Y(b, k)$ such that $x\,\mathcal{R}\,y$.
- If $\Diamond \in \theta_X(a, k)$ is a detectable exception $e \in V$, then $\Diamond \in \theta_Y(b, k)$.

5.2   State Initialisations and Distinctions

The global relator is quite fine-grained, testing for any possible initial state, and distinguishing between any two different final states. We can improve on this, formulating what constitutes as a good starting set of states, and a good relation on final states, such that we still get a relator. We do this in two steps: firstly we need to establish what features of the state we deem observable. This entails formulating a base relation on state which is preserved by runs over a program. Secondly, we need to establish which states can occur in a particular situation. In this subsection, we consider fixed a tree runner θ from S to (A, E) with state space K and a monadic relator Γ on $T_{A,E}$.

Distinguishing Final States. We study *preorders* on the state space K (reflexive and transitive relations). Given a preorder $\mathcal{R} \subseteq K \times K$, we define $\theta(\mathcal{R}) \subseteq K \times K$:

$$a\,\theta(\mathcal{R})\,b \quad \Longleftrightarrow \quad \forall p \in T X.\, \theta_X(p, a)\,\Gamma^{P_+}(\iota_X \times \mathcal{R})\,\theta_X(p, b)$$

The result $\theta(\mathcal{R})$ is also a preorder, and we say $\mathcal{R}$ is *preserved by runs* if $\mathcal{R} \subseteq \theta(\mathcal{R})$. In general, $\theta(\mathcal{R})$ is included in $\mathcal{R}$, as can be observed by taking $p = leaf(x)$ in the definition. If $\mathcal{R} \subseteq \mathcal{U}$, then $\theta(\mathcal{R}) \subseteq \theta(\mathcal{U})$.

Definition 13. *The θ-closure of a preorder $\mathcal{R} \subseteq K \times K$ is the preorder $\mathcal{R}^\theta$: $= \bigcup \{S \subseteq \mathcal{R} \mid S \subseteq \theta(S)\}$. This is the largest subrelation of $\mathcal{R}$ preserved by runs.*

The canonical choice would be to take $(K \times K)^\theta$, the θ-closure of the maximal relation on K. More generally though, one would start with $K \times K$, remove any pairs you would like to distinguish making sure the result stays a preorder, and take the θ-closure of whatever you have left. The identity relation is the smallest preorder preserved by runs, and is the one used in Definition 12.

In some cases, the θ-closure can be more easily constructed.

- If θ gives at most one result for each input (it is thin), then $\mathcal{R}^\theta = \theta(\mathcal{R})$.
- If θ gives a finite number of results for each input, then $\mathcal{R}^\theta = \cap_{n \in \mathbb{N}} \theta^n(\mathcal{R})$.

For establishing stateful relations, we fix one preorder $\prec$ preserved by runs. If we have no extra requirements, we take $(K \times K)^\theta$, the maximal option.

Limiting Initial States. It is a strong requirement to demand programs to be related for any possible initial state, especially when considering concurrent programs. For instance, the behavioural equivalence for global store programs will become as fine-grained as input/output programs if one can test it concurrently with any possible other global store program (this second program can simulate tests with its updates and lookups). Hence, for the verification of concurrent programs, it is important to limit the possible states that can occur.

We introduce the notion of *state world*. Given a trace $t \in T_{A,E}X$ and an element $x \in X$, we write $t \rhd x$ if x is a leaf of t. In other words, $[x] \rhd x$, $\diamondsuit \not\rhd x$ and $@t \rhd x$ if and only if $t \rhd x$. Let $\leadsto \subseteq K \times K$ be the relation such that $v \leadsto w$ when $\exists p \in MX, x \in X. \theta_X(p,v) \rhd (x,w)$. This is a preorder due to the unit and multiplication properties of the runner. A state world is a subset $W \subseteq K$ such that $v \in W \wedge v \leadsto w \implies w \in W$. In other words, it is a set closed under runs of programs. For each $s \in K$, we define the world $[s] = \{z \in K \mid s \leadsto z\}$.

Example 7. Considering Example 4, with as global state $\mathbb{N}$ the number of fees that can be paid, which determines how many possible results we may get. In this case, the θ-closure of $\mathbb{N} \times \mathbb{N}$ is the standard ordering $\leq$ on $\mathbb{N}$, since a higher number gives more possible results. The relation $\leadsto$ is the relation $\geq$ since the number can only go down, hence state worlds are down-closed subsets of $\mathbb{N}$.

We fix a tree runner θ and a preorder $\prec$ preserved by runs.

Definition 14. *We define the following relators on M_S:*

- *for each $s \in K$ a relator Γ^s where: $a\, \Gamma^s(\mathcal{R})\, b$ if $\theta(a,s)\, \Gamma^{\mathcal{P}_+}(\mathcal{R} \times \prec)\, \theta(b,s)$.*
- *for each subset $W \subseteq K$, a relator Γ^W where: $a\, \Gamma^W(\mathcal{R})\, b$ if $\forall s \in W,\ a\, \Gamma^s(\mathcal{R})\, b$.*

Lemma 13. *Given a state world $W \subseteq K$ and a state $s \in W$:*

- *$x\, \mathcal{R}\, y$ implies $\eta(x)\, \Gamma^W(\mathcal{R})\, \eta(y)$, which implies $\eta(x)\, \Gamma^s(\mathcal{R})\, \eta(y)$.*
- *$d\, \Gamma^s(\Gamma^W(\mathcal{R}))\, e \Rightarrow \mu(d)\, \Gamma^s(\mathcal{R})\, \mu(e)$, $d\, \Gamma^W(\Gamma^W(\mathcal{R}))\, e \Rightarrow \mu(d)\, \Gamma^W(\mathcal{R})\, \mu(e)$.*

Proof. Given $d\, \Gamma^s(\Gamma^W(\mathcal{R}))\, e$, we know that for any $t \in \theta(d,s)$ there is an $r \in \theta(e,s)$ such that $t\, \Gamma(\Gamma^W(\mathcal{R}) \times \prec)\, r$. Consider the sub-relation $\prec_W := (\prec) \cap (W \times W)$ of $\prec$, then $t\, \Gamma(\Gamma^W(\mathcal{R}) \times \prec_W)\, r$ since any state in a leaf of t and r are in W.

We prove: If $(a,u)\, \Gamma^W(\mathcal{R}) \times \prec_W\, (b,v)$, then $\theta(a,u)\, \Gamma^{\mathcal{P}_+}(\mathcal{R} \times \prec)\, \theta(b,v)$. Suppose $(a,u)\, \Gamma^W(\mathcal{R}) \times \prec_W\, (b,v)$, then $a\, \Gamma^W(\mathcal{R})\, b$, and $u \prec_W v$, hence 1) $u \prec v$ and 2) $v \in W$. By the former, $\theta(a,u)\, \Gamma^{\mathcal{P}_+}(\mathcal{I}_X \times \prec)\, \theta(a,v)$, since $\prec$ is preserved by runs. By the latter, $\theta(a,v)\, \Gamma^{\mathcal{P}_+}(\mathcal{R} \times \prec)\, \theta(b,v)$, since $a\, \Gamma^W(\mathcal{R})\, b$. So by the relator properties on $\Gamma^{\mathcal{P}_+}$, and transitivity on $\prec$, we get that $\theta(a,u)\, \Gamma^{\mathcal{P}_+}(\mathcal{R} \times \prec)\, \theta(b,v)$.

By naturality, $\mathcal{P}_+\mathsf{T}(\theta)(\theta(d,s))\, \Gamma^{\mathcal{P}_+}(\Gamma^{\mathcal{P}_+}(\mathcal{R} \times \prec))\, \mathcal{P}_+\mathsf{T}(\theta)(\theta(e,s))$, hence due to the multiplication property on $\overline{\mathcal{P}_+}\Gamma = \Gamma^{\mathcal{P}_+}$ and the multiplication property for runners, $\theta(\mu d, s)\, \overline{\mathcal{P}_+}(\Gamma(\mathcal{R} \times \prec))\, \theta(\mu e, s)$. Hence $\mu d\, \Gamma^s(\mathcal{R})\, \mu e$.

We conclude that for any state world $W \subseteq S$, Γ^W is monadic.

5.3 Algebraic Concurrent Theories

Taking a set of variables X, we can define for each state world $W \subseteq S$ the *stateful approximation* $\leq_W \subseteq MX \times MX$ as $\Gamma^W(\iota_X)$, and *stateful equivalence* $\equiv_W \subseteq MX \times MX$ as $a \equiv_W b \iff a \leq_W b \wedge b \leq_W a$. Both these relations are preorders. The fact that the relator is monadic consequently means these relations are *substitutive*:

Corollary 2. *Given a state world* $W \subseteq K$, $a \leq_W b$ *and* $f, g : X \to TX$ *s.t.* $\forall x \in X. f(x) \leq_W g(x)$, *then* $\mu_X^S(M(f)(a)) \leq_W \mu_X^S(M(g)(b))$. *Similarly for* $\equiv_W$.

Hence, the relators give rise to proper algebraic theories. The above results hold for any tree runner, including those implementing concurrency. Hence the relators give a notion of equivalence for effectful programs within concurrent environments containing other programs. We look at some concrete examples of such situations, and how this concurrency affects the stateful equivalences.

Example 8 (Printing with interference). Consider Example 1 of programs printing messages to an environment. Suppose some background process is printing messages at unpredictable times. We describe this with the runner ϕ, defining it to be the **1**-concurrent completion $\theta^{|1}$ of the runner θ from Example 1. This has as state space $\mathbf{T1} \times M^* \simeq M^* \times M^*$, containing the background process together with a history of printed messages. We want to distinguish between different histories, but not necessarily between different states of the background process. Hence we take as relation on state $< := ((\mathbf{T1})^2 \times \iota_{M^*})^\phi$, the largest relation preserved by runs which distinguishes different histories of printed messages.

Running a program in such an environment will intersperse the messages of the program with messages from the background process. Suppose the background process keeps printing $a \in M$. We can model this with an inductively defined set $U \subseteq \mathbf{T1}$, such that $[*] \in U$ and $t \in U$ implies $@(t) \in U$ (approximations of an infinite sequence of prints). Note that $U \times M^*$ is a state world, since it contains its own continuations. The notion of equivalence for running programs with this background process can be specified using the relator $\Gamma^{U \times M^*}$.

The algebraic theory resulting from this environment reflects the fact that, since output_a could be scheduled after any output action, any output_a produced by the program after the initial output can be ignored. So we have the equation: $\mathsf{output}_b(\mathsf{output}_a(\mathit{leaf}(x))) \equiv_{U \times M^*} \mathsf{output}_b(\mathit{leaf}(x))$.

Example 9 (Global Store). Consider Example 3 of the global store effect, where for simplicity we take as memory space $\{0, 1\}$, hence the lookup operation has arity $\{0, 1\}$, and we have two update operations. Let $t \in M_S X$ be the tree $\mathsf{update}_0(\mathsf{lookup}(0 \mapsto \bot, 1 \mapsto \mathit{leaf}(x)))$, which gives the set of branches $\beta(t) = \{(0!)(0?)\langle \bot \rangle, (0!)(1?)[x]\} \subseteq TX$. If t is run on its own with any initial state $i \in \{0, 1\}$, it must eventually yield the error message $\bot$, since 0 is saved to and subsequently read from the global memory. Hence, under standard global store semantics (implemented with the runner from Example 3), it holds that $t \equiv \bot$.

However, suppose t is run in an environment with a backup process which updates the global store to 1, e.g. $r = (1!)(r') \in TY$. Then $(0!)(1!)(1?)[x, r'] \in \rho(t, r)$, which under global store semantics will yield, for any initial state $i \in \{0, 1\}$, a result (x, r') with final state 1. Hence, in this environment, $t \not\equiv \bot$.

6   Conclusions

We have formulated an operation for interleaving concurrency satisfying the unit and multiplication equations for residual monad-comonad interaction laws in the sense of [13]. This operation can be used in at least two ways. Firstly, it can evaluate two programs concurrently, producing a process which returns a pair of return values. Secondly, we can run one program concurrently with another program, where this other program need only be evaluated partially. This forms a runner [29], which produces a return value of the former program and remainder of the latter program. Both together allow us to precisely schedule concurrent interleavings of higher-order programs.

The sequences of communications between a program and its environment are given by traces, which can be given a behavioural interpretation using stateful runners; a categorical formulation of how to handle and resolve effect operations in a state dependent manner. This can be implemented in practise using *Handlers* for algebraic effects [2,24]. One line of work for the future, is formulating a congruent notion of applicative bisimilarity for concrete higher-order concurrent languages, for example extending results from [15,26] for lambda-calculus style languages, or from [18,19] for a continuation-passing style languages.

It is difficult to generalise the interleaving operation to the monad of trees due to the lack of naturality of the strength operation for trees in any wide sub-category of **Rel** containing multi-valued (non-thin) relations. This is a problem, since the interleaving concurrency operation itself is multi-valued. By using the category of total relations **Rel**$_+$, we are still able to include nullary operations in our monad of traces. This is important, since many situations necessitate the use of exceptions; some effect examples need to exclude impossible sequences of events like reading the wrong state, and in case of infinite recursive processes we may have to mark the end of an approximation.

Models for alternative forms of concurrency could potentially be implemented by adapting the formalism of this paper. Firstly, we might want to run certain sequences of operations without being interrupted by other programs, for instance by only giving one program access to the environment at a time. This could be modelled by using lists of actions as our atomic actions. Secondly, we could look at models closer to *true concurrency* [11]. For instance, some operations may be executed at the exact same time, producing traces over some monoid of actions. Such a denotation would need to be endowed with appropriate notions of behaviour for simultaneously executed operations, which could be implemented by a runner. Lastly, concurrency itself could be described with algebraic effects, following [10], which may be combined with the approach of this paper.

References

1. Abramsky, S.: The Lazy Lambda Calculus, pp. 65–116. Addison-Wesley Longman Publishing Co., Inc. (1990)
2. Ahman, D., Bauer, A.: Runners in action. In: Müller, P. (ed.) ESOP 2020. LNCS, vol. 12075, pp. 29–55. Springer, Cham (2020). https://doi.org/10.1007/978-3-030-44914-8_2

3. Beck, J.: Distributive laws. In: Eckmann, B. (ed.) Seminar on Triples and Categorical Homology Theory. LNM, vol. 80, pp. 119–140. Springer, Heidelberg (1969). https://doi.org/10.1007/BFb0083084

4. Bergstra, J.A., Klop, J.W.: Algebra of communicating processes with abstraction. Theor. Comput. Sci. **37**, 77–121 (1985). https://doi.org/10.1016/0304-3975(85)90088-X

5. Bergstra, J.A., Klop, J.W., Tucker, J.V.: Process algebra with asynchronous communication mechanisms. In: Brookes, S.D., Roscoe, A.W., Winskel, G. (eds.) CONCURRENCY 1984. LNCS, vol. 197, pp. 76–95. Springer, Heidelberg (1985). https://doi.org/10.1007/3-540-15670-4_4

6. Busi, N., Gorrieri, R.: A survey on non-interference with Petri nets. In: Desel, J., Reisig, W., Rozenberg, G. (eds.) ACPN 2003. LNCS, vol. 3098, pp. 328–344. Springer, Heidelberg (2004). https://doi.org/10.1007/978-3-540-27755-2_8

7. Clinger, W.D.: Foundations of actor semantics. Technical report, Massachusetts Institute of Technology, USA (1981). http://hdl.handle.net/1721.1/6935

8. Fiore, M., Gambino, N., Hyland, M., Winskel, G.: The cartesian closed bicategory of generalised species of structures. J. Lond. Math. Soc. **77**, 203–220 (2008). https://doi.org/10.1112/jlms/jdm096

9. Fiore, M., Gambino, N., Hyland, M., Winskel, G.: Relative pseudomonads, Kleisli bicategories, and substitution monoidal structures. Sel. Math. New Ser. **24**(3), 2791–2830 (2017). https://doi.org/10.1007/s00029-017-0361-3

10. van Glabbeek, R., Plotkin, G.: On CSP and the algebraic theory of effects. In: Roscoe, A.W., Jones, C.B., Wood, K.R. (eds.) Reflections on the Work of C.A.R. Hoare, pp. 333–369. Springer, London (2010). https://doi.org/10.1007/978-1-84882-912-1_15

11. Gorrieri, R.: Interleaving vs true concurrency: some instructive security examples. In: Janicki, R., Sidorova, N., Chatain, T. (eds.) PETRI NETS 2020. LNCS, vol. 12152, pp. 131–152. Springer, Cham (2020). https://doi.org/10.1007/978-3-030-51831-8_7

12. Hasuo, I., Jacobs, B., Sokolova, A.: Generic trace semantics via coinduction. Logical Methods Comput. Sci. **3** (2007). https://doi.org/10.2168/LMCS-3(4:11)2007

13. Katsumata, S., Rivas, E., Uustalu, T.: Interaction laws of monads and comonads. In: Proceedings of the 35th Annual ACM/IEEE Symposium on Logic in Computer Science, LICS 2020, pp. 604–618. Association for Computing Machinery, New York (2020). https://doi.org/10.1145/3373718.3394808

14. Keller, R.M.: Formal verification of parallel programs. Commun. ACM **19**(7), 371–384 (1976). https://doi.org/10.1145/360248.360251

15. Lago, U.D., Gavazzo, F., Levy, P.B.: Effectful applicative bisimilarity: monads, relators, and Howe's method. In: Proceedings of 32nd Annual ACM/IEEE Symposium on Logic in Computer Science, LICS 2017, pp. 1–12. IEEE Computer Society (2017). https://doi.org/10.1109/LICS.2017.8005117

16. Levy, P.B.: Similarity quotients as final coalgebras. In: Hofmann, M. (ed.) FoSSaCS 2011. LNCS, vol. 6604, pp. 27–41. Springer, Heidelberg (2011). https://doi.org/10.1007/978-3-642-19805-2_3

17. MacLane, S.: Categories for the Working Mathematician. Graduate Texts in Mathematics, vol. 5. Springer, New York (1971). https://doi.org/10.1007/978-1-4612-9839-7

18. Matache, C.: Program equivalence for algebraic effects via modalities. Master's thesis, University of Oxford (2019)

19. Matache, C., Staton, S.: A sound and complete logic for algebraic effects. In: Bojańczyk, M., Simpson, A. (eds.) FoSSaCS 2019. LNCS, vol. 11425, pp. 382–399. Springer, Cham (2019). https://doi.org/10.1007/978-3-030-17127-8_22

20. Melliès, P.A.: Template games and differential linear logic. In: 2019 34th Annual ACM/IEEE Symposium on Logic in Computer Science (LICS), pp. 1–13 (2019). https://doi.org/10.1109/LICS.2019.8785830

21. Milner, R.: Communication and Concurrency. Prentice-Hall Inc., Hoboken (1989)

22. Moggi, E.: Notions of computation and monads. Inf. Comput. **93**(1), 55–92 (1991). https://doi.org/10.1016/0890-5401(91)90052-4

23. Plotkin, G., Power, J.: Adequacy for algebraic effects. In: Honsell, F., Miculan, M. (eds.) FoSSaCS 2001. LNCS, vol. 2030, pp. 1–24. Springer, Heidelberg (2001). https://doi.org/10.1007/3-540-45315-6_1

24. Plotkin, G.D., Pretnar, M.: Handling algebraic effects. Log. Methods Comput. Sci. **9**(4, Article 23), 1–36 (2013). https://doi.org/10.2168/lmcs-9(4:23)2013

25. Rivas, E., Jaskelioff, M.: Monads with merging (2019). https://hal.inria.fr/hal-02150199. Working paper or preprint

26. Simpson, A., Voorneveld, N.: Behavioural equivalence via modalities for algebraic effects. ACM Trans. Program. Lang. Syst. **42**(1), 4:1–4:45 (2020). https://doi.org/10.1145/3363518

27. Thijs, A.M.: Simulation and fixpoint semantics. Ph.D. thesis, University of Groningen (1996). https://research.rug.nl/en/publications/simulation-and-fixpoint-semantics

28. Turi, D., Plotkin, G.: Towards a mathematical operational semantics. In: Proceedings of Twelfth Annual IEEE Symposium on Logic in Computer Science, pp. 280–291 (1997). https://doi.org/10.1109/LICS.1997.614955

29. Uustalu, T.: Stateful runners of effectful computations. Electron. Notes Theor. Comput. Sci. **319**, 403–421 (2015). https://doi.org/10.1016/j.entcs.2015.12.024. The 31st Conference on the Mathematical Foundations of Programming Semantics

30. Uustalu, T., Vene, V.: Comonadic notions of computation. Electron. Notes Theor. Comput. Sci. **203**(5), 263–284 (2008). https://doi.org/10.1016/j.entcs.2008.05.029. Proceedings of the Ninth Workshop on Coalgebraic Methods in Computer Science (CMCS 2008)

Formal Grammars for Turn-Bounded Deterministic Context-Free Languages

Tomoyuki Yamakami[✉]

Faculty of Engineering, University of Fukui, 3-9-1, Bunkyo, Fukui 910-8507, Japan
TomoyukiYamakami@gmail.com

Abstract. As its computation proceeds, a one-way deterministic pushdown automaton (or a 1dpda) changes the height (or volume) of its stack (or pushdown store) by switching between a non-decreasing phase and a decreasing phase. Such a changing of the two different phases is referred to as a "turn" of the machine. Languages that are recognized by k-turn 1dpda's for each fixed number k are succinctly called k-turn deterministic context-free (dcf) languages. We first discuss closure properties of k-turn dcf languages. Such closure properties help us prove that finite-turn dcf languages are precisely characterized by a deterministic analogue of ultralinear grammars, called $LR(1)$-ultralinear grammars. In particular, when a 1dpda is further required to empty its stack at the beginning of each turn, the associated languages are characterized in terms of $LR(1)$-metalinear grammars. As an immediate application of these grammar characterizations, we prove a structural lemma, known as a pumping lemma, for finite-turn dcf languages.

Keywords: Deterministic context-free language · Finite turns · Ultralinear grammar · Metalinear grammar · Pumping lemma

1 Background and a Quick Overview

A *stack* (or a pushdown store) is a memory device restricted to FILO (first-in, last-out) accesses to its new and/or stored data. A *one-way nondeterministic pushdown automaton* (or a 1npda, for short) is equipped with such a memory device together with a read-once[1] input tape and such machines precisely characterize languages generated by *context-free grammars*. The *height* (or the volume) of a stack content in general varies during a computation of a 1npda. A single change of the stack height from a non-decreasing phase to a decreasing phase along each computation path of the 1npda is known as a *turn*.[2] There could be numerous turns being made along a computation to utilize the stack effectively

---

[1] A tape is said to be *read-once* if its tape head never moves back to the left and, whenever it scans a non-blank symbol, it must move to the right.

[2] Slightly differing from [8], in this paper, we define the number of "turns" by counting the times when a stack height changes from a nondecreasing phase to a decreasing phase (see [6,13]). The details will be given in Sect. 2.2.

H. Seidl et al. (Eds.): ICTAC 2022, LNCS 13572, pp. 425–441, 2022.
https://doi.org/10.1007/978-3-031-17715-6_27

because underlying 1npda's with no turn are merely equivalent to finite-state automata in recognition power. Since 1-turn 1npda's can recognize precisely linear languages [8], it is often easier to show that some languages are linear by simply constructing 1-turn 1npda's for them. One such example is the language $\{a^{n_1}ba^{n_2}b\cdots a^{n_k} \mid k \geq 2, \exists i, j \in \{1, 2, \ldots, k\}(i < j \wedge n_i \neq n_j)\}$ [1]. Ginsburg and Spanier [8] first discussed basic properties of *finite-turn* 1npda's from a viewpoint of parsing procedures of context-free languages. They introduced variants of linear grammars, called *ultralinear grammars*,[3] to characterize the language families induced by finite-turn 1npda's. For these languages, there exist relatively efficient parsing algorithms. A weaker variant of ultralinear grammar, known as a *metalinear grammar*, is related to 1npda's that empty their stacks at the beginning of each turn (we briefly refer to this situation as "making deep turns"). Those intriguing grammars were intensively studied in [13,15].

Here, we intend to pay special attention to *one-way deterministic pushdown automata* (or 1dpda's) instead of 1npda's. The 1dpda's were first studied in 1966 by Ginsburg and Greibach [7] and these machines induce *deterministic context-free (dcf) languages*. Surprisingly, little systematic and coherent study has been made intensively on turn-bounded 1dpda's. The past literature has discussed finite-turn 1dpda's only with respect to decidability by Valiant [18,19], simultaneously deterministic and linear languages [1], logarithmic-space simulation by Moriya and Tada [16], recursive-nonrecursive trade-offs by Malcher [14], and lately synchronization by Yamakami and Mikami [23] and Fernau, Wolf, and Yamakami [6]. As for a more restrictive model, nevertheless, there has been a fruitful study on deterministic (multi-)counter automata whose counters are k-*reversal bounded* [4,5] and also bounded context-switching visibly pushdown automata [17].

In this work, on the contrary, we intend to cast a new spotlight on an old but fundamental topic of turn-bounded pushdown automata from a new viewpoint of determinism and to set our focal point on the behaviors of 1dpda's when they make only a finite number of turns. The languages recognized by k-turn 1dpda's are called k-*turn dcf languages* and *finite-turn dcf languages* mean k-turn dcf languages for appropriate numbers $k \geq 0$. Those languages are defined by 1dpda's but no grammar-characterization is currently known. Therefore, the initial purpose of this paper is set to promote the basic understandings of finite-turn dcf languages by introducing appropriate formal grammars for them.

At this point, we introduce the useful notation, ktDCFL, to denote the family of all k-turn dcf languages whereas the notation ktCFL is reserved for k-turn context-free languages. We further denote by ωtDCFL the union of all ktDCFL for any integer $k \geq 1$. Similarly, the notation deep-ktDCFL addresses the family of deep-k-turn dcf languages and deep-ωtDCFL denotes $\bigcup_{k \in \mathbb{N}}$ deep-ktDCFL.

---

[3] These languages coincide with *quasi-rational languages* and are also characterized by context-free grammars of finite "indices", where the *index* of a derivation refers to the maximum number of occurrences of variables in the sentential forms used in the derivation (see, e.g., [1]).

Moriya and Tada [16] gave reasonable upper bounds on the necessary memory space to simulate finite-turn 1dpda's. As an immediate consequence of their simulation results, ωtDCFL is included in L (logarithmic-space complexity class), whereas the family DCFL of all dcf languages is only known to be in SC^2 (2nd level of Steve's Class). Furthermore, we can derive a few important "separation" results regarding ktDCFL and deep-ktDCFL, which are deducible from the past literature. A special language, T_{k+1}, which is recognized by a $(k+1)$-turn 1npda, cannot be recognized by any k-turn 1npda [9]; in other words, making more turns endows underlying 1npda's with more computational power. The fact that T_{k+1} belongs to deep-$(k+1)$tDCFL further leads to the conclusion that $\{k$tDCFL $\mid k \in \mathbb{N}^+\}$ forms an infinite hierarchy between DCFL and the family REG of all regular languages. In fact, it also follows that k-turn 1npda's are more powerful in general than k-turn 1dpda's, which turn out to be more powerful than deep-k-turn 1dpda's. These separation results are easily obtainable by combining the arguments in [8–10, 14]. See Sect. 2.2 for further details.

The main contribution of this paper is to introduce appropriately-defined "grammars" and characterize languages in ktDCFL in terms of these grammars. To lay out a road map to an introduction of such grammars, we first explore various closure/non-closure properties of ktDCFL as well as ωtDCFL in Sect. 3.1. These properties then help us establish a close connection between finite-turn dcf languages and a deterministic analogue of ultralinear grammars, which we call *LR(1)-ultralinear grammars* in Sect. 3.2. Similarly, we characterize deep-finite-turn dcf languages in terms of *LR(1)-metalinear grammars*. As a restricted case of 1-turn dcf languages, we obtain *LR(1)-linear grammars*. As remarked in [1], there is a language that is generated by both an *LR(1)* grammar and a linear grammar but actually requires 2 turns. Thus, no *LR(1)*-linear grammar can generate such a language. As a useful application of our grammar characterization of ωtDCFL, we prove a structural property of this class, known as a *pumping lemma* (or an *iteration theorem*) in Sect. 4. For ultralinear grammars, Magalini and Pighizzini [15] already proposed a pumping lemma. Our pumping lemma, by contrast, reflect the "deterministic" feature of *LR(1)*-ultralinear languages.

Language	Grammar
finite-turn context-free	ultralinear [8]
dcf	$LR(k)$ $(k \geq 1)$ [12]
finite-turn dcf	$LR(1)$-ultralinear
deep-finite-turn dcf	$LR(1)$-metalinear

2   Preparation: Notions and Notation

2.1   Numbers, Strings, and Grammars

The notation $\mathbb{N}$ indicates the set of all *natural numbers* (i.e., nonnegative integers) and $\mathbb{N}^+$ denotes the difference $\mathbb{N} - \{0\}$. For two integers m and n, when

$m \leq n$, we denote by $[m, n]_{\mathbb{Z}}$ the *integer interval* $\{m, m+1, m+2, \ldots, n\}$. For any number $n \in \mathbb{N}^+$, we abbreviate $[1, n]_{\mathbb{Z}}$ as $[n]$. Given a set A, $\mathcal{P}(A)$ expresses the *power set* of A. An *alphabet* is a finite set composed of "symbols" or "letters". A *string* over alphabet Σ is a finite sequence of symbols in Σ and a *language* A over Σ is a set of strings over Σ. The *length* of a string x, denoted $|x|$, is the total number of symbols in x. The *empty string* is a unique string of length 0 and is expressed as ε. Given a number $n \in \mathbb{N}$, Σ^n (resp., $\Sigma^{\leq n}$) denotes the set of all strings over Σ of length exactly n (resp., length at most n). Let $\Sigma^* = \bigcup_{n \in \mathbb{N}} \Sigma^n$. For any set Γ, the notation Γ_ε denotes $\Gamma \cup \{\varepsilon\}$. Given three strings $x, y, z \in \Sigma^*$, if $z = xy$, then x is a *prefix* of z and y is a *suffix* of z. A language L is called *prefix-free* if, for any $u, v \in L$, u cannot be a prefix of v. For any string w and any number $i \in [|w|]$, $(w)_{(0)} = \varepsilon$ and $(w)_{(i)}$ is the ith symbol of w. For convenience, whenever $i > |w|$, $(w)_{(i)}$ denotes ε. In particular, $(\varepsilon)_{(1)} = \varepsilon$ follows.

A *grammar* is of the form $\langle N, T, S, P \rangle$, where N is an alphabet of *non-terminals*, T is an alphabet of *terminals* satisfying $N \cap T = \varnothing$, S is the *axiom* (or *start symbol*) in N, and P is a finite set of *productions*, expressed using the single arrow $\rightarrow$. Each production induces a *derivation*, expressed using the double arrow $\Rightarrow$. A string $\alpha \in (N \cup T)^*$ is said to be *in a sentential form* if $S \Rightarrow^* \alpha$ holds, where $\Rightarrow^*$ is the transitive closure of $\Rightarrow$. In the case of a context-free grammar, the use of such derivations produces a *derivation tree*. In particular, the special notation $\Rightarrow_{rt}$ is used for the *rightmost derivation*. A derivation tree is *rightmost* if all derivations used to produce this tree are rightmost derivations. Without loss of generality, we assume that our grammars do not contain "useless" symbols; namely, for any symbol $A \in N \cup T$, there always exist $u, v \in (N \cup T)^*$ and $w \in T^*$ satisfying $S \Rightarrow^* uAv \Rightarrow^* w$. Following the formalism of [11, Section 12] as well as [24, Section 3], a context-free grammar $G = \langle N, T, P, S \rangle$ with $S \not\Rightarrow_{rt}^+ S$ is an *LR(1) grammar* if it satisfies the following condition: for any two derivations of the form $S \Rightarrow_{rt}^* \alpha_1 A_1 y_1 \Rightarrow_{rt} \alpha_1 \gamma_1 y_1$ and $S \Rightarrow_{rt}^* \alpha_2 A_2 y_2 \Rightarrow_{rt} \alpha_2 \gamma_2 y_2 = \alpha_1 \gamma_1 z_2$ with $\alpha_1, \alpha_2, \gamma_1, \gamma_2 \in (N \cup T)^*$, $A_1, A_2 \in N$, and $y_1, y_2, z_2 \in T^*$, if $(y_1)_{(1)} = (z_2)_{(1)}$ (including the case of $y_1 = z_2 = \varepsilon$), then $A_1 = A_2$, $\gamma_1 = \gamma_2$, and $y_2 = z_2$. The *language $L(G)$ generated* by such an $LR(1)$ grammar G is the set $\{w \mid S \Rightarrow^* w$ by $G\}$. In this paper, we deal only with $LR(1)$ grammars, and thus "language generation" is always understood in this sense. Notice that L is deterministic context-free (dcf) if and only if (iff) L is generated by a certain $LR(1)$ grammar [12].

2.2   Turns of Pushdown Automata

A *one-way deterministic pushdown automaton* (or a 1dpda, for short) M is formally a nonuple[4] $(Q, \Sigma, \{\triangleright, \triangleleft\}, \Gamma, \delta, q_0, \perp, Q_{acc}, Q_{rej})$, where Q is a finite set of inner states, Σ is an input alphabet, Γ is a stack alphabet, q_0 is the initial state in Q, $\perp$ is the bottom marker in Γ, Q_{acc} and Q_{rej} are respectively a set

---

[4] The use of endmarkers and a halting set pair (Q_{acc}, Q_{rej}) does not change the computational power of 1dpda's. In particular, the right endmarker helps a machine empty its stack at the end of its computation.

of accepting states in Q and that of rejecting states in Q with $Q_{acc} \cap Q_{rej} = \varnothing$, and a transition function δ maps $(Q - Q_{halt}) \times \check{\Sigma}_\varepsilon \times \Gamma$ to $\mathcal{P}(Q \times \Gamma^{\leq e})$ with $\check{\Sigma}_\varepsilon = \Sigma \cup \{\varepsilon, \triangleright, \triangleleft\}$, $Q_{halt} = Q_{acc} \cup Q_{rej}$, and $e \in \mathbb{N}^+$. The number e is called *push size*. The two symbols $\triangleright$ and $\triangleleft$ represent the left and the right endmarkers, respectively. For simplicity, this paper considers only 1dpda's that always terminate by entering appropriate halting states in Q_{halt} in the end of its computation. We further demand M to satisfy the following *deterministic requirement*: (i) $|\delta(p, \sigma, a)| \leq 1$ for all (q, σ, a) and (ii) if $\delta(q, \varepsilon, a) \neq \varnothing$, then $\delta(q, \sigma, a) = \varnothing$ for all $\sigma \in \check{\Sigma}$ ($= \Sigma \cup \{\triangleright, \triangleleft\}$). For convenience, we write $\delta(q, \sigma, a) = (p, w)$ in place of $\delta(q, \sigma, a) = \{(p, w)\}$. We assume that $\perp$ appears only at the bottom of the stack and it cannot be popped or replaced by any other symbol at any moment. We express the content of a stack (or a *stack content*) as $a_0 a_1 \cdots a_n$ with $a_n = \perp$, a topmost stack symbol a_0, and $a_i \in \Gamma^{(-)}$ for all $i \in [n]$, where $\Gamma^{(-)} = \Gamma - \{\perp\}$. For instance, assuming that M is scanning tape symbol σ in inner state q with stack content $a\gamma$, after M makes a transition of the form $\delta(q, \sigma, a) = (p, w)$, M's inner state becomes p and its stack content becomes $w\gamma$. The length of a stack content is called the *stack height*. Because $\perp$ is not removed, we conventionally say that the stack is *empty* if it contains only $\perp$.

To describe a computation of M, we introduce the notion of *configuration* of M as a triplet in $Q \times (\check{\Sigma})^* \times \Gamma^*$. A configuration (q, x, γ) indicates that M is in inner state q with stack content γ, scanning the leftmost symbol of x. Given two configurations (q, x, γ) and (p, y, ξ), we write $(q, x, \gamma) \vdash_M (p, y, \xi)$ if M changes (q, x, γ) to (p, y, ξ) in a single step. We use the notation $\vdash_M^*$ to denote the transitive closure of $\vdash_M$. A *computation* is a series of consecutive configurations starting at the initial configuration and ending at a certain halting configuration.

A string w is *accepted* (resp., *rejected*) by M if M starts with the input w, reads $\triangleright w \triangleleft$, eventually enters an inner state in Q_{acc} (resp., Q_{rej}), and halts. We say that M *recognizes* a language L if M accepts all strings in L and M rejects all strings in $\overline{L}$ ($= \Sigma^* - L$). For convenience, the notation $L(M)$ denotes the set of all strings accepted by M.

Since we are concerned with "turns" of 1dpda's, for clarity reason, we adopt the following convention: (i) a 1dpda always reads an entire input string as well as the right endmarker $\triangleleft$ and (ii) when $\triangleleft$ is read, if the stack still contains any non-$\perp$ symbol, then the 1dpda automatically pops all the non-$\perp$ symbols by a series of extra ε-moves and then enters an appropriate halting state. A "turn" roughly refers to a change of the behavior of the stack from non-decreasing to decreasing in volume. For later convenience, we define "turn" in the following fashion. On a given computation, a *stack history* refers to the series of stack contents produced at each step. Given a stack history $(\gamma_0, \gamma_1, \ldots, \gamma_n)$ produced on a computation, a *turn* is a contiguous subsequence $(\gamma_i, \gamma_{i+1}, \gamma_{i+2}, \ldots, \gamma_j, \gamma_{j+1})$ such that $|\gamma_i| < |\gamma_{i+1}| = |\gamma_{i+2}| = \cdots = |\gamma_j|$ and $|\gamma_j| > |\gamma_{j+1}|$. The moment j is referred to as a *turning point*. Recall that the stack must be empty after reading $\triangleleft$. Let us define $\tau_M(x)$ to be the number of turns made by M during the entire computation of M on input x. A 1dpda M *makes at most k turns* if, for any input $x \in \Sigma^*$, $\tau_M(x)$ is at most k. Such a machine is succinctly called a *k-turn 1dpda*.

A *finite-turn 1dpda* informally refers to any k-turn 1dpda for an appropriately chosen number $k \geq 0$, which is independent of inputs. Similarly to [13, Lemma 3], it is possible to start a new turn by first initializing inner states (to q_0). For convenience, we write ktDCFL to denote the family of all languages recognized by k-turn 1dpda's. In particular, a 1dpda is said to make a *deep turn* (or an empty-stack turn) if, before the start of each turn, it must empty the stack. We write deep-ktDCFL for the collection of all languages recognized by deep-k-turn 1dpda's for any $k \geq 1$. It follows by the definition that deep-1tDCFL = 1tDCFL. In a way similar to ktDCFL, we define ktCFL using the nondeterministic versions of k-turn 1dpda's (called *k-turn 1npda's*).

We can further consider the union of all ktDCFL for any number $k \geq 0$; for brevity, we denote this union by ωtDCFL. Similarly, we define deep-ωtDCFL to be $\bigcup_{k \in \mathbb{N}}$ deep-ktDCFL. It then follows that REG $\subseteq$ deep-ωtDCFL $\subseteq \omega$tDCFL $\subseteq$ DCFL, where REG is the set of all regular languages. Moreover, it follows that 0tDCFL = REG.

Example 1. *Let* $k \geq 1$. *The language* $T_k = \{a^{n_1}b^{n_1}a^{n_2}b^{n_2}\cdots a^{n_k}b^{n_k} \mid n_1, n_2, \ldots, n_k \in \mathbb{N}\}$ *belongs to* ktDCFL. *Moreover, the language* $L_k = \{c^n w d^n \mid n \geq 0, w \in T_k\}$ *is in* ktDCFL.

Since there is *no explicit reference* to class-separations concerning ktDCFL as well as deep-ktDCFL, we briefly state these class-separations, some of which are easily deducible from the past literature [8–10,14].

Lemma 2. *Let* k *be any number in* $\mathbb{N}^+$. *(1)* ktDCFL $\neq (k+1)$tDCFL. *(2)* deep-ktDCFL $\neq$ deep-$(k+1)$tDCFL. *(3)* deep-ktDCFL $\neq k$tDCFL. *(4)* ktDCFL $\neq k$tCFL. *(5)* ωtDCFL $\neq$ DCFL.

Proof. (1)–(2) Greibach [10, Lemma 3.2] demonstrated that the aforementioned language T_{k+1} is not in ktCFL. Since this language in fact belongs to deep-$(k+1)$tDCFL, we obtain the desired separations.

(3) Recall the language L_k from Example 1. Toward a contradiction, assume that $L_k \in$ deep-ktDCFL. For each input of the form $c^n w d^m$, an appropriately-chosen 1dpda M recognizing L_k must empty its stack before each turn. The information on n in c^n must be carried over to d^m using only inner states. When n is sufficiently large, that is impossible. Thus, M cannot make any deep turn.

(4) Consider the language $MPal_k = \{w_1 w_1^R \# w_2 w_2^R \# \cdots \# w_k w_k^R \mid w_1 w_2, \ldots, w_k \in \{0,1\}^*\}$ (multiple even-length palindromes), where x^R is the reverse of x. This $MPal_k$ belongs to ktCFL. However, even in the simple case of $k = 1$, $MPal_1$ is not in DCFL.

(5) Consider the language $L_\omega = \{a^{n_1}b^{n_1}\#a^{n_2}b^{n_2}\#\cdots\#a^{n_t}b^{n_t} \mid t \geq 1, n_1, n_2, \ldots, n_t \in \mathbb{N}\}$. Clearly, L_ω is in DCFL. It follows by Greibach [9] that L_ω cannot be in ktCFL for any $k \geq 1$; therefore, L_ω is outside of ωtDCFL. □

3   Grammar Characterizations

3.1   Useful Properties of ktDCFL and ωtDCFL

Before providing a new grammar for languages in the family ktDCFL, we state useful properties of ktDCFL for each $k \in \mathbb{N}^+$ as well as ωtDCFL. Those properties will be used in Sect. 3.3. By adapting a basic idea of [8], we use *one-way deterministic finite transducers* (or 1dft's, for short), which are one-way finite automata equipped with write-once output tapes. We here consider the following special type of 1dft's. On any input of the form ua, where $u = u_1 u_2 \cdots u_m$ with $u_i, a \in \Sigma$ and $u_i \neq a$, a 1dft M reads each symbol u_i from the input tape and writes a certain string v_i in Θ^* onto the output tape by applying M's transition function $\delta : (Q - Q_{fin}) \times \Sigma \to Q \times \Theta^*$, where Θ is an output alphabet and Q_{fin} is a set of final states. When M reads the last symbol a, it halts by writing symbol $b \in \Theta$ and then entering a certain final state. From M, we define the set that is composed of all ordered pairs (ua, bv) with $v = v_m v_{m-1} \cdots v_1$. We call this set *finite-state splitable*. As a quick example, the set $\{(c^n a, be^n) \mid n \geq 0\}$ is finite-state splitable. A language family $\mathcal{F}$ is said to be *closed under matching bilinear concatenation* if the following statement holds: for any two sets A and L, if $L \in \mathcal{F}$ and A is finite-state splitable, then the composite language $L[A] = \{uawbv \mid (ua, bv) \in A, awb \in L\}$ also belongs to $\mathcal{F}$. This property will be quite useful in proving Theorem 4.

Here, we intend to mention only the following closure properties.

Lemma 3. *Let $k \in \mathbb{N}^+$. The family ktDCFL is closed under all of the following operations: complementation, intersection with regular sets, inverse homomorphism, and matching bilinear concatenation.*

Proof Sketch. Let k denote any fixed constant in $\mathbb{N}^+$.

[matching bilinear concatenation] Take a finite-state splitable set A and a language L in ktDCFL. We consider $L[A]$. Take a 1dft M_A that witnesses "$(ua, bv) \in A$" and a 1dpda M_L that recognizes L. Let us consider the following 1dpda N. On input x of the form $uawbv$ with $u = u_1 \cdots u_n$ and $v = v_n \cdots v_1$, we first run M_A to generate v and store it into a stack until it reads a, writes b, and halts. We push a distinguished marker, say $\$$ into the stack. We then run M_L on awb. Note that M halts just after reading b. We then remove $\$$ and check whether v matches the stack content. This machine N recognizes $L[A]$ with at most k turns.   □

We remark that Lemma 3 also holds for deep-ktDCFL except for the matching bilinear concatenation.

3.2   LR(1)-Metalinear and LR(1)-Ultralinear Grammars

Ginsburg and Spanier [8] established a close connection between finite-turn 1npda's and ultralinear and metalinear grammars. A similar connection holds for finite-turn 1dpda's if we properly define a deterministic analogue of these grammars. We thus need to introduce the desired grammars.

Consider a context-free grammar $G = \langle N, T, P, S \rangle$. We say that G is $LR(1)$-*metalinear* if G is an $LR(1)$ grammar and all productions in P have the forms $S \rightarrow A_1 A_2 \cdots A_k$ with $A_i \in N^{(-)}$ and $A \rightarrow u$ with $k \in \mathbb{N}^+$, $A \in N^{(-)}$, and $u \in (T^* N^{(-)} T^*) \cup T^*$, where $N^{(-)} = N - \{S\}$. In particular, when $k = 1$, G is called $LR(1)$-*linear*. As a quick example, let us consider a grammar $G = \langle \{S, C, D\}, \{a, b\}, P, S \rangle$, where P consists of $S \rightarrow CD$, $C \rightarrow aCb$, $C \rightarrow \varepsilon$, $D \rightarrow Db$, and $D \rightarrow b$. This grammar G is $LR(1)$-metalinear.

It is important to note that the language $L_{OR,2} = \{a^n b^m a^p b^q \mid n, m, p, q \in \mathbb{N}^+, n = m \vee p = q\}$, for instance, is generated by both an $LR(1)$ grammar and a linear grammar but $L_{OR,2}$ requires at least two turns on any 1dpda [1, Section 6.1.1]. We thus conclude that no $LR(1)$-linear grammar generates this language because, otherwise, there exists a 1-turn 1dpda for $L_{OR,2}$, a contradiction.

A context-free grammar G is said to be $LR(1)$-*ultralinear* if G is an $LR(1)$ grammar and N is a finite union of disjoint (possibly empty) sets $N_0, N_1, \ldots, N_d$ such that, for any index $i \in [0, d]_{\mathbb{Z}}$ and any symbol $A \in N_i$, each production with A in its left-hand side has the form $A \rightarrow u$ for a certain string $u \in (T \cup N_0 \cup \cdots \cup N_{i-1})^* \cup (T^* N_i T^*)$, where we may assume that $S \in N_d$. The *level* of A is the index i satisfying $A \in N_i$ and we succinctly express this situation as $level(A) = i$. Clearly, $LR(1)$-metalinear grammars are $LR(1)$-ultralinear. Notice that there are $LR(1)$ grammars that are not $LR(1)$-ultralinear. For example, consider the grammar[5] whose productions are $S \rightarrow \varepsilon | aAbS | bBaS$, $A \rightarrow \varepsilon | aAbA$, and $B \rightarrow \varepsilon | bBaB$. This is an $LR(1)$ grammar but not $LR(1)$-ultralinear.

Recall from Sect. 2.1 that all grammars in this paper are assumed to contain no useless symbol.

Ginsburg and Spanier [8] proved that ωtCFL and deep-ωtCFL precisely contain all ultralinear languages and all metalinear languages, respectively. The following theorem is a deterministic analogue of the result of [8, Theorem 3.2] (see also [13, Theorem 1]). We remark that the characterization of dcf languages by $LR(1)$ grammars [12] does not instantly imply the theorem.

Theorem 4. *Let L be any language.*

1. *L is in ωtDCFL iff L is $LR(1)$-ultralinear.*
2. *L is in deep-ωtDCFL iff L is $LR(1)$-metalinear.*

3.3   Proof of Theorem 4

The purpose of this subsection is to prove Theorem 4. In the proof of [11, Theorem 12.8], it was shown that any $LR(k)$ grammar can be simulated by appropriate 1dpda's. This simulation, however, repeats a linear number of pushes and pops, and thus those 1dpda's are not finite-turn 1dpda's. We thus need to develop

---

[5] This grammar is also categorized to an expansive grammar (see, e.g., [1]).

a different technique for our purpose. As a preparation to the proof of the theorem, we show the following key lemma concerning $LR(1)$-linear grammars. This is a basis to the proof of Theorem 4.

Lemma 5. *Consider an $LR(1)$-linear grammar $G = \langle N, T, P, S \rangle$. Assume that P consists only of productions of the forms (i) $S \to C$ for $C \in N^{(-)}$, (ii) $A \to w$ for $A \in N^{(-)}$ and $w \in T^*$, and (iii) $A \to uCv$ for $A, C \in N^{(-)}$ and $u, v \in T^*$. There exists a 1-turn 1dpda M that recognizes $L(G)$.*

Proof. It is easy to see by the premise of the lemma that all strings x generated by G have the form $u_1 u_2 \cdots u_m w v_m \cdots v_2 v_1$ with $u_i, v_i, x \in T^*$ for any $i \in [m]$ by a derivation of the form (*) $S \Rightarrow C_0 \Rightarrow^* u_1 C_1 v_1 \Rightarrow u_1 u_2 C_2 v_2 v_1 \Rightarrow^* u_1 u_2 \cdots u_m C_m v_m \cdots v_2 v_1 \Rightarrow u_1 u_2 \cdots u_m w v_m \cdots v_2 v_1$.

It is possible to prove that the derivation (*) stated above is unique. This fact can be proven by induction on $i \in [0, m]_{\mathbb{Z}}$ that the ith derivation $u_1 \cdots u_i C_i v_i \cdots v_1 \Rightarrow u_1 \cdots u_i u_{i+1} C_{i+1} v_{i+1} v_i \cdots v_1$ is uniquely determined, provided that $C_{m+1} = w$. The proof follows from the definition of the $LR(1)$ grammar. Here, we omit the details of this proof.

In what follows, we construct a 1-turn 1dpda, say, M to accept all inputs x of the form $u_1 \cdots u_m w v_m \cdots v_1$. The desired 1dpda M is designed to simulate any derivation of G and accept such an x.

Let d denote the length of the longest string $\alpha \in T^* \cup (T^* N^{(-)} T^*)$ that appears in a production of the form $A \to \alpha$ for any symbol $A \in N^{(-)}$. We define $\Sigma = T$ and $\Gamma = (N \cup T)^{\leq d}$ for M. Let $t = |P|$ and assume that all productions are indexed by numbers in $[t]$. We begin with reading $\triangleright$ on an input tape and $\perp$ in a stack. We define B_i to denote a symbol C in $N^{(-)}$ corresponding to the ith production of the form $S \to C$ in (i) if any, and we set B_i to be $-$ (undefined) otherwise. We push a symbol $[B_1, B_2, \ldots, B_t]$ into the stack and move the tape head to the right.

(1) Assume that the stack contains $[B_1, B_2, \ldots, B_t]$, where B_i is of the form either $C_i u_i$ with $C_i \in N^{(-)}$ and $u_i \in T^{\leq d}$ or $-$ (undefined). Assume also that the tape head is rested on a cell that contains an input symbol σ.

(a) Assume that there exist three numbers $i, j, l \in [t]$ for which the ith production has the form $C_j \to u_j C_l v_j$ in (ii) for a certain string $v_j \in T^*$ and a symbol $C_l \in N^{(-)}$. We define $B_i' = v_j$ and $D_i = C_l$. If this is not he case, we set $B_i' = -$ and $D_i = B_i$. By making an ε-move, we replace $[B_1, \ldots, B_t]$ in the stack by two symbols of the form $[B_1', \ldots, B_t'][D_1, \ldots, D_t]$.

(b) Assume that there exist three numbers $i, j, l \in [t]$ for which the ith production has the form $C_j \to w_l$ in (iii) for a certain string $w_l \in T^*$. In this case, if B_j is of the from $C_j w_l$, then we pop $[B_1, B_2, \ldots, B_t]$ by making an ε-move. Otherwise, we reject. Go to Case (3).

(2) If Case (1) is not applicable, then we read an input symbol σ and replace $[B_1, \ldots, B_t]$ by $[B_1', \ldots, B_t']$, where $B_i' = -$ if B_i is not defined, and $B_i' = B_i \sigma$ otherwise. We then go back to Case (1).

(3) Assume that the stack contains $[B_1, B_2, \ldots, B_t]$, where B_i is of the form either $v_i \in T^{\leq d}$ or $-$ (undefined). Assume that the tape head scans an input symbol

σ. If v_i is of the form $\sigma v_i'$ for a nonempty string v_i', then we define $B_i' = v_i'$. We then replace $[B_1, B_2, \ldots, B_t]$ by $[B_1', B_2', \ldots, B_t']$. If $v_i = \sigma$, then we pop $[B_1, B_2, \ldots, B_t]$. Repeat Case (3) until we reach $\perp$.

If there is any procedural error during the above process, then we immediately reject. We remark that the stack height of M does not alter during the simulation of G except for the first and the last steps of M. This whole procedure is thus carried out with only one turn. Moreover, the uniqueness of the derivation (*) ensures that M is deterministic.   □

We return to Theorem 4 and present its proof below. We here prove only Theorem 4(1) and leave the proof of Theorem 4(2) to the avid reader. The closure property of ktDCFL under matching bilinear concatenation in Lemma 3 is partly necessary to prove the theorem.

As discussed in the literature (e.g., [20]), it is possible to assume that the push size e equals 2. We further consider an ε-extension of M and x, as in [21,22], which is a string obtained by supplementing a number of ε's as a new input symbol. We take an *extended 1dpda* M_ε taking an *ε-extended input string* $\hat{x}$ satisfying that M accepts (resp., rejects) x iff M_ε accepts (resp., rejects) $\hat{x}$.

Proof of Theorem 4(1). (If–part) Let $G = \langle N, T, P, S \rangle$ denote any $LR(1)$-ultralinear grammar with $N = \bigcup_{j \in [0,d]_\mathbb{Z}} N_j$ for a fixed constant $d \in \mathbb{N}$. For each index $i \in [0, d]_\mathbb{Z}$, we set $\tilde{N}_{(i)}$ to be $\bigcup_{j \in [0,i]_\mathbb{Z}} N_j$. Given a series of symbols $X \in (N \cup T)^*$ and a symbol $a \in T \cup \{\lhd\}$, we define $L_{X,a}$ to be the language $\{w \in T^* \mid Xa \Rightarrow_{rt}^* wa\}$. We first claim the following.

Claim 6. *For any index $i \in [0, d]_\mathbb{Z}$, for any symbol $X \in \tilde{N}_{(i)}$, and for any symbol $a \in T \cup \{\lhd\}$, $L_{X,a}$ is in ωtDCFL.*

Since $S \in N$ and $L_{S,\lhd} = L(G)$, Claim 6 concludes that $L(G)$ is in ωtDCFL.

Proof of Claim 6. Let us prove by induction on $i \in [0, d]_\mathbb{Z}$ that, for any $X \in \tilde{N}_{(i)}$ and any $a \in T \cup \{\lhd\}$, $L_{X,a} \in \omega$tDCFL. Firstly, we consider the basis case of $i = 0$. Fix a symbol $A \in \tilde{N}_{(0)}$ and a symbol $a \in T \cup \{\lhd\}$ arbitrarily. Notice that $\tilde{N}_{(0)} = N_0$ by definition. Consider a new $LR(1)$-linear grammar $\langle N_0, T, P_0, S_A \rangle$ whose P_0 consists of all productions of the forms $B \to w$ and $B \to uCv$ in P with $B, C \in N_0$ and $u, v, w \in T^*$ together with a new production $S_A \to A$. Note that $S_A a \Rightarrow_{rt}^* wa$ in this grammar is equivalent to $Aa \Rightarrow_{rt}^* wa$ in the original grammar. By Lemma 5, $L_{A,a}$ is in 1tDCFL and thus in ωtDCFL.

Let $i \geq 1$ and assume by induction hypothesis that $L_{X,a}$ is in ωtDCFL for every $X \in \tilde{N}_{(i-1)}$ and every $a \in T \cup \{\lhd\}$. Fix $A \in N_i$ and $a \in T \cup \{\lhd\}$ arbitrarily and focus on $L_{A,a}$. Our goal is to verify that $L_{A,a} \in \omega$tDCFL. Since $i \geq 1$, there may be productions of the forms (i) $A \to uCv$ and (ii) $A \to u_1 B_1 u_2 \cdots u_m B_m u_{m+1}$ in P for $C \in N_i$, $B_1, \ldots, B_m \in \tilde{N}_{(i-1)}$, and $u, v, u_1, \ldots, u_m \in T^*$.

We look into the case where (i) occurs and define a new $LR(1)$-linear grammar. We consider a chain of productions of the form: $A \to u_1 C_1 v_1$,

$C_i \rightarrow u_{i+1}C_{i+1}v_{i+1}$ for any $i \in [t-1]$, and $C_t \rightarrow u'_1 B_1 u'_2 \cdots u'_m B_m u'_{m+1}$ with $B_1, \ldots, B_m \in \tilde{N}_{(i-1)}$, where $t \geq 1$. We replace such a chain by $A \rightarrow u_1 u_2 \cdots u_t D v_t \cdots v_2 v_1$, where $D = u'_1 B_1 u'_2 \cdots u'_m B_m u'_{m+1}$. This case is then treated as (ii).

Next, assuming that (i) does not occur, we focus on (ii). For each of the productions of the form in (ii), we prepare a new terminal symbol, say, Y not in T and substitute Y for $u_1 B_1 u_2 \cdots u_m B_m u_{m+1}$. Let $T^{(ext)}$ denote the extension of T by adding all those new terminal symbols Y. Consider a new $LR(1)$-linear grammar $\langle N_i, T^{(ext)}, P_i, S_A \rangle$ whose P_i is composed of all productions of the forms $S_A \rightarrow A$, $B \rightarrow Y$, $B \rightarrow w$ in P with $w \in T^*$, and $B \rightarrow uCv$ in P with $C \in N_i$ and $u, v \in T^*$, provided that $B \in N_i$. For each Y, any string including Y generated by this grammar must have the form $\bar{u}_1 \cdots \bar{u}_m Y \bar{v}_m \cdots \bar{v}_1$ for $\bar{u}_j, \bar{v}_j \in T^*$ with $j \in [m]$ because of (ii). Associated with these strings, D denotes the collection of the form $(\bar{u}_1 \cdots \bar{u}_m a, b \bar{v}_m \cdots \bar{v}_1)$. By Lemma 5, the language generated by this grammar is in 1tDCFL, and thus the set D is finite-state splittable. Consider all productions of the form $B \rightarrow u_1 B_1 u_2 \cdots u_m B_m u_{m+1}$ with $B \in N_i$ and take the union of all $u_1 L_{B_1, a_1} u_2 \cdots u_m L_{B_m, a_m} u_{m+1}$, where each a_i is the first symbol of u_{i+1}. This union coincides with $L_{A,a}$. By the closure properties of ωtDCFL under matching bilinear concatenation, noted in Lemma 3, L_{B_j, a_j} is in ωtDCFL for all $j \in [m]$. This implies that $L_{A,a}$ belongs to ωtDCFL. Therefore, by induction, the claim is true.   □

(Only If–part) Let L denote any language in ktDCFL. For simplicity, we assume that either $k = 1$ or $L \notin (k-1)$tDCFL. Let $M = (Q, \Sigma, \{\rhd, \lhd\}, \Gamma, \delta, q_0, \bot, Q_{acc}, Q_{rej})$ denote a k-turn 1dpda that recognizes L. The use of endmarkers makes it possible to assume that $Q_{acc} = \{q_{acc}\}$ and $Q_{rej} = \{q_{rej}\}$ and that M empties its stack by making a consecutive series of ε-moves after reading $\lhd$. As noted in Sect. 2.2, the push size of M can be set to be 2. We partition Q into $Q_1, Q_2, \ldots, Q_k$ with $q_0 \in Q_1$ so that a nondecreasing move changes inner states in Q_i to those in Q_i and a decreasing move changes inner states in Q_i to those in Q_{i+1}.

Hereafter, we intend to describe how to construct the desired grammar. We first define $T = \check{\Sigma}_\varepsilon$ and $N = Q \times \Gamma \times Q \cup \{S\}$. We express each element of $N^{(-)}$ as $[q, A, r]$, where $q, r \in Q$ and $A \in \Gamma$. We then translate each transition of M_ε into a series of production rules as follows. Initially, we introduce $S \rightarrow [q_0, \bot, r]$ for any $r \in Q$. Let $N_k = \{S, [q_0, \bot, r] \mid r \in Q\}$. If $\delta(q, \sigma, A) = (p, B)$ with $A, B \in \Gamma$ and $p, q \in Q_i$, then we define $[q, A, r] \rightarrow \sigma[p, B, r]$ for any $r \in Q_n$ with $n \geq i$. If $[q, A, r] \in N_i$, then $[p, B, r] \in N_i$. If $\delta(q, \sigma, A) = (p, BC)$ with $A, B, C \in \Gamma$, and $p, q \in Q_i$, then we define $[q, A, r] \rightarrow \sigma[p, C, s][s, B, r]$ for any $r \in Q_n$ and $s \in Q_m$ with $n > m > i$. If $[q, A, r] \in N_i$, then $[p, C, s], [s, B, r] \in N_{i-1}$. If $\delta(q, \sigma, A) = (p, \varepsilon)$ with $q \in Q_i$ and $p \in Q_{i+1}$, then we introduce $[q, A, p] \rightarrow \sigma$. Those productions with T and N form a grammar, which we call by G.

Claim 7. *For any $p, q \in Q$, $A \in \Gamma$, and $x \in \Sigma^* \cup \rhd\Sigma^* \cup \Sigma^*\lhd \cup \rhd\Sigma^*\lhd$, $[q, A, p] \Rightarrow^*_{lt} \hat{x}$ iff $(q, \hat{x}, A\gamma) \vdash^*_{M_\varepsilon} (p, \varepsilon, \gamma)$ for any stack content $\gamma \in (\Gamma^{(-)})^*\bot \cup (\Gamma^{(-)})^*$, where $\hat{x}$ is an ε-extension of x and $\Rightarrow_{lt}$ is the leftmost derivation.*

Proof. Let $\hat{x} = x_1 x_2 \cdots x_n$ and, for any $i, j \in [n]$ with $i < j$, let $\hat{x}_{[i:j]}$ denote $x_i x_{i+1} \cdots x_j$. Notice that $\hat{x}_{[1:n]}$ coincides with $\hat{x}$.

(If–part) The proof proceeds by induction on the number of steps of M_ε. Assume that $(q, \hat{x}, A\gamma) \vdash_{M_\varepsilon} (q_1, \hat{x}_{[2:n]}, \alpha_1 \gamma) \vdash_{M_\varepsilon} (q_2, \hat{x}_{[3:n]}, \alpha_2 \gamma) \vdash_{M_\varepsilon} \cdots \vdash_{M_\varepsilon}$ $(q_n, \varepsilon, \alpha_n \gamma)$. When $n = 1$, since $\hat{x} \in \check{\Sigma}_\varepsilon \ (= \Sigma \cup \{\varepsilon, \triangleright, \triangleleft\})$, M_ε applies a transition $\delta(q, \hat{x}, A) = (p, \varepsilon)$ to obtain $(q, \hat{x}, A\gamma) \vdash_{M_\varepsilon}^* (p, \varepsilon, \gamma)$. By the definition of G, it must contain a production of the form $[q, A, p] \to \hat{x}$. Thus, we obtain $[q, A, p] \Rightarrow_{lt}^* \hat{x}$.

Next, we consider the case of $n \geq 2$ and assume that $(q, \hat{x}, A\gamma) \vdash_{M_\varepsilon}$ $(q_1, \hat{x}_{[2:n]}, \xi\gamma) \vdash_{M_\varepsilon}^* (p, \varepsilon, \gamma)$ for an appropriate string $\xi \in \Gamma \cup \Gamma^2$. (a) If $\xi = B \in \Gamma$, then $(q_1, \hat{x}_{[2:n]}, B\gamma) \vdash_{M_\varepsilon}^* (p, \varepsilon, \gamma)$ implies $[q_1, B, p] \Rightarrow_{lt}^* \hat{x}_{[2:n]}$ by induction hypothesis. Since δ has the transition $\delta(q, x_1, A) = (q_1, B)$, G must contain a production of the form $[q, A, p] \to x_1 [q_1, B, p]$. Thus, we obtain $[q, A, p] \Rightarrow_{lt}^* x_1 \hat{x}_{[2:n]} = \hat{x}$. (b) Similarly, if $\xi = BC \in \Gamma^2$, then we obtain $(q_1, \hat{x}_{[2:n]}, BC\gamma) \vdash_{M_\varepsilon}^* (p, \varepsilon, \gamma)$. Choose $q_2, q_3 \in Q$ such that $(q_1, x_2, B\gamma) \vdash_{M_\varepsilon}^* (q_2, \varepsilon, \gamma)$ and $(q_2, \hat{x}_{[3:n]}, C\gamma) \vdash_{M_\varepsilon}^* (p, \varepsilon, \gamma)$. By induction hypothesis, we obtain $[q_1, B, q_2] \Rightarrow_{lt}^* x_2$ and $[q_2, C, p] \Rightarrow_{lt}^* \hat{x}_{[3:n]}$. From $\delta(q, x_1, A) = (q_1, BC)$, G contains $[q, A, p] \to x_1 [q_1, B, q_2][q_2, C, p]$. This implies that $[q, A, p] \Rightarrow_{lt}^* x_1 x_2 \hat{x}_{[3:n]} = \hat{x}$.

(Only if–part) We prove this direction by induction on the length n of a derivation of G. If $n = 1$, then $\hat{x} \in \check{\Sigma}_\varepsilon$, and thus $[q, A, p] \Rightarrow_{lt}^* \hat{x}$ implies that G has the production $[q, A, p] \to \hat{x}$. This means that M makes a transition of the form $\delta(q, \hat{x}, A) = (p, \varepsilon)$, resulting in $(q, \hat{x}, A\gamma) \vdash_{M_\varepsilon}^* (p, \varepsilon, \gamma)$. Consider the other case of $n \geq 2$. Assume that $[q, A, p] \Rightarrow_{lt} x_1 [q_1, B, p] \Rightarrow_{lt}^* x_1 \hat{x}_{[2:n]}$ occurs for certain $q_1 \in Q$ and $B \in \Gamma$. Since $[q_1, B, p] \Rightarrow_{lt}^* \hat{x}_{[2:n]}$, by induction hypothesis, we obtain $(q_1, \hat{x}_{[2:n]}, B\gamma) \vdash_{M_\varepsilon}^* (p, \varepsilon, \gamma)$. From $[q, A, p] \Rightarrow_{lt} x_1 [q_1, B, p]$, G has the production $[q, A, p] \to x_1 [q_1, B, p]$. Thus, M_ε must apply $\delta(q, x_1, A) = (q_1, B)$ and we obtain $(q, x_1, A\gamma) \vdash_{M_\varepsilon} (q_1, \varepsilon, B\gamma)$. Therefore, $(q, \hat{x}, A\gamma) \vdash_{M_\varepsilon}^* (p, \varepsilon, \gamma)$ follows.

Next, we assume that $[q, A, p] \Rightarrow_{lt} x_1 [q_1, B, q_2][q_2, C, p]$, $[q_1, B, q_2] \Rightarrow_{lt}^* \hat{x}_{[2:m]}$, and $[q_2, C, p] \Rightarrow_{lt}^* \hat{x}_{[m:n]}$ for a certain number $m \in [3, n-1]_{\mathbb{Z}}$. Since G has $[q, A, p] \to x_1 [q_1, B, q_2][q_2, C, p]$, M_ε has $\delta(q, x_1, A) = (q_1, BC)$. By induction hypothesis, we obtain $(q_1, \hat{x}_{[2:m]}, B\gamma) \vdash_{M_\varepsilon}^* (q_2, \varepsilon, \gamma)$ and $(q_2, \hat{x}_{[m:n]}, C\gamma') \vdash_{M_\varepsilon}^* (p, \varepsilon, \gamma')$. By combining them, we conclude that $(q, \hat{x}, A\gamma) \vdash_{M_\varepsilon} (q_1, \hat{x}_{[2:n]}, BC\gamma) \vdash_{M_\varepsilon}^* (q_2, \hat{x}_{[m:n]}, C\gamma) \vdash_{M_\varepsilon}^* (p, \varepsilon, \gamma)$.   □

From Claim 7, it instantly follows that, for any x, $[q_0, \bot, q_{acc}] \Rightarrow_{lt}^* \triangleright x \triangleleft$ iff $(q_0, \triangleright x \triangleleft, \bot) \vdash_{M_\varepsilon}^* (q_{acc}, \varepsilon, \bot)$. This equivalence implies that $x \in L(G)$ iff $x \in L(M)$. Since x is arbitrary, we conclude that G generates $L(M)$.

It is obvious that G is ultralinear by its definition. The remaining claim is the $LR(1)$ property of G.

Claim 8. *The grammar G is an $LR(1)$ grammar.*

Proof. Assume that (i) $S \Rightarrow_{rt}^* \alpha_1 A_1 y_1 \Rightarrow_{rt} \alpha_1 \gamma_1 y_1$ and (ii) $S \Rightarrow_{rt}^* \alpha_2 A_2 y_2 \Rightarrow_{rt}$ $\alpha_2 \gamma_2 y_2 = \alpha_1 \gamma_1 z_2$ with $(y_1)_{(1)} = (z_2)_{(1)}$. Our goal is to show that $A_1 = A_2$, $\gamma_1 = \gamma_2$, and $y_2 = z_2$. Consider the case $|\alpha_1 \gamma_1| \geq |\alpha_2 \gamma_2|$. The other case of $|\alpha_1 \gamma_1| < |\alpha_2 \gamma_2|$ can be proven in a symmetric way. Since $\alpha_2 \gamma_2 y_2 = \alpha_1 \gamma_1 z_2$, we choose s to satisfy $\alpha_1 \gamma_1 = \alpha_2 \gamma_2 s$ and $y_2 = s z_2$. We further take strings x_1 and

w_1 in T^* for which $\alpha_1 \Rightarrow^*_{rt} x_1$ and $\gamma_1 \Rightarrow^*_{rt} w_1$ hold. We then obtain the derivation $S \Rightarrow^*_{rt} \alpha_1 A_1 y_1 \Rightarrow_{rt} \alpha_1 \gamma_1 y_1 \Rightarrow^*_{rt} x_1 w_1 y_1$.

Let us consider the leftmost derivation of the form (a) $S \Rightarrow^*_{lt} x_1 A_1 \eta_1 \Rightarrow_{lt} x_1 \gamma_1 \eta_1 \Rightarrow^*_{lt} x_1 w_1 \eta_1 \Rightarrow^*_{lt} x_1 w_1 y_1$, where η_1 in N satisfies $\eta_1 \Rightarrow^*_{lt} y_1$. Similarly, we choose x_2 and w_2 so that $\alpha_2 \Rightarrow^*_{lt} x_2$ and $\gamma_2 \Rightarrow^*_{lt} w_2$. Since $y_2 = sz_2$, we thus obtain (b) $S \Rightarrow^*_{rt} \alpha_2 A_2 y_2 = \alpha_2 A_2 sz_2 \Rightarrow_{rt} \alpha_2 \gamma_2 sz_2 \Rightarrow^*_{lt} x_2 w_2 sz_2 = x_1 w_1 y_1$. This can be rewritten using the leftmost derivation as (c) $S \Rightarrow^*_{lt} x_2 w_2 s\eta_2 = x_1 w_1 \eta_2 \Rightarrow^*_{lt} x_1 w_1 z_2$, where η_2 in N satisfies $\eta_2 \Rightarrow^*_{lt} z_2$. By the definition of G from M, (a) and (c) together imply that, after reading $x_1 w_1$, M must make the same behavior, producing the same symbol, and thus $\eta_1 = \eta_2$ holds. This implies that $y_1 = z_2$ and $y_2 = sy_1$. Since $\eta_1 = \eta_2$, (c) implies the derivation (d) $S \Rightarrow^*_{lt} x_2 w_2 s\eta_2 = x_2 w_2 s\eta_1 \Rightarrow^*_{lt} x_2 w_2 sy_1 = x_1 w_1 y_1$. Note that (a) and (d) must have the same derivation tree. From (b) follows the derivation (e) $S \Rightarrow^*_{rt} \alpha_2 A_2 sz_2 = \alpha_2 A_2 sy_1 \Rightarrow_{rt} \alpha_2 \gamma_2 sy_1 = \alpha_1 \gamma_1 y_1$. Compare (e) with (i). They must form the same derivation tree, and thus we conclude that $\alpha_1 = \alpha_2$, $A_1 = A_2$, $\gamma_1 = \gamma_2$, $s = \varepsilon$, and $y_2 = z_2$.   □

The above claim then implies that G is $LR(1)$-ultralinear. Therefore, we complete the first part of the theorem.   □

4   An Immediate Application of the Grammar Characterizations

Let us discuss an immediate application of the grammar characterizations of ωtDCFL and deep-ωtDCFL presented in Sect. 3.2. Here, we are particularly concerned with a "structural property," known as pumping lemmas or iteration theorems. In the past literature, numerous pumping lemmas for (subclasses of) DCFL have been proposed. Note that these pumping lemmas are highlighted in terms of "iterative pairs" [2].

As for ωtCFL, however, Magalini and Pighizzini already discussed a pumping lemma [15, Theorem 3]. We wish to distance ourselves from theirs and to focus solely on a "deterministic" nature of ωtDCFL.

We fix a language L. A quintuple $\tau = (x, y, z, u, v)$ of strings is said to *build* the string $xyzuv$ and, conversely, $xyzuv$ is said to be *factorized* into (x, y, z, u, v). This quintuple τ is called an *iterative pair* of L if $|yu| \geq 1$ and $xy^n zu^n v \in L$ holds for all $n \in \mathbb{N}$. In a vein similar to a "standard" pumping lemma (see, e.g., [11]), Yu [24] proved the following lemma.

Lemma 9 (Deterministic Pumping Lemma, [24]). *Let L be any infinite non-regular language in DCFL over an alphabet Σ. There exist two constants $k \in \mathbb{N}^+$ and $c > 0$ that satisfies the following condition. For any strings xy and xz, either there exists a factorization $(x_1, x_2, x_3, x_4, x_5)$ of x with $|x_2 x_3 x_4| \leq c$ that is also an iterative pair of L or there exist three factorizations $x = x_1 x_2 x_3$, $y = y_1 y_2 y_3$, and $z = z_1 z_2 z_3$ with $|x_2 x_3| \leq c$ such that $(x_1, x_2, x_3 y_1, y_2, y_3)$ and $(x_1, x_2, x_3 z_1, z_2, z_3)$ are both iterative pairs of L.*

For infinite languages in ωtDCFL $-$ REG, we propose a new pumping lemma.

Lemma 10 (Finite-Turn Pumping Lemma). *Let L be any infinite non-regular language in ωtDCFL over an alphabet Σ. There exist two constants $k \in \mathbb{N}^+$ and $c > 0$ that satisfy the following condition. For any number $l \geq 1$ and any string $w = w_1 w_2 \cdots w_l$ with $w_j = x_{j1}x_{j2}x_{j3}x_{j4}x_{j5}$ satisfying $|x_{j2}x_{j4}| \geq 1$ and $|x_{j2}x_{j3}x_{j4}| \leq c$ for each $i \in [l]$, if $w_1^{(i_1)} w_2^{(i_2)} \cdots w_l^{(i_l)} \in L$ for any $i_1, i_2, \ldots, i_l \in \mathbb{N}$, then $l \leq k$, where $w_j^{(i)} = x_{j1}x_{j2}^i x_{j3}x_{j4}^i x_{j5}$.*

Given a string w, we consider its rightmost derivation tree, say, H_w, which is generated by applying only rightmost derivations of G. For any subtree F of H_w generating a substring of w, F is said to contain a *repetitive subgraph* if there exist a path of F from its root to a leaf (of H_w) and a non-terminal symbol B such that B appears at least twice on this path.

Proof of Lemma 10. Given an infinite language L in ωtDCFL $-$ REG, let us consider an $LR(1)$-ultralinear grammar $G = \langle N, T, P, S \rangle$ that generates L. Let h denote the maximum length of the right-hand side of any production in P. We set $c = h2^{|N|+|T|}$.

We choose the maximum number k that satisfies the condition: for any $w \in \Sigma^*$, there is a factorization $w = w_1 w_2 \cdots w_k$ such that, for any index $j \in [k]$, a subtree of H_w generating w_j has a repetitive subgraph.

Let $l \geq 1$. Consider any string $w = w_1 w_2 \cdots w_l$ whose substrings w_j have the forms $x_{j1}x_{j2}x_{j3}x_{j4}x_{j5}$ with $|x_{j2}x_{j4}| \geq 1$ and $|x_{j2}x_{j3}x_{j4}| \leq c$ for every index $j \in [l]$. Assume that $w_1^{(i_1)} w_2^{(i_2)} \cdots w_l^{(i_l)} \in L$ for any $i_1, i_2, \ldots, i_l \in \mathbb{N}$, where $w_j^{(i)} = x_{j1}x_{j2}^i x_{j3}x_{j4}^i x_{j5}$. We further assume that l is maximal. We wish to assert that $l \leq k$. Toward a contradiction, we assume that $l \geq k+1$. We claim that, for each index $j \in [l]$, a subtree F of H_w generating w_j has a repetitive subgraph. The proof of this claim proceeds by induction on $j \in [l]$. We begin with the basis case of $j = l$. Let us focus on a unique subtree F of H_w that generates w_l. This subtree F is a derivation tree in which there is non-terminal symbol C satisfying $S \Rightarrow_{rt}^* \alpha C v$. Since $(x_{l1}, x_{l2}, x_{l3}, x_{l4}, x_{l5})$ is an iterative pair of L, by following the argument of the proof of [24, Lemma 1], there is a non-terminal symbol B such that, along an appropriate path from the root of F to its leaf, B appears at least twice. In short, F contains a repetitive subgraph. Because of the maximality of l, no prefix and no suffix of w_l can be factorized into any iterative pair.

For an induction step $j < l$, we consider the string $w_1 w_2 \cdots w_j$ and a subtree of H that generates $w_1 w_2 \cdots w_j$. We set this subtree as "new" H and follow an argument similar to the previous case of $j = l$. This shows the existence of a path that contains a repetitive subpath.

Overall, we conclude that there are l subtrees, each of which contains a repetitive subgraph. However, since $l \geq k+1$, this clearly contradicts the choice of k.   □

In what follows, we show how to apply Lemma 10. For this purpose, we first generalize $L_{OR,2}$ to $L_{OR,\omega}$ by setting $L_{OR,\omega}$ to be $\{a^{n_1}b^{m_1}a^{n_2}b^{m_2} \cdots a^{n_{k+1}}b^{m_{k+1}} \mid k \geq 1, n_1, n_2, \ldots, n_{k+1}, m_1, m_2, \ldots, m_{k+1} \geq 0, \exists i \in [k+1](n_i = m_i)\}$.

Lemma 11. $L_{OR,\omega} \notin \omega\text{tDCFL}$. *Thus,* $\text{DCFL} \cap 1\text{tCFL} \not\subseteq \omega\text{tDCFL}$.

Proof. We then intend to prove that (1) $L_{OR,\omega} \notin \omega\text{tDCFL}$ and, for the second assertion of the lemma, (2) $L_{OR,\omega} \in \text{DCFL} \cap 1\text{tCFL}$.

We begin with showing (1). Toward a contradiction, we assume that $L_{OR,\omega} \in \omega\text{tDCFL}$. We take two constants $k \in \mathbb{N}^+$ and $c > 0$ that satisfy Lemma 10. Choose prime numbers $p_1, p_2, \ldots, p_{k+1}$ with $c < p_1 < p_2 < \cdots < p_{k+1}$. Let $l = k+1$. Let us consider the string of the form $w = w_1 w_2 \cdots w_l$ with $w_j = a^{p_j} b^{p_j}$ for any index $j \in [l]$. We factorize each substring w_j into $(x_{j1}, x_{j2}, x_{j3}, x_{j4}, x_{j5})$ with $x_{j1} = a^{p_j - 1}$, $x_{j2} = a$, $x_{j3} = \varepsilon$, $x_{j4} = b$, and $x_{j5} = b^{p_j - 1}$. For each $i \in \mathbb{N}$, we write $w_j^{(i)}$ for the string $x_{j1} x_{j2}^i x_{j3} x_{j4}^i x_{j5}$. It immediately follows that $w_1^{(i_1)} w_2^{(i_2)} \cdots w_l^{(i_l)} \in L$ by the definition. Lemma 10 then implies $l \leq k$. Since $l = k + 1$, this leads to the desired contradiction.

As for (2), let us consider the following 1-turn 1npda N. On input w of the form $a^{n_1} b^{m_1} a^{n_2} b^{m_2} \cdots a^{n_{k+1}} b^{m_{k+1}}$, we guess (i.e., nondeterministically choose) an index $i \in [k + 1]$, skip $a^{n_1} b^{m_1} a^{n_2} b^{m_2} \cdots a^{n_{i-1}} b^{m_{i-1}}$, check if $n_i = m_i$ using a stack properly, and accept w whenever $n_i = m_i$. Note that N makes only one turn. Moreover, we modify N as follows. Instead of guessing i, we sequentially check whether at least one of the equalities $n_1 = m_1, n_2 = m_2, \ldots, n_{k+1} = m_{k+1}$ holds. If such an equation indeed exists, then we accept w; otherwise, we reject it. Clearly, we can perform this procedure deterministically.   □

5   A Short Discussion and Challenging Open Questions

Turn-bounded context-free languages were first discussed by Ginsburg and Spanier [8]. Here, we have taken a similar approach to capture finite-turn dcf languages. We have introduce new types of formal grammar, called $LR(1)$-*metalinear* and $LR(1)$-*ultralinear* grammars, for languages in ωtDCFL and deep-ωtDCFL, respectively. There still remain challenging open questions to answer. Is it possible to capture ωtDCFL as well as deep-ωtDCFL by different types of grammars whose definitions are simpler and more intuitive than the aforementioned grammars? What formal grammars naturally characterize "subclasses" of ωtDCFL? For each fixed $k \geq 1$, how can we grammatically generate languages in $k\text{tDCFL}$ and deep-$k\text{tDCFL}$?

References

1. Autebert, J.-M., Berstel, J., Boasson, L.: Context-Free Languages and Pushdown Automata. In: Rozenberg, G., Salomaa, A. (eds.) Handbook of Formal Languages, pp. 111–174. Springer, Heidelberg (1997). https://doi.org/10.1007/978-3-642-59136-5_3
2. Berstel, J.: Transductions and Context-Free Languages. Teubner Verlag, Wiesbaden (1979). https://doi.org/10.1007/978-3-663-09367-1
3. Boasson, L.: Two iteration theorems for some families of languages. J. Comput. Syst. Sci. **7**, 583–596 (1973)
4. Chan, T.: Reversal complexity of counter machines. In: Proceedings of the Thirteenth Annual ACM Symposium on Theory of Computing (STOC 1981), pp. 146–157 (1981)
5. Eremondi, J., Ibarra, O.H., McQuillan, I.: Insertion operations on deterministic reversal-bounded counter machines. J. Comput. Syst. Sci. **104**, 244–257 (2019)
6. Fernau, H., Wolf, P., Yamakami, T.: Synchronizing deterministic push-down automata can be really hard. In: Proceedings of the MFCS 2020. LIPIcs, pp. 33:1–33:15 (2020)
7. Ginsburg, S., Greibach, S.: Deterministic context free languages. Inform. Control **9**, 620–648 (1966)
8. Ginsburg, S., Spanier, E.H.: Finite-turn pushdown automata. SIAM J. Comput. **4**, 429–453 (1966)
9. Greibach, S.A.: The unsolvability of the recognition of linear context-free languages. J. ACM **13**, 582–587 (1966)
10. Greibach, S.A.: An infinite hierarchy of context-free languages. J. ACM **16**, 91–106 (1969)
11. Hopcroft, J. E., Ullman, J. D.: Formal Languages and Their Relation to Automata. Addison-Wesley Educational Publishers, Boston (1969)
12. Knuth, D.E.: On the translation of languages from left to right. Inform. Control **8**, 607–639 (1965)
13. Kutrib, M., Malcher, A.: Finite turns and the regular closure of linear context-free languages. Discret. Appl. Math. **155**, 2152–2164 (2007)
14. Malcher, A.: On recursive and non-recursive trade-offs between finite-turn pushdown automata. J. Autom. Lang. Comb. **12**, 265–277 (2007)
15. Magalini, E., Pighizzini, G.: A pumping condition for ultralinear languages. Int. J. Found. Comput. Sci. **18**, 1303–1312 (2007)
16. Moriya, E., Tada, T.: On the space complexity of turn bounded pushdown automata. Int. J. Comput. Math. **80**, 295–304 (2003)
17. La Torre, S., Madhusudan, P., Parlato, G.: The language theory of bounded context-switching. In: López-Ortiz, A. (ed.) LATIN 2010. LNCS, vol. 6034, pp. 96–107. Springer, Heidelberg (2010). https://doi.org/10.1007/978-3-642-12200-2_10
18. Valiant, L.G.: Decision procedures for families of determinsitic pushdown automata. Ph.D. Dissertation, University of Warwick (1973)
19. Valiant, L.G.: The equivalence problem for determinsitic finite-turn pushdown automata. Inform. Control **25**, 123–133 (1974)
20. Yamakami, T.: Behavioral strengths and weaknesses of various models of limited automata. In: Catania, B., Královič, R., Nawrocki, J., Pighizzini, G. (eds.) SOFSEM 2019. LNCS, vol. 11376, pp. 519–530. Springer, Cham (2019). https://doi.org/10.1007/978-3-030-10801-4_40

21. Yamakami, T.: Intersection and union hierarchies of deterministic context-free languages and pumping lemmas. In: Leporati, A., Martín-Vide, C., Shapira, D., Zandron, C. (eds.) LATA 2020. LNCS, vol. 12038, pp. 341–353. Springer, Cham (2020). https://doi.org/10.1007/978-3-030-40608-0_24

22. Yamakami, T.: The no endmarker theorem for one-way probabilistic pushdown automata. Manuscript, available at arXiv:2111.02688 (2021)

23. Yamakami, T., Mikami, E.: Synchronizing words for real-time deterministic pushdown automata. In: Giri, D., Raymond Choo, K.K., Ponnusamy, S., Meng, W., Akleylek, S., Prasad Maity, S. (eds.) Proceedings of the Seventh International Conference on Mathematics and Computing. AISC, vol. 1412, pp. 551–562. Springer, Singapore (2022). https://doi.org/10.1007/978-981-16-6890-6_41

24. Yu, S.: A pumping lemma for deterministic context-free languages. Inform. Process. Lett. **31**, 47–51 (1989)

Towards a Unifying Logical Framework
for Neural Networks

Xiyue Zhang[1], Xiaohong Chen[2(✉)], and Meng Sun[1(✉)]

[1] Peking University, Beijing, China
{zhangxiyue,sunm}@pku.edu.cn
[2] University of Illinois Urbana-Champaign, Champaign, USA
xc3@illinois.edu

Abstract. Neural networks are increasingly used in safety-critical applications such as medical diagnosis and autonomous driving, which calls for the need for formal specification of their behaviors. In this paper, we use matching logic—a unifying logic to specify and reason about programs and computing systems—to axiomatically define dynamic propagation and temporal operations in neural networks and to formally specify common properties about neural networks. As instances, we use matching logic to formalize a variety of neural networks, including generic feed-forward neural networks with different activation functions and recurrent neural networks. We define their formal semantics and several common properties in matching logic. This way, we obtain a unifying logical framework for specifying neural networks and their properties.

Keywords: Matching logic · Neural networks · Formal specifications

1   Introduction

Neural networks have been used in an increasing number of cutting-edge applications, especially safety-critical ones, such as autonomous vehicle control [2,10], healthcare [1], and cyber security [11,35]. Due to the impressive performance of neural networks in prediction accuracy and efficiency, a wide range of systems have incorporated them as decision-making components.

Feed-forward neural networks (FNNs) [33], which generally include *convolutional neural networks* (CNNs) [24], are the quintessential neural network models. As the name suggests, information in FNNs flows across the network, from the input layer, through the intermediate layers (also called hidden layers), to the output layer. Another popular type *recurrent neural networks* (RNNs) [16] are designed for processing sequential data [42], which have achieved tremendous success and powered many important commercial applications [37].

Along with the widespread application of neural networks to mission-critical domains, concerns with regard to their safety and reliability arise. This highlights the importance of providing a formal and rigorous specification framework for neural networks, wherein the neural network specification could further lend itself to proof certification and model checking for safety guarantees about

© The Author(s), under exclusive license to Springer Nature Switzerland AG 2022
H. Seidl et al. (Eds.): ICTAC 2022, LNCS 13572, pp. 442–461, 2022.
https://doi.org/10.1007/978-3-031-17715-6_28

the neural network behaviors. An ideal specification framework should support different activation functions, network architectures, and various properties dedicated to neural networks. In addition, it should admit the flexibility of incorporating new activation function designs, operations, and properties that arise in the rapidly developing field of machine learning.

Although the last few years witnessed a growing interest in formal verification of neural networks [3,4,13–15,17,22,32,38–40,44,45,47,49,51], there are few attempts in the development of specification frameworks to characterize neural network behaviors. [25] proposes a logical formalism, ReLU temporal logic (ReTL), for feed-forward networks using ReLU activation function [27], which extends linear temporal logic [30,31] with terms capturing data processing in ReLU networks. Albeit the popularity and piece-wise linear characteristic of ReLU networks, ReTL confined to a specific type of network falls short in providing a *unifying* logical framework for the specification of generic neural networks with different activation functions and architectures. [34] explores the specification of some properties dedicated to neural networks without considering the network itself, and organizes the properties along two dimensions: semantic classification and trace-theoretic classification. [36] introduces a framework DNNV focusing on standardizing the network and property format of verifiers by performing network simplification, property reduction, and translation. Therefore, the problem of finding *a unifying logic* that can serve as a specification framework for all types of neural networks, is yet to be addressed. In comparison with existing verification techniques, a unifying logical framework aims to provide rigorous definitions of formal semantics for different types of neural networks. On this basis, the behavior correctness of neural networks such as the robustness property can be specified as a logical formula and proved by generating machine-checkable proof certificates.

In this paper, we initiate an attempt to present a unifying logical framework for the formalization of neural networks using matching logic [7]. This framework builds on the patterns and pattern matching semantics of matching logic and leverages its key insight of capturing a new specification (also called a theory) based on a simple and minimal core. Specifically, we define a general logical framework to characterize the linear operations, dynamic propagation, and temporal behaviors of neural networks. It turns out the proposed logical framework not only subsumes ReTL (Sect. 4), but also offers good extensibility to neural network variants with different activation functions, as well as realistic neural network architectures such as RNNs (Sect. 5) and CNNs (see [52, Appendix C]). For the logical formalism ReTL, we prove equivalence theorems to show that our definitions are syntactically and semantically faithful. Based on this logical framework, the correctness of neural network behaviors can be further guaranteed by the existence of formal proofs for safety properties of interest, which are encoded as machine-checkable proof objects and generated leveraging existing verification practices.

To sum up, the primary contributions of this work are:

1. We present a unifying logical framework for specifying and reasoning about neural network behaviors based on matching logic (Sect. 3).

2. We define ReTL in our logical framework and prove the correctness of the definition by the equivalence theorems (Theorems 1 and 2). We establish formal semantics in the form of standard models for generic FNNs with a variety of activation functions (Sect. 4).
3. We define formal semantics for RNNs with specialized operations and architecture design to process sequential data (Sect. 5).
4. We show the formal specifications of common neural network properties, including robustness, interval, monotonicity, and fairness, based on our logical framework (Sect. 6).

2   Preliminaries

2.1   Neural Networks Preliminaries

Neural networks consist of layers of computation units, interconnected in a feed-forward manner or integrated with loops/cycles in the network. The former type is known as feed-forward neural networks and the representative of the latter type is recurrent neural networks. Convolutional neural networks are a specialized version of feed-forward neural networks with their operations and architectures designed for computer vision tasks.

A general feed-forward neural network containing $L + 1$ layers of interconnected neurons (with the first layer as the input layer) can be described by a set of matrices $\{M_i\}_{i=1}^{L}$ and bias vectors $\{b_i\}_{i=1}^{L}$ for the computation of affine transformations, followed by a pointwise activation function for nonlinear transformations. Activation functions allow effective backpropagation to learn the mappings between the network inputs and outputs. For classification tasks, *softmax* function is usually used as the activation function for the output layer, giving the probability of the input being classified in each label.

One of the most popular neural networks used in practice is the feed-forward neural network with the ReLU activation function (ReLU network in short). We present the mathematical description of layer-by-layer forward computation in ReLU networks in the following:

– The affine transformation is performed first to obtain an intermediate vector for each layer i from the previous layer $i - 1$: $v_i = M_i \cdot v_{i-1} + b_i$ for $1 \leq i \leq L$ where v_0 is the vector on the input layer.
– The pointwise application of ReLU is then performed on layer i except the output layer, which presents the final vector representation: $v_i' = relu(v_i)$ for $1 \leq i \leq L - 1$.

In the case of the output layer (i.e., $i = L$), $v_L' = softmax(v_L)$. The final predicted label is $y = \arg\max_{1 \leq j \leq n} v_L'[j]$. We often leave out the activation function *softmax* on the output layer in the prediction phase. It would not affect the predicted label as the value comparison results between the vector components stay the same without the application of *softmax*.

2.2 Matching Logic Preliminaries

In this section, we review the syntax and semantics of matching logic following [6], and then introduce the definitions of several important constructs.

Matching Logic Syntax. Matching logic is a logical formalism that specifies and reasons about structure by means of patterns and pattern matching. Matching logic formulas, called *patterns*, are built using variables, symbols, a binary construct called *application*, the standard FOL constructs $\bot$, $\rightarrow$, $\exists$, and the least fixpoint construct μ. Variables in matching logic include a set EV of *element variables* denoted $x, y, \ldots$, and a set SV of *set variables* denoted $Y, Z, \ldots$.

Definition 1. *A matching logic* signature Σ *is a set of* (constant) *symbols denoted* $\sigma, \sigma_1, \sigma_2, \ldots$. *The set of* ($\Sigma$-)patterns *is inductively defined as follows:*

$$\varphi ::= x \mid Y \mid \sigma \mid \varphi_1\, \varphi_2 \mid \bot \mid \varphi_1 \rightarrow \varphi_2 \mid \exists x\,.\,\varphi \mid \mu Y\,.\,\varphi$$

where in $\mu Y\,.\,\varphi$, *we require that* φ *is positive in* Y, *i.e.,* Y *is not nested in an odd number of times on the left-hand side of an implication* $\varphi_1 \rightarrow \varphi_2$.

Pattern $\varphi_1\, \varphi_2$ is called an application. For example, $\mathsf{succ\ zero}$ is a pattern matched by the successor of 0, i.e., 1, where $\mathsf{succ} \in \Sigma$ represents the *successor* function. Other connectives such as $\neg$ and $\vee$ are defined in the usual way.

Matching Logic Semantics. Matching logic has *pattern matching* semantics and each pattern is interpreted in a model as the set of elements that match it. We first define matching logic models.

Definition 2. *A matching logic* Σ-model *consists of*

1. *a nonempty* carrier set M;
2. *the interpretation of application: an* application function $\_\bullet\_ : M \times M \rightarrow \mathcal{P}(M)$, *where* $\mathcal{P}(M)$ *is the powerset of* M;
3. *the interpretation of symbols:* $M_\sigma \subseteq M$ *as a subset of* M *for* $\sigma \in \Sigma$.

Note that application and symbols are interpreted to return a set of elements in matching logic models. Next, we define variable and pattern valuations.

Definition 3. *Given a model* M, *a variable valuation is a function* $\rho \colon (EV \cup SV) \rightarrow (M \cup \mathcal{P}(M))$ *such that* $\rho(x) \in M$ *for* $x \in EV$ *and* $\rho(Y) \subseteq M$ *for* $Y \in SV$. *We define pattern valuation* $|\varphi|_{M,\rho}$ *inductively as follows:*

1. $|x|_{M,\rho} = \{\rho(x)\}$ *for* $x \in EV$
2. $|Y|_{M,\rho} = \rho(Y)$ *for* $Y \in SV$
3. $|\sigma|_{M,\rho} = M_\sigma$ *for* $\sigma \in \Sigma$
4. $|\varphi_1\, \varphi_2|_{M,\rho} = \bigcup_{a_i \in |\varphi_i|_{M,\rho}, i \in \{1,2\}} a_1 \bullet a_2$
5. $|\bot|_{M,\rho} = \emptyset$
6. $|\varphi_1 \rightarrow \varphi_2|_{M,\rho} = M \setminus (|\varphi_1|_{M,\rho} \setminus |\varphi_2|_{M,\rho})$

7. $|\exists x . \varphi|_{M,\rho} = \bigcup_{a \in M} |\varphi|_{M,\rho[a/x]}$

8. $|\mu Y . \varphi|_{M,\rho} = \mathbf{lfp}(A \mapsto |\varphi|_{M,\rho[A/Y]})$

Here, $\mathbf{lfp}(A \mapsto |\varphi|_{M,\rho[A/Y]})$ denotes the smallest set A such that $A = |\varphi|_{M,\rho[A/Y]}$, where the existence of the unique least fixpoint is guaranteed by the Knaster-Tarski theorem [43] (see also [7, Section IV.B]).

We now define the matching logic validity.

Definition 4. Given M and φ, $M \vDash \varphi$ iff $|\varphi|_{M,\rho} = M$ for all ρ. Let Γ be a theory; that is a set of patterns which we call axioms. $M \vDash \Gamma$ iff $M \vDash \varphi$ for all $\varphi \in \Gamma$. $\Gamma \vDash \varphi$ iff $M \vDash \Gamma$ implies $M \vDash \varphi$ for all M.

Important Constructs. Several mathematical constructs that are of practical importance, such as equality, membership, set inclusion, sorts, many-sorted functions and partial functions, can be defined in matching logic. Here we present the definitions of *many-sorted function* and *partial function*. Detailed definitions and notations of other mathematical constructs can be found in [52, Appendix A.2].

A many-sorted function $f : s_1 \times \cdots \times s_n \to s$ can be defined as a symbol, and axiomatized by the following axiom:

$$(\textsc{Function}) \quad \forall x_1 : s_1 \cdots \forall x_n : s_n . \exists y : s . f(x_1, \cdots, x_n) = y$$

Note that the (FUNCTION) axiom guarantees that there is exactly one element y because if there exists y' such that $f(x_1, \cdots, x_n) = y'$, then $y = y'$.

Similarly, a many-sorted partial function $f : s_1 \times \cdots \times s_n \rightharpoonup s$ can be defined as a symbol, and axiomatized by the following axiom:

$$(\textsc{Partial Function}) \quad \forall x_1 : s_1 \cdots \forall x_n : s_n . \exists y : s . f(x_1, \cdots, x_n) \subseteq y$$

3 Unifying Logical Framework for Neural Networks

In this section, we present our logical framework for unifying specification of neural network behaviors based on matching logic. We provide a complete formal definition of its main constructs for linear operations, dynamic propagation, and temporal behaviors in neural networks.

3.1 Defining Linear Operations

In this subsection, we show how the vector space in neural networks can be characterized and defined as patterns of matching logic. The most common computation operations in neural networks are linear operations on the vector space, which are defined as follows.

Definition 5. *Let* Nat, Vector *and* Matrix *be the sorts of natural numbers, vectors and matrices, respectively. We define the following symbols:*

$$\_[\_] : \text{Vector} \times \text{Nat} \rightharpoonup \text{Vector}$$
$$\_+\_ : \text{Vector} \times \text{Vector} \rightharpoonup \text{Vector}$$
$$\_\cdot\_ : \text{Matrix} \times \text{Vector} \rightharpoonup \text{Vector}$$

The *projection* symbol $\_[\_]$ takes a vector v and a natural number k, and returns the k-th component of v (as a vector of length 1) when $k \leq \text{len}(v)$. The *addition* symbol $\_+\_$ takes two vectors v, w, and returns $v + w$ when v and w are of the same length. The *matrix multiplication* symbol $\_\cdot\_$ takes a matrix M and a vector v, and returns $M \cdot x$ when the number of columns of M, denoted $col(M)$, equals the length of v. Note that the above symbols are partial functions as stated by the (PARTIAL FUNCTION) axioms. They are undefined in the cases of vector dimension exceedance, vector dimension inequality, matrix dimension mismatch, etc.

The comparison operators for the Vector sort are specified in the following way. For any two vectors $v = (v_i)_n$ and $w = (w_i)_n$ of length n, we denote $v = w$ iff $v_i = w_i$ for every $1 \leq i \leq n$. We denote $v \geq w$ iff $v_i \geq w_i$ for every $1 \leq i \leq n$. Other comparison operators are defined in a similar way.

Definition 6. *Let* Layer *be the sort of* network layers *and* Term *be the sort of functions that map a layer to a vector. We define the partial function*

$$\text{eval} : \text{Term} \times \text{Layer} \rightharpoonup \text{Vector}$$

to evaluate a term at a given layer.

The key insight of introducing the Term and Layer sorts, as well as the eval symbol is to fully capture the dynamic propagation in neural networks. Recall that in feed-forward neural networks, the transformation parameters in terms of matrices, bias vectors, and activation functions are configured differently at different layers. By introducing Term, the layer information is captured implicitly in the function term. The transformation can be configured accordingly given the element in the Layer sort. For example, when we compute one-step forward linear transformations in a network, matrix M_j and bias vector b_j can be configured according to the layer position j given by the (argument) sort Layer of symbol eval.

We declare a subsort relation Vector $\subseteq_{\text{subsort}}$ Term, since each vector v in Vector sort can be regarded as a constant term, which is axiomatized as:

$$(\text{CONSTANT TERM}) \quad \forall v : \text{Vector} \; \forall l : \text{Layer} . \, \text{eval}(v, l) = v$$

This allows us to characterize patterns of Vector sort as patterns of Term sort in a consistent manner, where the (CONSTANT TERM) axiom is automatically assumed for elements in Vector sort. The symbols for Vector sort are propagated and overloaded with respect to Term sort, which also leads us to the corresponding axiom for each symbol.

Definition 7. *Let* Layer *and* Term *be the sorts of layers and terms, and* eval *be the evaluation function in Definition 6. We define the following symbols:*

$$\_[\_]: \mathsf{Term} \times \mathsf{Nat} \rightharpoonup \mathsf{Term}$$
$$\_+\_: \mathsf{Term} \times \mathsf{Term} \rightharpoonup \mathsf{Term}$$
$$\_\cdot\_: \mathsf{Matrix} \times \mathsf{Term} \rightharpoonup \mathsf{Term}$$

as well as the following propagation axioms:

(PROJECTION)	$\mathsf{eval}(t[k], l) = \mathsf{eval}(t, l)[k]$
(ADDITION)	$\mathsf{eval}(t_1 + t_2, l) = \mathsf{eval}(t_1, l) + \mathsf{eval}(t_2, l)$
(MATMULT)	$\mathsf{eval}(M \cdot t, l) = M \cdot \mathsf{eval}(t, l)$

where the universal quantification with respect to sorts Term, Layer, Nat, *and* Matrix *are defined in the expected way.*

The above axioms state that a term t on the layer set can be lifted pointwise (i.e., layer-wise) to incorporate symbols for projection, addition, and matrix multiplication. Intuitively, (PROJECTION) states that pointwise projection $t[k]$ maps any layer l to the k-th vector component to which term t maps. (ADDITION) axiomatizes the pointwise addition $t_1 + t_2$, which maps any layer l to the sum of the vectors to which the (argument) terms t_1 and t_2 map. (MATMULT) axiomatizes the pointwise multiplication $M \cdot t$, which maps any layer l to the multiplication result of the constant matrix M and the vector to which term t maps.

3.2   Defining Dynamic Propagation

Neural networks achieve prediction by performing dynamic (forward) propagation from the input layer to the output layer. On each layer, a neural network computes a new vector through the layer-to-layer transformations. We show the mathematical description of the dynamic transformations for a feed-forward ReLU network in Sect. 2.1, where the vector of the successor layer is attained by first computing the affine (linear) transformations of the given vector and then applying the nonlinear activation function. This computation process continues until a vector representation reaches the output layer.

To capture such dynamic computation flows through the network layers, we define the following function:

$$\mathsf{next} : \mathsf{Term} \rightarrow \mathsf{Term}$$

Recall that the elements in Term sort are functions that map layers to vectors which are computed with properly configured transformations (dependent on the layer position). We introduce the next symbol to allow the function term to update; that is, the mapping from layers to the feature vectors, in order to specify the forward propagation across the network. We illustrate the mechanism of the next symbol in the following example. For a neural network with $L + 1$ layers, we denote the transformation functions between adjacent layers as $f_1, f_2, \cdots, f_L$ where f_i $(1 \leq i \leq L)$ is the transformation function from layer $i - 1$ to layer i. The next symbol satisfies that for all terms t, for layers $1 \leq l \leq L$:

$$\mathsf{eval}(\mathsf{next}(t), l) = f_l(\mathsf{eval}(t, l - 1))$$

Intuitively, the new term $\mathsf{next}(t)$ represents the updated function term that maps layers to the vector representation after one-layer forward computation with regard to the layer transformations. Specifically, for the feature vector v_l of layer l characterized by the updated term as $\mathsf{eval}(\mathsf{next}(t), l)$, it is the computation result of applying the transformation function f_l to the feature vector v_{l-1} of the previous layer specified as $\mathsf{eval}(t, l - 1)$. And the layer position l settles the configuration of the corresponding transformation function.

We have seen how the next function characterizes the forward flow of the vector representation across the layers. Other symbols that characterize the dynamic behaviors of neural networks can be defined in a similar way. For example, we define the function shift to allow the information to flow backward.

$$\mathsf{shift} : \mathsf{Term} \rightarrow \mathsf{Term}$$

$$(\textsc{Shift}) \quad \forall t : \mathsf{Term} \; \forall l : \mathsf{Layer} \, . \, \mathsf{eval}(\mathsf{shift}(t), l) = \mathsf{eval}(t, l + 1)$$

Intuitively, the symbol shift takes a term t and returns a new term that maps a layer to the vector representation originally configured on the successor layer after one-step backward shift. Note that shift makes no update to the feature vectors, but only changes the mapping from layer positions to feature vectors.

3.3   Defining Atomic Formulas and Temporal Operations

To reason about neural network behaviors, the framework needs to support constraint specifications on intermediate feature vectors and output vectors with respect to an oracle, which often comes in the form of a geometric region in the vector space. Therefore, we design the following constructs as atomic formulas to capture the vector constraints with regard to different layer positions.

$$t_1 = t_2 \equiv \exists l : \mathsf{Layer} \, . \, l \wedge \mathsf{eval}(t_1, l) = \mathsf{eval}(t_2, l)$$
$$t_1 \geq t_2 \equiv \exists l : \mathsf{Layer} \, . \, l \wedge \mathsf{eval}(t_1, l) \geq \mathsf{eval}(t_2, l)$$

The pattern $t_1 = t_2$ is matched by the layers such that the vectors to which t_1 corresponds are equal to the ones t_2 corresponds to. Note that we use existential quantification over layers to obtain the union set of layers of which the corresponding feature vectors satisfy the required constraints. We overload the equality notation to define patterns with respect to terms, which are interpreted as matching elements in the Layer sort. Similar interpretation applies to the pattern $t_1 \geq t_2$. The intuition behind the above definitions is to specify the constraint with regard to the vectors (on the intermediate and output layers) as membership inquiries on layers, that is, to determine whether a layer is a member of the set of layers that match the required constraint. Other atomic formulas in the form of comparison operators like $>, <, \leq, \neq$ can be derived by the propositional connectives, e.g., $t_1 < t_2 \equiv \neg(t_1 \geq t_2)$.

Neural networks can be regarded as transition systems whose states are the layers and the vector values on them. To specify layer transitions, we introduce the symbol $\mathsf{X} : \mathsf{Layer} \to \mathsf{Layer}$, which takes a layer and returns its predecessor layer in a neural network. The pattern $\mathsf{X}\varphi$ is matched by layers whose direct successor layers match φ. This construct allows us to specify and reason about behaviors of arbitrary layers. For example, we can reason about the i-th step unrolled recurrent layer we are interested in by transiting to this specific state through the X symbol. Other temporal operations can be derived from the symbol X and the μ-binder. $\varphi_1 \cup \varphi_2$ is defined as $\mu Y . \varphi_2 \vee (\varphi_1 \wedge \mathsf{X} Y)$ where Y is the set variable of Layer sort.

4   Instance: Feed-Forward Neural Networks

In this section, we instantiate the generic logical framework for neural networks in Sect. 3 with *feed-forward neural networks* (FNNs) and obtain a formal semantics of FNNs in matching logic. Among different types of FNNs, due to the computational simplicity and piece-wise linear property of the *ReLU* function, ReLU networks have rapidly become the most popular networks in practical applications. A recent logic design ReTL [25] is introduced to specify and reason about the behaviors of ReLU networks. We will first introduce the logical formalism ReTL. We then demonstrate how ReTL can be defined and subsumed in the proposed logical framework. We finally show the generalization of our framework to feed-forward network variants with different activation functions.

4.1   ReTL: A Logic for ReLU Networks

We give an overview of ReTL designed for specifying and reasoning about ReLU networks. The *syntax* of ReTL defines terms and formulas. Formally, ReTL terms are inductively defined by the following grammar:

$$\underline{ReTL\ terms}\ \ t ::= v \mid x \mid t[i] \mid t_1 + t_2 \mid Mt \mid \bigcirc_k t$$

where $t[i]$ is the projection of t on the i-th component; $t_1 + t_2$ is the addition of t_1 and t_2; Mt is the multiplication between a (concrete) matrix M and a term t; and $\bigcirc_k t$ denotes the transformed (future) value of t in k-th next layer.

ReTL formulas are then built from formulas such as $t_1 = t_2$ and $t_1 \geq t_2$ where t_1 and t_2 are terms of the same length, propositional connectives such as $\neg$ and $\wedge$, FOL-style quantification, and temporal operators $\mathsf{X}\varphi$ ("next" φ) and $\varphi_1 \cup \varphi_2$ (φ_1 "until" φ_2). Formally,

$$\underline{ReTL\ formulas}\ \ \varphi ::= t_1 = t_2 \mid t_1 \geq t_2 \mid \neg\varphi \mid \varphi_1 \wedge \varphi_2 \mid \exists x . \varphi \mid \mathsf{X}\varphi \mid \varphi_1 \cup \varphi_2$$

The *semantics* of ReTL is defined with regard to a ReLU network N (with $L + 1$ layers), a layer position $0 \leq l \leq L$, and a valuation ρ that assigns each vector variable to a vector of proper length. The semantics of ReTL terms are inductively defined as follows:

- $|v|_{N,\rho,l}^{\mathsf{ReTL}} = v$ for any vector constant v.
- $|x|_{N,\rho,l}^{\mathsf{ReTL}} = \rho(x)$ for any vector variable x.
- $|t[i]|_{N,\rho,l}^{\mathsf{ReTL}}$ is the i-th element of $|t|_{N,\rho,l}^{\mathsf{ReTL}}$.
- $|t_1 + t_2|_{N,\rho,l}^{\mathsf{ReTL}} = |t_1|_{N,\rho,l}^{\mathsf{ReTL}} + |t_2|_{N,\rho,l}^{\mathsf{ReTL}}$.
- $|Mt|_{N,\rho,l}^{\mathsf{ReTL}} = M|t|_{N,\rho,l}^{\mathsf{ReTL}}$.
- The semantics of $|\bigcirc_k t|_{N,\rho,l}^{\mathsf{ReTL}}$ are defined in several cases:
  (1) if $k = 0$, then $|\bigcirc_k t|_{N,\rho,l}^{\mathsf{ReTL}} = |t|_{N,\rho,l}^{\mathsf{ReTL}}$,
  (2) if $k > 0$ and $l + k < L$, then $|\bigcirc_k t|_{N,\rho,l}^{\mathsf{ReTL}} = relu(M_{l+k} |\bigcirc_{k-1} t|_{N,\rho,l}^{\mathsf{ReTL}} + b_{l+k})$,
  (3) if $k > 0$ and $l + k = L$, then $|\bigcirc_k t|_{N,\rho,l}^{\mathsf{ReTL}} = M_L |\bigcirc_{k-1} t|_{N,\rho,l}^{\mathsf{ReTL}} + b_L$,
  (4) if $l + k > L$, the term is undefined.

ReTL formulas $t_1 = t_2$ and $t_1 \geq t_2$ are interpreted as $|t_1|_{N,\rho,l}^{\mathsf{ReTL}} = |t_2|_{N,\rho,l}^{\mathsf{ReTL}}$ and $|t_1|_{N,\rho,l}^{\mathsf{ReTL}} \geq |t_2|_{N,\rho,l}^{\mathsf{ReTL}}$, respectively. The satisfaction relation $\models_{\mathsf{ReTL}}$ of ReTL formulas is defined as follows:

- $N, \rho, l \models_{\mathsf{ReTL}} t_1 = t_2$ iff $|t_1|_{N,\rho,l}^{\mathsf{ReTL}} = |t_2|_{N,\rho,l}^{\mathsf{ReTL}}$.
- $N, \rho, l \models_{\mathsf{ReTL}} t_1 \geq t_2$ iff $|t_1|_{N,\rho,l}^{\mathsf{ReTL}} \geq |t_2|_{N,\rho,l}^{\mathsf{ReTL}}$.
- $N, \rho, l \models_{\mathsf{ReTL}} \neg\varphi$ iff $N, \rho, l \nvDash_{\mathsf{ReTL}} \varphi$.
- $N, \rho, l \models_{\mathsf{ReTL}} \varphi_1 \wedge \varphi_2$ iff $N, \rho, l \models_{\mathsf{ReTL}} \varphi_1$ and $N, \rho, l \models_{\mathsf{ReTL}} \varphi_2$.
- $N, \rho, l \models_{\mathsf{ReTL}} \exists x \in \mathbb{R}^n . \varphi$ iff there exists $v \in \mathbb{R}^n$ such that $N, \rho[v/x], l \models_{\mathsf{ReTL}} \varphi$, where $\rho[v/x]$ denotes the valuation with $\rho[v/x](x) = v$ and $\rho[v/x](y) = \rho(y)$ for all $y \neq x$.
- $N, \rho, l \models_{\mathsf{ReTL}} X\varphi$ iff $l < L$ and $N, \rho, l+1 \models_{\mathsf{ReTL}} \varphi$.
- $N, \rho, l \models_{\mathsf{ReTL}} \varphi_1 U \varphi_2$ iff there exists some $k \geq l$ and $k \leq L$ such that $N, \rho, k \models_{\mathsf{ReTL}} \varphi_2$ and $N, \rho, j \models_{\mathsf{ReTL}} \varphi_1$ for $l \leq j < k$.

4.2 Defining ReTL in Matching Logic

The syntax and semantics of *ReTL terms* can be subsumed by the Term sort (including Vector as the subsort), the symbols for linear operations and dynamic propagation in our logical framework. However, the definition of $\bigcirc_k t$ in ReTL for k-step forward transformations is not trivial. In the following, we show how to capture the syntax and semantics of the operation $\bigcirc_k t$ for k-step dynamic computation using the next and shift symbols. We use next^k and shift^k as the shortcut for k continuous application of next and shift in the following context.

With the next symbol defined for the forward propagation of feature vectors and the shift symbol for the backward layer shift, the $\bigcirc_k t$ operation can be defined as:

$$\bigcirc_k t \equiv \mathsf{shift}^k(\mathsf{next}^k(t))$$

Thus, for a given layer l, we have

$$eval(\bigcirc_k t, l) = eval(\mathsf{next}^k(t), l + k)$$

Recall that the satisfaction relation in ReTL is evaluated with regard to a certain layer l. Through defining $\bigcirc_k t$ with k-step forward propagation and k-step backward shift, the interpretation of $\bigcirc_k t$ is consistent with the semantics in ReTL, where the forward propagation of the vector representation from l to $l + k$ is followed by backward shift from layer $l + k$ to l. This way, the satisfaction relation can be evaluated with regard to layer l.

The forward propagation for arbitrary steps can be captured by repeating the application of next accordingly without introducing a variable indicating how many forward steps to take. As the next symbol involves no layer shift operations, the updated vector representation is taken on layer $l + k$, which also indicates the correct configuration of next step forward transformations (from layer $l+k$).

Note that in ReTL, $\bigcirc_k t$ is *not* equivalent to $\underbrace{\bigcirc_1 \cdots \bigcirc_1}_{k} t$. It can be seen more evidently in matching logic, where $\bigcirc_k t \equiv \mathsf{shift}^k(\mathsf{next}^k(t))$, but

$$\underbrace{\bigcirc_1 \cdots \bigcirc_1}_{k} t = \underbrace{\mathsf{shift}(\mathsf{next}(\cdots \mathsf{shift}(\mathsf{next}(t)) \cdots))}_{k}$$

Since next and shift are not commutable when shift changes the configured layer transformation to the predecessor layer, the equivalence does not hold when the linear mappings of network layers are different from each other, which is common in practice.

To sum up, we showed that the syntax and semantics of ReTL terms and formulas are *precisely captured* by matching logic patterns, using the built-in constructs for propositional connectives, quantification, and temporal operators in matching logic, without needing to introduce additional logical symbols.

4.3   Defining Standard Models of Feed-Forward ReLU Networks

In this subsection, we establish formal semantics of feed-forward ReLU networks, which are defined in the form of standard models.

Definition 8. *Let N be a ReLU network with $L + 1$ layers. A* standard model M^N *for N consists of:*

1. *Carrier set, which is the disjoint union of the following:*
   - *The carrier sets of the* Nat, Vector, *and* Matrix *sorts are defined in the usual way.*
   - *The carrier set of sort* Layer *is $M^N_{\mathsf{Layer}} = \{0, 1, \cdots, L\}$, i.e., the set of the network layers.*
   - *The carrier set of sort* Term *is the set of functions M^N_{Term} that map network layers to vectors.*
2. *Symbol interpretations:*
   - *The projection, addition, and matrix multiplication symbols are interpreted in the usual way.*

- *The* eval *and* shift *symbols are interpreted as functions* M_{eval}^N *and* M_{shift}^N *straightforward from their definitions.* M_{eval}^N *is the partial function mapping a term and a layer (arguments) to a vector;* M_{shift}^N *is the function that maps a term to a new term satisfying Axiom* (SHIFT).
- *The* next *symbol is interpreted as* M_{next}^N, *the unique function that satisfies the following property*

$$M_{\text{eval}}^N(M_{\text{next}}^N(t), l) = \begin{cases} M_{\text{eval}}^N(t, 0) & \text{if } = 0 \\ relu(M_l \cdot M_{\text{eval}}^N(t, l-1) + b_l) & \text{if } \leq l < L \\ M_L \cdot M_{\text{eval}}^N(t, L-1) + b_L & \text{if } = L \end{cases}$$

- *The* X *symbol is interpreted as the function that satisfies*

$$M_X^N(l) = \begin{cases} \{l-1\} & \text{if } 1 \leq l \leq L \\ \emptyset & \text{if } l = 0 \end{cases}$$

Recall that any ReTL term t and formula φ can be defined as a matching logic pattern. Theorems 1 and 2 show that the definitions of ReTL terms and formulas in our logical framework are syntactically and semantically faithful.

Theorem 1. *Let t be an ReTL term. Then* $|\text{eval}(t, l)|_{M^N, \rho} = \{|t|_{N, \rho, l}^{\text{ReTL}}\}$.

Theorem 2. *Let φ be an ReTL formula. Then* $l \in |\varphi|_{M^N, \rho}$ *iff* $N, \rho, l \models_{\text{ReTL}} \varphi$.

Note that $|\text{eval}(t, l)|_{M^N, \rho}$ evaluates to a singleton set, while $|t|_{N, \rho, l}^{\text{ReTL}}$ evaluates to a single element. Please refer to [52, Appendix B] for proof details.

4.4   Instances of Neural Networks Using Other Activation Functions

We have established that ReTL can be subsumed in the proposed logical framework. In this subsection, we show that this framework allows us to generalize to neural networks using other nonlinear activation functions, without the need to define a new logical formalism specialized for neural networks with new activation function design as nonlinear mapping [9,23]. In the following, we present an example of FNNs that use *tanh* as the nonlinear activation function [20].

Definition 9. *Let N be a feed-forward neural network with tanh as the activation function and $L+1$ layers. A standard model M^N for N consists of:*

1. *The* next *symbol is interpreted as* M_{next}^N, *the unique function satisfying that*

$$M_{\text{eval}}^N(M_{\text{next}}^N(t), l) = \begin{cases} M_{\text{eval}}^N(t, 0) & \text{if } = 0 \\ tanh(M_l \cdot M_{\text{eval}}^N(t, l-1) + b_l) & \text{if } \leq l < L \\ M_L \cdot M_{\text{eval}}^N(t, L-1) + b_L & \text{if } l = L \end{cases}$$

2. *Everything else is the same as Definition 8.*

Formal semantics of all the variants of FNNs [9,23,26,28], including CNNs [52, Appendix C], can be similarly defined in our framework.

5   Instance: Recurrent Neural Networks

In this section, we define *recurrent neural networks* (RNNs) [16] in our logical framework. RNNs are often used to process sequential data or time series data such as natural language [42]. A typical RNN consists of an input layer, a recurrent layer, and a fully-connected layer, in which the recurrent layer enables the RNN to process sequential inputs of any length with shared parameters. The main challenge to characterize the dynamic computation of RNNs is to specify the propagation on the recurrent layer.

Propagation on the Recurrent Layer. The computation flow on the recurrent layer, in the form of hidden state vectors, can be regarded the same as feature vectors in FNNs by unrolling the recurrent layer step by step. The recurrent layer processes the information from the sequential input by incorporating it into the hidden state which is passed forward through time steps.

We can formulate the unrolled recurrence after l steps as $h_l = f(h_{l-1}, x_l)$ where h_l and h_{l-1} represent the hidden state vectors at step l and the previous step $l-1$, x_l indicates the input vector at step l, and f represents the transformation function on the recurrent layer. The number of unrolled hidden layers then depends on the length of the input sequence. However, unlike FNNs, the RNN transformations across the unrolled hidden layers are shared with (1) fixed weight matrices: hidden-to-hidden matrix M_{hh} and input-to-hidden matrix M_{xh}, (2) fixed bias vector b_h, and (3) fixed activation function σ_h.

The challenge to characterize the propagation on the recurrent layer is that for each unrolled hidden layer, different input vectors corresponding to one specific token (or word) of the input sequence are involved. The Term sort is useful to address this challenge, since it is designed to capture the vector representation at different layer positions. For an input sequence $t^{in} = (t_1^{in}, t_2^{in}, \cdots, t_L^{in})$, we use $\mathsf{eval}(t^{in}, l)$ to specify the input vector t_l^{in} fed to the recurrent layer at time step l (i.e., unrolled hidden layer l).

The forward propagation of hidden state vectors can then be specified by adding the transformation of a proper input vector at each layer position. Generally, for an input sequence t^{in}, the forward propagation to hidden layer l for $1 \leq l \leq \mathsf{len}(t^{in})$ is defined as:

$$h_l = \sigma_h(M_{hh} \cdot h_{l-1} + M_{xh} \cdot t_l^{in} + b_h)$$

Propagation on the Fully-Connected Layer. The dynamic propagation of the hidden state vector on the recurrent layer is generally followed by a fully-connected output layer for many-to-one prediction tasks. The forward propagation from the last hidden layer position $\mathsf{len}(t^{in})$ (decided by the length of the sequential input) to the output layer demonstrates the same behaviors as FNNs.

Specifically, the forward propagation to the output layer in RNNs is characterized by a hidden-to-output weight matrix M_{hy} and a bias vector b_y. Generally, the dynamic transformation to the output layer can be defined as:

$$y_l = M_{hy} \cdot h_{l-1} + b_y$$

The same as FNNs, only linear transformations are involved in the computation on the output layer. The projection, addition and matrix multiplication symbols naturally accommodate hidden state vectors of the unrolled recurrent layer.

Standard Models. Here we define the standard models of RNNs.

Definition 10. *Let N be a recurrent neural network with an input layer, a recurrent layer, and a fully-connected layer. A standard model M^N for N with respect to a sequential data t^{in} consists of:*

1. $M^N_{\mathsf{Layer}} = \{0, 1, \cdots, \mathsf{len}(t^{in}) + 1\}$ *is the carrier set of the* Layer *sort where layer* 0 *indicates the input layer, layers* 1, $\cdots$, $\mathsf{len}(t^{in})$ *are the unrolled hidden layers, and layer* $\mathsf{len}(t^{in}) + 1$ *indicates the output layer.*
2. *The* next *symbol is interpreted as* M^N_{next}, *the unique function satisfying that*

$$M^N_{\mathsf{eval}}(M^N_{\mathsf{next}}(t), l) = \begin{cases} h_0 & \text{if } l = 0 \\ \sigma_h(M_{hh} \cdot M^N_{\mathsf{eval}}(t, l-1) + M_{xh} \cdot M^N_{\mathsf{eval}}(t^{in}, l) + b_h) & \\ & \text{if } 1 \le l \le \mathsf{len}(t^{in}) \\ M_{hy} \cdot M^N_{\mathsf{eval}}(t, \mathsf{len}(t^{in})) + b_y & \text{if } l = \mathsf{len}(t^{in}) + 1 \end{cases}$$

3. *Everything else is the same as Definition 8.*

Now we have shown that RNNs integrated with loops/cycles can be defined in the proposed logical framework in a consistent manner with FNNs, with slight change to the carrier set of Layer sort and the interpretation of the next symbol.

6   Specifying Neural Network Properties

In this section, we present some common properties of neural networks and how to formally specify them as patterns, in our unifying framework.

6.1   Robustness

The robustness of neural networks against adversarial perturbations has been extensively investigated [5,12,18,21,29,48]. In general, the robustness property states that, given an input x, a distance function L_p, and a distance bound ϵ, the prediction of the neural network on the ϵ-neighborhood $\eta(x, L_p, \epsilon)$ of x where $\eta(x, L_p, \epsilon) = \{x' \mid \|x' - x\|_p \le \epsilon\}$ is the same as the prediction of input x. This is often referred to as local robustness. Note that in the following we formalize the local robustness property in terms of vector constraints instead of using the *argmax* function.

Example 1. Consider a neural network N with $L+1$ layers, input dimension s_0, and output dimension s_L. Given an input-label pair (x_0, y_0), the local robustness of N on the input $x_0 \in \mathbb{R}^{s_0}$ with respect to an $\epsilon_0 \in \mathbb{R}^{s_0}$ neighborhood in terms of L_∞ norm can be specified as:

$$\forall x \in \mathbb{R}^{s_0} . (x \leq x_0 + \epsilon_0) \wedge (x \geq x_0 - \epsilon_0) \rightarrow$$
$$\forall 1 \leq j \leq s_L . \mathsf{eval}(\mathsf{next}^L(x)[y_0], L) \geq \mathsf{eval}(\mathsf{next}^L(x)[j], L)$$

6.2 Interval Property

The interval property [21,46] aims to analyze whether the outputs of a neural network are restricted in a geometric region. A simple interval property is to determine whether a real number ub or lb is a valid upper or lower bound for a specific dimension of the output vectors on an input region.

Example 2. Consider a neural network N with $L+1$ layers, input dimension s_0, and output dimension s_L. Given an input region $[0,1]^{s_0}$, the interval property is to check whether lb is a valid lower bound for the k_0-th component of the network outputs on the input region. This interval property can be specified as:

$$\forall x \in \mathbb{R}^{s_0} . x \leq 1 \wedge x \geq 0 \rightarrow \mathsf{eval}(\mathsf{next}^L(x)[k_0], L) \geq lb$$

where $\mathbf{1}$ and $\mathbf{0}$ denote the vectors in $\mathbb{R}^{s_0}$ where all the components are 1 and 0.

Neural networks can be regarded as programs that compute the function results of the inputs. From this perspective, the aforementioned robustness and interval properties can be viewed as special cases of functional correctness which specifies the input-output constraints of the programs (neural networks). The specifications of such properties can be formulated in a unified manner with respect to a pair of pre- and post-conditions in the form of $\forall x . P(x) \rightarrow Q(\mathsf{next}^L(x))$.

6.3 Monotonicity

The monotonicity property [50] focuses on the output monotonicity of a network with respect to a user-specified subset of the inputs. Assuming that a neural network is used to predict whether to give an applicant the loan, the network is expected to guarantee that the prediction will be monotonically increasing when the value of the applicant's income increases and the other values are the same.

Example 3. Consider a neural network N with $L+1$ layers, input dimension s_0, and output dimension s_L. Given that the domain-specific feature dimension is i_0, and the monotonic label dimension is k_0, the monotonicity property is to check whether the k_0-th component of the network outputs is monotonic with respect to the value of input feature i_0. This monotonicity property can be specified as:

$$\forall x_1, x_2 \in \mathbb{R}^{s_0} . (x_1[i_0] \leq x_2[i_0] \wedge (\forall 1 \leq i \leq s_0 . i \neq i_0 \rightarrow x_1[i] = x_2[i])) \rightarrow$$
$$\mathsf{eval}(\mathsf{next}^L(x_1)[k_0], L) \leq \mathsf{eval}(\mathsf{next}^L(x_2)[k_0], L)$$

6.4   Fairness

The fairness property [19,41] generally constrains that the neural network's pre-diction should not be influenced by protected features such as gender, age and race. There are many different formulations of neural network fairness. Here we focus on the independence-based fairness, which states that the neural network's prediction is independent of the values of protected features. Note that we specify the values of protected features explicitly in the following to formalize the independence-based fairness in a more straightforward manner.

Example 4. Consider a neural network N with $L + 1$ layers, whose input and output dimensions are s_0 and s_L, respectively. Suppose i_0 is the protected feature dimension, Q is the set of protected feature values, and k_0 is the specified label. *Fairness* states that the k_0-th component of the network outputs is independent of the value of the protected feature i_0, which can be specified as:

$$\forall x_1, x_2 \in \mathbb{R}^{s_0} . ((\forall q_1, q_2 \in Q . x_1[i_0] = q_1 \wedge x_2[i_0] = q_2) \wedge (\forall 1 \leq i \leq s_0 .$$
$$i \neq i_0 \rightarrow x_1[i] = x_2[i])) \rightarrow \mathsf{eval}(\mathsf{next}^L(x_1)[k_0], L) = \mathsf{eval}(\mathsf{next}^L(x_2)[k_0], L)$$

The exact equivalence on the prediction can be relaxed by introducing a positive tolerance ϵ to the output difference, which is specified as:

$$\forall x_1, x_2 \in \mathbb{R}^{s_0} . ((\forall q_1, q_2 \in Q . x_1[i_0] = q_1 \wedge x_2[i_0] = q_2) \wedge$$
$$(\forall 1 \leq i \leq s_0 . i \neq i_0 \rightarrow x_1[i] = x_2[i])) \rightarrow$$
$$(\mathsf{eval}(\mathsf{next}^L(x_1)[k_0], L) \leq \mathsf{eval}(\mathsf{next}^L(x_2)[k_0], L) + \epsilon \wedge$$
$$\mathsf{eval}(\mathsf{next}^L(x_1)[k_0], L) \geq \mathsf{eval}(\mathsf{next}^L(x_2)[k_0], L) - \epsilon)$$

Neural networks can be viewed as data-driven systems, of which the execution on an input forms a trace, i.e., a sequence of vectors on the layers. We have been familiar with ordinary properties that reason over a single execution of a system. In contrast, the hyperproperty [8] reasons over a set of executions of a system, instead of over a single one. The monotonicity and fairness properties both involve examining pairs of executions, which renders them both as hyper-properties. Compared with ordinary properties, hyperproperties are capable of constraining complex relations among multiple execution traces of a system.

7   Conclusion

We present a unifying logical framework for the specification of neural network behaviors by defining the linear operations, dynamic propagation, and temporal operations as a matching logic theory. The key insight is to provide a general framework to define formal semantics of neural networks with different activation functions and network architectures, so as to offer good extensibility and flexibility in the rapidly developing field of machine learning. We prove that existing logic design ReTL can be faithfully defined in our framework. We also show that the logical framework can serve as the specification formalism of important network properties, such as robustness, interval, monotonicity, and fairness.

Acknowledgements. This research was sponsored by the National Natural Science Foundation of China under Grant No. 62172019, 61772038, and CCF-Huawei Formal Verification Innovation Research Plan. The work presented in this paper was supported in part by NSF CNS 16-19275. This material is based upon work supported by the United States Air Force and DARPA under Contract No. FA8750-18-C-0092.

References

1. Babak, A., Delong, A., Weirauch, M.T., Frey, B.J.: Predicting the sequence specificities of DNA- and RNA-binding proteins by deep learning. Nat. Biotechnol. **33**(8), 831–838 (2015). https://doi.org/10.1038/nbt.3300
2. Bojarski, M., et al.: End to end learning for self-driving cars. CoRR abs/1604.07316 (2016). http://arxiv.org/abs/1604.07316
3. Boopathy, A., Weng, T., Chen, P., Liu, S., Daniel, L.: CNN-Cert: an efficient framework for certifying robustness of convolutional neural networks. In: Proceedings of the 33rd AAAI Conference on Artificial Intelligence, Honolulu, Hawaii, USA, pp. 3240–3247. AAAI Press (2019). https://doi.org/10.1609/aaai.v33i01.33013240
4. Bunel, R., Turkaslan, I., Torr, P.H.S., Kohli, P., Mudigonda, P.K.: A unified view of piecewise linear neural network verification. In: Proceedings of the 32nd Annual Conference on Neural Information Processing Systems, Montréal, Canada, pp. 4795–4804. Curran Associates Inc. (2018)
5. Carlini, N., Wagner, D.A.: Towards evaluating the robustness of neural networks. In: Proceedings of the 38th IEEE Symposium on Security and Privacy, San Jose, California, USA, pp. 39–57. IEEE Computer Society (2017). https://doi.org/10.1109/SP.2017.49
6. Chen, X., Lucanu, D., Roşu, G.: Matching logic explained. J. Logical Algebraic Methods Program. **120**, 1–36 (2021). https://doi.org/10.1016/j.jlamp.2021.100638
7. Chen, X., Roşu, G.: Matching μ-logic. In: Proceedings of the 34th Annual ACM/IEEE Symposium on Logic in Computer Science, Vancouver, Canada, pp. 1–13. IEEE (2019). https://doi.org/10.1109/LICS.2019.8785675
8. Clarkson, M.R., Schneider, F.B.: Hyperproperties. J. Comput. Secur. **18**(6), 1157–1210 (2010). https://doi.org/10.3233/JCS-2009-0393
9. Clevert, D., Unterthiner, T., Hochreiter, S.: Fast and accurate deep network learning by exponential linear units (ELUs). In: Proceedings of the 4th International Conference on Learning Representations, San Juan, Puerto Rico. OpenReview.net (2016)
10. Codevilla, F., Müller, M., López, A.M., Koltun, V., Dosovitskiy, A.: End-to-end driving via conditional imitation learning. In: Proceedings of the 2018 IEEE International Conference on Robotics and Automation, Brisbane, Australia, pp. 1–9. IEEE (2018). https://doi.org/10.1109/ICRA.2018.8460487
11. Dahl, G.E., Stokes, J.W., Deng, L., Yu, D.: Large-scale malware classification using random projections and neural networks. In: Proceedings of the 38th IEEE International Conference on Acoustics, Speech and Signal Processing, Vancouver, British Columbia, Canada, pp. 3422–3426. IEEE (2013). https://doi.org/10.1109/ICASSP.2013.6638293
12. Dreossi, T., Jha, S., Seshia, S.A.: Semantic adversarial deep learning. In: Chockler, H., Weissenbacher, G. (eds.) CAV 2018. LNCS, vol. 10981, pp. 3–26. Springer, Cham (2018). https://doi.org/10.1007/978-3-319-96145-3_1

13. Dutta, S., Jha, S., Sankaranarayanan, S., Tiwari, A.: Output range analysis for deep feedforward neural networks. In: Dutle, A., Muñoz, C., Narkawicz, A. (eds.) NFM 2018. LNCS, vol. 10811, pp. 121–138. Springer, Cham (2018). https://doi.org/10.1007/978-3-319-77935-5_9

14. Dvijotham, K., Stanforth, R., Gowal, S., Mann, T.A., Kohli, P.: A dual approach to scalable verification of deep networks. In: Proceedings of the 34th Conference on Uncertainty in Artificial Intelligence, Monterey, California, USA, pp. 550–559. AUAI Press (2018)

15. Ehlers, R.: Formal verification of piece-wise linear feed-forward neural networks. In: D'Souza, D., Narayan Kumar, K. (eds.) ATVA 2017. LNCS, vol. 10482, pp. 269–286. Springer, Cham (2017). https://doi.org/10.1007/978-3-319-68167-2_19

16. Elman, J.L.: Finding structure in time. Cogn. Sci. **14**(2), 179–211 (1990). https://doi.org/10.1207/s15516709cog1402_1

17. Gehr, T., Mirman, M., Drachsler-Cohen, D., Tsankov, P., Chaudhuri, S., Vechev, M.T.: AI2: safety and robustness certification of neural networks with abstract interpretation. In: Proceedings of the 39th IEEE Symposium on Security and Privacy, San Francisco, California, USA, pp. 3–18. IEEE Computer Society (2018). https://doi.org/10.1109/SP.2018.00058

18. Goodfellow, I.J., Shlens, J., Szegedy, C.: Explaining and harnessing adversarial examples. In: Proceedings of the 3rd International Conference on Learning Representations, San Diego, California, USA. OpenReview.net (2015)

19. Hardt, M., Price, E., Srebro, N.: Equality of opportunity in supervised learning. In: Proceedings of the 30th Annual Conference on Neural Information Processing Systems, Barcelona, Spain, pp. 3315–3323. Curran Associates Inc. (2016)

20. Hayou, S., Doucet, A., Rousseau, J.: On the selection of initialization and activation function for deep neural networks. CoRR abs/1805.08266 (2018). http://arxiv.org/abs/1805.08266

21. Huang, X., et al.: A survey of safety and trustworthiness of deep neural networks: verification, testing, adversarial attack and defence, and interpretability. Comput. Sci. Rev. **37**, 100270 (2020). https://doi.org/10.1016/j.cosrev.2020.100270

22. Huang, X., Kwiatkowska, M., Wang, S., Wu, M.: Safety verification of deep neural networks. In: Majumdar, R., Kunčak, V. (eds.) CAV 2017. LNCS, vol. 10426, pp. 3–29. Springer, Cham (2017). https://doi.org/10.1007/978-3-319-63387-9_1

23. Klambauer, G., Unterthiner, T., Mayr, A., Hochreiter, S.: Self-normalizing neural networks. In: Proceedings of the 31st Annual Conference on Neural Information Processing Systems, Long Beach, California, USA, pp. 971–980. Curran Associates Inc. (2017)

24. LeCun, Y., Bengio, Y.: Convolutional Networks for Images, Speech, and Time Series, pp. 255–258. MIT Press, Cambridge (1998)

25. Liu, W.-W., Song, F., Zhang, T.-H.-R., Wang, J.: Verifying ReLU neural networks from a model checking perspective. J. Comput. Sci. Technol. **35**(6), 1365–1381 (2020). https://doi.org/10.1007/s11390-020-0546-7

26. Maas, A.L., Hannun, A.Y., Ng, A.Y.: Rectifier nonlinearities improve neural network acoustic models. In: Proceedings of the 30th International Conference on Machine Learning, Atlanta, Georgia, USA, vol. 30. PMLR (2013)

27. Nair, V., Hinton, G.E.: Rectified linear units improve restricted Boltzmann machines. In: Proceedings of the 27th International Conference on Machine Learning, Haifa, Israel, pp. 807–814. Omnipress (2010)

28. Narayan, S.: The generalized sigmoid activation function: competitive supervised learning. Inf. Sci. **99**(1), 69–82 (1997). https://doi.org/10.1016/S0020-0255(96)00200-9

29. Papernot, N., McDaniel, P.D., Jha, S., Fredrikson, M., Celik, Z.B., Swami, A.: The limitations of deep learning in adversarial settings. In: Proceedings of the 1st IEEE European Symposium on Security and Privacy, Saarbrücken, Germany, pp. 372–387. IEEE (2016). https://doi.org/10.1109/EuroSP.2016.36

30. Pnueli, A.: The temporal logic of programs. In: Proceedings of the 18th Annual Symposium on Foundations of Computer Science, Providence, Rhode Island, USA, pp. 46–57. IEEE Computer Society (1977). https://doi.org/10.1109/SFCS.1977.32

31. Roşu, G.: Finite-trace linear temporal logic: coinductive completeness. Formal Methods Syst. Des. **53**(1), 138–163 (2018). https://doi.org/10.1007/s10703-018-0321-3

32. Ruan, W., Huang, X., Kwiatkowska, M.: Reachability analysis of deep neural networks with provable guarantees. In: Proceedings of the 27th International Joint Conference on Artificial Intelligence, Stockholm, Sweden, pp. 2651–2659. ijcai.org (2018). https://doi.org/10.24963/ijcai.2018/368

33. Schmidhuber, J.: Deep learning in neural networks: an overview. Neural Netw. **61**, 85–117 (2015). https://doi.org/10.1016/j.neunet.2014.09.003

34. Seshia, S.A., et al.: Formal specification for deep neural networks. In: Lahiri, S.K., Wang, C. (eds.) ATVA 2018. LNCS, vol. 11138, pp. 20–34. Springer, Cham (2018). https://doi.org/10.1007/978-3-030-01090-4_2

35. Shin, E.C.R., Song, D., Moazzezi, R.: Recognizing functions in binaries with neural networks. In: Proceedings of the 24th USENIX Security Symposium, Washington, D.C., USA, pp. 611–626. USENIX Association (2015)

36. Shriver, D., Elbaum, S., Dwyer, M.B.: DNNV: a framework for deep neural network verification. In: Silva, A., Leino, K.R.M. (eds.) CAV 2021. LNCS, vol. 12759, pp. 137–150. Springer, Cham (2021). https://doi.org/10.1007/978-3-030-81685-8_6

37. Simard, P.Y., Steinkraus, D., Platt, J.C.: Best practices for convolutional neural networks applied to visual document analysis. In: Proceedings of the 7th International Conference on Document Analysis and Recognition, Edinburgh, Scotland, UK, pp. 958–962. IEEE Computer Society (2003). https://doi.org/10.1109/ICDAR.2003.1227801

38. Singh, G., Ganvir, R., Püschel, M., Vechev, M.T.: Beyond the single neuron convex barrier for neural network certification. In: Proceedings of the 33rd Annual Conference on Neural Information Processing Systems, Vancouver, British Columbia, Canada, pp. 15072–15083. Curran Associates Inc. (2019)

39. Singh, G., Gehr, T., Püschel, M., Vechev, M.T.: An abstract domain for certifying neural networks. Proc. ACM Program. Lang. **3**(POPL), 41:1–41:30 (2019). https://doi.org/10.1145/3290354

40. Singh, G., Gehr, T., Püschel, M., Vechev, M.T.: Boosting robustness certification of neural networks. In: Proceedings of the 7th International Conference on Learning Representations, New Orleans, LA, USA. OpenReview.net (2019)

41. Sun, B., Sun, J., Dai, T., Zhang, L.: Probabilistic verification of neural networks against group fairness. In: Huisman, M., Păsăreanu, C., Zhan, N. (eds.) FM 2021. LNCS, vol. 13047, pp. 83–102. Springer, Cham (2021). https://doi.org/10.1007/978-3-030-90870-6_5

42. Sutskever, I., Vinyals, O., Le, Q.V.: Sequence to sequence learning with neural networks. In: Proceedings of the 28th Annual Conference on Neural Information Processing Systems, Montreal, Quebec, Canada, pp. 3104–3112. Curran Associates Inc. (2014)

43. Tarski, A.: A lattice-theoretical fixpoint theorem and its applications. Pac. J. Math. **5**(2), 285–309 (1955). pjm/1103044538

44. Tjeng, V., Xiao, K.Y., Tedrake, R.: Evaluating robustness of neural networks with mixed integer programming. In: Proceedings of the 7th International Conference on Learning Representations, New Orleans, LA, USA. OpenReview.net (2019)

45. Wang, S., Pei, K., Whitehouse, J., Yang, J., Jana, S.: Efficient formal safety analysis of neural networks. In: Proceedings of the 32nd Annual Conference on Neural Information Processing Systems, Montréal, Canada, pp. 6369–6379. Curran Associates Inc. (2018)

46. Wang, S., Pei, K., Whitehouse, J., Yang, J., Jana, S.: Formal security analysis of neural networks using symbolic intervals. In: Proceedings of the 27th USENIX Security Symposium, Baltimore, Maryland, USA, pp. 1599–1614. USENIX Association (2018)

47. Weng, T., et al.: Towards fast computation of certified robustness for ReLU networks. In: Proceedings of the 35th International Conference on Machine Learning. Proceedings of Machine Learning Research, Stockholmsmässan, Stockholm, Sweden, vol. 80, pp. 5273–5282. PMLR (2018)

48. Weng, T., et al.: Evaluating the robustness of neural networks: an extreme value theory approach. In: Proceedings of the 6th International Conference on Learning Representations, Vancouver, British Columbia, Canada. OpenReview.net (2018)

49. Xiang, W., Tran, H., Johnson, T.T.: Output reachable set estimation and verification for multilayer neural networks. IEEE Trans. Neural Netw. Learn. Syst. **29**(11), 5777–5783 (2018). https://doi.org/10.1109/TNNLS.2018.2808470

50. You, S., Ding, D., Canini, K.R., Pfeifer, J., Gupta, M.R.: Deep lattice networks and partial monotonic functions. In: Proceedings of the 31st Annual Conference on Neural Information Processing Systems, Long Beach, California, USA, pp. 2981–2989. Curran Associates Inc. (2017)

51. Zhang, H., Weng, T., Chen, P., Hsieh, C., Daniel, L.: Efficient neural network robustness certification with general activation functions. In: Proceedings of the 32nd Annual Conference on Neural Information Processing Systems, Montréal, Canada, pp. 4944–4953. Curran Associates Inc. (2018)

52. Zhang, X., Chen, X., Sun, M.: Towards a unifying logical framework for neural networks. Technical report, Peking University and University of Illinois Urbana-Champaign (2022). https://hdl.handle.net/2142/114412

Type Inference for Rank-2 Intersection Types Using Set Unification

Pedro Ângelo[✉] and Mário Florido

LIACC, Departamento de Ciência de Computadores, Faculdade de Ciências, Universidade do Porto, Rua do Campo Alegre s/n, 4169-007 Porto, Portugal
{pedro.angelo,amflorid}@fc.up.pt

Abstract. Several type inference approaches for rank-2 idempotent and commutative intersection types have been presented in the literature. Type inference relies on two stages: type constraint generation and solving. Defining constraint generation rules is rather straightforward, with one exception. To infer the type of an application, several derivations of the argument are required, one for each instance of the domain type of the function. The types of these derivations are then constrained against the instances. Noting that these derivations are isomorphic, by renaming of type variables, they can be obtained via a duplication operation on a single derivation of the argument. The application rule then constrains the intersection type resulting from duplication against the domain type of the function, resulting in an equality constraint between intersections. By treating intersections as sets, these constraints can be solved by solving a set unification problem, thus ensuring the types of the argument unify with the domain type of the function. Here we present a new type inference algorithm for rank-2 intersection types, which relies on set unification to solve equality constraints between intersections, and show it is both sound and complete.

Keywords: Intersection types · Type inference · Set unification

1 Introduction

The benefits (and the costs) of strong static typing in programming languages are now generally recognized. Languages such as ML, Haskell or Java are examples of the use of strong typing. To avoid the extra effort of declaring types for every part of the program, compilers should infer types as much as possible. And to avoid rejecting well-behaved programs as much as possible, type inference should be able to support some form of polymorphism. Two of the main options for polymorphism are universally quantified types (such as the Damas-Milner type system [17] and System $\mathcal{F}$ [28,29,41]), and intersection types [13].

Intersection types originate in the works of Barendregt, Coppo and Dezani [6,13,15], and give us a characterization of the strongly normalizable terms. New attention was given to intersection type systems due to a result of Kfoury and

H. Seidl et al. (Eds.): ICTAC 2022, LNCS 13572, pp. 462–480, 2022.
https://doi.org/10.1007/978-3-031-17715-6_29

Wells [35,36] which proved that these systems are decidable for restrictions of finite rank, which correspond to a large class of typable terms. Consider the following example: in intersection type systems λx . x x has type $(\alpha \wedge (\alpha \to \beta)) \to \beta$. Note that the two (non-unifiable) types of the variable x belong to the domain type of the abstraction linked by the intersection operator. A more interesting example is the term $(\lambda x$. x $x)$ I, where $I = \lambda y$. y. This term has type $\alpha \to \alpha$ which does not involve intersections, although it is not typable in the simply typed lambda calculus [16,31] because it has a non-typable subterm.

Intersection type systems characterise the set of strongly normalising terms and have huge expressive power, typing more terms than the simply typed lambda calculus or the type system of pure ML or core Haskell. Applications of intersection types in programming language theory cover diverse topics, including the design of programming languages [7,42], program analysis [38], program synthesis [26], and extensions such as refinement, union and gradual types [3,11,12,23,24,27]. But expressive power comes with a price: type theoretic problems such as type inference and inhabitation are undecidable in general [5,45].

In [35] Wells and Kfoury define an intersection type system which types exactly the strongly normalizable terms and shows that every finite-rank restriction of this system, using Leivant's notion of rank [37], has principal typings and also decidable type inference. This system uses expansion variables [10,36], which are subject to substitution as are ordinary variables, and a unification-based type inference algorithm using a new form of unification called β-unification. Due to the complexity of type inference algorithms for higher finite ranks, the most successful decidable fragments of intersection type systems have focused on the rank-2 restriction. Indeed, we rely on the same argument to motivate our rank-2 restriction of the type inference algorithm presented in this paper. The rank of a type is easily determined by its syntactic tree. A type is of rank n if no path from the root of the syntactic tree of the type to an intersection passes to the left of n arrows. Rank 0 and 1 are equivalent to the simple typed lambda-calculus. But starting from rank 2, the systems type more terms than the type system of pure ML or Core Haskell.

Van Bakel presents a unification algorithm as the basis of type inference for a rank-2 system [46]. Later, independent work by Trevor Jim also solves the same problem for practical programming language issues such as recursive definitions and separate compilation [33]. Damiani [18] also studied rank-2 principal typings with intersection types and focus his work on rank-2 typable recursive definitions.

All these previous algorithms rely on extensions to first-order unification [43], either explicit [35,36,46], or implicit [32,33]. In these, a more general form of subtyping type constraints is first generated, and subsequently, in the constraint solving phase, further simplified by rewriting subtyping into equalities.

Several authors have also explored intersection type inference systems using unification theory. Approaches focus on relating β-reduction with unification [8], and more similarly to our work, building type inference algorithms using set unification theory [14,22,44]. However, we relate the properties of intersection types with set unification, which as far as we know, is novel work.

Originally [13, 15], intersection types were denoted by finite sets of types:

"The main idea is to define from an arbitrary set of types $\{\tau_1, \cdots, \tau_n\}$ a "sequence" $[\tau_1, \cdots, \tau_n]$ whose underlying set of terms can be interpreted as the intersection of those of $\tau_1, \cdots, \tau_n$" [13].

Picking up on this original motivation, we here define a new type inference algorithm for rank-2 intersection types which relies on *set unification* [20, 21] to solve the type constraints generated by function applications. The main contributions of this paper are the following:

- A unification-based type inference algorithm for rank-2 intersection types using set unification. The algorithm is terminating, always returning principal typings. A nice feature of this algorithm is its similarity with type inference for simple types [39] - just replace first-order unification by set unification.
- Proofs of soundness and completeness of the algorithm, meaning that the outputs of type inference are types which are derivable in a rank-2 intersection type system, and more, they are principal typings in the sense that every other type derivable in the type system may be obtained from them using substitution.

It is important to note that the majority of the discussed results can be obtained by the other previously defined rank-2 intersection type inference algorithms. Nonetheless, it is our belief that the work in this paper constitutes further a step towards a better understanding of the role of set unification as the base of type inference algorithms for intersection types and may highlight how intersections at different depth are related to different restrictions of set unification in the type inference mechanism. Complete proofs for theorems introduced in this paper are presented in the technical report [4].

The paper is organized as follows. Section 2 introduces the syntax of the system. A rank-2 intersection type system, where every type declared in the context is used in the type derivation, is presented in Sect. 3. The formalization of the type inference algorithm, along with its components, follows in Sect. 4. The first phase of the algorithm consists of the constraint generation rules, which are detailed in Subsect. 4.1. In particular, we present an alternative design to the rule for applications: by requiring only one derivation and then duplicating it, there is a derivation of the argument for each instance in the domain type of the function. Set unification, explained in Subsect. 4.2, will be required to solve equality constraints between intersection types. The general constraint solving rules are presented in Subsect. 4.3. We finally produce the type inference algorithm, along with important properties, in Subsect. 4.4. The conclusion follows in Sect. 5.

2   Types and Terms

Our language is an intersection typed lambda calculus á la Curry, which supports term constants, such as integers and booleans, and built-in addition. Other arithmetic operations can be defined similarly. The syntax of our language is given by the following grammar:

Definition 1 (Syntax).

monotypes	τ, ρ	$::=$	$B \mid \alpha \mid \sigma \to \tau$
sequences	σ, υ	$::=$	$\tau_1 \wedge \ldots \wedge \tau_n \mid \phi$
terms	M, N	$::=$	$k \mid x \mid \lambda x . M \mid M\,M \mid M + M$
typing context	Γ	$::=$	$\emptyset \mid \Gamma, x : \sigma \qquad \text{with } \sigma \in \mathcal{T}_1$
constraint	C	$::=$	$\sigma \doteq \sigma$
constraints	C^*	$::=$	$\emptyset \mid C^* \cup C$

B ranges over base types such as Int and Bool, α and β range over type variables and ϕ ranges over sequence variables. τ and ρ range over monotypes i.e. the top level constructor is not the intersection type connective, and σ and υ range over sequences. M and N range over terms, x, y and z range over term variables and k ranges over constants, such as integers and booleans. Γ ranges over typing contexts, and $\emptyset$ represents an empty context. C ranges over equality constraints, written as $\sigma \doteq \sigma$, and C^* ranges over multisets of equality constraints C. χ ranges over sets of type, and sequence, variables.

Remark 1. The indexes i, j, m, n, p and q range over the set $\mathbb{Z}_0^+$.

Remark 2. We distinguish meta-variables with different subscript natural numbers, and also with superscript apostrophe.

As in the original system [13,40], we consider the intersection connective $\wedge$ as commutative, e.g. $\tau \wedge \rho = \rho \wedge \tau$, and idempotent, e.g. $\tau \wedge \tau = \tau$. We do not consider associativity, since we are not dealing with a binary operator. Therefore, an intersection type $\tau_1 \wedge \ldots \wedge \tau_n$ is seen as the set of types $\tau_1, \ldots, \tau_n$. Given a sequence $\tau_1 \wedge \ldots \wedge \tau_n$, each τ_i is called an *instance* of the intersection. We allow sequences of size one, so σ and υ also range over monotypes. Sequences can only appear in the left-hand side of the arrow type constructor, therefore the shape of a (valid) arrow type is $\sigma \to \tau$. The intersection type connective $\wedge$ has a higher precedence than the arrow type constructor $\to$, and $\to$ associates to the right.

Definition 2 (Type Variables). *The function $tvars(.)$, which returns the set of type, and sequence, variables occurring in a given type, is defined as follows:*
$$tvars(\sigma) \overset{def}{=} \{\alpha \mid \alpha \text{ occurs in } \sigma\} \cup \{\phi \mid \phi \text{ occurs in } \sigma\}.$$

Definition 3 (Free Variables). *The function $fvars(.)$, which returns the set of free term variables occurring in a given term, is defined as follows:*
$$fvars(M) \overset{def}{=} \{x \mid x \text{ occurs free in } M\}.$$

Definition 4 (Atomic Type Sets). *Atomic types in our language are categorized according to the following sets:*

$$
\begin{aligned}
\mathcal{T}_{base} &= \{B \mid B \text{ is a base type}\} \\
\mathcal{T}_{tvar} &= \{\alpha \mid \alpha \text{ is a type variable}\} \\
\mathcal{T}_{svar} &= \{\phi \mid \phi \text{ is a sequence variable}\}
\end{aligned}
$$

According to the definition of rank restriction [33,37], a *rank n intersection type* can have no intersection type connective $\wedge$ to the left of n or more arrow type constructors $\rightarrow$:

Definition 5 (Rank). *Types of our language are categorized according to rank:*

simple types	$\mathcal{T}_0$	$= \mathcal{T}_{base} \cup \mathcal{T}_{tvar} \cup \{\tau \rightarrow \rho \mid \tau, \rho \in \mathcal{T}_0\}$
rank 1 types	$\mathcal{T}_1$	$= \mathcal{T}_0 \cup \mathcal{T}_{svar} \cup \{\tau_1 \wedge \ldots \wedge \tau_n \mid \tau_1, \ldots, \tau_n \in \mathcal{T}_0\}$
rank 2 types	$\mathcal{T}_2$	$= \mathcal{T}_0 \cup \{\sigma \rightarrow \tau \mid \sigma \in \mathcal{T}_1, \tau \in \mathcal{T}_2\}$

We restrict types in our system to be only of up to rank 2, so the only possible types are those belonging to $\mathcal{T}_1 \cup \mathcal{T}_2$, e.g. $(((\tau \rightarrow \rho) \wedge \tau) \rightarrow \rho) \rightarrow \tau$ is not a valid type.

Remark 3. We denote the singleton context, which contains only one type binding, as $x : \sigma$. We write Γ_1, Γ_2 for the union of contexts Γ_1 and Γ_2, assuming Γ_1 and Γ_2 are disjoint.

Definition 6 (Joining Typing Contexts). *Let Γ_1 and Γ_2 be two typing contexts. $\Gamma_1 \wedge \Gamma_2$ is a typing context, where $x : \sigma \in \Gamma_1 \wedge \Gamma_2$ if and only if σ is defined as follows:*

$$
\sigma = \begin{cases}
\sigma_1 \wedge \sigma_2, & \text{if } x : \sigma_1 \in \Gamma_1 \text{ and } x : \sigma_2 \in \Gamma_2 \\
\sigma_1, & \text{if } x : \sigma_1 \in \Gamma_1 \text{ and } \neg \exists \sigma_2 . x : \sigma_2 \in \Gamma_2 \\
\sigma_2, & \text{if } \neg \exists \sigma_1 . x : \sigma_1 \in \Gamma_1 \text{ and } x : \sigma_2 \in \Gamma_2
\end{cases}
$$

3   Type System

In Fig. 1 we define an intersection type system where every type declared in the context is used in the type derivation, a property which is going to be quite useful in subsequent results.

The two rules for abstractions, [T-ABSI] and [T-ABSK], are necessary because if there is a derivation of $\Gamma \vdash_\wedge M : \sigma$ and x does not occur free in M, then there is not a type declaration for x in Γ. The set of types for a given term M in this system is strictly included in the set of types for M in the original intersection type system of Coppo and Dezani [13,15]. For example, the type $(\alpha_1 \wedge \alpha_2) \rightarrow \alpha_1$ types $\lambda x . x$ in the Coppo-Dezani type system but not in our system. The reason for this is that types for free variables, which are introduced by rule [T-VAR], can only be included in an intersection via rules [T-APP] or

$$[\text{T-Con}] \ \frac{k \text{ is a constant of base type } B}{\emptyset \vdash_\wedge k : B} \qquad\qquad [\text{T-Var}] \ \frac{}{x : \tau \vdash_\wedge x : \tau}$$

$$[\text{T-AbsI}] \ \frac{\Gamma, x : \sigma \vdash_\wedge M : \tau}{\Gamma \vdash_\wedge \lambda x . M : \sigma \to \tau} \qquad [\text{T-AbsK}] \ \frac{\Gamma \vdash_\wedge M : \tau}{\Gamma \vdash_\wedge \lambda x . M : \sigma \to \tau} \ x \notin fvars(M)$$

$$[\text{T-App}] \ \frac{\Gamma \vdash_\wedge M : \tau_1 \wedge \ldots \wedge \tau_n \to \tau \qquad \forall i \in 1..n \ . \ \Gamma_i \vdash_\wedge N : \tau_i}{\Gamma \wedge \Gamma_1 \wedge \ldots \wedge \Gamma_n \vdash_\wedge M \ N : \tau}$$

$$[\text{T-Add}] \ \frac{\Gamma_1 \vdash_\wedge M : Int \qquad \Gamma_2 \vdash_\wedge N : Int}{\Gamma_1 \wedge \Gamma_2 \vdash_\wedge M + N : Int}$$

Fig. 1. Intersection type system $(\Gamma \vdash_\wedge M : \sigma)$

[T-Add]. Thus each element of the intersection corresponds to a type that is actually used in the type derivation. However, the set of terms typable in both systems is the same and corresponds to the strongly normalizable terms (a proof of this for a similar type system can be found in [25]).

One peculiarity of this type system is that it does not satisfy the property of *subject reduction* as it is shown by the following example:

Example 1. In this system, the following two statements hold:

$$z : \alpha_2 \to \beta \vdash_\wedge \lambda x . (\lambda y . z) \ x \ x : \alpha_1 \wedge \alpha_2 \to \beta$$

$$\lambda x . (\lambda y . z) \ x \ x \underset{\beta}{\to} \lambda x . z \ x$$

But we also have that

$$z : \alpha_2 \to \beta \nvdash_\wedge \lambda x . z \ x : \alpha_1 \wedge \alpha_2 \to \beta$$

because type $\alpha_1 \wedge \alpha_2$ can't be assigned to x, since only one occurrence of x (typed with α_2) exists.

The lack of subject reduction also happens in other restrictions of intersection type systems where every type in the environment has to be used in the type derivation [19,35]. The reason for the lack of subject reduction is that there is no weakening introducing unneeded type assumptions. Note that the lack of subject reduction is not a problem, because derivations in this system can be easily translated into derivations on more standard systems of intersection types which have subject reduction. Defining the system without a weakening mechanism makes the later analysis about type inference much easier.

Consider the following example of a type derivation for $(\lambda x . x \ x) (\lambda y . y)$:

Example 2. We abbreviate $\tau = \rho \rightarrow \rho$. We have the following derivations by applying the last rule as follows:

$$[\text{T-AbsI}] \quad \emptyset \vdash_\wedge \lambda x \,.\, x \; x : (\tau \rightarrow \tau) \wedge \tau \rightarrow \tau \tag{1}$$

$$[\text{T-AbsI}] \quad \emptyset \vdash_\wedge \lambda y \,.\, y : \tau \rightarrow \tau \tag{2}$$

$$[\text{T-AbsI}] \quad \emptyset \vdash_\wedge \lambda y \,.\, y : \tau \tag{3}$$

By rule [T-App] on derivations (1), (2) and (3), we have:

$$[\text{T-App}] \quad \emptyset \vdash_\wedge (\lambda x \,.\, x \; x) \, (\lambda y \,.\, y) : \tau$$

4   Type Inference

We follow a conventional approach to type inference [47]: a constraint generation phase generates type constraints from the term, and a constraint solving phase solves these constraints to generate type substitutions.

Substitution on types is defined in the standard way [39], extended to allow intersections.

Definition 7 (Substitution). *Let S range over standard type substitutions [39]. We write $[\alpha \mapsto \tau]$ for a type substitution on monotypes that maps a type variable α into a monotype τ; and $[\phi \mapsto \sigma]$ for a type substitution on sequences that maps a sequence variable ϕ into a sequence σ.*

For each type system rule in Fig. 1, an analogous constraint generation rule is required. Deriving these from the type system is rather straightforward: convert judgments in the premises to constraint generation judgments, making the type opaque; then convert the judgment in the conclusion, adding constraints that reflect how types relate to each other in the type system.

Deriving a constraint generation rule from [T-App] is not as straightforward. In the type system rule for applications, the function is assumed to be typed with an arrow type. However, the same assumption cannot be made for the constraint generation rules. Therefore, two constraint generation rules for applications are required: one where this assumption holds, and another where it does not, leading to an opaque type being inferred for the function. In standard systems [32], the application rule which assumes the type of the function is an arrow type behaves similarly to rule [T-App]. The rule ensures there are distinct type derivations of the argument, exactly one for each instance of the domain type of the function. By having distinct type derivations, the rule ensures the argument fits into each occurrence of the bound variable in the body of the lambda abstraction.

We follow a different approach: the application rule features a single type derivation of the argument. Then, the type obtained from this derivation is duplicated, and each copy is constrained to each instance in the domain type of the function. The duplication operation is defined as in [46]:

Definition 8 (Duplication). *Let $\chi = \{\alpha_1, \ldots, \alpha_j\} \cup \{\phi_{j+1}, \ldots, \phi_m\}$ be a set of type and sequence variables; let $\beta_{11}, \ldots, \beta_{1n}, \ldots, \beta_{m1}, \ldots, \beta_{mn}$ be fresh type* *variables; and let* $S_i = [\alpha_1 \mapsto \beta_{1i}, \ldots, \alpha_j \mapsto \beta_{ji}, \phi_{j+1} \mapsto \beta_{(j+1)i}, \ldots, \phi_m \mapsto \beta_{mi}]$, *for* $1 \leq i \leq n$. *The duplication function* $duplicate_\chi^n(\tau)$ *is defined as follows:*

$$duplicate_\chi^n(\tau) \stackrel{def}{=} S_1(\tau) \wedge \ldots \wedge S_n(\tau).$$

The argument χ represents the set of variables that will be duplicated, and the argument n represents the number of duplications. Therefore, n fresh variables β are required for each type variable in χ, to ensure new duplications. Only simple types ($\tau \in \mathcal{T}_0$) are duplicated, so sequence variables ϕ that might appear in the type are treated as simple types and replaced by type variables β. Note that if duplication is applied to a type without type variables, due to idempotence, duplication will return the same type, e.g. $duplicate_\emptyset^2(Int \rightarrow Int) = (Int \rightarrow Int) \wedge (Int \rightarrow Int)$, which is the same as $Int \rightarrow Int$. On the other hand, if type variables are considered, duplication will generate n many copies of the type, e.g. $duplicate_{\{\alpha_1,\alpha_2\}}^2(\alpha_1 \rightarrow \alpha_2) = (\beta_{11} \rightarrow \beta_{21}) \wedge (\beta_{12} \rightarrow \beta_{22})$.

We give meaning to constraints through a satisfaction relation $\models$. A substitution S satisfies a constraint $\sigma \stackrel{.}{=} v$ if and only if applying the substitution to both types in the constraint yields an equality. Taking into account that intersection types are idempotent and commutative, two sequences are equal if both share the same set of instances. Since sequences of size one are allowed, the equality constraint between monotypes $\tau \stackrel{.}{=} \rho$ is an instance of $\sigma \stackrel{.}{=} v$, i.e. $S \models \tau \stackrel{.}{=} \rho \iff S(\tau) = S(\rho)$.

Definition 9 (Constraint Satisfaction).

1. $S \models \emptyset$
2. $S \models \sigma \stackrel{.}{=} v \iff S(\sigma) = S(v)$
3. $S \models C^* \iff S \models C$ *for all* $C \in C^*$

Definition 10 (Lifting Type Variables). *We lift function* $tvars(.)$, *from Definition 2, to typing contexts* Γ *and equality constraints* C^* *in the obvious way.*

Definition 11 (Lifting Substitution). *We lift substitutions, from Definition 7, to:*

- *typing contexts* Γ *in the obvious way;*
- *constraints in the following way:* $S(\sigma \stackrel{.}{=} v) \stackrel{def}{=} S(\sigma) \stackrel{.}{=} S(v)$. *Also,* $S(C^* \cup C) \stackrel{def}{=} S(C^*) \cup S(C)$ *and* $S(\emptyset) \stackrel{def}{=} \emptyset$.

Definition 12 (Lifting Duplication). *Assuming* $S_1, \ldots, S_n$ *are type substitutions generated from* χ *according to Definition 8, we lift function* $duplicate_\chi^n(.)$, *from Definition 8, to:*

- *typing contexts in the following way:* $duplicate_\chi^n(\Gamma) \stackrel{def}{=} S_1(\Gamma) \wedge \ldots \wedge S_n(\Gamma)$;
- *constraints in the following way:* $duplicate_\chi^n(C^*) \stackrel{def}{=} S_1(C^*) \cup \ldots \cup S_n(C^*)$.

Besides duplicating the type of argument derivations in the application rule, the typing context and constraints must also be duplicated, thus simulating several derivations of the same term. These derivations are just renamings of type variables of the original derivation.

$$[\text{G-CON}] \ \frac{k \text{ is a constant of base type B}}{\emptyset \vdash_\wedge k : B \mid \emptyset} \qquad [\text{G-VAR}] \ \frac{\alpha \text{ fresh}}{x : \alpha \vdash_\wedge x : \alpha \mid \emptyset}$$

$$[\text{G-ABSI}] \ \frac{\Gamma, x : \sigma \vdash_\wedge M : \tau \mid C^*}{\Gamma \vdash_\wedge \lambda x . \ M : \sigma \to \tau \mid C^*}$$

$$[\text{G-ABSK}] \ \frac{\Gamma \vdash_\wedge M : \tau \mid C^* \qquad \phi \text{ fresh}}{\Gamma \vdash_\wedge \lambda x . \ M : \phi \to \tau \mid C^*} \ x \notin fvars(M)$$

$$[\text{G-APP}\wedge] \ \frac{\begin{array}{c} \Gamma_1 \vdash_\wedge M : \tau_1 \wedge \ldots \wedge \tau_n \to \tau \mid C_1^* \qquad \Gamma_2 \vdash_\wedge N : \rho \mid C_2^* \\ duplicate^n(\langle \Gamma_2, \rho, C_2^* \rangle) = \langle [\Gamma_{21}, \ldots, \Gamma_{2n}], [\rho_1, \ldots, \rho_n], [C_{21}^*, \ldots, C_{2n}^*] \rangle \\ C = \tau_1 \wedge \ldots \wedge \tau_n \doteq \rho_1 \wedge \ldots \wedge \rho_n \end{array}}{\Gamma_1 \wedge \Gamma_{21} \wedge \ldots \wedge \Gamma_{2n} \vdash_\wedge M \ N : \tau \mid C_1^* \cup C_{21}^* \cup \ldots \cup C_{2n}^* \cup C}$$

$$[\text{G-APP}] \ \frac{\Gamma_1 \vdash_\wedge M : \tau \mid C_1^* \qquad \Gamma_2 \vdash_\wedge N : \rho \mid C_2^* \qquad \alpha \text{ fresh}}{\Gamma_1 \wedge \Gamma_2 \vdash_\wedge M \ N : \alpha \mid C_1^* \cup C_2^* \cup \{\tau \doteq \rho \to \alpha\}}$$

$$[\text{G-ADD}] \ \frac{\Gamma_1 \vdash_\wedge M : \tau \mid C_1^* \qquad \Gamma_2 \vdash_\wedge N : \rho \mid C_2^*}{\Gamma_1 \wedge \Gamma_2 \vdash_\wedge M + N : Int \mid C_1^* \cup \{\tau \doteq Int\} \cup C_2^* \cup \{\rho \doteq Int\}}$$

Fig. 2. Constraint generation ($\Gamma \vdash_\wedge M : \tau \mid C^*$)

Definition 13 (Duplication). *Let $\langle \Gamma, \tau, C^* \rangle$ be a triple composed of a typing context Γ, a type τ and constraints C^*. The duplication function is defined as $duplicate^n(\langle \Gamma, \tau, C^* \rangle) = \langle [\Gamma_1, \ldots, \Gamma_n], [\tau_1, \ldots, \tau_n], [C_1^*, \ldots, C_n^*] \rangle$ where:*

- $\chi = tvars(\Gamma) \cup tvars(\tau) \cup tvars(C^*)$;
- $duplicate_\chi^n(\Gamma) \equiv \Gamma_1 \wedge \ldots \wedge \Gamma_n$;
- $duplicate_\chi^n(\tau) \equiv \tau_1 \wedge \ldots \wedge \tau_n$;
- $duplicate_\chi^n(C^*) \equiv C_1^* \cup \ldots \cup C_n^*$.

4.1   Constraint Generation

We define the constraint generation rules in Fig. 2. The constraint generation judgment is written as $\Gamma \vdash_\wedge M : \tau \mid C^*$, where given a term M, the rules generate a typing context Γ, type τ and constraints C^*. We follow [32], assigning fresh type variables to variables in [G-VAR]. No assumptions are made for the type of the term variable, allowing it to be constrained to the correct type according to the context. Similarly to the type system, there are two constraint generation rules for lambda abstractions: [G-ABSI], when the bound variable occurs free in the body, and [G-ABSK], when it does not. When the bound variable occurs free in the body, rule [G-VAR] will gather type assumptions in the context. Then, rules containing several premises, [G-APP], [G-APP∧] and [G-ADD], join the contexts under an intersection (Definition 6). Due to this, the domain of the function type in the conclusion of rule [G-ABSI] corresponds to the intersection of the types of all ocurrences of the bound variable, which is given by the context in the premise of the rule. When the bound variable does not occur free in the body, there is no information regarding the type for the domain. Rule [G-ABsK] then returns an arrow type whose domain is a fresh sequence variable.

Whereas in the type system, there's a single application rule, two constraint generation rules are required: [G-APP∧] and [G-APP]. In [G-APP∧], the type of the function term is an arrow and its domain is an intersection. Then, the type of the function term, particularly the domain $\tau_1 \wedge \ldots \wedge \tau_n$, constrains how many derivations are needed of the argument term. For each instance in the domain type of the function, a derivation of the argument is required. Furthermore, each instance must unify with its corresponding argument's type.

However, instead of following the standard approach [32] of ensuring multiple derivations of the argument, we explore a different approach. In fact, generating multiple derivations of the argument amounts to duplicating type variables found in the context, type and constraints. We made this explicit in rule [G-APP∧].

If the type of the function term is not an arrow, then there is no information on the number of derivations required of the argument term, so only one is needed. Furthermore, the type of the function is constrained to be an arrow type, and its domain to match the argument's type, as specified in [G-APP].

Taking the previous example in Sect. 3, constraints are now generated for the expression:

Example 3. We have the following derivations by applying the rule:

$$[\text{G-ABsI}] \quad \emptyset \vdash_\wedge \lambda x . x\, x : \alpha_1 \wedge \alpha_2 \to \alpha_3 \mid \{\alpha_1 \doteq \alpha_2 \to \alpha_3\} \tag{4}$$

$$[\text{G-ABsI}] \quad \emptyset \vdash_\wedge \lambda y . y : \alpha_4 \to \alpha_4 \mid \emptyset \tag{5}$$

By rule [G-APP∧] on derivations (4), (5) and premises (6) and (7) we have:

$$duplicate^2(\langle \emptyset, \alpha_4 \to \alpha_4, \emptyset \rangle) = \langle [\emptyset, \emptyset], [\alpha_5 \to \alpha_5, \alpha_6 \to \alpha_6], [\emptyset, \emptyset] \rangle \tag{6}$$

$$C = \alpha_1 \wedge \alpha_2 \doteq \alpha_5 \to \alpha_5 \wedge \alpha_6 \to \alpha_6 \tag{7}$$

$$[\text{G-APP∧}] \quad \emptyset \vdash_\wedge (\lambda x . x\, x)\,(\lambda y . y) : \alpha_3 \mid \{\alpha_1 \doteq \alpha_2 \to \alpha_3\} \cup C$$

We show the following properties of our constraint generation algorithm:

Lemma 1 (Soundness of Constraint Generation). *If* $\Gamma \vdash_\wedge M : \tau \mid C^*$ *and* $S \models C^*$ *then* $S(\Gamma) \vdash_\wedge M : S(\tau)$.

Proof. Proof by induction on the length of the derivation tree of $\Gamma \vdash_\wedge M : \tau \mid C^*$.

Lemma 2 (Completeness of Constraint Generation). *If* $S_1(\Gamma) \vdash_\wedge M : \tau$ *then* $\Gamma \vdash_\wedge M : \rho \mid C^*$ *s.t. the domain of* S_1 *is disjoint from* χ, *and* $\exists S_2$ *s.t.* S_2 *agrees with* S_1 *except at* χ, $S_2 \models C^*$ *and* $S_2(\rho) = \tau$, *where* χ *are the fresh variables introduced in the derivation of* $\Gamma \vdash_\wedge M : \rho \mid C^*$.

Proof. Proof by induction on the length of the derivation tree of $S_1(\Gamma) \vdash_\wedge M : \tau$.

4.2 Set Unification

Type inference for simple types relies on first-order unification. However, equality constraints between idempotent and commutative intersection types are not so easy to solve. Solving such constraints involves finding the correct association between instances in both sequences. If we consider sequences as sets, this problem is equivalent to solving a set unification problem [20, 21].

According to [21], a set is an arbitrary, unordered collection of elements, i.e. the order and repetition of elements do not matter. Since we consider the intersection type operator $\wedge$ as idempotent and commutative, a sequence $\tau_1 \wedge \ldots \wedge \tau_n$ can be interpreted as a set $\{\tau_1, \ldots, \tau_n\}$, whose elements are the instances of the sequence. By Definition 1, a sequence can have as instances base types B, type variables α, and arrows $\sigma \to \tau$. These are the building blocks of sequences, so we define their counterparts for sets:

Definition 14 (Individuals). *The set of individuals $\mathcal{U}$ is defined as follows:*

- *if $B \in \mathcal{T}_{base}$ then $B \in \mathcal{U}$;*
- *if s, t are abstract set terms, then $\to (s, t) \in \mathcal{U}$.*

Individuals are essentially ground terms that make up our sets. Besides base types B, the arrow type is also considered an individual, however, one with two arguments.

Now we can define sets, that will act as a counterpart for sequences. According to [20, 21], the full class of sets is defined as follows. For $m, n, p, q \geq 0$, the class $set(m, n, p, q)$ represents the collection of all abstract set terms $\{X_1, \ldots, X_{m'}, a_1, \ldots, a_{n'}, s_1, \ldots, s_{p'}\} \cup Y_1 \cup \ldots \cup Y_{q'}$ such that $0 \geq m' \geq m, 0 \geq n' \geq n, 0 \geq p' \geq p, 0 \geq q' \geq q$, where X_i, Y_i are variables, a_i are individuals and s_i, t_i are abstract set terms (distinct from variables).

However, the full class of sets has more expressive power than what we need to encode sequences. The language of types, as well the rank restriction (Definition 5), restricts the expressive power of sequences to be less than that of sets. Only rank 1 sequences are allowed, therefore sequences cannot contain other sequences as elements. This restriction means that abstract set terms s_i inside sets are not permitted. Furthermore, extra variables Y_i have no counterpart in our sequences. Therefore, we only need a restricted fragment of the class $set(m, n, p, q)$: the class $flat(0) = \bigcup_{m \geq 0, n \geq 0} set(m, n, 0, 0)$. We then define our sets under this class:

Definition 15 (Abstract Set Terms). *An abstract set term is a term of the form: $\{X_1, \ldots, X_m, a_1, \ldots, a_n\}$, with $m, n \geq 0$.*

Therefore, rank 1 sequence solving is equivalent to the Set Unification Decision [21] problem between two $flat(0)$ sets.

We now define the translation, allowing sequences to be encoded as abstract set terms, which can be then passed onto the unification algorithm:

Definition 16 (Types as Abstract Set Terms). *The translation function* $(\![.]\!)$ *is defined according to the following rules:*

$$\frac{B \in \mathcal{T}_{base}}{(\![B]\!) = B} \qquad \overline{(\![\alpha]\!) = X} \qquad \frac{(\![\sigma]\!) = s \quad (\![v]\!) = t}{(\![\sigma \to \tau]\!) = \to (s,t)}$$

$$\frac{(\![\tau_1]\!) = t_1 \quad \ldots \quad (\![\tau_n]\!) = t_n}{(\![\tau_1 \wedge \ldots \wedge \tau_n]\!) = \{t_1, \ldots, t_n\}}$$

The translation function is bijective, and its inverse is defined as follows: assuming $(\![\sigma]\!) = s$, *then* $(\![s]\!)^{inv} = \sigma$.

With an encoding of sequences as sets, we can unify two sets with algorithm `AbCl_unify` [20,21]. Generally, algorithm `AbCl_unify` takes a system of equations as input and returns either fail or a collection of systems in solved form. However, since the constraint solving algorithm only needs to solve one equality constraint between sequences at a time, `AbCl_unify` is only ever called with a single equation as input. The algorithm then essentially tries to find a match between the elements of the two sets, non-deterministically checking different permutations. As two sets can be unified in several ways, this algorithm is non-deterministic, i.e. provides various solutions, albeit all correct. Therefore, due to relying on `AbCl_unify`, the constraint solving algorithm is also non-deterministic. We encapsulate the unification algorithm as well as the necessary translation, and define the sequence solving procedure $C \xRightarrow{s} S$:

Definition 17 (Sequence Solving). *Let* $\sigma \doteq v$ *be an equality constraint between two rank 1 sequences* σ *and* v. *The sequence solving procedure* $(\sigma \doteq v) \xRightarrow{s} S_i$, *that non-deterministically returns a set of substitutions* $S_1, \ldots, S_n$, *is defined by the following steps.*

Let $(\sigma \doteq v) \xRightarrow{s} S_i$, *such that:*

1. *let* t, s *be abstract set terms such that* $(\![\sigma]\!) = t$ *and* $(\![v]\!) = s$;
2. *choose an arbitrary solution* $\mathcal{E}_i$ *returned by* `AbCl_unify`$(\{t = s\})$:
   (a) *for every solved form equation* $X = t' \in \mathcal{E}_i$, *if* $(\![X]\!)^{inv} = \alpha$ *and* $(\![t']\!)^{inv} = \sigma'$, *then* $[\alpha \mapsto \sigma'] \in S_i$

We transcribe the soundness and completeness result from [20], from which we can then derive our own:

Theorem 1 (Soundness and Completeness of `AbCl_unify` [20]). *Given a system* $\mathcal{E}$, *let* $\mathcal{E}_1, \ldots, \mathcal{E}_n$ *be all the systems in solved form produced by the unification algorithm. Then* $Soln(\mathcal{E}) = Soln(\mathcal{E}_1)|_{vars(\mathcal{E})} \cup \ldots \cup Soln(\mathcal{E}_n)|_{vars(\mathcal{E})}$ *where* $Soln(X)$ *is the set of all ground set-unifiers of* X *and* $Soln(\mathcal{E}_i)|_{vars(\mathcal{E})}$ *is* $Soln(\mathcal{E}_i)$ *restricted to the variables of* $\mathcal{E}$.

Lemma 3 (Soundness of Sequence Solving). *If* $(\sigma \doteq v) \xRightarrow{s} S$ *then* $S \models \sigma \doteq v$.

Proof. If $(\sigma \doteq \upsilon) \overset{s}{\Rightarrow} S_i$, for all $i \in 1..n$, then by Definition 17: $(\!|\sigma|\!) = t$ and $(\!|\upsilon|\!) = s$; AbCl_unify($\{t = s\}$) returns solutions $\mathcal{E}_1, \ldots, \mathcal{E}_n$; and for every solved form equation $X = t' \in \mathcal{E}_i$, if $(\!|X|\!)^{inv} = \alpha$ and $(\!|t'|\!)^{inv} = \sigma'$, then $[\alpha \mapsto \sigma'] \in S_i$. By Theorem 1, $Soln(\{t = s\}) = Soln(\mathcal{E}_1)|_{vars(\{t=s\})} \cup \ldots \cup Soln(\mathcal{E}_n)|_{vars(\{t=s\})}$. We then have that $\mathcal{E}_i$ is a solution for $\{t = s\}$. By Definition 16, $(\!|t|\!)^{inv} = \sigma$ and $(\!|s|\!)^{inv} = \upsilon$. Therefore, S_i is a solution to $\sigma \doteq \upsilon$, or rather, $S_i(\sigma) = S_i(\upsilon)$. By Definition 9, $S_i \models \sigma \doteq \upsilon$.

Lemma 4. (Completeness of Sequence Solving). *If $S_1 \models \sigma \doteq \upsilon$ then $\exists S, S_2$ s.t. $(\sigma \doteq \upsilon) \overset{s}{\Rightarrow} S_2$ and $S_1 = S \circ S_2$.*

Proof. If $S_1 \models \sigma \doteq \upsilon$, then by Definition 16, (1) $(\!|\sigma|\!) = t$ and $(\!|\upsilon|\!) = s$. We then have that (2) AbCl_unify($\{t = s\}$) returns solutions $\mathcal{E}_1, \ldots, \mathcal{E}_n$, with $i \in 1..n$. By Theorem 1, we have that $Soln(\{t = s\}) = Soln(\mathcal{E}_1)|_{vars(\mathcal{E})} \cup \ldots \cup Soln(\mathcal{E}_n)|_{vars(\mathcal{E})}$. Therefore, the set of solved form equations of $\mathcal{E}_i$, for all $i \in 1..n$, represents all possible solutions of $\{t = s\}$, and each solution $\mathcal{E}_i$ is a minimal solution. (2a) For every solved form equation $X = t' \in \mathcal{E}_i$, if $(\!|X|\!)^{inv} = \alpha$ and $(\!|t'|\!)^{inv} = \sigma'$, then $[\alpha \mapsto \sigma'] \in S_i'$. By Definition 17, since we have (1), (2), and (2a), then $(\sigma \doteq \upsilon) \overset{s}{\Rightarrow} S_i'$, non-deterministically for all $i \in 1..n$. One of these solutions S_i' agrees with S_1, and is a most general solution to $\sigma \doteq \upsilon$. Therefore, $\exists S, S_i'$ s.t. $S_1 = S \circ S_i'$.

4.3 Constraint Solving

The constraint solving rules are defined in Fig. 2. The constraint solving judgment is written as $C^* \Rightarrow S$, where given constraints C^* the rules generate substitutions S. Most rules are straightforward, following standard formulations for type inference. Rule [S-EMPTY] allows constraint solving to terminate: when no constraints are left, the algorithm returns the substitutions. Rule [S-SAME] discards equality constraints between the same types. Rule [S-ARROW] deconstructs an equality constraint between two arrows, by constraining both the domains to each other, and both the codomains to each other.

Rule [S-SEQ] solves equality constraints between two sequences by calling the sequence solving algorithm $C \overset{s}{\Rightarrow} S'$, which in turn calls the solving algorithm AbCl_unify from [20,21]. Resulting substitutions are then applied to the remaining constraints, and solving proceeds as usual. Due to non-determinism of AbCl_unify, and consequently, $C \overset{s}{\Rightarrow} S'$, this rule introduces non-determinism in the constraint solving algorithm. However, every parallel solution is either correct, or constraint solving fails.

The remaining rules are standard rules to deal with type variables. Rules [S-TVARR] and [S-SVARR] apply when the type (and sequence) variables appear on the right side, swapping the positions of the constrained types. Rules [S-TVARL] and [S-SVARL] then produce a substitution between the type (and sequence) variable and the type on the right of the constraint.

Continuing the example from Sect. 4.1, constraints are solved:

$$[\text{S-EMPTY}] \ \frac{}{\emptyset \Rightarrow \emptyset} \qquad\qquad [\text{S-SAME}] \ \frac{C^* \Rightarrow S}{\{\tau \doteq \tau\} \cup C^* \Rightarrow S} \ \tau \in \mathcal{T}_{base} \cup \mathcal{T}_{tvar}$$

$$[\text{S-ARROW}] \ \frac{\{\sigma \doteq \upsilon, \tau \doteq \rho\} \cup C^* \Rightarrow S}{\{\sigma \to \tau \doteq \upsilon \to \rho\} \cup C^* \Rightarrow S}$$

$$[\text{S-SEQ}] \ \frac{(\tau_1 \wedge \ldots \wedge \tau_n \doteq \rho_1 \wedge \ldots \wedge \rho_m) \overset{s}{\Rightarrow} S' \qquad S'(C^*) \Rightarrow S}{\{\tau_1 \wedge \ldots \wedge \tau_n \doteq \rho_1 \wedge \ldots \wedge \rho_m\} \cup C^* \Rightarrow S \circ S'}$$

$$[\text{S-TVARR}] \ \frac{\{\alpha \doteq \tau\} \cup C^* \Rightarrow S}{\{\tau \doteq \alpha\} \cup C^* \Rightarrow S} \ \tau \notin \mathcal{T}_{tvar}$$

$$[\text{S-TVARL}] \ \frac{[\alpha \mapsto \tau]C^* \Rightarrow S}{\{\alpha \doteq \tau\} \cup C^* \Rightarrow S \circ [\alpha \mapsto \tau]} \ \tau \in \mathcal{T}_0 \ and \ \alpha \notin tvars(\tau)$$

$$[\text{S-SVARR}] \ \frac{\{\phi \doteq \sigma\} \cup C^* \Rightarrow S}{\{\sigma \doteq \phi\} \cup C^* \Rightarrow S} \ \sigma \notin \mathcal{T}_{svar}$$

$$[\text{S-SVARL}] \ \frac{[\phi \mapsto \sigma]C^* \Rightarrow S}{\{\phi \doteq \sigma\} \cup C^* \Rightarrow S \circ [\phi \mapsto \sigma]} \ \sigma \in \mathcal{T}_1 \ and \ \phi \notin tvars(\sigma)$$

Fig. 3. Constraint solving $(C^* \Rightarrow S)$

Example 4. We now have the following constraints to solve:

$$\{\alpha_1 \doteq \alpha_2 \to \alpha_3, \alpha_1 \wedge \alpha_2 \doteq \alpha_5 \to \alpha_5 \wedge \alpha_6 \to \alpha_6\} \Rightarrow \emptyset$$

$$[\text{S-TVARL}] \quad \{\alpha_2 \to \alpha_3 \wedge \alpha_2 \doteq \alpha_5 \to \alpha_5 \wedge \alpha_6 \to \alpha_6\} \Rightarrow [\alpha_1 \mapsto \alpha_2 \to \alpha_3]$$

Due to non-determinism of $C \overset{s}{\Rightarrow} S$, there are two solutions:

$$[\text{S-SEQ}] \quad \emptyset \Rightarrow [\alpha_5 \mapsto \alpha_6 \to \alpha_6] \circ [\alpha_2 \mapsto \alpha_5, \alpha_3 \mapsto \alpha_5] \circ [\alpha_1 \mapsto \alpha_2 \to \alpha_3]$$
$$[\text{S-SEQ}] \quad \emptyset \Rightarrow [\alpha_6 \mapsto \alpha_5 \to \alpha_5] \circ [\alpha_2 \mapsto \alpha_6, \alpha_3 \mapsto \alpha_6] \circ [\alpha_1 \mapsto \alpha_2 \to \alpha_3]$$

Choosing the first solution, our expression is typed as follows:

$$[\text{T-ABSI}] \quad \emptyset \vdash_\wedge \lambda x . x \ x : ((\alpha_6 \to \alpha_6) \to \alpha_6 \to \alpha_6) \wedge (\alpha_6 \to \alpha_6) \to \alpha_6 \to \alpha_6$$
$$[\text{T-ABSI}] \quad \emptyset \vdash_\wedge \lambda y . y : (\alpha_6 \to \alpha_6) \to \alpha_6 \to \alpha_6$$
$$[\text{T-ABSI}] \quad \emptyset \vdash_\wedge \lambda y . y : \alpha_6 \to \alpha_6$$
$$[\text{T-APP}] \quad \emptyset \vdash_\wedge (\lambda x . x \ x) \ (\lambda y . y) : \alpha_6 \to \alpha_6$$

We show our constraint solving algorithm is both sound and complete:

Lemma 5 (Soundness of Constraint Solving). *If $C^* \Rightarrow S$ then $S \models C^*$.*

Proof. Proof by induction on the length of the derivation tree of $C^* \Rightarrow S$.

Lemma 6 (Completeness of Constraint Solving). *If $S_1 \models C^*$ then $\exists S, S_2$ s.t. $C^* \Rightarrow S_2$ and $S_1 = S \circ S_2$.*

Proof. Proof by induction on the breakdown of constraint sets C^* by the solving rules.

4.4   Algorithm

Having defined both a constraint generation and solving algorithm, we now include both in the main type inference algorithm. We also show our type inference is sound and complete.

Definition 18 (Type Inference). *The type inference procedure infer$(M) \overset{def}{=} (\Gamma, \tau, S)$, that given an expression M, non-deterministically returns a triple (Γ, τ, S) composed of a typing context Γ, type τ and substitutions S, is defined by the following steps:*

Let infer$(M) \overset{def}{=} (\Gamma, \tau, S)$, such that:

1. *let Γ, τ and C^* such that $\Gamma \vdash_\wedge M : \tau \mid C^*$;*
2. *let S such that $C^* \Rightarrow S$;*

Theorem 2 (Soundness). *If infer$(M) = (\Gamma, \tau, S)$ then $S(\Gamma) \vdash_\wedge M : S(\tau)$.*

Proof. By Definition 18, we have Γ, τ and C^* such that $\Gamma \vdash_\wedge M : \tau \mid C^*$, and S such that $C^* \Rightarrow S$. By Lemma 5, since $C^* \Rightarrow S$ then $S \models C^*$. By Lemma 1, since $\Gamma \vdash_\wedge M : \tau \mid C^*$ and $S \models C^*$ then $S(\Gamma) \vdash_\wedge M : S(\tau)$.

Theorem 3 (Completeness). *If $S_1(\Gamma) \vdash_\wedge M : \tau$ then $\exists S_2, \rho, S$ s.t. infer$(M) = (\Gamma, \rho, S_2)$ and $\tau = S \circ S_2(\rho)$.*

Proof. If $S_1(\Gamma) \vdash_\wedge M : \tau$ then by Lemma 2, $\Gamma \vdash_\wedge M : \rho \mid C^*$ and $\exists S_2$ s.t. S_2 agrees with S_1 except at χ, $S_2 \models C^*$ and $S_2(\rho) = \tau$, where χ are the fresh variables introduced in the derivation of $\Gamma \vdash_\wedge M : \rho \mid C^*$. By Lemma 6, $\exists S, S_3$ s.t $C^* \Rightarrow S_3$ and $S_2 = S \circ S_3$. By Definition 18, infer$(M) = (\Gamma, \rho, S_3)$. Then, we have that $\tau = S \circ S_3(\rho)$.

5   Conclusion and Future Work

In this paper we present a sound and complete unification-based type inference algorithm for rank-2 intersection types using set unification. One nice feature of this algorithm is its similarity with type inference for simple types, it is basically the same algorithm, replacing first-order unification by set unification.

5.1   Future Work

Using Set-Unification Based Type Inference in Practice. This work is carried out in the context of a larger research project, focused in the use of intersection types and gradual types for programming language design and implementation. This larger project assumes the implementation and evaluation of intersection gradual types in a functional programming language compiler. Several points need to be further developed to enable the use of the algorithm presented here in the overall project goals. Some important points to address are:

1. Extension of the term language with recursive definitions. This will enable to apply our algorithm to a more realistic language and will address the known problems related with decidability for recursive definitions [30,34].
2. Add support to let expressions and conditional expressions. Most likely, in the case of conditional expressions, this will mean extending the type language with union types.

Theoretical Issues. The work presented here inspires the following possible future work:

1. Types here use associative, commutative and idempotent intersections. In the last years non-idempotent intersections have been successfully used to obtain quantitative information of program behaviour [1,2,9]. We believe it is rather promising to use multiset unification (usually based on solving diophantine equations) in the same way we use set unification, to infer types in this particular setting.
2. Investigate the complexity of our type inference algorithm. Being exponential for sure, because this is the complexity of the type inference problem for rank-2 intersection types, we want to study the exact complexity of our type inference algorithm and investigate if using set-unification may have some impact on the overall efficiency of type inference.
3. Extension to higher rank intersection types. Here we use a simple form of set unification where there cannot be sets inside sets. We conjecture that using those nested sets limited to a fixed level of nesting will result in type inference algorithms for higher (but finite) rank intersection types.
4. Study the relation of our approach with β-unification [35] and other forms of unification. Unification theory is a wide research field and studying in detail the relations between different unification algorithms, which, in this case, are used for the same purpose may shed some light on their relations and also contribute to the area of unification theory.

Acknowledgements. This work was partially financially supported by the portuguese Fundação para a Ciência e a Tecnologia, under the PhD grant number SFRH/BD/145183/2019 and by Base Funding - UIDB/00027/2020 of the Artificial Intelligence and Computer Science Laboratory – LIACC - funded by national funds through the FCT/MCTES (PIDDAC).

References

1. Accattoli, B., Graham-Lengrand, S., Kesner, D.: Tight typings and split bounds. In: Proceeding ACM Programming Language, vol. 2(ICFP), pp. 94:1–94:30 (2018)
2. Alves, S., Kesner, D., Ventura, D.: A quantitative understanding of pattern matching. In: 25th International Conference on Types for Proofs and Programs, TYPES 2019, 11–14 June 2019, Oslo, Norway. LIPIcs, vol. 175, pp. 3:1–3:36. Schloss Dagstuhl - Leibniz-Zentrum für Informatik (2019)
3. Ângelo, P., Florido, M.: Type inference for rank 2 gradual intersection types. In: Bowman, W.J., Garcia, R. (eds.) Trends in Functional Programming, pp. 84–120. Springer International Publishing, Cham (2020). https://doi.org/10.1007/978-3-030-47147-7_5
4. Ângelo, P., Florido, M.: Type inference for rank-2 intersection types using set unification. Technical report, Faculdade de Ciências & LIACC, Universidade do Porto (2022). https://raw.githubusercontent.com/pedroangelo/papers/master/angelo2022type_complete.pdf
5. Barendregt, H.P., Dekkers, W., Statman, R.: Lambda Calculus with Types. Perspectives in logic, Cambridge University Press (2013)
6. Barendregt, H., Coppo, M., Dezani-Ciancaglini, M.: A filter lambda model and the completeness of type assignment. J. Symb. Log. **48**(4), 931–940 (1983). https://doi.org/10.2307/2273659
7. Bettini, L., Bono, V., Dezani-Ciancaglini, M., Giannini, P., Venneri, B.: Java & lambda: a featherweight story. Log. Methods Comput. Sci. **14**(3) (2018)
8. Boudol, G., Zimmer, P.: On type inference in the intersection type discipline. Electron. Notes Theor. Comput. Sci. **136**, 23–42 (2005). https://doi.org/10.1016/j.entcs.2005.06.016, https://www.sciencedirect.com/science/article/pii/S1571066105050589. Proceedings of the Third International Workshop on Intersection Types and Related Systems (ITRS 2004)
9. Bucciarelli, A., Kesner, D., Ventura, D.: Non-idempotent intersection types for the Lambda-Calculus. Logic J. IGPL **25**(4), 431–464 (2017). https://doi.org/10.1093/jigpal/jzx018
10. Carlier, S., Wells, J.B.: Type inference with expansion variables and intersection types in system e and an exact correspondence with β-reduction. In: Proceedings of the 6th ACM SIGPLAN International Conference on Principles and Practice of Declarative Programming, pp. 132–143. PPDP 2004. Association for Computing Machinery, New York, NY, USA (2004). https://doi.org/10.1145/1013963.1013980
11. Castagna, G., Lanvin, V.: Gradual typing with union and intersection types. Proc. ACM Program. Lang. 1(ICFP), **1**, 41:1–41:28 (2017). https://doi.org/10.1145/3110285
12. Castagna, G., Lanvin, V., Petrucciani, T., Siek, J.G.: Gradual typing: a new perspective. Proc. ACM Program. Lang. 3(POPL), 16:1–16:32 (2019). https://doi.org/10.1145/3290329
13. Coppo, M., Dezani-Ciancaglini, M.: An extension of the basic functionality theory for the λ-calculus. Notre Dame J. Formal Logic **21**(4), 685–693 (1980). https://doi.org/10.1305/ndjfl/1093883253
14. Coppo, M., Giannini, P.: Principal types and unification for simple intersection type systems. Inf. Comput. **122**(1), 70–96 (1995). https://doi.org/10.1006/inco.1995.1141
15. Coppo, M.: An extended polymorphic type system for applicative languages. In: Dembiński, P. (ed.) MFCS 1980. LNCS, vol. 88, pp. 194–204. Springer, Heidelberg (1980). https://doi.org/10.1007/BFb0022505

16. Curry, H.B.: Functionality in combinatory logic. Proc. Nat. Acad. Sci. **20**(11), 584–590 (1934). https://doi.org/10.1073/pnas.20.11.584
17. Damas, L., Milner, R.: Principal type-schemes for functional programs. In: Proceedings of the 9th ACM SIGPLAN-SIGACT Symposium on Principles of Programming Languages, pp. 207–212. POPL 1982. ACM, New York, NY, USA (1982). https://doi.org/10.1145/582153.582176
18. Damiani, F.: Rank 2 intersection types for modules. In: Proceedings of the 5th ACM SIGPLAN International Conference on Principles and Practice of Declaritive Programming, pp. 67–78. PPDP 2003. Association for Computing Machinery, New York, NY, USA (2003). https://doi.org/10.1145/888251.888259
19. Damiani, F., Giannini, P.: A decidable intersection type system based on relevance. In: Hagiya, M., Mitchell, J.C. (eds.) TACS 1994. LNCS, vol. 789, pp. 707–725. Springer, Heidelberg (1994). https://doi.org/10.1007/3-540-57887-0_122
20. Dovier, A., Omodeo, E., Pontelli, E., Rossi, G.: A language for programming in logic with finite sets. J. Log. Program. **28**, 1–44 (1996)
21. Dovier, A., Pontelli, E., Rossi, G.: Set unification. Theory Pract. Logic Program. **6**(6), 645–701 (2006). https://doi.org/10.1017/S1471068406002730
22. Dudenhefner, A., Martens, M., Rehof, J.: The algebraic intersection type unification problem. Log. Meth. Comput. Sci. **13** (2017)
23. Dunfield, J.: Elaborating intersection and union types. In: Proceedings of the 17th ACM SIGPLAN International Conference on Functional Programming, pp. 17–28. ICFP 2012. Association for Computing Machinery, New York, NY, USA (2012). https://doi.org/10.1145/2364527.2364534
24. Dunfield, J., Pfenning, F.: Type assignment for intersections and unions in call-by-value languages. In: Gordon, A.D. (ed.) FoSSaCS 2003. LNCS, vol. 2620, pp. 250–266. Springer, Heidelberg (2003). https://doi.org/10.1007/3-540-36576-1_16
25. Florido, M., Damas, L.: Linearization of the lambda-calculus and its relation with intersection type systems. J. Funct. Program. **14**(5), 519–546 (2004). https://doi.org/10.1017/S0956796803004970
26. Frankle, J., Osera, P.M., Walker, D., Zdancewic, S.: Example-directed synthesis: a type-theoretic interpretation. In: Proceedings of the 43rd Annual ACM SIGPLAN-SIGACT Symposium on Principles of Programming Languages, pp. 802–815. POPL 2016. Association for Computing Machinery, New York, NY, USA (2016). https://doi.org/10.1145/2837614.2837629
27. Freeman, T., Pfenning, F.: Refinement types for ml. In: Proceedings of the ACM SIGPLAN 1991 Conference on Programming Language Design and Implementation, pp. 268–277. PLDI 1991. Association for Computing Machinery, New York, NY, USA (1991). https://doi.org/10.1145/113445.113468
28. Girard, J.Y.: Une extension de Linterpretation de gödel a Lanalyse, et son application a Lelimination des coupures dans Lanalyse et la theorie des types. In: Fenstad, J. (ed.) Proceedings of the Second Scandinavian Logic Symposium, Studies in Logic and the Foundations of Mathematics, vol. 63, pp. 63–92. Elsevier (1971). https://doi.org/10.1016/S0049-237X(08)70843-7, https://www.sciencedirect.com/science/article/pii/S0049237X08708437
29. Girard, J.Y., Taylor, P., Lafont, Y.: Proofs and Types. Cambridge University Press, Cambridge (1989)
30. Henglein, F.: Type inference with polymorphic recursion. ACM Trans. Program. Lang. Syst. **15**(2), 253–289 (1993). https://doi.org/10.1145/169701.169692
31. Hindley, J.R.: Basic Simple Type Theory. Cambridge University Press (1997)
32. Jim, T.: Rank 2 type systems and recursive definitions. Technical report, Cambridge, MA, USA (1995)

33. Jim, T.: What are principal typings and what are they good for ? In: Proceedings of the 23rd ACM SIGPLAN-SIGACT Symposium on Principles of Programming Languages, pp. 42–53. POPL 1996. ACM, New York, NY, USA (1996). https://doi.org/10.1145/237721.237728

34. Kfoury, A.J., Tiuryn, J., Urzyczyn, P.: Type reconstruction in the presence of polymorphic recursion. ACM Trans. Program. Lang. Syst. **15**(2), 290–311 (1993)

35. Kfoury, A.J., Wells, J.B.: Principality and decidable type inference for finite-rank intersection types. In: Proceedings of the 26th ACM SIGPLAN-SIGACT Symposium on Principles of Programming Languages, pp. 161–174. POPL 1999. ACM, New York, NY, USA (1999). https://doi.org/10.1145/292540.292556

36. Kfoury, A., Wells, J.: Principality and type inference for intersection types using expansion variables. Theoret. Comput. Sci. **311**(1), 1–70 (2004). https://doi.org/10.1016/j.tcs.2003.10.032

37. Leivant, D.: Polymorphic type inference. In: Proceedings of the 10th ACM SIGACT-SIGPLAN Symposium on Principles of Programming Languages, pp. 88–98. POPL 1983. Association for Computing Machinery, New York, NY, USA (1983). https://doi.org/10.1145/567067.567077

38. Palsberg, J., Pavlopoulou, C.: From polyvariant flow information to intersection and union types. J. Funct. Program. **11**(3), 263–317 (2001). https://doi.org/10.1017/S095679680100394X

39. Pierce, B.C.: Types and Programming Languages. The MIT Press, 1st edn. (2002)

40. Pottinger, G.: A type assignment for the strongly normalizable lambda-terms. In: Hindley, J., Seldin, J. (eds.) To H. B. Curry: Essays on Combinatory Logic, Lambda Calculus and Formalism, pp. 561–577. Academic Press (1980)

41. Reynolds, J.C.: Towards a theory of type structure. In: Programming Symposium, Proceedings Colloque Sur La Programmation, pp. 408–423. Springer-Verlag, Berlin, Heidelberg (1974). https://doi.org/10.1007/3-540-06859-7_148

42. Reynolds, J.C.: Design of the Programming Language Forsythe, pp. 173–233. Birkhäuser Boston, Boston, MA (1997). https://doi.org/10.1007/978-1-4612-4118-8_9

43. Robinson, J.A.: A machine-oriented logic based on the resolution principle. J. ACM **12**(1), 23–41 (1965). https://doi.org/10.1145/321250.321253

44. Ronchi Della Rocca, S.: Principal type scheme and unification for intersection type discipline. Theor. Comput. Sci. 59(1–2), 181–209 (1988). https://doi.org/10.1016/0304-3975(88)90101-6

45. Urzyczyn, P.: The emptiness problem for intersection types. In: Proceedings Ninth Annual IEEE Symposium on Logic in Computer Science, pp. 300–309 (1994). https://doi.org/10.1109/LICS.1994.316059

46. Van Bakel, S.J.: Intersection Type Disciplines in Lambda Calculus and Applicative Term Rewriting Systems. Mathematisch Centrum, Amsterdam (1993)

47. Wand, M.: A simple algorithm and proof for type inference. Fund. Inform. **10**(2), 115–121 (1987)

Author Index